Born in New York in 1904, Joseph Campbell earned his B.A. and M.A. degrees at Columbia in 1925 and 1927. He went on to study medieval French and Sanskrit at the universities of Paris and Munich, and it was in the latter city that he became acquainted with the work of Jung. Returning to the United States at the time of the great Depression, he visited California (where he met John Steinbeck and the biologist Ed Ricketts), taught at the Canterbury School, and, in 1934, joined the literature department at Sarah Lawrence College, a post he retained for many years. During the 1940s and '50s, he helped Swami Nikhilananda to translate the Upanishads and *The Gospel of Sri Ramakrishna*. Professor Campbell's numerous books include *The Hero with a Thousand Faces; Myths to Live By; The Flight of the Wild Gander;* a four-volume study, *The Masks of God;* and *The Mythic Image*. In addition to *The Portable Jung*, he has edited *The Portable Arabian Nights*.

# The Portable
# ❧ JUNG ❧

*Edited, with an Introduction, by*

J O S E P H  C A M P B E L L

*Translated by R. F. C. Hull*

PENGUIN BOOKS

Penguin Books Ltd, Harmondsworth,
Middlesex, England
Penguin Books, 40 West 23rd Street,
New York, New York 10010, U.S.A.
Penguin Books Australia Ltd, Ringwood,
Victoria, Australia
Penguin Books Canada Limited, 2801 John Street,
Markham, Ontario, Canada L3R 1B4
Penguin Books (N.Z.) Ltd, 182–190 Wairau Road,
Auckland 10, New Zealand

First published in the United States of America
by The Viking Press 1971
Reprinted 1972 (twice), 1973 (twice), 1974 (twice), 1975, 1976
Published in Penguin Books 1976
Reprinted 1977, 1978, 1980, 1981 (twice), 1982, 1983, 1984 (twice), 1985

# Contents

# Editor's Introduction

The first task, on approaching such a mobile model of the living psyche as Carl G. Jung's, must be to become familiar as quickly as possible with its variables. To this end I have opened this anthology with papers introducing the elementary terms and themes of Jung's psychology. Once acquainted with these, the reader will be prepared to range at will through *The Collected Works*; and my second aim, consequently, has been to provide a usable guide to that treasury of learning. For Jung was not only a medical man but a scholar in the grand style, whose researches, particularly in comparative mythology, alchemy, and the psychology of religion, have inspired and augmented the findings of an astonishing number of the leading creative scholars of our time. Evidence of this will be found in the forty-odd volumes already published of the continuing *Eranos-Jahrbuch* series,[1] where stand the

[1] *Eranos-Jahrbücher* (Zurich: Rhein-Verlag, 1933———). Six volumes of selected papers have been published in English, under my editorship, translated by Ralph Manheim, *Papers from the Eranos Yearbooks*, Bollingen Series XXX (New York: Pantheon Books, 1954, 1955, 1957, 1960, 1964, 1969).

contributions of some two hundred major scholars, render-
ing matters of their special fields in the light of—and as
relevant to—the culture-historical studies of Carl G. Jung.
My final aim, accordingly, has been to provide such a
primer and handbook to Jung's writings that if a reader
will proceed faithfully from the first page to the last, he
will emerge not only with a substantial understanding of
Analytical Psychology, but also with a new realization
of the relevance of the mythic lore of all peoples to his
own psychological *opus magnum* of Individuation.

## *1. Childhood and Student Years (1875–1900)*

Carl Gustav Jung was born July 26, 1875, in Kesswil,
Switzerland, on Lake Constance. His paternal grandfather,
after whom he was named, had moved from Germany in
1822, when Alexander von Humboldt obtained an appoint-
ment for him as professor of surgery at the University of
Basel. His father, Johann Paul Achilles Jung (1842–
1896), was a clergyman, and his mother, Emilie Preiswerk
Jung (1848–1923), was the daughter of a long-established
Basel family. When the boy was four, his parents moved
to Klein-Hüningen, near Basel, and it was there his education began. His father taught him Latin, and his mother,
as he tells in a volume of old-age reminiscences, *Memories,
Dreams, Reflections*, read to him of exotic religions from
an illustrated children's book, to which he constantly returned to view with fascination its pictures of Hindu gods.

During early youth, Jung thought of archaeology as
a career. Theology, too, interested him, though not in his
father's sense; for the concept of Christ's life as the sole
decisive feature in the drama of God and man he regarded
as belying Christ's own teaching that the Holy Ghost
would take his place among men after his death. He
regarded Jesus as a man; hence, either fallible or a mere
mouthpiece of the Holy Ghost, who, in turn, was "a manifestation of the inconceivable God."

One day, in the library of a college classmate's father, the questing youth chanced on a small book on spiritualistic phenomena that immediately caught and absorbed him; for the phenomena described were like those of stories he had been hearing in the Swiss countryside since childhood. Furthermore, he knew that similar tales were reported from all parts of the world. They could not be the products of religious superstition, since religious teachings differ and these accounts were alike. They must be connected, he thought, with the objective behavior of the psyche. Interest ignited, he read ravenously; but among his friends he encountered only resistance to the subject, a curious, hard resistance that amazed him.

"I had the feeling," he declares, "that I had pushed to the brink of the world; what was of burning interest to me was null and void for others, and even a cause of dread. Dread of what? I could find no explanation for this. After all, there was nothing preposterous and world-shaking in the idea that there might be events which overstepped the limited categories of space, time, and causality. Animals were known to sense beforehand storms and earthquakes. There were dreams which foresaw the death of certain persons, clocks which stopped at the moment of death, glasses which shattered at the critical moment. All these things had been taken for granted in the world of my childhood. And now I was apparently the only person who had ever heard of them. In all earnestness I asked myself what kind of world I had stumbled into. Plainly the urban world knew nothing about the country world, the real world of mountains, woods, and rivers, of animals and 'God's thoughts' (plants and crystals). I found this explanation comforting. At all events, it bolstered my self-esteem."

What decided this young scholar of philosophical bent to enter medicine has not, as far as I know, been told. It was possibly the imposing model of his very distinguished grandfather of Humboldt's time. But he has himself described the strange events that turned him, in the last months of his medical schooling, from medicine and surgery to psychiatry.

While following his required courses, he had been avidly reading, on Sundays, in Kant and Goethe, Hartmann, Schopenhauer and Nietzsche; but again had found, when he thought to talk of such authors to his friends, that no one wanted to hear of them. All his friends wanted were facts, and all he had for them was talk—until, one day, there came to him something as solid and cold as steel.

He was in his room, studying, with the door half open to the dining room, where his widowed mother was knitting by the window, when a loud report sounded, like a pistol shot, and the circular walnut table beside her had split from the rim to beyond the center—a table of solid walnut, dried and seasoned for some seventy years. Two weeks later, the young medical student, returning home at evening, found his mother, his fourteen-year-old sister, and the maid in high agitation. About an hour earlier, another deafening crack had come from the neighborhood of a heavy nineteenth-century sideboard, which the women had then examined without finding any sign. Nearby, in the cupboard containing the breadbasket, however, Jung discovered the breadknife with its steel blade broken to pieces: in one corner of the basket, its handle; in each of the others, a fraction of the blade. To the end of his life Jung preserved the fragments of that concrete fact.

A few weeks later he learned of certain relatives engaged in table-turning, who had a medium, a young girl of fifteen and a half, who produced somnambulistic states and spiritualistic phenomena. Invited to participate, Jung immediately conjectured that the manifestations in his mother's house might be connected with that medium. He joined the sessions and, for the next two years, meticulously took notes, until, in the end, the medium, feeling her powers failing, began to cheat, and Jung departed.

Meanwhile, he was still at medical school, and in due season the time arrived for the state examination. His professor in psychology had been "not exactly," in his judgment, "stimulating." Moreover, in the medical world of that time, psychiatry was held in contempt. So in preparing himself he had reserved for the last his psychiatric textbook, Krafft-Ebing's *Lehrbuch der Psychiatrie,* which he opened with the unpromising thought, "Well, now let's see what a psychiatrist has to say for himself."

Beginning with the preface, he read: "It is probably due to the peculiarity of the subject and its incomplete state of development that psychiatric textbooks are stamped with a more or less subjective character." A few lines further on, Krafft-Ebing termed psychoses "diseases of the personality," and the reader's heart began suddenly to pound. He had to stand and draw a deep breath. His excitement was intense; for, as he tells, "it had become clear to me in a flash of illumination, that for me the only possible goal was psychiatry." Here, and here alone, was the empirical field common to spiritual and biological facts.


### 2. The Scholar Physician: First Period (1900–1907)

COLLECTED WORKS:  Volume 1. *Psychiatric Studies*
                                (1902–1906)
                                Volume 2. *Experimental Researches*
                                (1904–1907)


December 10, 1900, the twenty-five-year-old Carl Jung assumed his post as First Assistant Physician at the Burghölzli Psychiatric Clinic in Zurich, under Eugen Bleuler, whom he recognized gratefully all his life as the first of his only two teachers; Pierre Janet, at the Salpêtrière in Paris, with whom he studied for a term in 1902, being the second. Under Bleuler he completed in 1902 his doctoral dissertation, "On the Psychology and Pathology of So-Called Occult Phenomena" (*Collected Works,* Vol. 1), analyzing the medium and séances of his two-year adventure in the occult, with a review of earlier published studies of somnambulism, hystero-epilepsy, amnesia, and other related twilight states. And what is here remarkable is that already in this earliest work there appear at least five major themes that were to recur as leitmotifs through all of Jung's later thinking.

The first is of the autonomy of unconscious psychic contents. During states of semi-somnambulism or preoccupation, such autonomous elements may assume control, producing "automatisms" of various sorts: hallucinatory visions, sensations, or voices (which may be interpreted as of spirits), automatic movements, writings, etc. If the composition of such an autonomous complex becomes, in the course of time, reinforced, a second, "unconscious" personality can be built up, which can then, under releasing conditions, take over. In the case of his medium, Jung was able to identify in her recent experiences the sources of many of her fantasies; noting that even normally in adolescence, which is when the future ego-complex is being formed, analogous splittings occur.

And this enabled him to put forward a second idea destined to remain fundamental in his thinking, namely, of such a psychological disturbance as having teleological significance, i.e. as transitional under crisis, protective yet pointing forward, giving the individual, who would otherwise inevitably succumb to threatening circumstance, "the means of victory."

A third and a fourth point demonstrated in this paper were not only that the unconscious is a carrier of memories lost to consciousness, but also that it is an intuiting agent of a receptivity "far exceeding that of the conscious mind"; to which latter point Jung quoted the French psychiatrist Alfred Binet, to the effect that, according to his calculations, "the unconscious sensibility of an hysterical patient is at certain moments *fifty times* more acute than that of a normal person."

Finally, Jung remarked in this first paper of his long career that a curious mythological concept of the cosmos which the young medium one day brought forth with joyful face as having been "revealed" to her by the spirits, resembled other occult "systems" scattered about in works to which this girl would have had no access. Constructed of fragmentary components received from various identifiable sources, her system had been put together below or beyond the field of her conscious mind and presented to her as an image already formed. Jung's conclusion, to be developed in his later writings, was that, inherent in the human psyche, there is a patterning force, which may, at various times and in places out of touch with each other, spontaneously put forth similar constellations of fantasy; so that, as he states in a later volume: "One could almost say that if all the world's traditions were cut off at a single blow, the whole mythology and the whole history of religion would start all over again with the next generation."

In 1903 this brilliant youth set up in the Burghölzli Clinic a laboratory for experimental psychopathology, where, with a number of students and with Dr. Franz Riklin as collaborator, he undertook to investigate psychic reactions by means of association tests. The basic concept supporting this method was of the "feeling tone" (Bleuler's term: "an affective state accompanied by somatic innervations") as a binding force by which constellations of ideas are held together, whether in the conscious or in the unconscious mind, the conscious ego itself and the whole mass of ideas pertaining to it being but one such "feeling-toned complex."

"The ego," Jung states in the culminating paper of this period, a work on "The Psychology of Dementia Praecox" (*Collected Works*, Vol. 3), which he later sent to Freud, "is the psychological expression of the firmly associated combinations of all body sensations. One's own personality is therefore the firmest and strongest complex, and (good health permitting) it weathers all psychological storms." However: "Reality sees to it that the peaceful cycle of egocentric ideas is constantly interrupted by ideas with a strong feeling-tone, that is, by affects. A situation threatening danger pushes aside the tranquil play of ideas and puts in their place a complex of other ideas with a very strong feeling-tone. The new complex then crowds everything else into the background. For the time being it is the most distinct because it totally inhibits all other ideas." It was by touching and activating a subject's feeling-toned associations that the word test exposed the hidden "facts" of his life. And it was in response to Jung's early publications on this topic that he acquired his first professional reputation.

Jung in 1903 had married Emma Rauschenbach, who was to become the mother of four daughters and a son, and to remain his close collaborator until the day of her death in 1955. Two years after the marriage he became Senior Physician at the clinic and was appointed Lecturer in Psychiatry at the University of Zurich, where he dealt chiefly with hypnosis and researches in somnambulism, automatism, hysteria, etc. It was largely as the result of a little miracle that occurred in this lecture class that his private practice suddenly acquired dimension.

A middle-aged woman on crutches came into the room one day, led by a maid. She had for seventeen years been suffering a painful paralysis of the left leg; and when he had placed her in a comfortable chair, bidding her tell her story, she went on at such interminable length that he had finally to interrupt. "Well now," he said, "we have no more time for so much talk. I am now going to hypnotize you." Whereupon she closed her eyes and fell into a profound trance without any hypnosis at all, continuing, meanwhile, her talking, relating the most remarkable dreams. The situation for the baffled young instructor, before his twenty students, was becoming increasingly uncomfortable; and when he tried to wake her, without success, he became alarmed. It took some ten minutes to bring her to, and when she woke, she was giddy and confused. He said to her, "I am the doctor; everything is all right." At which she cried out, "But I am cured!" threw away her crutches, and was able to walk. Flushed with embarrassment, Jung said to the students, "Now you've seen what can be done with hypnosis!" whereas, in fact, he had not the slightest

idea what had happened. The woman departed in the best
of spirits to proclaim her cure, and himself as a wizard,
far and wide.

## 3. *The Scholar Physician: Second Period* (*1907–1912*)

COLLECTED WORKS:

Jung's acquaintance with the writings of Freud commenced in 1900, the year of publication of *The Interpretation of Dreams,* which he read at Bleuler's suggestion but
was not yet prepared to appreciate. Three years later,
returning to the book, he realized that it offered the best
explanation he had found of the *mechanism* of the repressions observed in his word-association experiments. He
could not, however, accept Freud's identification of the
*content* of repression as invariably a sexual trauma, since
from his own practice he was familiar with cases in which
(to quote his words) "the question of sexuality played a
subordinate part, other factors standing in the foreground—
for example, the problem of social adaptation, of oppres-
sion by tragic circumstances of life, prestige considerations,
and so on."

Jung opened an exchange with Freud by sending him
in 1906 a collection of his early papers entitled *Studies
in Word Association,*[2] to which Freud graciously re-

[2] These were: "The Association of Normal Subjects" (1904);
"Reaction-Time in Association Experiments" (1905); "Experimen-
tal Observations on Memory" (1905); and "Psychoanalysis and
Association Experiments" (1905). All are assigned to *Collected
Works,* Vol. 2, "Experimental Researches."

sponded; and Jung went to visit him in Vienna. They met at one in the afternoon and talked for thirteen hours, almost without let.

The next year Jung sent his monograph on "The Psychology of Dementia Praecox" and again was invited to Vienna, but with his wife this time, and affairs took another turn.

"When I arrived in Vienna with my young and happy wife," Jung told a visitor, Dr. John M. Billinsky,[3] in 1957, "Freud came to see us at the hotel and brought some flowers for my wife. He was trying to be very considerate and at one point said to me, 'I am sorry that I can give you no real hospitality. I have nothing at home but an elderly wife.' When my wife heard him say that, she looked perplexed and embarrassed. At Freud's home that evening, during dinner, I tried to talk to Freud and his wife about psychoanalysis and Freud's activities, but I soon discovered that Mrs. Freud knew absolutely nothing about what Freud was doing. It was very obvious that there was a very superficial relationship between Freud and his wife.

"Soon I met Freud's wife's younger sister. She was very good-looking, and she not only knew enough about psychoanalysis but also about everything Freud was doing. When, a few days later, I was visiting Freud's laboratory, his sister-in-law asked me if she could talk with me. She was very much bothered by her relationship with Freud and felt guilty about it. From her I learned that Freud was in love with her and that their friendship was indeed very intimate. It was a shocking discovery to me, and even now I recall the agony I felt at the time."

The following year, 1908, Jung attended in Vienna the First International Congress of Psycho-Analysis; and it

[3] Guiles Professor of Psychology and Clinical Studies at Andover Newton Theological School, Newton Center, Mass. His article, "Jung and Freud," from which I quote, appeared in the *Andover Newton Quarterly*, Vol. 10, No. 2 (November 1969), pp. 39–43.

was there that he met the greater part of that distinguished company which, in the next years, was to make the psychoanalytic movement known to the world. The next spring, 1909, found Jung once again in Vienna, and on this occasion Freud—his elder by nineteen years—confided to him kindly that he was adopting him "as an eldest son, anointing him as successor and crown prince." However, when the anointed later asked what his adopting elder's views might be on precognition and parapsychology, Freud replied abruptly: Sheer nonsense!—"and in terms," states Jung, "of so shallow a positivism that I had difficulty in checking the sharp retort on the tip of my tongue."

"I had a curious sensation," Jung continues in his account of this first real crisis in their friendship. "It was as if my diaphragm were made of iron and were becoming red-hot—a glowing vault. And at that moment there was such a loud report in the bookcase, which stood right next to us, that we started up in alarm, fearing the thing was going to topple over on us. I said to Freud: 'There, that is an example of a so-called catalytic exteriorization phenomenon.'

" 'Oh come!' he exclaimed. 'That is sheer bosh.'

" 'It is not,' I replied. 'You are mistaken, Herr Professor. And to prove my point I now predict that in a moment there will be another such loud report!' Sure enough, no sooner had I said the words than the same detonation went off in the bookcase. . . . Freud only stared aghast at me. I do not know what was in his mind, or what his look meant. In any case, this incident aroused his mistrust of me, and I had the feeling that I had done something against him." [4]

It is hardly surprising, after such a display of shamanism on the part of his newly adopted "son," that the "father"

---

[4] C. G. Jung, *Memories, Dreams, Reflections,* recorded and edited by Aniela Jaffé, translated by Richard and Clara Winston (New York: Pantheon Books, 1963), pp. 155–56; see Freud's letter of attempted interpretation, ibid., pp. 361–63.

(with his *idée fixe* about Oedipus) should, on their next occasion, have suffered a hysterical crisis. This occurred that fall, in Bremen, where they had met to embark for America, invited, both, to Clark University to receive honorary degrees. Jung had been reading of the peat-bog corpses brought to light in Denmark: bodies from the Iron Age, perfectly preserved, which he had hoped to see while in the North. And when he began talking of these, there was something about his persistence that began to get on Freud's nerves. Several times Freud asked why he was so concerned about those corpses; and when, at dinner, Jung went on, Freud suddenly fainted—having conceived the idea, as he later explained, that Jung had death wishes against him.

"From the very beginning of our trip," Jung confided to Dr. Billinsky, fifty years later, "we started to analyze each other's dreams. Freud had some dreams that bothered him very much. The dreams were about the triangle—Freud, his wife, and wife's younger sister. Freud had no idea that I knew about the triangle and his intimate relationship with his sister-in-law. And so, when Freud told me about the dream in which his wife and her sister played important parts, I asked him to tell me some of his personal associations with the dream. He looked at me with bitterness and said, 'I could tell you more, but I cannot risk my authority.' That, of course, finished my attempt to deal with his dreams. . . . If Freud had tried to understand consciously the triangle, he would have been much, much better off."

The next traumatic event occurred in 1910, the year of the Second Congress of the Association of Psycho-Analysis, where Freud proposed, and even insisted against organized opposition, that Jung should be appointed Permanent President. "My dear Jung," he urged on this occasion, as Jung tells, "promise me never to abandon the sexual theory. That is the most essential thing of all. You see, we must make a dogma of it, an unshakable bulwark." He said this with great emotion, in the tone (states Jung) of a father saying, "And promise me this one thing, my dear son: that you will go to church every Sunday." In some astonishment Jung asked him, "A bulwark—against what?" To which he replied, "Against the black tide of mud"—and here he hesitated for a moment, then added—"of occultism."

"First of all," comments Jung on this episode, "it was the words 'bulwark' and 'dogma' that alarmed me; for a dogma, that is to say, an undisputable confession of faith, is set up only when the aim is to suppress doubts once and for all. But that no longer has anything to do with scientific judgment; only with a personal power drive.

"This was the thing that struck at the heart of our friendship. I knew that I would never be able to accept such an attitude. What Freud seemed to mean by 'occultism' was virtually everything that philosophy and religion, including the rising contemporary science of parapsychology, had learned about the psyche. To me the sexual theory was just as occult, that is to say, just as unproven a hypothesis, as many other speculative views. As I saw it, a scientific truth was a hypothesis that might be adequate for the moment but was not to be preserved as an article of faith for all time."

The incompatibility of the two minds was clear; yet they contrived to work together until the next congress, in 1912, in Munich, where Freud was again overwhelmed by his oedipal myth. Someone had turned the talk to Ikhnaton, suggesting that because of a negative attitude toward his father he had destroyed his father's cartouches on the steles, and that in back of his creation of a monotheistic religion there lay, therefore, a father complex. Jung, irritated by such talk, responded that Ikhnaton had held his father's memory in honor and that what his zeal had been directed against was the name of the god Amon: other pharaohs had replaced their fathers' names with their own, feeling they had a right to do so as incarnations of the same god; yet they had not inaugurated a new religion. . . . On hearing which words, Freud slid off his chair in a faint.

Many have held that the break in the friendship of these two was caused by Jung's publication of his altogether non-Freudian work, *Symbols of Transformation* (*Collected Works,* Vol. 5; Part I, 1911; Part II, 1912). However, this was not quite Jung's own view, although the book certainly played a part. "The only thing he saw in my work," Jung said in his talk with Dr. Billinsky, "was 'resistance to the father'—my wish to destroy the father. When I tried to point out to him my reasoning about the libido, his attitude toward me was one of bitterness and rejection." More deeply, however, as Jung went on to explain: "It was my knowledge of Freud's triangle that became a very important factor in my break with Freud. And then," he continued, "I could not accept Freud's placing authority above truth."

Jung's approach to the writing of his decisive—and divisive—work, *Symbols of Transformation,* commenced in 1909, the year of that trip to America. He had just begun his study of mythology and in the course of the readings came across Friedrich Creuzer's *Symbolik und Mythologie der alten Völker* (1810–1823), which, as he declares, "fired" him. He worked like mad through a mountain of mythological material, continued through the Gnostic writers, and ended in total confusion; then chanced on a series of fantasies of a certain Miss Miller of New York, published in the *Archives de Psychologie* by his revered friend Théodore Flournoy. He was immediately struck by the mythological character of the fantasies and found that they operated as a catalyst on the stored-up ideas within him. He commenced writing, and, as he told in later years of the composition of this pivotal work of his career: "It was the explosion of all those psychic contents which could find no room, no breathing space, in the constricting atmosphere of Freudian psychology and its narrow outlook." "It was written at top speed, amid the rush and press of my medical practice, without regard to time or method. I had to fling my material hastily together, just as I found it. There was no opportunity to let my thoughts mature. The whole thing came upon me like a landslide that cannot be stopped." Egyptian, Babylonian, Hindu, Classical and Gnostic, Germanic and American Indian materials came clustering about the fantasies of a modern American woman on the brink of a schizophrenic breakdown. And Jung's experience in the course of this labor transformed his entire point of view with respect to the task of interpreting psychological symbols.

"Hardly had I finished the manuscript," he states, "when it struck me what it means to live with a myth, and what it means to live without one. Myth, says a Church Father, is 'what is believed always, everywhere, by everybody'; hence the man who thinks he can live without myth, or outside it, is an exception. He is like one uprooted, having no true link either with the past, or with the ancestral life which continues within him, or yet with contemporary human society. This plaything of his reason never grips his vitals. It may occasionally be heavy on his stomach, for that organ is apt to reject the products of reason as indigestible. The psyche is not of today; its ancestry goes back many millions of years. Individual consciousness is only the flower and the fruit of a season, sprung from the perennial rhizome beneath the earth; and it would find itself in better accord with the truth if it took the existence of the rhizome into its calculations. For the root matter is the mother of all things."

It was this radical shift of ground from a subjective and personalistic, essentially *biographical* approach to the reading of the symbolism of the psyche, to a larger, culture-historical, *mythological* orientation, that then became the characteristic of Jung's psychology. He asked himself, "What is the myth *you* are living?" and found that he did not know. "So, in the most natural way, I took it upon myself to get to know 'my myth, and I regarded this as the task of tasks; for—so I told myself—how could I, when treating my patients, make due allowance for the personal factor, for my personal equation, which is yet so necessary for a knowledge of the other person, if I was unconscious of it? I simply had to know what unconscious or preconscious myth was forming me, from what rhizome I sprang. This resolve led me to devote many years of my life to investigating the subjective contents which are the products of unconscious processes, and to work out methods which would enable us, or at any rate help us, to explore the manifestations of the unconscious."

Briefly summarized, the essential realizations of this pivotal work of Jung's career were, first, that since the archetypes or norms of myth are common to the human species, they are inherently expressive neither of local social circumstance nor of any individual's singular experience, but of common human needs, instincts, and potentials; second, that in the traditions of any specific folk, local circumstance will have provided the imagery through which the archetypal themes are displayed in the supporting myths of the culture; third, that if the manner of life and thought of an individual so departs from the norms of the species that a pathological state of imbalance ensues, of neurosis or psychosis, dreams and fantasies analogous to fragmented myths will appear; and fourth, that such dreams are best interpreted, not by reference backward to repressed infantile memories (reduction to autobiography), but by comparison outward with the analogous mythic forms (amplification to mythology), so that the disturbed individual may learn to see himself depersonalized in the mirror of the human spirit and discover by analogy the way to his own larger fulfillment. Dreams, in Jung's view, are the natural reaction of the self-regulating psychic system and, as such, point forward to a higher, potential health, not simply backward to past crises. The posture of the unconscious is compensatory to consciousness, and its productions, dreams, and fantasies, consequently, are not only corrective but also prospective, giving clues, if properly read, to those functions and archetypes of the psyche pressing, at the moment, for recognition.

### 4. The Scholar Physician: Master Period (1912–1946)

The years from the opening of World War I to the close of World War II were the prime of Jung's maturity—and, as the reader possibly has noted, all but three of the papers of this *Portable* are from the writings of those years. The period began, however, with a season of profound disorientation. Even before the break with Freud, Jung's readings in mythology had turned his center of concern from the daylight world of time, space, and personalities to a timeless eviternity of satyrs, nymphs, centaurs, and dragons to be slain. In 1909 he resigned his post at the Burghölzli Clinic; largely, as he tells, because he was over his head in work, having so large a private practice he could no longer keep up with his tasks. Then, when he had renounced Freud's dogma, the whole psychoanalytic community turned against him, launching even a paranoiac campaign of character assassination. Cut off in these several ways from all his earlier professional associates and even many of his former friends, he was left to wallow in a mercurial sea of fantasies and mythologies, his patients' dreams and his own. And, as he tells, in this condition of uncertainty he decided that in his work with patients he should not bring theoretical premises to bear, but only wait and see what they would tell of their own accord. They spontaneously recounted dreams, and he would ask, simply, "What occurs to you in connection with that?" or "How do you mean that, where does it come from, what do you think about it?"—leaving everything open to chance. In his own fantasying he was being reminded, meanwhile, that in childhood he had enjoyed building-blocks and had gone on to constructing little towns and castles of stones and mud: accordingly, he decided to try going back to that childhood game; and what he presently found was that it was releasing in him streams of fantasy, which he soon began to record. Next he began embellishing his chronicle of these fantasies with ornamental designs, which soon led to larger pictorial figurations, which, for a time, he was led to believe might be "Art," but then realized were not. They were X-rays of his spiritual state.

Toward the autumn of 1913, Jung was overcome and deeply troubled by a series of appalling visions of the whole of Europe drowning in blood. The World War broke out the following August: and it was as though a general schizophrenic eruption of autonomous feeling-toned complexes had shattered forever the rationalized surface of Occidental thought and civilization. On the one remaining island of peace, Jung, like a number of others in those years, set himself the task of exploring deeply the spiritual history of European man, in order to identify, and if possible transcend, the compulsions of irrational self-destruction. His fantasies and dreams, meanwhile, were revealing to him the same archetypes from within that he had already come to know as of world mythology, and his ornamental designs were developing into mandalas, magic circles, "cryptograms concerning the state of the self," such as in the Orient had been used for centuries as supports for meditation. "In what myth," he was asking, "does man live nowadays? Or do we no longer have any myth?"

It is in point to remark that James Joyce, during those years, was also in Zurich, composing *Ulysses*; Lenin, too, was there, incubating world revolution; Hugo Ball, Richard Huelsenbeck, Hans Arp, and Tristan Tzara, likewise, inventing Dada as a protest against rationalized organization; while in Germany Thomas Mann was at work on the materials of *The Magic Mountain,* and Oswald Spengler was revising and augmenting his prophetic *Decline of the West.* The fruit of Jung's thinking appeared in 1921 in the monumental tome (now Volume 6 of *The Collected Works*), *Psychological Types, or The Psychology of Individuation.*

This was a work of more than 700 pages, the first 470 dealing with an astounding range of philosophical speculations from India, China and Japan, Classical antiquity, Gnosticism and the Early Fathers, the Middle Ages, Reformation, Renaissance, Baroque and Enlightenment, Kant, Goethe, Schiller, Hegel, Schopenhauer, Wagner, Nietzsche, and assorted moderns: all concerned with the single theme of psychological types. And in the last 240 pages Jung's own formulation appears (in the present volume, Selection 8), along with a glossary of basic Jungian terms and a conclusion discussing the relevance of a recognition of psychological differences to an appreciation of the relativity of all so-called "truths" and "facts" to the organs of their perceivers.

Jung assigns the leading part in the differentiation of types to what he terms the "Four Functions of Consciousness"; noticing that whereas one person may favor *thought* as a guide to judgment, another will follow *feeling;* and whereas one will tend to experience both the world and his friends through impressions made directly on his *senses,* another will be given, rather, to *intuiting* potentialities, hidden relationships, intentions, and possible sources. Sensation and Intuition are the two functions, according to this view, by which "facts" and the "fact world" are apprehended; Feeling and Thinking, those of judging and evaluating. But as Jung observes and shows—and here is the crux of his argument—only *one* of these four functions takes the lead in the governance of a person's life, and it is seconded, normally, by only one (not both) from the other duad; as, for example, Thinking supported by Sensation, or Sensation supported by Thinking: both of which combinations (characteristic of modern Western man) leave Feeling and Intuition disregarded, undeveloped, or even repressed and, consequently, in the unconscious, susceptible to activation and outburst as autonomous complexes, either in the way of demoniacal seizures, or, more mildly, uncontrollable moods.

Jung names such a turnover, such a transfer of leadership from conscious to unconscious factors, *enantiodromia,* a "running the other way," which is a term borrowed from Heraclitus, who taught that everything in time turns into its opposite. "Out of life," Heraclitus wrote, "comes death and out of death life, out of the young the old, and out of the old the young, out of waking sleep and out of sleep waking, the stream of creation and dissolution never stops." The idea is fundamental to Jung's psychology, and applies, furthermore, to *all* pairs-of-opposites: interchanges not only of the four functions but also of those two contrary dispositions of psychic energy that Jung has termed Extraversion and Introversion.

Jung recalls in his autobiographical volume, *Memories,*

*Dreams, Reflections,* that even while associated with the psychoanalytic movement he had remarked that, where Freud named sexuality as the controlling psychological force, Alfred Adler (who soon left the movement to develop in his own direction) put the Will to Power; and each was such a monotheist that he could brook no contradiction. Jung, on the other hand, had been a polytheist all his life; that is to say, had always known that the ultimate "One" which cannot be named (the "inconceivable God") is manifest in many forms, these appearing as pairs-of-opposites; so that anybody fixing his eyes on but one is left open at the back to the other; whereas the art is to learn of both, to recognize and come to a knowledge of both: again, in the words of Heraclitus, "Good and evil are one," and, "God is day and night, summer and winter, war and peace, surfeit and hunger."

Jung terms Extraversion the trend of libido recognized by Freud, which is characterized by an openness—one might even say vulnerability—of the subject to the object: thinking, feeling, and acting in relation, willy-nilly, to the claims or appeal of the object. Introversion, on the other hand, is the trend recognized by Adler, which is characterized by a concentration of interest in the subject: thinking, feeling, and acting in relation primarily to the interests—concerns, aims, feelings, and thought processes—of oneself. Each attitude, however, is susceptible to *enantiodromia,* and when that occurs there emerge all the other unconscious contents, contaminating, reinforcing, and bewildering one another in such a pell-mell of feeling-toned complexes as to put one, literally, "beside oneself."

Jung's concept is that the aim of one's life, psychologically speaking, should be not to suppress or repress, but to come to know one's other side, and so both to enjoy and to control the whole range of one's capacities; i.e., in the full sense, to "know oneself." And he terms that faculty of the psyche by which one is rendered capable of this work of gaining release from the claims of but one or the other of any pair-of-opposites, the Transcendent Function, which may be thought of as a fifth, at the crossing of the

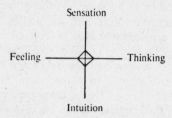

pairs of the other four. The Transcendent Function works through Symbolization, Mythologization; that is, by releasing names and things from their perceived and conceived associations, it recognizes them and their contexts as delimited representations to our faculties (Sensation, Thinking, Feeling, and Intuition) of an undelimited unknown.

Jung distinguishes symbols from signs. Living symbols become signs when read as referring to something known; as, for instance, the cross, to the Church or to a *historical* crucifixion. A sign becomes, on the other hand, a symbol when it is read as pointing to an unknown—the inconceivable "God" beyond the four beams of the cross—to which Jesus went when he left his body on the beams; or better, which was already immanent in the body on the beams; or better still, which is immanent within all bodies at the crossing points of lines drawn from the four directions. "Individuation" is Jung's term for the process of achieving such command of all four functions that, even while bound to the cross of this limiting earth (Saint Paul's "body of this death"), one might open one's eyes at the center, to see, think, feel and intuit transcendence, and to act out of such knowledge. This, I would say, is the final good, the Summum Bonum, of all his thought and work.

In 1920, the year before the publication of *Psychological Types,* Jung visited Tunis and Algiers, where for the first time he experienced the great world of people living without clocks and watches. Deeply moved, he came to new realizations there concerning the psyche of the modern European. And this insight into other worlds was amplified when, in 1924 and 1925, he met and talked long at Taos Pueblo, New Mexico, with Indians for whom the sun, the local mountains, and the local waters still were divine. His most important voyage, however, was in 1926, to Kenya, Mount Elgon, and the sources of the Nile, where both the timeless charm and nobility and the night terrors of the primitive condition were made known to him directly, and his return trip down the Nile to Egypt became, as he described it, a "drama of the birth of light."

The following year one of the leading Sinologists of the period, Richard Wilhelm, sent Jung the manuscript of a Chinese Taoist alchemical text entitled *The Secret of the Golden Flower,* which dealt with the problem of a centering amidst opposites; and it was, Jung declares, through this Chinese text that light on the nature of European as well as Far Eastern alchemy first came to him. "Grounded in the natural philosophy of the Middle Ages, alchemy formed a bridge," he found, "on the one hand into the past, to Gnosticism, and on the other into the future, to the modern psychology of the unconscious." Moreover, in European thought alchemy represented a balancing tradition to what Jung had always felt to be an excessively masculine, patriarchal emphasis in the usually accepted forms of the Jewish and Christian faiths, since in philosophical alchemy the feminine principle plays a no less important part than the masculine.

Then it came to pass, amid the circle of Jung's now numerous company of friends, that there was fashioned for him in those last decades of his life a new and very modern sort of alchemical retort, in the form of a lecture hall, open to the fair sky, blue waters, and sublime peaks of upper Lago Maggiore. Commencing in 1933, constellations of scholars from all over the world were annually invited to read and discuss, from their various learned disciplines, papers relevant to the questions of Jungian thought. These are the annual Eranos Lectures, delivered on the Ascona estate of the foundress, Frau Olga Froebe-Kapteyn. Many of the principal papers of Jung's later years were first presented at those meetings; and even a passing glance at the names of the scholars contributing will suffice to make Jung's great point, that "dividing walls are transparent," and where insight rules beyond differences, all the pairs-of-opposites come together.

### 5. *Old Age and Retirement* (*1946–1961*)

COLLECTED WORKS:
  Volume 9.ii. *Aion* (1951)
  Volume 14. *Mysterium Coniunctionis* (1955–56)
  Late items, also, in Vols. 3, 8, 9.i., 10, and 11

The childhood game of building-blocks had developed in the middle years of Jung's life into an actual work of house-building. In Bollingen, at the waterside of Lake Zurich, he bought in 1922 a piece of land and there began the unhurried hobby of constructing for himself a castle of stone, The Tower, which continued to alter in form with the years; and it was largely to that castle of dream—or castle-window to eternity—that he repaired when, after 1946, he resigned the last of his teaching posts, at the University of Basel, and turned to the final tasks of his still developing career.

Already in 1909, but increasingly during his lonely and (as he knew) dangerous descent into the image-producing abyss, he had been impressed by the recurrence of certain stereotypes among the figures of his dream-fantasies, suggesting those with which he was already acquainted through his studies of mythology. "I took great care," he states, "to try to understand every single image, every item of my psychic inventory, and to classify them scientifically—so far as this was possible—and, above all, to realize them in actual life." During his sessions with patients, when they brought dreams to him, day after day, he again was identifying, classifying, and striving to evaluate roles: all of which led, finally, to his recognition of a cast of inevitable stock characters that have played through all time, through the dreams and myths of all mankind, in ever-changing situations, confrontations, and costumes, yet, for all that, are as predictable in their company as the characters of a *Punch and Judy* stage.

These are the figures that he variously terms, "primordial images" and "archetypes of the unconscious." Like the Kantian *a priori* Forms of Sensibility (space and time), which condition all perception, and Categories of Logic (quantity, quality, relation, and modality), which precondition all thought, these Jungian "archetypes" are the *a priori* Forms of Mythic Fantasy. They "are not determined as regards their content," he states, "but only as regards their form, and then only to a very limited degree. A primordial image is determined as to its content only when it has become conscious and is therefore filled out with the material of conscious experience. Its form, however, . . . might perhaps be compared to the axial system of a crystal, which, as it were, preforms the crystalline structure in the mother liquid, although it has no material existence of its own. This first appears according to the specific way in which the ions and molecules aggregate. The archetype in itself is empty and purely formal, nothing but a *facultas praeformandi,* a possibility of representation which is given *a priori.* The representations themselves are not inherited, only the forms, and in that respect they correspond in every way to the instincts, which are also determined in form only."

Throughout the pages of Jung's long life-work the manifestations of those archetypes ever appear and reappear; and in his old age he summarized their roles in the tidy volume *Aion* (1951), where he treated also, at some length, of the Christ image as symbolized in the fish. I have chosen from that volume, for Selection 6, the chapters introducing four of Jung's company of archetypes; and have given also, from this period, his speculative essay "On Synchronicity" (1951), as well as, finally, his wonderful "Answer to Job" (1952).

After his wife's death in 1955, which smote him hard, Jung went to work on a new idea for the further building of his Tower, that is to say, of himself, signifying "an extension of consciousness achieved in old age." And he rounded out, as well, his thirty-year study of alchemy in his final masterwork, *Mysterium Coniunctionis,* where, as he states with satisfaction, "my psychology was at last given its place in reality and established upon its historical foundations. Thus my task was finished, my work done, and now it can stand."

Jung died, after a brief illness, at his home in Küsnacht Zurich, June 6, 1961.

# Chronology

Major publications are marked with asterisks. Numbers in brackets indicate sources of selections in this volume.

## 1. Boyhood and Student Years (1875–1900)

1875   Born in Kesswil (Thurgau Canton), Switzerland
1879   Family moves to Klein-Hüningen, near Basel
1881   Schooling commences, in Basel
1884   Birth of sister
1896   Death of father
1898   Investigations of occult phenomena
1900   Decides to become a psychiatrist

## 2. The Scholar Physician: First Period (1900–1907)

1900   Appointed Assistant Staff Physician, Burghölzli Mental Clinic, under Eugen Bleuler
1902   Studies theoretical psychopathology at the Salpêtrière, Paris, under Pierre Janet

Research experiments in word association, at Burghölzli

First publications:

    * On the Psychology and Pathology of So-Called Occult Phenomena (CW 1)

    A Case of Hysterical Stupor in a Prisoner in Detention (CW 1)

1903    Marries Emma Rauschenbach (1882–1955)
      *On Manic Mood Disorder (CW 1)*
      *On Simulated Insanity (CW 1)*
1904    *A Medical Opinion on a Case of Simulated Insanity (CW 1)*
      *On Hysterical Misreading (CW 1)*
      (With F. Riklin) *The Associations of Normal Subjects (CW 2)*
1905    Promoted to Senior Staff Physician, Burghölzli
      Appointed Lecturer in Psychiatry, University of Zurich.
      *Cryptomnesia (CW 1)*
      *On the Psychological Diagnosis of Facts (CW 1)*
      *An Analysis of the Associations of an Epileptic (CW 2)*
      *Reaction-Time in Association Experiments (CW 2)*
      *Experimental Observations on Memory (CW 2)*
      *Psychoanalysis and Association Experiments (CW 2)*
1906    First meeting with Freud, in Vienna
      *A Third and Final Opinion on Two Contradictory Diagnoses (CW 1)*
      *On the Determination of Facts by Psychological Means (CW 2)*
      *Association, Dream, and Hysterical Symptoms (CW 2)*
      *The Significance of Association Experiments for Psychopathology (CW 2)*
      * *The Psychology of Dementia Praecox (CW 3)*
      *Freud's Theory of Hysteria: A Reply to Aschaffenburg (CW 4)*
1907    *On Disturbances in Reproduction in Association Experiments (CW 2)*
      *On Psychophysical Relations of the Associative Experiment (CW 2)*
      (With F. Peterson) *Psychophysical Investigations with the Galvanometer and Pneumograph in Normal and Insane Individuals (CW 2)*

*3. The Scholar Physician: Second Period (1908–1912)*

1908    Attends First International Congress of Psycho-Analysis, Vienna

(With C. Ricksher) *Further Investigations on the Galvanic Phenomenon and Respiration in Normal and Insane Individuals* (*CW* 2)
*The Content of Psychoses* (*CW* 3)
*The Freudian Theory of Hysteria* (*CW* 4)

1909 Beginning of intense studies in mythology
Private practice flourishing; Resigns from Burghölzli post
Journey with Freud to U.S.A.; receives honorary degree, Clark University
*The Significance of the Father in the Destiny of the Individual* (*CW* 4)
*The Analysis of Dreams* (*CW* 4)

1910 Attends Second International Congress of Psycho-Analysis, Nuremberg; appointed Permanent President
*The Association Method* (*CW* 2)
*A Contribution to the Psychology of Rumour* (*CW* 4)
*On the Criticism of Psychoanalysis* (*CW* 4)
*Psychic Conflicts in a Child* (*CW* 17)

1911 *A Criticism of Bleuler's Theory of Schizophrenic Negativism* (*CW* 3)
*On the Significance of Number Dreams* (*CW* 4)
*Morton Prince, "Mechanism and Interpretation of Dreams: A Critical Review"* (*CW* 4)
\* *Symbols of Transformation*, Part I (*CW* 5)

1912 Dreams are summoning him to an inward awakening
*Concerning Psychoanalysis* (*CW* 4)
\* *Symbols of Transformation*, Part II (*CW* 5)
*New Paths in Psychology* (*CW* 7)

## 4. The Scholar Physician: Master Period (1913–1946)

1913 Break with Freud and Psychoanalytic School
Resigns Professorship, University of Zurich
Intense preoccupation with images of the unconscious
*The Theory of Psychoanalysis* (*CW* 4)
*General Aspects of Psychoanalysis* (*CW* 4)

1914 Resigns Presidency of International Congress of Psycho-Analysis
Outbreak of World War I

1933    Commences lecturing at Eidgenössische Technische Hochschule, Zurich

Becomes President, General Medical Society for Psychotherapy: Editorial, on becoming President, in *Zentralblatt für Psychotherapie und ihre Grenzgebiete* (Leipzig) VI: 3 (December 1933) (*CW* 10)

First Eranos Meeting, Ascona, Switzerland. Jung's paper:

> \* *A Study in the Process of Individuation* (*CW* 9.i)
> *The Real and the Surreal* (*CW* 8)
> *The Meaning of Psychology for Modern Man* (*CW* 10)
> *Brother Klaus* (*CW* 11)

1934    Founds and becomes first President of International General Medical Society for Psychotherapy

Second Eranos Meeting, Ascona. Jung's paper:

> \* *Archetypes of the Collective Unconscious* (*CW* 9.i)
> *A Review of the Complex Theory* (*CW* 8)
> *The Soul and Death* (*CW* 8)
> *The State of Psychotherapy Today* (*CW* 10)
> *Review of Keyserling's "La Revolution Mondiale"* (*CW* 10)
> *A Rejoinder to Dr. Bally* (*CW* 10)
> *Circular Letter on the Founding of the International General Medical Society for Psychotherapy* (*CW* 10)
> *The Practical Use of Dream Analysis* (*CW* 16)
> *The Development of the Personality* (*CW* 17)

1935    Third Eranos Meeting, Ascona. Jung's paper:

> \* *Dream Symbols of the Individuation Process* (revised as *Individual Dream Symbolism in Relation to Alchemy*, 1936: *CW* 12)
> Editorial in *Zentralblatt* VIII: 1; Editorial Note, ibid. VII: 2 (both in *CW 10*)
> Presidential Address, 8th General Medical Congress for Psychotherapy, Bad Nauheim (*CW* 10)
> *Contribution to a Discussion of Psychotherapy* (*CW* 10)
> *Psychological Commentary on "The Tibetan Book of the Dead"* (*CW* 11)
> *Principles of Practical Psychotherapy* (*CW* 16)

*What Is Psychotherapy* (*CW* 16)
*Analytical Psychology: Its Theory and Practice* (The Tavistock Lectures, London. Published New York: Pantheon Books; London: Routledge & Kegan Paul, 1968)

1936    Received honorary doctorate, Harvard University
Fourth Eranos Meeting, Ascona. Jung's paper:
* *Religious Ideas in Alchemy* (published as Part III of *Psychology and Alchemy: CW* 12)

[4]    *The Concept of the Collective Unconscious* (*CW* 9.i)
*Concerning the Archetypes, with Special Reference to the Anima Concept* (*CW* 9.i)
*Wotan* (*CW* 10)
*Yoga and the West* (*CW* 11)

[11]    * *Individual Dream Symbolism in Relation to Alchemy* (*CW* 12)

1937    Fifth Eranos Meeting, Ascona. Jung's paper:
*The Visions of Zosimus* (*CW* 13)
Seminars and lectures in U.S.A.
*Psychological Factors Determining Human Behavior* (*CW* 8)
*Presidential Address:* 9th International Medical Congress for Psychotherapy, Copenhagen (*CW* 10)
*The Realities of Practical Psychotherapy* (*CW* 16)

1938    Receives honorary doctorate, Oxford; becomes member, Royal Society of Medicine
Journey to India on invitation of British Government of India for 25th Anniversary of University of Calcutta
Sixth Eranos Meeting, Ascona. Jung's paper:
*Psychological Aspects of the Mother Archetype* (*CW* 9.i)
Presidential Address: 10th International Medical Congress for Psychotherapy, Oxford, 1938 (*CW* 10)
*Psychology and Religion* (The Terry Lectures, Yale University: *CW* 11)

1939    Outbreak of World War II
Appointed Editor, *Zentralblatt für Psychotherapie und ihre Grenzgebiete*
Seventh Eranos Meeting, Ascona. Jung's paper:
*Concerning Rebirth* (*CW* 9.i)
*Conscious, Unconscious, and Individuation* (*CW* 9.i)

> *The Dreamlike World of India* (*CW* 10)
> *What Can India Teach Us?* (*CW* 10)
>
> [13] *Psychological Commentary to "The Tibetan Book of the Great Liberation"* (*CW* 11)
> *Foreword to Suzuki's "Introduction to Zen Buddhism"* (*CW* 11)
> *In Memory of Sigmund Freud* (*CW* 15)
> *Richard Wilhelm: In Memoriam* (*CW* 15)

1940    Eighth Eranos Meeting, Ascona. Jung's paper:
> *A Psychological Approach to the Idea of the Trinity* (*CW* 11)
> *The Psychology of the Child Archetype* (*CW* 9.i)

1941    Ninth Eranos Meeting, Ascona. Jung's paper:
> *Transformation Symbol in the Mass* (*CW* 11)
> *The Psychological Aspects of Kore* (*CW* 9.i)
> *Paracelsus the Physician* (*CW* 15)

1942    Resigns post at Eidgenössische Technische Hochschule (1933–1942)
Tenth Eranos Meeting, Ascona. Jung's paper:
> *The Spirit Mercurius* (*CW* 13)
> *Paracelsus as a Spiritual Phenomenon* (*CW* 13)

1943    Becomes honorary member, Swiss Academy of Sciences
Eleventh Eranos Meeting, Ascona. Jung absent, illness
> *The Psychology of Eastern Meditation* (*CW* 11)
> *Psychotherapy and a Philosophy of Life* (*CW* 16)
> *The Gifted Child* (*CW* 17)

1944    Occupies Chair in Medical Psychology, founded for him at University of Basel; illness forces resignation the following year
Suffers broken foot; heart attack; had new series of visions
Twelfth Eranos Meeting, Ascona. Jung absent, illness
> *The Holy Men of India: Introduction to Heinrich Zimmer's "Der Weg zum Selbst"* (*CW* 11). Jung editor of this posthumous work
> * *Psychology and Alchemy* (*CW* 12). Based on two papers delivered at Eranos Meetings, 1935, 1936.

1945    Received honorary doctorate, University of Geneva (honoring seventieth birthday)
Thirteenth Eranos Meeting, Ascona. Jung's paper:

*The Phenomenology of the Spirit in Fairytales* (*CW* 9.i)
*On the Nature of Dreams* (*CW* 8)
*After the Catastrophe* (*CW* 10)
*The Philosophical Tree* (*CW* 13)
*Medicine and Psychotherapy* (*CW* 16)
*Psychology Today* (*CW* 16)

1946   Fourteenth Eranos Meeting, Ascona. Jung's paper:
*The Spirit of Psychology* (published, enlarged, under new title: *On the Nature of the Psyche: CW* 8)
*Preface and Epilogue to "Essays on Contemporary Events"* (*CW* 10)
*The Fight with the Shadow* (*CW* 10)
\* *The Psychology of the Transference* (*CW* 16)

## 5. Retirement and Old Age (*1947–1961*)

1947   Retirement to Bollingen Tower
Fifteenth Eranos Meeting, Ascona. Jung absent
1948   Sixteenth Eranos Meeting, Ascona. Jung's paper:
*On the Self* (later incorporated as Chap. IV, *CW* 9.ii)
Reworking of many earlier papers
1949   Seventeenth Eranos Meeting, Ascona. Jung absent
1950   Eighteenth Eranos Meeting, Ascona. Jung absent
Reworking of earlier papers
*Concerning Mandala Symbolism* (*CW* 9.i)
*Foreword to "I Ching"* (*CW* 11)
1951   Nineteenth Eranos Meeting, Ascona.[1] Jung's paper:
[14]   *On Synchronicity* (*CW* 8)
[6]   \* *Aion: Researches into the Phenomenology of the Self* (*CW* 9.ii)
*Prefatory Note to English Edition of Psychology and Alchemy* (*CW* 12)
*Fundamental Questions of Psychotherapy* (*CW* 16)
1952   *Synchronicity: An Acausal Connecting Principle* (*CW* 8)

[1] Eranos Meetings have continued to the present. Jung's participation ceased in 1951.

Foreword to White's *"God and the Unconscious"*
(*CW* 11)
Foreword to Werblowsky's *"Lucifer and Prometheus"*
(*CW* 11)
[15] * *Answer to Job* (*CW* 11)

1953    Foreword to John Weir Perry's *"The Self in Psychotic Process. Its Symbolization in Schizophrenia"* (Berkeley and Los Angeles: University of California Press; London: Cambridge University Press)

1954    Reworking of earlier papers
*On the Psychology of the Trickster Figure* (*CW* 9.i)

1955    Death of Emma Rauschenbach Jung
Receives honorary doctorate, Eidgenössische Technische Hochschule, Zurich (honoring eightieth birthday)
Culmination and conclusion of alchemical studies
*Mandalas* (*CW* 9.i)
* *Mysterium Coniunctionis* (*CW* 14)

1956    *Why and How I Wrote My "Answer to Job"* (*CW* 11)

1957    Conversation with John M. Billinsky, quoted above, pp. *xvi–xvii*
*The Undiscovered Self* (*Present and Future*) (*CW* 10)

1958    Work on autobiographical *Memories, Dreams, Reflections*
*Flying Saucers: A Modern Myth* (*CW* 10)
*A Psychological View of Conscience* (*CW* 10)

1959    *Good and Evil in Analytical Psychology* (*CW* 10)
*Introduction to Wolff's "Studies in Jungian Psychology"* (*CW* 10)

1960    Foreword to Miguel Serrano's *"The Visits of the Queen of Sheba"* (Bombay and London: Asia Publishing House)

1961    Death, after brief illness, June 6, at his home in Küsnacht, Zurich

# Part I

# ❧ 1 ❧

## The Stages of Life[1]

To discuss the problems connected with the stages of human development is an exacting task, for it means nothing less than unfolding a picture of psychic life in its entirety from the cradle to the grave. Within the framework of a lecture such a task can be carried out only on the broadest lines, and it must be well understood that no attempt will be made to describe the normal psychic occurrences within the various stages. We shall restrict ourselves, rather, to certain "problems," that is, to things that are difficult, questionable, or ambiguous; in a word, to questions which allow of more than one answer—and, moreover, answers that are always open to doubt. For this reason there will be much to which we must add a question-mark in our thoughts. Worse still, there will be some things we must accept on faith, while now and then we must even indulge in speculations.

[1] From *The Structure and Dynamics of the Psyche. Collected Works*, Vol. 8, pars. 749–795. [Originally published as "Die seelischen Probleme der menschlichen Alterstufen," *Neue Zürcher Zeitung*, March 14 and 16, 1930. Revised and largely rewritten, it was republished as "Die Lebenswende," *Seelenprobleme der Gegenwart* (Psychologische Abhandlunger, III; Zurich, 1931), which version was translated by W. S. Dell and Cary F. Baynes as "The Stages of Life," *Modern Man in Search of a Soul* (London and New York, 1933). The present translation by R. F. C. Hull is based on this.—EDITORS OF *The Collected Works*.]

If psychic life consisted only of self-evident matters of fact—which on a primitive level is still the case—we could content ourselves with a sturdy empiricism. The psychic life of civilized man, however, is full of problems; we cannot even think of it except in terms of problems. Our psychic processes are made up to a large extent of reflections, doubts, experiments, all of which are almost completely foreign to the unconscious, instinctive mind of primitive man. It is the growth of consciousness which we must thank for the existence of problems; they are the Danaän gift of civilization. It is just man's turning away from instinct—his opposing himself to instinct—that creates consciousness. Instinct is nature and seeks to perpetuate nature, whereas consciousness can only seek culture or its denial. Even when we turn back to nature, inspired by a Rousseauesque longing, we "cultivate" nature. As long as we are still submerged in nature we are unconscious, and we live in the security of instinct which knows no problems. Everything in us that still belongs to nature shrinks away from a problem, for its name is doubt, and wherever doubt holds sway there is uncertainty and the possibility of divergent ways. And where several ways seem possible, there we have turned away from the certain guidance of instinct and are handed over to fear. For consciousness is now called upon to do that which nature has always done for her children—namely, to give a certain, unquestionable, and unequivocal decision. And here we are beset by an all-too-human fear that consciousness—our Promethean conquest—may in the end not be able to serve us as well as nature.

Problems thus draw us into an orphaned and isolated state where we are abandoned by nature and are driven to consciousness. There is no other way open to us; we are forced to resort to conscious decisions and solutions where formerly we trusted ourselves to natural happenings. Every problem, therefore, brings the possibility of a widening of consciousness, but also the necessity of saying goodbye to childlike unconsciousness and trust in nature. This necessity is a psychic fact of such importance that it constitutes one of the most essential symbolic teachings of the Christian religion. It is the sacrifice of the merely natural man, of the unconscious, ingenuous being whose tragic career began with the eating of the apple in Paradise. The biblical fall of man presents the dawn of consciousness as a curse. And as a matter of fact it is in this light that we first look upon every problem that forces us to greater consciousness and separates us even further from the paradise of unconscious childhood. Every one of us gladly turns away from his problems; if possible, they must not be mentioned, or, better still, their existence is denied. We wish to make our lives simple, certain, and smooth, and for that reason problems are taboo. We want to have certainties and no doubts—results and no experiments—without even seeing that certainties can arise only through doubt and results only through experiment. The artful denial of a problem will not produce conviction; on the contrary, a wider and higher consciousness is required to give us the certainty and clarity we need.

This introduction, long as it is, seemed to me necessary in order to make clear the nature of our subject. When we must deal with problems, we instinctively resist trying the way that leads through obscurity and darkness. We wish to hear only of unequivocal results, and completely forget that these results can only be brought about when we have ventured into and emerged again from the darkness. But to penetrate the darkness we must summon all the powers of enlightenment that consciousness can offer; as I have already said, we must even indulge in speculations. For in treating the problems of psychic life we perpetually stumble upon questions of principle belonging to the private domains of the most heterogeneous branches of knowledge. We disturb and anger the theologian no less than the philosopher, the physician no less than the educator; we even grope about in the field of the biologist and of the historian. This extravagant behaviour is due not to arrogance but to the circumstance that man's psyche is a unique combination of factors which are at the same time the special subjects of far-reaching lines of research. For it is out of himself and out of his peculiar constitution that man has produced his sciences. They are *symptoms* of his psyche.

If, therefore, we ask ourselves the unavoidable question, "Why does man, in obvious contrast to the animal world, have problems at all?" we run into that inextricable tangle of thoughts which many thousands of incisive minds have woven in the course of the centuries. I shall not perform the labours of a Sisyphus upon this masterpiece of confusion, but will try to present quite simply my contribution toward man's attempt to answer this basic question.

There are no problems without consciousness. We must therefore put the question in another way and ask, "How does consciousness arise in the first place?" Nobody can say with certainty; but we can observe small children in the process of becoming conscious. Every parent can see it if he pays attention. And what we see is this: when the child recognizes someone or something—when he "knows" a person or a thing—then we feel that the child has consciousness. That, no doubt, is also why in Paradise it was the tree of knowledge which bore such fateful fruit.

But what is recognition or "knowledge" in this sense? We speak of "knowing" something when we succeed in linking a new perception to an already existing context, in such a way that we hold in consciousness not only the perception but parts of this context as well. "Knowing" is based, therefore, upon the perceived connection between psychic contents. We can have no knowledge of a content that is not connected with anything, and we cannot even be conscious of it should our consciousness still be on this low initial level. Accordingly the first stage of consciousness which we can observe consists in the mere connection between two or more psychic contents. At this level, consciousness is merely sporadic, being limited to the perception of a few connections, and the content is not remembered later on. It is a fact that in the early years of life there is no continuous memory; at most there are islands of consciousness which are like single lamps or lighted objects in the far-flung darkness. But these islands of memory are not the same as those earliest connections which are merely perceived; they contain a new, very important series of contents belonging to the perceiving subject himself, the so-called ego. This series, like the initial series of contents, is at first merely perceived, and for this reason the child logically begins by speaking of itself objectively, in the third person. Only later, when the ego-contents—the so-called ego-complex—have acquired an energy of their own (very likely as a result of training and practice) does the feeling of subjectivity or "I-ness" arise. This may well be the moment when the child begins to speak of itself in the first person. The continuity of memory probably begins at this stage. Essentially, therefore, it would be a continuity of ego-memories.

In the childish stage of consciousness there are as yet no problems; nothing depends upon the subject, for the child itself is still wholly dependent on its parents. It is as though it were not yet completely born, but were still enclosed in the psychic atmosphere of its parents. Psychic birth, and with it the conscious differentiation from the parents, normally takes place only at puberty, with the eruption of sexuality. The physiological change is attended by a psychic revolution. For the various bodily manifestations give such an emphasis to the ego that it often asserts itself without stint or moderation. This is sometimes called "the unbearable age."

Until this period is reached the psychic life of the individual is governed largely by instinct, and few or no problems arise. Even when external limitations oppose his subjective impulses, these restraints do not put the individual at variance with himself. He submits to them or cir-

cumvents them, remaining quite at one with himself. He
does not yet know the state of inner tension induced by
a problem. This state only arises when what was an external limitation becomes an inner one; when one impulse
is opposed by another. In psychological language we would
say: the problematical state, the inner division with oneself, arises when, side by side with the series of ego-contents, a second series of equal intensity comes into being.
This second series, because of its energy value, has a functional significance equal to that of the ego-complex; we
might call it another, second ego which can on occasion
even wrest the leadership from the first. This produces the
division with oneself, the state that betokens a problem.

To recapitulate what we have said: the first stage of
consciousness, consisting in merely recognizing or "knowing," is an anarchic or chaotic state. The second, that of
the developed ego-complex, is monarchic or monistic. The
third brings another step forward in consciousness, and
consists in an awareness of the divided, or dualistic, state.

And here we come to our real theme—the problem of
the stages of life. First of all we must deal with the period
of youth. It extends roughly from the years just after puberty to middle life, which itself begins between the thirty-
fifth and fortieth year.

I might well be asked why I begin with the second stage,
as though there were no problems connected with childhood. The complex psychic life of the child is, of course,
a problem of the first magnitude to parents, educators, and
doctors, but when normal the child has no real problems of
its own. It is only the adult human being who can have
doubts about himself and be at variance with himself.

We are all familiar with the sources of the problems
that arise in the period of youth. For most people it is the
demands of life which harshly put an end to the dream of
childhood. If the individual is sufficiently well prepared,
the transition to a profession or career can take place
smoothly. But if he clings to illusions that are contrary to

reality, then problems will surely arise. No one can take the step into life without making certain assumptions, and occasionally these assumptions are false—that is, they do not fit the conditions into which one is thrown. Often it is a question of exaggerated expectations, underestimation of difficulties, unjustified optimism, or a negative attitude. One could compile quite a list of the false assumptions that give rise to the first conscious problems.

But it is not always the contradiction between subjective assumptions and external facts that gives rise to problems; it may just as often be inner, psychic difficulties. They may exist even when things run smoothly in the outside world. Very often it is the disturbance of psychic equilibrium caused by the sexual instinct; equally often it is the feeling of inferiority which springs from an unbearable sensitivity. These inner conflicts may exist even when adaptation to the outer world has been achieved without apparent effort. It even seems as if young people who have had a hard struggle for existence are spared inner problems, while those who for some reason or other have no difficulty with adaptation run into problems of sex or conflicts arising from a sense of inferiority.

People whose own temperaments offer problems are often neurotic, but it would be a serious misunderstanding to confuse the existence of problems with neurosis. There is a marked difference between the two in that the neurotic is ill because he is unconscious of his problems, while the person with a difficult temperament suffers from his conscious problems without being ill.

If we try to extract the common and essential factors from the almost inexhaustible variety of individual problems found in the period of youth, we meet in all cases with one particular feature: a more or less patent clinging to the childhood level of consciousness, a resistance to the fateful forces in and around us which would involve us in the world. Something in us wishes to remain a child, to be unconscious or, at most, conscious only of the ego; to reject everything strange, or else subject it to our will; to do nothing, or else indulge our own craving for pleasure or power. In all this there is something of the inertia of matter; it is a persistence in the previous state whose range of consciousness is smaller, narrower, and more egoistic than that of the dualistic phase. For here the individual is faced with the necessity of recognizing and accepting what is different and strange as a part of his own life, as a kind of "also-I."

The essential feature of the dualistic phase is the widening of the horizon of life, and it is this that is so vigorously resisted. To be sure, this expansion—or diastole, as Goethe called it—had started long before this. It begins at birth, when the child abandons the narrow confinement of the mother's body; and from then on it steadily increases until it reaches a climax in the problematical state, when the individual begins to struggle against it.

What would happen to him if he simply changed himself into that foreign-seeming "also-I" and allowed the earlier ego to vanish into the past? We might suppose this to be a quite practical course. The very aim of religious education, from the exhortation to put off the old Adam right back to the rebirth rituals of primitive races, is to transform the human being into the new, future man, and to allow the old to die away.

Psychology teaches us that, in a certain sense, there is nothing in the psyche that is old; nothing that can really, finally die away. Even Paul was left with a thorn in the flesh. Whoever protects himself against what is new and strange and regresses to the past falls into the same neurotic condition as the man who identifies himself with the new and runs away from the past. The only difference is that the one has estranged himself from the past and the other from the future. In principle both are doing the same thing: they are reinforcing their narrow range of consciousness instead of shattering it in the tension of opposites and building up a state of wider and higher consciousness.

This outcome would be ideal if it could be brought about in the second stage of life—but there's the rub. For one thing, nature cares nothing whatsoever about a higher level of consciousness; quite the contrary. And then society does not value these feats of the psyche very highly; its prizes are always given for achievement and not for personality, the latter being rewarded for the most part posthumously. These facts compel us towards a particular solution: we are forced to limit ourselves to the attainable, and to differentiate particular aptitudes in which the socially effective individual discovers his true self.

Achievement, usefulness and so forth are the ideals that seem to point the way out of the confusions of the problematical state. They are the lodestars that guide us in the adventure of broadening and consolidating our physical existence; they help us to strike our roots in the world, but they cannot guide us in the development of that wider consciousness to which we give the name of culture. In the period of youth, however, this course is the normal one and in all circumstances preferable to merely tossing about in a welter of problems.

The dilemma is often solved, therefore, in this way: whatever is given to us by the past is adapted to the possibilities and demands of the future. We limit ourselves to the attainable, and this means renouncing all our other psychic potentialities. One man loses a valuable piece of his past, another a valuable piece of his future. Everyone can call to mind friends or schoolmates who were promising and idealistic youngsters, but who, when we meet them again years later, seem to have grown dry and cramped in a narrow mould. These are examples of the solution mentioned above.

The serious problems in life, however, are never fully solved. If ever they should appear to be so it is a sure sign that something has been lost. The meaning and purpose of a problem seem to lie not in its solution but in our working at it incessantly. This alone preserves us from stultification and petrifaction. So also the solution 'of the problems of youth by restricting ourselves to the attainable is only temporarily valid and not lasting in a deeper sense. Of course, to win for oneself a place in society and to transform one's nature so that it is more or less fitted to this kind of existence is in all cases a considerable achievement. It is a fight waged within oneself as well as outside, comparable to the struggle of the child for an ego. That struggle is for the most part unobserved because it happens in the dark; but when we see how stubbornly childish illusions and assumptions and egoistic habits are still clung to in later years we can gain some idea of the energies that were needed to form them. And so it is with the ideals, convictions, guiding ideas and attitudes which in the period of youth lead us out into life, for which we struggle, suffer, and win victories: they grow together with our own being, we apparently change into them, we seek to perpetuate them indefinitely and as a matter of course, just as the young person asserts his ego in spite of the world and often in spite of himself.

The nearer we approach to the middle of life, and the better we have succeeded in entrenching ourselves in our personal attitudes and social positions, the more it appears as if we had discovered the right course and the right ideals and principles of behaviour. For this reason we suppose them to be eternally valid, and make a virtue of unchangeably clinging to them. We overlook the essential fact that the social goal is attained only at the cost of a diminution of personality. Many—far too many—aspects of life which should also have been experienced lie in the lumber-room among dusty memories; but sometimes, too, they are glowing coals under grey ashes.

Statistics show a rise in the frequency of mental depressions in men about forty. In women the neurotic difficulties generally begin somewhat earlier. We see that in this phase of life—between thirty-five and forty—an important change in the human psyche is in preparation. At first it is not a conscious and striking change; it is rather a matter of indirect signs of a change which seems to take its rise in the unconscious. Often it is something like a slow change in a person's character; in another case certain traits may come to light which had disappeared since childhood; or again, one's previous inclinations and interests begin to weaken and others take their place. Conversely—and this happens very frequently—one's cherished convictions and principles, especially the moral ones, begin to harden and to grow increasingly rigid until, somewhere around the age of fifty, a period of intolerance and fanaticism is reached. It is as if the existence of these principles were endangered and it were therefore necessary to emphasize them all the more.

The wine of youth does not always clear with advancing years; sometimes it grows turbid. All the phenomena mentioned above can best be seen in rather one-sided people, turning up sometimes sooner and sometimes later. Their appearance, it seems to me, is often delayed by the fact that the parents of the person in question are still alive. It is then as if the period of youth were being unduly drawn out. I have seen this especially in the case of men whose fathers were long-lived. The death of the father then has the effect of a precipitate and almost catastrophic ripening.

I know of a pious man who was a churchwarden and who, from the age of forty onward, showed a growing and finally unbearable intolerance in matters of morality and religion. At the same time his moods grew visibly worse. At last he was nothing more than a darkly lowering pillar of the Church. In this way he got along until the age of fifty-five, when suddenly, sitting up in bed in the middle of the night, he said to his wife: "Now at last I've got it! I'm just a plain rascal." Nor did this realization remain without results. He spent his declining years in riotous living and squandered a goodly part of his fortune. Obviously quite a likable fellow, capable of both extremes!

The very frequent neurotic disturbances of adult years all have one thing in common: they want to carry the psychology of the youthful phase over the threshold of the so-called years of discretion. Who does not know those touching old gentlemen who must always warm up the dish of their student days, who can fan the flame of life only by reminiscences of their heroic youth, but who, for the rest, are stuck in a hopelessly wooden Philistinism? As a rule, to be sure, they have this one merit which it would be wrong to undervalue: they are not neurotic, but only boring and stereotyped. The neurotic is rather a person who can never have things as he would like them in the present, and who can therefore never enjoy the past either.

As formerly the neurotic could not escape from childhood, so now he cannot part with his youth. He shrinks from the grey thoughts of approaching age, and, feeling the prospect before him unbearable, is always straining to look behind him. Just as the childish person shrinks back from the unknown in the world and in human existence, so the grown man shrinks back from the second half of life. It is as if unknown and dangerous tasks awaited him, or as if he were threatened with sacrifices and losses which he does not wish to accept, or as if his life up to now seemed to him so fair and precious that he could not relinquish it.

Is it perhaps at bottom the fear of death? That does not seem to me very probable, because as a rule death is still far in the distance and therefore somewhat abstract. Experience shows us, rather, that the basic cause of all the difficulties of this transition is to be found in a deep-seated and peculiar change within the psyche. In order to characterize it I must take for comparison the daily course of the sun—but a sun that is endowed with human feeling and man's limited consciousness. In the morning it rises from the nocturnal sea of unconsciousness and looks upon the wide, bright world which lies before it in an expanse that steadily widens the higher it climbs in the firmament. In this extension of its field of action caused by its own rising, the sun will discover its significance; it will see the attainment of the greatest possible height, and the widest possible dissemination of its blessings, as its goal. In this conviction the sun pursues its course to the unforeseen zenith—unforeseen, because its career is unique and individual, and the culminating point could not be calculated in advance. At the stroke of noon the descent begins. And the descent means the reversal of all the ideals and values that were cherished in the morning. The sun falls into contradiction with itself. It is as though it should draw in its rays instead of emitting them. Light and warmth decline and are at last extinguished.

All comparisons are lame, but this simile is at least not lamer than others. A French aphorism sums it up with cynical resignation: *Si jeunesse savait, si vieillesse pouvait.*

Fortunately we are not rising and setting suns, for then it would fare badly with our cultural values. But there is something sunlike within us, and to speak of the morning and spring, of the evening and autumn of life is not mere sentimental jargon. We thus give expression to psychological truths and, even more, to physiological facts, for the reversal of the sun at noon changes even bodily characteristics. Especially among southern races one can observe that older women develop deep, rough voices, incipient moustaches, rather hard features and other masculine traits. On the other hand the masculine physique is toned down by feminine features, such as adiposity and softer facial expressions.

There is an interesting report in the ethnological literature about an Indian warrior chief to whom in middle life the Great Spirit appeared in a dream. The spirit announced to him that from then on he must sit among the women and children, wear women's clothes, and eat the food of women. He obeyed the dream without suffering a loss of prestige. This vision is a true expression of the psychic revolution of life's noon, of the beginning of life's decline. Man's values, and even his body, do tend to change into their opposites.

We might compare masculinity and femininity and their psychic components to a definite store of substances of which, in the first half of life, unequal use is made. A man consumes his large supply of masculine substance and has left over only the smaller amount of feminine substance, which must now be put to use. Conversely, the woman allows her hitherto unused supply of masculinity to become active.

This change is even more noticeable in the psychic realm than in the physical. How often it happens that a man of forty-five or fifty winds up his business, and the wife then dons the trousers and opens a little shop where he perhaps performs the duties of a handyman. There are many women who only awaken to social responsibility and to social consciousness after their fortieth year. In modern business life, especially in America, nervous breakdowns in the forties are a very common occurrence. If one examines the victims one finds that what has broken down is the masculine style of life which held the field up to now, and that what is left over is an effeminate man. Contrariwise, one can observe women in these selfsame business spheres who have developed in the second half of life an uncommonly masculine tough-mindedness which thrusts the feelings and the heart aside. Very often these changes are accompanied by all sorts of catastrophes in marriage, for it is not hard to imagine what will happen when the husband discovers his tender feelings and the wife her sharpness of mind.

The worst of it all is that intelligent and cultivated people live their lives without even knowing of the possibility of such transformations. Wholly unprepared, they embark upon the second half of life. Or are there perhaps colleges for forty-year-olds which prepare them for their coming life and its demands as the ordinary colleges introduce our young people to a knowledge of the world? No, thoroughly unprepared we take the step into the afternoon of life; worse still, we take this step with the false assumption that our truths and ideals will serve us as hitherto. But we cannot live the afternoon of life according to the programme of life's morning; for what was great in the morning will be little at evening, and what in the morning was true will at evening have become a lie. I have given psychological treatment to too many people of advancing years, and have looked too often into the secret chambers of their souls, not to be moved by this fundamental truth.

Ageing people should know that their lives are not mounting and expanding, but that an inexorable inner process enforces the contraction of life. For a young person it is almost a sin, or at least a danger, to be too preoccupied with himself; but for the ageing person it is a duty and a necessity to devote serious attention to himself. After having lavished its light upon the world, the sun withdraws its rays in order to illuminate itself. Instead of doing likewise, many old people prefer to be hypochondriacs, niggards, pedants, applauders of the past or else eternal adolescents—all lamentable substitutes for the illumination of the self, but inevitable consequences of the delusion that the second half of life must be governed by the principles of the first.

I said just now that we have no schools for forty-year-olds. That is not quite true. Our religions were always such schools in the past, but how many people regard them as such today? How many of us older ones have been brought up in such a school and really prepared for the second half of life, for old age, death and eternity?

A human being would certainly not grow to be seventy or eighty years old if this longevity had no meaning for the species. The afternoon of human life must also have a significance of its own and cannot be merely a pitiful appendage to life's morning. The significance of the morning undoubtedly lies in the development of the individual, our entrenchment in the outer world, the propagation of our kind, and the care of our children. This is the obvious purpose of nature. But when this purpose has been attained —and more than attained—shall the earning of money, the extension of conquests, and the expansion of life go steadily on beyond the bounds of all reason and sense? Whoever carries over into the afternoon the law of the morning, or the natural aim, must pay for it with damage to his soul, just as surely as a growing youth who tries to carry over his childish egoism into adult life must pay for this mistake with social failure. Money-making, social achievement, family and posterity are nothing but plain nature, not culture. Culture lies outside the purpose of nature. Could by any chance culture be the meaning and purpose of the second half of life?

In primitive tribes we observe that the old people are almost always the guardians of the mysteries and the laws, and it is in these that the cultural heritage of the tribe is expressed. How does the matter stand with us? Where is the wisdom of our old people, where are their precious secrets and their visions? For the most part our old people try to compete with the young. In the United States it is almost an ideal for a father to be the brother of his sons, and for the mother to be if possible the younger sister of her daughter.

I do not know how much of this confusion is a reaction against an earlier exaggeration of the dignity of age, and how much is to be charged to false ideals. These undoubtedly exist, and the goal of those who hold them lies behind, and not ahead. Therefore they are always striving to turn back. We have to grant these people that it is hard to see what other goal the second half of life can offer than the well-known aims of the first. Expansion of life, usefulness, efficiency, the cutting of a figure in society, the shrewd steering of offspring into suitable marriages and good positions—are not these purposes enough? Unfortunately not enough meaning and purpose for those who see in the approach of old age a mere diminution of life and can feel their earlier ideals only as something faded and worn out. Of course, if these persons had filled up the beaker of life earlier and emptied it to the lees, they would feel quite differently about everything now; they would have kept nothing back, everything that wanted to catch fire would have been consumed, and the quiet of old age would be very welcome to them. But we must not forget that only a very few people are artists in life; that the art of life is the most distinguished and rarest of all the arts. Who ever succeeded in draining the whole cup with grace? So for many people all too much unlived life remains over—sometimes potentialities which they could never have lived with the best of wills, so that they approach the threshold of old age with unsatisfied demands which inevitably turn their glances backwards.

It is particularly fatal for such people to look back. For them a prospect and a goal in the future are absolutely necessary. That is why all great religions hold out the promise of a life beyond, of a supramundane goal which makes it possible for mortal man to live the second half of life with as much purpose and aim as the first. For the man of today the expansion of life and its culmination are plausible goals, but the idea of life after death seems to him questionable or beyond belief. Life's cessation, that is, death, can only be accepted as a reasonable goal either when existence is so wretched that we are only too glad for it to end, or when we are convinced that the sun strives to its setting "to illuminate distant races" with the same logical consistency it showed in rising to the zenith. But to believe has become such a difficult art today that it is beyond the capacity of most people, particularly the educated part of humanity. They have become too accustomed to the thought that, with regard to immortality and such questions, there are innumerable contradictory opinions and no convincing proofs. And since "science" is the catchword that seems to carry the weight of absolute conviction in the contemporary world, we ask for "scientific" proofs. But educated people who can think know very well that proof of this kind is a philosophical impossibility. We simply cannot know anything whatever about such things.

May I remark that for the same reasons we cannot know, either, whether something *does* happen to a person after death? No answer of any kind is permissible, either for or against. We simply have no definite scientific knowledge about it one way or the other, and are therefore in the same position as when we ask whether the planet Mars is inhabited or not. And the inhabitants of Mars, if there are any, are certainly not concerned whether we affirm or deny their existence. They may exist or they may not. And that is how it stands with so-called immortality—with which we may shelve the problem.

But here my medical conscience awakens and urges me to say a word which has an important bearing on this question. I have observed that a life directed to an aim is in general better, richer, and healthier than an aimless one, and that it is better to go forwards with the stream of time than backwards against it. To the psychotherapist an old man who cannot bid farewell to life appears as feeble and sickly as a young man who is unable to embrace it. And as a matter of fact, it is in many cases a question of the selfsame childish greediness, the same fear, the same defiance and wilfulness, in the one as in the other. As a doctor I am convinced that it is hygienic—if I may use the word—to discover in death a goal towards which one can strive, and that shrinking away from it is something unhealthy and abnormal which robs the second half of life of its purpose. I therefore consider that all religions with a supramundane goal are eminently reasonable from the point of view of psychic hygiene. When I live in a house which I know will fall about my head within the next two weeks, all my vital functions will be impaired by this thought; but if on the contrary I feel myself to be safe, I can dwell there in a normal and comfortable way. From the standpoint of psychotherapy it would therefore be desirable to think of death as only a transition, as part of a life process whose extent and duration are beyond our knowledge.

In spite of the fact that the majority of people do not know why the body needs salt, everyone demands it nonetheless because of an instinctive need. It is the same with the things of the psyche. By far the greater portion of mankind have from time immemorial felt the need of believing in a continuance of life. The demands of therapy, therefore, do not lead us into any bypaths but down the middle of the highway trodden by humanity. For this reason we are thinking correctly, and in harmony with life, even though we do not understand what we think.

Do we ever understand what we think? We only understand that kind of thinking which is a mere equation, from which nothing comes out but what we have put in. That is the working of the intellect. But besides that there is a thinking in primordial images, in symbols which are older than the historical man, which are inborn in him from the earliest times, and, eternally living, outlasting all generations, still make up the groundwork of the human psyche. It is only possible to live the fullest life when we are in harmony with these symbols; wisdom is a return to them. It is a question neither of belief nor of knowledge, but of the agreement of our thinking with the primordial images of the unconscious. They are the unthinkable matrices of all our thoughts, no matter what our conscious mind may cogitate. One of these primordial thoughts is the idea of life after death. Science and these primordial images are incommensurables. They are irrational data, *a priori* conditions of the imagination which are simply there, and whose purpose and justification science can only investigate *a posteriori*, much as it investigates a function like that of the thyroid gland. Before the nineteenth century the thyroid was regarded as a meaningless organ merely because it was not understood.

It would be equally shortsighted of us today to call the primordial images senseless. For me these images are something like psychic organs, and I treat them with the very greatest respect. It happens sometimes that I must say to an older patient: "Your picture of God or your idea of immortality is atrophied, consequently your psychic metabolism is out of gear." The ancient *athanasias pharmakon,* the medicine of immortality, is more profound and meaningful than we supposed.

In conclusion I would like to come back for a moment to the comparison with the sun. The one hundred and eighty degrees of the arc of life are divisible into four parts. The first quarter, lying to the east, is childhood, that state in which we are a problem for others but are not yet conscious of any problems of our own. Conscious problems fill out the second and third quarters; while in the last, in extreme old age, we descend again into that condition where, regardless of our state of consciousness, we once more become something of a problem for others. Childhood and extreme old age are, of course, utterly different, and yet they have one thing in common: submersion in unconscious psychic happenings. Since the mind of a child grows out of the unconscious its psychic processes, though not easily accessible, are not as difficult to discern as those of a very old person who is sinking again into the unconscious, and who progressively vanishes within it. Childhood and old age are the stages of life without any conscious problems, for which reason I have not taken them into consideration here.

# ❧ 2 ❧

## The Structure of
## the Psyche[1]

The psyche, as a reflection of the world and man, is a thing of such infinite complexity that it can be observed and studied from a great many sides. It faces us with the same problem that the world does: because a systematic study of the world is beyond our powers, we have to content ourselves with mere rules of thumb and with aspects that particularly interest us. Everyone makes for himself his own segment of world and constructs his own private system, often with air-tight compartments, so that after a time it seems to him that he has grasped the meaning and structure of the whole. But the finite will never be able to

[1] From *The Structure and Dynamics of the Psyche. Collected Works,* Vol. 8, pars. 283–342. [Originally published as part of "Die Erdbedingtheit der Psyche," in the symposium *Mensch und Erde,* edited by Count Hermann Keyserling (Darmstadt, 1927). (The other part became the essay "Seele und Erde," which is now published as "Mind and Earth" in Vol. 10 of the *Collected Works.*) The present work, constituting about the first half of the 1927 publication, was published as "Die Struktur der Seele," *Europäische Revue* (Berlin), IV (1928), 1 and 2. It was later revised and expanded in *Seelenprobleme der Gegenwart* (Psychologische Abhandlungen, III; Zurich, 1931), and this version is translated here.—EDITORS OF *The Collected Works.*]

grasp the infinite. Although the world of psychic phenomena is only a part of the world as a whole, it may seem
easier to grasp precisely for that reason. But one would
be forgetting that the psyche is the only phenomenon that
is given to us immediately and, therefore, is the *sine qua
non* of all experience.

The only things we experience immediately are the contents of consciousness. In saying this I am not attempting
to reduce the "world" to our "idea" of it. What I am
trying to emphasize could be expressed from another point
of view by saying: Life is a function of the carbon atom.
This analogy reveals the limitations of the specialist point
of view, to which I succumb as soon as I attempt to say
anything explanatory about the world, or even a part of it.

My point of view is naturally a psychological one, and
moreover that of a practising psychologist whose task it is
to find the quickest road through the chaotic muddle of
complicated psychic states. This view must needs be very
different from that of the psychologist who can study an
isolated psychic process at his leisure, in the quiet of his
laboratory. The difference is roughly that between a surgeon
and an histologist. I also differ from the metaphysician,
who feels he has to say how things are "in themselves," and
whether they are absolute or not. My subject lies wholly
within the bounds of experience.

My prime need is to grasp complicated conditions and be
able to talk about them. I must be able to differentiate
between various groups of psychic facts. The distinctions
so made must not be arbitrary, since I have to reach an
understanding with my patient. I therefore have to rely on
simple schemata which on the one hand satisfactorily reflect
the empirical facts, and on the other hand link up with
what is generally known and so finds acceptance.

If we now set out to classify the contents of consciousness, we shall begin, according to tradition, with the prop-
osition: *Nihil est in intellectu quod non antea fuerit in
sensu.*

Consciousness seems to stream into us from outside in the form of *sense-perceptions*. We see, hear, taste, and smell the world, and so are conscious of the world. Sense-perceptions tell us that something *is*. But they do not tell us *what* it is. This is told us not by the process of perception but by the process of *apperception,* and this has a highly complex structure. Not that sense-perception is anything simple; only, its complex nature is not so much psychic as physiological. The complexity of apperception, on the other hand, is psychic. We can detect in it the co-operation of a number of psychic processes. Supposing we hear a noise whose nature seems to us unknown. After a while it becomes clear to us that the peculiar noise must come from air-bubbles rising in the pipes of the central heating: we have *recognized* the noise. This recognition derives from a process which we call thinking. Thinking tells us *what* a thing is.

I have just called the noise "peculiar." When I characterize something as "peculiar," I am referring to the special *feeling-tone* which that thing has. The feeling-tone implies an *evaluation*.

The *process of recognition* can be conceived in essence as comparison and differentiation with the help of memory. When I see a fire, for instance, the light-stimulus conveys to me the idea "fire." As there are countless memory-images of fire lying ready in my memory, these images enter into combination with the fire-image I have just received, and the process of comparing it with and differentiating it from these memory-images produces the recognition; that is to say, I finally establish in my mind the peculiarity of this particular image. In ordinary speech this process is called *thinking*.

The *process of evaluation* is different. The fire I see arouses emotional reactions of a pleasant or unpleasant nature, and the memory-images thus stimulated bring with them concomitant emotional phenomena which are known as *feeling-tones*. In this way an object appears to us as pleasant, desirable, and beautiful, or as unpleasant, disgusting, ugly, and so on. In ordinary speech this process is called *feeling*.

The *intuitive process* is neither one of sense-perception, nor of thinking, nor yet of feeling, although language shows a regrettable lack of discrimination in this respect. One person will exclaim: "I can see the whole house burning down already!" Another will say: "It is as certain as two and two make four that there will be a disaster if a fire breaks out here." A third will say: "I have the feeling that this fire will lead to catastrophe." According to their respective temperaments, the one speaks of his intuition as a distinct *seeing*, that is, he makes a sense-perception of it. The other designates it as *thinking*: "One has only to reflect, and then it is quite clear what the consequences will be." The third, under the stress of emotion, calls his intuition a process of *feeling*. But intuition, as I conceive it, is one of the basic functions of the psyche, namely, *perception of the possibilities inherent in a situation*. It is probably due to the insufficient development of language that "feeling," "sensation," and "intuition" are still confused in German, while *sentiment* and *sensation* in French, and "feeling" and "sensation" in English, are absolutely distinct, in contrast to *sentiment* and "feeling," which are sometimes used as auxiliary words for "intuition." Recently, however, "intuition" has begun to be commonly used in English speech.

As further contents of consciousness, we can also distinguish *volitional* processes and *instinctual* processes. The former are defined as directed impulses, based on apperception, which are at the disposal of so-called free will. The latter are impulses originating in the unconscious or directly in the body and are characterized by lack of freedom and by compulsiveness.

Apperceptive processes may be either *directed* or *undirected*. In the former case we speak of "attention," in the latter case of "fantasy" or "dreaming." The directed processes are rational, the undirected irrational. To these last-named processes we must add—as the seventh category of contents of consciousness—*dreams*. In some respects dreams are like conscious fantasies in that they have an undirected, irrational character. But they differ inasmuch as their cause, course, and aim are, at first, very obscure. I accord them the dignity of coming into the category of conscious contents because they are the most important and most obvious results of unconscious psychic processes obtruding themselves upon consciousness. These seven categories probably give a somewhat superficial survey of the contents of consciousness, but they are sufficient for our purpose.

There are, as we know, certain views which would restrict everything psychic to consciousness, as being identical with it. I do not believe this is sufficient. If we assume that there is anything at all beyond our sense-perception, then we are entitled to speak of psychic elements whose existence is only indirectly accessible to us. For anybody acquainted with the psychology of hypnotism and somnambulism, it is a well-known fact that though an artificially or morbidly restricted consciousness of this kind does not contain certain ideas, it nevertheless behaves exactly as if it did. For instance, there was an hysterically deaf patient who was fond of singing. One day the doctor unobtrusively sat down at the piano and accompanied the next verse in another key, whereupon the patient went on singing in the new key. Another patient always fell into "hystero-epileptic" convulsions at the sight of a naked flame. He had a markedly restricted field of vision, that is, he suffered from peripheral blindness (having what is known as a "tubular" field of vision). If one now held a lighted match in the blind zone, the attack followed just as if he had seen the flame. In the symptomatology of such states there are innumerable cases of this kind, where with the best will in the world one can only say that these people perceive, think, feel, remember, decide, and act unconsciously, doing unconsciously what others do consciously. These processes occur regardless of whether consciousness registers them or not.

These unconscious psychic processes also include the not inconsiderable labour of composition that goes into a dream. Though sleep is a state in which consciousness is greatly restricted, the psyche by no means ceases to exist and to act. Consciousness has merely withdrawn from it and, lacking any objects to hold its attention, lapsed into a state of comparative unconsciousness. But psychic life obviously goes on, just as there is unconscious psychic activity during the waking state. Evidence for this is not difficult to find; indeed, Freud has described this particular field of experience in *The Psychopathology of Everyday Life*. He shows that our conscious intentions and actions are often frustrated by unconscious processes whose very existence is a continual surprise to us. We make slips of the tongue and slips in writing and unconsciously do things that betray our most closely guarded secrets—which are sometimes unknown even to ourselves. "Lingua lapsa verum dicit," says an old proverb. These phenomena can also be demonstrated experimentally by the association tests, which are very useful for finding out things that people cannot or will not speak about.

But the classic examples of unconscious psychic activity are to be found in pathological states. Almost the whole symptomatology of hysteria, of the compulsion neuroses, of phobias, and very largely of schizophrenia, the commonest mental illness, has its roots in unconscious psychic activity. We are therefore fully justified in speaking of an unconscious psyche. It is not directly accessible to observation—otherwise it would not be unconscious—but can only be inferred. Our inferences can never go beyond: "it is as if."

The unconscious, then, is part of the psyche. Can we now, on the analogy of the different contents of consciousness, also speak of contents of the unconscious?

That would be postulating another consciousness, so to speak, in the unconscious. I will not go into this delicate question here, since I have discussed it in another connection, but will confine myself to inquiring whether we can differentiate anything in the unconscious or not. This question can only be answered empirically, that is, by the counter-question whether there are any plausible grounds for such a differentiation.

To my mind there is no doubt that all the activities ordinarily taking place in consciousness can also proceed in the unconscious. There are numerous instances of an intellectual problem, unsolved in the waking state, being solved in a dream. I know, for instance, of an expert accountant who had tried in vain for many days to clear up a fraudulent bankruptcy. One day he had worked on it till midnight, without success, and then went to bed. At three in the morning his wife heard him get up and go into his study. She followed, and saw him industriously making notes at his desk. After about a quarter of an hour he came back. In the morning he remembered nothing. He began working again and discovered, in his own handwriting, a number of notes which straightened out the whole tangle finally and completely.

In my practical work I have been dealing with dreams for more than twenty years. Over and over again I have seen how thoughts that were not thought and feelings that were not felt by day afterwards appeared in dreams, and in this way reached consciousness indirectly. The dream as such is undoubtedly a content of consciousness, otherwise it could not be an object of immediate experience. But in so far as it brings up material that was unconscious before, we are forced to assume that these contents already had some kind of psychic existence in an unconscious state and appeared to the "remnant" of consciousness only in the dream. The dream belongs to the normal contents of the psyche and may be regarded as a resultant of unconscious processes obtruding on consciousness.

Now if, with these experiences in mind, we are driven to asume that all the categories of conscious contents can on occasion also be unconscious, and can act on the conscious mind as unconscious processes, we find ourselves faced with the somewhat unexpected question whether the unconscious has dreams too. In other words, are there resultants of still deeper and—if that be possible—still more unconscious processes which infiltrate into the dark regions of the psyche? I should have to dismiss this paradoxical question as altogether too adventurous were there not, in fact, grounds which bring such an hypothesis within the realm of possibility.

We must first see what sort of evidence is required to prove that the unconscious has dreams. If we wish to prove that dreams appear as contents of consciousness, we have simply to show that there are certain contents which, in character and meaning, are strange and not to be compared with the other contents which can be rationally explained and understood. If we are to show that the unconscious also has dreams, we must treat its contents in a similar way. It will be simplest if I give a practical example:

The case is that of an officer, twenty-seven years of age. He was suffering from severe attacks of pain in the region of the heart and from a choking sensation in the throat, as though a lump were stuck there. He also had piercing pains in the left heel. There was nothing organically the matter with him. The attacks had begun about two months previously, and the patient had been exempted from military service on account of his occasional inability to walk. Various cures had availed nothing. Close investigation into the previous history of his illness gave no clue, and he himself had no idea what the cause might be. He gave the impression of having a cheerful, rather light-hearted nature, perhaps a bit on the tough side, as though saying theatrically: "You can't keep us down." As the anamnesis revealed nothing, I asked about his dreams. It at once became apparent what the cause was. Just before the beginning of

his neurosis the girl with whom he was in love jilted him
and got engaged to another man. In talking to me he dis-
missed this whole story as irrelevant—"a stupid girl, if
she doesn't want me it's easy enough to get another one.
A man like me isn't upset by a thing like that." That was
the way he treated his disappointment and his real grief.
But now the affects came to the surface. The pains in his
heart soon disappeared, and the lump in his throat vanished
after a few bouts of weeping. "Heartache" is a poeticism,
but here it became an actual fact because his pride would
not allow him to suffer the pain in his soul. The "lump in
the throat," the so-called *globus hystericus,* comes, as
everyone knows, from swallowed tears. His consciousness
had simply withdrawn from contents that were too painful
to him, and these, left to themselves, could reach consciousness only indirectly, as symptoms. All this was a
rationally understandable and perfectly intelligible process,
which could just as well have passed off consciously, had
it not been for his masculine pride.

But now for the third symptom. The pains in the heel
did not disappear. They do not belong in the picture we
have just sketched, for the heart is in no way connected
with the heel, nor does one express sorrow through the
heel. From the rational point of view, one cannot see why
the other two syndromes should not have sufficed. Theoretically, it would have been entirely satisfactory if the
conscious realization of the repressed psychic pain had
resulted in normal grief and hence in a cure.

As I could get no clue to the heel symptom from the
patient's conscious mind, I turned once more to the previous method—to the dreams. The patient now had a
dream in which *he was bitten in the heel by a snake and
instantly paralyzed.* This dream plainly offered an interpretation of the heel symptom. His heel hurt him because
he had been bitten there by a snake. This is a very strange
content, and one can make nothing of it rationally. We
could understand at once why his heart ached, but that

his heel should ache too is beyond all rational expectation. The patient was completely mystified.

Here, then, we have a content that propels itself into the unconscious zone in a singular manner, and probably derives from some deeper layer that cannot be fathomed rationally. The nearest analogy to this dream is obviously the neurosis itself. When the girl jilted him, she gave him a wound that paralyzed him and made him ill. Further analysis of the dream elicited something from his previous history that now became clear to the patient for the first time: He had been the darling of a somewhat hysterical mother. She had pitied him, admired him, pampered him so much that he never got along properly at school because he was too girlish. Later he suddenly swung over to the masculine side and went into the army, where he was able to hide his inner weakness by a display of "toughness." Thus, in a sense, his mother too had lamed him.

We are evidently dealing here with that same old serpent who had been the special friend of Eve. "And I will put enmity between thee and the woman, and between thy seed and her seed; it shall bruise thy head, and thou shalt bruise his heel," runs the saying in Genesis, an echo of the much more ancient Egyptian hymn that used to be recited or chanted for the cure of snake-bite:

> The mouth of the god trembled with age,
> His spittle fell to the earth,
> And what he spat forth fell upon the ground.
> Then Isis kneaded it with her hands
> Together with the earth which was there;
> And she made it like a spear.
> She wound not the living snake about her face,
> But threw it in a coil upon the path
> Where the great god was wont to wander
> At his pleasure through his two kingdoms.
> The noble god stepped forth in splendour,
> The gods serving Pharaoh bore him company,
> And he went forth as was each day his wont.
> Then the noble worm stung him . . .

His jawbones chattered,
He trembled in all his limbs,
And the poison invaded his flesh
As the Nile invades his territory.[2]

The patient's conscious knowledge of the Bible was at a lamentable minimum. Probably he had once heard of the serpent biting the heel and then quickly forgotten it. But something deep in his unconscious heard it and did not forget; it remembered this story at a suitable opportunity. This part of the unconscious evidently likes to express itself mythologically, because this way of expression is in keeping with its nature.

But to what kind of mentality does the symbolical or metaphorical way of expression correspond? It corresponds to the mentality of the primitive, whose language possesses no abstractions but only natural and "unnatural" analogies. This primeval mentality is as foreign to the psyche that produced the heartache and the lump in the throat as a brontosaurus is to a racehorse. The dream of the snake reveals a fragment of psychic activity that has nothing whatever to do with the dreamer as a modern individual. It functions at a deeper level, so to speak, and only the results of this activity rise up into the upper layer where the repressed affects lie, as foreign to them as a dream is to waking consciousness. Just as some kind of analytical technique is needed to understand a dream, so a knowledge of mythology is needed in order to grasp the meaning of a content deriving from the deeper levels of the psyche.

The snake-motif was certainly not an individual acquisition of the dreamer, for snake-dreams are very common even among city-dwellers who have probably never seen a real snake.

It might be objected that the snake in the dream is nothing but a concretized figure of speech. We say of certain women that they are treacherous as snakes, wily as

[2] Adolf Erman, *Life in Ancient Egypt,* translated by H. M. Tirard (London, 1894), pp. 265–67, modified.

serpents; we speak of the snake of temptation, etc. This objection does not seem to me to hold good in the present instance, though it would be difficult to prove this because the snake is in fact a common figure of speech. A more certain proof would be possible only if we succeeded in finding a case where the mythological symbolism is neither a common figure of speech nor an instance of cryptomnesia —that is to say, where the dreamer had not read, seen, or heard the motif somewhere, and then forgotten it and remembered it unconsciously. This proof seems to me of great importance, since it would show that the rationally explicable unconscious, which consists of material that has been made unconscious artificially, as it were, is only a top layer, and that underneath is an absolute unconscious which has nothing to do with our personal experience. This absolute unconscious would then be a psychic activity which goes on independently of the conscious mind and is not dependent even on the upper layers of the unconscious, untouched—and perhaps untouchable—by personal experience. It would be a kind of supra-individual psychic activity, a *collective unconscious,* as I have called it, as distinct from a superficial, relative, or personal unconscious.

But before we go in search of this proof, I would like, for the sake of completeness, to make a few more remarks about the snake-dream. It seems as if this hypothetical deeper layer of the unconscious—the collective unconscious, as I shall now call it—had translated the patient's experiences with women into the snake-bite dream and thus turned them into a regular mythological motif. The reason—or rather, the purpose—of this is at first somewhat obscure. But if we remember the fundamental principle that the symptomatology of an illness is at the same time a natural attempt at healing—the heartaches, for example, being an attempt to produce an emotional outburst—then we must regard the heel symptom as an attempt at healing too. As the dream shows, not only the recent disappointment in love, but all other disappointments, in school and elsewhere, are raised by this symptom to the level of a mythological event, as though this would in some way help the patient.

This may strike us as flatly incredible. But the ancient Egyptian priest-physicians, who intoned the hymn to the Isis-serpent over the snake-bite, did not find this theory at all incredible; and not only they, but the whole world believed, as the primitive today still believes, in magic by analogy or "sympathetic magic."

We are concerned here, then, with the psychological phenomenon that lies at the root of magic by analogy. We should not think that this is an ancient superstition which we have long since outgrown. If you read the Latin text of the Mass carefully, you will constantly come upon the famous "sicut"; this always introduces an analogy by means of which a change is to be produced. Another striking example of analogy is the making of fire on Holy Saturday. In former times, the new fire was struck from the stone, and still earlier it was obtained by boring into a piece of wood, which was the prerogative of the Church. Therefore in the prayer of the priest it is said: "Deus, qui per Filium tuum, angularem scilicet lapidem, claritatis tuae fidelibus ignem contulisti productum ex silice, nostris pro-futurum usibus, novum hunc ignem sanctifica."—"O God, who through thy Son, who is called the cornerstone, hast brought the fire of thy light to the faithful, make holy for our future use this new fire struck from the firestone." By the analogy of Christ with the cornerstone, the firestone is raised to the level of Christ himself, who again kindles a new fire.

The rationalist may laugh at this. But something deep in us is stirred, and not in us alone but in millions of Christian men and women, though we may call it only a feeling for beauty. What is stirred in us is that faraway background, those immemorial patterns of the human mind, which we have not acquired but have inherited from the dim ages of the past.

If this supra-individual psyche exists, everything that is

translated into its picture-language would be depersonalized, and if this became conscious would appear to us
*sub specie aeternitatis*. Not as my sorrow, but as the sorrow of the world; not a personal isolating pain, but a pain
without bitterness that unites all humanity. The healing
effect of this needs no proof.

But as to whether this supra-individual psychic activity
actually exists, I have so far given no proof that satisfies all
the requirements. I should now like to do this once more
in the form of an example. The case is that of a man in
his thirties, who was suffering from a paranoid form of
schizophrenia. He became ill in his early twenties. He had
always presented a strange mixture of intelligence, wrong-
headedness, and fantastic ideas. He was an ordinary clerk,
employed in a consulate. Evidently as a compensation for
his very modest existence he was seized with megalomania
and believed himself to be the Saviour. He suffered from
frequent hallucinations and was at times very much disturbed. In his quiet periods he was allowed to go unat-
tended in the corridor. One day I came across him there,
blinking through the window up at the sun, and moving
his head from side to side in a curious manner. He took
me by the arm and said he wanted to show me something.
He said I must look at the sun with eyes half shut, and
then I could see the sun's phallus. If I moved my head
from side to side the sun-phallus would move too, and
that was the origin of the wind.

I made this observation about 1906. In the course of
the year 1910, when I was engrossed in mythological studies, a book of Dieterich's came into my hands. It was part
of the so-called Paris magic papyrus and was thought by
Dieterich to be a liturgy of the Mithraic cult.[3] It consisted
of a series of instructions, invocations, and visions. One of

---

[3] [Albrecht Dieterich, *Eine Mithrasliturgie* (London, 1903; 2nd ed.,
1910), pp. 6–7. As the author subsequently learned, the 1910 edition was actually the second, there having been a first edition in
1903. The patient had, however, been committed some years before
1903.

these visions is described in the following words: "And likewise the so-called tube, the origin of the ministering wind. For you will see hanging down from the disc of the sun something that looks like a tube. And towards the regions westward it is as though there were an infinite east wind. But if the other wind should prevail towards the regions of the east, you will in like manner see the vision veering in that direction." The Greek word for "tube," αὐλός, means a wind-instrument, and the combination αὐλὸς παχύς in Homer means "a thick jet of blood." So evidently a stream of wind is blowing through the tube out of the sun.

The vision of my patient in 1906, and the Greek text first edited in 1910, should be sufficiently far apart to rule out the possibility of cryptomnesia on his side and of thought-transference on mine. The obvious parallelism of the two visions cannot be disputed, though one might object that the similarity is purely fortuitous. In that case we should expect the vision to have no connections with analogous ideas, nor any inner meaning. But this expectation is not fulfilled, for in certain medieval paintings this tube is actually depicted as a sort of hose-pipe reaching down from heaven under the robe of Mary. In it the Holy Ghost flies down in the form of a dove to impregnate the Virgin. As we know from the miracle of Pentecost, the Holy Ghost was originally conceived as a mighty rushing wind, the πνεῦμα, "the wind that bloweth where it listeth." In a Latin text we read: "Animo descensus per orbem solis tribuitur" (They say that the spirit descends through the disc of the sun). This conception is common to the whole of late classical and medieval philosophy.

I cannot, therefore, discover anything fortuitous in these visions, but simply the revival of possibilities of ideas that have always existed, that can be found again in the most diverse minds and in all epochs, and are therefore not to be mistaken for inherited ideas.

I have purposely gone into the details of this case in

order to give you a concrete picture of that deeper psychic activity which I call the collective unconscious. Summing up, I would like to emphasize that we must distinguish three psychic levels: (1) consciousness, (2) the personal unconscious, and (3) the collective unconscious. The personal unconscious consists firstly of all those contents that became unconscious either because they lost their intensity and were forgotten or because consciousness was withdrawn from them (repression), and secondly of contents, some of them sense-impressions, which never had sufficient intensity to reach consciousness but have somehow entered the psyche. The collective unconscious, however, as the ancestral heritage of possibilities of representation, is not individual but common to all men, and perhaps even to all animals, and is the true basis of the individual psyche.

This whole psychic organism corresponds exactly to the body, which, though individually varied, is in all essential features the specifically human body which all men have. In its development and structure, it still preserves elements that connect it with the invertebrates and ultimately with the protozoa. Theoretically it should be possible to "peel" the collective unconscious, layer by layer, until we came to the psychology of the worm, and even of the amoeba.

We are all agreed that it would be quite impossible to understand the living organism apart from its relation to the environment. There are countless biological facts that can only be explained as reactions to environmental conditions, e.g., the blindness of *Proteus anguinus,* the peculiarities of intestinal parasites, the anatomy of vertebrates that have reverted to aquatic life.

The same is true of the psyche. Its peculiar organization must be intimately connected with environmental conditions. We should expect consciousness to react and adapt itself to the present, because it is that part of the psyche which is concerned chiefly with events of the moment. But from the collective unconscious, as a timeless and universal psyche, we should expect reactions to universal and constant conditions, whether psychological, physiological, or physical.

The collective unconscious—so far as we can say anything about it at all—appears to consist of mythological motifs or primordial images, for which reason the myths of all nations are its real exponents. In fact, the whole of mythology could be taken as a sort of projection of the collective unconscious. We can see this most clearly if we look at the heavenly constellations, whose originally chaotic forms were organized through the projection of images. This explains the influence of the stars as asserted by astrologers. These influences are nothing but unconscious, introspective perceptions of the activity of the collective unconscious. Just as the constellations were projected into the heavens, similar figures were projected into legends and fairy tales or upon historical persons. We can therefore study the collective unconscious in two ways, either in mythology or in the analysis of the individual. As I cannot make the latter material available here, I must confine myself to mythology. This is such a wide field that we can select from it only a few types. Similarly, environmental conditions are endlessly varied, so here too only a few of the more typical can be discussed.

Just as the living body with its special characteristics is a system of functions for adapting to environmental conditions, so the psyche must exhibit organs or functional systems that correspond to regular physical events. By this I do not mean sense-functions dependent on organs, but rather a sort of psychic parallel to regular physical occurrences. To take an example, the daily course of the sun and the regular alternation of day and night must have imprinted themselves on the psyche in the form of an image from primordial times. We cannot demonstrate the existence of this image, but we find instead more or less fantastic analogies of the physical process. Every morning a divine hero is born from the sea and mounts the chariot of the sun. In the West a Great Mother awaits him, and he is devoured by her in the evening. In the belly of a dragon he traverses the depths of the midnight sea. After a frightful combat with the serpent of night he is born again in the morning.

This conglomerate myth undoubtedly contains a reflection of the physical process. Indeed this is so obvious that many investigators assume that primitives invent such myths merely to explain physical processes. There can be no doubt that science and philosophy have grown from this matrix, but that primitives think up such things merely from a need for explanation, as a sort of physical or astronomical theory, seems to me highly improbable.

What we can safely say about mythical images is that the physical process imprinted itself on the psyche in this fantastic, distorted form and was preserved there, so that the unconscious still reproduces similar images today. Naturally the question now arises: why does the psyche not register the actual process, instead of mere fantasies about the physical process?

If you can put yourself in the mind of the primitive, you will at once understand why this is so. He lives in such "participation mystique" with his world, as Lévy-Bruhl calls it, that there is nothing like that absolute distinction between subject and object which exists in our minds. What happens outside also happens in him, and what happens in him also happens outside. I witnessed a very fine example of this when I was with the Elgonyi, a primitive tribe living on Mount Elgon, in East Africa. At sunrise they spit on their hands and then hold the palms towards the sun as it comes over the horizon. "We are happy that the night is past," they say. Since the word for sun, *adhista,* also means God, I asked: "Is the sun God?" They said "No" to this and laughed, as if I had said something especially stupid. As the sun was just then high in the heavens, I pointed to it and asked: "When the sun is there you say it is not God, but when it is in the east you say it is God. How is that?" There was an embarrassed silence till an old chief began to explain. "It is so," he said. "When the sun is up there it is not God, but when it rises, that is God [or: then it is God]." To the primitive mind it is immaterial which of these two versions is correct. Sunrise and his own feeling of deliverance are for him the same divine experience, just as night and his fear are the same thing. Naturally his emotions are more important to him than physics; therefore what he registers is his emotional fantasies. For him night means snakes and the cold breath of spirits, whereas morning means the birth of a beautiful god.

There are mythological theories that explain everything as coming from the sun and lunar theories that do the same for the moon. This is due to the simple fact that there are countless myths about the moon, among them a whole host in which the moon is the wife of the sun. The moon is the changing experience of the night, and thus coincides with the primitive's sexual experience of woman, who for him is also the experience of the night. But the moon can equally well be the injured brother of the sun, for at night affect-laden and evil thoughts of power and revenge may disturb sleep. The moon, too, is a disturber of sleep, and is also the abode of departed souls, for at night the dead return in dreams and the phantoms of the past terrify the sleepless. Thus the moon also signifies madness ("lunacy"). It is such experiences as these that have impressed themselves on the mind, rather than the changing image of the moon.

It is not storms, not thunder and lightning, not rain and cloud that remain as images in the psyche, but the fantasies caused by the affects they arouse. I once experienced a violent earthquake, and my first, immediate feeling was that I no longer stood on the solid and familiar earth, but on the skin of a gigantic animal that was heaving under my feet. It was this image that impressed itself on me, not the physical fact. Man's curses against devastating thunderstorms, his terror of the unchained elements—

these affects anthropomorphize the passion of nature, and the purely physical element becomes an angry god.

Like the physical conditions of his environment, the physiological conditions, glandular secretions, etc., also can arouse fantasies charged with affect. Sexuality appears as a god of fertility, as a fiercely sensual, feminine daemon, as the devil himself with Dionysian goat's legs and obscene gestures, or as a terrifying serpent that squeezes its victims to death.

Hunger makes food into gods. Certain Mexican tribes even give their food-gods an annual holiday to allow them to recuperate, and during this time the staple food is not eaten. The ancient Pharaohs were worshipped as eaters of gods. Osiris is the wheat, the son of the earth, and to this day the Host must be made of wheat-meal, i.e., a god to be eaten, as also was Iacchos, the mysterious god of the Eleusinian mysteries. The bull of Mithras is the edible fruitfulness of the earth.

The psychological conditions of the environment naturally leave similar mythical traces behind them. Dangerous situations, be they dangers to the body or to the soul, arouse affect-laden fantasies, and, in so far as such situations typically repeat themselves, they give rise to *archetypes,* as I have termed myth-motifs in general.

Dragons make their lairs by watercourses, preferably near a ford or some such dangerous crossing; jinn and other devils are to be found in waterless deserts or in dangerous gorges; spirits of the dead haunt the eerie thickets of the bamboo forest; treacherous nixies and sea-serpents live in the depths of the ocean and its whirlpools. Mighty ancestor-spirits or gods dwell in the man of importance; deadly fetish-power resides in anyone strange or extraordinary. Sickness and death are never due to natural causes, but are invariably caused by spirits, witches, or wizards. Even the weapon that has killed a man is *mana,* endowed with extraordinary power.

How is it then, you may ask, with the most ordinary

everyday events, with immediate realities like husband, wife, father, mother, child? These ordinary everyday facts, which are eternally repeated, create the mightiest archetypes of all, whose ceaseless activity is everywhere apparent even in a rationalistic age like ours. Let us take as an example the Christian dogma. The Trinity consists of Father, Son, and Holy Ghost, who is represented by the bird of Astarte, the dove, and who in early Christian times was called Sophia and thought of as feminine. The worship of Mary in the later Church is an obvious substitute for this. Here we have the archetype of the family ἐν ὑπερουρανίῳ τόπῳ, "in a supracelestial place," as Plato expresses it, enthroned as a formulation of the ultimate mystery. Christ is the bridegroom, the Church is the bride, the baptismal font is the womb of the Church, as it is still called in the text of the *Benedictio fontis*. The holy water has salt put into it, with the idea of making it like the amniotic fluid, or like sea-water. A *hieros gamos* or sacred wedding is performed on Holy Saturday before Easter, which I have just mentioned, and a burning candle as a phallic symbol is plunged three times into the font, in order to fertilize it and lend it the power to bear the baptized child anew (*quasimodo genitus*). The *mana* personality, the medicine-man, is the *pontifex maximus,* the *Papa;* the Church is *mater ecclesia,* the *magna mater* of magical power, and mankind are children in need of help and grace.

The deposit of mankind's whole ancestral experience—so rich in emotional imagery—of father, mother, child, husband and wife, of the magic personality, of dangers to body and soul, has exalted this group of archetypes into the supreme regulating principles of religious and even of political life, in unconscious recognition of their tremendous psychic power.

I have found that a rational understanding of these things in no way detracts from their value; on the contrary, it helps us not only to feel but to gain insight into

their immense significance. These mighty projections enable the Catholic to experience large tracts of his collective
unconscious in tangible reality. He has no need to go in
search of authority, superior power, revelation, or something that would link him with the eternal and the timeless.
These are always present and available for him: there, in
the Holy of Holies on every altar, dwells the presence of
God. It is the Protestant and the Jew who have to seek,
the one because he has, in a manner of speaking, destroyed
the earthly body of the Deity, the other because he can
never find it. For both of them the archetypes, which to
the Catholic world have become a visible and living reality,
lie in the unconscious. Unfortunately I cannot enter here
into the remarkable differences of attitude towards the
unconscious in our culture, but would only point out that
this question is one of the greatest problems confronting
humanity.

That this is so is immediately understandable when we
consider that the unconscious, as the totality of all archetypes, is the deposit of all human experience right back to
its remotest beginnings. Not, indeed, a dead deposit, a
sort of abandoned rubbish-heap, but a living system of
reactions and aptitudes that determine the individual's life
in invisible ways—all the more effective because invisible.
It is not just a gigantic historical prejudice, so to speak, an
*a priori* historical condition; it is also the source of the
instincts, for the archetypes are simply the forms which
the instincts assume. From the living fountain of instinct
flows everything that is creative; hence the unconscious
is not merely conditioned by history, but is the very source
of the creative impulse. It is like Nature herself—prodi-
giously conservative, and yet transcending her own historical conditions in her acts of creation. No wonder, then,
that it has always been a burning question for humanity
how best to adapt to these invisible determinants. If consciousness had never split off from the unconscious—an
eternally repeated event symbolized as the fall of the angels

and the disobedience of the first parents—this problem would never have arisen, any more than would the question of environmental adaptation.

The existence of an individual consciousness makes man aware of the difficulties of his inner as well as his outer life. Just as the world about him takes on a friendly or a hostile aspect to the eyes of primitive man, so the influences of his unconscious seem to him like an opposing power, with which he has to come to terms just as with the visible world. His countless magical practices serve this end. On higher levels of civilization, religion and philosophy fulfil the same purpose. Whenever such a system of adaptation breaks down a general unrest begins to appear, and attempts are made to find a suitable new form of relationship to the unconscious.

These things seem very remote to our modern, "enlightened" eyes. When I speak of this hinterland of the mind, the unconscious, and compare its reality with that of the visible world, I often meet with an incredulous smile. But then I must ask how many people there are in our civilized world who still believe in *mana* and spirits and suchlike theories—in other words, how many millions of Christian Scientists and spiritualists are there? I will not add to this list of questions. They are merely intended to illustrate the fact that the problem of invisible psychic determinants is as alive today as ever it was.

The collective unconscious contains the whole spiritual heritage of mankind's evolution, born anew in the brain structure of every individual. His conscious mind is an ephemeral phenomenon that accomplishes all provisional adaptations and orientations, for which reason one can best compare its function to orientation in space. The unconscious, on the other hand, is the source of the instinctual forces of the psyche and of the forms or categories that regulate them, namely the archetypes. All the most powerful ideas in history go back to archetypes. This is particularly true of religious ideas, but the central concepts of science, philosophy, and ethics are no exception to this rule. In their present form they are variants of archetypal ideas, created by consciously applying and adapting these ideas to reality. For it is the function of consciousness not only to recognize and assimilate the external world through the gateway of the senses, but to translate into visible reality the world within us.

## 3

### Instinct and the
### Unconscious[1]

The theme of this symposium concerns a problem that is of great importance for biology as well as for psychology and philosophy. But if we are to discuss the relation between instinct and the unconscious, it is essential that we start out with a clear definition of our terms.

With regard to the definition of instinct, I would like to stress the significance of the "all-or-none" reaction formulated by Rivers; indeed, it seems to me that this peculiarity of instinctive activity is of special importance for the

[1] From *The Structure and Dynamics of the Psyche. Collected Works,* Vol. 8, pars. 263–282. A contribution to the symposium of the same name, presented, in an English translation by C. F. and H. G. Baynes, at a joint meeting of the Aristotelian Society, the Mind Association, and the British Psychological Society, at Bedford College, London University, July, 1919. [First published in the *British Journal of Psychology* (General Section) (London), X (1919): 1, 15–26; republished in *Contributions to Analytical Psychology* (London and New York, 1928). The original ms. was subsequently published as "Instinkt und Unbewusstes" in *Über die Energetik der Seele* (Psychologische Abhandlungen, II; Zurich, 1928); republished, with a short concluding note, in *Über psychische Energetik und das Wesen der Träume* (Zurich, 1948). The Baynes version has been consulted in the preparation of the present translation.—EDITORS OF *The Collected Works.*]

psychological side of the problem. I must naturally confine myself to this aspect of the question, because I do not
feel competent to treat the problem of instinct under its
biological aspect. But when I attempt to give a psychological definition of instinctive activity, I find I cannot rely
solely on Rivers' criterion of the "all-or-none" reaction,
and for the following reason: Rivers defines this reaction
as a process that shows no gradation of intensity in respect
of the circumstances which provoke it. It is a reaction that
takes place with its own specific intensity under all circumstances and is not proportional to the precipitating
stimulus. But when we examine the psychological processes
of consciousness in order to determine whether there are
any whose intensity is out of all proportion to the stimulus,
we can easily find a great many of them in everybody, for
instance disproportionate affects, impressions, exaggerated
impulses, intentions that go too far, and others of the kind.
It follows that all these processes cannot possibly be classed
as instinctive processes, and we must therefore look round
for another criterion.

We use the word "instinct" very frequently in ordinary
speech. We speak of "instinctive actions," meaning by
that a mode of behaviour of which neither the motive nor
the aim is fully conscious and which is prompted only by
obscure inner necessity. This peculiarity has already been
stressed by an older English writer, Thomas Reid, who
says: "By instinct, I mean a natural impulse to certain
actions, without having any end in view, without deliberation and without any conception of what we do." [2] Thus
instinctive action is characterized by an *unconsciousness*
of the psychological motive behind it, in contrast to the
strictly conscious processes which are distinguished by the
conscious continuity of their motives. Instinctive action
appears to be a more or less abrupt psychic occurrence, a
sort of interruption of the continuity of consciousness. On

[2] Thomas Reid, *Essays on the Active Powers of Man* (Edinburgh,
1788), p. 103.

this account, it is felt as an inner necessity—which is, in fact, the definition of instinct given by Kant.[3]

Accordingly, instinctive activity would have to be included among the specifically unconscious processes, which are accessible to consciousness only through their results. But were we to rest content with this conception of instinct, we should soon discover its insufficiency: it merely marks off instinct from the conscious processes and characterizes it as unconscious. If, on the other hand, we survey the unconscious processes as a whole, we find it impossible to class them all as instinctive, even though no differentiation is made between them in ordinary speech. If you suddenly meet a snake and get a violent fright, you can legitimately call this impulse instinctive because it is no different from the instinctive fear of snakes in monkeys. It is just the uniformity of the phenomenon and the regularity of its recurrence which are the most characteristic qualities of instinctive action. As Lloyd Morgan aptly remarks, it would be as uninteresting to bet on an instinctive reaction as on the rising of the sun tomorrow. On the other hand, it may also happen that someone is regularly seized with fright whenever he meets a perfectly harmless hen. Although the mechanism of fright in this case is just as much an unconscious impulse as the instinct, we must nevertheless distinguish between the two processes. In the former case the fear of snakes is a purposive process of general occurrence; the latter, when habitual, is a phobia and not an instinct, since it occurs only in isolation and is not a general peculiarity. There are many other unconscious compulsions of this kind—for instance, obsessive thoughts, musical obsessions, sudden ideas and moods, impulsive affects, depressions, anxiety states, etc. These phenomena are met with in normal as well as abnormal individuals. In so far as they occur only in isolation and are not repeated regularly they must be distinguished from instinc-

[3] Immanuel Kant, *Anthropologie,* in *Werke,* Ernst Cassirer, ed. (Berlin, 1912–22), Vol. VIII, p. 156.

tive processes, even though their psychological mechanism seems to correspond to that of an instinct. They may even be characterized by the all-or-none reaction, as can easily be observed in pathological cases. In psychopathology there are many such cases where a given stimulus is followed by a definite and relatively disproportionate reaction comparable to an instinctive reaction.

All these processes must be distinguished from instinctive ones. Only those unconscious processes which are inherited, and occur uniformly and regularly, can be called instinctive. At the same time they must show the mark of compelling necessity, a reflex character of the kind pointed out by Herbert Spencer. Such a process differs from a mere sensory-motor reflex only because it is more complicated. William James therefore calls instinct, not unjustly, "a mere excito-motor impulse, due to the pre-existence of a certain 'reflex-arc' in the nerve-centres." [4] Instincts share with reflexes their uniformity and regularity as well as the unconsciousness of their motivations.

The question of where instincts come from and how they were acquired is extraordinarily complicated. The fact that they are invariably inherited does nothing to explain their origin; it merely shifts the problem back to our ancestors. The view is widely held that instincts originated in individual, and then general, acts of will that were frequently repeated. This explanation is plausible in so far as we can observe every day how certain laboriously learnt activities gradually become automatic through constant practice. But if we consider the marvellous instincts to be found in the animal world, we must admit that the element of learning is sometimes totally absent. In certain cases it is impossible to conceive how any learning and practice could ever have come about. Let us take as an example the incredibly refined instinct of propagation in the yucca moth (*Pronuba*

---

[4] William James, *Principles of Psychology* (New York, 1890, 2 vols.), Vol. II, p. 391.

*yuccasella*).[5] The flowers of the yucca plant open for one night only. The moth takes the pollen from one of the flowers and kneads it into a little pellet. Then it visits a second flower, cuts open the pistil, lays its eggs between the ovules and then stuffs the pellet into the funnel-shaped opening of the pistil. Only once in its life does the moth carry out this complicated operation.

Such cases are difficult to explain on the hypothesis of learning and practice. Hence other ways of explanation, deriving from Bergson's philosophy, have recently been put forward, laying stress on the factor of intuition. Intuition is an unconscious process in that its result is the irruption into consciousness of an unconscious content, a sudden idea or "hunch." [6] It resembles a process of perception, but unlike the conscious activity of the senses and introspection the perception is unconscious. That is why we speak of intuition as an "instinctive" act of comprehension. It is a process analogous to instinct, with the difference that whereas instinct is a purposive impulse to carry out some highly complicated action, intuition is the unconscious, purposive apprehension of a highly complicated situation. In a sense, therefore, intuition is the reverse of instinct, neither more nor less wonderful than it. But we should never forget that what we call complicated or even wonderful is not at all wonderful for Nature, but quite ordinary. We always tend to project into things our own difficulties of understanding and to call them complicated, when in reality they are very simple and know nothing of our intellectual problems.

A discussion of the problem of instinct without reference to the concept of the unconscious would be incomplete, because it is just the instinctive processes which make the supplementary concept of the unconscious necessary. I de-

[5] Anton Kerner von Marilaun, *The Natural History of Plants*, translated by F. W. Oliver and others (London, 1902, 2 vols.), Vol. II, p. 156.
[6] Cf. supra, p. 26; also infra, pp. 220–23, 258–61.

fine the unconscious as the totality of all psychic phenomena that lack the quality of consciousness. These psychic
contents might fittingly be called "subliminal," on the assumption that every psychic content must possess a certain
energy value in order to become conscious at all. The
lower the value of a conscious content falls, the more
easily it disappears below the threshold. From this it follows that the unconscious is the receptacle of all lost memories and of all contents that are still too weak to become
conscious. These contents are products of an unconscious
associative activity which also gives rise to dreams. Besides these we must include all more or less intentional
repressions of painful thoughts and feelings. I call the sum
of all these contents the "personal unconscious." But, over
and above that, we also find in the unconscious qualities
that are not individually acquired but are inherited, e.g.,
instincts as impulses to carry out actions from necessity,
without conscious motivation. In this "deeper" stratum we
also find the *a priori,* inborn forms of "intuition," namely
the *archetypes*[7] of perception and apprehension, which
are the necessary *a priori* determinants of all psychic processes. Just as his instincts compel man to a specifically
human mode of existence, so the archetypes force his ways
of perception and apprehension into specifically human
patterns. The instincts and the archetypes together form
the "collective unconscious." I call it "collective" because,
unlike the personal unconscious, it is not made up of in-

---

[7] [This is the first occasion on which Jung uses the term "archetype"
(*Archetypus*). Previously, in his publications, he had discussed the
same concept under the term "primordial image" (*Urbild*), which
he derived from Burckhardt (cf. *Symbols of Transformation* [*Collected Works,* Vol. 5], par. 45, n. 45; *Two Essays on Analytical
Psychology* [*Collected Works,* Vol. 7], par. 101). The primordial
image, be it observed, is here and elsewhere used as the equivalent
of the archetype; this has given rise to some confusion and to the
belief that Jung's theory of hereditary elements involves the inher-
itance of representations (ideas or images), a view against which
Jung repeatedly protests.—EDITORS OF *The Collected Works.*] See
discussion supra, in Editor's Introduction, pp. *xxxi–xxxii.*—J.C.

dividual and more or less unique contents but of those which are universal and of regular occurrence. Instinct is an essentially collective, i.e., universal and regularly occurring phenomenon which has nothing to do with individuality. Archetypes have this quality in common with the instincts and are likewise collective phenomena.

In my view the question of instinct cannot be dealt with psychologically without considering the archetypes, because at bottom they determine one another. It is, however, extremely difficult to discuss this problem, as opinions about the role of instinct in human psychology are extraordinarily divided. Thus William James is of the opinion that man is swarming with instincts, while others restrict them to a very few processes barely distinguishable from reflexes, namely to certain movements executed by the infant, to particular reactions of its arms and legs, of the larynx, the use of the right hand, and the formation of syllabized sounds. In my opinion, this restriction goes too far, though it is very characteristic of human psychology in general. Above all, we should always remember that in discussing human instincts we are speaking of ourselves and, therefore, are doubtless prejudiced.

We are in a far better position to observe instincts in animals or in primitives than in ourselves. This is due to the fact that we have grown accustomed to scrutinizing our own actions and to seeking rational explanations for them. But it is by no means certain that our explanations will hold water, indeed it is highly unlikely. No superhuman intellect is needed to see through the shallowness of many of our rationalizations and to detect the real motive, the compelling instinct behind them. As a result of our artificial rationalizations it may seem to us that we were actuated not by instinct but by conscious motives. Naturally I do not mean to say that by careful training man has not succeeded in partially converting his instincts into acts of the will. Instinct has been domesticated, but the basic motive still remains instinct. There is no doubt that we have succeeded in enveloping a large number of instincts in rational explanations to the point where we can no longer recognize the original motive behind so many veils. In this way it seems as though we possessed practically no instincts any more. But if we apply the Rivers criterion of the disproportionate all-or-none reaction to human behaviour, we find innumerable cases where exaggerated reactions occur. Exaggeration, indeed, is a universal human peculiarity, although everybody carefully tries to explain his reactions in terms of rational motives. There is never any lack of good arguments, but the fact of exaggeration remains. And why is it that a man does not do or say, give or take, just as much as is needed, or reasonable, or justifiable in a given situation, but frequently so much more or less? Precisely because an unconscious process is released in him that runs its course without the aid of reason and therefore falls short of, or exceeds, the degree of rational motivation. This phenomenon is so uniform and so regular that we can only call it instinctive, though no one in this situation likes to admit the instinctive nature of his behaviour. I am therefore inclined to believe that human behaviour is influenced by instinct to a far higher degree than is generally supposed, and that we are prone to a great many falsifications of judgment in this respect, again as a result of an instinctive exaggeration of the rationalistic standpoint.

*Instincts are typical modes of action, and wherever we meet with uniform and regularly recurring modes of action and reaction we are dealing with instinct, no matter whether it is associated with a conscious motive or not.*

Just as it may be asked whether man possesses many instincts or only a few, so we must also raise the still unbroached question of whether he possesses many or few primordial forms, or archetypes, of psychic reaction. Here we are faced with the same difficulty I mentioned above: we are so accustomed to operating with conventional and self-evident concepts that we are no longer conscious of the extent to which they are based on archetypal modes of perception. Like the instincts, the primordial images have been obscured by the extraordinary differentiation of our thinking. Just as certain biological views attribute only a few instincts to man, so the theory of cognition reduces the archetypes to a few, logically limited categories of understanding.

In Plato, however, an extraordinarily high value is set on the archetypes as metaphysical ideas, as "paradigms" or models, while real things are held to be only the copies of these model ideas. Medieval philosophy, from the time of St. Augustine—from whom I have borrowed the idea of the archetype[8]—down to Malebranche and Bacon, still stands on a Platonic footing in this respect. But in scholasticism we find the notion that archetypes are natural images engraved on the human mind, helping it to form its judgments. Thus Herbert of Cherbury says: "Natural instincts are expressions of those faculties which are found in every normal man, through which the Common Notions touching the internal conformity of things, such as the cause, means and purpose of things, the good, bad, beautiful, pleasing, etc. . . . are brought into conformity independently of discursive thought." [9]

From Descartes and Malebranche onward, the metaphysical value of the "idea" or archetype steadily deteriorated. It became a "thought," an internal condition of cognition, as clearly formulated by Spinoza: "By 'idea' I understand a conception of the mind which the mind forms by reason of its being a thinking thing." [10] Finally Kant reduced the archetypes to a limited number of categories of understanding. Schopenhauer carried the process of

[8] The actual term "archetype," however, is to be found in Dionysius the Areopagite and in the *Corpus Hermeticum.*
[9] Edward, Baron Herbert of Cherbury, *De veritate,* originally published 1624, translated by Meyrick H. Carré, University of Bristol Studies, 6 (Bristol, 1937), p. 122.
[10] Cf. Benedict Spinoza, *Ethics,* translated by Andrew Boyle (London and New York, 1934, Everyman's Library), p. 37.

simplification still further, while at the same time endow-
ing the archetypes with an almost Platonic significance.

In this all-too-summary sketch we can see once again
that same psychological process at work which disguises
the instincts under the cloak of rational motivations and
transforms the archetypes into rational concepts. It is
hardly possible to recognize the archetype under this guise.
And yet the way in which man inwardly pictures the world
is still, despite all differences of detail, as uniform and as
regular as his instinctive actions. Just as we have been
compelled to postulate the concept of an instinct determining or regulating our conscious actions, so, in order
to account for the uniformity and regularity of our perceptions, we must have recourse to the correlated concept
of a factor determining the mode of apprehension. It is
this factor which I call the archetype or primordial image.
The primordial image might suitably be described as the
*instinct's perception of itself,* or as the self-portrait of the
instinct, in exactly the same way as consciousness is an
inward perception of the objective life-process. Just as
conscious apprehension gives our actions form and direction, so unconscious apprehension through the archetype
determines the form and direction of instinct. If we call
instinct "refined," then the "intuition" which brings the
instinct into play, in other words the apprehension by
means of the archetype, must be something incredibly
precise. Thus the yucca moth must carry within it an image, as it were, of the situation that "triggers off" its instinct. This image enables it to "recognize" the yucca flower
and its structure.

The criterion of the all-or-none reaction proposed by
Rivers has helped us to discover the operation of instinct
everywhere in human psychology, and it may be that the
concept of the primordial image will perform a similar
service with regard to acts of intuitive apprehension. In-
tuitional activity can be observed most easily among primitives. There we constantly meet with certain typical images

and motifs which are the foundations of their mythologies. These images are autochthonous and occur with great regularity; everywhere we find the idea of a magic power or substance, of spirits and their doings, of heroes and gods and their legends. In the great religions of the world we see the perfection of those images and at the same time their progressive incrustation with rational forms. They even appear in the exact sciences, as the foundation of certain indispensable auxiliary concepts such as energy, ether, and the atom.[11] In philosophy, Bergson affords an example of the revival of a primordial image with his conception of "durée créatrice," which can be found in Proclus and, in its original form, in Heraclitus.

Analytical psychology is daily concerned, in the normal and sick alike, with disturbances of conscious apprehension caused by the admixture of archetypal images. The exaggerated actions due to the interference of instinct are caused by intuitive modes of apprehension actuated by archetypes and all too likely to lead to over-intense and often distorted impressions.

*Archetypes are typical modes of apprehension, and wherever we meet with uniform and regularly recurring modes of apprehension we are dealing with an archetype, no matter whether its mythological character is recognized or not.*

The collective unconscious consists of the sum of the instincts and their correlates, the archetypes. Just as everybody possesses instincts, so he also possesses a stock of archetypal images. The most striking proof of this is the psychopathology of mental disturbances that are characterized by an irruption of the collective unconscious. Such is the case in schizophrenia; here we can often observe the

[11] Like the now obsolete concept of ether, energy and the atom are primitive intuitions. A primitive form of the one is *mana*, and of the other the atom of Democritus and the "soul-sparks" of the Australian aborigines. [Cf. *Two Essays on Analytical Psychology* (*Collected Works*, Vol. 7), pars. 108f.—EDITORS OF *The Collected Works.*]

emergence of archaic impulses in conjunction with unmistakable mythological images.

In my view it is impossible to say which comes first—apprehension of the situation, or the impulse to act. It seems to me that both are aspects of the same vital activity, which we have to think of as two distinct processes simply for the purpose of better understanding.[12]

---

[12] In the course of my life I have often reflected on the theme of this short essay, and the conclusions I have come to are set down in a paper entitled "On the Nature of the Psyche" [in *The Structure and Dynamics of the Psyche* (*Collected Works*, Vol. 8), pars. 343ff.], where the problem of instinct and archetype in its later developments is dealt with in considerable detail. The biological side of the problem is discussed in Alverdes, "Die Wirksamkeit von Archetypen in den Instinkthandlungen der Tiere," *Zoologischer Anzeiger* (Leipzig), CXIX: 9/10 (1937), 225-36.

## ⚜ 4 ⚜

# The Concept of the
# Collective Unconscious[1]

Probably none of my empirical concepts has met with so much misunderstanding as the idea of the collective unconscious. In what follows I shall try to give (1) a definition of the concept, (2) a description of what it means for psychology, (3) an explanation of the method of proof, and (4) an example.[2]

## 1. *Definition*

The collective unconscious is a part of the psyche which can be negatively distinguished from a personal unconscious by the fact that it does not, like the latter, owe its existence to personal experience and consequently is not

[1] From *The Archetypes and the Collective Unconscious. Collected Works,* Vol. 9.i, pars. 87–110. [Originally given as a lecture to the Abernethian Society at St. Bartholomew's Hospital, London, on Oct. 19, 1936, and published in the hospital's *Journal,* XLIV (1936/37), 46–49, 64–66. The present version has been slighty revised by the author and edited in terminology.—EDITORS OF *The Collected Works.*]
[2] The example will here be omitted, since it is again that reported supra, p. 36, of the man who saw the phallus of the sun.—J.C.

a personal acquisition. While the personal unconscious is made up essentially of contents which have at one time been conscious but which have disappeared from consciousness through having been forgotten or repressed, the contents of the collective unconscious have never been in consciousness, and therefore have never been individually acquired, but owe their existence exclusively to heredity. Whereas the personal unconscious consists for the most part of *complexes,* the content of the collective unconscious is made up essentially of *archetypes.*

The concept of the archetype, which is an indispensable correlate of the idea of the collective unconscious, indicates the existence of definite forms in the psyche which seem to be present always and everywhere. Mythological research calls them "motifs"; in the psychology of primitives they correspond to Lévy-Bruhl's concept of "représentations collectives," and in the field of comparative religion they have been defined by Hubert and Mauss as "categories of the imagination." Adolf Bastian long ago called them "elementary" or "primordial thoughts." From these references it should be clear enough that my idea of the archetype—literally a pre-existent form—does not stand alone but is something that is recognized and named in other fields of knowledge.

My thesis, then, is as follows: In addition to our immediate consciousness, which is of a thoroughly personal nature and which we believe to be the only empirical psyche (even if we tack on the personal unconscious as an appendix), there exists a second psychic system of a collective, universal, and impersonal nature which is identical in all individuals. This collective unconscious does not develop individually but is inherited. It consists of pre-existent forms, the archetypes, which can only become conscious secondarily and which give definite form to certain psychic contents.

## 2. The Psychological Meaning of the Collective Unconscious

Medical psychology, growing as it did out of professional practice, insists on the *personal* nature of the psyche. By this I mean the views of Freud and Adler. It is a *psychology of the person,* and its aetiological or causal factors are regarded almost wholly as personal in nature. Nonetheless, even this psychology is based on certain general biological factors, for instance on the sexual instinct or on the urge for self-assertion, which are by no means merely personal peculiarities. It is forced to do this because it lays claim to being an explanatory science. Neither of these views would deny the existence of *a priori* instincts common to man and animals alike, or that they have a significant influence on personal psychology. Yet instincts are impersonal, universally distributed, hereditary factors of a dynamic or motivating character, which very often fail so completely to reach consciousness that modern psychotherapy is faced with the task of helping the patient to become conscious of them. Moreover, the instincts are not vague and indefinite by nature, but are specifically formed motive forces which, long before there is any consciousness, and in spite of any degree of consciousness later on, pursue their inherent goals. Consequently they form very close analogies to the archetypes, so close, in fact, that there is good reason for supposing that the archetypes are the unconscious images of the instincts themselves, in other words, that they are *patterns of instinctual behaviour.*

The hypothesis of the collective unconscious is, therefore, no more daring than to assume there are instincts. One admits readily that human activity is influenced to a high degree by instincts, quite apart from the rational motivations of the conscious mind. So if the assertion is made that our imagination, perception, and thinking are likewise influenced by inborn and universally present formal elements, it seems to me that a normally functioning intelligence can discover in this idea just as much or just as little mysticism as in the theory of instincts. Although this reproach of mysticism has frequently been levelled at my concept, I must emphasize yet again that the concept of the collective unconscious is neither a speculative nor a philosophical but an empirical matter. The question is simply this: are there or are there not unconscious, universal forms of this kind? If they exist, then there is a region of the psyche which one can call the collective unconscious. It is true that the diagnosis of the collective unconscious is not always an easy task. It is not sufficient to point out the often obviously archetypal nature of unconscious products, for these can just as well be derived from acquisitions through language and education. Cryptomnesia should also be ruled out, which it is almost impossible to do in certain cases. In spite of all these difficulties, there remain enough individual instances showing the autochthonous revival of mythological motifs to put the matter beyond any reasonable doubt. But if such an unconscious exists at all, psychological explanation must take account of it and submit certain alleged personal aetiologies to sharper criticism.

What I mean can perhaps best be made clear by a concrete example. You have probably read Freud's discussion[3] of a certain picture by Leonardo da Vinci: St. Anne with the Virgin Mary and the Christ-child. Freud interprets this remarkable picture in terms of the fact that Leonardo himself had two mothers. This causality is personal. We shall not linger over the fact that this picture is far from unique, nor over the minor inaccuracy that St. Anne happens to be the grandmother of Christ and not, as required by Freud's interpretation, the mother, but shall simply point out that interwoven with the apparently personal

[3] *Leonardo da Vinci and a Memory of His Childhood*, sec. IV. Translated by Alan Tyson in Sigmund Freud, *Standard Edition of the Complete Psychological Works*, II (London, 1957).

psychology there is an impersonal motif well known to us from other fields. This is the motif of the *dual mother,* an archetype to be found in many variants in the field of mythology and comparative religion and forming the basis of numerous "représentations collectives." I might mention, for instance, the motif of the *dual descent,* that is, descent from human and divine parents, as in the case of Heracles, who received immortality through being unwittingly adopted by Hera. What was a myth in Greece was actually a ritual in Egypt: Pharaoh was both human and divine by nature. In the birth chambers of the Egyptian temples Pharaoh's second, divine conception and birth is depicted on the walls; he is "twice-born." It is an idea that underlies all rebirth mysteries, Christianity included. Christ himself is "twice-born": through his baptism in the Jordan he was regenerated and reborn from water and spirit. Consequently, in the Roman liturgy the font is designated the "uterus ecclesiae," and, as you can read in the Roman missal, it is called this even today, in the "benediction of the font" on Holy Saturday before Easter. Further, according to an early Christian-Gnostic idea, the spirit which appeared in the form of a dove was interpreted as Sophia-Sapientia—Wisdom and the Mother of Christ. Thanks to this motif of the dual birth, children today, instead of having good and evil fairies who magically "adopt" them at birth with blessings or curses, are given sponsors—a "godfather" and a "godmother."

The idea of a second birth is found at all times and in all places. In the earliest beginnings of medicine it was a magical means of healing; in many religions it is the central mystical experience; it is the key idea in medieval, occult philosophy, and, last but not least, it is an infantile fantasy occurring in numberless children, large and small, who believe that their parents are not their real parents but merely foster-parents to whom they were handed over. Benvenuto Cellini also had this idea, as he himself relates in his autobiography.

Now it is absolutely out of the question that all the individuals who believe in a dual descent have in reality always had two mothers, or conversely that those few who shared Leonardo's fate have infected the rest of humanity with their complex. Rather, one cannot avoid the assumption that the universal occurrence of the dual-birth motif together with the fantasy of the two mothers answers an omnipresent human need which is reflected in these motifs. If Leonardo da Vinci did in fact portray his two mothers in St. Anne and Mary—which I doubt—he nonetheless was only expressing something which countless millions of people before and after him have believed. The vulture symbol (which Freud also discusses in the work mentioned) makes this view all the more plausible. With some justification he quotes as the source of the symbol the *Hieroglyphica* of Horapollo, a book much in use in Leonardo's time. There you read that vultures are female only and symbolize the mother. They conceive through the wind (*pneuma*). This word took on the meaning of "spirit" chiefly under the influence of Christianity. Even in the account of the miracle at Pentecost the pneuma still has the double meaning of wind and spirit. This fact, in my opinion, points without doubt to Mary, who, a virgin by nature, conceived through the pneuma, like a vulture. Furthermore, according to Horapollo, the vulture also symbolizes Athene, who sprang, unbegotten, directly from the head of Zeus, was a virgin, and knew only spiritual motherhood. All this is really an allusion to Mary and the rebirth motif. There is not a shadow of evidence that Leonardo meant anything else by his picture. Even if it is correct to assume that he identified himself with the Christ-child, he was in all probability representing the mythological dual-mother motif and by no means his own personal prehistory. And what about all the other artists who painted the same theme? Surely not all of them had two mothers?

Let us now transpose Leonardo's case to the field of the neuroses, and assume that a patient with a mother complex is suffering from the delusion that the cause of his neurosis lies in his having really had two mothers. The personal interpretation would have to admit that he is right—and yet it would be quite wrong. For in reality the cause of his neurosis would lie in the reactivation of the dual-mother archetype, quite regardless of whether he had one mother or two mothers, because, as we have seen, this archetype functions individually and historically without any reference to the relatively rare occurrence of dual motherhood.

In such a case, it is of course tempting to presuppose so simple and personal a cause, yet the hypothesis is not only inexact but totally false. It is admittedly difficult to understand how a dual-mother motif—unknown to a physician trained only in medicine—could have so great a determining power as to produce the effect of a traumatic condition. But if we consider the tremendous powers that lie hidden in the mythological and religious sphere in man, the aetiological significance of the archetype appears less fantastic. In numerous cases of neurosis the cause of the disturbance lies in the very fact that the psychic life of the patient lacks the co-operation of these motive forces. Nevertheless a purely personalistic psychology, by reducing everything to personal causes, tries its level best to deny the existence of archetypal motifs and even seeks to destroy them by personal analysis. I consider this a rather dangerous procedure which cannot be justified medically. Today you can judge better than you could twenty years ago the nature of the forces involved. Can we not see how a whole nation is reviving an archaic symbol, yes, even archaic religious forms, and how this mass emotion is influencing and revolutionizing the life of the individual in a catastrophic manner? [4] The man of the past is alive in us today to a degree undreamt of before the war, and in the last analysis what is the fate of great nations but a summation of the psychic changes in individuals?

[4] The reference, of course, is to Hitler's Germany.—J.C.

So far as a neurosis is really only a private affair, having its roots exclusively in personal causes, archetypes play no role at all. But if it is a question of a general incompatibility or an otherwise injurious condition productive of neuroses in relatively large numbers of individuals, then we must assume the presence of constellated archetypes. Since neuroses are in most cases not just private concerns, but *social* phenomena, we must assume that archetypes are constellated in these cases too. The archetype corresponding to the situation is activated, and as a result those explosive and dangerous forces hidden in the archetype come into action, frequently with unpredictable consequences. There is no lunacy people under the domination of an archetype will not fall a prey to. If thirty years ago anyone had dared to predict that our psychological development was tending towards a revival of the medieval persecutions of the Jews, that Europe would again tremble before the Roman fasces and the tramp of legions, that people would once more give the Roman salute, as two thousand years ago, and that instead of the Christian Cross an archaic swastika would lure onward millions of warriors ready for death—why, that man would have been hooted at as a mystical fool. And today? Surprising as it may seem, all this absurdity is a horrible reality. Private life, private aetiologies, and private neuroses have become almost a fiction in the world of today. The man of the past who lived in a world of archaic "représentations collectives" has risen again into very visible and painfully real life, and this not only in a few unbalanced individuals but in many millions of people.

There are as many archetypes as there are typical situations in life. Endless repetition has engraved these experiences into our psychic constitution, not in the form of images filled with content, but at first only as *forms without content,* representing merely the possibility of a certain type of perception and action. When a situation occurs which corresponds to a given archetype, that archetype becomes activated and a compulsiveness appears, which, like an instinctual drive, gains its way against all reason and will, or else produces a conflict of pathological dimensions, that is to say, a neurosis.

### 3. *Method of Proof*

We must now turn to the question of how the existence of archetypes can be proved. Since archetypes are supposed to produce certain psychic forms, we must discuss how and where one can get hold of the material demonstrating these forms. The main source, then, is *dreams,* which have the advantage of being involuntary, spontaneous products of the unconscious psyche and are therefore pure products of nature not falsified by any conscious purpose. By questioning the individual one can ascertain which of the motifs appearing in the dream are known to him. From those which are unknown to him we must naturally exclude all motifs which *might* be known to him, as for instance—to revert to the case of Leonardo—the vulture symbol. We are not sure whether Leonardo took this symbol from Horapollo or not, although it would have been perfectly possible for an educated person of that time, because in those days artists were distinguished for their wide knowledge of the humanities. Therefore, although the bird motif is an archetype par excellence, its existence in Leonardo's fantasy would still prove nothing. Consequently, we must look for motifs which could not possibly be known to the dreamer and yet behave functionally in his dream in such a manner as to coincide with the functioning of the archetype known from historical sources.

Another source for the material we need is to be found in "active imagination." By this I mean a sequence of fantasies produced by deliberate concentration. I have found that the existence of unrealized, unconscious fantasies increases the frequency and intensity of dreams, and that when these fantasies are made conscious the dreams change their character and become weaker and less frequent. From this I have drawn the conclusion that dreams often contain fantasies which "want" to become conscious. The sources of dreams are often repressed instincts which have a natural tendency to influence the conscious mind. In cases of this sort, the patient is simply given the task of contemplating any one fragment of fantasy that seems significant to him—a chance idea, perhaps, or something he has become conscious of in a dream—until its context becomes visible, that is to say, the relevant associative material in which it is embedded. It is not a question of the "free association" recommended by Freud for the purpose of dream-analysis, but of elaborating the fantasy by observing the further fantasy material that adds itself to the fragment in a natural manner.

This is not the place to enter upon a technical discussion of the method. Suffice it to say that the resultant sequence of fantasies relieves the unconscious and produces material rich in archetypal images and associations. Obviously, this is a method that can only be used in certain carefully selected cases. The method is not entirely without danger, because it may carry the patient too far away from reality. A warning against thoughtless application is therefore in place.

Finally, very interesting sources of archetypal material are to be found in the delusions of paranoiacs, the fantasies observed in trance-states, and the dreams of early childhood, from the third to the fifth year. Such material is available in profusion, but it is valueless unless one can adduce convincing mythological parallels. It does not, of course, suffice simply to connect a dream about a snake with the mythological occurrence of snakes, for who is to guarantee that the functional meaning of the snake in the dream is the same as in the mythological setting? In order to draw a valid parallel, it is necessary to know the functional meaning of the individual symbol, and then to find out whether the apparently parallel mythological symbol has a similar context and therefore the same functional meaning. Establishing such facts not only requires lengthy and wearisome researches, but is also an ungrateful subject for demonstration. As the symbols must not be torn out of their context, one has to launch forth into exhaustive descriptions, personal as well as symbological, and this is practically impossible in the framework of a lecture. I have repeatedly tried it at the risk of sending one half of my audience to sleep.

## 4. *An Example*

[The example given is again that of the paranoid schizophrenic who thought he saw the phallus of the sun. Supra, p. 36.]

## ❧ 5 ❧

# The Relations Between the
# Ego and the Unconscious[1]

### Part One
### THE EFFECTS OF THE UNCONSCIOUS
### UPON CONSCIOUSNESS

### I
### The Personal and the Collective
### Unconscious

In Freud's view, as most people know, the contents of the unconscious are reducible to infantile tendencies which are repressed because of their incompatible character. Repression is a process that begins in early childhood under the moral influence of the environment and continues throughout life. By means of analysis the repressions are removed and the repressed wishes made conscious.

According to this theory, the unconscious contains only those parts of the personality which could just as well be conscious, and have been suppressed only through

[1] From *Two Essays on Analytical Psychology. Collected Works,* Vol. 7, Second Essay, pars. 202–295; translated from *Die Beziehungen zwischen dem Ich und dem Unbewussten* (2nd ed.; 1928, 1935), published by Rascher Verlag, Zurich.

the process of education. Although from one point of view the infantile tendencies of the unconscious are the most conspicuous, it would nonetheless be a mistake to define or evaluate the unconscious entirely in these terms. The unconscious has still another side to it: it includes not only repressed contents, but all psychic material that lies below the threshold of consciousness. It is impossible to explain the subliminal nature of all this material on the principle of repression, for in that case the removal of repression ought to endow a person with a prodigious memory which would thenceforth forget nothing.

We therefore emphatically affirm that in addition to the repressed material the unconscious contains all those psychic components that have fallen below the threshold, as well as subliminal sense-perceptions. Moreover we know, from abundant experience as well as for theoretical reasons, that the unconscious also contains all the material that has *not yet* reached the threshold of consciousness. These are the seeds of future conscious contents. Equally we have reason to suppose that the unconscious is never quiescent in the sense of being inactive, but is ceaselessly engaged in grouping and regrouping its contents. This activity should be thought of as completely autonomous only in pathological cases; normally it is co-ordinated with the conscious mind in a compensatory relationship.

It is to be assumed that all these contents are of a personal nature in so far as they are acquired during the individual's life. Since this life is limited, the number of acquired contents in the unconscious must also be limited. This being so, it might be thought possible to empty the unconscious either by analysis or by making a complete inventory of the unconscious contents, on the ground that the unconscious cannot produce anything more than what is already known and assimilated into consciousness. We should also have to suppose, as already said, that if one could arrest the descent of conscious contents into the unconscious by doing away with repression, unconscious productivity would be paralyzed. This is possible only to a very limited extent, as we know from experience. We urge our patients to hold fast to repressed contents that have been re-associated with consciousness, and to assimilate them into their plan of life. But this procedure, as we may daily convince ourselves, makes no impression on the unconscious, since it calmly goes on producing dreams and fantasies which, according to Freud's original theory, must arise from personal repressions. If in such cases we pursue our observations systematically and without prejudice, we shall find material which, although similar in form to the previous personal contents, yet seems to contain allusions that go far beyond the personal sphere.

Casting about in my mind for an example to illustrate what I have just said, I have a particularly vivid memory of a woman patient with a mild hysterical neurosis which, as we expressed it in those days [about 1910], had its principal cause in a "father-complex." By this we wanted to denote the fact that the patient's peculiar relationship to her father stood in her way. She had been on very good terms with her father, who had since died. It was a relationship chiefly of feeling. In such cases it is usually the intellectual function that is developed, and this later becomes the bridge to the world. Accordingly our patient became a student of philosophy. Her energetic pursuit of knowledge was motivated by her need to extricate herself from the emotional entanglement with her father. This operation may succeed if her feelings can find an outlet on the new intellectual level, perhaps in the formation of an emotional tie with a suitable man, equivalent to the former tie. In this particular case, however, the transition refused to take place, because the patient's feelings remained suspended, oscillating between her father and a man who was not altogether suitable. The progress of her life was thus held up, and that inner disunity so characteristic of a neurosis promptly made its appearance. The so-called normal person would probably be able to break the

emotional bond in one or the other direction by a powerful act of will, or else—and this is perhaps the more usual
thing—he would come through the difficulty unconsciously,
on the smooth path of instinct, without ever being aware
of the sort of conflict that lay behind his headaches or
other physical discomforts. But any weakness of instinct
(which may have many causes) is enough to hinder a
smooth unconscious transition. Then all progress is delayed
by conflict, and the resulting stasis of life is equivalent to
a neurosis. In consequence of the standstill, psychic energy
flows off in every conceivable direction, apparently quite
uselessly. For instance, there are excessive innervations
of the sympathetic system, which lead to nervous disorders
of the stomach and intestines; or the vagus (and consequently the heart) is stimulated; or fantasies and memories, uninteresting enough in themselves, become overvalued and prey on the conscious mind (mountains out
of molehills). In this state a new motive is needed to put
an end to the morbid suspension. Nature herself paves the
way for this, unconsciously and indirectly, through the
phenomenon of the transference (Freud). In the course
of treatment the patient transfers the father-imago to the
doctor, thus making him, in a sense, the father, and in the
sense that he is *not* the father, also making him a substitute for the man she cannot reach. The doctor therefore
becomes both a father and a kind of lover—in other words,
an object of conflict. In him the opposites are united, and
for this reason he stands for a quasi-ideal solution of the
conflict. Without in the least wishing it, he draws upon himself an over-valuation that is almost incredible to the outsider, for to the patient he seems like a saviour or a god.
This way of speaking is not altogether so laughable as it
sounds. It is indeed a bit much to be a father and lover
at once. Nobody could possibly stand up to it in the long
run, precisely because it is too much of a good thing. One
would have to be a demigod at least to sustain such a role
without a break, for all the time one would have to be

the giver. To the patient in the state of transference, this provisional solution naturally seems ideal, but only at first; in the end she comes to a standstill that is just as bad as the neurotic conflict was. Fundamentally, nothing has yet happened that might lead to a real solution. The conflict has merely been transferred. Nevertheless a successful transference can—at least temporarily—cause the whole neurosis to disappear, and for this reason it has been very rightly recognized by Freud as a healing factor of first-rate importance, but, at the same time, as a provisional state only, for although it holds out the possibility of a cure, it is far from being the cure itself.

This somewhat lengthy discussion seemed to me essential if my example was to be understood, for my patient had arrived at the state of transference and had already reached the upper limit where the standstill begins to make itself disagreeable. The question now arose: what next? I had of course become the complete saviour, and the thought of having to give me up was not only exceedingly distasteful to the patient, but positively terrifying. In such a situation "sound common sense" generally comes out with a whole repertory of admonitions: "you simply must," "you really ought," "you just cannot," etc. So far as sound common sense is, happily, not too rare and not entirely without effect (pessimists, I know, exist), a rational motive can, in the exuberant feeling of buoyancy you get from the transference, release so much enthusiasm that a painful sacrifice can be risked with a mighty effort of will. If successful—and these things sometimes are—the sacrifice bears blessed fruit, and the erstwhile patient leaps at one bound into the state of being practically cured. The doctor is generally so delighted that he fails to tackle the theoretical difficulties connected with this little miracle.

If the leap does not succeed—and it did not succeed with my patient—one is then faced with the problem of resolving the transference. Here "psychoanalytic" theory shrouds itself in a thick darkness. Apparently we are to fall back on some nebulous trust in fate: somehow or other the matter will settle itself. "The transference stops automatically when the patient runs out of money," as a slightly cynical colleague once remarked to me. Or the ineluctable demands of life make it impossible for the patient to linger on in the transference—demands which compel the involuntary sacrifice, sometimes with a more or less complete relapse as a result. (One may look in vain for accounts of such cases in the books that sing the praises of psychoanalysis!)

To be sure, there are hopeless cases where nothing helps; but there are also cases that do not get stuck and do not inevitably leave the transference situation with bitter hearts and sore heads. I told myself, at this juncture with my patient, that there must be a clear and respectable way out of the impasse. My patient had long since run out of money—if indeed she ever possessed any—but I was curious to know what means nature would devise for a satisfactory way out of the transference deadlock. Since I never imagined that I was blessed with that "sound common sense" which always knows exactly what to do in every quandary, and since my patient knew as little as I, I suggested to her that we could at least keep an eye open for any movements coming from a sphere of the psyche uncontaminated by our superior wisdom and our conscious plannings. That meant first and foremost her dreams.

Dreams contain images and thought-associations which we do not create with conscious intent. They arise spontaneously without our assistance and are representatives of a psychic activity withdrawn from our arbitrary will. Therefore the dream is, properly speaking, a highly objective, natural product of the psyche, from which we might expect indications, or at least hints, about certain basic trends in the psychic process. Now, since the psychic process, like any other life-process, is not just a causal sequence, but is also a process with a teleological orientation, we might expect dreams to give us certain *indicia* about the objective causality as well as about the objective tendencies, precisely because dreams are nothing less than self-representations of the psychic life-process.

On the basis of these reflections, then, we subjected the dreams to a careful examination. It would lead too far to quote word for word all the dreams that now followed. Let it suffice to sketch their main character: the majority referred to the person of the doctor, that is to say, the actors were unmistakably the dreamer herself and her doctor. The latter, however, seldom appeared in his natural shape, but was generally distorted in a remarkable way. Sometimes his figure was of supernatural size, sometimes he seemed to be extremely aged, then again he resembled her father, but was at the same time curiously woven into nature, as in the following dream: *Her father (who in reality was of small stature) was standing with her on a hill that was covered with wheat-fields. She was quite tiny beside him, and he seemed to her like a giant. He lifted her up from the ground and held her in his arms like a little child. The wind swept over the wheat-fields, and as the wheat swayed in the wind, he rocked her in his arms.*

From this dream and from others like it I could discern various things. Above all I got the impression that her unconscious was holding unshakably to the idea of my being the father-lover, so that the fatal tie we were trying to undo appeared to be doubly strengthened. Moreover one could hardly avoid seeing that the unconscious placed a special emphasis on the supernatural, almost "divine" nature of the father-lover, thus accentuating still further the over-valuation occasioned by the transference. I therefore asked myself whether the patient had still not understood the wholly fantastic character of her transference, or whether perhaps the unconscious could never be reached by understanding at all, but must blindly and idiotically pursue some nonsensical chimera. Freud's idea that the unconscious can "do nothing but wish," Schopenhauer's blind and aimless Will, the gnostic demiurge who

in his vanity deems himself perfect and then in the blindness of his limitation creates something lamentably imperfect—all these pessimistic suspicions of an essentially
negative background to the world and the soul came threateningly near. And there would indeed be nothing to set
against this except a well-meaning "you ought," reinforced
by a stroke of the axe that would cut down the whole
phantasmagoria for good and all.

But, as I turned the dreams over and over in my mind,
there dawned on me another possibility. I said to myself: it
cannot be denied that the dreams continue to speak in the
same old metaphors with which our conversations have
made the patient as well as myself sickeningly familiar.
But the patient has an undoubted understanding of her
transference fantasy. She knows that I appear to her as
a semi-divine father-lover, and she can, at least intellectually, distinguish this from my factual reality. Therefore
the dreams are obviously reiterating the conscious standpoint minus the conscious criticism, which they completely
ignore. They reiterate the conscious contents, not *in toto,*
but insist on the fantastic standpoint as opposed to "sound
common sense."

I naturally asked myself what was the source of this
obstinacy and what was its purpose? That it must have
some purposive meaning I was convinced, for there is no
truly living thing that does not have a final meaning, that
can in other words be explained as a mere left-over from
antecedent facts. But the energy of the transference is so
strong that it gives one the impression of a vital instinct.
That being so, what is the purpose of such fantasies? A
careful examination and analysis of the dreams, especially
of the one just quoted, revealed a very marked tendency
—in contrast to conscious criticism, which always seeks
to reduce things to human proportions—to endow the
person of the doctor with superhuman attributes. He had
to be gigantic, primordial, huger than the father, like the
wind that sweeps over the earth—was he then to be made

into a god? Or, I said to myself, was it rather the case that the unconscious was trying to *create* a god out of the person of the doctor, as it were to free a vision of God from the veils of the personal, so that the transference to the person of the doctor was no more than a misunderstanding on the part of the conscious mind, a stupid trick played by "sound common sense"? Was the urge of the unconscious perhaps only apparently reaching out towards the person, but in a deeper sense towards a god? Could the longing for a god be a *passion* welling up from our darkest, instinctual nature, a passion unswayed by any outside influences, deeper and stronger perhaps than the love for a human person? Or was it perhaps the highest and truest meaning of that inappropriate love we call "transference," a little bit of real *Gottesminne,* that has been lost to consciousness ever since the fifteenth century?

No one will doubt the reality of a passionate longing for a human person; but that a fragment of religious psychology, an historical anachronism, indeed something of a medieval curiosity—we are reminded of Mechtild of Magdeburg—should come to light as an immediate living reality in the middle of the consulting-room, and be expressed in the prosaic figure of the doctor, seems almost too fantastic to be taken seriously.

A genuinely scientific attitude must be unprejudiced. The sole criterion for the validity of an hypothesis is whether or not it possesses an heuristic—i.e., explanatory—value. The question now is, can we regard the possibilities set forth above as a valid hypothesis? There is no *a priori* reason why it should not be just as possible that the unconscious tendencies have a goal beyond the human person, as that the unconscious can "do nothing but wish." Experience alone can decide which is the more suitable hypothesis. This new hypothesis was not entirely plausible to my very critical patient. The earlier view that I was the father-lover, and as such presented an ideal solution of the conflict, was incomparably more attractive to her way of feeling. Nevertheless her intellect was sufficiently keen to appreciate the theoretical possibility of the new hypothesis. Meanwhile the dreams continued to disintegrate the person of the doctor and swell him to ever vaster proportions. Concurrently with this there now occurred something which at first I alone perceived, and with the utmost astonishment, namely a kind of subterranean undermining of the transference. Her relations with a certain friend deepened perceptibly, notwithstanding the fact that consciously she still clung to the transference. So that when the time came for leaving me, it was no catastrophe, but a perfectly reasonable parting. I had the privilege of being the only witness during the process of severance. I saw how the transpersonal control-point developed—I cannot call it anything else—a *guiding function* and step by step gathered to itself all the former personal over-valuations; how, with this afflux of energy, it gained influence over the resisting conscious mind without the patient's consciously noticing what was happening. From this I realized that the dreams were not just fantasies, but self-representations of unconscious developments which allowed the psyche of the patient gradually to grow out of the pointless personal tie.

This change took place, as I showed, through the unconscious development of a transpersonal control-point; a virtual goal, as it were, that expressed itself symbolically in a form which can only be described as a vision of God. The dreams swelled the human person of the doctor to superhuman proportions, making him a gigantic primordial father who is at the same time the wind, and in whose protecting arms the dreamer rests like an infant. If we try to make the patient's conscious, and traditionally Christian, idea of God responsible for the divine image in the dreams, we would still have to lay stress on the distortion. In religious matters the patient had a critical and agnostic attitude, and her idea of a possible deity had long since passed into the realm of the inconceivable, i.e., had dwindled into a complete abstraction. In contrast to this, the god-image of the dreams corresponded to the archaic conception of a nature-daemon, something like Wotan. θεὸς τὸ πνεῦμα, "God is spirit," is here translated back into its original form where πνεῦμα means "wind": God is the wind, stronger and mightier than man, an invisible breath-spirit. As in Hebrew *ruah,* so in Arabic *ruh* means breath and spirit.[2] Out of the purely personal form the dreams develop an archaic god-image that is infinitely far from the conscious idea of God. It might be objected that this is simply an infantile image, a childhood memory. I would have no quarrel with this assumption if we were dealing with an old man sitting on a golden throne in heaven. But there is no trace of any sentimentality of that kind; instead, we have a primordial idea that can correspond only to an archaic mentality.

These primordial ideas, of which I have given a great many examples in my *Symbols of Transformation,* oblige one to make, in regard to unconscious material, a distinction of quite a different character from that between "preconscious" and "unconscious" or "subconscious" and "unconscious." The justification for these distinctions need not be discussed here. They have their specific value and are worth elaborating further as points of view. The fundamental distinction which experience has forced upon me claims to be no more than that. It should be evident from the foregoing that we have to distinguish in the unconscious a layer which we may call the *personal unconscious.* The materials contained in this layer are of a personal nature in so far as they have the character partly of acquisitions derived from the individual's life and partly of psychological factors which could just as well be conscious. It can readily be understood that incompatible psychological elements are liable to repression and therefore become unconscious. But on the other hand this implies the possibility of making and keeping the repressed contents con-

[2] For a fuller elaboration of this theme see *Symbols of Transformation (Collected Works,* Vol. 5), index, s.v. "wind."

scious once they have been recognized. We recognize them as personal contents because their effects, or their partial manifestation, or their source can be discovered in our personal past. They are the integral components of the personality, they belong to its inventory, and their loss to consciousness produces an inferiority in one respect or another—an inferiority, moreover, that has the psychological character not so much of an organic lesion or an inborn defect as of a lack which gives rise to a feeling of moral resentment. The sense of moral inferiority always indicates that the missing element is something which, to judge by this feeling about it, really ought not be missing, or which could be made conscious if only one took sufficient trouble. The moral inferiority does not come from a collision with the generally accepted and, in a sense, arbitrary moral law, but from the conflict with one's own self which, for reasons of psychic equilibrium, demands that the deficit be redressed. Whenever a sense of moral inferiority appears, it indicates not only a need to assimilate an unconscious component, but also the possibility of such assimilation. In the last resort it is a man's moral qualities which force him, either through direct recognition of the need or indirectly through a painful neurosis, to assimilate his unconscious self and to keep himself fully conscious. Whoever progresses along this road of self-realization must inevitably bring into consciousness the contents of the personal unconscious, thus enlarging the scope of his personality. I should add at once that this enlargement has to do primarily with one's moral consciousness, one's knowledge of oneself, for the unconscious contents that are released and brought into consciousness by analysis are usually unpleasant—which is precisely why these wishes, memories, tendencies, plans, etc. were repressed. These are the contents that are brought to light in much the same way by a thorough confession, though to a much more limited extent. The rest comes out as a rule in dream analysis. It is often very interesting to watch how the dreams fetch up the essential points, bit by bit and with the nicest choice. The total material that is added to consciousness causes a considerable widening of the horizon, a deepened self-knowledge which, more than anything else, one would think, is calculated to humanize a man and make him modest. But even self-knowledge, assumed by all wise men to be the best and most efficacious, has different effects on different characters. We make very remarkable discoveries in this respect in practical analysis, but I shall deal with this question in the next chapter.

As my example of the archaic idea of God shows, the unconscious seems to contain other things besides personal acquisitions and belongings. My patient was quite unconscious of the derivation of "spirit" from "wind," or of the parallelism between the two. This content was not the product of her thinking, nor had she ever been taught it. The critical passage in the New Testament was inaccessible to her—τὸ πνεῦμα πνεῖ ὅπου θέλει—since she knew no Greek. If we must take it as a wholly personal acquisition, it might be a case of so-called cryptomnesia,[3] the unconscious recollection of a thought which the dreamer had once read somewhere. I have nothing against such a possibility in this particular case; but I have seen a sufficient number of other cases—many of them are to be found in the book mentioned above—where cryptomnesia can be excluded with certainty. Even if it were a case of cryptomnesia, which seems to me very improbable, we should still have to explain what the predisposition was that caused just this image to be retained and later, as Semon puts it, "ecphorated" (ἐκφορεῖν, Latin *efferre*, 'to produce'). In any case, cryptomnesia or no cryptomnesia, we are dealing with a genuine and thoroughly primitive god-image that grew up in the unconscious of a civilized person and produced

[3] Cf. Théodore Flournoy, *Des Indes à la planète Mars: Étude sur un cas de somnambulisme avec Glossolalie* (Paris and Geneva, 1900), translated by D. B. Vermilye as *From India to the Planet Mars* (New York, 1900), and Jung, "Psychology and Pathology of So-called Occult Phenomena"(*Collected Works*, Vol. 1), pars. 138ff.

a living effect—an effect which might well give the psychologist of religion food for reflection. There is nothing about this image that could be called personal: it is a wholly collective image, the ethnic origin of which has long been known to us. Here is an historical image of world-wide distribution that has come into existence again through a natural psychic function. This is not so very surprising, since my patient was born into the world with a human brain which presumably still functions today much as it did of old. We are dealing with a reactivated *archetype,* as I have elsewhere called these primordial images.[4] These ancient images are restored to life by the primitive, analogical mode of thinking peculiar to dreams. It is not a question of inherited ideas, but of inherited thought-patterns.[5]

In view of these facts we must assume that the unconscious contains not only personal, but also impersonal collective components in the form of inherited categories[6] or archetypes. I have therefore advanced the hypothesis that at its deeper levels the unconscious possesses collective contents in a relatively active state. That is why I speak of a collective unconscious.

# II
## *Phenomena Resulting from the Assimilation of the Unconscious*

The process of assimilating the unconscious leads to some very remarkable phenomena. It produces in some patients an unmistakable and often unpleasant increase of self-confidence and conceit: they are full of themselves,

[4] Cf. *Psychological Types (Collected Works,* Vol. 6), Def. 26. [See also supra pp. *xxxi–xxxii,* 39–46, and 50–58.—J.C.
[5] Consequently, the accusation of "fanciful mysticism" levelled at my ideas is lacking in foundation.
[6] Henry Hubert and Marcel Mauss, *Mélanges d'histoire des religions* (Paris, 1909), p. xxix.

they know everything, they imagine themselves to be fully informed of everything concerning their unconscious, and are persuaded that they understand perfectly everything that comes out of it. At every interview with the doctor they get more and more above themselves. Others on the contrary feel themselves more and more crushed under the contents of the unconscious, they lose their self-confidence and abandon themselves with dull resignation to all the extraordinary things that the unconscious produces. The former, overflowing with feelings of their own importance, assume a responsibility for the unconscious that goes much too far, beyond all reasonable bounds; the others finally give up all sense of responsibility, overcome by a sense of the powerlessness of the ego against the fate working through the unconscious.

If we analyze these two modes of reaction more deeply, we find that the optimistic self-confidence of the first conceals a profound sense of impotence, for which their conscious optimism acts as an unsuccessful compensation; while the pessimistic resignation of the others masks a defiant will to power, far surpassing in cocksureness the conscious optimism of the first type.

With these two modes of reaction I have sketched only two crude extremes. A finer shading would have been truer to reality. As I have said elsewhere, every analysand starts by unconsciously misusing his newly won knowledge in the interests of his abnormal, neurotic attitude, unless he is sufficiently freed from his symptoms in the early stages to be able to dispense with further treatment altogether. A very important contributory factor is that in the early stages everything is still understood on the objective level, i.e., without distinction between imago and object, so that everything is referred directly to the object. Hence the man for whom "other people" are the objects of prime importance will conclude from any self-knowledge he may have imbibed at this stage of the analysis: "Aha! so that is what other people are like!" He will therefore feel it his duty, according to his nature, tolerant or otherwise, to enlighten the world. But the other man, who feels himself to be more the object of his fellows than their subject, will be weighed down by this self-knowledge and become correspondingly depressed. (I am naturally leaving out of account those numerous and more superficial natures who experience these problems only by the way.) In both cases the relation to the object is reinforced—in the first case in an active, in the second case in a reactive sense. The collective element is markedly accentuated. The one extends the sphere of his action, the other the sphere of his suffering.

Adler has employed the term "godlikeness" to characterize certain basic features of neurotic power psychology. If I likewise borrow the same term from *Faust,* I use it here more in the sense of that well-known passage where Mephisto writes "Eritis sicut Deus, scientes bonum et malum" in the student's album, and makes the following aside:

> Just follow the old advice
> And my cousin the snake.
> There'll come a time when your godlikeness
> Will make you quiver and quake.[7]

The godlikeness evidently refers to knowledge, the knowledge of good and evil. The analysis and conscious realization of unconscious contents engender a certain superior tolerance, thanks to which even relatively indigestible portions of one's unconscious characterology can be accepted. This tolerance may look very wise and superior, but often it is no more than a grand gesture that brings all sorts of consequences in its train. Two spheres have been brought together which before were kept anxiously apart. After considerable resistances have been overcome, the union of opposites is successfully achieved, at least to all appearances. The deeper understanding thus gained, the juxtaposition of what was before separated, and hence the apparent over-

---

[7] *Faust,* Part I, 3rd scene in Faust's study.

coming of the moral conflict, give rise to a feeling of superiority that may well be expressed by the term "god-likeness." But this same juxtaposition of good and evil can have a very different effect on a different kind of temperament. Not everyone will feel himself a superman, holding in his hands the scales of good and evil. It may also seem as though he were a helpless object caught between hammer and anvil; not in the least a Hercules at the parting of the ways, but rather a rudderless ship buffeted between Scylla and Charybdis. For without knowing it, he is caught up in perhaps the greatest and most ancient of human conflicts, experiencing the throes of eternal principles in collision. Well might he feel himself like a Prometheus chained to the Caucasus, or as one crucified. This would be a "godlikeness" in suffering. Godlikeness is certainly not a scientific concept, although it aptly characterizes the psychological state in question. Nor do I imagine that every reader will immediately grasp the peculiar state of mind implied by "godlikeness." The term belongs too exclusively to the sphere of *belles-lettres*. So I should probably be better advised to give a more circumspect description of this state. The insight and understanding, then, gained by the analysand usually reveal much to him that was before unconscious. He naturally applies this knowledge to his environment; in consequence he sees, or thinks he sees, many things that before were invisible. Since his knowledge was helpful to him, he readily assumes that it would be useful also to others. In this way he is liable to become arrogant; it may be well meant, but it is nonetheless annoying to other people. He feels as though he possesses a key that opens many, perhaps even all, doors. Psychoanalysis itself has this same bland unconsciousness of its limitations, as can clearly be seen from the way it meddles with works of art.

Since human nature is not compounded wholly of light, but also abounds in shadows, the insight gained in practical analysis is often somewhat painful, the more so if, as is generally the case, one has previously neglected the other side. Hence there are people who take their newly won insight very much to heart, far too much in fact, quite forgetting that they are not unique in having a shadow-side. They allow themselves to get unduly depressed and are then inclined to doubt everything, finding nothing right anywhere. That is why many excellent analysts with very good ideas can never bring themselves to publish them, because the psychic problem, as they see it, is so overwhelmingly vast that it seems to them almost impossible to tackle it scientifically. One man's optimism makes him overweening, while another's pessimism makes him over-anxious and despondent. Such are the forms which the great conflict takes when reduced to a smaller scale. But even in these lesser proportions the essence of the conflict is easily recognized: the arrogance of the one and the despondency of the other share a common uncertainty as to their boundaries. The one is excessively expanded, the other excessively contracted. Their individual boundaries are in some way obliterated. If we now consider the fact that, as a result of psychic compensation, great humility stands very close to pride, and that "pride goeth before a fall," we can easily discover behind the haughtiness certain traits of an anxious sense of inferiority. In fact we shall see clearly how his uncertainty forces the enthusiast to puff up his truths, of which he feels none too sure, and to win proselytes to his side in order that his followers may prove to himself the value and trustworthiness of his own convictions. Nor is he altogether so happy in his fund of knowledge as to be able to hold out alone; at bottom he feels isolated by it, and the secret fear of being left alone with it induces him to trot out his opinions and interpretations in and out of season, because only when convincing someone else does he feel safe from gnawing doubts.

It is just the reverse with our despondent friend. The more he withdraws and hides himself, the greater becomes his secret need to be understood and recognized. Although he speaks of his inferiority he does not really believe it. There arises within him a defiant conviction of his unrecognized merits, and in consequence he is sensitive to the slightest disapprobation, always wearing the stricken air of one who is misunderstood and deprived of his rightful due. In this way he nurses a morbid pride and an insolent discontent—which is the very last thing he wants and for which his environment has to pay all the more dearly.

Both are at once too small and too big; their individual mean, never very secure, now becomes shakier than ever. It sounds almost grotesque to describe such a state as "godlike." But since each in his way steps beyond his human proportions, both of them are a little "superhuman" and therefore, figuratively speaking, godlike. If we wish to avoid the use of this metaphor, I would suggest that we speak instead of "psychic inflation." The term seems to me appropriate in so far as the state we are discussing involves an extension of the personality beyond individual limits, in other words, a state of being puffed up. In such a state a man fills a space which normally he cannot fill. He can only fill it by appropriating to himself contents and qualities which properly exist for themselves alone and should therefore remain outside our bounds. What lies outside ourselves belongs either to someone else, or to everyone, or to no one. Since psychic inflation is by no means a phenomenon induced exclusively by analysis, but occurs just as often in ordinary life, we can investigate it equally well in other cases. A very common instance is the humourless way in which many men identify themselves with their business or their titles. The office I hold is certainly my special activity; but it is also a collective factor that has come into existence historically through the co-operation of many people and whose dignity rests solely on collective approval. When, therefore, I identify myself with my office or title, I behave as though I myself were the

whole complex of social factors of which that office consists, or as though I were not only the bearer of the office,
but also and at the same time the approval of society. I
have made an extraordinary extension of myself and have
usurped qualities which are not in me but outside me.
*L'état c'est moi* is the motto for such people.

In the case of inflation through knowledge we are dealing with something similar in principle, though psychologically more subtle. Here it is not the dignity of an office
that causes the inflation, but very significant fantasies. I
will explain what I mean by a practical example, choosing
a mental case whom I happened to know personally and
who is also mentioned in a publication by Maeder.[8] The
case is characterized by a high degree of inflation. (In
mental cases we can observe all the phenomena that are
present only fleetingly in normal people, in a cruder and
enlarged form.)[9] The patient suffered from paranoid dementia with megalomania. He was in telephonic communication with the Mother of God and other great ones.
In human reality he was a wretched locksmith's apprentice
who at the age of nineteen had become incurably insane.
He had never been blessed with intelligence, but he had,
among other things, hit upon the magnificent idea that
the world was his picture-book, the pages of which he
could turn at will. The proof was quite simple: he had
only to turn round, and there was a new page for him to
see.

This is Schopenhauer's "world as will and idea" in un-

[8] A. Maeder, "Psychologische Untersuchungen an Dementia-Praecox-
Kranken," *Jahrbuch für psychoanalytische und psychopathologische
Forschungen,* II (1910), 209ff.
[9] When I was still a doctor at the psychiatric clinic in Zurich, I
once took an intelligent layman through the sick-wards. He had
never seen a lunatic asylum from the inside before. When we had
finished our round, he exclaimed, "I tell you, it's just like Zurich in
miniature! A quintessence of the population. It is as though all the
types one meets every day on the streets had been assembled here
in their classical purity. Nothing but oddities and picked specimens
from top to bottom of society!" I had never looked at it from this
angle before, but my friend was not far wrong.

adorned, primitive concreteness of vision. A shattering idea indeed, born of extreme alienation and seclusion from the world, but so naïvely and simply expressed that at first one can only smile at the grotesqueness of it. And yet this primitive way of looking lies at the very heart of Schopenhauer's brilliant vision of the world. Only a genius or a madman could so disentangle himself from the bonds of reality as to see the world as his picture-book. Did the patient actually work out or build up such a vision, or did it just befall him? Or did he perhaps fall into it? His pathological disintegration and inflation point rather to the latter. It is no longer *he* that thinks and speaks, but *it* thinks and speaks within him: he hears voices. So the difference between him and Schopenhauer is that, in him, the vision remained at the stage of a mere spontaneous growth, while Schopenhauer abstracted it and expressed it in language of universal validity. In so doing he raised it out of its subterranean beginnings into the clear light of collective consciousness. But it would be quite wrong to suppose that the patient's vision had a purely personal character or value, as though it were something that belonged to him. If that were so, he would be a philosopher. A man is a philosopher of genius only when he succeeds in transmuting the primitive and merely natural vision into an abstract idea belonging to the common stock of consciousness. This achievement, and this alone, constitutes his personal value, for which he may take credit without necessarily succumbing to inflation. But the sick man's vision is an impersonal value, a natural growth against which he is powerless to defend himself, by which he is actually swallowed up and "wafted" clean out of the world. Far from *his* mastering the idea and expanding *it* into a philosophical view of the world, it is truer to say that the undoubted grandeur of his vision blew *him* up to pathological proportions. The personal value lies entirely in the philosophical achievement, not in the primary vision. To the philosopher as well this vision comes as so much increment, and is simply a part of the common property of mankind, in which, in principle, everyone has a share. The golden apples drop from the same tree, whether they be gathered by an imbecile locksmith's apprentice or by a Schopenhauer.

There is, however, yet another thing to be learnt from this example, namely that these transpersonal contents are not just inert or dead matter that can be annexed at will. Rather they are living entities which exert an attractive force upon the conscious mind. Identification with one's office or one's title is very attractive indeed, which is precisely why so many men are nothing more than the decorum accorded to them by society. In vain would one look for a personality behind the husk. Underneath all the padding one would find a very pitiable little creature. That is why the office—or whatever this outer husk may be— is so attractive: it offers easy compensation for personal deficiencies.

Outer attractions, such as offices, titles, and other social regalia are not the only things that cause inflation. These are simply impersonal quantities that lie outside in society, in the collective consciousness. But just as there is a society outside the individual, so there is a collective psyche outside the personal psyche, namely the collective unconscious, concealing, as the above example shows, elements that are no whit less attractive. And just as a man may suddenly step into the world on his professional dignity ("Messieurs, à présent je suis Roy"), so another may disappear out of it equally suddenly when it is his lot to behold one of those mighty images that put a new face upon the world. These are the magical *représentations collectives* which underlie the slogan, the catchword, and, on a higher level, the language of the poet and mystic. I am reminded of another mental case who was neither a poet nor anything very outstanding, just a naturally quiet and rather sentimental youth. He had fallen in love with a girl and, as so often happens, had failed to ascertain whether his love was requited. His primitive *participation mystique* took it for granted that his agitations were plainly the agitations of the other, which on the lower levels of human psychology is naturally very often the case. Thus he built up a sentimental love-fantasy which precipitately collapsed when he discovered that the girl would have none of him. He was so desperate that he went straight to the river to drown himself. It was late at night, and the stars gleamed up at him from the dark water. It seemed to him that the stars were swimming two by two down the river, and a wonderful feeling came over him. He forgot his suicidal intentions and gazed fascinated at the strange, sweet drama. And gradually he became aware that every star was a face, and that all these pairs were lovers, who were carried along locked in a dreaming embrace. An entirely new understanding came to him: all had changed —his fate, his disappointment, even his love, receded and fell away. The memory of the girl grew distant, blurred; but instead, he felt with complete certainty that untold riches were promised him. He knew that an immense treasure lay hidden for him in the neighbouring observatory. The result was that he was arrested by the police at four o'clock in the morning, attempting to break into the observatory.

What had happened? His poor head had glimpsed a Dantesque vision, whose loveliness he could never have grasped had he read it in a poem. But he saw it, and it transformed him. What had hurt him most was now far away; a new and undreamed-of world of stars, tracing their silent courses far beyond this grievous earth, had opened out to him the moment he crossed "Proserpine's threshold." The intuition of untold wealth—and could any fail to be touched by this thought?—came to him like a revelation. For his poor turnip-head it was too much. He did not drown in the river, but in an eternal image, and its beauty perished with him.

Just as one man may disappear in his social role, so

another may be engulfed in an inner vision and be lost to his surroundings. Many fathomless transformations of personality, like sudden conversions and other far-reaching changes of mind, originate in the attractive power of a collective image,[10] which, as the present example shows, can cause such a high degree of inflation that the entire personality is disintegrated. This disintegration is a mental disease, of a transitory or a permanent nature, a "splitting of the mind" or "schizophrenia," in Bleuler's term.[11] The pathological inflation naturally depends on some innate weakness of the personality against the autonomy of collective unconscious contents.

We shall probably get nearest to the truth if we think of the conscious and personal psyche as resting upon the broad basis of an inherited and universal psychic disposition which is as such unconscious, and that our personal psyche bears the same relation to the collective psyche as the individual to society.

But equally, just as the individual is not merely a unique and separate being, but is also a social being, so the human psyche is not a self-contained and wholly individual phenomenon, but also a collective one. And just as certain social functions or instincts are opposed to the interests of single individuals, so the human psyche exhibits certain functions or tendencies which, on account of their collective nature, are opposed to individual needs. The reason for this is that every man is born with a highly differentiated brain and is thus assured of a wide range of mental functioning which is neither developed ontogenetically nor acquired. But, to the degree that human brains are uniformly differentiated, the mental functioning thereby made possible is also collective and universal. This explains, for example, the interesting fact that the unconscious processes

[10] Léon Daudet, in *L'Hérédo* (Paris, 1916), calls this process "autofécondation intérieure," by which he means the reawakening of an ancestral soul.
[11] Eugen Bleuler, *Dementia Praecox or the Group of Schizophrenias*, originally published 1911, translated by J. Zinkin (New York, 1950).

of the most widely separated peoples and races show a quite remarkable correspondence, which displays itself, among other things, in the extraordinary but well-authenticated analogies between the forms and motifs of autochthonous myths. The universal similarity of human brains leads to the universal possibility of a uniform mental functioning. This functioning is the *collective psyche.* Inasmuch as there are differentiations corresponding to race, tribe, and even family, there is also a collective psyche limited to race, tribe, and family over and above the "universal" collective psyche. To borrow an expression from Pierre Janet,[12] the collective psyche comprises the *parties inférieures* of the psychic functions, that is to say those deep-rooted, well-nigh automatic portions of the individual psyche which are inherited and are to be found everywhere, and are thus impersonal or suprapersonal. Consciousness plus the personal unconscious constitutes the *parties supérieures* of the psychic functions, those portions, therefore, that are developed ontogenetically and acquired. Consequently, the individual who annexes the unconscious heritage of the collective psyche to what has accrued to him in the course of his ontogenetic development, as though it were part of the latter, enlarges the scope of his personality in an illegitimate way and suffers the consequences. In so far as the collective psyche comprises the *parties inférieures* of the psychic functions and thus forms the basis of every personality, it has the effect of crushing and devaluing the personality. This shows itself either in the aforementioned stifling of self-confidence or else in an unconscious heightening of the ego's importance to the point of a pathological will to power.

By raising the personal unconscious to consciousness, the analysis makes the subject aware of things which he is generally aware of in others, but never in himself. This discovery makes him therefore less individually unique, and more collective. His collectivization is not always a

[12] Pierre Janet, *Les Névroses* (Paris, 1898).

step to the bad; it may sometimes be a step to the good. There are people who repress their good qualities and consciously give free rein to their infantile desires. The lifting of personal repressions at first brings purely personal contents into consciousness; but attached to them are the collective elements of the unconscious, the ever-present instincts, qualities, and ideas (images) as well as all those "statistical" quotas of average virtue and average vice which we recognize when we say, "Everyone has in him something of the criminal, the genius, and the saint." Thus a living picture emerges, containing pretty well everything that moves upon the checkerboard of the world, the good and the bad, the fair and the foul. A sense of solidarity with the world is gradually built up, which is felt by many natures as something very positive and in certain cases actually is the deciding factor in the treatment of neurosis. I have myself seen cases who, in this condition, managed for the first time in their lives to arouse love, and even to experience it themselves; or, by daring to leap into the unknown, they get involved in the very fate for which they were suited. I have seen not a few who, taking this condition as final, remained for years in a state of enterprising euphoria. I have often heard such cases referred to as shining examples of analytical therapy. But I must point out that cases of this euphoric and enterprising type are so utterly lacking in differentiation from the world that nobody could pass them as fundamentally cured. To my way of thinking they are as much cured as not cured. I have had occasion to follow up the lives of such patients, and it must be owned that many of them showed symptoms of maladjustment, which, if persisted in, gradually leads to the sterility and monotony so characteristic of those who have divested themselves of their egos. Here too I am speaking of the border-line cases, and not of the less valuable, normal, average folk for whom the question of adaptation is more technical than problematical. If I were more of a therapist than an investigator, I would naturally be unable to check a certain optimism of judgment, because my eyes would then be glued to the number of cures. But my conscience as an investigator is concerned not with quantity but with quality. Nature is aristocratic, and one person of value outweighs ten lesser ones. My eye followed the valuable people, and from them I learned the dubiousness of the results of a purely personal analysis, and also to understand the reasons for this dubiousness.

If, through assimilation of the unconscious, we make the mistake of including the collective psyche in the inventory of personal psychic functions, a dissolution of the personality into its paired opposites inevitably follows. Besides the pair of opposites already discussed, megalomania and the sense of inferiority, which are so painfully evident in neurosis, there are many others, from which I will single out only the specifically moral pair of opposites, namely good and evil. The specific virtues and vices of humanity are contained in the collective psyche like everything else. One man arrogates collective virtue to himself as his personal merit, another takes collective vice as his personal guilt. Both are as illusory as the megalomania and the inferiority, because the imaginary virtues and the imaginary wickednesses are simply the moral pair of opposites contained in the collective psyche, which have become perceptible or have been rendered conscious artificially. How much these paired opposites are contained in the collective psyche is exemplified by primitives: one observer will extol the greatest virtues in them, while another will record the very worst impressions of the selfsame tribe. For the primitive, whose personal differentiation is, as we know, only just beginning, both judgments are true, because his psyche is essentially collective and therefore for the most part unconscious. He is still more or less identical with the collective psyche, and for that reason shares equally in the collective virtues and vices, without any personal attribution and without inner contradiction. The contradiction arises only when the personal development of the psyche begins, and when reason discovers the irreconcilable nature of the opposites. The consequence of this discovery is the conflict of repression. We want to be good, and therefore must repress evil; and with that the paradise of the collective psyche comes to an end. Repression of the collective psyche was absolutely necessary for the development of personality. In primitives, development of personality, or more accurately, development of the person, is a question of magical prestige. The figure of the medicine-man or chief leads the way: both make themselves conspicuous by the singularity of their ornaments and their mode of life, expressive of their social roles. The singularity of his outward tokens marks the individual off from the rest, and the segregation is still further enhanced by the possession of special ritual secrets. By these and similar means the primitive creates around him a shell, which might be called a persona (mask). Masks, as we know, are actually used among primitives in totem ceremonies—for instance, as a means of enhancing or changing the personality. In this way the outstanding individual is apparently removed from the sphere of the collective psyche, and to the degree that he succeeds in identifying himself with his persona, he actually is removed. This removal means magical prestige. One could easily assert that the impelling motive in this development is the will to power. But that would be to forget that the building up of prestige is always a product of collective compromise: not only must there be one who wants prestige, there must also be a public seeking somebody on whom to confer prestige. That being so, it would be incorrect to say that a man creates prestige for himself out of his individual will to power; it is on the contrary an entirely collective affair. Since society as a whole needs the magically effective figure, it uses this need of the will to power in the individual, and the will to submit in the mass, as a vehicle, and thus brings about the creation of personal prestige. The latter is a phenomenon which, as the history of political institutions shows, is of the utmost importance for the comity of nations.

The importance of personal prestige can hardly be overestimated, because the possibility of regressive dissolution in the collective psyche is a very real danger, not only for the outstanding individual but also for his followers. This possibility is most likely to occur when the goal of prestige —universal recognition—has been reached. The person then becomes a collective truth, and that is always the beginning of the end. To gain prestige is a positive achievement not only for the outstanding individual but also for the clan. The individual distinguishes himself by his deeds, the many by their renunciation of power. So long as this attitude needs to be fought for and defended against hostile influences, the achievement remains positive; but as soon as there are no more obstacles and universal recognition has been attained, prestige loses its positive value and usually becomes a dead letter. A schismatic movement then sets in, and the whole process begins again from the beginning.

Because personality is of such paramount importance for the life of the community, everything likely to disturb its development is sensed as a danger. But the greatest danger of all is the premature dissolution of prestige by an invasion of the collective psyche. Absolute secrecy is one of the best known primitive means of exorcising this danger. Collective thinking and feeling and collective effort are far less of a strain than individual functioning and effort; hence there is always a great temptation to allow collective functioning to take the place of individual differentiation of the personality. Once the personality has been differentiated and safeguarded by magical prestige, its levelling down and eventual dissolution in the collective psyche (e.g., Peter's denial) occasion a "loss of soul" in the individual, because an important personal achievement has been either neglected or allowed to slip into regression. For this reason taboo infringements are followed by Dra-

conian punishments altogether in keeping with the seriousness of the situation. So long as we regard these things
from the causal point of view, as mere historical survivals
and metastases of the incest taboo,[13] it is impossible to
understand what all these measures are for. If, however,
we approach the problem from the teleological point of
view, much that was quite inexplicable becomes clear.

For the development of personality, then, strict differentiation from the collective psyche is absolutely necessary,
since partial or blurred differentiation leads to an immediate melting away of the individual in the collective. There
is now a danger that in the analysis of the unconscious
the collective and the personal psyche may be fused together, with, as I have intimated, highly unfortunate results. These results are injurious both to the patient's life-
feeling and to his fellow men, if he has any influence at
all on his environment. Through his identification with
the collective psyche he will infallibly try to force the demands of his unconscious upon others, for identity with
the collective psyche always brings with it a feeling of
universal validity—"godlikeness"—which completely ignores all differences in the personal psyche of his fellows.
(The feeling of universal validity comes, of course, from
the universality of the collective psyche.) A collective attitude naturally presupposes this same collective psyche in
others. But that means a ruthless disregard not only of
individual differences but also of differences of a more
general kind within the collective psyche itself, as for example differences of race.[14] This disregard for individuality

---

[13] Sigmund Freud, *Totem and Taboo*, translated by J. Strachey (London, 1950).
[14] Thus it is a quite unpardonable mistake to accept the conclusions
of a Jewish psychology as generally valid. Nobody would dream of
taking Chinese or Indian psychology as binding upon ourselves. The
cheap accusation of anti-Semitism that has been levelled at me on
the ground of this criticism is about as intelligent as accusing me of
an anti-Chinese prejudice. No doubt, on an earlier and deeper level
of psychic development, where it is still impossible to distinguish
between an Aryan, Semitic, Hamitic, or Mongolian mentality, all

obviously means the suffocation of the single individual, as a consequence of which the element of differentiation is obliterated from the community. The element of differentiation is the individual. All the highest achievements of virtue, as well as the blackest villainies, are individual. The larger a community is, and the more the sum total of collective factors peculiar to every large community rests on conservative prejudices detrimental to individuality, the more will the individual be morally and spiritually crushed, and, as a result, the one source of moral and spiritual progress for society is choked up. Naturally the only thing that can thrive in such an atmosphere is sociality and whatever is collective in the individual. Everything individual in him goes under, i.e., is doomed to repression. The individual elements lapse into the unconscious, where, by the law of necessity, they are transformed into something essentially baleful, destructive, and anarchical. Socially, this evil principle shows itself in the spectacular crimes—regicide and the like—perpetrated by certain prophetically-inclined individuals; but in the great mass of the community it remains in the background, and only manifests itself indirectly in the inexorable moral degeneration of society. It is a notorious fact that the morality of society as a whole is in inverse ratio to its size; for the greater the aggregation of individuals, the more the individual factors are blotted out, and with them morality, which rests entirely on the moral sense of the individual and the freedom necessary for this. Hence every man is, in a certain sense, unconsciously a worse man when he is in society than when acting alone; for he is carried by society and to that extent relieved of his individual responsibility. Any large company composed of wholly admirable persons has the moral-

human races have a common collective psyche. But with the beginning of racial differentiation essential differences are developed in the collective psyche as well. For this reason we cannot transplant the spirit of a foreign race *in globo* into our own mentality without sensible injury to the latter, a fact which does not, however, deter sundry natures of feeble instinct from affecting Indian philosophy and the like.

ity and intelligence of an unwieldy, stupid, and violent animal. The bigger the organization, the more unavoidable is its immorality and blind stupidity (*Senatus bestia, senatores boni viri*). Society, by automatically stressing all the collective qualities in its individual representatives, puts a premium on mediocrity, on everything that settles down to vegetate in an easy, irresponsible way. Individuality will inevitably be driven to the wall. This process begins in school, continues at the university, and rules all departments in which the State has a hand. In a small social body, the individuality of its members is better safeguarded, and the greater is their relative freedom and the possibility of conscious responsibility. Without freedom there can be no morality. Our admiration for great organizations dwindles when once we become aware of the other side of the wonder: the tremendous piling up and accentuation of all that is primitive in man, and the unavoidable destruction of his individuality in the interests of the monstrosity that every great organization in fact is. The man of today, who resembles more or less the collective ideal, has made his heart into a den of murderers, as can easily be proved by the analysis of his unconscious, even though he himself is not in the least disturbed by it. And in so far as he is normally "adapted" [15] to his environment, it is true that the greatest infamy on the part of his group will not disturb him, so long as the majority of his fellows steadfastly believe in the exalted morality of their social organization. Now, all that I have said here about the influence of society upon the individual is identically true of the influence of the collective unconscious upon the individual psyche. But, as is apparent from my examples, the latter influence is as invisible as the former is visible. Hence it is not surprising that its inner effects are not understood, and that those to whom such things happen are called pathological freaks and treated as crazy. If one of them happened to

---

[15] Cf. "adjustment" and "adaptation" in *Psychological Types* (*Collected Works*, Vol. 6), par. 564.

be a real genius, the fact would not be noted until the next generation or the one after. So obvious does it seem to us that a man should drown in his own dignity, so utterly incomprehensible that he should seek anything other than what the mob wants, and that he should vanish permanently from view in this other. One could wish both of them a sense of humour, that—according to Schopenhauer—truly "divine" attribute of man which alone befits him to maintain his soul in freedom.

The collective instincts and fundamental forms of thinking and feeling whose activity is revealed by the analysis of the unconscious constitute, for the conscious personality, an acquisition which it cannot assimilate without considerable disturbance. It is therefore of the utmost importance in practical treatment to keep the integrity of the personality constantly in mind. For, if the collective psyche is taken to be the personal possession of the individual, it will result in a distortion or an overloading of the personality which is very difficult to deal with. Hence it is imperative to make a clear distinction between personal contents and those of the collective psyche. This distinction is far from easy, because the personal grows out of the collective psyche and is intimately bound up with it. So it is difficult to say exactly what contents are to be called personal and what collective. There is no doubt, for instance, that archaic symbolisms such as we frequently find in fantasies and dreams are collective factors. All basic instincts and basic forms of thinking and feeling are collective. Everything that all men agree in regarding as universal is collective, likewise everything that is universally understood, universally found, universally said and done. On closer examination one is always astonished to see how much of our so-called individual psychology is really collective. So much, indeed, that the individual traits are completely overshadowed by it. Since, however, individuation[16] is an ineluctable psychological necessity, we

[16] Ibid., Def. 29: "Individuation is a process of differentiation, having for its goal the development of the individual personality."

can see from the ascendancy of the collective what very special attention must be paid to this delicate plant "individuality" if it is not to be completely smothered.

Human beings have one faculty which, though it is of the greatest utility for collective purposes, is most pernicious for individuation, and that is the faculty of imitation. Collective psychology cannot dispense with imitation, for without it all mass organizations, the State and the social order, are impossible. Society is organized, indeed, less by law than by the propensity to imitation, implying equally suggestibility, suggestion, and mental contagion. But we see every day how people use, or rather abuse, the mechanism of imitation for the purpose of personal differentiation: they are content to ape some eminent personality, some striking characteristic or mode of behaviour, thereby achieving an outward distinction from the circle in which they move. We could almost say that as a punishment for this the uniformity of their minds with those of their neighbours, already real enough, is intensified into an unconscious, compulsive bondage to the environment. As a rule these specious attempts at individual differentiation stiffen into a pose, and the imitator remains at the same level as he always was, only several degrees more sterile than before. To find out what is truly individual in ourselves, profound reflection is needed; and suddenly we realize how uncommonly difficult the discovery of individuality is.

# III
## *The Persona as a Segment of the Collective Psyche*

In this chapter we come to a problem which, if overlooked, is liable to cause the greatest confusion. It will be remembered that in the analysis of the personal uncon-

---

—"Since the individual is not only a single entity, but also, by his very existence, presupposes a collective relationship, the process of individuation does not lead to isolation, but to an intenser and more universal collective solidarity."

scious the first things to be added to consciousness are the personal contents, and I suggested that these contents, which have been repressed but are capable of becoming conscious, should be called the *personal unconscious.* I also showed that to annex the deeper layers of the unconscious, which I have called the *collective unconscious,* produces an enlargement of the personality leading to the state of inflation. This state is reached by simply continuing the analytical work, as in the case of the young woman discussed above. By continuing the analysis we add to the personal consciousness certain fundamental, general, and impersonal characteristics of humanity, thereby bringing about the inflation[17] I have just described, which might be regarded as one of the unpleasant consequences of becoming fully conscious.

[17] This phenomenon, which results from the extension of consciousness, is in no sense specific to analytical treatment. It occurs whenever people are overpowered by knowledge or by some new realization. "Knowledge puffeth up," Paul writes to the Corinthians, for the new knowledge had turned the heads of many, as indeed constantly happens. The inflation has nothing to do with the *kind* of knowledge, but simply and solely with the fact that any new knowledge can so seize hold of a weak head that he no longer sees and hears anything else. He is hypnotized by it, and instantly believes he has solved the riddle of the universe. But that is equivalent to almighty self-conceit. This process is such a general reaction that, in Genesis 2:17, eating of the tree of knowledge is represented as a deadly sin. It may not be immediately apparent why greater consciousness followed by self-conceit should be such a dangerous thing. Genesis represents the act of becoming conscious as a taboo infringement, as though knowledge meant that a sacrosanct barrier had been impiously overstepped. I think that Genesis is right in so far as every step towards greater consciousness is a kind of Promethean guilt: through knowledge, the gods are as it were robbed of their fire, that is, something that was the property of the unconscious powers is torn out of its natural context and subordinated to the whims of the conscious mind. The man who has usurped the new knowledge suffers, however, a transformation or enlargement of consciousness, which no longer resembles that of his fellow men. He has raised himself above the human level of his age ("ye shall become like unto God"), but in so doing has alienated himself from humanity. The pain of this loneliness is the vengeance of the gods, for never again can he return to mankind. He is, as the myth says, chained to the lonely cliffs of the Caucasus, forsaken of God and man.

From this point of view the conscious personality is a more or less arbitrary segment of the collective psyche. It consists in a sum of psychic facts that are felt to be personal. The attribute "personal" means: pertaining exclusively to this particular person. A consciousness that is purely personal stresses its proprietary and original right to its contents with a certain anxiety, and in this way seeks to create a whole. But all those contents that refuse to fit into this whole are either overlooked and forgotten or repressed and denied. This is one way of educating oneself, but it is too arbitrary and too much of a violation. Far too much of our common humanity has to be sacrificed in the interests of an ideal image into which one tries to mould oneself. Hence these purely "personal" people are always very sensitive, for something may easily happen that will bring into consciousness an unwelcome portion of their real ("individual") character.

This arbitrary segment of collective psyche—often fashioned with considerable pains—I have called the *persona*. The term *persona* is really a very appropriate expression for this, for originally it meant the mask once worn by actors to indicate the role they played. If we endeavour to draw a precise distinction between what psychic material should be considered personal, and what impersonal, we soon find ourselves in the greatest dilemma, for by definition we have to say of the persona's contents what we have said of the impersonal unconscious, namely, that it is collective. It is only because the persona represents a more or less arbitrary and fortuitous segment of the collective psyche that we can make the mistake of regarding it *in toto* as something individual. It is, as its name implies, only a mask of the collective psyche, a mask that *feigns individuality,* making others and oneself believe that one is individual, whereas one is simply acting a role through which the collective psyche speaks.

When we analyze the persona we strip off the mask, and discover that what seemed to be individual is at bottom collective; in other words, that the persona was only a mask of the collective psyche. Fundamentally the persona is nothing real: it is a compromise between individual and society as to what a man should appear to be. He takes a name, earns a title, exercises a function, he is this or that. In a certain sense all this is real, yet in relation to the essential individuality of the person concerned it is only a secondary reality, a compromise formation, in making which others often have a greater share than he. The persona is a semblance, a two-dimensional reality, to give it a nickname.

It would be wrong to leave the matter as it stands without at the same time recognizing that there is, after all, something individual in the peculiar choice and delineation of the persona, and that despite the exclusive identity of the ego-consciousness with the persona the unconscious self, one's real individuality, is always present and makes itself felt indirectly if not directly. Although the ego-consciousness is at first identical with the persona—that compromise role in which we parade before the community—yet the unconscious self can never be repressed to the point of extinction. Its influence is chiefly manifest in the special nature of the contrasting and compensating contents of the unconscious. The purely personal attitude of the conscious mind evokes reactions on the part of the unconscious, and these, together with personal repressions, contain the seeds of individual development in the guise of collective fantasies. Through the analysis of the personal unconscious, the conscious mind becomes suffused with collective material which brings with it the elements of individuality. I am well aware that this conclusion must be almost unintelligible to anyone not familiar with my views and technique, and particularly so to those who habitually regard the unconscious from the standpoint of Freudian theory. But if the reader will recall my example of the philosophy student, he can form a rough idea of what I mean. At the beginning of the treatment the patient was quite unconscious of the fact that her relation to her father was a fixation, and that she was therefore seeking a man like her father, whom she could then meet with her intellect. This in itself would not have been a mistake if her intellect had not had that peculiarly protesting character such as is unfortunately often encountered in intellectual women. Such an intellect is always trying to point out mistakes in others; it is pre-eminently critical, with a disagreeably personal undertone, yet it always wants to be considered objective. This invariably makes a man bad-tempered, particularly if, as so often happens, the criticism touches on some weak spot which, in the interests of fruitful discussion, were better avoided. But far from wishing the discussion to be fruitful, it is the unfortunate peculiarity of this feminine intellect to seek out a man's weak spots, fasten on them, and exasperate him. This is not usually a conscious aim, but rather has the unconscious purpose of forcing a man into a superior position and thus making him an object of admiration. The man does not as a rule notice that he is having the role of the hero thrust upon him; he merely finds her taunts so odious that in future he will go a long way to avoid meeting the lady. In the end the only man who can stand her is the one who gives in at the start, and therefore has nothing wonderful about him.

My patient naturally found much to reflect upon in all this, for she had no notion of the game she was playing. Moreover she still had to gain insight into the regular romance that had been enacted between her and her father ever since childhood. It would lead us too far to describe in detail how, from her earliest years, with unconscious sympathy, she had played upon the shadow-side of her father which her mother never saw, and how, far in advance of her years, she became her mother's rival. All this came to light in the analysis of the personal unconscious. Since, if only for professional reasons, I could not allow myself to be irritated, I inevitably became the hero and father-lover. The transference too consisted at first of contents from the personal unconscious. My role as a hero was just a sham, and so, as it turned me into the merest phantom, she was able to play her traditional role of the supremely wise, very grown-up, all-understanding mother-daughter-beloved—an empty role, a persona behind which her real and authentic being, her individual self, lay hidden. Indeed, to the extent that she at first completely identified herself with her role, she was altogether unconscious of her real self. She was still in her nebulous infantile world and had not yet discovered the real world at all. But as, through progressive analysis, she became conscious of the nature of her transference, the dreams I spoke of in Chapter I began to materialize. They brought up bits of the collective unconscious, and that was the end of her infantile world and of all the heroics. She came to herself and to her own real potentialities. This is roughly the way things go in most cases, if the analysis is carried far enough. That the consciousness of her individuality should coincide exactly with the reactivation of an archaic god-image is not just an isolated coincidence, but a very frequent occurrence which, in my view, corresponds to an unconscious law.

After this digression, let us turn back to our earlier reflections.

Once the personal repressions are lifted, the individuality and the collective psyche begin to emerge in a coalescent state, thus releasing the hitherto repressed personal fantasies. The fantasies and dreams which now appear assume a somewhat different aspect. An infallible sign of collective images seems to be the appearance of the "cosmic" element, i.e., the images in the dream or fantasy are connected with cosmic qualities, such as temporal and spatial infinity, enormous speed and extension of movement, "astrological" associations, telluric, lunar, and solar analogies, changes in the proportions of the body, etc. The obvious occurrence of mythological and religious motifs in a dream also points to the activity of the collective unconscious. The collective element is very often announced by peculiar symptoms,[18] as for example by dreams where the dreamer is flying through space like a comet, or feels that he is the earth, or the sun, or a star; or else is of immense size, or dwarfishly small; or that he is dead, is in a strange place, is a stranger to himself, confused, mad, etc. Similarly, feelings of disorientation, of dizziness and the like, may appear along with symptoms of inflation.

The forces that burst out of the collective psyche have a confusing and blinding effect. One result of the dissolution of the persona is a release of involuntary fantasy, which is apparently nothing else than the specific activity of the collective psyche. This activity throws up contents whose existence one had never suspected before. But as the influence of the collective unconscious increases, so the conscious mind loses its power of leadership. Imperceptibly it becomes the led, while an unconscious and impersonal process gradually takes control. Thus, without noticing it, the conscious personality is pushed about like a figure on a chess-board by an invisible player. It is this player who decides the game of fate, not the conscious mind and its plans. This is how the resolution of the transference, apparently so impossible to the conscious mind, was brought about in my earlier example.

The plunge into this process becomes unavoidable whenever the necessity arises of overcoming an apparently insuperable difficulty. It goes without saying that this necessity does not occur in every case of neurosis, since perhaps in the majority the prime consideration is only the removal of temporary difficulties of adaptation. Certainly severe cases cannot be cured without a far-reaching change of character or of attitude. In by far the greater number,

[18] It may not be superfluous to note that collective elements in dreams are not restricted to this stage of the analytical treatment. There are many psychological situations in which the activity of the collective unconscious can come to the surface. But this is not the place to enlarge upon these conditions.

adaptation to external reality demands so much work that inner adaptation to the collective unconscious cannot be considered for a very long time. But when this inner adaptation becomes a problem, a strange, irresistible attraction proceeds from the unconscious and exerts a powerful influence on the conscious direction of life. The predominance of unconscious influences, together with the associated disintegration of the persona and the deposition of the conscious mind from power, constitute a state of psychic disequilibrium which, in analytical treatment, is artificially induced for the therapeutic purpose of resolving a difficulty that might block further development. There are of course innumerable obstacles that can be overcome with good advice and a little moral support, aided by goodwill and understanding on the part of the patient. Excellent curative results can be obtained in this way. Cases are not uncommon where there is no need to breathe a word about the unconscious. But again, there are difficulties for which one can foresee no satisfactory solution. If in these cases the psychic equilibrium is not already disturbed before treatment begins, it will certainly be upset during the analysis, and sometimes without any interference by the doctor. It often seems as though these patients had only been waiting to find a trustworthy person in order to give up and collapse. Such a loss of balance is similar in principle to a psychotic disturbance; that is, it differs from the initial stages of mental illness only by the fact that it leads in the end to greater health, while the latter leads to yet greater destruction. It is a condition of panic, a letting go in face of apparently hopeless complications. Mostly it was preceded by desperate efforts to master the difficulty by force of will; then came the collapse, and the once guiding will crumbles completely. The energy thus freed disappears from consciousness and falls into the unconscious. As a matter of fact, it is at these moments that the first signs of unconscious activity appear. (I am thinking of the example of that young man who was weak in

the head.) Obviously the energy that fell away from consciousness has activated the unconscious. The immediate
result is a change of attitude. One can easily imagine that
a stronger head would have taken that vision of the stars
as a healing apparition, and would have looked upon human suffering *sub specie aeternitatis,* in which case his
senses would have been restored.[19]

Had this happened, an apparently insurmountable obstacle would have been removed. Hence I regard the loss
of balance as purposive, since it replaces a defective consciousness by the automatic and instinctive activity of the
unconscious, which is aiming all the time at the creation
of a new balance and will moreover achieve this aim, provided that the conscious mind is capable of assimilating
the contents produced by the unconscious, i.e., of understanding and digesting them. If the unconscious simply
rides roughshod over the conscious mind, a psychotic condition develops. If it can neither completely prevail nor
yet be understood, the result is a conflict that cripples all
further advance. But with this question, namely the understanding of the collective unconscious, we come to a formidable difficulty which I have made the theme of my next
chapter.

# IV
## Negative Attempts to Free
## the Individuality from
## the Collective Psyche

### a. Regressive Restoration of the Persona

A collapse of the conscious attitude is no small matter.
It always feels like the end of the world, as though every-

---

[19] Cf. Théodore Flournoy, "Automatisme téléologique antisuicide:
un cas de suicide empêché par une hallucination," *Archives de
Psychologie,* VIII (1907), 113–37; and Jung, "The Psychology of
Dementia Praecox" (*Collected Works,* Vol. 3), pars. 304ff.

thing had tumbled back into original chaos. One feels delivered up, disoriented, like a rudderless ship that is abandoned to the moods of the elements. So at least it seems.
In reality, however, one has fallen back upon the collective
unconscious, which now takes over the leadership. We
could multiply examples of cases where, at the critical
moment, a "saving" thought, a vision, an "inner voice,"
came with an irresistible power of conviction and gave
life a new direction. Probably we could mention just as
many cases where the collapse meant a catastrophe that
destroyed life, for at such moments morbid ideas are also
liable to take root, or ideals wither away, which is no less
disastrous. In the one case some psychic oddity develops,
or a psychosis; in the other, a state of disorientation and
demoralization. But once the unconscious contents break
through into consciousness, filling it with their uncanny
power of conviction, the question arises of how the individual will react. Will he be overpowered by these contents? Will he credulously accept them? Or will he reject
them? (I am disregarding the ideal reaction, namely critical
understanding.) The first case signifies paranoia or schizophrenia; the second may either become an eccentric with
a taste for prophecy, or he may revert to an infantile attitude and be cut off from human society; the third signifies
the *regressive restoration of the persona*. This formulation
sounds very technical, and the reader may justifiably suppose that it has something to do with a complicated psychic reaction such as can be observed in the course of
analytical treatment. It would, however, be a mistake to
think that cases of this kind make their appearance only
in analytical treatment. The process can be observed just
as well, and often better, in other situations of life, namely
in all those careers where there has been some violent and
destructive intervention of fate. Every one, presumably,
has suffered adverse turns of fortune, but mostly they are
wounds that heal and leave no crippling mark. But here
we are concerned with experiences that are destructive,

that can smash a man completely or at least cripple him for good. Let us take as an example a businessman who takes too great a risk and consequently becomes bankrupt. If he does not allow himself to be discouraged by this depressing experience, but, undismayed, keeps his former daring, perhaps with a little salutary caution added, his wound will be healed without permanent injury. But if, on the other hand, he goes to pieces, abjures all further risks, and laboriously tries to patch up his social reputation within the confines of a much more limited personality, doing inferior work with the mentality of a scared child, in a post far below him, then, technically speaking, he will have restored his persona in a regressive way. He will as a result of his fright have slipped back to an earlier phase of his personality; he will have demeaned himself, pretending that he is as he was *before* the crucial experience, though utterly unable even to think of repeating such a risk. Formerly perhaps he wanted more than he could accomplish; now he does not even dare to attempt what he has it in him to do.

Such experiences occur in every walk of life and in every possible form, hence in psychological treatment also. Here again it is a question of widening the personality, of taking a risk on one's circumstances or on one's nature. What the critical experience is in actual treatment can be seen from the case of our philosophy student: it is the transference. As I have already indicated, it is possible for the patient to slip over the reef of the transference unconsciously, in which case it does not become an experience and nothing fundamental happens. The doctor, for the sake of mere convenience, might well wish for such patients. But if they are intelligent, the patients soon discover the existence of this problem for themselves. If then the doctor, as in the above case, is exalted into the father-lover and consequently has a flood of demands let loose against him, he must perforce think out ways and means of parrying the onslaught, without himself getting drawn into the maelstrom and without injury to the patient. A violent rupture of the transference may bring on a complete relapse, or worse; so the problem must be handled with great tact and foresight. Another possibility is the pious hope that "in time" the "nonsense" will stop of its own accord. Certainly everything stops in time, but it may be an unconscionably long time, and the difficulties may be so unbearable for both sides that one might as well give up the idea of time as a healing factor at once.

A far better instrument for "combatting" the transference would seem to be offered by the Freudian theory of neurosis. The dependence of the patient is explained as an infantile sexual demand that takes the place of a rational application of sexuality. Similar advantages are offered by the Adlerian theory,[20] which explains the transference as an infantile power-aim, and as a "security measure." Both theories fit the neurotic mentality so neatly that every case of neurosis can be explained by both theories at once.[21] This highly remarkable fact, which any unprejudiced observer is bound to corroborate, can only rest on the circumstance that Freud's "infantile eroticism" and Adler's "power drive" are one and the same thing, regardless of the clash of opinions between the two schools. It is simply a fragment of uncontrolled, and at first uncontrollable, primordial instinct that comes to light in the phenomenon of transference. The archaic fantasy-forms that gradually reach the surface of consciousness are only a further proof of this.

We can try both theories to make the patient see how infantile, impossible, and absurd his demands are, and perhaps in the end he will actually come to his senses again. My patient, however, was not the only one who did not do this. True enough, the doctor can always save his face with these theories and extricate himself from a pain-

---

[20] Alfred Adler, *The Neurotic Constitution*, originally published 1912, translated by B. Glueck and J. E. Lind (London, 1921).
[21] Cf. "On the Psychology of the Unconscious" (*Collected Works*, Vol. 7), pars. 44ff., for an example of such a case.

ful situation more or less humanely. There are indeed patients with whom it is, or seems to be, unrewarding to go to greater lengths; but there are also cases where these procedures cause senseless psychic injury. In the case of my student I dimly felt something of the sort, and I therefore abandoned my rationalistic attempts in order—with ill-concealed mistrust—to give nature a chance to correct what seemed to me to be her own foolishness. As already mentioned, this taught me something extraordinarily important, namely the existence of an unconscious self-regulation. Not only can the unconscious "wish," it can also cancel its own wishes. This realization, of such immense importance for the integrity of the personality, must remain sealed to anyone who cannot get over the idea that it is simply a question of infantilism. He will turn round on the threshold of this realization and tell himself: "It was all nonsense of course. I am a crazy visionary! The best thing to do would be to bury the unconscious or throw it overboard with all its works." The meaning and purpose he so eagerly desired he will see only as infantile maunderings. He will understand that his longing was absurd; he learns to be tolerant with himself, resigned. What can he do? Rather than face the conflict he will turn back and, as best he can, regressively restore his shattered persona, discounting all those hopes and expectations that had blossomed under the transference. He will become smaller, more limited, more rationalistic than he was before. One could not say that this result would be an unqualified misfortune in all cases, for there are all too many who, on account of their notorious ineptitude, thrive better in a rationalistic system than in freedom. Freedom is one of the more difficult things. Those who can stomach this way out can say with Faust:

> This earthly circle I know well enough.
> Towards the Beyond the view has been cut off;
> Fool—who directs that way his dazzled eye,
> Contrives himself a double in the sky!

Let him look round him here, not stray beyond;
To a sound man this world must needs respond.
To roam into eternity is vain!
What he perceives, he can attain.
Thus let him walk along his earthlong day;
Though phantoms haunt him, let him go his way.[22]

Such a solution would be perfect if a man were really
able to shake off the unconscious, drain it of its energy
and render it inactive. But experience shows that the unconscious can be deprived of its energy only in part: it
remains continually active, for it not only contains but is
itself the source of the libido from which the psychic elements flow. It is therefore a delusion to think that by some
kind of magical theory or method the unconscious can
be finally emptied of libido and thus, as it were, eliminated.
One may for a while play with this delusion, but the day
comes when one is forced to say with Faust:

But now such spectredom so throngs the air
That none knows how to dodge it, none knows where.
Though one day greet us with a rational gleam,
The night entangles us in webs of dream.
We come back happy from the fields of spring—
And a bird croaks. Croaks what? Some evil thing.
Enmeshed in superstition night and morn,
It forms and shows itself and comes to warn.
And we, so scared, stand without friend or kin,
And the door creaks—and nobody comes in.[23]

Nobody, of his own free will, can strip the unconscious of
its effective power. At best, one can merely deceive oneself
on this point. For, as Goethe says:

Unheard by the outward ear
In the heart I whisper fear;
Changing shape from hour to hour
I employ my savage power.[24]

---

[22] *Faust,* translated by Louis MacNeice (London, 1951), p. 283
(Part II, Act V).
[23] Ibid., p. 281 (Part II, Act V).
[24] Ibid., p. 282 (Part II, Act V), modified.

Only one thing is effective against the unconscious, and that is hard outer necessity. (Those with rather more knowledge of the unconscious will see behind the outer necessity the same face which once gazed at them from within.) An inner necessity can change into an outer one, and so long as the outer necessity is real, and not just faked, psychic problems remain more or less ineffective. This is why Mephisto offers Faust, who is sick of the "madness of magic," the following advice:

> Right. There is one way that needs
> No money, no physician, and no witch.
> Pack up your things and get back to the land
> And there begin to dig and ditch;
> Keep to the narrow round, confine your mind,
> And live on fodder of the simplest kind,
> A beast among the beasts; and don't forget
> To use your own dung on the crops you set! [25]

It is a well-known fact that the "simple life" cannot be faked, and therefore the unproblematical existence of a poor man, who really is delivered over to fate, cannot be bought by such cheap imitations. Only the man who lives such a life not as a mere possibility, but is actually driven to it by the necessity of his own nature, will blindly pass over the problem of his soul, since he lacks the capacity to grasp it. But once he has seen the Faustian problem, the escape into the "simple life" is closed for ever. There is of course nothing to stop him from taking a two-room cottage in the country, or from pottering about in a garden and eating raw turnips. But his soul laughs at the deception. Only what is really oneself has the power to heal.

The regressive restoration of the persona is a possible course only for the man who owes the critical failure of his life to his own inflatedness. With diminished personality, he turns back to the measure he can fill. But in every other case resignation and self-belittlement are an evasion, which in the long run can be kept up only at the cost of neurotic

[25] Ibid., p. 67 (Part I, Witch's Kitchen scene), modified.

sickliness. From the conscious point of view of the person concerned, his condition does not look like an evasion at all, but seems to be due to the impossibility of coping with the problem. Usually he is a lonely figure, with little or nothing to help him in our present-day culture. Even psychology has only purely reductive interpretations to offer, since it inevitably underlines the archaic and infantile character of these transitional states and makes them unacceptable to him. The fact that a medical theory may also serve the purpose of enabling the doctor to pull his own head more or less elegantly out of the noose does not occur to him. That is precisely why these reductive theories fit the essence of neurosis so beautifully—because they are of such great service to the doctor.

### b. *Identification with the Collective Psyche*

The second way leads to identification with the collective psyche. This would amount to an acceptance of inflation, but now exalted into a system. That is to say, one would be the fortunate possessor of *the* great truth which was only waiting to be discovered, of the eschatological knowledge which spells the healing of the nations. This attitude is not necessarily megalomania in direct form, but in the milder and more familiar form of prophetic inspiration and desire for martyrdom. For weak-minded persons, who as often as not possess more than their fair share of ambition, vanity, and misplaced naïveté, the danger of yielding to this temptation is very great. Access to the collective psyche means a renewal of life for the individual, no matter whether this renewal is felt as pleasant or unpleasant. Everybody would like to hold fast to this renewal: one man because it enhances his life-feeling, another because it promises a rich harvest of knowledge, a third because he has discovered the key that will transform his whole life. Therefore all those who do not wish to deprive themselves of the great treasures that lie buried in the collective psyche will strive by every means possible to maintain their newly won connection with the primal source of life.[26] Identification would seem to be the shortest road to this, for the dissolution of the persona in the collective psyche positively invites one to wed oneself with the abyss and blot out all memory in its embrace. This piece of mysticism is innate in all better men as the "longing for the mother," the nostalgia for the source from which we came.

As I have shown in my book on libido [*Symbols of Transformation* (*Collected Works*, Vol. 5)], there lie at the root of the regressive longing, which Freud conceives as "infantile fixation" or the "incest wish," a specific value and a specific need which are made explicit in myths. It is precisely the strongest and best among men, the heroes, who give way to their regressive longing and purposely expose themselves to the danger of being devoured by the monster of the maternal abyss. But if a man is a hero, he is a hero because, in the final reckoning, he did not let the monster devour him, but subdued it, not once but many times. Victory over the collective psyche alone yields the true value—the capture of the hoard, the invincible weapon, the magic talisman, or whatever it be that the myth deems most desirable. Anyone who identifies with the collective psyche—or, in mythological terms, lets himself be devoured by the monster—and vanishes in it, attains the treasure that the dragon guards, but he does so in spite of himself and to his own greatest harm.

Probably no one who was conscious of the absurdity of this identification would have the courage to make a principle of it. But the danger is that very many people lack

[26] I would like to call attention here to an interesting remark of Kant's. In his lectures on psychology (*Vorlesungen über Psychologie*, Leipzig, 1889) he speaks of the "treasure lying within the field of dim representations, that deep abyss of human knowledge forever beyond our reach." This treasure, as I have demonstrated in my *Symbols of Transformation* (*Collected Works*, Vol. 5), is the aggregate of all those primordial images in which the libido is invested, or rather, which are self-representations of the libido.

the necessary humour, or else it fails them at this particular juncture; they are seized by a sort of pathos, everything seems pregnant with meaning, and all effective self-
criticism is checked. I would not deny in general the existence of genuine prophets, but in the name of caution I
would begin by doubting each individual case; for it is
far too serious a matter for us lightly to accept a man as a
genuine prophet. Every respectable prophet strives man-
fully against the unconscious pretensions of his role. When
therefore a prophet appears at a moment's notice, we would
be better advised to contemplate a possible psychic disequilibrium.

But besides the possibility of becoming a prophet, there
is another alluring joy, subtler and apparently more legitimate: the joy of becoming a prophet's disciple. This, for
the vast majority of people, is an altogether ideal technique. Its advantages are: the *odium dignitatis,* the superhuman responsibility of the prophet, turns into the so
much sweeter *otium indignitatis.* The disciple is unworthy;
modestly he sits at the Master's feet and guards against
having ideas of his own. Mental laziness becomes a virtue;
one can at least bask in the sun of a semidivine being. He
can enjoy the archaism and infantilism of his unconscious
fantasies without loss to himself, for all responsibility is
laid at the Master's door. Through his deification of the
Master, the disciple, apparently without noticing it, waxes
in stature; moreover, does he not possess the great truth
—not his own discovery, of course, but received straight
from the Master's hands? Naturally the disciples always
stick together, not out of love, but for the very understandable purpose of effortlessly confirming their own
convictions by engendering an air of collective agreement.

Now this is an identification with the collective psyche
that seems altogether more commendable: somebody else
has the honour of being a prophet, but also the dangerous
responsibility. For one's own part, one is a mere disciple,
but nonetheless a joint guardian of the great treasure

which the Master has found. One feels the full dignity and burden of such a position, deeming it a solemn duty and a moral necessity to revile others not of a like mind, to enrol proselytes and to hold up a light to the Gentiles, exactly as though one were the prophet oneself. And these people, who creep about behind an apparently modest persona, are the very ones who, when inflated by identification with the collective psyche, suddenly burst upon the world scene. For, just as the prophet is a primordial image from the collective psyche, so also is the disciple of the prophet.

In both cases inflation is brought about by the collective unconscious, and the independence of the individuality suffers injury. But since by no means all individualities have the strength to be independent, the disciple-fantasy is perhaps the best they can accomplish. The gratifications of the accompanying inflation at least do something to make up for the loss of spiritual freedom. Nor should we underestimate the fact that the life of a real or imagined prophet is full of sorrows, disappointments, and privations, so that the hosanna-shouting band of disciples has the value of a compensation. All this is so humanly understandable that it would be a matter for astonishment if it led to any further destination whatever.

## Part Two
### INDIVIDUATION

### I
### *The Function of the Unconscious*

There is a destination, a possible goal, beyond the alternative stages dealt with in our last chapter. That is the way of individuation. Individuation means becoming an "in-dividual," and, in so far as "individuality" embraces our innermost, last, and incomparable uniqueness, it also implies becoming one's own self. We could therefore translate individuation as "coming to selfhood" or "self-realization."

The possibilities of development discussed in the preceding chapters were, at bottom, alienations of the self, ways of divesting the self of its reality in favour of an external role or in favour of an imagined meaning. In the former case the self retires into the background and gives place to social recognition; in the latter, to the auto-suggestive meaning of a primordial image. In both cases the collective has the upper hand. Self-alienation in favour of the collective corresponds to a social ideal; it even passes for social duty and virtue, although it can also be misused for egotistical purposes. Egoists are called "selfish," but this, naturally, has nothing to do with the concept of "self" as I am using it here. On the other hand, self-realization seems to stand in opposition to self-alienation. This misunderstanding is quite general, because we do not sufficiently distinguish between individualism and individuation. Individualism means deliberately stressing and giving prominence to some supposed peculiarity rather than to collective considerations and obligations. But individuation means precisely the better and more complete fulfilment of the collective qualities of the human being, since adequate consideration of the peculiarity of the individual is more conducive to a better social performance than when the peculiarity is neglected or suppressed. The idiosyncrasy of an individual is not to be understood as any strangeness in his substance or in his components, but rather as a unique combination, or gradual differentiation, of functions and faculties which in themselves are universal. Every human face has a nose, two eyes, etc., but these universal factors are variable, and it is this variability which makes individual peculiarities possible. Individuation, therefore, can only mean a process of psychological development that fulfils the individual qualities given; in other words, it is a process by which a man becomes the definite, unique being he in fact is. In so doing he does not become "selfish" in the ordinary sense of the word, but is merely fulfilling the peculiarity of his nature, and this, as we have said, is vastly different from egotism or individualism.

Now in so far as the human individual, as a living unit, is composed of purely universal factors, he is wholly collective and therefore in no sense opposed to collectivity. Hence the individualistic emphasis on one's own peculiarity is a contradiction of this basic fact of the living being. Individuation, on the other hand, aims at a living co-operation of all factors. But since the universal factors always appear only in individual form, a full consideration of them will also produce an individual effect, and one which cannot be surpassed by anything else, least of all by individualism.

The aim of individuation is nothing less than to divest the self of the false wrappings of the persona on the one hand, and of the suggestive power of primordial images on the other. From what has been said in the previous chapters it should be sufficiently clear what the persona means psychologically. But when we turn to the other side, namely to the influence of the collective unconscious, we find we are moving in a dark interior world that is vastly more difficult to understand than the psychology of the persona, which is accessible to everyone. Everyone knows what is meant by "putting on official airs" or "playing a social role." Through the persona a man tries to appear as this or that, or he hides behind a mask, or he may even build up a definite persona as a barricade. So the problem of the persona should present no great intellectual difficulties.

It is, however, another thing to describe, in a way that can be generally understood, those subtle inner processes which invade the conscious mind with such suggestive force. Perhaps we can best portray these influences with the help of examples of mental illness, creative inspiration, and religious conversion. A most excellent account—taken from life, so to speak—of such an inner transformation is to be found in H. G. Wells' *Christina Alberta's Father*. Changes of a similar kind are described in Léon Daudet's

eminently readable *L'Hérédo*. A wide range of material is
contained in William James' *Varieties of Religious Experience*. Although in many cases of this kind there are certain
external factors which either directly condition the change,
or at least provide the occasion for it, yet it is not always
the case that the external factor offers a sufficient explanation of these changes of personality. We must recognize
the fact that they can also arise from subjective inner
causes, opinions, convictions, where external stimuli play
no part at all, or a very insignificant one. In pathological
changes of personality this can even be said to be the rule.
The cases of psychosis that present a clear and simple
reaction to some overwhelming outside event belong to the
exceptions. Hence, for psychiatry, the essential aetiological
factor is the inherited or acquired pathological disposition.
The same is probably true of most creative intuitions, for
we are hardly likely to suppose a purely causal connection
between the falling apple and Newton's theory of gravitation. Similarly all religious conversions that cannot be
traced back directly to suggestion and contagious example
rest upon independent interior processes culminating in a
change of personality. As a rule these processes have the
peculiarity of being subliminal, i.e., unconscious, in the
first place and of reaching consciousness only gradually.
The moment of irruption can, however, be very sudden, so
that consciousness is instantaneously flooded with extremely
strange and apparently quite unsuspected contents. That is
how it looks to the layman and even to the person concerned, but the experienced observer knows that psychological events are never sudden. In reality the irruption
has been preparing for many years, often for half a lifetime, and already in childhood all sorts of remarkable signs
could have been detected which, in more or less symbolic
fashion, hinted at abnormal future developments. I am
reminded, for instance, of a mental case who refused all
nourishment and created quite extraordinary difficulties in
connection with nasal feeding. In fact an anaesthetic was

necessary before the tube could be inserted. The patient was able in some remarkable way to swallow his tongue by pressing it back into the throat, a fact that was quite new and unknown to me at the time. In a lucid interval I obtained the following history from the man. As a boy he had often revolved in his mind the idea of how he could take his life, even if every conceivable measure were employed to prevent him. He first tried to do it by holding his breath, until he found that by the time he was in a semiconscious state he had already begun to breathe again. So he gave up these attempts and thought: perhaps it would work if he refused food. This fantasy satisfied him until he discovered that food could be poured into him through the nasal cavity. He therefore considered how this entrance might be closed, and thus it was that he hit upon the idea of pressing his tongue backwards. At first he was unsuccessful, and so he began a regular training, until at last he succeeded in swallowing his tongue in much the same way as sometimes happens accidentally during anaesthesia, evidently in his case by artificially relaxing the muscles at the root of the tongue.

In this strange manner the boy paved the way for his future psychosis. After the second attack he became incurably insane. This is only one example among many others, but it suffices to show how the subsequent, apparently sudden irruption of alien contents is really not sudden at all, but is rather the result of an unconscious development that has been going on for years.

The great question now is: in what do these unconscious processes consist? And how are they constituted? Naturally, so long as they are unconscious, nothing can be said about them. But sometimes they manifest themselves, partly through symptoms, partly through actions, opinions, affects, fantasies, and dreams. Aided by such observational material we can draw indirect conclusions as to the momentary state and constitution of the unconscious processes and their development. We should not, however, labour under the illusion that we have now discovered the real nature of the unconscious processes. We never succeed in getting further than the hypothetical "as if."

"No mortal mind can plumb the depths of nature"—nor even the depths of the unconscious. We do know, however, that the unconscious never rests. It seems to be always at work, for even when asleep we dream. There are many people who declare that they never dream, but the probability is that they simply do not remember their dreams. It is significant that people who talk in their sleep mostly have no recollection either of the dream which started them talking, or even of the fact that they dreamed at all. Not a day passes but we make some slip of the tongue, or something slips our memory which at other times we know perfectly well, or we are seized by a mood whose cause we cannot trace, etc. These things are all symptoms of some consistent unconscious activity which becomes directly visible at night in dreams, but only occasionally breaks through the inhibitions imposed by our daytime consciousness.

So far as our present experience goes, we can lay it down that the unconscious processes stand in a compensatory relation to the conscious mind. I expressly use the word "compensatory" and not the word "contrary" because conscious and unconscious are not necessarily in opposition to one another, but complement one another to form a totality, which is the *self*. According to this definition the self is a quantity that is supraordinate to the conscious ego. It embraces not only the conscious but also the unconscious psyche, and is therefore, so to speak, a personality which we *also* are. It is easy enough to think of ourselves as possessing part-souls. Thus we can, for instance, see ourselves as a persona without too much difficulty. But it transcends our powers of imagination to form a clear picture of what we are as a self, for in this operation the part would have to comprehend the whole. There is little hope of our ever being able to reach even approximate consciousness of the self, since however much we may make conscious there will always exist an indeterminate and indeterminable amount of unconscious material which belongs to the totality of the self. Hence the self will always remain a supraordinate quantity.

The unconscious processes that compensate the conscious ego contain all those elements that are necessary for the self-regulation of the psyche as a whole. On the personal level, these are the not consciously recognized personal motives which appear in dreams, or the meanings of daily situations which we have overlooked, or conclusions we have failed to draw, or affects we have not permitted, or criticisms we have spared ourselves. But the more we become conscious of ourselves through self-knowledge, and act accordingly, the more the layer of the personal unconscious that is superimposed on the collective unconscious will be diminished. In this way there arises a consciousness which is no longer imprisoned in the petty, oversensitive, personal world of the ego, but participates freely in the wider world of objective interests. This widened consciousness is no longer that touchy, egotistical bundle of personal wishes, fears, hopes, and ambitions which always has to be compensated or corrected by unconscious counter-tendencies; instead, it is a function of relationship to the world of objects, bringing the individual into absolute, binding, and indissoluble communion with the world at large. The complications arising at this stage are no longer egotistic wish-conflicts, but difficulties that concern others as much as oneself. At this stage it is fundamentally a question of collective problems, which have activated the collective unconscious because they require collective rather than personal compensation. We can now see that the unconscious produces contents which are valid not only for the person concerned, but for others as well, in fact for a great many people and possibly for all.

The Elgonyi, natives of the Elgon forests, of central

Africa, explained to me that there are two kinds of dreams: the ordinary dream of the little man, and the "big vision" that only the great man has, e.g., the medicine-man or chief. Little dreams are of no account, but if a man has a "big dream" he summons the whole tribe in order to tell it to everybody.

How is a man to know whether his dream is a "big" or a "little" one? He knows it by an instinctive feeling of significance. He feels so overwhelmed by the impression it makes that he would never think of keeping the dream to himself. He *has* to tell it, on the psychologically correct assumption that it is of general significance. Even with us the collective dream has a feeling of importance about it that impels communication. It springs from a conflict of relationship and must therefore be built into our conscious relations, because it compensates these and not just some inner personal quirk.

The processes of the collective unconscious are concerned not only with the more or less personal relations of an individual to his family or to a wider social group, but with his relations to society and to the human community in general. The more general and impersonal the condition that releases the unconscious reaction, the more significant, bizarre, and overwhelming will be the compensatory manifestation. It impels not just private communication, but drives people to revelations and confessions, and even to a dramatic representation of their fantasies.

I will explain by an example how the unconscious manages to compensate relationships. A somewhat arrogant gentleman once came to me for treatment. He ran a business in partnership with his younger brother. Relations between the two brothers were very strained, and this was one of the essential causes of my patient's neurosis. From the information he gave me, the real reason for the tension was not altogether clear. He had all kinds of criticisms to make of his brother, whose gifts he certainly did not show in a very favourable light. The brother frequently came into his dreams, always in the role of a Bismarck, Napoleon, or Julius Caesar. His house looked like the Vatican or Yildiz Kiosk. My patient's unconscious evidently had the need to exalt the rank of the younger brother. From this I concluded that he was setting himself too high and his brother too low. The further course of analysis entirely justified this inference.

Another patient, a young woman who clung to her mother in an extremely sentimental way, always had very sinister dreams about her. She appeared in the dreams as a witch, as a ghost, as a pursuing demon. The mother had spoilt her beyond all reason and had so blinded her by tenderness that the daughter had no conscious idea of her mother's harmful influence. Hence the compensatory criticism exercised by the unconscious.

I myself once happened to put too low a value on a patient, both intellectually and morally. In a dream I saw a castle perched on a high cliff, and on the topmost tower was a balcony, and there sat my patient. I did not hesitate to tell her this dream at once, naturally with the best results.

We all know how apt we are to make fools of ourselves in front of the very people we have unjustly underrated. Naturally the case can also be reversed, as once happened to a friend of mine. While still a callow student he had written to Virchow, the pathologist, craving an audience with "His Excellency." When, quaking with fear, he presented himself and tried to give his name, he blurted out, "My name is Virchow." Whereupon His Excellency, smiling mischievously, said, "Ah! So your name is Virchow too?" The feeling of his own nullity was evidently too much for the unconscious of my friend, and in consequence it instantly prompted him to present himself as equal to Virchow in grandeur.

In these more personal relations there is of course no need for any very collective compensations. On the other hand, the figures employed by the unconscious in our first case are of a definitely collective nature: they are universally recognized heroes. Here there are two possible interpretations: either my patient's younger brother is a man of acknowledged and far-reaching collective importance, or my patient is overestimating his own importance not merely in relation to his brother but in relation to everybody else as well. For the first assumption there was no support at all, while for the second there was the evidence of one's own eyes. Since the man's extreme arrogance affected not only himself, but a far wider social group, the compensation availed itself of a collective image.

The same is true of the second case. The "witch" is a collective image; hence we must conclude that the blind dependence of the young woman applied as much to the wider social group as it did to her mother personally. This was indeed the case, in so far as she was still living in an exclusively infantile world, where the world was identical with her parents. These examples deal with relations within the personal orbit. There are, however, impersonal relations which occasionally need unconscious compensation. In such cases collective images appear with a more or less mythological character. Moral, philosophical, and religious problems are, on account of their universal validity, the most likely to call for mythological compensation. In the aforementioned novel by H. G. Wells we find a classical type of compensation: Mr. Preemby, a midget personality, discovers that he is really a reincarnation of Sargon, King of Kings. Happily, the genius of the author rescues poor old Sargon from pathological absurdity, and even gives the reader a chance to appreciate the tragic and eternal meaning in this lamentable affray. Mr. Preemby, a complete nonentity, recognizes himself as the point of intersection of all ages past and future. This knowledge is not too dearly bought at the cost of a little madness, provided that Preemby is not in the end devoured by that monster of a primordial image—which is in fact what nearly happens to him.

The universal problem of evil and sin is another aspect

of our impersonal relations to the world. Almost more than any other, therefore, this problem produces collective compensations. One of my patients, aged sixteen, had as the initial symptom of a severe compulsion neurosis the following dream: *He is walking along an unfamiliar street. It is dark, and he hears steps coming behind him. With a feeling of fear he quickens his pace. The footsteps come nearer, and his fear increases. He begins to run. But the footsteps seem to be overtaking him. Finally he turns round, and there he sees the devil. In deathly terror he leaps into the air and hangs there suspended.* This dream was repeated twice, a sign of its special urgency.

It is a notorious fact that the compulsion neuroses, by reason of their meticulousness and ceremonial punctilio, not only have the surface appearance of a moral problem but are indeed brim-full of inhuman beastliness and ruthless evil, against the integration of which the very delicately organized personality puts up a desperate struggle. This explains why so many things have to be performed in ceremonially "correct" style, as though to counteract the evil hovering in the background. After this dream the neurosis started, and its essential feature was that the patient had, as he put it, to keep himself in a "provisional" or "uncontaminated" state of purity. For this purpose he either severed or made "invalid" all contact with the world and with everything that reminded him of the transitoriness of human existence, by means of lunatic formalities, scrupulous cleansing ceremonies, and the anxious observance of innumerable rules and regulations of an unbelievable complexity. Even before the patient had any suspicion of the hellish existence that lay before him, the dream showed him that if he wanted to come down to earth again there would have to be a pact with evil.

Elsewhere I have described a dream that illustrates the compensation of a religious problem in a young theological student.[27] He was involved in all sorts of difficulties of

---

[27] "Archetypes of the Collective Unconscious" (*Collected Works,* Vol. 9.i), par. 71.

belief, a not uncommon occurrence in the man of today. In his dream he was the pupil of the "white magician," who, however, was dressed in black. After having instructed him up to a certain point, the white magician told him that they now needed the "black magician." The black magician appeared, but clad in a white robe. He declared that he had found the keys of paradise, but needed the wisdom of the white magician in order to understand how to use them. This dream obviously contains the problem of opposites which, as we know, has found in Taoist philosophy a solution very different from the views prevailing in the West. The figures employed by the dream are impersonal collective images corresponding to the nature of the impersonal religious problem. In contrast to the Christian view, the dream stresses the relativity of good and evil in a way that immediately calls to mind the Taoist symbol of Yin and Yang.

We should certainly not conclude from these compensations that, as the conscious mind becomes more deeply engrossed in universal problems, the unconscious will bring forth correspondingly far-reaching compensations. There is what one might call a legitimate and an illegitimate interest in impersonal problems. Excursions of this kind are legitimate only when they arise from the deepest and truest needs of the individual; illegitimate when they are either mere intellectual curiosity or a flight from unpleasant reality. In the latter case the unconscious produces all too human and purely personal compensations, whose manifest aim is to bring the conscious mind back to ordinary reality. People who go illegitimately mooning after the infinite often have absurdly banal dreams which endeavour to damp down their ebullience. Thus, from the nature of the compensation, we can at once draw conclusions as to the seriousness and rightness of the conscious strivings.

There are certainly not a few people who are afraid to admit that the unconscious could ever have "big" ideas. They will object, "But do you really believe that the unconscious is capable of offering anything like a constructive criticism of our Western mentality?" Of course, if we take the problem intellectually and impute rational intentions to the unconscious, the thing becomes absurd. But it would never do to foist our conscious psychology upon the unconscious. Its mentality is an instinctive one; it has no differentiated functions, and it does not "think" as we understand "thinking." It simply creates an image that answers to the conscious situation. This image contains as much thought as feeling, and is anything rather than a product of rationalistic reflection. Such an image would be better described as an artist's vision. We tend to forget that a problem like the one which underlies the dream last mentioned cannot, even to the conscious mind of the dreamer, be an intellectual problem, but is profoundly emotional. For a moral man the ethical problem is a passionate question which has its roots in the deepest instinctual processes as well as in his most idealistic aspirations. The problem for him is devastatingly real. It is not surprising, therefore, that the answer likewise springs from the depths of his nature. The fact that everyone thinks his psychology is the measure of all things, and, if he also happens to be a fool, will inevitably think that such a problem is beneath his notice, should not trouble the psychologist in the least, for he has to take things objectively, as he finds them, without twisting them to fit his subjective suppositions. The richer and more capacious natures may legitimately be gripped by an impersonal problem, and to the extent that this is so, their unconscious can answer in the same style. And just as the conscious mind can put the question, "Why is there this frightful conflict between good and evil?," so the unconscious can reply, "Look closer! Each needs the other. The best, just because it is the best, holds the seed of evil, and there is nothing so bad but good can come of it."

It might then dawn on the dreamer that the apparently insoluble conflict is, perhaps, a prejudice, a frame of mind conditioned by time and place. The seemingly complex dream-image might easily reveal itself as plain, instinctive common sense, as the tiny germ of a rational idea, which a maturer mind could just as well have thought consciously. At all events Chinese philosophy thought of it ages ago. The singularly apt, plastic configuration of thought is the prerogative of that primitive, natural spirit which is alive in all of us and is only obscured by a one-sided conscious development. If we consider the unconscious compensations from this angle, we might justifiably be accused of judging the unconscious too much from the conscious standpoint. And indeed, in pursuing these reflections, I have always started from the view that the unconscious simply reacts to the conscious contents, albeit in a very significant way, but that it lacks initiative. It is, however, far from my intention to give the impression that the unconscious is merely reactive in all cases. On the contrary, there is a host of experiences which seem to prove that the unconscious is not only spontaneous but can actually take the lead. There are innumerable cases of people who lingered on in a pettifogging unconsciousness, only to become neurotic in the end. Thanks to the neurosis contrived by the unconscious, they are shaken out of their apathy, and this in spite of their own laziness and often desperate resistance.

Yet it would, in my view, be wrong to suppose that in such cases the unconscious is working to a deliberate and concerted plan and is striving to realize certain definite ends. I have found nothing to support this assumption. The driving force, so far as it is possible for us to grasp it, seems to be in essence only an urge towards self-realization. If it were a matter of some general teleological plan, then all individuals who enjoy a surplus of unconsciousness would necessarily be driven towards higher consciousness by an irresistible urge. That is plainly not the case. There are vast masses of the population who, despite their notorious unconsciousness, never get anywhere near a neurosis.

The few who are smitten by such a fate are really persons of the "higher" type who, for one reason or another, have remained too long on a primitive level. Their nature does not in the long run tolerate persistence in what is for them an unnatural torpor. As a result of their narrow conscious outlook and their cramped existence they save energy; bit by bit it accumulates in the unconscious and finally explodes in the form of a more or less acute neurosis. This simple mechanism does not necessarily conceal a "plan." A perfectly understandable urge towards self-realization would provide a quite satisfactory explanation. We could also speak of a retarded maturation of the personality.

Since it is highly probable that we are still a long way from the summit of absolute consciousness, presumably everyone is capable of wider consciousness, and we may assume accordingly that the unconscious processes are constantly supplying us with contents which, if consciously recognized, would extend the range of consciousness. Looked at in this way, the unconscious appears as a field of experience of unlimited extent. If it were merely reactive to the conscious mind, we might aptly call it a psychic mirror-world. In that case, the real source of all contents and activities would lie in the conscious mind, and there would be absolutely nothing in the unconscious except the distorted reflections of conscious contents. The creative process would be shut up in the conscious mind, and anything new would be nothing but conscious invention or cleverness. The empirical facts give the lie to this. Every creative man knows that spontaneity is the very essence of creative thought. Because the unconscious is not just a reactive mirror-reflection, but an independent, productive activity, its realm of experience is a self-contained world, having its own reality, of which we can only say that it affects us as we affect it—precisely what we say about our experience of the outer world. And just as material objects are the constituent elements of this world, so psychic factors constitute the objects of that other world.

The idea of psychic objectivity is by no means a new discovery. It is in fact one of the earliest and most universal acquisitions of humanity: it is nothing less than the conviction as to the concrete existence of a spirit-world. The spirit-world was certainly never an invention in the sense that fire-boring was an invention; it was far rather the experience, the conscious acceptance of a reality in no way inferior to that of the material world. I doubt whether primitives exist anywhere who are not acquainted with magical influence or a magical substance. ("Magical" is simply another word for "psychic.") It would also appear that practically all primitives are aware of the existence of spirits.[28] "Spirit" is a psychic fact. Just as we distinguish our own bodiliness from bodies that are strange to us, so primitives—if they have any notion of "souls" at all— distinguish between their own souls and the spirits, which are felt as strange and as "not belonging." They are objects of outward perception, whereas their own soul (or one of several souls where a plurality is assumed), though believed to be essentially akin to the spirits, is not usually an object of so-called sensible perception. After death the soul (or one of the plurality of souls) becomes a spirit which survives the dead man, and often it shows a marked deterioration of character that partly contradicts the notion of personal immortality. The Bataks,[29] of Sumatra, go so far as to assert that the people who were good in this life turn into malign and dangerous spirits. Nearly everything that the primitives say about the tricks which the spirits play on the living, and the general picture they give of the *revenants,* corresponds down to the last detail with the phenomena established by spiritualistic experience. And just as the communications from the "Beyond" can be

[28] In cases of reports to the contrary, it must always be borne in mind that the fear of spirits is sometimes so great that people will actually deny that there are any spirits to fear. I have come across this myself among the dwellers on Mount Elgon.
[29] Joh. Warnecke, "Die Religion der Batak," in Julius Boehmen, ed., *Religions-Urkunden der Völker* (Leipzig, 1909), Part IV, Vol. I.

seen to be the activities of broken-off bits of the psyche, so these primitive spirits are manifestations of unconscious complexes.[30] The importance that modern psychology attaches to the "parental complex" is a direct continuation of primitive man's experience of the dangerous power of the ancestral spirits. Even the error of judgment which leads him unthinkingly to assume that the spirits are realities of the external world is carried on in our assumption (which is only partially correct) that the real parents are responsible for the parental complex. In the old trauma theory of Freudian psychoanalysis, and in other quarters as well, this assumption even passed for a scientific explanation. (It was in order to avoid this confusion that I advocated the term "parental imago.")[31]

The simple soul is of course quite unaware of the fact that his nearest relations, who exercise immediate influence over him, create in him an image which is only partly a replica of themselves, while its other part is compounded of elements derived from himself. The imago is built up of parental influences plus the specific reactions of the child; it is therefore an image that reflects the object with very considerable qualifications. Naturally, the simple soul believes that his parents are as he sees them. The image is unconsciously projected, and when the parents die, the projected image goes on working as though it were a spirit existing on its own. The primitive then speaks of parental spirits who return by night (*revenants*), while the modern man calls it a father or mother complex.

The more limited a man's field of consciousness is, the more numerous the psychic contents (imagos) which meet him as quasi-external apparitions, either in the form of spirits, or as magical potencies projected upon living people

[30] Cf. "The Psychological Foundations of Belief in Spirits," in *The Structure and Dynamics of the Psyche* (*Collected Works*, Vol. 8). [31] [This term was taken up by psychoanalysis, but in analytical psychology it has been largely replaced by "primordial image of the parent" or "parental archetype."—EDITORS OF *The Collected Works*.]

(magicians, witches, etc.). At a rather higher stage of development, where the idea of the soul already exists, not all the imagos continue to be projected (where this happens, even trees and stones talk), but one or the other complex has come near enough to consciousness to be felt as no longer strange, but as somehow "belonging." Nevertheless, the feeling that it "belongs" is not at first sufficiently strong for the complex to be sensed as a subjective content of consciousness. It remains in a sort of no man's land between conscious and unconscious, in the half-shadow, in part belonging or akin to the conscious subject, in part an autonomous being, and meeting consciousness as such. At all events it is not necessarily obedient to the subject's intentions, it may even be of a higher order, more often than not a source of inspiration or warning, or of "supernatural" information. Psychologically such a content could be explained as a partly autonomous complex that is not yet fully integrated. The archaic souls, the *ba* and *ka* of the Egyptians, are complexes of this kind. At a still higher level, and particularly among the civilized peoples of the West, this complex is invariably of the feminine gender—anima and ψυχή—a fact for which deeper and cogent reasons are not lacking.

# ❦ 6 ❧

## *Aion: Phenomenology of the Self*[1]

### I
### *The Ego*

Investigation of the psychology of the unconscious confronted me with facts which required the formulation of new concepts. One of these concepts is the *self*. The entity so denoted is not meant to take the place of the one that has always been known as the *ego,* but includes it in a supraordinate concept. We understand the ego as the complex factor to which all conscious contents are related. It forms, as it were, the centre of the field of consciousness; and, in so far as this comprises the empirical personality, the ego is the subject of all personal acts of consciousness. The relation of a psychic content to the ego forms the criterion of its consciousness, for no content can be conscious unless it is represented to a subject.

With this definition we have described and delimited the *scope* of the subject. Theoretically, no limits can be

[1] From *Aion: Researches into the Phenomenology of the Self. Collected Works,* Vol. 9.ii, pars. 1–42; translated from the first part of *Aion: Untersuchungen zur Symbolgeschichte* (Psychologische Abhandlungen, VIII; Zurich, Rascher Verlag, 1951).

set to the field of consciousness, since it is capable of indefinite extension. Empirically, however, it always finds its limit when it comes up against the *unknown*. This consists of everything we do not know, which, therefore, is not related to the ego as the centre of the field of consciousness. The unknown falls into two groups of objects: those which are outside and can be experienced by the senses, and those which are inside and are experienced immediately. The first group comprises the unknown in the outer world; the second the unknown in the inner world. We call this latter territory the *unconscious*.

The ego, as a specific content of consciousness, is not a simple or elementary factor but a complex one which, as such, cannot be described exhaustively. Experience shows that it rests on two seemingly different bases: the *somatic* and the *psychic*. The somatic basis is inferred from the totality of endosomatic perceptions, which for their part are already of a psychic nature and are associated with the ego, and are therefore conscious. They are produced by endosomatic stimuli, only some of which cross the threshold of consciousness. A considerable proportion of these stimuli occur unconsciously, that is, subliminally. The fact that they are subliminal does not necessarily mean that their status is merely physiological, any more than this would be true of a psychic content. Sometimes they are capable of crossing the threshold, that is, of becoming perceptions. But there is no doubt that a large proportion of these endosomatic stimuli are simply incapable of consciousness and are so elementary that there is no reason to assign them a psychic nature—unless of course one favours the philosophical view that all life-processes are psychic anyway. The chief objection to this hardly demonstrable hypothesis is that it enlarges the concept of the psyche beyond all bounds and interprets the life-process in a way not absolutely warranted by the facts. Concepts that are too broad usually prove to be unsuitable instruments because they are too vague and nebulous. I have therefore suggested that the term "psychic" be used only where there is evidence of a will capable of modifying reflex or instinctual processes. Here I must refer the reader to my paper "On the Nature of the Psyche," [2] where I have discussed this definition of the "psychic" at somewhat greater length.

The somatic basis of the ego consists, then, of conscious and unconscious factors. The same is true of the psychic basis: on the one hand the ego rests on the *total field of consciousness*, and on the other, on the *sum total of unconscious contents*. These fall into three groups: first, temporarily subliminal contents that can be reproduced voluntarily (memory); second, unconscious contents that cannot be reproduced voluntarily; third, contents that are not capable of becoming conscious at all. Group two can be inferred from the spontaneous irruption of subliminal contents into consciousness. Group three is hypothetical; it is a logical inference from the facts underlying group two. It contains contents which have *not yet* irrupted into consciousness, or which never will.

When I said that the ego "rests" on the total field of consciousness I do not mean that it *consists* of this. Were that so, it would be indistinguishable from the field of consciousness as a whole. The ego is only the latter's point of reference, grounded on and limited by the somatic factor described above.

Although its bases are in themselves relatively unknown and unconscious, the ego is a conscious factor par excellence. It is even acquired, empirically speaking, during the individual's lifetime. It seems to arise in the first place from the collision between the somatic factor and the environment, and, once established as a subject, it goes on developing from further collisions with the outer world and the inner.

Despite the unlimited extent of its bases, the ego is never more and never less than consciousness as a whole. As a conscious factor the ego could, theoretically at least,

[2] *Collected Works,* Vol. 8, pars. 371ff.

be described completely. But this would never amount to more than a picture of the *conscious personality;* all those features which are unknown or unconscious to the subject would be missing. A total picture would have to include these. But a total description of the personality is, even in theory, absolutely impossible, because the unconscious portion of it cannot be grasped cognitively. This unconscious portion, as experience has abundantly shown, is by no means unimportant. On the contrary, the most decisive qualities in a person are often unconscious and can be perceived only by others, or have to be laboriously discovered with outside help.

Clearly, then, the *personality as a total phenomenon* does not coincide with the ego, that is, with the conscious personality, but forms an entity that has to be distinguished from the ego. Naturally the need to do this is incumbent only on a psychology that reckons with the fact of the unconscious, but for such a psychology the distinction is of paramount importance. Even for jurisprudence it should be of some importance whether certain psychic facts are conscious or not—for instance, in adjudging the question of responsibility.

I have suggested calling the total personality which, though present, cannot be fully known, the *self*. The ego is, by definition, subordinate to the self and is related to it like a part to the whole. Inside the field of consciousness it has, as we say, free will. By this I do not mean anything philosophical, only the well-known psychological fact of "free choice," or rather the subjective feeling of freedom. But, just as our free will clashes with necessity in the outside world, so also it finds its limits outside the field of consciousness in the subjective inner world, where it comes into conflict with the facts of the self. And just as circumstances or outside events "happen" to us and limit our freedom, so the self acts upon the ego like an *objective occurrence* which free will can do very little to alter. It is, indeed, well known that the ego not only can do nothing against the self, but is sometimes actually assimilated by unconscious components of the personality that are in the process of development and is greatly altered by them.

It is, in the nature of the case, impossible to give any general description of the ego except a formal one. Any other mode of observation would have to take account of the *individuality* which attaches to the ego as one of its main characteristics. Although the numerous elements composing this complex factor are, in themselves, everywhere the same, they are infinitely varied as regards clarity, emotional colouring, and scope. The result of their combination—the ego—is therefore, so far as one can judge, individual and unique, and retains its identity up to a certain point. Its stability is relative, because far-reaching changes of personality can sometimes occur. Alterations of this kind need not always be pathological; they can also be developmental and hence fall within the scope of the normal.

Since it is the point of reference for the field of consciousness, the ego is the subject of all successful attempts at adaptation so far as these are achieved by the will. The ego therefore has a significant part to play in the psychic economy. Its position there is so important that there are good grounds for the prejudice that the ego is the centre of the personality, and that the field of consciousness is the psyche *per se*. If we discount certain suggestive ideas in Leibniz, Kant, Schelling, and Schopenhauer, and the philosophical excursions of Carus and von Hartmann, it is only since the end of the nineteenth century that modern psychology, with its inductive methods, has discovered the foundations of consciousness and proved empirically the existence of a psyche outside consciousness. With this discovery the position of the ego, till then absolute, became relativized; that is to say, though it retains its quality as the centre of the field of consciousness, it is questionable whether it is the centre of the personality. It is part of the personality but not the whole of it. As I have said, it is simply impossible to estimate how large or how small its share is; how free or how dependent it is on the qualities of this extra-conscious" psyche. We can only say that its freedom is limited and its dependence proved in ways that are often decisive. In my experience one would do well not to underestimate its dependence on the unconscious. Naturally there is no need to say this to persons who already overestimate the latter's importance. Some criterion for the right measure is afforded by the psychic consequences of a wrong estimate, a point to which we shall return later on.

We have seen that, from the standpoint of the psychology of consciousness, the unconscious can be divided into three groups of contents. But from the standpoint of the psychology of the personality a twofold division ensues: an "extra-conscious" psyche whose contents are *personal,* and an "extra-conscious" psyche whose contents are *impersonal* and *collective.* The first group comprises contents which are integral components of the individual personality and could therefore just as well be conscious; the second group forms, as it were, an omnipresent, unchanging, and everywhere identical *quality or substrate of the psyche per se.* This is, of course, no more than a hypothesis. But we are driven to it by the peculiar nature of the empirical material, not to mention the high probability that the general similarity of psychic processes in all individuals must be based on an equally general and impersonal principle that conforms to law, just as the instinct manifesting itself in the individual is only the partial manifestation of an instinctual substrate common to all men.

II

*The Shadow*

Whereas the contents of the personal unconscious are acquired during the individual's lifetime, the contents of the collective unconscious are invariably archetypes that were present from the beginning. Their relation to the instincts has been discussed elsewhere.[3] The archetypes most clearly characterized from the empirical point of view are those which have the most frequent and the most disturbing influence on the ego. These are the *shadow*, the *anima*, and the *animus*.[4] The most accessible of these, and the easiest to experience, is the shadow, for its nature can in large measure be inferred from the contents of the personal unconscious. The only exceptions to this rule are those rather rare cases where the positive qualities of the personality are repressed, and the ego in consequence plays an essentially negative or unfavourable role.

The shadow is a moral problem that challenges the whole ego-personality, for no one can become conscious of the shadow without considerable moral effort. To become conscious of it involves recognizing the dark aspects of the personality as present and real. This act is the essential condition for any kind of self-knowledge, and it therefore, as a rule, meets with considerable resistance. Indeed, self-knowledge as a psychotherapeutic measure frequently requires much painstaking work extending over a long period.

Closer examination of the dark characteristics—that is, the inferiorities constituting the shadow—reveals that they have an *emotional* nature, a kind of autonomy, and accordingly an obsessive or, better, possessive quality. Emotion, incidentally, is not an activity of the individual but something that happens to him. Affects occur usually where adaptation is weakest, and at the same time they reveal the reason for its weakness, namely a certain de-

[3] "Instinct and the Unconscious" (supra, pp. 47–58) and "On the Nature of the Psyche," in *The Structure and Dynamics of the Psyche* (*Collected Works*, Vol. 8), pars. 397ff.
[4] The contents of this and the following chapter are taken from a lecture delivered to the Swiss Society for Practical Psychology, in Zurich, 1948. The material was first published in the *Wiener Zeitschrift für Nervenheilkunde und deren Grenzgebiete*, I (1948), 4.

gree of inferiority and the existence of a lower level of personality. On this lower level with its uncontrolled or scarcely controlled emotions one behaves more or less like a primitive, who is not only the passive victim of his affects but also singularly incapable of moral judgment.

Although, with insight and good will, the shadow can to some extent be assimilated into the conscious personality, experience shows that there are certain features which offer the most obstinate resistance to moral control and prove almost impossible to influence. These resistances are usually bound up with *projections,* which are not recognized as such, and their recognition is a moral achievement beyond the ordinary. While some traits peculiar to the shadow can be recognized without too much difficulty as one's own personal qualities, in this case both insight and good will are unavailing because the cause of the emotion appears to lie, beyond all possibility of doubt, in the *other person*. No matter how obvious it may be to the neutral observer that it is a matter of projections, there is little hope that the subject will perceive this himself. He must be convinced that he throws a very long shadow before he is willing to withdraw his emotionally-toned projections from their object.

Let us suppose that a certain individual shows no inclination whatever to recognize his projections. The projection-making factor then has a free hand and can realize its object—if it has one—or bring about some other situation characteristic of its power. As we know, it is not the conscious subject but the unconscious which does the projecting. Hence one meets with projections, one does not make them. The effect of projection is to isolate the subject from his environment, since instead of a real relation to it there is now only an illusory one. Projections change the world into the replica of one's own unknown face. In the last analysis, therefore, they lead to an auto-erotic or autistic condition in which one dreams a world whose reality remains forever unattainable. The resultant *sentiment d'incomplétude* and the still worse feeling of sterility are in their turn explained by projection as the malevolence of the environment, and by means of this vicious circle the isolation is intensified. The more projections are thrust in between the subject and the environment, the harder it is for the ego to see through its illusions. A forty-five-year-old patient who had suffered from a compulsion neurosis since he was twenty and had become completely cut off from the world once said to me: "But I can never admit to myself that I've wasted the best twenty-five years of my life!"

It is often tragic to see how blatantly a man bungles his own life and the lives of others yet remains totally incapable of seeing how much the whole tragedy originates in himself, and how he continually feeds it and keeps it going. Not *consciously*, of course—for consciously he is engaged in bewailing and cursing a faithless world that recedes further and further into the distance. Rather, it is an unconscious factor which spins the illusions that veil his world. And what is being spun is a cocoon, which in the end will completely envelop him.

One might assume that projections like these, which are so very difficult if not impossible to dissolve, would belong to the realm of the shadow—that is, to the negative side of the personality. This assumption becomes untenable after a certain point, because the symbols that then appear no longer refer to the same but to the opposite sex, in a man's case to a woman and vice versa. The source of projections is no longer the shadow—which is always of the same sex as the subject—but a contrasexual figure. Here we meet the animus of a woman and the anima of a man, two corresponding archetypes whose autonomy and unconsciousness explain the stubbornness of their projections. Though the shadow is a motif as well known to mythology as anima and animus, it represents first and foremost the personal unconscious, and its content can therefore be made conscious without too much difficulty. In this it differs from anima and animus, for whereas the shadow can be seen through and recognized fairly easily, the anima and animus are much further away from consciousness and in normal circumstances are seldom if ever realized. With a little self-criticism one can see through the shadow—so far as its nature is personal. But when it appears as an archetype, one encounters the same difficulties as with anima and animus. In other words, it is quite within the bounds of possibility for a man to recognize the relative evil of his nature, but it is a rare and shattering experience for him to gaze into the face of absolute evil.

# III
## *The Syzygy: Anima and Animus*

What, then, is this projection-making factor? The East calls it the "Spinning Woman" [5]—Maya, who creates illusion by her dancing. Had we not long since known it from the symbolism of dreams, this hint from the Orient would put us on the right track: the enveloping, embracing, and devouring element points unmistakably to the mother,[6] that is, to the son's relation to the real mother, to her imago, and to the woman who is to become a mother for him. His Eros is passive like a child's; he hopes to be caught, sucked in, enveloped, and devoured. He seeks, as it were, the protecting, nourishing, charmed circle of the mother, the condition of the infant released from every care, in which the outside world bends over him and even forces happiness upon him. No wonder the real world vanishes from sight!

If this situation is dramatized, as the unconscious usually

[5] Erwin Rousselle, "Spiritual Guidance in Contemporary Taoism," translated by Ralph Mannheim, in Joseph Campbell, ed., *Papers from the Eranos Yearbooks,* Bollingen Series XXX (New York, 1954–68, 6 vols.), Vol. 4, p. 82.
[6] Here and in what follows, the word "mother" is not meant in the literal sense but as a symbol of everything that functions as a mother.

dramatizes it, then there appears before you on the psychological stage a man living regressively, seeking his childhood and his mother, fleeing from a cold cruel world which denies him understanding. Often a mother appears beside him who apparently shows not the slightest concern that her little son should become a man, but who, with tireless and self-immolating effort, neglects nothing that might hinder him from growing up and marrying. You behold the secret conspiracy between mother and son, and how each helps the other to betray life.

Where does the guilt lie? With the mother, or with the son? Probably with both. The unsatisfied longing of the son for life and the world ought to be taken seriously. There is in him a desire to touch reality, to embrace the earth and fructify the field of the world. But he makes no more than a series of fitful starts, for his initiative as well as his staying power are crippled by the secret memory that the world and happiness may be had as a gift—from the mother. The fragment of world which he, like every man, must encounter again and again is never quite the right one, since it does not fall into his lap, does not meet him half way, but remains resistant, has to be conquered, and submits only to force. It makes demands on the masculinity of a man, on his ardour, above all on his courage and resolution when it comes to throwing his whole being into the scales. For this he would need a faithless Eros, one capable of forgetting his mother and undergoing the pain of relinquishing the first love of his life. The mother, foreseeing this danger, has carefully inculcated into him the virtues of faithfulness, devotion, loyalty, so as to protect him from the moral disruption which is the risk of every life adventure. He has learnt these lessons only too well, and remains true to his mother. This naturally causes her the deepest anxiety (when, to her greater glory, he turns out to be a homosexual, for example) and at the same time affords her an unconscious satisfaction that is positively mythological. For, in the relationship now reigning between them, there is consummated the immemorial and most sacred archetype of the marriage of mother and son. What, after all, has commonplace reality to offer, with its registry offices, pay envelopes, and monthly rent, that could outweigh the mystic awe of the *hieros gamos?* Or the star-crowned woman whom the dragon pursues, or the pious obscurities veiling the marriage of the Lamb?

This myth, better than any other, illustrates the nature of the collective unconscious. At this level the mother is both old and young, Demeter and Persephone, and the son is spouse and sleeping suckling rolled into one. The imperfections of real life, with its laborious adaptations and manifold disappointments, naturally cannot compete with such a state of indescribable fulfilment.

In the case of the son, the projection-making factor is identical with the mother-imago, and this is consequently taken to be the real mother. The projection can only be dissolved when the son sees that in the realm of his psyche there is an imago not only of the mother but of the daughter, the sister, the beloved, the heavenly goddess, and the chthonic Baubo. Every mother and every beloved is forced to become the carrier and embodiment of this omnipresent and ageless image, which corresponds to the deepest reality in a man. It belongs to him, this perilous image of Woman; she stands for the loyalty which in the interests of life he must sometimes forgo; she is the much needed compensation for the risks, struggles, sacrifices that all end in disappointment; she is the solace for all the bitterness of life. And, at the same time, she is the great illusionist, the seductress, who draws him into life with her Maya—and not only into life's reasonable and useful aspects, but into its frightful paradoxes and ambivalences where good and evil, success and ruin, hope and despair, counterbalance one another. Because she is his greatest danger she demands from a man his greatest, and if he has it in him she will receive it.

This image is "My Lady Soul," as Spitteler called her. I

have suggested instead the term "anima," as indicating something specific, for which the expression "soul" is too general and too vague. The empirical reality summed up under the concept of the anima forms an extremely dramatic content of the unconscious. It is possible to describe this content in rational, scientific language, but in this way one entirely fails to express its living character. Therefore, in describing the living processes of the psyche, I deliberately and consciously give preference to a dramatic, mythological way of thinking and speaking, because this is not only more expressive but also more exact than an abstract scientific terminology, which is wont to toy with the notion that its theoretic formulations may one fine day be resolved into algebraic equations.

The projection-making factor is the anima, or rather the unconscious as represented by the anima. Whenever she appears, in dreams, visions, and fantasies, she takes on personified form, thus demonstrating that the factor she embodies possesses all the outstanding characteristics of a feminine being.[7] She is not an invention of the conscious, but a spontaneous product of the unconscious. Nor is she a substitute figure for the mother. On the contrary, there is every likelihood that the numinous qualities which make the mother-imago so dangerously powerful derive from the collective archetype of the anima, which is incarnated anew in every male child.

Since the anima is an archetype that is found in men, it is reasonable to suppose that an equivalent archetype must be present in women; for just as the man is compensated by a feminine element, so woman is compensated by a masculine one. I do not, however, wish this argument

---

[7] Naturally, she is a typical figure in *belles-lettres*. Recent publications on the subject of the anima include Linda Fierz-David, *The Dream of Poliphilo*, translated by Mary Hottinger, Bollingen Series XXV (New York, 1950), and my "Psychology of the Transference" (*Collected Works*, Vol. 16). The anima as a psychological idea first appears in the sixteenth-century humanist Richardus Vitus. Cf. my *Mysterium Coniunctionis* (*Collected Works*, Vol. 14), pars. 91ff.

to give the impression that these compensatory relationships were arrived at by deduction. On the contrary, long and varied experience was needed in order to grasp the nature of anima and animus empirically. Whatever we have to say about these archetypes, therefore, is either directly verifiable or at least rendered probable by the facts. At the same time, I am fully aware that we are discussing pioneer work which by its very nature can only be provisional.

Just as the mother seems to be the first carrier of the projection-making factor for the son, so is the father for the daughter. Practical experience of these relationships is made up of many individual cases presenting all kinds of variations on the same basic theme. A concise description of them can, therefore, be no more than schematic.

Woman is compensated by a masculine element and therefore her unconscious has, so to speak, a masculine imprint. This results in a considerable psychological difference between men and women, and accordingly I have called the projection-making factor in women the animus, which means mind or spirit. The animus corresponds to the paternal Logos just as the anima corresponds to the maternal Eros. But I do not wish or intend to give these two intuitive concepts too specific a definition. I use Eros and Logos merely as conceptual aids to describe the fact that woman's consciousness is characterized more by the connective quality of Eros than by the discrimination and cognition associated with Logos. In men, Eros, the function of relationship, is usually less developed than Logos. In women, on the other hand, Eros is an expression of their true nature, while their Logos is often only a regrettable accident. It gives rise to misunderstandings and annoying interpretations in the family circle and among friends. This is because it consists of *opinions* instead of reflections, and by opinions I mean *a priori* assumptions that lay claim to absolute truth. Such assumptions, as everyone knows, can be extremely irritating. As the animus is partial to argument, he can best be seen at work in disputes where both parties know they are right. Men can argue in a very womanish way, too, when they are anima-possessed and have thus been transformed into the animus of their own anima. With them the question becomes one of personal vanity and touchiness (as if they were females); with women it is a question of *power,* whether of truth or justice or some other "ism"—for the dressmaker and hairdresser have already taken care of their vanity. The "Father" (i.e., the sum of conventional opinions) always plays a great role in female argumentation. No matter how friendly and obliging a woman's Eros may be, no logic on earth can shake her if she is ridden by the animus. Often the man has the feeling—and he is not altogether wrong—that only seduction or a beating or rape would have the necessary power of persuasion. He is unaware that this highly dramatic situation would instantly come to a banal and unexciting end if he were to quit the field and let a second woman carry on the battle (his wife, for instance, if she herself is not the fiery war horse). This sound idea seldom or never occurs to him, because no man can converse with an animus for five minutes without becoming the victim of his own anima. Anyone who still had enough sense of humour to listen objectively to the ensuing dialogue would be staggered by the vast number of commonplaces, misapplied truisms, clichés from newspapers and novels, shop-soiled platitudes of every description interspersed with vulgar abuse and brain-splitting lack of logic. It is a dialogue which, irrespective of its participants, is repeated millions and millions of times in all the languages of the world and always remains essentially the same.

This singular fact is due to the following circumstance: when animus and anima meet, the animus draws his sword of power and the anima ejects her poison of illusion and seduction. The outcome need not always be negative, since the two are equally likely to fall in love (a special instance of love at first sight). The language of love is of astonishing uniformity, using the well-worn formulas with the utmost devotion and fidelity, so that once again the two partners find themselves in a banal collective situation. Yet they live in the illusion that they are related to one another in a most individual way.

In both its positive and its negative aspects the anima/animus relationship is always full of "animosity," i.e., it is emotional, and hence collective. Affects lower the level of the relationship and bring it closer to the common instinctual basis, which no longer has anything individual about it. Very often the relationship runs its course heedless of its human performers, who afterwards do not know what happened to them.

Whereas the cloud of "animosity" surrounding the man is composed chiefly of sentimentality and resentment, in woman it expresses itself in the form of opinionated views, interpretations, insinuations, and misconstructions, which all have the purpose (sometimes attained) of severing the relation between two human beings. The woman, like the man, becomes wrapped in a veil of illusions by her demon-familiar, and, as the daughter who alone understands her father (that is, is eternally right in everything), she is translated to the land of sheep, where she is put to graze by the shepherd of her soul, the animus.

Like the anima, the animus too has a positive aspect. Through the figure of the father he expresses not only conventional opinion but—equally—what we call "spirit," philosophical or religious ideas in particular, or rather the attitude resulting from them. Thus the animus is a psychopomp, a mediator between the conscious and the unconscious and a personification of the latter. Just as the anima becomes, through integration, the Eros of consciousness, so the animus becomes a Logos; and in the same way that the anima gives relationship and relatedness to a man's consciousness, the animus gives to woman's consciousness a capacity for reflection, deliberation, and self-knowledge.

The effect of anima and animus on the ego is in principle the same. This effect is extremely difficult to eliminate because, in the first place, it is uncommonly strong and immediately fills the ego-personality with an unshakable feeling of rightness and righteousness. In the second place, the cause of the effect is projected and appears to lie in objects and objective situations. Both these characteristics can, I believe, be traced back to the peculiarities of the archetype. For the archetype, of course, exists *a priori*. This may possibly explain the often totally irrational yet undisputed and indisputable existence of certain moods and opinions. Perhaps these are so notoriously difficult to influence because of the powerfully suggestive effect emanating from the archetype. Consciousness is fascinated by it, held captive, as if hypnotized. Very often the ego experiences a vague feeling of moral defeat and then behaves all the more defensively, defiantly, and self-righteously, thus setting up a vicious circle which only increases its feeling of inferiority. The bottom is then knocked out of the human relationship, for, like megalomania, a feeling of inferiority makes mutual recognition impossible, and without this there is no relationship.

As I said, it is easier to gain insight into the shadow than into the anima or animus. With the shadow, we have the advantage of being prepared in some sort by our education, which has always endeavoured to convince people that they are not one-hundred-per-cent pure gold. So everyone immediately understands what is meant by "shadow," "inferior personality," etc. And if he has forgotten, his memory can easily be refreshed by a Sunday sermon, his wife, or the tax collector. With the anima and animus, however, things are by no means so simple. Firstly, there is no moral education in this respect, and secondly, most people are content to be self-righteous and prefer mutual vilification (if nothing worse!) to the recognition of their projections. Indeed, it seems a very natural state of affairs for men to have irrational moods and women irrational opinions. Presumably this situation is grounded on instinct and must remain as it is to ensure that the Empedoclean game of the hate and love of the elements shall continue for all eternity. Nature is conservative and does not easily allow her courses to be altered; she defends in the most stubborn way the inviolability of the preserves where anima and animus roam. Hence it is much more difficult to become conscious of one's anima/animus projections than to acknowledge one's shadow side. One has, of course, to overcome certain moral obstacles, such as vanity, ambition, conceit, resentment, etc., but in the case of projections all sorts of purely intellectual difficulties are added, quite apart from the contents of the projection which one simply doesn't know how to cope with. And on top of all this there arises a profound doubt as to whether one is not meddling too much with nature's business by prodding into consciousness things which it would have been better to leave asleep.

Although there are, in my experience, a fair number of people who can understand without special intellectual or moral difficulties what is meant by anima and animus, one finds very many more who have the greatest trouble in visualizing these empirical concepts as anything concrete. This shows that they fall a little outside the usual range of experience. They are unpopular precisely because they seem unfamiliar. The consequence is that they mobilize prejudice and become taboo like everything else that is unexpected.

So if we set it up as a kind of requirement that projections should be dissolved, because it is wholesomer that way and in every respect more advantageous, we are entering upon new ground. Up till now everybody has been convinced that the idea "my father," "my mother," etc., is nothing but a faithful reflection of the real parent, corresponding in every detail to the original, so that when someone says "my father" he means no more and no less than what his father is in reality. This is actually what he supposes he does mean, but a supposition of identity by no means brings that identity about. This is where the fallacy of the *enkekalymmenos* ("the veiled one") comes in.[8] If one includes in the psychological equation X's picture of his father, which he takes for the real father, the equation will not work out, because the unknown quantity he has introduced does not tally with reality. X has overlooked the fact that his idea of a person consists, in the first place, of the possibly very incomplete picture he has received of the real person and, in the second place, of the subjective modifications he has imposed upon this picture. X's idea of his father is a complex quantity for which the real father is only in part responsible, an indefinitely larger share falling to the son. So true is this that every time he criticizes or praises his father he is unconsciously hitting back at himself, thereby bringing about those psychic consequences that overtake people who habitually disparage or overpraise themselves. If, however, X carefully compares his reactions with reality, he stands a chance of noticing that he has miscalculated somewhere by not realizing long ago from his father's behaviour that the picture he has of him is a false one. But as a rule X is convinced that he is right, and if anybody is wrong it must be the other fellow. Should X have a poorly developed Eros, he will be either indifferent to the inadequate relationship he has with his father or else annoyed by the inconsistency and general incomprehensibility of a father whose behaviour never really corresponds to the picture X has of him. Therefore X thinks he has every right to feel hurt, misunderstood, and even betrayed.

One can imagine how desirable it would be in such cases to dissolve the projection. And there are always optimists who believe that the golden age can be ushered in simply

---

[8] The fallacy, which stems from Eubulides the Megarian, runs: "Can you recognize your father?" Yes. "Can you recoginze this veiled one?" No. "This veiled one is your father. Hence you can recognize your father and not recognize him."

by telling people the right way to go. But just let them try to explain to these people that they are acting like a dog chasing its own tail. To make a person see the short-comings of his attitude considerably more than mere "telling" is needed, for more is involved than ordinary common sense can allow. What one is up against here is the kind of fateful misunderstanding which, under ordinary conditions, remains forever inaccessible to insight. It is rather like expecting the average respectable citizen to recognize himself as a criminal.

I mention all this just to illustrate the order of magnitude to which the anima/animus projections belong, and the moral and intellectual exertions that are needed to dissolve them. Not all the contents of the anima and animus are projected, however. Many of them appear spontaneously in dreams and so on, and many more can be made conscious through active imagination. In this way we find that thoughts, feelings, and affects are alive in us which we would never have believed possible. Naturally, possibilities of this sort seem utterly fantastic to anyone who has not experienced them himself, for a normal person "knows what he thinks." Such a childish attitude on the part of the "normal person" is simply the rule, so that no one without experience in this field can be expected to understand the real nature of anima and animus. With these reflections one gets into an entirely new world of psychological experience, provided of course that one succeeds in realizing it in practice. Those who do succeed can hardly fail to be impressed by all that the ego does not know and never has known. This increase in self-knowledge is still very rare nowadays and is usually paid for in advance with a neurosis, if not with something worse.

The autonomy of the collective unconscious expresses itself in the figures of anima and animus. They personify those of its contents which, when withdrawn from projection, can be integrated into consciousness. To this extent, both figures represent *functions* which filter the contents of the collective unconscious through to the conscious mind. They appear or behave as such, however, only so long as the tendencies of the conscious and unconscious do not diverge too greatly. Should any tension arise, these functions, harmless till then, confront the conscious mind in personified form and behave rather like systems split off from the personality, or like part souls. This comparison is inadequate in so far as nothing previously belonging to the ego-personality has split off from it; on the contrary, the two figures represent a disturbing accretion. The reason for their behaving in this way is that though the *contents* of anima and animus can be integrated they themselves cannot, since they are archetypes. As such they are the foundation stones of the psychic structure, which in its totality exceeds the limits of consciousness and therefore can never become the object of direct cognition. Though the effects of anima and animus can be made conscious, they themselves are factors transcending consciousness and beyond the reach of perception and volition. Hence they remain autonomous despite the integration of their contents, and for this reason they should be borne constantly in mind. This is extremely important from the therapeutic standpoint, because constant observation pays the unconscious a tribute that more or less guarantees its co-operation. The unconscious as we know can never be "done with" once and for all. It is, in fact, one of the most important tasks of psychic hygiene to pay continual attention to the symptomatology of unconscious contents and processes, for the good reason that the conscious mind is always in danger of becoming one-sided, of keeping to well-worn paths and getting stuck in blind alleys. The complementary and compensating function of the unconscious ensures that these dangers, which are especially great in neurosis, can in some measure be avoided. It is only under ideal conditions, when life is still simple and unconscious enough to follow the serpentine path of instinct without hesitation or misgiving, that the compensation works with entire success. The more civilized, the more unconscious and complicated a man is, the less he is able to follow his instincts. His complicated living conditions and the influence of his environment are so strong that they drown the quiet voice of nature. Opinions, beliefs, theories, and collective tendencies appear in its stead and back up all the aberrations of the conscious mind. Deliberate attention should then be given to the unconscious so that the compensation can set to work. Hence it is especially important to picture the archetypes of the unconscious not as a rushing phantasmagoria of fugitive images but as constant, autonomous factors, which indeed they are.

Both these archetypes, as practical experience shows, possess a fatality that can on occasion produce tragic results. They are quite literally the father and mother of all the disastrous entanglements of fate and have long been recognized as such by the whole world. Together they form a divine pair,[9] one of whom, in accordance with his Logos nature, is characterized by *pneuma* and *nous*, rather like Hermes with his ever-shifting hues, while the other, in accordance with her Eros nature, wears the features of Aphrodite, Helen (Selene), Persephone, and Hecate. Both of them are unconscious powers, "gods" in fact, as the ancient world quite rightly conceived them to be. To call them by this name is to give them that central position in the scale of psychological values which has always been theirs whether consciously acknowledged or not; for their power grows in proportion to the degree that they remain unconscious. Those who do not see them are in their hands, just as a typhus epidemic flourishes best

[9] Naturally this is not meant as a psychological definition, let alone a metaphysical one. As I pointed out in "The Relations between the Ego and the Unconscious" (*Collected Works*, Vol. 7, pars. 296ff.), the syzygy consists of three elements: the femininity pertaining to the man and the masculinity pertaining to the woman; the experience which man has of woman and vice versa; and, finally, the masculine and feminine archetypal image. The first element can be integrated into the personality by the process of conscious realization, but the last one cannot.

when its source is undiscovered. Even in Christianity the divine syzygy has not become obsolete, but occupies the highest place as Christ and his bride the Church.[10] Parallels like these prove extremely helpful in our attempts to find the right criterion for gauging the significance of these two archetypes. What we can discover about them from the conscious side is so slight as to be almost imperceptible. It is only when we throw light into the dark depths of the psyche and explore the strange and tortuous paths of human fate that it gradually becomes clear to us how immense is the influence wielded by these two factors that complement our conscious life.

Recapitulating, I should like to emphasize that the integration of the shadow, or the realization of the personal unconscious, marks the first stage in the analytic process, and that without it a recognition of anima and animus is impossible. The shadow can be realized only through a relation to a partner, and anima and animus only through a relation to a partner of the opposite sex, because only in such a relation do their projections become operative. The recognition of the anima gives rise, in a man, to a triad, one third of which is transcendent: the masculine subject, the opposing feminine subject, and the transcendent anima. With a woman the situation is reversed. The missing fourth element that would make the triad a quaternity is, in a man, the archetype of the Wise Old Man, which I have not discussed here, and in a woman the Chthonic Mother. These four constitute a half immanent and half transcendent quaternity, an archetype which I have called the *marriage quaternio*.[11] The marriage quaternio provides a

[10] "For the Scripture says, God made man male and female; the male is Christ, the female is the Church." Second Epistle of Clement to the Corinthians, xiv, 2 (translated by Kirsopp Lake, *The Apostolic Fathers*, Loeb Classical Library [London and New York, 1912–13, 2 vols.], Vol. I, p. 151). In pictorial representations, Mary often takes the place of the Church.

[11] "The Psychology of the Transference" (*Collected Works*, Vol. 16), pars. 425ff. Cf. "The Structure and Dynamics of the Self" (*Collected Works*, Vol. 9.ii), pars. 358ff., the Naassene quaternio.

schema not only for the self but also for the structure of primitive society with its cross-cousin marriage, marriage classes, and division of settlements into quarters. The self, on the other hand, is a God-image, or at least cannot be distinguished from one. Of this the early Christian spirit was not ignorant, otherwise Clement of Alexandria could never have said that he who knows himself knows God.[12]

[12] Cf. "The Structure and Dynamics of the Self" (*Collected Works,* Vol. 9.ii), par. 347.

# ❧ 7 ❧

## *Marriage as a Psychological Relationship*[1]

Regarded as a psychological relationship, marriage is a highly complex structure made up of a whole series of subjective and objective factors, mostly of a very heterogeneous nature. As I wish to confine myself here to the purely psychological problems of marriage, I must disregard in the main the objective factors of a legal and social nature, although these cannot fail to have a pronounced influence on the psychological relationship between the marriage partners.

Whenever we speak of a "psychological relationship" we presuppose one that is *conscious,* for there is no such thing as a psychological relationship between two people who are in a state of unconsciousness. From the psychological point of view they would be wholly without

[1] From *The Development of Personality. Collected Works,* Vol. 17, pars. 324–345. [First published as "Die Ehe als psychologische Beziehung," in *Das Ehebuch* (Celle, 1925), a volume edited by Count Hermann Keyserling; translated by Theresa Duerr in the English version, *The Book of Marriage* (New York, 1926). The original was reprinted in *Seelenprobleme der Gegenwart* (Zurich, 1931). The essay was again translated into English by H. G. and Cary F. Baynes in *Contributions to Analytical Psychology* (London and New York, 1928), and this version has been freely consulted in the present translation.—EDITORS OF *The Collected Works.*]

relationship. From any other point of view, the physiological for example, they could be regarded as related, but one
could not call their relationship psychological. It must be
admitted that though such total unconsciousness as I have
assumed does not occur, there is nevertheless a not inconsiderable degree of partial unconsciousness, and the
psychological relationship is limited in the degree to which
that unconsciousness exists.

In the child, consciousness rises out of the depths of
unconscious psychic life, at first like separate islands, which
gradually unite to form a "continent," a continuous land-
mass of consciousness. Progressive mental development
means, in effect, extension of consciousness. With the
rise of a continuous consciousness, and not before, psychological relationship becomes possible. So far as we
know, consciousness is always ego-consciousness. In order
to be conscious of myself, I must be able to distinguish
myself from others. Relationship can only take place where
this distinction exists. But although the distinction may
be made in a general way, normally it is incomplete, because large areas of psychic life still remain unconscious.
As no distinction can be made with regard to unconscious
contents, on this terrain no relationship can be established;
here there still reigns the original unconscious condition
of the ego's primitive identity with others, in other words
a complete absence of relationship.

The young person of marriageable age does, of course,
possess an ego-consciousness (girls more than men, as a
rule), but, since he has only recently emerged from the
mists of original unconsciousness, he is certain to have
wide areas which still lie in the shadow and which preclude
to that extent the formation of psychological relationship.
This means, in practice, that the young man (or woman)
can have only an incomplete understanding of himself and
others, and is therefore imperfectly informed as to his, and
their, motives. As a rule the motives he acts from are
largely unconscious. Subjectively, of course, he thinks him-

self very conscious and knowing, for we constantly over-estimate the existing content of consciousness, and it is a great and surprising discovery when we find that what we had supposed to be the final peak is nothing but the first step in a very long climb. The greater the area of uncon-sciousness, the less is marriage a matter of free choice, as is shown subjectively in the fatal compulsion one feels so acutely when one is in love. The compulsion can exist even when one is not in love, though in less agreeable form.

Unconscious motivations are of a personal and of a general nature. First of all, there are the motives deriving from parental influence. The relationship of the young man to his mother, and of the girl to her father, is the deter-mining factor in this respect. It is the strength of the bond to the parents that unconsciously influences the choice of husband or wife, either positively or negatively. Con-scious love for either parent favours the choice of a like mate, while an unconscious tie (which need not by any means express itself consciously as love) makes the choice difficult and imposes characteristic modifications. In order to understand them, one must know first of all the cause of the unconscious tie to the parents, and under what condi-tions it forcibly modifies, or even prevents, the conscious choice. Generally speaking, all the life which the parents could have lived, but of which they thwarted themselves for artificial motives, is passed on to the children in sub-stitute form. That is to say, the children are driven un-consciously in a direction that is intended to compensate for everything that was left unfulfilled in the lives of their parents. Hence it is that excessively moral-minded parents have what are called "unmoral" children, or an irrespon-sible wastrel of a father has a son with a positively morbid amount of ambition, and so on. The worst results flow from parents who have kept themselves artificially uncon-scious. Take the case of a mother who deliberately keeps herself unconscious so as not to disturb the pretence of a "satisfactory" marriage. Unconsciously she will bind her son to her, more or less as a substitute for a husband. The son, if not forced directly into homosexuality, is compelled to modify his choice in a way that is contrary to his true nature. He may, for instance, marry a girl who is obviously inferior to his mother and therefore unable to compete with her; or he will fall for a woman of a tyrannical and overbearing disposition, who may perhaps succeed in tearing him away from his mother. The choice of a mate, if the instincts have not been vitiated, may remain free from these influences, but sooner or later they will make themselves felt as obstacles. A more or less instinctive choice might be considered the best from the point of view of maintaining the species, but it is not always fortunate psychologically, because there is often an uncommonly large difference between the purely instinctive personality and one that is individually differentiated. And though in such cases the race might be improved and invigorated by a purely instinctive choice, individual happiness would be bound to suffer. (The idea of "instinct" is of course nothing more than a collective term for all kinds of organic and psychic factors whose nature is for the most part unknown.)

If the individual is to be regarded solely as an instrument for maintaining the species, then the purely instinctive choice of a mate is by far the best. But since the foundations of such a choice are unconscious, only a kind of impersonal liaison can be built upon them, such as can be observed to perfection among primitives. If we can speak here of a "relationship" at all, it is, at best, only a pale reflection of what we mean, a very distant state of affairs with a decidedly impersonal character, wholly regulated by traditional customs and prejudices, the prototype of every conventional marriage.

So far as reason or calculation or the so-called loving care of the parents does not arrange the marriage, and the pristine instincts of the children are not vitiated either by false education or by the hidden influence of accumulated and neglected parental complexes, the marriage choice will normally follow the unconscious motivations of instinct. Unconsciousness results in non-differentiation, or unconscious identity. The practical consequence of this is that one person presupposes in the other a psychological structure similar to his own. Normal sex life, as a shared experience with apparently similar aims, further strengthens the feeling of unity and identity. This state is described as one of complete harmony, and is extolled as a great happiness ("one heart and one soul")—not without good reason, since the return to that original condition of unconscious oneness is like a return to childhood. Hence the childish gestures of all lovers. Even more is it a return to the mother's womb, into the teeming depths of an as yet unconscious creativity. It is, in truth, a genuine and incontestable experience of the Divine, whose transcendent force obliterates and consumes everything individual; a real communion with life and the impersonal power of fate. The individual will for self-possession is broken: the woman becomes the mother, the man the father, and thus both are robbed of their freedom and made instruments of the life urge.

Here the relationship remains within the bounds of the biological instinctive goal, the preservation of the species. Since this goal is of a collective nature, the psychological link between husband and wife will also be essentially collective, and cannot be regarded as an individual relationship in the psychological sense. We can only speak of this when the nature of the unconscious motivations has been recognized and the original identity broken down. Seldom or never does a marriage develop into an individual relationship smoothly and without crises. There is no birth of consciousness without pain.

The ways that lead to conscious realization are many, but they follow definite laws. In general, the change begins with the onset of the second half of life. The middle period of life is a time of enormous psychological importance.

The child begins its psychological life within very narrow limits, inside the magic circle of the mother and the family. With progressive maturation it widens its horizon and its own sphere of influence; its hopes and intentions are directed to extending the scope of personal power and possessions; desire reaches out to the world in ever-widening range; the will of the individual becomes more and more identical with the natural goals pursued by unconscious motivations. Thus man breathes his own life into things, until finally they begin to live of themselves and to multiply; and imperceptibly he is overgrown by them. Mothers are overtaken by their children, men by their own creations, and what was originally brought into being only with labour and the greatest effort can no longer be held in check. First it was passion, then it became duty, and finally an intolerable burden, a vampire that battens on the life of its creator. Middle life is the moment of greatest unfolding, when a man still gives himself to his work with his whole strength and his whole will. But in this very moment evening is born, and the second half of life begins. Passion now changes her face and is called duty; "I want" becomes the inexorable "I must," and the turnings of the pathway that once brought surprise and discovery become dulled by custom. The wine has fermented and begins to settle and clear. Conservative tendencies develop if all goes well; instead of looking forward one looks backward, most of the time involuntarily, and one begins to take stock, to see how one's life has developed up to this point. The real motivations are sought and real discoveries are made. The critical survey of himself and his fate enables a man to recognize his peculiarities. But these insights do not come to him easily; they are gained only through the severest shocks.

Since the aims of the second half of life are different from those of the first, to linger too long in the youthful attitude produces a division of the will. Consciousness still presses forward, in obedience, as it were, to its own inertia, but the unconscious lags behind, because the strength and inner resolve needed for further expansion have been sapped. This disunity with oneself begets discontent, and since one is not conscious of the real state of things one generally projects the reasons for it upon one's partner. A critical atmosphere thus develops, the necessary prelude to conscious realization. Usually this state does not begin simultaneously for both partners. Even the best of marriages cannot expunge individual differences so completely that the state of mind of the partners is absolutely identical. In most cases one of them will adapt to marriage more quickly than the other. The one who is grounded on a positive relationship to the parents will find little or no difficulty in adjusting to his or her partner, while the other may be hindered by a deep-seated unconscious tie to the parents. He will therefore achieve complete adaptation only later, and, because it is won with greater difficulty, it may even prove the more durable.

These differences in tempo, and in the degree of spiritual development, are the chief causes of a typical difficulty which makes its appearance at critical moments. In speaking of "the degree of spiritual development" of a personality, I do not wish to imply an especially rich or magnanimous nature. Such is not the case at all. I mean, rather, a certain complexity of mind or nature, comparable to a gem with many facets as opposed to the simple cube. There are many-sided and rather problematical natures burdened with hereditary traits that are sometimes very difficult to reconcile. Adaptation to such natures, or their adaptation to simpler personalities, is always a problem. These people, having a certain tendency to dissociation, generally have the capacity to split off irreconcilable traits of character for considerable periods, thus passing themselves off as much simpler than they are; or it may happen that their many-sidedness, their very versatility, lends them a peculiar charm. Their partners can easily lose themselves in such a labyrinthine nature, finding in it such an abundance of possible experiences that their personal interests are completely absorbed, sometimes in a not very agreeable way, since their sole occupation then consists in tracking the other through all the twists and turns of his character. There is always so much experience available that the simpler personality is surrounded, if not actually swamped, by it; he is swallowed up in his more complex partner and cannot see his way out. It is an almost regular occurrence for a woman to be wholly contained, spiritually, in her husband, and for a husband to be wholly contained, emotionally, in his wife. One could describe this as the problem of the "contained" and the "container."

The one who is contained feels himself to be living entirely within the confines of his marriage; his attitude to the marriage partner is undivided; outside the marriage there exist no essential obligations and no binding interests. The unpleasant side of this otherwise ideal partnership is the disquieting dependence upon a personality that can never be seen in its entirety, and is therefore not altogether credible or dependable. The great advantage lies in his own undividedness, and this is a factor not to be underrated in the psychic economy.

The container, on the other hand, who in accordance with his tendency to dissociation has an especial need to unify himself in undivided love for another, will be left far behind in this effort, which is naturally very difficult for him, by the simpler personality. While he is seeking in the latter all the subtleties and complexities that would complement and correspond to his own facets, he is disturbing the other's simplicity. Since in normal circumstances simplicity always has the advantage over complexity, he will very soon be obliged to abandon his efforts to arouse subtle and intricate reactions in a simpler nature. And soon enough his partner, who in accordance with her[2] simpler nature expects simple answers from him, will give

[2] [In translating this and the following passages, I have, for the sake of clarity, assumed that the container is the man and the contained woman. This assumption is due entirely to the exigencies of English grammar, and is not implied in the German text. Needless to say, the situation could just as easily be reversed.—TRANSLATOR.]

him plenty to do by constellating his complexities with her everlasting insistence on simple answers. Willy-nilly, he must withdraw into himself before the suasions of simplicity. Any mental effort, like the conscious process itself, is so much of a strain for the ordinary man that he invariably prefers the simple, even when it does not happen to be the truth. And when it represents at least a half-truth, then it is all up with him. The simpler nature works on the more complicated like a room that is too small, that does not allow him enough space. The complicated nature, on the other hand, gives the simpler one too many rooms with too much space, so that she never knows where she really belongs. So it comes about quite naturally that the more complicated contains the simpler. The former cannot be absorbed in the latter, but encompasses it without being itself contained. Yet, since the more complicated has perhaps a greater need of being contained than the other, he feels himself outside the marriage and accordingly always plays the problematical role. The more the contained clings, the more the container feels shut out of the relationship. The contained pushes into it by her clinging, and the more she pushes, the less the container is able to respond. He therefore tends to spy out of the window, no doubt unconsciously at first; but with the onset of middle age there awakens in him a more insistent longing for that unity and undividedness which is especially necessary to him on account of his dissociated nature. At this juncture things are apt to occur that bring the conflict to a head. He becomes conscious of the fact that he is seeking completion, seeking the contentedness and undividedness that have always been lacking. For the contained this is only a confirmation of the insecurity she has always felt so painfully; she discovers that in the rooms which apparently belonged to her there dwell other, unwished-for guests. The hope of security vanishes, and this disappointment drives her in on herself, unless by desperate and violent efforts she can succeed in forcing her partner to capitulate, and in extort-

ing a confession that his longing for unity was nothing but
a childish or morbid fantasy. If these tactics do not succeed, her acceptance of failure may do her a real good, by
forcing her to recognize that the security she was so desperately seeking in the other is to be found in herself. In
this way she finds herself and discovers in her own simpler
nature all those complexities which the container had
sought for in vain.

If the container does not break down in face of what
we are wont to call "unfaithfulness," but goes on believing
in the inner justification of his longing for unity, he will
have to put up with his self-division for the time being. A
dissociation is not healed by being split off, but by more
complete disintegration. All the powers that strive for
unity, all healthy desire for selfhood, will resist the disintegration, and in this way he will become conscious of the
possibility of an inner integration, which before he had
always sought outside himself. He will then find his reward
in an undivided self.

This is what happens very frequently about the midday
of life, and in this wise our miraculous human nature enforces the transition that leads from the first half of life
to the second. It is a metamorphosis from a state in which
man is only a tool of instinctive nature, to another in which
he is no longer a tool, but himself: a transformation of
nature into culture, of instinct into spirit.

One should take great care not to interrupt this necessary
development by acts of moral violence, for any attempt
to create a spiritual attitude by splitting off and suppressing
the instincts is a falsification. Nothing is more repulsive
than a furtively prurient spirituality; it is just as unsavoury
as gross sensuality. But the transition takes a long time,
and the great majority of people get stuck in the first stages.
If only we could, like the primitives, leave the unconscious
to look after this whole psychological development which
marriage entails, these transformations could be worked
out more completely and without too much friction. So
often among so-called "primitives" one comes across spirit-

ual personalities who immediately inspire respect, as though they were the fully matured products of an undisturbed fate. I speak here from personal experience. But where among present-day Europeans can one find people not deformed by acts of moral violence? We are still barbarous enough to believe in both asceticism and its opposite. But the wheel of history cannot be put back; we can only strive towards an attitude that will allow us to live out our fate as undisturbedly as the primitive pagan in us really wants. Only on this condition can we be sure of not perverting spirituality into sensuality, and vice versa; for both must live, each drawing life from the other.

The transformation I have briefly described above is the very essence of the psychological marriage relationship. Much could be said about the illusions that serve the ends of nature and bring about the transformations that are characteristic of middle life. The peculiar harmony that characterizes marriage during the first half of life—provided the adjustment is successful—is largely based on the projection of certain archetypal images, as the critical phase makes clear.

Every man carries within him the eternal image of woman, not the image of this or that particular woman, but a definite feminine image. This image is fundamentally unconscious, an hereditary factor of primordial origin engraved in the living organic system of the man, an imprint or "archetype" of all the ancestral experiences of the female, a deposit, as it were, of all the impressions ever made by woman—in short, an inherited system of psychic adaptation. Even if no women existed, it would still be possible, at any given time, to deduce from this unconscious image exactly how a woman would have to be constituted psychically. The same is true of the woman: she too has her inborn image of man. Actually, we know from experience that it would be more accurate to describe it as an image of *men,* whereas in the case of the man it is rather the image of *woman.* Since this image is unconscious, it is always unconsciously projected upon the person of the beloved, and is one of the chief reasons for passionate attraction or aversion. I have called this image the "anima," and I find the scholastic question *Habet mulier animam?* especially interesting, since in my view it is an intelligent one inasmuch as the doubt seems justified. Woman has no anima, no soul, but she has an *animus*. The anima has an erotic, emotional character, the animus a rationalizing one. Hence most of what men say about feminine eroticism, and particularly about the emotional life of women, is derived from their own anima projections and distorted accordingly. On the other hand, the astonishing assumptions and fantasies that women make about men come from the activity of the animus, who produces an inexhaustible supply of illogical arguments and false explanations.

Anima and animus are both characterized by an extraordinary many-sidedness. In a marriage it is always the contained who projects this image upon the container, while the latter is only partially able to project his unconscious image upon his partner. The more unified and simple this partner is, the less complete the projection. In which case, this highly fascinating image hangs as it were in mid air, as though waiting to be filled out by a living person. There are certain types of women who seem to be made by nature to attract anima projections; indeed one could almost speak of a definite "anima type." The so-called "sphinx-like" character is an indispensable part of their equipment, also an equivocalness, an intriguing elusiveness—not an indefinite blur that offers nothing, but an indefiniteness that seems full of promises, like the speaking silence of a Mona Lisa. A woman of this kind is both old and young, mother and daughter, of more than doubtful chastity, childlike, and yet endowed with a naïve cunning that is extremely disarming to men.[3] Not every man of real intellectual power can be an animus, for the animus must be a master

[3] There are excellent descriptions of this type in H. Rider Haggard's *She* (London, 1887) and Pierre Benoît's *L'Atlantide* (Paris, 1920; translated by Mary C. Tongue and Mary Ross as *Atlantida*, New York, 1920).

not so much of fine ideas as of fine words—words seemingly full of meaning which purport to leave a great deal
unsaid. He must also belong to the "misunderstood" class,
or be in some way at odds with his environment, so that
the idea of self-sacrifice can insinuate itself. He must be
a rather questionable hero, a man with possibilities, which is
not to say that an animus projection may not discover a
real hero long before he has become perceptible to the
sluggish wits of the man of "average intelligence." [4]

For man as well as for woman, in so far as they are
"containers," the filling out of this image is an experience
fraught with consequences, for it holds the possibility of
finding one's own complexities answered by a corresponding diversity. Wide vistas seem to open up in which one
feels oneself embraced and contained. I say "seem" ad-
visedly, because the experience may be two-faced. Just as
the animus projection of a woman can often pick on a man
of real significance who is not recognized by the mass, and
can actually help him to achieve his true destiny with her
moral support, so a man can create for himself a *femme in-
spiratrice* by his anima projection. But more often it turns
out to be an illusion with destructive consequences, a
failure because his faith was not sufficiently strong. To the
pessimists I would say that these primordial psychic images
have an extraordinarily positive value, but I must warn
the optimists against blinding fantasies and the likelihood
of the most absurd aberrations.

One should on no account take this projection for an
individual and conscious relationship. In its first stages it is
far from that, for it creates a compulsive dependence based
on unconscious motives other than the biological ones.
Rider Haggard's *She* gives some indication of the curious
world of ideas that underlies the anima projection. They

[4] A passably good account of the animus is to be found in Marie
Hay's book *The Evil Vineyard* (New York, 1923), also in Elinor
Wylie's *Jennifer Lorn* (New York, 1923) and Selma Lagerlöf's
*Gösta Berlings Saga* (1891; English translation by P. B. Flach, *The
Story of Gösta Berling*, 1898).

are in essence spiritual contents, often in erotic disguise, obvious fragments of a primitive mythological mentality that consists of archetypes, and whose totality constitutes the collective unconscious. Accordingly, such a relationship is at bottom collective and not individual. (Benoît, who created in *L'Atlantide* a fantasy figure similar even in details to "She," denies having plagiarized Rider Haggard.)

If such a projection fastens on to one of the marriage partners, a collective spiritual relationship conflicts with the collective biological one and produces in the container the division or disintegration I have described above. If he is able to hold his head above water, he will find himself through this very conflict. In that case the projection, though dangerous in itself, will have helped him to pass from a collective to an individual relationship. This amounts to full conscious realization of the relationship that marriage brings. Since the aim of this paper is a discussion of the psychology of marriage, the psychology of projection cannot concern us here. It is sufficient to mention it as a fact.

One can hardly deal with the psychological marriage relationship without mentioning, even at the risk of misunderstanding, the nature of its critical transitions. As is well known, one understands nothing psychological unless one has experienced it oneself. Not that this ever prevents anyone from feeling convinced that his own judgment is the only true and competent one. This disconcerting fact comes from the necessary overvaluation of the momentary content of consciousness, for without this concentration of attention one could not be conscious at all. Thus it is that every period of life has its own psychological truth, and the same applies to every stage of psychological development. There are even stages which only the few can reach, it being a question of race, family, education, talent, and passion. Nature is aristocratic. The normal man is a fiction, although certain generally valid laws do exist. Psychic life is a development that can easily be arrested on the lowest levels. It is as though every individual had a specific gravity, in accordance with which he either rises, or sinks down, to the level where he reaches his limit. His views and convictions will be determined accordingly. No wonder, then, that by far the greater number of marriages reach their upper psychological limit in fulfilment of the biological aim, without injury to spiritual or moral health. Relatively few people fall into deeper disharmony with themselves. Where there is a great deal of pressure from outside, the conflict is unable to develop much dramatic tension for sheer lack of energy. Psychological insecurity, however, increases in proportion to social security, unconsciously at first, causing neuroses, then consciously, bringing with it separations, discord, divorces, and other marital disorders. On still higher levels, new possibilities of psychological development are discerned, touching on the sphere of religion where critical judgment comes to a halt.

Progress may be permanently arrested on any of these levels, with complete unconsciousness of what might have followed at the next stage of development. As a rule graduation to the next stage is barred by violent prejudices and superstitious fears. This, however, serves a most useful purpose, since a man who is compelled by accident to live at a level too high for him becomes a fool and a menace.

Nature is not only aristocratic, she is also esoteric. Yet no man of understanding will thereby be induced to make a secret of what he knows, for he realizes only too well that the secret of psychic development can never be betrayed, simply because that development is a question of individual capacity.

# ❧ 8 ❧

## Psychological Types

### General Description of the Types

#### 1. Introduction

In the following pages I shall attempt a general description of the psychology of the types, starting with the two basic types I have termed introverted and extraverted. This will be followed by a description of those more special types whose peculiarities are due to the fact that the individual adapts and orients himself chiefly by means of his most differentiated function. The former I would call *attitude-types*, distinguished by the direction of their interest, or of the movement of libido; the latter I would call *function-types*.

The attitude-types, as I have repeatedly emphasized in the preceding chapters,[1] are distinguished by their attitude

[1] Chapters of *Psychological Types* (*Collected Works*, Vol. 6), Part I. The present selection is from Part II, pars. 556–671. [Originally published in German as *Psychologische Typen*, Rascher Verlag, Zurich, 1921, and as Volume 6 in the *Gesammelte Werke*, Rascher Verlag, Zurich, 1960; 2nd edition, 1967. The H. G. Baynes translation of *Psychological Types* was published in 1923 by Kegan Paul, London, and Harcourt, Brace and Co., New York. The present translation by R. F. C. Hull is based on this.—EDITORS OF *The Collected Works*.]

to the object. The introvert's attitude is an abstracting one; at bottom, he is always intent on withdrawing libido from the object, as though he had to prevent the object from gaining power over him. The extravert, on the contrary, has a positive relation to the object. He affirms its importance to such an extent that his subjective attitude is constantly related to and oriented by the object. The object can never have enough value for him, and its importance must always be increased. The two types are so different and present such a striking contrast that their existence becomes quite obvious even to the layman once it has been pointed out. Everyone knows those reserved, inscrutable, rather shy people who form the strongest possible contrast to the open, sociable, jovial, or at least friendly and approachable characters who are on good terms with everybody, or quarrel with everybody, but always relate to them in some way and in turn are affected by them.

One is naturally inclined, at first, to regard such differences as mere idiosyncrasies of character peculiar to individuals. But anyone with a thorough knowledge of human nature will soon discover that the contrast is by no means a matter of isolated individual instances but of typical attitudes which are far more common than one with limited psychological experience would assume. Indeed, as the preceding chapters may have shown, it is a fundamental contrast, sometimes quite clear, sometimes obscured, but always apparent when one is dealing with individuals whose personality is in any way pronounced. Such people are found not merely among the educated, but in all ranks of society, so that our types can be discovered among labourers and peasants no less than among the most highly differentiated members of a community. Sex makes no difference either; one finds the same contrast among women of all classes. Such a widespread distribution could hardly have come about if it were merely a question of a conscious and deliberate choice of attitude. In that case, one would surely find one particular attitude in one particular class of people linked together by a common education and background and localized accordingly. But that is not so at all; on the contrary, the types seem to be distributed quite at random. In the same family one child is introverted, the other extraverted. Since the facts show that the attitude-type is a general phenomenon having an apparently random distribution, it cannot be a matter of conscious judgment or conscious intention, but must be due to some unconscious, instinctive cause. As a general psychological phenomenon, therefore, the type-antithesis must have some kind of biological foundation.

The relation between subject and object, biologically considered, is always one of adaptation, since every relation between subject and object presupposes the modification of one by the other through reciprocal influence. Adaptation consists in these constant modifications. The typical attitudes to the object, therefore, are processes of adaptation. There are in nature two fundamentally different modes of adaptation which ensure the continued existence of the living organism. The one consists in a high rate of fertility, with low powers of defence and short duration of life for the single individual; the other consists in equipping the individual with numerous means of self-preservation plus a low fertility rate. This biological difference, it seems to me, is not merely analogous to, but the actual foundation of, our two psychological modes of adaptation. I must content myself with this broad hint. It is sufficient to note that the peculiar nature of the extravert constantly urges him to expend and propagate himself in every way, while the tendency of the introvert is to defend himself against all demands from outside, to conserve his energy by withdrawing it from objects, thereby consolidating his own position. Blake's intuition did not err when he described the two classes of men as "prolific" and "devouring." [2] Just as, biologically, the two modes of adaptation work

[2] William Blake, "The Marriage of Heaven and Hell," G. Keynes, ed., *Complete Writings of William Blake* (London, 1925), p. 155.

equally well and are successful in their own way, so too with the typical attitudes. The one achieves its end by a multiplicity of relationships, the other by monopoly.

The fact that children often exhibit a typical attitude quite unmistakably even in their earliest years forces us to assume that it cannot be the struggle for existence in the ordinary sense that determines a particular attitude. It might be objected, cogently enough, that even the infant at the breast has to perform an unconscious act of psychological adaptation, in that the mother's influence leads to specific reactions in the child. This argument, while supported by incontestable evidence, becomes rather flimsy in face of the equally incontestable fact that two children of the same mother may exhibit contrary attitudes at an early age, though no change in the mother's attitude can be demonstrated. Although nothing would induce me to underrate the incalculable importance of parental influence, this familiar experience compels me to conclude that the decisive factor must be looked for in the disposition of the child. Ultimately, it must be the individual disposition which decides whether the child will belong to this or that type despite the constancy of external conditions. Naturally I am thinking only of normal cases. Under abnormal conditions, i.e., when the mother's own attitude is extreme, a similar attitude can be forced on the children too, thus violating their individual disposition, which might have opted for another type if no abnormal external influences had intervened. As a rule, whenever such a falsification of type takes place as a result of parental influence, the individual becomes neurotic later, and can be cured only by developing the attitude consonant with his nature.

As to the individual disposition, I have nothing to say except that there are obviously individuals who have a greater capacity, or to whom it is more congenial, to adapt in one way and not in another. It may well be that physiological causes of which we have no knowledge play a part in this. I do not think it improbable, in view of one's experience that a reversal of type often proves exceedingly harmful to the physiological well-being of the organism, usually causing acute exhaustion.

## 2. The Extraverted Type

In our description of this and the following types it is necessary, for the sake of clarity, to distinguish between the psychology of consciousness and the psychology of the unconscious. We shall first describe the phenomena of consciousness.

### a) The General Attitude of Consciousness

Although it is true that everyone orients himself in accordance with the data supplied by the outside world, we see every day that the data in themselves are only relatively decisive. The fact that it is cold outside prompts one man to put on his overcoat, while another, who wants to get hardened, finds this superfluous. One man admires the latest tenor because everybody else does, another refuses to do so, not because he dislikes him, but because in his view the subject of universal admiration is far from having been proved admirable. One man resigns himself to circumstances because experience has shown him that nothing else is possible, another is convinced that though things have gone the same way a thousand times before, the thousand and first time will be different. The one allows himself to be oriented by the given facts, the other holds in reserve a view which interposes itself between him and the objective data. Now, when orientation by the object predominates in such a way that decisions and actions are determined not by subjective views but by objective conditions, we speak of an extraverted attitude. When this is habitual, we speak of an extraverted type. If a man thinks, feels, acts, and actually lives in a way that is *directly* correlated with the objective conditions and their demands, he is extraverted. His life makes it perfectly clear that it is the object and not his subjective view that plays the determining role in his consciousness. Naturally he has subjective views too, but their determining value is less than that of the objective conditions. Consequently, he never expects to find any absolute factors in his own inner life, since the only ones he knows are outside himself. Like Epimetheus, his inner life is subordinated to external necessity, though not without a struggle; but it is always the objective determinant that wins in the end. His whole consciousness looks outward, because the essential and decisive determinant always comes from outside. But it comes from outside only because that is where he expects it to come from. All the peculiarities of his psychology, except those that depend on the primacy of one particular psychological function or on idiosyncrasies of character, follow from this basic attitude. His interest and attention are directed to objective happenings, particularly those in his immediate environment. Not only people but things seize and rivet his attention. Accordingly, they also determine his actions, which are fully explicable on those grounds. The actions of the extravert are recognizably related to external conditions. In so far as they are not merely reactive to environmental stimuli, they have a character that is always adapted to the actual circumstances, and they find sufficient play within the limits of the objective situation. No serious effort is made to transcend these bounds. It is the same with his interest: objective happenings have an almost inexhaustible fascination for him, so that ordinarily he never looks for anything else.

The moral laws governing his actions coincide with the demands of society, that is, with the prevailing moral standpoint. If this were to change, the extravert's subjective moral guidelines would change accordingly, without this altering his general psychological habits in any way. This strict determination by objective factors does not mean, as one might suppose, a complete let alone ideal adaptation to the general conditions of life. In the eyes of the extravert, of course, an *adjustment* of this kind to the objective situation must seem like complete adaptation, since for him no other criterion exists. But from a higher point of view it by no means follows that the objective situation is in all circumstances a normal one. It can quite well be temporarily or locally abnormal. An individual who adjusts himself to it is admittedly conforming to the style of his environment, but together with his whole surroundings he is in an abnormal situation with respect to the universally valid laws of life. He may indeed thrive in such surroundings, but only up to the point where he and his milieu meet with disaster for transgressing these laws. He will share the general collapse to exactly the same extent as he was adjusted to the previous situation. Adjustment is not adaptation; adaptation requires far more than merely going along smoothly with the conditions of the moment. (Once again I would remind the reader of Spitteler's Epimetheus.) It requires observance of laws more universal than the immediate conditions of time and place. The very adjustment of the normal extraverted type is his limitation. He owes his normality on the one hand to his ability to fit into existing conditions with comparative ease. His requirements are limited to the objectively possible, for instance to the career that holds out good prospects at this particular moment; he does what is needed of him, or what is expected of him, and refrains from all innovations that are not entirely self-evident or that in any way exceed the expectations of those around him. On the other hand, his normality must also depend essentially on whether he takes account of his subjective needs and requirements, and this is just his weak point, for the tendency of his type is so outer-directed that even the most obvious of all subjective facts, the condition of his own body, receives scant attention. The body is not sufficiently objective or "outside," so that the satisfaction of elementary needs which are indispensable to physical well-being is no longer given its due. The body accordingly suffers, to say nothing of the psyche. The extravert is usually unaware of this latter fact, but it is all the more apparent to his household. He feels his loss of equilibrium only when it announces itself in abnormal body sensations. These he cannot ignore. It is quite natural that he should regard them as concrete and "objective," since with his type of mentality they cannot be anything else—for him. In others he at once sees "imagination" at work. A too extraverted attitude can also become so oblivious of the subject that the latter is sacrificed completely to so-called objective demands—to the demands, for instance, of a continually expanding business, because orders are piling up and profitable opportunities have to be exploited.

This is the extravert's danger: he gets sucked into objects and completely loses himself in them. The resultant functional disorders, nervous or physical, have a compensatory value, as they force him into an involuntary self-restraint. Should the symptoms be functional, their peculiar character may express his psychological situation in symbolic form; for instance, a singer whose fame has risen to dangerous heights that tempt him to expend too much energy suddenly finds he cannot sing high notes because of some nervous inhibition. Or a man of modest beginnings who rapidly reaches a social position of great influence with wide prospects is suddenly afflicted with all the symptoms of a mountain sickness.[3] Again, a man about to marry a woman of doubtful character whom he adores and vastly overestimates is seized with a nervous spasm of the oesophagus and has to restrict himself to two cups of milk a day, each of which takes him three hours to consume. All visits to the adored are effectively stopped, and he

---

[3] For a detailed discussion of this case see Jung, *Analytical Psychology: Its Theory and Practice* (New York and London, 1968), pp. 87ff.—J. C.

has no choice but to devote himself to the nourishment of his body. Or a man who can no longer carry the weight of the huge business he has built up is afflicted with nervous attacks of thirst and speedily falls a victim to hysterical alcoholism.

Hysteria is, in my view, by far the most frequent neurosis of the extraverted type. The hallmark of classic hysteria is an exaggerated rapport with persons in the immediate environment and an adjustment to surrounding conditions that amounts to imitation. A constant tendency to make himself interesting and to produce an impression is a basic feature of the hysteric. The corollary of this is his proverbial suggestibility, his proneness to another person's influence. Another unmistakable sign of the extraverted hysteric is his effusiveness, which occasionally carries him into the realm of fantasy, so that he is accused of the "hysterical lie." The hysterical character begins as an exaggeration of the normal attitude; it is then complicated by compensatory reactions from the unconscious, which counteract the exaggerated extraversion by means of physical symptoms that force the libido to introvert. The reaction of the unconscious produces another class of symptoms having a more introverted character, one of the most typical being a morbid intensification of fantasy activity.

After this general outline of the extraverted attitude we shall now turn to a description of the modifications which the basic psychological functions undergo as a result of this attitude.

### b) The Attitude of the Unconscious

It may perhaps seem odd that I should speak of an "attitude of the unconscious." As I have repeatedly indicated, I regard the attitude of the unconscious as compensatory to consciousness. According to this view, the unconscious has as good a claim to an "attitude" as the latter.

In the preceding section I emphasized the tendency to one-sidedness in the extraverted attitude, due to the ascendency of the object over the course of psychic events. The extraverted type is constantly tempted to expend himself for the apparent benefit of the object, to assimilate subject to object. I have discussed in some detail the harmful consequences of an exaggeration of the extraverted attitude, namely, the suppression of the subjective factor. It is only to be expected, therefore, that the psychic compensation of the conscious extraverted attitude will lay special weight on the subjective factor, and that we shall find a markedly egocentric tendency in the unconscious. Practical experience proves this to be the case. I do not wish to cite case material at this point, so must refer my readers to the ensuing sections, where I try to present the characteristic attitude of the unconscious in each function-type. In this section we are concerned simply with the compensation of the extraverted attitude in general, so I shall confine myself to describing the attitude of the unconscious in equally general terms.

The attitude of the unconscious as an effective complement to the conscious extraverted attitude has a definitely introverting character. It concentrates the libido on the subjective factor, that is, on all those needs and demands that are stifled or repressed by the conscious attitude. As may be gathered from what was said in the previous section, a purely objective orientation does violence to a multitude of subjective impulses, intentions, needs, and desires and deprives them of the libido that is their natural right. Man is not a machine that can be remodelled for quite other purposes as occasion demands, in the hope that it will go on functioning as regularly as before but in a quite different way. He carries his whole history with him; in his very structure is written the history of mankind. This historical element in man represents a vital need to which a wise psychic economy must respond. Somehow the past must come alive and participate in the present. Total assimilation to the object will always arouse the protest of the suppressed minority of those elements that belong to the past and have existed from the very beginning.

From these general considerations it is easy to see why the unconscious demands of the extravert have an essentially primitive, infantile, egocentric character. When Freud says that the unconscious "can do nothing but wish" this is very largely true of the unconscious of the extravert. His adjustment to the objective situation and his assimilation to the object prevent low-powered subjective impulses from reaching consciousness. These impulses (thoughts, wishes, affects, needs, feelings, etc.) take on a regressive character according to the degree of repression; the less they are acknowledged, the more infantile and archaic they become. The conscious attitude robs them of all energy that is readily disposable, only leaving them the energy of which it cannot deprive them. This residue, which still possesses a potency not to be underestimated, can be described only as primordial instinct. Instinct can never be eradicated in an individual by arbitrary measures; it requires the slow, organic transformation of many generations to effect a radical change, for instinct is the energic expression of the organism's make-up.

Thus with every repressed impulse a considerable amount of energy ultimately remains, of an instinctive character, and preserves its potency despite the deprivation that made it unconscious. The more complete the conscious attitude of extraversion is, the more infantile and archaic the unconscious attitude will be. The egoism which characterizes the extravert's unconscious attitude goes far beyond mere childish selfishness; it verges on the ruthless and the brutal. Here we find in full flower the incest-wish described by Freud. It goes without saying that these things are entirely unconscious and remain hidden from the layman so long as the extraversion of the conscious attitude is not extreme.

But whenever it is exaggerated, the unconscious comes to light in symptomatic form; its egoism, infantilism, and archaism lose their original compensatory character and appear in more or less open opposition to the conscious attitude. This begins as an absurd exaggeration of the conscious standpoint, aiming at a further repression of the unconscious, but usually it ends in a *reductio ad absurdum* of the conscious attitude and hence in catastrophe. The catastrophe may take an objective form, since the objective aims gradually become falsified by the subjective. I remember the case of a printer who, starting as a mere employee, worked his way up after years of hard struggle till at last he became the owner of a flourishing business. The more it expanded, the more it tightened its hold on him, until finally it swallowed up all his other interests. This proved his ruin. As an unconscious compensation of his exclusive interest in the business, certain memories of his childhood came to life. As a child he had taken great delight in painting and drawing. But instead of renewing this capacity for its own sake as a compensating hobby, he channelled it into his business and began wondering how he might embellish his products in an "artistic" way. Unfortunately his fantasies materialized: he actually turned out stuff that suited his own primitive and infantile taste, with the result that after a very few years his business went to pieces. He acted in accordance with one of our "cultural ideals," which says that any enterprising person has to concentrate everything on the one aim in view. But he went too far, and merely fell a victim to the power of his infantile demands.

The catastrophe can, however, also be subjective and take the form of a nervous breakdown. This invariably happens when the influence of the unconscious finally paralyzes all conscious action. The demands of the unconscious then force themselves imperiously on consciousness and bring about a disastrous split which shows itself in one of two ways: either the subject no longer knows what he really wants and nothing interests him, or he wants too much at once and has too many interests, but in impossible things. The suppression of infantile and primitive demands for cultural reasons easily leads to a neurosis or to the abuse of narcotics such as alcohol, morphine, cocaine, etc. In more extreme cases the split ends in suicide.

It is an outstanding peculiarity of unconscious impulses that, when deprived of energy by lack of conscious recognition, they take on a destructive character, and this happens as soon as they cease to be compensatory. Their compensatory function ceases as soon as they reach a depth corresponding to a cultural level absolutely incompatible with our own. From this moment the unconscious impulses form a block in every way opposed to the conscious attitude, and its very existence leads to open conflict.

Generally speaking, the compensating attitude of the unconscious finds expression in the maintenance of the psychic equilibrium. A normal extraverted attitude does not, of course, mean that the individual invariably behaves in accordance with the extraverted schema. Even in the same individual many psychological processes may be observed that involve the mechanism of introversion. We call a mode of behaviour extraverted only when the mechanism of extraversion predominates. In these cases the most differentiated function is always employed in an extraverted way, whereas the inferior functions are introverted;[4] in other words, the superior function is the most conscious one and completely under conscious control, whereas the less differentiated functions are in part unconscious and far less under the control of consciousness. The superior function is always an expression of the conscious personality, of its aims, will, and general performance, whereas the less differentiated functions fall into the category of

[4] The "psychological functions" here referred to are those named in Selection 2, "The Structure of the Psyche," and discussed at length below, namely, Sensation, Thinking, Feeling, and Intuition. See also supra, Editor's Introduction, pp. *xxvi–xxviii.*—J.C.

things that simply "happen" to one. These things need not be mere slips of the tongue or pen and other such oversights, they can equally well be half or three-quarters intended, for the less differentiated functions also possess a slight degree of consciousness. A classic example of this is the extraverted feeling type, who enjoys an excellent feeling rapport with the people around him, yet occasionally "happens" to express opinions of unsurpassable tactlessness. These opinions spring from his inferior and half-conscious thinking, which, being only partly under his control and insufficiently related to the object, can be quite ruthless in its effects.

The less differentiated functions of the extravert always show a highly subjective colouring with pronounced egocentricity and personal bias, thus revealing their close connection with the unconscious. The unconscious is continually coming to light through them. It should not be imagined that the unconscious lies permanently buried under so many overlying strata that it can only be uncovered, so to speak, by a laborious process of excavation. On the contrary, there is a constant influx of unconscious contents into the conscious psychological process, to such a degree that at times it is hard for the observer to decide which character traits belong to the conscious and which to the unconscious personality. This difficulty is met with mainly in people who are given to express themselves more profusely than others. Naturally it also depends very largely on the attitude of the observer whether he seizes hold of the conscious or the unconscious character of the personality. Generally speaking, a judging observer will tend to seize on the conscious character, while a perceptive observer will be more influenced by the unconscious character, since judgment is chiefly concerned with the conscious motivation of the psychic process, while perception registers the process itself. But in so far as we apply judgment and perception in equal measure, it may easily happen that a personality appears to us as both introverted and extraverted, so that we cannot decide at first to which attitude the superior function belongs. In such cases only a thorough analysis of the qualities of each function can help us to form a valid judgment. We must observe which function is completely under conscious control, and which functions have a haphazard and spontaneous character. The former is always more highly differentiated than the latter, which also possess infantile and primitive traits. Occasionally the superior function gives the impression of normality, while the others have something abnormal or pathological about them.

### c) The Peculiarities of the Basic Psychological Functions in the Extraverted Attitude

#### Thinking

As a consequence of the general attitude of extraversion, thinking is oriented by the object and objective data. This gives rise to a noticeable peculiarity. Thinking in general is fed on the one hand from subjective and in the last resort unconscious sources, and on the other hand from objective data transmitted by sense-perception. Extraverted thinking is conditioned in a larger measure by the latter than by the former. Judgment always presupposes a criterion; for the extraverted judgment, the criterion supplied by external conditions is the valid and determining one, no matter whether it be represented directly by an objective, perceptible fact or by an objective idea; for an objective idea is equally determined by external data or borrowed from outside even when it is subjectively sanctioned. Extraverted thinking, therefore, need not necessarily be purely concretistic thinking; it can just as well be purely ideal thinking, if for instance it can be shown that the ideas it operates with are largely borrowed from outside, i.e., have been transmitted by tradition and education. So in judging whether a particular thinking is extraverted or not we must first ask: by what criterion does it judge—does it come from outside, or is its origin subjective? A further criterion is the direction the thinking takes in drawing conclusions —whether it is principally directed outwards or not. It is no proof of its extraverted nature that it is preoccupied with concrete objects, since my thinking may be preoccupied with a concrete object either because I am abstracting my thought from it or because I am concretizing my thought through it. Even when my thinking is preoccupied with concrete things and could be described as extraverted to that extent, the direction it will take still remains an essential characteristic and an open question— namely, whether or not in its further course it leads back again to objective data, external facts, or generally accepted ideas. So far as the practical thinking of the business man, the technician, or the scientific investigator is concerned, its outer-directedness is obvious enough. But in the case of the philosopher it remains open to doubt when his thinking is directed to ideas. We then have to inquire whether these ideas are simply abstractions from objective experience, in which case they would represent higher collective concepts comprising a sum of objective facts, or whether (if they are clearly not abstractions from immediate experience) they may not be derived from tradition or borrowed from the intellectual atmosphere of the time. In the latter case, they fall into the category of objective data, and accordingly this thinking should be called extraverted.

Although I do not propose to discuss the nature of introverted thinking at this point, reserving it for a later section (infra, pp. 237–45), it is essential that I should say a few words about it before proceeding further. For if one reflects on what I have just said about extraverted thinking, one might easily conclude that this covers everything that is ordinarily understood as thinking. A thinking that is directed neither to objective facts nor to general ideas, one might argue, scarcely deserves the name "thinking" at all. I am fully aware that our age and its most eminent representatives know and acknowledge only the extra-verted type of thinking. This is largely because all the thinking that appears visibly on the surface in the form of science or philosophy or even art either derives directly from objects or else flows into general ideas. For both these reasons it appears essentially understandable, even though it may not always be self-evident, and it is there-fore regarded as valid. In this sense it might be said that the extraverted intellect oriented by objective data is actually the only one that is recognized. But—and now I come to the question of the introverted intellect—there also exists an entirely different kind of thinking, to which the term "thinking" can hardly be denied: it is a kind that is oriented neither by immediate experience of objects nor by tradi-tional ideas. I reach this other kind of thinking in the following manner: when my thoughts are preoccupied with a concrete object or a general idea, in such a way that the course of my thinking eventually leads me back to my starting-point, this intellectual process is not the only psychic process that is going on in me. I will disregard all those sensations and feelings which become noticeable as a more or less disturbing accompaniment to my train of thought, and will merely point out that this very thinking process which starts from the object and returns to the object also stands in a constant relation to the subject. This relation is a *sine qua non,* without which no thinking process whatsoever could take place. Even though my think-ing process is directed, as far as possible, to objective data, it is still *my* subjective process, and it can neither avoid nor dispense with this admixture of subjectivity. Struggle as I may to give an objective orientation to my train of thought, I cannot shut out the parallel subjective process and its running accompaniment without extinguishing the very spark of life from my thought. This parallel process has a natural and hardly avoidable tendency to subjectify the objective data and assimilate them to the subject.

Now when the main accent lies on the subjective process,

that other kind of thinking arises which is opposed to extra-verted thinking, namely, that purely subjective orientation which I call introverted. This thinking is neither determined by objective data nor directed to them; it is a thinking that starts from the subject and is directed to subjective ideas or subjective facts. I do not wish to enter more fully into this kind of thinking here; I have merely established its exist-ence as the necessary complement of extraverted thinking and brought it into clearer focus.

Extraverted thinking, then, comes into existence only when the objective orientation predominates. This fact does nothing to alter the logic of thinking; it merely constitutes that difference between thinkers which James considered a matter of temperament.[5] Orientation to the object, as already explained, makes no essential change in the thinking function; only its appearance is altered. It has the appearance of being captivated by the object, as though without the external orientation it simply could not exist. It almost seems as though it were a mere sequela of external facts, or as though it could reach its highest point only when flowing into some general idea. It seems to be constantly affected by the objective data and to draw con-clusions only with their consent. Hence it gives one the impression of a certain lack of freedom, of occasional short-sightedness, in spite of all its adroitness within the area circumscribed by the objects. What I am describing is simply the impression this sort of thinking makes on the observer, who must himself have a different standpoint, otherwise it would be impossible for him to observe the phenomenon of extraverted thinking at all. But because of his different standpoint he sees only its outward aspect, not its essence, whereas the thinker himself can apprehend its essence but not its outward aspect. Judging by appear-ances can never do justice to the essence of the thing, hence the verdict is in most cases depreciatory.

In its essence this thinking is no less fruitful and creative

---

[5] William James, *Pragmatism* (London, 1911): the "tough minded" and the "tender minded" temperaments.

than introverted thinking, it merely serves other ends. This difference becomes quite palpable when extraverted thinking appropriates material that is the special province of introverted thinking; when, for instance, a subjective conviction is explained analytically in terms of objective data or as being derived from objective ideas. For our scientific consciousness, however, the difference becomes even more obvious when introverted thinking attempts to bring objective data into connections not warranted by the object—in other words, to subordinate them to a subjective idea. Each type of thinking senses the other as an encroachment on its own province, and hence a sort of shadow effect is produced, each revealing to the other its least favourable aspect. Introverted thinking then appears as something quite arbitrary, while extraverted thinking seems dull and banal. Thus the two orientations are incessantly at war.

One might think it easy enough to put an end to this conflict by making a clear distinction between objective and subjective data. Unfortunately, this is impossible, though not a few have attempted it. And even if it were possible it would be a disastrous proceeding, since in themselves both orientations are one-sided and of limited validity, so that each needs the influence of the other. When objective data predominate over thinking to any great extent, thinking is sterilized, becoming a mere appendage of the object and no longer capable of abstracting itself into an independent concept. It is then reduced to a kind of "after-thought," by which I do not mean "reflection" but a purely imitative thinking which affirms nothing beyond what was visibly and immediately present in the objective data in the first place. This thinking naturally leads directly back to the object, but never beyond it, not even to a linking of experience with an objective idea. Conversely, when it has an idea for an object, it is quite unable to experience its practical, individual value, but remains stuck in a more or less tautological position. The materialistic mentality is an instructive example of this.

When extraverted thinking is subordinated to objective data as a result of over-determination by the object, it engrosses itself entirely in the individual experience and accumulates a mass of undigested empirical material. The oppressive weight of individual experiences having little or no connection with one another produces a dissociation of thought which usually requires psychological compensation. This must consist in some simple, general idea that gives coherence to the disordered whole, or at least affords the possibility of such. Ideas like "matter" or "energy" serve this purpose. But when the thinking depends primarily not on objective data but on some second-hand idea, the very poverty of this thinking is compensated by an all the more impressive accumulation of facts congregating round a narrow and sterile point of view, with the result that many valuable and meaningful aspects are completely lost sight of. Many of the allegedly scientific outpourings of our own day owe their existence to this wrong orientation.

## The Extraverted Thinking Type

It is a fact of experience that the basic psychological functions seldom or never all have the same strength or degree of development in the same individual. As a rule, one or the other function predominates in both strength and development. When thinking holds prior place among the psychological functions, i.e., when the life of an individual is mainly governed by reflective thinking so that every important action proceeds, or is intended to proceed, from intellectually considered motives, we may fairly call this a thinking type. Such a type may be either introverted or extraverted. We will first discuss the extraverted thinking type.

This type will, by definition, be a man whose constant endeavour—in so far, of course, as he is a pure type—is to make all his activities dependent on intellectual conclusions, which in the last resort are always oriented by objective data, whether these be external facts or generally accepted ideas. This type of man elevates objective reality, or an objectively oriented intellectual formula, into the ruling principle not only for himself but for his whole environment. By this formula good and evil are measured, and beauty and ugliness determined. Everything that agrees with this formula is right, everything that contradicts it is wrong, and anything that passes by it indifferently is merely incidental. Because this formula seems to embody the entire meaning of life, it is made into a universal law which must be put into effect everywhere all the time, both individually and collectively. Just as the extraverted thinking type subordinates himself to his formula, so, for their own good, everybody round him must obey it too, for whoever refuses to obey it is wrong—he is resisting the universal law, and is therefore unreasonable, immoral, and without a conscience. His moral code forbids him to tolerate exceptions; his ideal must under all circumstances be realized, for in his eyes it is the purest conceivable formulation of objective reality, and therefore must also be a universally valid truth, quite indispensable for the salvation of mankind. This is not from any great love for his neighbour, but from the higher standpoint of justice and truth. Anything in his own nature that appears to invalidate this formula is a mere imperfection, an accidental failure, something to be eliminated on the next occasion, or, in the event of further failure, clearly pathological. If tolerance for the sick, the suffering, or the abnormal should chance to be an ingredient of the formula, special provisions will be made for humane societies, hospitals, prisons, missions, etc., or at least extensive plans will be drawn up. Generally the motive of justice and truth is not sufficient to ensure the actual execution of such projects; for this, real Christian charity is needed, and this has more to do with feeling than with any intellectual formula. "Oughts" and "musts" bulk large in this programme. If the formula is broad enough, this type

may play a very useful role in social life as a reformer or
public prosecutor or purifier of conscience, or as the prop-
agator of important innovations. But the more rigid the
formula, the more he develops into a martinet, a quibbler,
and a prig, who would like to force himself and others into
one mould. Here we have the two extremes between
which the majority of these types move.

In accordance with the nature of the extraverted attitude,
the influence and activities of these personalities are the
more favourable and beneficial the further from the centre
their radius extends. Their best aspect is to be found at the
periphery of their sphere of influence. The deeper we penetrate into their own power province, the more we feel the
unfavourable effects of their tyranny. A quite different life
pulses at the periphery, where the truth of the formula can
be felt as a vaulable adjunct to the rest. But the closer we
come to centre of power where the formula operates, the
more life withers away from everything that does not
conform to its dictates. Usually it is the nearest relatives
who have to taste the unpleasant consequences of the
extraverted formula, since they are the first to receive its
relentless benefits. But in the end it is the subject himself
who suffers most—and this brings us to the reverse side
of the psychology of this type.

The fact that an intellectual formula never has been
and never will be devised which could embrace and express
the manifold possibilities of life must lead to the inhibition
or exclusion of other activities and ways of living that are
just as important. In the first place, all those activities that
are dependent on feeling will become repressed in such a
type—for instance, aesthetic activities, taste, artistic sense,
cultivation of friends, etc. Irrational phenomena such as
religious experiences, passions, and suchlike are often
repressed to the point of complete unconsciousness. Doubtless there are exceptional people who are able to sacrifice
their entire life to a particular formula, but for most of us
such exclusiveness is impossible in the long run. Sooner

or later, depending on outer circumstances or inner disposition, the potentialities repressed by the intellectual attitude will make themselves indirectly felt by disturbing the conscious conduct of life. When the disturbance reaches a definite pitch, we speak of a neurosis. In most cases it does not go so far, because the individual instinctively allows himself extenuating modifications of his formula in a suitably rationalistic guise, thus creating a safety valve.

The relative or total unconsciousness of the tendencies and functions excluded by the conscious attitude keeps them in an undeveloped state. In comparison with the conscious function they are inferior. To the extent that they are unconscious, they become merged with the rest of the unconscious contents and acquire a bizarre character. To the extent that they are conscious, they play only a secondary role, though one of considerable importance for the over-all psychological picture. The first function to be affected by the conscious inhibition is feeling, since it is the most opposed to the rigid intellectual formula and is therefore repressed the most intensely. No function can be entirely eliminated—it can only be greatly distorted. In so far as feeling is compliant and lets itself be subordinated, it has to support the conscious attitude and adapt to its aims. But this is possible only up to a point; part of it remains refractory and has to be repressed. If the repression is successful, the subliminal feeling then functions in a way that is opposed to the conscious aims, even producing effects whose cause is a complete enigma to the individual. For example, the conscious altruism of this type, which is often quite extraordinary, may be thwarted by a secret self-seeking which gives a selfish twist to actions that in themselves are disinterested. Purely ethical intentions may lead him into critical situations which sometimes have more than a semblance of being the outcome of motives far from ethical. There are guardians of public morals who suddenly find themselves in compromising situations, or rescue workers who are themselves in dire need of rescue. Their desire to save others leads them to employ means which are calculated to bring about the very thing they wished to avoid. There are extraverted idealists so consumed by their desire for the salvation of mankind that they will not shrink from any lie or trickery in pursuit of their ideal. In science there are not a few painful examples of highly respected investigators who are so convinced of the truth and general validity of their formula that they have not scrupled to falsify evidence in its favour. Their sanction is: the end justifies the means. Only an inferior feeling function, operating unconsciously and in secret, could seduce otherwise reputable men into such aberrations.

The inferiority of feeling in this type also manifests itself in other ways. In keeping with the objective formula, the conscious attitude becomes more or less impersonal, often to such a degree that personal interests suffer. If the attitude is extreme, all personal considerations are lost sight of, even those affecting the subject's own person. His health is neglected, his social position deteriorates, the most vital interests of his family—health, finances, morals—are violated for the sake of the ideal. Personal sympathy with others must in any case suffer unless they too happen to espouse the same ideal. Often the closest members of his family, his own children, know such a father only as a cruel tyrant, while the outside world resounds with the fame of his humanity. Because of the highly impersonal character of the conscious attitude, the unconscious feelings are extremely personal and oversensitive, giving rise to secret prejudices, a readiness, for instance, to misconstrue any opposition to his formula as personal ill-will, or a constant tendency to make negative assumptions about other people in order to invalidate their arguments in advance—in defence, naturally, of his own touchiness. His unconscious sensitivity makes him sharp in tone, acrimonious, aggressive. Insinuations multiply. His feelings have a sultry and resentful character—always a mark of the inferior function. Magnanimous as he may be in sacrificing himself to his intellectual goal, his feelings are petty, mistrustful, crotchety, and conservative. Anything new that is not already contained in his formula is seen through a veil of unconscious hatred and condemned accordingly. As late as the middle of the last century a certain doctor, famed for his humanitarianism, threatened to dismiss an assistant for daring to use a thermometer, because the formula decreed that temperature must be taken by the pulse.

The more the feelings are repressed, the more deleterious is their secret influence on thinking that is otherwise beyond reproach. The intellectual formula, which because of its intrinsic value might justifiably claim general recognition, undergoes a characteristic alteration as a result of this unconscious personal sensitiveness: it becomes rigidly dogmatic. The self-assertion of the personality is transferred to the formula. Truth is no longer allowed to speak for itself; it is identified with the subject and treated like a sensitive darling whom an evil-minded critic has wronged. The critic is demolished, if possible with personal invective, and no argument is too gross to be used against him. The truth must be trotted out, until finally it begins to dawn on the public that it is not so much a question of truth as of its personal begetter.

The dogmatism of the intellectual formula sometimes undergoes further characteristic alterations, due not so much to the unconscious admixture of repressed personal feelings as to a contamination with other unconscious factors which have become fused with them. Although reason itself tells us that every intellectual formula can never be anything more than a partial truth and can never claim general validity, in practice the formula gains such an ascendency that all other possible standpoints are thrust into the background. It usurps the place of all more general, less definite, more modest and therefore more truthful views of life. It even supplants that general view of life we call religion. Thus the formula becomes a religion, although in essentials it has not the slightest connection with anything religious. At the same time, it assumes the essentially religious quality of absoluteness. It becomes an intellectual superstition. But now all the psychological tendencies it has repressed build up a counter-position in the unconscious and give rise to paroxysms of doubt. The more it tries to fend off the doubt, the more fanatical the conscious attitude becomes, for fanaticism is nothing but over-compensated doubt. This development ultimately leads to an exaggerated defence of the conscious position and to the formation of a counter-position in the unconscious absolutely opposed to it; for instance, conscious rationalism is opposed by an extreme irrationality, and a scientific attitude by one that is archaic and superstitious. This explains those bigoted and ridiculous views well-known in the history of science which have proved stumbling-blocks to many an eminent investigator. Frequently the unconscious counter-position is embodied in a woman. In my experience this type is found chiefly among men, since, in general, thinking tends more often to be a dominant function in men than in women. When thinking dominates in a woman it is usually associated with a predominantly *intuitive* cast of mind.

The thinking of the extraverted type is *positive,* i.e., productive. It leads to the discovery of new facts or to general conceptions based on disparate empirical material. It is usually synthetic too. Even when it analyzes it constructs, because it is always advancing beyond the analysis to a new combination, to a further conception which reunites the analyzed material in a different way or adds something to it. One could call this kind of judgment *predicative.* A characteristic feature, at any rate, is that it is never absolutely depreciative or destructive, since it always substitutes a fresh value for the one destroyed. This is because the thinking of this type is the main channel into which his vital energy flows. The steady flow of life manifests itself in his thinking, so that his thought has a progressive, creative quality. It is not stagnant or regressive. But it can become so if it fails to retain prior place in his consciousness. In that case it loses the quality of a positive, vital activity. It follows in the wake of other functions and becomes Epimethean, plagued by afterthoughts, contenting itself with constant broodings on things past and gone, chewing them over in an effort to analyze and digest them. Since the creative element is now lodged in another function, thinking no longer progresses: it stagnates. Judgment takes on a distinct quality of *inherence:* it confines itself entirely to the range of the given material, nowhere overstepping it. It is satisfied with more or less abstract statements which do not impart any value to the material that is not already inherent in it. Such judgments are always oriented to the object, and they affirm nothing more about an experience than its objective and intrinsic meaning. We may easily observe this type of thinking in people who cannot refrain from tacking on to an impression or experience some rational and doubtless very valid remark which in no way ventures beyond the charmed circle of the objective datum. At bottom such a remark merely says: "I have understood it because afterwards I can think it." And there the matter ends. At best such a judgment amounts to no more than putting the experience in an objective setting, where it quite obviously belonged in the first place.

But whenever a function other than thinking predominates in consciousness to any marked degree, thinking, so far as it is conscious at all and not directly dependent on the dominant function, assumes a negative character. If it is subordinated to the dominant function it may actually wear a positive aspect, but closer scrutiny will show that it simply mimics the dominant function, supporting it with arguments that clearly contradict the laws of logic proper to thinking. This kind of thinking is of no interest for our present discussion. Our concern is rather with the nature of a thinking which cannot subordinate itself to another function but remains true to its own principle. To observe and investigate this thinking is not easy, because it is more or less constantly repressed by the conscious attitude. Hence, in the majority of cases, it must first be retrieved from the background of consciousness, unless it should come to the surface accidently in some unguarded moment. As a rule it has to be enticed with some such question as "Now what do you *really* think?" or "What is your private view of the matter?" Or perhaps one may have to use a little cunning, framing the question something like this: "What do you imagine, then, that *I* really think about it?" One should adopt this device when the real thinking is unconscious and therefore projected. The thinking that is enticed to the surface in this way has characteristic qualities, and it was these I had in mind when I described it as negative. Its habitual mode is best expressed by the two words "nothing but." Goethe personified this thinking in the figure of Mephistopheles. Above all it shows a distinct tendency to trace the object of its judgment back to some banality or other, thus stripping it of any significance in its own right. The trick is to make it appear dependent on something quite commonplace. Whenever a conflict arises between two men over something apparently objective and impersonal, negative thinking mutters "Cherchez la femme." Whenever somebody defends or advocates a cause, negative thinking never asks about its importance but simply: "What does *he* get out of it?" The dictum ascribed to Moleschott, "Der Mensch ist, was er isst" (man is what he eats, or, rendered more freely, what you eat you are), likewise comes under this heading, as do many other aphorisms I need not quote here.

The destructive quality of this thinking, as well as its limited usefulness on occasion, does not need stressing. But there is still another form of negative thinking, which at first glance might not be recognized as such, and that is *theosophical* thinking, which today is rapidly spreading in all parts of the world, presumably in reaction to the materialism of the recent past. Theosophical thinking has an air that is not in the least reductive, since it exalts everything to a transcendental and world-embracing idea. A dream, for instance, is no longer just a dream, but an experience "on another plane." The hitherto inexplicable fact of telepathy is very simply explained as "vibrations" passing from one person to another. An ordinary nervous complaint is explained by the fact that something has collided with the "astral body." Certain ethnological peculiarities of the dwellers on the Atlantic seaboard are easily accounted for by the submergence of Atlantis, and so on. We have only to open a theosophical book to be overwhelmed by the realization that everything is already explained, and that "spiritual science" has left no enigmas unsolved. But, at bottom, this kind of thinking is just as negative as materialistic thinking. When the latter regards psychology as chemical changes in the ganglia or as the extrusion and retraction of cell-pseudopodia or as an internal secretion, this is just as much a superstition as theosophy. The only difference is that materialism reduces everything to physiology, whereas theosophy reduces everything to Indian metaphysics. When a dream is traced back to an overloaded stomach, this is no explanation of the dream, and when we explain telepathy as vibrations we have said just as little. For what are "vibrations"? Not only are both methods of explanation futile, they are actually destructive, because by diverting interest away from the main issue, in one case to the stomach and in the other to imaginary vibrations, they hamper any serious investigation of the problem by a bogus explanation. Either kind of thinking is sterile and sterilizing. Its negative quality is due to the fact that it is so indescribably cheap, impoverished, and lacking in creative energy. It is a thinking taken in tow by other functions.

Feeling

Feeling in the extraverted attitude is likewise oriented by objective data, the object being the indispensable determinant of the quality of feeling. The extravert's feeling is always in harmony with objective values. For anyone who has known feeling only as something subjective, the nature of extraverted feeling will be difficult to grasp, because it has detached itself as much as possible from the subjective factor and subordinated itself entirely to the influence of the object. Even when it appears not to be qualified by a concrete object, it is none the less still under the spell of traditional or generally accepted values of some kind. I may feel moved, for instance, to say that something is "beautiful" or "good," not because I find it "beautiful" or "good" from my own subjective feeling about it, but because it is fitting and politic to call it so, since a contrary judgment would upset the general feeling situation. A feeling judgment of this kind is not by any means a pretence or a lie, it is simply an act of adjustment. A painting, for instance, is called "beautiful" because a painting hung in a drawing room and bearing a well-known signature is generally assumed to be beautiful, or because to call it "hideous" would presumably offend the family of its fortunate possessor, or because the visitor wants to create a pleasant feeling atmosphere, for which purpose everything must be felt as agreeable. These feelings are governed by an objective criterion. As such they are genuine, and represent the feeling function as a whole.

In precisely the same way as extraverted thinking strives to rid itself of subjective influences, extraverted feeling has to undergo a process of differentiation before it is finally denuded of every subjective trimming. The valuations resulting from the act of feeling either correspond directly with objective values or accord with traditional and generally accepted standards. This kind of feeling is very largely responsible for the fact that so many people flock to the theatre or to concerts, or go to church, and do so moreover with their feelings correctly adjusted. Fashions, too, owe their whole existence to it, and, what is far more valuable, the positive support of social, philanthropic, and other such cultural institutions. In these matters extraverted feeling proves itself a creative factor. Without it, a harmonious social life would be impossible. To that extent extraverted feeling is just as beneficial and sweetly reasonable in its effects as extraverted thinking. But these salutary effects are lost as soon as the object gains ascendency. The force of extraverted feeling then pulls the personality into the object, the object assimilates him, whereupon the personal quality of the feeling, which constitutes its chief charm, disappears. It becomes cold, "unfeeling," untrustworthy. It has ulterior motives, or at least makes an impartial observer suspect them. It no longer makes that agreeable and refreshing impression which invariably accompanies genuine feeling; instead, one suspects a pose, or that the person is acting, even though he may be quite unconscious of any egocentric motives. Overextraverted feeling may satisfy aesthetic expectations, but it does not speak to the heart; it appeals merely to the senses or—worse still—only to reason. It can provide the aesthetic padding for a situation, but there it stops, and beyond that its effect is nil. It has become sterile. If this process goes any further, a curiously contradictory dissociation of feeling results: everything becomes an object of feeling valuations, and innumerable relationships are entered into which are all at variance with each other. As this situation would become quite impossible if the subject received anything like due emphasis, even the last vestiges of a real personal standpoint are suppressed. The subject becomes so enmeshed in the network of individual feelings processes that to the observer it seems as though there were merely a feeling process and no longer a subject of feeling. Feeling in this state has lost all human warmth; it gives the impression of being put on, fickle, unreliable, and in the worst cases hysterical.

### The Extraverted Feeling Type

As feeling is undeniably a more obvious characteristic of feminine psychology than thinking, the most pronounced feeling types are to be found among women. When extraverted feeling predominates we speak of an extraverted feeling type. Examples of this type that I can call to mind are, almost without exception, women. The woman of this type follows her feeling as a guide throughout life. As a result of upbringing her feeling has developed into an adjusted function subject to conscious control. Except in extreme cases, her feeling has a personal quality, even though she may have repressed the subjective factor to a large extent. Her personality appears adjusted in relation to external conditions. Her feelings harmonize with objective situations and general values. This is seen nowhere more clearly than in her love choice: the "suitable" man is loved, and no one else; he is suitable not because he appeals to her hidden subjective nature—about which she usually knows nothing—but because he comes up to all reasonable expectations in the matter of age, position, income, size and respectability of his family, etc. One could easily reject such a picture as ironical or cynical, but I am fully convinced that the love feeling of this type of woman is in perfect accord with her choice. It is genuine and not just shrewd. There are countless "reasonable" marriages of this kind and they are by no means the worst. These women are good companions and excellent mothers so long as the husbands and children are blessed with the conventional psychic constitution.

But one can feel "correctly" only when feeling is not disturbed by anything else. Nothing disturbs feeling so much as thinking. It is therefore understandable that in this type thinking will be kept in abeyance as much as possible. This does not mean that the woman does not think at all; on the contrary, she may think a great deal and very cleverly, but her thinking is never *sui generis*— it is an Epimethean appendage to her feeling. What she cannot feel, she cannot consciously think. "But I can't think what I don't feel," such a type said to me once in indignant tones. So far as her feeling allows, she can think very well, but every conclusion, however logical, that might lead to a disturbance of feeling is rejected at the outset. It is simply not thought. Thus everything that fits in with objective values is good, and is loved, and everything else seems to her to exist in a world apart.

But a change comes over the picture when the importance of the object reaches a still higher level. As already explained, the subject then becomes so assimilated to the object that the subject of feeling is completely engulfed. Feeling loses its personal quality, and becomes feeling for its own sake; the personality seems wholly dissolved in the feeling of the moment. But since actual life is a constant succession of situations that evoke different and even contradictory feelings, the personality gets split up into as many different feeling states. At one moment one is this, at another something quite different—to all appearances, for in reality such a multiple personality is impossible. The basis of the ego always remains the same and consequently finds itself at odds with the changing feeling states. To the observer, therefore, the display of feeling no longer appears as a personal expression of the subject but as an alteration of the ego—a mood, in other words. Depending on the degree of dissociation between the ego and the momentary state of feeling, signs of self-disunity will become clearly apparent, because the originally compensatory attitude of the unconscious has turned into open opposition. This shows itself first of all in extravagant displays of feeling, gushing talk, loud expostulations, etc., which ring hollow: "The lady doth protest too much." It is at once apparent that some kind of resistance is being overcompensated, and one begins to wonder whether these demonstrations might not turn out quite different. And a little later they do. Only a very slight alteration in the situation is needed to call forth at once just the opposite pronouncement on the selfsame object. As a result of these experiences the observer is unable to take either pronouncement seriously. He begins to reserve judgment. But since, for this type, it is of the highest importance to establish an intense feeling of rapport with the environment, redoubled efforts are now required to overcome this reserve. Thus, in the manner of a vicious circle, the situation goes from bad to worse. The stronger the feeling relation to the object, the more the unconscious opposition comes to the surface.

We have already seen that the extraverted feeling type suppresses thinking most of all because this is the function most liable to disturb feeling. For the same reason, thinking totally shuts out feeling if ever it wants to reach any kind of pure results, for nothing is more liable to prejudice and falsify thinking than feeling values. But, as I have said, though the thinking of the extraverted feeling type is repressed as an independent function, the repression is not complete; it is repressed only so far as its inexorable logic drives it to conclusions that are incompatible with feeling. It is suffered to exist as a servant of feeling, or rather as its slave. Its backbone is broken; it may not operate on its own account, in accordance with its own laws. But since logic nevertheless exists and enforces its inexorable conclusions, this must take place somewhere, and it takes place outside consciousness, namely in the unconscious. Accordingly the unconscious of this type contains first and foremost a peculiar kind of thinking, a thinking that is infantile, archaic, negative. So long as the conscious feeling preserves its personal quality, or, to put it another way, so long as the personality is not swallowed up in successive states of feeling, this unconscious thinking remains compensatory. But as soon as the personality is dissociated and dissolves into a succession of contradictory feeling states, the identity of the ego is lost and the subject lapses into the unconscious. When this happens, it gets associated with the unconscious thinking processes and occasionally helps them to the surface. The stronger the conscious feeling is and the more ego-less it becomes, the stronger grows the unconscious opposition. The unconscious thoughts gravitate round just the most valued objects and mercilessly strip them of their value. The "nothing but" type of thinking comes into its own here, since it effectively depotentiates all feelings that are bound to the object. The unconscious thinking reaches the surface in the form of obsessive ideas which are invariably of a negative and depreciatory character. Women of this type have moments when the most hideous thoughts fasten on the very objects most valued by their feelings. This negative thinking utilizes every infantile prejudice or comparison for the deliberate purpose of casting aspersions on the feeling value, and musters every primitive instinct in the attempt to come out with "nothing but" interpretations. It need hardly be remarked that this procedure also mobilizes the collective unconscious and activates its store of primordial images, thus bringing with it the possibility of a regeneration of attitude on a different basis. Hysteria, with the characteristic infantile sexuality of its unconscious world of ideas, is the principal form of neurosis in this type.

## Summary of the Extraverted Rational Types

I call the two preceding types rational or judging types because they are characterized by the supremacy of the reasoning and judging functions. It is a general distinguishing mark of both types that their life is, to a great extent, subordinated to rational judgment. But we have to consider whether by "rational" we are speaking from the standpoint of the individual's subjective psychology or from that of the observer, who perceives and judges from without. This observer could easily arrive at a contrary judgment, especially if he intuitively apprehended merely the outward behaviour of the person observed and judged accordingly. On the whole, the life of this type is never dependent on rational judgment alone; it is influenced in almost equal degree by unconscious irrationality. If observation is restricted to outward behaviour, without any concern for the internal economy of the individual's consciousness, one may get an even stronger impression of the irrational and fortuitous nature of certain unconscious manifestations than of the reasonableness of his conscious intentions and motivations. I therefore base my judgment on what the individual feels to be his conscious psychology. But I am willing to grant that one could equally well conceive and present such a psychology from precisely the opposite angle. I am also convinced that, had I myself chanced to possess a different psychology, I would have described the rational types in the reverse way, from the standpoint of the unconscious—as irrational, therefore. This aggravates the difficulty of a lucid presentation of psychological matters and immeasurably increases the possibility of misunderstandings. The arguments provoked by these misunderstandings are, as a rule, quite hopeless because each side is speaking at cross purposes. This experience is one reason the more for basing my presentation on the conscious psychology of the individual, since there at least we have a definite objective footing, which completely drops away the moment we try to base our psychological rationale on the unconscious. For in that case the observed object would have no voice in the matter at all, because there is nothing about which he is more uninformed than his own unconscious. The judgment is then left entirely to the subjective observer—a sure guarantee that it will be based on his own individual psychology, which would be forcibly imposed on the observed. To my mind, this is the case with the psychologies of both Freud and Adler. The individual is completely at the mercy of the judging observer, which can never be the case when the conscious psychology of the observed is accepted as a basis. He after all is the only competent judge, since he alone knows his conscious motives.

The rationality that characterizes the conscious conduct of life in both these types involves a deliberate exclusion of everything irrational and accidental. Rational judgment, in such a psychology, is a force that coerces the untidiness and fortuitousness of life into a definite pattern, or at least tries to do so. A definite choice is made from among all the possibilities it offers, only the rational ones being accepted; but on the other hand the independence and influence of the psychic functions which aid the perception of life's happenings are consequently restricted. Naturally this restriction of sensation and intuition is not absolute. These functions exist as before, but their products are subject to the choice made by rational judgment. It is not the intensity of a sensation as such that decides action, for instance, but judgment. Thus, in a sense, the functions of perception share the same fate as feeling in the case of the first type, or thinking in that of the second. They are relatively repressed, and therefore in an inferior state of differentiation. This gives a peculiar stamp to the unconscious of both our types: what they consciously and intentionally do accords with reason (*their* reason, of course), but what happens to them accords with the nature of infantile, primitive sensations and intuitions. At all events, what happens to these types is irrational (from their standpoint). But since there are vast numbers of people whose lives consist more of what happens to them than of actions governed by rational intentions, such a person, after observing them closely, might easily describe both our types as irrational. And one has to admit that only too often a man's unconscious makes a far stronger impression on an observer than his consciousness does, and that his actions are of considerably more importance than his rational intentions.

The rationality of both types is object-oriented and dependent on objective data. It accords with what is collectively considered to be rational. For them, nothing is rational save what is generally considered as such. Reason, however, is in large part subjective and individual. In our types this part is repressed, and increasingly so as the object gains in importance. Both the subject and his subjective reason, therefore, are in constant danger of repression, and when they succumb to it they fall under the tyranny of the unconscious, which in this case possesses very unpleasant qualities. Of its peculiar thinking we have already spoken. But, besides that, there are primitive sensations that express themselves compulsively, for instance in the form of compulsive pleasure-seeking in every conceivable form; there are also primitive intuitions that can become a positive torture to the person concerned and to everybody in his vicinity. Everything that is unpleasant and painful, everything that is disgusting, hateful, and evil, is sniffed out or suspected, and in most cases it is a half-truth calculated to provoke misunderstandings of the most poisonous kind. The antagonistic unconscious elements are so strong that they frequently disrupt the conscious rule of reason; the individual becomes the victim of chance happenings, which exercise a compulsive influence over him either because they pander to his sensations or because he intuits their unconscious significance.

## Sensation

Sensation, in the extraverted attitude, is pre-eminently conditioned by the object. As sense perception, sensation is naturally dependent on objects. But, just as naturally, it is also dependent on the subject, for which reason there is subjective sensation of a kind entirely different from objective sensation. In the extraverted attitude the subjective component of sensation, so far as its conscious application is concerned, is either inhibited or repressed. Similarly, as an irrational function, sensation is largely repressed when thinking or feeling holds prior place; that is to say, it is a conscious function only to the extent that the rational attitude of consciousness permits accidental perceptions to become conscious contents—in a word, registers them. The sensory function is, of course, absolute in the stricter sense; everything is seen or heard, for instance, to the physiological limit, but not everything attains the threshold value a perception must have in order to be apperceived. It is different when sensation itself is paramount instead of merely seconding another function. In this case no element of objective sensation is excluded and nothing is repressed (except the subjective component already mentioned).

As sensation is chiefly conditioned by the object, those objects that excite the strongest sensations will be decisive for the individual's psychology. The result is a strong sensuous tie to the object. Sensation is therefore a vital function equipped with the strongest vital instinct. Objects are valued in so far as they excite sensations, and, so far as lies within the power of sensation, they are fully accepted into consciousness whether they are compatible with rational judgments or not. The sole criterion of their value is the intensity of the sensation produced by their objective qualities. Accordingly, all objective processes which excite any sensations at all make their appearance in consciousness. However, it is only concrete, sensuously perceived objects or processes that excite sensations; those, exclusively, which everyone everywhere would sense as concrete. Hence the orientation of such an individual accords with purely sensuous reality. The judging, rational functions are subordinated to the concrete facts of sensation, and thus have all the qualities of the less differentiated functions, exhibiting negative, infantile, and archaic traits. The function most repressed is naturally the opposite of sensation—intuition, the function of unconscious perception.

### The Extraverted Sensation Type

No other human type can equal the extraverted sensation type in realism. His sense for objective facts is extraordinarily developed. His life is an accumulation of actual experiences of concrete objects, and the more pronounced his type, the less use does he make of his experience. In certain cases the events of his life hardly deserve the name "experience" at all. What he experiences serves at most as a guide to fresh sensations; anything new that comes within his range of interest is acquired by way of sensation and has to serve its ends. Since one is inclined to regard a highly developed reality-sense as a sign of rationality, such people will be esteemed as very rational. But in actual fact this is not the case, since they are just as much at the mercy of their sensations in the face of irrational, chance happenings as they are in the face of rational ones. This type—the majority appear to be men— naturally does not think he is at the "mercy" of sensation. He would ridicule this view as quite beside the point, because sensation for him is a concrete expression of life— it is simply real life lived to the full. His whole aim is concrete enjoyment, and his morality is oriented accordingly. Indeed, true enjoyment has its own special morality, its own moderation and lawfulness, its own unselfishness and willingness to make sacrifices. It by no means follows that he is just sensual or gross, for he may differentiate his sensation to the finest pitch of aesthetic purity without ever deviating from his principle of concrete sensation however abstract his sensations may be. Wulfen's *Der Genussmensch: ein Cicerone im rücksichtslosen Lebens-*

genuss[6] is the unvarnished confession of a type of this sort, and the book seems to me worth reading on that account alone.

On the lower levels, this type is the lover of tangible reality, with little inclination for reflection and no desire to dominate. To feel the object, to have sensations and if possible enjoy them—that is his constant aim. He is by no means unlovable; on the contrary, his lively capacity for enjoyment makes him very good company; he is usually a jolly fellow, and sometimes a refined aesthete. In the former case the great problems of life hang on a good or indifferent dinner; in the latter, it's all a question of good taste. Once an object has given him a sensation, nothing more remains to be said or done about it. It cannot be anything except concrete and real; conjectures that go beyond the concrete are admitted only on condition that they enhance sensation. The intensification does not necessarily have to be pleasurable, for this type need not be a common voluptuary; he is merely desirous of the strongest sensations, and these, by his very nature, he can receive only from outside. What comes from inside seems to him morbid and suspect. He always reduces his thoughts and feelings to objective causes, to influences emanating from objects, quite unperturbed by the most glaring violations of logic. Once he can get back to tangible reality in any form he can breathe again. In this respect he is surprisingly credulous. He will unhesitatingly connect a psychogenic symptom with a drop in the barometer, while on the other hand the existence of a psychic conflict seems to him morbid imagination. His love is unquestionably rooted in the physical attractions of its object. If normal, he is conspicuously well adjusted to reality. That is his ideal, and it even makes him considerate of others. As he has no ideals connected with ideas, he has no reason to act in any way contrary to the reality of things as they are. This manifests itself in all the externals of his life. He

[6] "The Sybarite: A Guide to the Ruthless Enjoyment of Life."

dresses well, as befits the occasion; he keeps a good table with plenty of drink for his friends, making them feel very grand, or at least giving them to understand that his refined taste entitles him to make a few demands of them. He may even convince them that certain sacrifices are decidedly worth while for the sake of style.

The more sensation predominates, however, so that the subject disappears behind the sensation, the less agreeable does this type become. He develops into a crude pleasure-seeker, or else degenerates into an unscrupulous, effete aesthete. Although the object has become quite indispensable to him, yet, as something existing in its own right, it is none the less devalued. It is ruthlessly exploited and squeezed dry, since now its sole use is to stimulate sensation. The bondage to the object is carried to the extreme limit. In consequence, the unconscious is forced out of its compensatory role into open opposition. Above all, the repressed intuitions begin to assert themselves in the form of projections. The wildest suspicions arise; if the object is a sexual one, jealous fantasies and anxiety states gain the upper hand. More acute cases develop every sort of phobia, and, in particular, compulsion symptoms. The pathological contents have a markedly unreal character, with a frequent moral or religious streak. A pettifogging captiousness follows, or a grotesquely punctilious morality combined with primitive, "magical" superstitions that fall back on abstruse rites. All these things have their source in the repressed inferior functions which have been driven into harsh opposition to the conscious attitude, and they appear in a guise that is all the more striking because they rest on the most absurd assumptions, in complete contrast to the conscious sense of reality. The whole structure of thought and feeling seems, in this second personality, to be twisted into a pathological parody: reason turns into hair-splitting pedantry, morality into dreary moralizing and blatant Pharisaism, religion into ridiculous superstition, and intuition, the noblest gift of man, into meddlesome officiousness, poking into every corner; instead of gazing into the far distance, it descends to the lowest level of human meanness.

The specifically compulsive character of the neurotic symptoms is the unconscious counterpart of the easy-going attitude of the pure sensation type, who, from the standpoint of rational judgment, accepts indiscriminately everything that happens. Although this does not by any means imply an absolute lawlessness and lack of restraint, it nevertheless deprives him of the essential restraining power of judgment. But rational judgment is a conscious coercion which the rational type appears to impose on himself of his own free will. This coercion overtakes the sensation type from the unconscious, in the form of compulsion. Moreover, the very existence of a judgment means that the rational type's relation to the object will never become an absolute tie, as it is in the case of the sensation type. When his attitude attains an abnormal degree of one-sidedness, therefore, he is in danger of being overpowered by the unconscious in the same measure as he is consciously in the grip of the object. If he should become neurotic, it is much harder to treat him by rational means because the functions which the analyst must turn to are in a relatively undifferentiated state, and little or no reliance can be placed on them. Special techniques for bringing emotional pressure to bear are often needed in order to make him at all conscious.

## Intuition

In the extraverted attitude, intuition as the function of unconscious perception is wholly directed to external objects. Because intuition is in the main an unconscious process, its nature is very difficult to grasp. The intuitive function is represented in consciousness by an attitude of expectancy, by vision and penetration; but only from the subsequent result can it be established how much of what was "seen" was actually in the object, and how much was "read into" it. Just as sensation, when it is the dominant function, is not a mere reactive process of no further significance for the object, but an activity that seizes and shapes its object, so intuition is not mere perception, or vision, but an active, creative process that puts into the object just as much as it takes out. Since it does this unconsciously, it also has an unconscious effect on the object.

The primary function of intuition, however, is simply to transmit images, or perceptions of relations between things, which could not be transmitted by the other functions or only in a very roundabout way. These images have the value of specific insights which have a decisive influence on action whenever intuition is given priority. In this case, psychic adaptation will be grounded almost entirely on intuitions. Thinking, feeling, and sensation are then largely repressed, sensation being the one most affected, because, as the conscious sense function, it offers the greatest obstacle to intuition. Sensation is a hindrance to clear, unbiassed, naïve perception; its intrusive sensory stimuli direct attention to the physical surface, to the very things round and beyond which intuition tries to peer. But since extraverted intuition is directed predominantly to objects, it actually comes very close to sensation; indeed, the expectant attitude to external objects is just as likely to make use of sensation. Hence, if intuition is to function properly, sensation must to a large extent be suppressed. By sensation I mean in this instance the simple and immediate sense-impression understood as a clearly defined physiological and psychic datum. This must be expressly established beforehand because, if I ask an intuitive how he orients himself, he will speak of things that are almost indistinguishable from sense-impressions. Very often he will even use the word "sensation." He does have sensations, of course, but he is not guided by them as such; he uses them merely as starting-points for his perceptions. He selects them by unconscious predilection. It is not the strongest sensation, in the physiological sense, that is accorded the chief value, but any sensation whatsoever whose value is enhanced by the intuitive's unconscious attitude. In this way it may eventually come to acquire the chief value, and to his conscious mind it appears to be pure sensation. But actually it is not so.

Just as extraverted sensation strives to reach the highest pitch of actuality, because this alone can give the appearance of a full life, so intuition tries to apprehend the widest range of *possibilities*, since only through envisioning possibilities is intuition fully satisfied. It seeks to discover what possibilities the objective situation holds in store; hence, as a subordinate function (i.e., when not in the position of priority), it is the auxiliary that automatically comes into play when no other function can find a way out of a hopelessly blocked situation. When it is the dominant function, every ordinary situation in life seems like a locked room which intuition has to open. It is constantly seeking fresh outlets and new possibilities in external life. In a very short time every existing situation becomes a prison for the intuitive, a chain that has to be broken. For a time objects appear to have an exaggerated value, if they should serve to bring about a solution, a deliverance, or lead to the discovery of a new possibility. Yet no sooner have they served their purpose as stepping-stones or bridges than they lose their value altogether and are discarded as burdensome appendages. Facts are acknowledged only if they open new possibilities of advancing beyond them and delivering the individual from their power. Nascent possibilities are compelling motives from which intuition cannot escape and to which all else must be sacrificed.

### The Extraverted Intuitive Type

Whenever intuition predominates, a peculiar and unmistakable psychology results. Because extraverted intuition is oriented by the object, there is a marked dependence on external situations, but it is altogether different from the dependence of the sensation type. The intuitive is never to be found in the world of accepted reality-values, but he has a keen nose for anything new and in the making. Because he is always seeking out new possibilities, stable conditions suffocate him. He seizes on new objects or situations with great intensity, sometimes with extraordinary enthusiasm, only to abandon them cold-bloodedly, without any compunction and apparently without remembering them, as soon as their range is known and no further developments can be divined. So long as a new possibility is in the offing, the intuitive is bound to it with the shackles of fate. It is as though his whole life vanished in the new situation. One gets the impression, which he himself shares, that he has always just reached a final turning-point, and that from now on he can think and feel nothing else. No matter how reasonable and suitable it may be, and although every conceivable argument speaks for its stability, a day will come when nothing will deter him from regarding as a prison the very situation that seemed to promise him freedom and deliverance, and from acting accordingly. Neither reason nor feeling can restrain him or frighten him away from a new possibility, even though it goes against all his previous convictions. Thinking and feeling, the indispensable components of conviction, are his inferior functions, carrying no weight and hence incapable of effectively withstanding the power of intuition. And yet these functions are the only ones that could compensate its supremacy by supplying the *judgment* which the intuitive type totally lacks. The intuitive's morality is governed neither by thinking nor by feeling; he has his own characteristic morality, which consists in a loyalty to his vision and in voluntary submission to its authority. Consideration for the welfare of others is weak. Their psychic well-being counts as little with him as does his own. He has equally little regard for their convictions and way of life, and on this account he is often put down as an immoral and unscrupulous adventurer. Since his intuition is concerned with externals and with ferreting out their possibilities, he readily turns to professions in which he can exploit these capacities to the full. Many business tycoons, entrepreneurs, speculators, stockbrokers, politicians, etc., belong to this type. It would seem to be more common among women, however, than among men. In women the intuitive capacity shows itself not so much in the professional as in the social sphere. Such women understand the art of exploiting every social occasion, they make the right social connections, they seek out men with prospects only to abandon everything again for the sake of a new possibility.

It goes without saying that such a type is uncommonly important both economically and culturally. If his intentions are good, i.e., if his attitude is not too egocentric, he can render exceptional service as the initiator or promoter of new enterprises. He is the natural champion of all minorities with a future. Because he is able, when oriented more to people than things, to make an intuitive diagnosis of their abilities and potentialities, he can also "make" men. His capacity to inspire courage or to kindle enthusiasm for anything new is unrivalled, although he may already have dropped it by the morrow. The stronger his intuition, the more his ego becomes fused with all the possibilities he envisions. He brings his vision to life, he presents it convincingly and with dramatic fire, he embodies it, so to speak. But this is not play-acting, it is a kind of fate.

Naturally this attitude holds great dangers, for all too easily the intuitive may fritter away his life on things and people, spreading about him an abundance of life which others live and not he himself. If only he could stay put, he would reap the fruits of his labours; but always he must be running after a new possibility, quitting his newly planted fields while others gather in the harvest. In the end he goes away empty. But when the intuitive lets things come to such a pass, he also has his own unconscious against him. The unconscious of the intuitive bears some resemblance to that of the sensation type. Thinking and feeling, being largely repressed, come up with infantile, archaic thoughts and feelings similar to those of the countertype. They take the form of intense projections which are just as absurd as his, though they seem to lack the "magical" character of the latter and are chiefly concerned with quasi-realities such as sexual suspicions, financial hazards, forebodings of illness, etc. The difference seems to be due to the repression of real sensations. These make themselves felt when, for instance, the intuitive suddenly finds himself entangled with a highly unsuitable woman— or, in the case of a woman, with an unsuitable man— because these persons have stirred up the archaic sensations. This leads to an unconscious, compulsive tie which bodes nobody any good. Cases of this kind are themselves symptomatic of compulsion, to which the intuitive is as prone as the sensation type. He claims a similar freedom and exemption from restraint, submitting his decisions to no rational judgment and relying entirely on his nose for the possibilities that chance throws in his way. He exempts himself from the restrictions of reason only to fall victim to neurotic compulsions in the form of over-subtle ratiocinations, hair-splitting dialectics, and a compulsive tie to the sensation aroused by the object. His conscious attitude towards both sensation and object is one of ruthless superiority. Not that he means to be ruthless or superior—he simply does not see the object that everyone else sees and rides roughshod over it, just as the sensation type has no eyes for its soul. But sooner or later the object takes revenge in the form of compulsive hypochondriacal ideas, phobias, and every imaginable kind of absurd bodily sensation.

## Summary of the Extraverted Irrational Types

I call the two preceding types irrational for the reasons previously discussed, namely that whatever they do or do not do is based not on rational judgment but on the sheer intensity of perception. Their perception is directed simply and solely to events as they happen, no selection being made by judgment. In this respect they have a decided advantage over the two judging types. Objective events both conform to law and are accidental. In so far as they conform to law, they are accessible to reason; in so far as they are accidental, they are not. Conversely, we might also say that an event conforms to law when it presents an aspect accessible to reason, and that when it presents an aspect for which we can find no law we call it accidental. The postulate of universal lawfulness is a postulate of reason alone, but in no sense is it a postulate of our perceptive functions. Since these are in no way based on the principle of reason and its postulates, they are by their very nature irrational. That is why I call the perception types "irrational" by nature. But merely because they subordinate judgment to perception, it would be quite wrong to regard them as "unreasonable." It would be truer to say that they are in the highest degree *empirical*. They base themselves exclusively on experience—so exclusively that, as a rule, their judgment cannot keep pace with their experience. But the judging functions are none the less present, although they eke out a largely unconscious existence. Since the unconscious, in spite of its separation from the conscious subject, is always appearing on the scene, we notice in the actual life of the irrational types striking judgments and acts of choice, but they take the form of apparent sophistries, cold-hearted criticisms, and a seemingly calculating selection of persons and situations. These traits have a rather infantile and even primitive character; both types can on occasion be astonishingly naïve, as well as ruthless, brusque, and violent.

To the rational types the real character of these people might well appear rationalistic and calculating in the worst sense. But this judgment would be valid only for their unconscious, and therefore quite incorrect for their conscious psychology, which is entirely oriented by perception, and because of its irrational nature is quite unintelligible to any rational judgment. To the rational mind it might even seem that such a hodge-podge of accidentals hardly deserves the name "psychology" at all. The irrational type ripostes with an equally contemptuous opinion of his opposite number: he sees him as something only half alive, whose sole aim is to fasten the fetters of reason on everything living and strangle it with judgments. These are crass extremes, but they nevertheless occur.

From the standpoint of the rational type, the other might easily be represented as an inferior kind of rationalist—when, that is to say, he is judged by what happens to him. For what happens to him is not accidental—here he is the master—instead, the accidents that befall him take the form of rational judgments and rational intentions, and these are the things he stumbles over. To the rational mind this is something almost unthinkable, but its unthinkableness merely equals the astonishment of the irrational type when he comes up against someone who puts rational ideas above actual and living happenings. Such a thing seems to him scarcely credible. As a rule it is quite hopeless to discuss these things with him as questions of principle, for all rational communication is just as alien and repellent to him as it would be unthinkable for the rationalist to enter into a contract without mutual consultation and obligation.

This brings me to the problem of the psychic relationship between the two types. Following the terminology of the French school of hypnotists, psychic relationship is known in modern psychiatry as "rapport." Rapport consists essentially in a feeling of agreement in spite of acknowledged differences. Indeed, the recognition of existing differences, if it be mutual, is itself a rapport, a feeling of agreement. If in a given case we make this feeling conscious to a higher degree than usual, we discover that it is not just a feeling whose nature cannot be analyzed further, but at the same time an insight or a content of cognition which presents the point of agreement in conceptual form. This rational presentation is valid only for the rational types, but not for the irrational, whose rapport is based not on judgment but on the parallelism of living events. His feeling of agreement comes from the common perception of a sensation or intuition. The rational type would say that rapport with the irrational depends purely on chance. If, by some accident, the objective situations are exactly in tune, something like a human relationship takes place, but nobody can tell how valid it is or how long it will last. To the rational type it is often a painful thought that the relationship will last just as long as external circumstances and chance provide a common interest. This does not seem to him particularly human, whereas it is precisely in this that the irrational type sees a human situation of particular beauty. The result is that each regards the other as a man destitute of relationships, who cannot be relied upon, and with whom one can never get on decent terms. This unhappy outcome, however, is reached only when one makes a conscious effort to assess the nature of one's relationships with others. But since this kind of psychological conscientiousness is not very common, it frequently happens that despite an absolute difference of standpoint a rapport nevertheless comes about, and in the following way: one party, by unspoken projection, assumes that the other is, in all essentials, of the same opinion as himself, while the other divines or senses an objective community of interest, of which, however, the former has no conscious inkling and whose existence he would at once dispute, just as it would never occur to the other that his relationship should be based on a common point of view. A rapport of this kind is by far the most frequent; it rests on mutual projection, which later becomes the source of many misunderstandings.

Psychic relationship, in the extraverted attitude, is always governed by objective factors and external determinants. What a man is within himself is never of any decisive significance. For our present-day culture the extraverted attitude to the problem of human relationships is the principle that counts; naturally the introverted principle occurs too, but it is still the exception and has to appeal to the tolerance of the age.

### 3. *The Introverted Type*

#### a) *The General Attitude of Consciousness*

As I have already explained in the previous section, the introvert is distinguished from the extravert by the fact that he does not, like the latter, orient himself by the object and by objective data, but by subjective factors. I also mentioned [7] that the introvert interposes a subjective view between the perception of the object and his own action, which prevents the action from assuming a character that fits the objective situation. Naturally this is a special instance, mentioned by way of example and intended to serve only as a simple illustration. We must now attempt a formulation on a broader basis.

Although the introverted consciousness is naturally aware of external conditions, it selects the subjective determinants as the decisive ones. It is therefore oriented by the factor in perception and cognition which responds to the sense stimulus in accordance with the individual's subjective disposition. For example, two people see the same object, but they never see it in such a way that the images they receive are absolutely identical. Quite apart from the variable acute-

[7] Supra, p. 182.

ness of the sense organs and the personal equation, there often exists a radical difference, both in kind and in degree, in the psychic assimilation of the perceptual image. Whereas the extravert continually appeals to what comes to him from the object, the introvert relies principally on what the sense impression constellates in the subject. The difference in the case of a single apperception may, of course, be very delicate, but in the total psychic economy it makes itself felt in the highest degree, particularly in the effect in has on the ego. If I may anticipate, I consider the viewpoint which inclines, with Weininger, to describe the introverted attitude as philautic, autoerotic, egocentric, subjectivistic, egotistic, etc., to be misleading in principle and thoroughly depreciatory. It reflects the normal bias of the extraverted attitude in regard to the nature of the introvert. We must not forget—although the extravert is only too prone to do so— that perception and cognition are not purely objective, but are also subjectively conditioned. The world exists not merely in itself, but also as it appears to me. Indeed, at bottom, we have absolutely no criterion that could help us to form a judgment of a world which was unassimilable by the subject. If we were to ignore the subjective factor, it would be a complete denial of the great doubt as to the possibility of absolute cognition. And this would mean a relapse into the stale and hollow positivism that marred the turn of the century—an attitude of intellectual arrogance accompanied by crudeness of feeling, a violation of life as stupid as it is presumptuous. By overvaluing our capacity for objective cognition we repress the importance of the subjective factor, which simply means a denial of the subject. But what is the subject? The subject is man himself—we are the subject. Only a sick mind could forget that cognition must have a subject, and that there is no knowledge whatever and therefore no world at all unless "I know" has been said, though with this statement one has already expressed the subjective limitation of all knowledge.

This applies to all the psychic functions: they have a subject which is just as indispensable as the object. It is characteristic of our present extraverted sense of values that the word "subjective" usually sounds like a reproof; at all events the epithet "merely subjective" is brandished like a weapon over the head of anyone who is not boundlessly convinced of the absolute superiority of the object. We must therefore be quite clear as to what "subjective" means in this inquiry. By the subjective factor I understand that psychological action or reaction which merges with the effect produced by the object and so gives rise to a new psychic datum. In so far as the subjective factor has, from the earliest times and among all peoples, remained in large measure constant, elementary perceptions and cognitions being almost universally the same, it is a reality that is just as firmly established as the external object. If this were not so, any sort of permanent and essentially unchanging reality would be simply inconceivable, and any understanding of the past would be impossible. In this sense, therefore, the subjective factor is as ineluctable a datum as the extent of the sea and the radius of the earth. By the same token, the subjective factor has all the value of a co-determinant of the world we live in, a factor that can on no account be left out of our calculations. It is another universal law, and whoever bases himself on it has a foundation as secure, as permanent, and as valid as the man who relies on the object. But just as the object and objective data do not remain permanently the same, being perishable and subject to chance, so too the subjective factor is subject to variation and individual hazards. For this reason its value is also merely relative. That is to say, the excessive development of the introverted standpoint does not lead to a better and sounder use of the subjective factor, but rather to an artificial subjectivizing of consciousness which can hardly escape the reproach "merely subjective." This is then counterbalanced by a de-subjectivization which takes the form of an exaggerated extraverted attitude, an attitude aptly described by Weininger as "misautic." But since the introverted attitude is based on the ever-present, extremely real, and absolutely indispensable fact of psychic adaptation, expressions like "philautic," "egocentric," and so on are out of place and objectionable because they arouse the prejudice that it is always a question of the beloved ego. Nothing could be more mistaken than such an assumption. Yet one is continually meeting it in the judgments of the extravert on the introvert. Not, of course, that I wish to ascribe this error to individual extraverts; it is rather to be put down to the generally accepted extraverted view which is by no means restricted to the extraverted type, for it has just as many representatives among introverts, very much to their own detriment. The reproach of being untrue to their own nature can justly be levelled at the latter, whereas this at least cannot be held against the former.

The introverted attitude is normally oriented by the psychic structure, which is in principle hereditary and is inborn in the subject. This must not be assumed, however, to be simply identical with the subject's ego, as is implied by the above designations of Weininger; it is rather the psychic structure of the subject prior to any ego-development. The really fundamental subject, the self, is far more comprehensive than the ego, since the former includes the unconscious whereas the latter is essentially the focal point of consciousness. Were the ego identical with the self, it would be inconceivable how we could sometimes see ourselves in dreams in quite different forms and with entirely different meanings. But it is a characteristic peculiarity of the introvert, which is as much in keeping with his own inclination as with the general bias, to confuse his ego with the self, and to exalt it as the subject of the psychic process, thus bringing about the aforementioned subjectivization of consciousness which alienates him from the object.

The psychic structure is the same as what Semon calls

"mneme" [8] and what I call the "collective unconscious."
The individual self is a portion or segment or representative of something present in all living creatures, an exponent
of the specific mode of psychological behaviour, which
varies from species to species and is inborn in each of its
members. The inborn mode of *acting* has long been known
as *instinct,* and for the inborn mode of psychic apprehension I have proposed the term *archetype.*[9] I may assume
that what is understood by instinct is familiar to everyone.
It is another matter with the archetype. What I understand
by it is identical with the "primordial image," a term bor-
rcwed from Jacob Burckhardt,[10] and I describe it as such
in the Definitions that conclude this book. I must here
refer the reader to the definition "Image." [11]

The archetype is a symbolic formula which always begins
to function when there are no conscious ideas present, or
when conscious ideas are inhibited for internal or external
reasons. The contents of the collective unconscious are
represented in consciousness in the form of pronounced
preferences and definite ways of looking at things. These
subjective tendencies and views are generally regarded by
the individual as being determined by the object—incorrectly, since they have their source in the unconscious
structure of the psyche and are merely released by the
effect of the object. They are stronger than the object's
influence, their psychic value is higher, so that they super-
impose themselves on all impressions. Thus, just as it seems
incomprehensible to the introvert that the object should
always be the decisive factor, it remains an enigma to the
extravert how a subjective standpoint can be superior to

[8] Richard Semon, *Die Mneme als erhaltendes Prinzip im Wechsel
des organischen Geschehens* (Leipzig, 1904); translated by L. Simon,
*The Mneme* (London, 1921).
[9] "Instinct and the Unconscious," supra, pp. 47–58.
[10] Cf. *Symbols of Transformation* (*Collected Works,* Vol. 5), par.
45, n. 45.
[11] These references are to the volume *Psychological Types* (*Collected
Works,* Vol. 6), Ch. xi.

the objective situation. He inevitably comes to the conclusion that the introvert is either a conceited egoist or crack-brained bigot. Today he would be suspected of harbouring an unconscious power complex. The introvert certainly lays himself open to these suspicions, for his positive, highly generalizing manner of expression, which appears to rule out every other opinion from the start, lends countenance to all the extravert's prejudices. Moreover the inflexibility of his subjective judgment, setting itself above all objective data, is sufficient in itself to create the impression of marked egocentricity. Faced with this prejudice the introvert is usually at a loss for the right argument, for he is quite unaware of the unconscious but generally quite valid assumptions on which his subjective judgment and his subjective perceptions are based. In the fashion of the times he looks outside for an answer, instead of seeking it behind his own consciousness. Should he become neurotic, it is the sign of an almost complete identity of the ego with the self; the importance of the self is reduced to nil, while the ego is inflated beyond measure. The whole world-creating force of the subjective factor becomes concentrated in the ego, producing a boundless power-complex and a fatuous egocentricity. Every psychology which reduces the essence of man to the unconscious power drive springs from this kind of disposition. Many of Nietzsche's lapses in taste, for example, are due to this subjectivization of consciousness.

## b) The Attitude of the Unconscious

The predominance of the subjective factor in consciousness naturally involves a devaluation of the object. The object is not given the importance that belongs to it by right. Just as it plays too great a role in the extraverted attitude, it has too little meaning for the introvert. To the extent that his consciousness is subjectivized and excessive importance attached to the ego, the object is put in a position which in the end becomes untenable. The object is a factor whose power cannot be denied, whereas the ego is a very limited and fragile thing. It would be a very different matter if the self opposed the object. Self and world are commensurable factors; hence a normal introverted attitude is as justifiable and valid as a normal extraverted attitude. But if the ego has usurped the claims of the subject, this naturally produces, by way of compensation, an unconscious reinforcement of the influence of the object. In spite of positively convulsive efforts to ensure the superiority of the ego, the object comes to exert an overwhelming influence, which is all the more invincible because it seizes on the individual unawares and forcibly obtrudes itself on his consciousness. As a result of the ego's unadapted relation to the object—for a desire to dominate it is not adaptation —a compensatory relation arises in the unconscious which makes itself felt as an absolute and irrepressible tie to the object. The more the ego struggles to preserve its independence, freedom from obligation, and superiority, the more it becomes enslaved to the objective data. The individual's freedom of mind is fettered by the ignominy of his financial dependence, his freedom of action trembles in the face of public opinion, his moral superiority collapses in a morass of inferior relationships, and his desire to dominate ends in a pitiful craving to be loved. It is now the unconscious that takes care of the relation to the object, and it does so in a way that is calculated to bring the illusion of power and the fantasy of superiority to utter ruin. The object assumes terrifying proportions in spite of the conscious attempt to degrade it. In consequence, the ego's efforts to detach itself from the object and get it under control become all the more violent. In the end it surrounds itself with a regular system of defences (aptly described by Adler) for the purpose of preserving at least the illusion of superiority. The introvert's alienation from the object is now complete; he wears himself out with defence measures on the one hand, while on the other he makes fruitless attempts to impose his will on the object and assert himself. These efforts are constantly being frustrated by the overwhelming impressions received from the object. It continually imposes itself on him against his will, it arouses in him the most disagreeable and intractable affects and persecutes him at every step. A tremendous inner struggle is needed all the time in order to "keep going." The typical form his neurosis takes is psychasthenia, a malady characterized on the one hand by extreme sensitivity and on the other by great proneness to exhaustion and chronic fatigue.

An analysis of the personal unconscious reveals a mass of power fantasies coupled with fear of objects which he himself has forcibly activated, and of which he is often enough the victim. His fear of objects develops into a peculiar kind of cowardliness; he shrinks from making himself or his opinions felt, fearing that this will only increase the object's power. He is terrified of strong affects in others, and is hardly ever free from the dread of falling under hostile influences. Objects possess puissant and terrifying qualities for him—qualities he cannot consciously discern in them, but which he imagines he sees through his unconscious perception. As his relation to the object is very largely repressed, it takes place via the unconscious, where it becomes charged with the latter's qualities. These qualities are mostly infantile and archaic, so that the relation to the object becomes primitive too, and the object seems endowed with magical powers. Anything strange and new arouses fear and mistrust, as though concealing unknown perils; heirlooms and suchlike are attached to his soul as by invisible threads; any change is upsetting, if not positively dangerous, as it seems to denote a magical animation of the object. His ideal is a lonely island where nothing moves except what he permits to move. Vischer's novel, *Auch Einer,* affords deep insight into this side of the introvert's psychology, and also into the underlying symbolism of the collective unconscious. But this latter question I must leave to one side, since it is not specific to a description of types but is a general phenomenon.

### c) *The Peculiarities of the Basic Psychological Functions in the Introverted Attitude*

#### Thinking

In the section on extraverted thinking I gave a brief description of introverted thinking (supra, pp. 193–95) and must refer to it again here. Introverted thinking is primarily oriented by the subjective factor. At the very least the subjective factor expresses itself as a feeling of guidance which ultimately determines judgment. Sometimes it appears as a more or less complete image which serves as a criterion. But whether introverted thinking is concerned with concrete or with abstract objects, always at the decisive points it is oriented by subjective data. It does not lead from concrete experience back again to the object, but always to the subjective content. External facts are not the aim and origin of this thinking, though the introvert would often like to make his thinking appear so. It begins with the subject and leads back to the subject, far though it may range into the realm of actual reality. With regard to the establishment of new facts it is only indirectly of value, since new views rather than knowledge of new facts are its main concern. It formulates questions and creates theories, it opens up new prospects and insights, but with regard to facts its attitude is one of reserve. They are all very well as illustrative examples, but they must not be allowed to predominate. Facts are collected as evidence for a theory, never for their own sake. If ever this happens, it is merely a concession to the extraverted style. Facts are of secondary importance for this kind of thinking; what seems to it of paramount importance is the development

238 : Psychological Types

and presentation of the subjective idea, of the initial symbolic image hovering darkly before the mind's eye. Its aim
is never an intellectual reconstruction of the concrete fact,
but a shaping of that dark image into a luminous idea. It
wants to reach reality to see how the external fact will fit
into and fill the framework of the idea, and the creative
power of this thinking shows itself when it actually creates
an idea which, though not inherent in the concrete fact, is
yet the most suitable abstract expression of it. Its task is
completed when the idea it has fashioned seems to emerge
so inevitably from the external facts that they actually
prove its validity.

But no more than extraverted thinking can wrest a
sound empirical concept from concrete facts or create new
ones can introverted thinking translate the initial image into
an idea adequately adapted to the facts. For, as in the
former case the purely empirical accumulation of facts
paralyzes thought and smothers their meaning, so in the
latter case introverted thinking shows a dangerous tendency
to force the facts into the shape of its image, or to ignore
them altogether in order to give fantasy free play. In that
event it will be impossible for the finished product—the
idea—to repudiate its derivation from the dim archaic
image. It will have a mythological streak which one is apt
to interpret as "originality" or, in more pronounced cases,
as mere whimsicality, since its archaic character is not
immediately apparent to specialists unfamiliar with mythological motifs. The subjective power of conviction ex-
erted by an idea of this kind is usually very great, and
it is all the greater the less it comes into contact with
external facts. Although it may seem to the originator of
the idea that his meagre store of facts is the actual source
of its truth and validity, in reality this is not so, for the
idea derives its convincing power from the unconscious
archetype, which, as such, is eternally valid and true. But
this truth is so universal and so symbolic that it must first
be assimilated to the recognized and recognizable knowl-

edge of the time before it can become a practical truth of any value for life. What would causality be, for instance, if it could nowhere be recognized in practical causes and practical effects?

This kind of thinking easily gets lost in the immense truth of the subjective factor. It creates theories for their own sake, apparently with an eye to real or at least possible facts, but always with a distinct tendency to slip over from the world of ideas into mere imagery. Accordingly, visions of numerous possibilties appear on the scene, but none of them ever becomes a reality until finally images are produced which no longer express anything externally real, being mere symbols of the ineffable and unknowable. It is now merely a mystical thinking and quite as unfruitful as thinking that remains bound to objective data. Whereas the latter sinks to the level of a mere representation of facts, the former evaporates into a representation of the irrepresentable, far beyond anything that could be expressed in an image. The representation of facts has an incontestable truth because the subjective factor is excluded and the facts speak for themselves. Similarly, the representation of the irrepresentable has an immediate, subjective power of conviction because it demonstrates its own existence. The one says "Est, ergo est"; the other says "Cogito, ergo cogito." Introverted thinking carried to extremes arrives at the evidence of its own subjective existence, and extraverted thinking at the evidence of its complete identity with the objective fact. Just as the latter abnegates itself by evaporating into the object, the former empties itself of each and every content and has to be satisfied with merely existing. In both cases the further development of life is crowded out of the thinking function into the domain of the other psychic functions, which till then had existed in a state of relative unconsciousness. The extraordinary impoverishment of introverted thinking is compensated by a wealth of unconscious facts. The more consciousness is impelled by the thinking function to confine itself within the smallest and emptiest circle—which seems, however, to contain all the riches of the gods—the more the unconscious fantasies will be enriched by a multitude of archaic contents, a veritable "pandaemonium" of irrational and magical figures, whose physiognomy will accord with the nature of the function that will supersede the thinking function as the vehicle of life. If it should be the intuitive function, then the "other side" will be viewed through the eyes of a Kubin or a Meyrink.[12] If it is the feeling function, then quite unheard-of and fantastic feeling relationships will be formed, coupled with contradictory and unintelligible value judgments. If it is the sensation function, the senses will nose up something new and never experienced before, in and outside the body. Closer examination of these permutations will easily demonstrate a recrudescence of primitive psychology with all its characteristic features. Naturally, such experiences are not merely primitive, they are also symbolic; in fact, the more primordial and aboriginal they are, the more they represent a future truth. For everything old in the unconscious hints at something coming.

Under ordinary circumstances, not even the attempt to get to the "other side" will be successful—and still less the redeeming journey through the unconscious. The passage across is usually blocked by conscious resistance to any subjection of the ego to the realities of the unconscious and their determining power. It is a state of dissociation, in other words a neurosis characterized by inner debility and increasing cerebral exhaustion—the symptoms of psychasthenia.

### The Introverted Thinking Type

Just as we might take Darwin as an example of the normal extraverted thinking type, the normal introverted

[12] Alfred Kubin, *The Other Side,* translated by Denver Lindley (New York, 1968), and Gustav Meyrink, *Das grüne Gesicht* (Leipzig, 1915).

thinking type could be represented by Kant. The one speaks with facts, the other relies on the subjective factor. Darwin ranges over the wide field of objective reality, Kant restricts himself to a critique of knowledge. Cuvier and Nietzsche would form an even sharper contrast.

The introverted thinking type is characterized by the primacy of the kind of thinking I have just described. Like his extraverted counterpart, he is strongly influenced by ideas, though his ideas have their origin not in objective data but in his subjective foundation. He will follow his ideas like the extravert, but in the reverse direction: inwards and not outwards. Intensity is his aim, not extensity. In these fundamental respects he differs quite unmistakably from his extraverted counterpart. What distinguishes the other, namely, his intense relation to objects, is almost completely lacking in him as in every introverted type. If the object is a person, this person has a distinct feeling that he matters only in a negative way; in milder cases he is merely conscious of being *de trop*, but with a more extreme type he feels himself warded off as something definitely disturbing. This negative relation to the object, ranging from indifference to aversion, characterizes every introvert and makes a description of the type exceedingly difficult. Everything about him tends to disappear and get concealed. His judgment appears cold, inflexible, arbitrary, and ruthless, because it relates far less to the object than to the subject. One can feel nothing in it that might possibly confer a higher value on the object; it always bypasses the object and leaves one with a feeling of the subject's superiority. He may be polite, amiable, and kind, but one is constantly aware of a certain uneasiness betraying an ulterior motive—the disarming of an opponent, who must at all costs be pacified and placated lest he prove himself a nuisance. In no sense, of course, is he an opponent, but if he is at all sensitive he will feel himself repulsed, and even belittled.

Invariably the object has to submit to a certain amount of neglect, and in pathological cases it is even surrounded with quite unnecessary precautionary measures. Thus this type tends to vanish behind a cloud of misunderstanding, which gets all the thicker the more he attempts to assume, by way of compensation and with the help of his inferior functions, an air of urbanity which contrasts glaringly with his real nature. Although he will shrink from no danger in building up his world of ideas, and never shrinks from thinking a thought because it might prove to be dangerous, subversive, heretical, or wounding to other people's feelings, he is none the less beset by the greatest anxiety if ever he has to make it an objective reality. That goes against the grain. And when he does put his ideas into the world, he never introduces them like a mother solicitous for her children, but simply dumps them there and gets extremely annoyed if they fail to thrive on their own account. His amazing unpracticalness and horror of publicity in any form have a hand in this. If in his eyes his product appears correct and true, then it must be so in practice, and others have got to bow to its truth. Hardly ever will he go out of his way to win anyone's appreciation of it, especially anyone of influence. And if ever he brings himself to do so, he generally sets about it so clumsily that it has just the opposite of the effect intended. He usually has bad experiences with rivals in his own field because he never understands how to curry their favour; as a rule he only succeeds in showing them how entirely superfluous they are to him. In the pursuit of his ideas he is generally stubborn, headstrong, and quite unamenable to influence. His suggestibility to personal influences is in strange contrast to this. He has only to be convinced of a person's seeming innocuousness to lay himself open to the most undesirable elements. They seize hold of him from the unconscious. He lets himself be brutalized and exploited in the most ignominious way if only he can be left in peace to pursue his ideas. He simply does not see when he is being plundered behind his back and wronged in practice, for to him the relation to people and things is secondary and the objective evaluation of his product is something he remains unconscious of. Because he thinks out his problems to the limit, he complicates them and constantly gets entangled in his own scruples and misgivings. However clear to him the inner structure of his thoughts may be, he is not in the least clear where or how they link up with the world of reality. Only with the greatest difficulty will he bring himself to admit that what is clear to him may not be equally clear to everyone. His style is cluttered with all sorts of adjuncts, accessories, qualifications, retractions, saving clauses, doubts, etc., which all come from his scrupulosity. His work goes slowly and with difficulty.

In his personal relations he is taciturn or else throws himself on people who cannot understand him, and for him this is one more proof of the abysmal stupidity of man. If for once he is understood, he easily succumbs to credulous overestimation of his prowess. Ambitious women have only to know how to take advantage of his cluelessness in practical matters to make an easy prey of him; or he may develop into a misanthropic bachelor with a childlike heart. Often he is gauche in his behaviour, painfully anxious to escape notice, or else remarkably unconcerned and childishly naïve. In his own special field of work he provokes the most violent opposition, which he has no notion how to deal with, unless he happens to be seduced by his primitive affects into acrimonious and fruitless polemics. Casual acquaintances think him inconsiderate and domineering. But the better one knows him, the more favourable one's judgment becomes, and his closest friends value his intimacy very highly. To outsiders he seems prickly, unapproachable, and arrogant, and sometimes soured as a result of his anti-social prejudices. As a personal teacher he has little influence, since the mentality of his students is strange to him. Besides, teaching has, at bottom, no interest for him unless it happens to provide him with a theoretical problem. He is a poor teacher, because all the time he is teaching his thought is occupied with the material itself and not with its presentation.

With the intensification of his type, his convictions become all the more rigid and unbending. Outside influences are shut off; as a person, too, he becomes more unsympathetic to his wider circle of acquaintances, and therefore more dependent on his intimates. His tone becomes personal and surly, and though his ideas may gain in profundity they can no longer be adequately expressed in the material at hand. To compensate for this, he falls back on emotionality and touchiness. The outside influences he has brusquely fended off attack him from within, from the unconscious, and in his efforts to defend himself he attacks things that to outsiders seem utterly unimportant. Because of the subjectivization of consciousness resulting from his lack of relationship to the object, what secretly concerns his own person now seems to him of extreme importance. He begins to confuse his subjective truth with his own personality. Although he will not try to press his convictions on anyone personally, he will burst out with vicious, personal retorts against every criticism, however just. Thus his isolation gradually increases. His originally fertilizing ideas become destructive, poisoned by the sediment of bitterness. His struggle against the influences emanating from the unconscious increases with his external isolation, until finally they begin to cripple him. He thinks his withdrawal into ever-increasing solitude will protect him from the unconscious influences, but as a rule it only plunges him deeper into the conflict that is destroying him from within.

The thinking of the introverted type is positive and synthetic in developing ideas which approximate more and more to the eternal validity of the primordial images. But as their connection with objective experience becomes more and more tenuous, they take on a mythological colouring and no longer hold true for the contemporary situation. Hence his thinking is of value for his contemporaries only so long as it is manifestly and intelligibly related to the known facts of the time. Once it has become mythological, it ceases to be relevant and runs on in itself. The counterbalancing functions of feeling, intuition, and sensation are comparatively unconscious and inferior, and therefore have a primitive extraverted character that accounts for all the troublesome influences from outside to which the introverted thinker is prone. The various protective devices and psychological minefields which such people surround themselves with are known to everyone, and I can spare myself a description of them. They all serve as a defence against "magical" influences—and among them is a vague fear of the feminine sex.

## Feeling

Introverted feeling is determined principally by the subjective factor. It differs quite as essentially from extraverted feeling as introverted from extraverted thinking. It is extremely difficult to give an intellectual account of the introverted feeling process, or even an approximate description of it, although the peculiar nature of this kind of feeling is very noticeable once one has become aware of it. Since it is conditioned subjectively and is only secondarily concerned with the object, it seldom appears on the surface and is generally misunderstood. It is a feeling which seems to devalue the object, and it therefore manifests itself for the most part negatively. The existence of positive feeling can be inferred only indirectly. Its aim is not to adjust itself to the object, but to subordinate it in an unconscious effort to realize the underlying images. It is continually seeking an image which has no existence in reality, but which it has seen in a kind of vision. It glides unheedingly over all objects that do not fit in with its aim. It strives after inner intensity, for which the object serves at most as a stimulus. The depth of this feeling can only be guessed —it can never be clearly grasped. It makes people silent and difficult of access; it shrinks back like a violet from the brute nature of the object in order to fill the depths of the subject. It comes out with negative judgments or assumes an air of profound indifference as a means of defence.

The primordial images are, of course, just as much ideas as feelings. Fundamental ideas, ideas like God, freedom, and immortality, are just as much feeling-values as they are significant ideas. Everything, therefore, that we have said about introverted thinking is equally true of introverted feeling, only here everything is felt while there it was thought. But the very fact that thoughts can generally be expressed more intelligibly than feelings demands a more than ordinary descriptive or artistic ability before the real wealth of this feeling can be even approximately presented or communicated to the world. If subjective thinking can be understood only with difficulty because of its unrelatedness, this is true in even higher degree of subjective feeling. In order to communicate with others, it has to find an external form not only acceptable to itself, but capable also of arousing a parallel feeling in them. Thanks to the relatively great inner (as well as outer) uniformity of human beings, it is actually possible to do this, though the form acceptable to feeling is extraordinarily difficult to find so long as it is still mainly oriented to the fathomless store of primordial images. If, however, feeling is falsified by an egocentric attitude, it at once becomes unsympathetic, because it is then concerned mainly with the ego. It inevitably creates the impression of sentimental self-love, of trying to make itself interesting, and even of morbid self-admiration. Just as the subjectivized consciousness of the introverted thinker, striving after abstraction to the nth degree, only succeeds in intensifying a thought-process that is in itself empty, the intensification of egocentric feeling only leads to inane transports of feeling for their own sake. This is the mystical, ecstatic stage which opens the way for the extraverted functions that feeling has repressed. Just as introverted thinking is counterbalanced by a primitive feeling, to which objects attach themselves with magical force, introverted feeling is counterbalanced by a primitive thinking, whose concretism and slavery to facts surpass all bounds. Feeling progressively emancipates itself from the object and creates for itself a freedom of action and conscience that is purely subjective, and may even renounce all traditional values. But so much the more does unconscious thinking fall a victim to the power of objective reality.

## The Introverted Feeling Type

It is principally among women that I have found the predominance of introverted feeling. "Still waters run deep" is very true of such women. They are mostly silent, inaccessible, hard to understand; often they hide behind a childish or banal mask, and their temperament is inclined to melancholy. They neither shine nor reveal themselves. As they are mainly guided by their subjective feelings, their true motives generally remain hidden. Their outward demeanour is harmonious, inconspicuous, giving an impression of pleasing repose, or of sympathetic response, with no desire to affect others, to impress, influence, or change them in any way. If this outward aspect is more pronounced, it arouses a suspicion of indifference and coldness, which may actually turn into a disregard for the comfort and well-being of others. One is distinctly aware then of the movement of feeling away from the object. With the normal type, however, this happens only when the influence of the object is too strong. The feeling of harmony, therefore, lasts only so long as the object goes its own moderate way and makes no attempt to cross the other's path. There is little effort to respond to the real emotions of the other person; they are more often damped down and rebuffed, or cooled off by a negative value judgment. Although there is a constant readiness for peaceful and harmonious co-existence, strangers are shown no touch of amiability, no gleam of responsive warmth, but are met with apparent indifference or a repelling coldness. Often they are made to feel entirely superfluous. Faced with anything that might carry her away or arouse enthusiasm, this type observes a benevolent though critical neutrality, coupled with a faint trace of superiority that soon takes the wind out of the sails of a sensitive person. Any stormy emotion, however, will be struck down with murderous coldness, unless it happens to catch the woman on her unconscious side—that is, unless it hits her feelings by arousing a primordial image. In that case she simply feels paralyzed for the moment, and this in due course invariably produces an even more obstinate resistance which will hit the other person in his most vulnerable spot. As far as possible, the feeling relationship is kept to the safe middle path, all intemperate passions being resolutely tabooed. Expressions of feeling therefore remain niggardly, and the other person has a permanent sense of being undervalued once he becomes conscious of it. But this need not always be so, because very often he remains unconscious of the lack of feeling shown to him, in which case the unconscious demands of feeling will produce symptoms designed to compel attention.

Since this type appears rather cold and reserved, it might seem on a superficial view that such women have no feelings at all. But this would be quite wrong; the truth is, their feelings are intensive rather than extensive. They develop in depth. While an extensive feeling of sympathy can express itself in appropriate words and deeds, and thus quickly gets back to normal again, an intensive sympathy, being shut off from every means of expression, acquires a passionate depth that comprises a whole world of misery and simply gets benumbed. It may perhaps break out in some extravagant form and lead to an astounding act of almost heroic character, quite unrelated either to the subject herself or to the object that provoked the outburst. To the outside world, or to the blind eyes of the extravert, this intensive sympathy looks like coldness, because usually it does nothing visible, and an extraverted consciousness is unable to believe in invisible forces. Such a misunderstanding is a common occurrence in the life of this type, and is used as a weighty argument against the possibility of any deeper feeling relation with the object. But the real object of this feeling is only dimly divined by the normal type herself. It may express itself in a secret religiosity anxiously guarded from profane eyes, or in intimate poetic forms that are kept equally well hidden, not without the secret ambition of displaying some kind of superiority over the other person by this means. Women often express a good deal of their feelings through their children, letting their passion flow secretly into them.

Although this tendency to overpower or coerce the other person with her secret feelings rarely plays a disturbing role in the normal type, and never leads to a serious attempt of this kind, some trace of it nevertheless seeps through into the personal effect they have on him, in the form of a domineering influence often difficult to define. It is sensed as a sort of stifling or oppressive feeling which holds everybody around her under a spell. It gives a woman of this type a mysterious power that may prove terribly fascinating to the extraverted man, for it touches his unconscious. This power comes from the deeply felt, unconscious images, but consciously she is apt to relate it to the ego, whereupon her influence becomes debased into a personal tyranny. Whenever the unconscious subject is identified with the ego, the mysterious power of intensive feeling turns into a banal and overweening desire to dominate, into vanity and despotic bossiness. This produces a type of woman notorious for her unscrupulous ambition and mischievous cruelty. It is a change, however, that leads to neurosis.

So long as the ego feels subordinate to the unconscious subject, and feeling is aware of something higher and mightier than the ego, the type is normal. Although the unconscious thinking is archaic, its reductive tendencies help to compensate the occasional fits of trying to exalt the ego into the subject. If this should nevertheless happen as a result of complete suppression of the counterbalancing subliminal processes, the unconscious thinking goes over into open opposition and gets projected. The egocentrized subject now comes to feel the power and importance of the devalued object. She begins consciously to feel "what other people think." Naturally, other people are thinking all sorts of mean things, scheming evil, contriving plots, secret intrigues, etc. In order to forestall them, she herself is obliged to start counter-intrigues, to suspect others and sound them out, and weave counterplots. Beset by rumours, she must make frantic efforts to get her own back and be top dog. Endless clandestine rivalries spring up, and in these embittered struggles she will shrink from no baseness or meanness, and will even prostitute her virtues in order to play the trump card. Such a state of affairs must end in exhaustion. The form of neurosis is neurasthenic rather than hysterical, often with severe physical complications, such as anaemia and its sequelae.

## Summary of the Introverted Rational Types

Both the foregoing types may be termed rational, since they are grounded on the functions of rational judgment. Rational judgment is based not merely on objective but also on subjective data. The predominance of one or the other factor, however, as a result of a psychic disposition often existing from early youth, will give the judgment a corresponding bias. A judgment that is truly rational will appeal to the objective and the subjective factor equally and do justice to both. But that would be an ideal case and would presuppose an equal development of both extraversion and introversion. In practice, however, either movement excludes the other, and, so long as this dilemma remains, they cannot exist side by side but at best successively. Under ordinary conditions, therefore, an ideal rationality is impossible. The rationality of a rational type always has a typical bias. Thus, the judgment of the introverted rational types is undoubtedly rational, only it is oriented more by the subjective factor. This does not necessarily imply any logical bias, since the bias lies in the premise. The premise consists in the predominance of the subjective factor prior to all conclusions and judgments. The superior value of the subjective as compared with the objective factor appears self-evident from the beginning. It is not a question of *assigning* this value, but, as we have said, of a natural disposition existing before all rational valuation. Hence, to the introvert, rational judgment has many nuances which differentiate it from that of the extravert. To mention only the most general instance, the chain of reasoning that leads to the subjective factor seems to the introvert somewhat more rational than the one that leads to the object. This difference, though slight and practically unnoticeable in individual cases, builds up in the end to unbridgeable discrepancies which are the more irritating the less one is aware of the minimal shift of standpoint occasioned by the psychological premise. A capital error regularly creeps in here, for instead of recognizing the difference in the premise one tries to demonstrate a fallacy in the conclusion. This recognition is a difficult matter for every rational type, since it undermines the apparently absolute validity of his own principle and delivers him over to its antithesis, which for him amounts to a catastrophe.

The introvert is far more subject to misunderstanding than the extravert, not so much because the extravert is a more merciless or critical adversary than he himself might be, but because the style of the times which he himself imitates works against him. He finds himself in the minority, not in numerical relation to the extravert, but in relation to the general Western view of the world as judged by his feeling. In so far as he is a convinced participator in the general style, he undermines his own foundations;

for the general style, acknowledging as it does only the visible and tangible values, is opposed to his specific principle. Because of its invisibility, he is obliged to depreciate the subjective factor, and must force himself to join in the extraverted overvaluation of the object. He himself sets the subjective factor at too low a value, and his feelings of inferiority are his chastisement for this sin. Little wonder, therefore, that it is precisely in the present epoch, and particularly in those movements which are somewhat ahead of the time, that the subjective factor reveals itself in exaggerated, tasteless forms of expression bordering on caricature. I refer to the art of the present day.

The undervaluation of his own principle makes the introvert egotistical and forces on him the psychology of the underdog. The more egotistical he becomes, the more it seems to him that the others, who are apparently able, without qualms, to conform to the general style, are the oppressors against whom he must defend himself. He generally does not see that his chief error lies in not depending on the subjective factor with the same trust and devotion with which the extravert relies on the object. His undervaluation of his own principle makes his leanings towards egotism unavoidable, and because of this he fully deserves the censure of the extravert. If he remained true to his own principle, the charge of egotism would be altogether false, for his attitude would be justified by its effects in general, and the misunderstanding would be dissipated.

### Sensation

Sensation, which by its very nature is dependent on the object and on objective stimuli, undergoes considerable modification in the introverted attitude. It, too, has a subjective factor, for besides the sensed object there is a sensing subject who adds his subjective disposition to the objective stimulus. In the introverted attitude sensation is based predominantly on the subjective component of perception. What I mean by this is best illustrated by works of art which reproduce external objects. If, for instance, several painters were to paint the same landscape, each trying to reproduce it faithfully, each painting will be different from the others, not merely because of differences in ability, but chiefly because of different ways of seeing; indeed, in some of the paintings there will be a distinct psychic difference in mood and the treatment of colour and form. These qualities betray the influence of the subjective factor. The subjective factor in sensation is essentially the same as in the other functions we have discussed. It is an unconscious disposition which alters the sense-perception at its source, thus depriving it of the character of a purely objective influence. In this case, sensation is related primarily to the subject and only secondarily to the object. How extraordinarily strong the subjective factor can be is shown most clearly in art. Its predominance sometimes amounts to a complete suppression of the object's influence, and yet the sensation remains sensation even though it has become a perception of the subjective factor and the object has sunk to the level of a mere stimulus. Introverted sensation is oriented accordingly. True sense-perception certainly exists, but it always looks as though the object did not penetrate into the subject in its own right, but as though the subject were seeing it quite differently, or saw quite other things than other people see. Actually, he perceives the same things as everybody else, only he does not stop at the purely objective influence, but concerns himself with the subjective perception excited by the objective stimulus.

Subjective perception is markedly different from the objective. What is perceived is either not found at all in the object, or is, at most, merely suggested by it. That is, although the perception can be similar to that of other men, it is not immediately derived from the objective behaviour of things. It does not impress one as a mere product of consciousness—it is too genuine for that. But it makes a definite psychic impression because elements of a higher psychic order are discernible in it. This order, however, does not coincide with the contents of consciousness. It has to do with presuppositions or dispositions of the collective unconscious, with mythological images, with primordial possibilities of ideas. Subjective perception is characterized by the meaning that clings to it. It means more than the mere image of the object, though naturally only to one for whom the subjective factor means anything at all. To another, the reproduced subjective impression seems to suffer from the defect of not being sufficiently like the object and therefore to have failed in its purpose.

Introverted sensation apprehends the background of the physical world rather than its surface. The decisive thing is not the reality of the object, but the reality of the subjective factor, of the primordial images which, in their totality, constitute a psychic mirror-world. It is a mirror with the peculiar faculty of reflecting the existing contents of consciousness not in their known and customary form but, as it were, *sub specie aeternitatis*, somewhat as a million-year-old consciousness might see them. Such a consciousness would see the becoming and passing away of things simultaneously with their momentary existence in the present, and not only that, it would also see what was before their becoming and will be after their passing hence. Naturally this is only a figure of speech, but one that I needed in order to illustrate in some way the peculiar nature of introverted sensation. We could say that introverted sensation transmits an image which does not so much reproduce the object as spread over it the patina of age-old subjective experience and the shimmer of events still unborn. The bare sense impression develops in depth, reaching into the past and future, while extraverted sensation seizes on the momentary existence of things open to the light of day.

### The Introverted Sensation Type

The predominance of introverted sensation produces a definite type, which is characterized by certain peculiarities. It is an irrational type, because it is oriented amid the flux of events not by rational judgment but simply by what happens. Whereas the extraverted sensation type is guided by the intensity of objective influences, the introverted type is guided by the intensity of the subjective sensation excited by the objective stimulus. Obviously, therefore, no proportional relation exists between object and sensation, but one that is apparently quite unpredictable and arbitrary. What will make an impression and what will not can never be seen in advance, and from outside. Did there exist an aptitude for expression in any way proportional to the intensity of his sensations, the irrationality of this type would be extraordinarily striking. This is the case, for instance, when an individual is a creative artist. But since this is the exception, the introvert's characteristic difficulty in expressing himself also conceals his irrationality. On the contrary, he may be conspicuous for his calmness and passivity, or for his rational self-control. This peculiarity, which often leads a superficial judgment astray, is really due to his unrelatedness to objects. Normally the object is not consciously devalued in the least, but its stimulus is removed from it and immediately replaced by a subjective reaction no longer related to the reality of the object. This naturally has the same effect as devaluation. Such a type can easily make one question why one should exist at all, or why objects in general should have any justification for their existence since everything essential still goes on happening without them. This doubt may be justified in extreme cases, but not in the normal, since the objective stimulus is absolutely necessary to sensation and merely produces something different from what the external situation might lead one to expect.

Seen from the outside, it looks as though the effect of the object did not penetrate into the subject at all. This impression is correct inasmuch as a subjective content does, in fact, intervene from the unconscious and intercept the effect of the object. The intervention may be so abrupt that the individual appears to be shielding himself directly from all objective influences. In more serious cases, such a protective defence actually does exist. Even with only a slight increase in the power of the unconscious, the subjective component of sensation becomes so alive that it almost completely obscures the influence of the object. If the object is a person, he feels completely devalued, while the subject has an illusory conception of reality, which in pathological cases goes so far that he is no longer able to distinguish between the real object and the subjective perception. Although so vital a distinction reaches the vanishing point only in near-psychotic states, yet long before that the subjective perception can influence thought, feeling, and action to an excessive degree despite the fact that the object is clearly seen in all its reality. When its influence does succeed in penetrating into the subject— because of its special intensity or because of its complete analogy with the unconscious image—even the normal type will be compelled to *act* in accordance with the unconscious model. Such action has an illusory character unrelated to objective reality and is extremely disconcerting. It instantly reveals the reality-alienating subjectivity of this type. But when the influence of the object does not break through completely, it is met with a well-intentioned neutrality, disclosing little sympathy yet constantly striving to soothe and adjust. The too low is raised a little, the too high is lowered, enthusiasm is damped down, extravagance restrained, and anything out of the ordinary reduced to the right formula—all this in order to keep the influence of the object within the necessary bounds. In this way the type becomes a menace to his environment because his total innocuousness is not altogether above suspicion. In that case he easily becomes a victim of the aggressive-

ness and domineeringness of others. Such men allow themselves to be abused and then take their revenge on the
most unsuitable occasions with redoubled obtuseness and
stubbornness.

If no capacity for artistic expression is present, all impressions sink into the depths and hold consciousness under
a spell, so that it becomes impossible to master their fascination by giving them conscious expression. In general,
this type can organize his impressions only in archaic
ways, because thinking and feeling are relatively unconscious and, if conscious at all, have at their disposal only
the most necessary, banal, everyday means of expression.
As conscious functions, they are wholly incapable of adequately reproducing his subjective perceptions. This type,
therefore, is uncommonly inaccessible to objective understanding, and he usually fares no better in understanding
himself.

Above all, his development alienates him from the reality
of the object, leaving him at the mercy of his subjective
perceptions, which orient his consciousness to an archaic
reality, although his lack of comparative judgment keeps
him wholly unconscious of this fact. Actually he lives in
a mythological world, where men, animals, locomotives,
houses, rivers, and mountains appear either as benevolent
deities or as malevolent demons. That they appear thus
to him never enters his head, though that is just the effect
they have on his judgments and actions. He judges and
acts as though he had such powers to deal with; but this
begins to strike him only when he discovers that his sensations are totally different from reality. If he has any aptitude for objective reason, he will sense this difference as
morbid; but if he remains faithful to his irrationality, and
is ready to grant his sensations reality value, the objective
world will appear a mere make-believe and a comedy.
Only in extreme cases, however, is this dilemma reached.
As a rule he resigns himself to his isolation and the banality
of the world, which he has unconsciously made archaic.

His unconscious is distinguished chiefly by the repression

of intuition, which consequently acquires an extraverted and archaic character. Whereas true extraverted intuition is possessed of a singular resourcefulness, a "good nose" for objectively real possibilities, this archaicized intuition has an amazing flair for all the ambiguous, shadowy, sordid, dangerous possibilities lurking in the background. The real and conscious intentions of the object mean nothing to it; instead, it sniffs out every conceivable archaic motive underlying such an intention. It therefore has a dangerous and destructive quality that contrasts glaringly with the well-meaning innocuousness of the conscious attitude. So long as the individual does not hold too aloof from the object, his unconscious intuition has a salutary compensating effect on the rather fantastic and overcredulous attitude of consciousness. But as soon as the unconscious becomes antagonistic, the archaic intuitions come to the surface and exert their pernicious influence, forcing themselves on the individual and producing compulsive ideas of the most perverse kind. The result is usually a compulsion neurosis, in which the hysterical features are masked by symptoms of exhaustion.

### Intuition

Introverted intuition is directed to the inner object, a term that might justly be applied to the contents of the unconscious. The relation of inner objects to consciousness is entirely analogous to that of outer objects, though their reality is not physical but psychic. They appear to intuitive perception as subjective images of things which, though not to be met with in the outside world, constitute the contents of the unconscious, and of the collective unconscious in particular. These contents *per se* are naturally not accessible to experience, a quality they have in common with external objects. For just as external objects correspond only relatively to our perception of them, so

the phenomenal forms of the inner objects are also relative—products of their (to us) inaccessible essence and of
the peculiar nature of the intuitive function.

Like sensation, intuition has its subjective factor, which
is suppressed as much as possible in the extraverted attitude but is the decisive factor in the intuition of the introvert. Although his intuition may be stimulated by external objects, it does not concern itself with external
possibilities but with what the external object has released
within him. Whereas introverted sensation is mainly restricted to the perception, via the unconscious, of the
phenomena of innervation and is arrested there, introverted intuition suppresses this side of the subjective factor
and perceives the image that caused the innervation. Supposing, for instance, a man is overtaken by an attack of
psychogenic vertigo. Sensation is arrested by the peculiar
nature of this disturbance of innervation, perceiving all
its qualities, its intensity, its course, how it arose and how
it passed, but not advancing beyond that to its content,
to the thing that caused the disturbance. Intuition, on the
other hand, receives from sensation only the impetus to its
own immediate activity; it peers behind the scenes, quickly
perceiving the inner image that gave rise to this particular
form of expression—the attack of vertigo. It sees the
image of a tottering man pierced through the heart by an
arrow. This image fascinates the intuitive activity; it is
arrested by it, and seeks to explore every detail of it. It
holds fast to the vision, observing with the liveliest interest
how the picture changes, unfolds, and finally fades.

In this way introverted intuition perceives all the background processes of consciousness with almost the same
distinctness as extraverted sensation registers external objects. For intuition, therefore, unconscious images acquire
the dignity of things. But, because intuition excludes the
co-operation of sensation, it obtains little or no knowledge
of the disturbances of innervation or of the physical effects
produced by the unconscious images. The images appear

as though detached from the subject, as though existing in themselves without any relation to him. Consequently, in the above-mentioned example, the introverted intuitive, if attacked by vertigo, would never imagine that the image he perceived might in some way refer to himself. To a judging type this naturally seems almost inconceivable, but it is none the less a fact which I have often come across in my dealings with intuitives.

The remarkable indifference of the extraverted intuitive to external objects is shared by the introverted intuitive in relation to inner objects. Just as the extraverted intuitive is continually scenting out new possibilities, which he pursues with equal unconcern for his own welfare and for that of others, pressing on quite heedless of human considerations and tearing down what has just been built in his everlasting search for change, so the introverted intuitive moves from image to image, chasing after every possibility in the teeming womb of the unconscious, without establishing any connection between them and himself. Just as the world of appearances can never become a moral problem for the man who merely senses it, the world of inner images is never a moral problem for the intuitive. For both of them it is an aesthetic problem, a matter of perception, a "sensation." Because of this, the introverted intuitive has little consciousness of his own bodily existence or of its effect on others. The extravert would say: "Reality does not exist for him, he gives himself up to fruitless fantasies." The perception of the images of the unconscious, produced in such inexhaustible abundance by the creative energy of life, is of course fruitless from the standpoint of immediate utility. But since these images represent possible views of the world which may give life a new potential, this function, which to the outside world is the strangest of all, is as indispensable to the total psychic economy as is the corresponding human type to the psychic life of a people. Had this type not existed, there would have been no prophets in Israel.

Introverted intuition apprehends the images arising from

the *a priori* inherited foundations of the unconscious. These archetypes, whose innermost nature is inaccessible to experience, are the precipitate of the psychic functioning of the whole ancestral line; the accumulated experiences of organic life in general, a million times repeated, and condensed into types. In these archetypes, therefore, all experiences are represented which have happened on this planet since primeval times. The more frequent and the more intense they were, the more clearly focussed they become in the archetype. The archetype would thus be, to borrow from Kant, the noumenon of the image which intuition perceives and, in perceiving, creates.

Since the unconscious is not just something that lies there like a psychic *caput mortuum,* but co-exists with us and is constantly undergoing transformations which are inwardly connected with the general run of events, introverted intuition, through its perception of these inner processes, can supply certain data which may be of the utmost importance for understanding what is going on in the world. It can even foresee new possibilities in more or less clear outline, as well as events which later actually do happen. Its prophetic foresight is explained by its relation to the archetypes, which represent the laws governing the course of all experienceable things.

### The Introverted Intuitive Type

The peculiar nature of introverted intuition, if it gains the ascendency, produces a peculiar type of man: the mystical dreamer and seer on the one hand, the artist and the crank on the other. The artist might be regarded as the normal representative of this type, which tends to confine itself to the perceptive character of intuition. As a rule, the intuitive stops at perception; perception is his main problem, and—in the case of a creative artist—the shaping of his perception. But the crank is content with a visionary idea by which he himself is shaped and determined. Naturally the intensification of intuition often results in an extraordinary aloofness of the individual from tangible reality; he may even become a complete enigma to his immediate circle. If he is an artist, he reveals strange, far-off things in his art, shimmering in all colours, at once portentous and banal, beautiful and grotesque, sublime and whimsical. If not an artist, he is frequently a misunderstood genius, a great man "gone wrong," a sort of wise simpleton, a figure for "psychological" novels.

Although the intuitive type has little inclination to make a moral problem of perception, since a strengthening of the judging functions is required for this, only a slight differentiation of judgment is sufficient to shift intuitive perception from the purely aesthetic into the moral sphere. A variety of this type is thus produced which differs essentially from the aesthetic, although it is none the less characteristic of the introverted intuitive. The moral problem arises when the intuitive tries to relate himself to his vision, when he is no longer satisfied with mere perception and its aesthetic configuration and evaluation, when he confronts the questions: What does this mean for me or the world? What emerges from this vision in the way of a duty or a task, for me or the world? The pure intuitive who represses his judgment, or whose judgment is held in thrall by his perceptive faculties, never faces this question squarely, since his only problem is the "know-how" of perception. He finds the moral problem unintelligible or even absurd, and as far as possible forbids his thoughts to dwell on the disconcerting vision. It is different with the morally oriented intuitive. He reflects on the meaning of his vision, and is less concerned with developing its aesthetic possibilities than with the moral effects which emerge from its intrinsic significance. His judgment allows him to discern, though often only darkly, that he, as a man and a whole human being, is somehow involved in his vision, that it is not just an object to be perceived, but wants to participate in the life of the subject. Through this realization he feels bound to transform his vision into his own life. But since he tends to rely most predominately on his vision, his moral efforts become one-sided; he makes himself and his life symbolic—adapted, it is true, to the inner and eternal meaning of events, but unadapted to present-day reality. He thus deprives himself of any influence upon it because he remains uncomprehended. His language is not the one currently spoken—it has become too subjective. His arguments lack the convincing power of reason. He can only profess or proclaim. His is "the voice of one crying in the wilderness."

What the introverted intuitive represses most of all is the sensation of the object, and this colours his whole unconscious. It gives rise to a compensatory extraverted sensation function of an archaic character. The unconscious personality can best be described as an extraverted sensation type of a rather low and primitive order. Instinctuality and intemperance are the hallmarks of this sensation, combined with an extraordinary dependence on sense-impressions. This compensates the rarefied air of the intuitive's conscious attitude, giving it a certain weight, so that complete "sublimation" is prevented. But if, through a forced exaggeration of the conscious attitude, there should be a complete subordination to inner perceptions, the unconscious goes over to the opposition, giving rise to compulsive sensations whose excessive dependence on the object directly contradicts the conscious attitude. The form of neurosis is a compulsion neurosis with hypochondriacal symptoms, hypersensitivity of the sense organs, and compulsive ties to particular persons or objects.

## Summary of the Introverted Irrational Types

The two types just described are almost inaccessible to judgment from outside. Being introverted, and having in consequence little capacity or desire for expression, they offer but a frail handle in this respect. As their main activity is directed inwards, nothing is outwardly visible but reserve, secretiveness, lack of sympathy, uncertainty, and an apparently groundless embarrassment. When anything does come to the surface, it is generally an indirect manifestation of the inferior and relatively unconscious functions. Such manifestations naturally arouse all the current prejudices against this type. Accordingly they are mostly underestimated, or at least misunderstood. To the extent that they do not understand themselves—because they very largely lack judgment—they are also powerless to understand why they are so constantly underestimated by the public. They cannot see that their efforts to be forthcoming are, as a matter of fact, of an inferior character. Their vision is enthralled by the richness of subjective events. What is going on inside them is so captivating, and of such inexhaustible charm, that they simply do not notice that the little they do manage to communicate contains hardly anything of what they themselves have experienced. The fragmentary and episodic character of their communications makes too great a demand on the understanding and good will of those around them; also, their communications are without the personal warmth that alone carries the power of conviction. On the contrary, these types have very often a harsh, repelling manner, though of this they are quite unaware and they did not intend it. We shall form a fairer judgment of such people, and show them greater forbearance, when we begin to realize how hard it is to translate into intelligible language what is perceived within. Yet this forbearance must not go so far as to exempt them altogether from the need to communicate. This would only do them the greatest harm. Fate itself prepares for them, perhaps even more than for other men, overwhelming external difficulties which have a very sobering effect on those intoxicated by the inner vision. Often it is only an intense personal need that can wring from them a human confession.

From an extraverted and rationalistic standpoint, these types are indeed the most useless of men. But, viewed from a higher standpoint, they are living evidence that this rich and varied world with its overflowing and intoxicating life is not purely external, but also exists within. These types are admittedly one-sided specimens of nature, but they are an object-lesson for the man who refuses to be blinded by the intellectual fashion of the day. In their own way, they are educators and promoters of culture. Their life teaches more than their words. From their lives, and not least from their greatest fault—their inability to communicate—we may understand one of the greatest errors of our civilization, that is, the superstitious belief in verbal statements, the boundless overestimation of instruction by means of words and methods. A child certainly allows himself to be impressed by the grand talk of his parents, but is it really imagined that he is educated by it? Actually it is the parents' lives that educate the child, and what they add by word and gesture serves at best only to confuse him. The same holds good for the teacher. But we have such a belief in method that, if only the method be good, the practice of it seems to sanctify the teacher. An inferior man is never a good teacher. But he can conceal his pernicious inferiority, which secretly poisons the pupil, behind an excellent method or an equally brilliant intellectual gift of the gab. Naturally the pupil of riper years desires nothing better than the knowledge of useful methods, because he is already defeated by the general attitude, which believes in the all-conquering method. He has learnt that the emptiest head, correctly parroting a method, is the best pupil. His whole environment is an optical demonstration that all success and all happiness are outside, and that only the right method is needed to attain the haven of one's desires. Or does, perchance, the life of his religious instructor demonstrate the happiness which radiates from the treasure of the inner vision? The irrational introverted types are certainly no teachers of a more perfect humanity; they lack reason and the ethics of reason. But their lives teach the other possibility, the interior life which is so painfully wanting in our civilization.

### d) *The Principal and Auxiliary Functions*

In the foregoing descriptions I have no desire to give my readers the impression that these types occur at all frequently in such pure form in actual life. They are, as it were, only Galtonesque family portraits, which single out the common and therefore typical features, stressing them disproportionately, while the individual features are just as disproportionately effaced. Closer investigation shows with great regularity that, besides the most differentiated function, another, less differentiated function of secondary importance is invariably present in consciousness and exerts a co-determining influence.

To recapitulate for the sake of clarity: the products of all functions can be conscious, but we speak of the "consciousness" of a function only when its use is under the control of the will and, at the same time, its governing principle is the decisive one for the orientation of consciousness. This is true when, for instance, thinking is not a mere afterthought, or rumination, and when its conclusions possess an absolute validity, so that the logical result holds good both as a motive and as a guarantee of practical action without the backing of any further evidence. This absolute sovereignty always belongs, empirically, to one function alone, and *can* belong only to one function, because the equally independent intervention of another function would necessarily produce a different orientation which, partially at least, would contradict the first. But since it is a vital condition for the conscious process of adaptation always to have clear and unambiguous aims, the presence of a second function of equal

power is naturally ruled out. This other function, therefore, can have only a secondary importance, as has been
found to be the case in practice. Its secondary importance
is due to the fact that it is not, like the primary function,
valid in its own right as an absolutely reliable and decisive factor, but comes into play more as an auxiliary or
complementary function. Naturally only those functions
can appear as auxiliary whose nature is not opposed to
the dominant function. For instance, feeling can never
act as the second function alongside thinking, because it
is by its very nature too strongly opposed to thinking.
Thinking, if it is to be real thinking and true to its own
principle, must rigorously exclude feeling. This, of course,
does not do away with the fact that there are individuals
whose thinking and feeling are on the same level, both
being of equal motive power for consciousness. But in
these cases there is also no question of a differentiated
type, but merely of relatively undeveloped thinking and
feeling. The uniformly conscious or uniformly unconscious
state of the functions is, therefore, the mark of a primitive
mentality.

Experience shows that the secondary function is always
one whose nature is different from, though not antagonistic
to, the primary function. Thus, thinking as the primary
function can readily pair with intuition as the auxiliary, or
indeed equally well with sensation, but, as already observed, never with feeling. Neither intuition nor sensation
is antagonistic to thinking; they need not be absolutely excluded, for they are not of a nature equal and opposite to
thinking, as feeling is—which, as a judging function, successfully competes with thinking—but are functions of
perception, affording welcome assistance to thought. But
as soon as they reached the same level of differentiation
as thinking, they would bring about a change of attitude
which would contradict the whole trend of thinking. They
would change the judging attitude into a perceiving one;
whereupon the principle of rationality indispensable to

thought would be suppressed in favour of the irrationality of perception. Hence the auxiliary function is possible and useful only in so far as it *serves* the dominant function, without making any claim to the autonomy of its own principle.

For all the types met with in practice, the rule holds good that besides the conscious, primary function there is a relatively unconscious, auxiliary function which is in every respect different from the nature of the primary function. The resulting combinations present the familiar picture of, for instance, practical thinking allied with sensation, speculative thinking forging ahead with intuition, artistic intuition selecting and presenting its images with the help of feeling-values, philosophical intuition systematizing its vision into comprehensible thought by means of a powerful intellect, and so on.

The unconscious functions likewise group themselves in patterns correlated with the conscious ones. Thus, the correlative of conscious, practical thinking may be an unconscious, intuitive-feeling attitude, with feeling under a stronger inhibition than intuition. These peculiarities are of interest only for one who is concerned with the practical treatment of such cases, but it is important that he should know about them. I have frequently observed how an analyst, confronted with a terrific thinking type, for instance, will do his utmost to develop the feeling function directly out of the unconscious. Such an attempt is foredoomed to failure, because it involves too great a violation of the conscious standpoint. Should the violation nevertheless be successful, a really compulsive dependence of the patient on the analyst ensues, a transference that can only be brutally terminated, because, having been left without a standpoint, the patient has made his standpoint the analyst. But the approach to the unconscious and to the most repressed function is disclosed, as it were, of its own accord, and with adequate protection of the conscious standpoint, when the way of development proceeds via the auxiliary function—in the case of a rational type via one of the irrational functions. This gives the patient a broader view of what is happening, and of what is possible, so that his consciousness is sufficiently protected against the inroads of the unconscious. Conversely, in order to cushion the impact of the unconscious, an irrational type needs a stronger development of the rational auxiliary function present in consciousness.

The unconscious functions exist in an archaic, animal state. Hence their symbolic appearance in dreams and fantasies is usually represented as the battle or encounter between two animals or monsters.

# ❧ Part II ❧

# ❧ 9 ❧

## *The Transcendent Function*[1]

There is nothing mysterious or metaphysical about the term "transcendent function." It means a psychological function comparable in its way to a mathematical function of the same name, which is a function of real and imaginary numbers. The psychological "transcendent function" arises from the union of conscious and unconscious contents.

Experience in analytical psychology has amply shown that the conscious and the unconscious seldom agree as to their contents and their tendencies. This lack of parallelism is not just accidental or purposeless, but is due to the fact that the unconscious behaves in a compensatory or complementary manner towards the conscious. We can also put it the other way round and say that the conscious behaves

[1] From *The Structure and Dynamics of the Psyche. Collected Works,* Vol. 8. [Written in 1916 under the title "Die Transzendente Funktion," the ms. lay in Professor Jung's files until 1953. First published in 1957 by the Students Association, C. G. Jung Institute, Zurich, in an English translation by A. R. Pope. The German original, considerably revised by the author, was published in *Geist und Werk . . . zum 75. Geburtstag von Dr. Daniel Brody* (Zurich, 1958), together with a prefatory note of more general import specially written for that volume. The author has partially rewritten the note for publication here. The present translation is based on the revised German version, and Mr. Pope's translation has been consulted.— EDITORS OF *The Collected Works.*]

in a complementary manner towards the unconscious. The reasons for this relationship are:

(1) Consciousness possesses a threshold intensity which its contents must have attained, so that all elements that are too weak remain in the unconscious.

(2) Consciousness, because of its directed functions, exercises an inhibition (which Freud calls censorship) on all incompatible material, with the result that it sinks into the unconscious.

(3) Consciousness constitutes the momentary process of adaptation, whereas the unconscious contains not only all the forgotten material of the individual's own past, but all the inherited behaviour traces constituting the structure of the mind.

(4) The unconscious contains all the fantasy combinations which have not yet attained the threshold intensity, but which in the course of time and under suitable conditions will enter the light of consciousness.

This readily explains the complementary attitude of the unconscious towards the conscious.

The definiteness and directedness of the conscious mind are qualities that have been acquired relatively late in the history of the human race, and are for instance largely lacking among primitives today. These qualities are often impaired in the neurotic patient, who differs from the normal person in that his threshold of consciousness gets shifted more easily; in other words, the partition between conscious and unconscious is much more permeable. The psychotic, on the other hand, is under the direct influence of the unconscious.

The definiteness and directedness of the conscious mind are extremely important acquisitions which humanity has bought at a very heavy sacrifice, and which in turn have rendered humanity the highest service. Without them science, technology, and civilization would be impossible, for they all presuppose the reliable continuity and directedness of the conscious process. For the statesman, doctor, and engineer as well as for the simplest labourer, these qualities are absolutely indispensable. We may say in general that social worthlessness increases to the degree that these qualities are impaired by the unconscious. Great artists and others distinguished by creative gifts are, of course, exceptions to this rule. The very advantage that such individuals enjoy consists precisely in the permeability of the partition separating the conscious and the unconscious. But, for those professions and social activities which require just this continuity and reliability, these exceptional human beings are as a rule of little value.

It is therefore understandable, and even necessary, that in each individual the psychic process should be as stable and definite as possible, since the exigencies of life demand it. But this involves a certain disadvantage: the quality of directedness makes for the inhibition or exclusion of all those psychic elements which appear to be, or really are, incompatible with it, i.e., likely to bias the intended direction to suit their purpose and so lead to an undesired goal. But how do we know that the concurrent psychic material is "incompatible"? We know it by an act of judgment which determines the direction of the path that is chosen and desired. This judgment is partial and prejudiced, since it chooses one particular possibility at the cost of all the others. The judgment in its turn is always based on experience, i.e., on what is already known. As a rule it is never based on what is new, what is still unknown, and what under certain conditions might considerably enrich the directed process. It is evident that it cannot be, for the very reason that the unconscious contents are excluded from consciousness.

Through such acts of judgment the directed process necessarily becomes one-sided, even though the rational judgment may appear many-sided and unprejudiced. The very rationality of the judgment may even be the worst prejudice, since we call reasonable what appears reasonable to us. What appears to us unreasonable is therefore doomed to be excluded because of its irrational character. It may really be irrational, but may equally well merely appear irrational without actually being so when seen from another standpoint.

One-sidedness is an unavoidable and necessary characteristic of the directed process, for direction implies one-sidedness. It is an advantage and a drawback at the same time. Even when no outwardly visible drawback seems to be present, there is always an equally pronounced counter-position in the unconscious, unless it happens to be the ideal case where all the psychic components are tending in one and the same direction. This possibility cannot be disputed in theory, but in practice it very rarely happens. The counter-position in the unconscious is not dangerous so long as it does not possess any high energy-value. But if the tension increases as a result of too great one-sidedness, the counter-tendency breaks through into consciousness, usually just at the moment when it is most important to maintain the conscious direction. Thus the speaker makes a slip of the tongue just when he particularly wishes not to say anything stupid. This moment is critical because it possesses a high energy tension which, when the unconscious is already charged, may easily "spark" and release the unconscious content.

Civilized life today demands concentrated, directed conscious functioning, and this entails the risk of a considerable dissociation from the unconscious. The further we are able to remove ourselves from the unconscious through directed functioning, the more readily a powerful counter-position can build up in the unconscious, and when this breaks out it may have disagreeable consequences.

Analysis has given us a profound insight into the importance of unconscious influences, and we have learnt so much from this for our practical life that we deem it unwise to expect an elimination or standstill of the unconscious after the so-called completion of the treatment. Many patients, obscurely recognizing this state of affairs, have great difficulty in deciding to give up the analysis, although both they and the analyst find the feeling of dependency irksome. Often they are afraid to risk standing on their own feet, because they know from experience that the unconscious can intervene again and again in their lives in a disturbing and apparently unpredictable manner.

It was formerly assumed that patients were ready to cope with normal life as soon as they had acquired enough practical self-knowledge to understand their own dreams. Experience has shown, however, that even professional analysts, who might be expected to have mastered the art of dream interpretation, often capitulate before their own dreams and have to call in the help of a colleague. If even one who purports to be an expert in the method proves unable to interpret his own dreams satisfactorily, how much less can this be expected of the patient. Freud's hope that the unconscious could be "exhausted" has not been fulfilled. Dream-life and intrusions from the unconscious continue— *mutatis mutandis*—unimpeded.

There is a widespread prejudice that analysis is something like a "cure," to which one submits for a time and is then discharged healed. That is a layman's error left over from the early days of psychoanalysis. Analytical treatment could be described as a readjustment of psychological attitude achieved with the help of the doctor. Naturally this newly won attitude, which is better suited to the inner and outer conditions, can last a considerable time, but there are very few cases where a single "cure" is permanently successful. It is true that medical optimism has never stinted itself of publicity and has always been able to report definitive cures. We must, however, not let ourselves be deceived by the all-too-human attitude of the practitioner, but should always remember that the life of the unconscious goes on and continually produces problematical situations. There is no need for pessimism; we have seen too many excellent results achieved with good luck and honest work for that. But this need not prevent us from recognizing that analysis is no once-and-for-all "cure"; it is no more, at first, than a more or less thorough readjustment. There is no change that is unconditionally valid over a long period of time. Life has always to be tackled anew. There are, of course, extremely durable collective attitudes which permit the solution of typical conflicts. A collective attitude enables the individual to fit into society without friction, since it acts upon him like any other condition of life. But the patient's difficulty consists precisely in the fact that his individual problem cannot be fitted without friction into a collective norm; it requires the solution of an individual conflict if the whole of his personality is to remain viable. No rational solution can do justice to this task, and there is absolutely no collective norm that could replace an individual solution without loss.

The new attitude gained in the course of analysis tends sooner or later to become inadequate in one way or another, and necessarily so, because the constant flow of life again and again demands fresh adaptation. Adaptation is never achieved once and for all. One might certainly demand of analysis that it should enable the patient to gain new orientations in later life, too, without undue difficulty. And experience shows that this is true up to a point. We often find that patients who have gone through a thorough analysis have considerably less difficulty with new adjustments later on. Nevertheless, these difficulties prove to be fairly frequent and may at times be really troublesome. That is why even patients who have had a thorough analysis often turn to their old analyst for help at some later period. In the light of medical practice in general there is nothing very unusual about this, but it does contradict a certain misplaced enthusiasm on the part of the therapist as well as the view that analysis constitutes a unique "cure." In the last resort it is highly improbable that there could ever be a therapy that got rid of all difficulties. Man needs difficulties; they are necessary for health. What concerns us here is only an excessive amount of them.

The basic question for the therapist is not how to get rid of the momentary difficulty, but how future difficulties may be successfully countered. The question is: what kind of mental and moral attitude is it necessary to have towards the disturbing influences of the unconscious, and how can it be conveyed to the patient?

The answer obviously consists in getting rid of the separation between conscious and unconscious. This cannot be done by condemning the contents of the unconscious in a one-sided way, but rather by recognizing their significance in compensating the one-sidedness of consciousness and by taking this significance into account. The tendencies of the conscious and the unconscious are the two factors that together make up the transcendent function. It is called "transcendent" because it makes the transition from one attitude to another organically possible, without loss of the unconscious. The constructive or synthetic method of treatment presupposes insights which are at least potentially present in the patient and can therefore be made conscious. If the analyst knows nothing of these potentialities he cannot help the patient to develop them either, unless analyst and patient together devote proper scientific study to this problem, which as a rule is out of the question.

In actual practice, therefore, the suitably trained analyst mediates the transcendent function for the patient, i.e., helps him to bring conscious and unconscious together and so arrive at a new attitude. In this function of the analyst lies one of the many important meanings of the *transference*. The patient clings by means of the transference to the person who seems to promise him a renewal of attitude; through it he seeks this change, which is vital to him, even though he may not be conscious of doing so. For the patient, therefore, the analyst has the character of an indispensable figure absolutely necessary for life. However infantile this dependence may appear to be, it expresses an extremely important demand which, if disappointed, often turns to bitter hatred of the analyst. It is therefore important to know what this demand concealed in the transference is really aiming at; there is a tendency to understand it in the reductive sense only, as an erotic infantile fantasy. But that would mean taking this fantasy, which is usually concerned with the parents, literally, as though the patient, or rather his unconscious, still had the expectations the child once had towards the parents. Outwardly it still is the same expectation of the child for the help and protection of the parents, but in the meantime the child has become an adult, and what was normal for a child is improper in an adult. It has become a metaphorical expression of the not consciously realized need for help in a crisis. Historically it is correct to explain the erotic character of the transference in terms of the infantile *eros*. But in that way the meaning and purpose of the transference are not understood, and its interpretation as an infantile sexual fantasy leads away from the real problem. The understanding of the transference is to be sought not in its historical antecedents but in its purpose. The one-sided, reductive explanation becomes in the end nonsensical, especially when absolutely nothing new comes out of it except the increased resistances of the patient. The sense of boredom which then appears in the analysis is simply an expression of the monotony and poverty of ideas—not of the unconscious, as is sometimes supposed, but of the analyst, who does not understand that these fantasies should not be taken merely in a concretistic-reductive sense, but rather in a constructive one. When this is realized, the standstill is often overcome at a single stroke.

Constructive treatment of the unconscious, that is, the question of meaning and purpose, paves the way for the patient's insight into that process which I call the transcendent function.

It may not be superfluous, at this point, to say a few words about the frequently heard objection that the constructive method is simply "suggestion." The method is based, rather, on evaluating the symbol (i.e., dream-image or fantasy) not *semiotically,* as a sign for elementary instinctual processes, but symbolically in the true sense, the word "symbol" being taken to mean the best possible expression for a complex fact not yet clearly apprehended by consciousness. Through reductive analysis of this expression nothing is gained but a clearer view of the elements originally composing it, and though I would not deny that increased insight into these elements may have its advantages, it nevertheless bypasses the question of purpose. Dissolution of the symbol at this stage of analysis is therefore a mistake. To begin with, however, the method for working out the complex meanings suggested by the symbol is the same as in reductive analysis. The associations of the patient are obtained, and as a rule they are plentiful enough to be used in the synthetic method. Here again they are evaluated not semiotically but symbolically. The question we must ask is: to what meaning do the individual associations A, B, C point, when taken in conjunction with the manifest dream-content?

An unmarried woman patient dreamt that *someone gave her a wonderful, richly ornamented, antique sword dug up out of a tumulus.*

#### ASSOCIATIONS

Her *father's* dagger, which he once flashed in the sun in front of her. It made a great impression on her. Her father was in every respect an energetic, strong-willed man, with an impetuous temperament, and adventurous in love affairs. A *Celtic* bronze sword: Patient is proud of her Celtic ancestry. The Celts are full of temperament, impetuous, passionate. The ornamentation has a mysterious look about it, ancient tradition, runes, signs of ancient wisdom, ancient civilizations, heritage of mankind, brought to light again out of the grave.

#### ANALYTICAL INTERPRETATION

Patient has a pronounced father complex and a rich tissue of sexual fantasies about her father, whom she lost early. She always put herself in her mother's place, although with strong resistances towards her father. She has never been able to accept a man like her father and has therefore chosen weakly, neurotic men against her will. Also in the analysis violent resistance towards the physician-father. The dream digs up her wish for her father's "weapon." The rest is clear. In theory, this would immediately point to a phallic fantasy.

CONSTRUCTIVE INTERPRETATION

It is as if the patient needed such a weapon. Her father had the weapon. He was energetic, lived accordingly, and also took upon himself the difficulties inherent in his temperament. Therefore, though living a passionate, exciting life he was not neurotic. This weapon is a very ancient heritage of mankind, which lay buried in the patient and was brought to light through excavation (analysis). The weapon has to do with insight, with wisdom. It is a means of attack and defence. Her father's weapon was a passionate, unbending will, with which he made his way through life. Up till now the patient has been the opposite in every respect. She is just on the point of realizing that a person can also will something and need not merely be driven, as she had always believed. The will based on a knowledge of life and on insight is an ancient heritage of the human race, which also is in her, but till now lay buried, for in this respect, too, she is her father's daughter. But she had not appreciated this till now, because her character had been that of a perpetually whining, pampered, spoilt child. She was extremely passive and completely given to sexual fantasies.

In this case there was no need of any supplementary analogies on the part of the analyst. The patient's associations provided all that was necessary. It might be objected that this treatment of the dream involves suggestion. But this ignores the fact that a suggestion is never accepted without an inner readiness for it, or if after great insistence it is accepted, it is immediately lost again. A suggestion that is accepted for any length of time always presupposes a marked psychological readiness which is merely brought into play by the so-called suggestion. This objection is therefore thoughtless and credits suggestion with a magical power it in no way possesses, otherwise suggestion therapy would have an enormous effect and would render analytical procedures quite superfluous. But this is far from being the case. Furthermore, the charge of suggestion does not take account of the fact that the patient's own associations point to the cultural significance of the sword.

After this digression, let us return to the question of the transcendent function. We have seen that during treatment the transcendent function is, in a sense, an "artificial" product because it is largely supported by the analyst. But if the patient is to stand on his own feet he must not depend permanently on outside help. The interpretation of dreams would be an ideal method for synthesizing the conscious and unconscious data, but in practice the difficulties of analyzing one's own dreams are too great.

We must now make clear what is required to produce the transcendent function. First and foremost, we need the unconscious material. The most readily accessible expression of unconscious processes is undoubtedly dreams. The dream is, so to speak, a pure product of the unconscious. The alterations which the dream undergoes in the process of reaching consciousness, although undeniable, can be considered irrelevant, since they too derive from the unconscious and are not intentional distortions. Possible modifications of the original dream-image derive from a more superficial layer of the unconscious and therefore contain valuable material too. They are further fantasy-products following the general trend of the dream. The same applies to the subsequent images and ideas which frequently occur while dozing or rise up spontaneously on waking. Since the dream originates in sleep, it bears all the characteristics of an "abaissement du niveau mental" (Janet), or of low energy-tension: logical discontinuity, fragmentary character, analogy formations, superficial associations of the verbal, clang, or visual type, condensations, irrational expressions, confusion, etc. With an increase of energy-tension, the dreams acquire a more ordered character; they become dramatically composed and reveal clear sense-connections, and the valency of the associations increases.

Since the energy-tension in sleep is usually very low, dreams, compared with conscious material, are inferior expressions of unconscious contents and are very difficult to understand from a constructive point of view, but are usually easier to understand reductively. In general, dreams are unsuitable or difficult to make use of in developing the transcendent function, because they make too great demands on the subject.

We must therefore look to other sources for the unconscious material. There are, for instance, the unconscious interferences in the waking state, ideas "out of the blue," slips, deceptions and lapses of memory, symptomatic actions, etc. This material is generally more useful for the reductive method than for the constructive one; it is too fragmentary and lacks continuity, which is indispensable for a meaningful synthesis.

Another source is spontaneous fantasies. They usually have a more composed and coherent character and often contain much that is obviously significant. Some patients are able to produce fantasies at any time, allowing them to rise up freely simply by eliminating critical attention. Such fantasies can be used, though this particular talent is none too common. The capacity to produce free fantasies can, however, be developed with practice. The training consists first of all in systematic exercises for eliminating critical attention, thus producing a vacuum in consciousness. This encourages the emergence of any fantasies that are lying in readiness. A prerequisite, of course, is that fantasies with a high libido-charge are actually lying ready. This is naturally not always the case. Where this is not so, special measures are required.

Before entering upon a discussion of these, I must yield to an uncomfortable feeling which tells me that the reader may be asking dubiously, what really is the point of all this? And why is it so absolutely necessary to bring up the unconscious contents? Is it not sufficient if from time to time they come up of their own accord and make themselves unpleasantly felt? Does one have to drag the unconscious to the surface by force? On the contrary, should it not be the job of analysis to empty the unconscious of fantasies and in this way render it ineffective?

It may be as well to consider these misgivings in somewhat more detail, since the methods for bringing the unconscious to consciousness may strike the reader as novel, unusual, and perhaps even rather weird. We must therefore first discuss these natural objections, so that they shall not hold us up when we begin demonstrating the methods in question.

As we have seen, we need the unconscious contents to supplement the conscious attitude. If the conscious attitude were only to a slight degree "directed," the unconscious could flow in quite of its own accord. This is what does in fact happen with all those people who have a low level of conscious tension, as for instance primitives. Among primitives, no special measures are required to bring up the unconscious. Nowhere, really, are special measures required for this, because those people who are least aware of their unconscious side are the most influenced by it. But they are unconscious of what is happening. The secret participation of the unconscious is everywhere present without our having to search for it, but as it remains unconscious we never really know what is going on or what to expect. What we are searching for is a way to make conscious those contents which are about to influence our actions, so that the secret interference of the unconscious and its unpleasant consequences can be avoided.

The reader will no doubt ask: why cannot the unconscious be left to its own devices? Those who have not already had a few bad experiences in this respect will naturally see no reason to control the unconscious. But anyone with sufficiently bad experience will eagerly welcome the bare possibility of doing so. Directedness is absolutely necessary for the conscious process, but as we have seen it entails an unavoidable one-sidedness. Since the psyche is a self-regulating system, just as the body is, the regulating counteraction will always develop in the unconscious. Were it not for the directedness of the conscious function, the counteracting influences of the unconscious could set in unhindered. It is just this directedness that excludes them. This, of course, does not inhibit the counteraction, which goes on in spite of everything. Its regulating influence, however, is eliminated by critical attention and the directed will, because the counteraction as such seems incompatible with 'the conscious direction. To this extent the psyche of civilized man is no longer a self-regulating system but could rather be compared to a machine whose speed-regulation is so insensitive that it can continue to function to the point of self-injury, while on the other hand it is subject to the arbitrary manipulations of a one-sided will.

Now it is a peculiarity of psychic functioning that when the unconscious counteraction is suppressed it loses its regulating influence. It then begins to have an accelerating and intensifying effect on the conscious process. It is as though the counteraction had lost its regulating influence, and hence its energy, altogether; for a condition then arises in which not only no inhibiting counteraction takes place, but in which its energy seems to add itself to that of the conscious direction. To begin with, this naturally facilitates the execution of the conscious intentions, but because they are unchecked, they may easily assert themselves at the cost of the whole. For instance, when someone makes a rather bold assertion and suppresses the counteraction, namely a well-placed doubt, he will insist on it all the more, to his own detriment.

The ease with which the counteraction can be eliminated is proportional to the degree of dissociability of the psyche and leads to loss of instinct. This is characteristic of, as well as very necessary for, civilized man, since instincts in their original strength can render social adaptation almost impossible. It is not a real atrophy of instinct but, in most cases, only a relatively lasting product of education, and would never have struck such deep roots had it not served the interests of the individual.

Apart from the everyday cases met with in practice, a good example of the suppression of the unconscious regulating influence can be found in Nietzsche's *Zarathustra*.

The discovery of the "higher" man, and also of the "ugliest" man, expresses the regulating influence, for the "higher" men want to drag Zarathustra down to the collective sphere of average humanity as it always has been, while the "ugliest" man is actually the personification of the counteraction. But the roaring lion of Zarathustra's moral conviction forces all these influences, above all the feeling of pity, back again into the cave of the unconscious. Thus the regulating influence is suppressed, but not the secret counteraction of the unconscious, which from now on becomes clearly noticeable in Nietzsche's writings. First he seeks his adversary in Wagner, whom he cannot forgive for *Parsifal,* but soon his whole wrath turns against Christianity and in particular against St. Paul, who in some ways suffered a fate similar to Nietzsche's. As is well known, Nietzsche's psychosis first produced an identification with the "Crucified Christ" and then with the dismembered Dionysus. With this catastrophe the counteraction at last broke through to the surface.

Another example is the classic case of megalomania preserved for us in the fourth chapter of the Book of Daniel. Nebuchadnezzar at the height of his power had a dream which foretold disaster if he did not humble himself. Daniel interpreted the dream quite expertly, but without getting a hearing. Subsequent events showed that his interpretation was correct, for Nebuchadnezzar, after suppressing the unconscious regulating influence, fell victim to a psychosis that contained the very counteraction he had sought to escape: he, the lord of the earth, was degraded to an animal.

An acquaintance of mine once told me a dream in which *he stepped out into space from the top of a mountain.* I explained to him something of the influence of the unconscious and warned him against dangerous mountaineering expeditions, for which he had a regular passion. But he laughed at such ideas. A few months later while climbing a mountain he actually did step off into space and was killed.

Anyone who has seen these things happen over and over again in every conceivable shade of dramatic intensity is bound to ponder. He becomes aware how easy it is to overlook the regulating influences, and that he should endeavour to pay attention to the unconscious regulation which is so necessary for our mental and physical health. Accordingly he will try to help himself by practising self-observation and self-criticism. But mere self-observation and intellectual self-analysis are entirely inadequate as a means to establishing contact with the unconscious. Although no human being can be spared bad experiences, everyone shrinks from risking them, especially if he sees any way by which they might be circumvented. Knowledge of the regulating influences of the unconscious offers just such a possibility and actually does render much bad experience unnecessary. We can avoid a great many detours that are distinguished by no particular attraction but only by tiresome conflicts. It is bad enough to make detours and painful mistakes in unknown and unexplored territory, but to get lost in inhabited country on broad highways is merely exasperating. What, then, are the means at our disposal of obtaining knowledge of the regulating factors?

If there is no capacity to produce fantasies freely, we have to resort to artificial aid. The reason for invoking such aid is generally a depressed or disturbed state of mind for which no adequate cause can be found. Naturally the patient can give any number of rationalistic reasons—the bad weather alone suffices as a reason. But none of them is really satisfying as an explanation, for a causal explanation of these states is usually satisfying only to an outsider, and then only up to a point. The outsider is content if his causal requirements are more or less satisfied; it is sufficient for him to know where the thing comes from; he does not feel the challenge which, for the patient, lies in the depression. The patient would like to know what it is all for and how to gain relief. *In the intensity of the emotional disturbance itself lies the value, the energy which he should have at his*

*disposal in order to remedy the state of reduced adaptation.*
Nothing is achieved by repressing this state or devaluing it
rationally.

In order, therefore, to gain possession of the energy that
is in the wrong place, he must make the emotional state the
basis or starting point of the procedure. He must make himself as conscious as possible of the mood he is in, sinking
himself in it without reserve and noting down on paper all
the fantasies and other associations that come up. Fantasy
must be allowed the freest possible play, yet not in such a
manner that it leaves the orbit of its object, namely the
affect, by setting off a kind of "chain-reaction" association
process. This "free association," as Freud called it, leads
away from the object to all sorts of complexes, and one can
never be sure that they relate to the affect and are not dis-
placements which have appeared in its stead. Out of this
preoccupation with the object there comes a more or less
complete expression of the mood, which reproduces the
content of the depression in some way, either concretely or
symbolically. Since the depression was not manufactured by
the conscious mind but is an unwelcome intrusion from the
unconscious, the elaboration of the mood is, as it were, a
picture of the contents and tendencies of the unconscious
that were massed together in the depression. The whole
procedure is a kind of enrichment and clarification of the
affect, whereby the affect and its contents are brought
nearer to consciousness, becoming at the same time more
impressive and more understandable. This work by itself
can have a favourable and vitalizing influence. At all
events, it creates a new situation, since the previously unrelated affect has become a more or less clear and articulate
idea, thanks to the assistance and co-operation of the conscious mind. This is the beginning of the transcendent function, i.e., of the collaboration of conscious and unconscious
data.

The emotional disturbance can also be dealt with in another way, not by clarifying it intellectually but by giving it

visible shape. Patients who possess some talent for drawing or painting can give expression to their mood by means of a picture. It is not important for the picture to be technically or aesthetically satisfying, but merely for the fantasy to have free play and for the whole thing to be done as well as possible. In principle this procedure agrees with the one first described. Here too a product is created which is influenced by both conscious and unconscious, embodying the striving of the unconscious for the light and the striving of the conscious for substance.

Often, however, we find cases where there is no tangible mood or depression at all, but just a general, dull discontent, a feeling of resistance to everything, a sort of boredom or vague disgust, an indefinable but excruciating emptiness. In these cases no definite starting point exists—it would first have to be created. Here a special introversion of libido is necessary, supported perhaps by favourable external conditions, such as complete rest, especially at night, when the libido has in any case a tendency to introversion. (" 'Tis night: now do all fountains speak louder. And my soul also is a bubbling fountain." [2])

Critical attention must be eliminated. Visual types should concentrate on the expectation that an inner image will be produced. As a rule such a fantasy-picture will actually appear—perhaps hypnagogically—and should be carefully observed and noted down in writing. Audio-verbal types usually hear inner words, perhaps mere fragments of apparently meaningless sentences to begin with, which however should be carefully noted down too. Others at such times simply hear their "other" voice. There are, indeed, not a few people who are well aware that they possess a sort of inner critic or judge who immediately comments on everything they say or do. Insane people hear this voice directly as auditory hallucinations. But normal people too, if their inner life is fairly well developed, are able to repro-

[2] [Nietzsche, *Thus Spake Zarathustra*, XXXI; Common translation, p. 156.—EDITORS OF *The Collected Works*.]

duce this inaudible voice without difficulty, though as it is notoriously irritating and refractory it is almost always repressed. Such persons have little difficulty in procuring the unconscious material and thus laying the foundation of the transcendent function.

There are others, again, who neither see nor hear anything inside themselves, but whose hands have the knack of giving expression to the contents of the unconscious. Such people can profitably work with plastic materials. Those who are able to express the unconscious by means of bodily movements are rather rare. The disadvantage that movements cannot easily be fixed in the mind must be met by making careful drawings of the movements afterwards, so that they shall not be lost to the memory. Still rarer, but equally valuable, is automatic writing, direct or with the planchette. This, too, yields useful results.

We now come to the next question: what is to be done with the material obtained in one of the manners described. To this question there is no *a priori* answer; it is only when the conscious mind confronts the products of the unconscious that a provisional reaction will ensue which determines the subsequent procedure. Practical experience alone can give us a clue. So far as my experience goes, there appear to be two main tendencies. One is the way of *creative formulation,* the other the way of *understanding.*

Where the principle of creative formulation predominates, the material is continually varied and increased until a kind of condensation of motifs into more or less stereotyped symbols takes place. These stimulate the creative fantasy and serve chiefly as aesthetic motifs. This tendency leads to the aesthetic problem of artistic formulation.

Where, on the other hand, the principle of understanding predominates, the aesthetic aspect is of relatively little interest and may occasionally even be felt as a hindrance. Instead, there is an intensive struggle to understand the *meaning* of the unconscious product.

Whereas aesthetic formulation tends to concentrate on

the formal aspect of the motif, an intuitive understanding often tries to catch the meaning from barely adequate hints in the material, without considering those elements which would come to light in a more careful formulation.

Neither of these tendencies can be brought about by an arbitrary effort of will; they are far more the result of the peculiar make-up of the individual personality. Both have their typical dangers and may lead one astray. The danger of the aesthetic tendency is overvaluation of the formal or "artistic" worth of the fantasy-productions; the libido is diverted from the real goal of the transcendent function and sidetracked into purely aesthetic problems of artistic expression. The danger of wanting to understand the meaning is overvaluation of the content, which is subjected to intellectual analysis and interpretation, so that the essentially symbolic character of the product is lost. Up to a point these bypaths must be followed in order to satisfy aesthetic or intellectual requirements, whichever predominate in the individual case. But the danger of both these bypaths is worth stressing, for, after a certain point of psychic development has been reached, the products of the unconscious are greatly overvalued precisely because they were boundlessly undervalued before. This undervaluation is one of the greatest obstacles in formulating the unconscious material. It reveals the collective standards by which anything individual is judged: nothing is considered good or beautiful that does not fit into the collective schema, though it is true that contemporary art is beginning to make compensatory efforts in this respect. What is lacking is not the collective recognition of the individual product but its subjective appreciation, the understanding of its meaning and value for the *subject*. This feeling of inferiority for one's own product is of course not the rule everywhere. Sometimes we find the exact opposite: a naïve and uncritical overvaluation coupled with the demand for collective recognition once the initial feeling of inferiority has been overcome. Conversely, an initial overvaluation can easily turn into depreciatory scepticism. These erroneous judgments are due to the individual's unconsciousness and lack of self-reliance: either he is able to judge only by collective standards, or else, owing to ego-inflation, he loses his capacity for judgment altogether.

*One tendency seems to be the regulating principle of the other;* both are bound together in a compensatory relationship. Experience bears out this formula. So far as it is possible at this stage to draw more general conclusions, we could say that aesthetic formulation needs understanding of the meaning, and understanding needs aesthetic formulation. The two supplement each other to form the transcendent function.

The first steps along both paths follow the same principle: consciousness puts its media of expression at the disposal of the unconscious content. It must not do more than this at first, so as not to exert undue influence. In giving the content form, the lead must be left as far as possible to the chance ideas and associations thrown up by the unconscious. This is naturally something of a setback for the conscious standpoint and is often felt as painful. It is not difficult to understand this when we remember how the contents of the unconscious usually present themselves: as things which are too weak by nature to cross the threshold, or as incompatible elements that were repressed for a variety of reasons. Mostly they are unwelcome, unexpected, irrational contents, disregard or repression of which seems altogether understandable. Only a small part of them has any unusual value, either from the collective or from the subjective standpoint. But contents that are collectively valueless may be exceedingly valuable when seen from the standpoint of the individual. This fact expresses itself in their affective tone, no matter whether the subject feels it as negative or positive. Society, too, is divided in its acceptance of new and unknown ideas which obtrude their emotionality. The purpose of the initial procedure is to discover the feeling-toned contents, for in these cases we are always

294 : *The Structure and Dynamics of the Psyche*

dealing with situations where the one-sidedness of consciousness meets with the resistance of the instinctual
sphere.

The two ways do not divide until the aesthetic problem
becomes decisive for the one type of person and the intel-
lectual-moral problem for the other. The ideal case would
be if these two aspects could exist side by side or rhythmi-
cally succeed each other; that is, if there were an alternation of creation and understanding. It hardly seems possible
for the one to exist without the other, though it sometimes
does happen in practice: the creative urge seizes possession
of the object at the cost of its meaning, or the urge to
understand overrides the necessity of giving it form. The
unconscious contents want first of all to be seen clearly,
which can only be done by giving them shape, and to be
judged only when everything they have to say is tangibly
present. It was for this reason that Freud got the dream-
contents, as it were, to express themselves in the form of
"free associations" before he began interpreting them.

It does not suffice in all cases to elucidate only the conceptual context of a dream-content. Often it is necessary to
clarify a vague content by giving it a visible form. This can
be done by drawing, painting, or modelling. Often the
hands know how to solve a riddle with which the intellect
has wrestled in vain. By shaping it, one goes on dreaming
the dream in greater detail in the waking state, and the
initially incomprehensible, isolated event is integrated into
the sphere of the total personality, even though it remains
at first unconscious to the subject. Aesthetic formulation
leaves it at that and gives up any idea of discovering a
meaning. This sometimes leads patients to fancy themselves
artists—misunderstood ones, naturally. The desire to understand, if it dispenses with careful formulation, starts with
the chance idea or association and therefore lacks an adequate basis. It has better prospects of success if it begins
only with the formulated product. The less the initial material is shaped and developed, the greater is the danger that

understanding will be governed not by the empirical facts but by theoretical and moral considerations. The kind of understanding with which we are concerned at this stage consists in a reconstruction of the meaning that seems to be immanent in the original "chance" idea.

It is evident that such a procedure can legitimately take place only when there is a sufficient motive for it. Equally, the lead can be left to the unconscious only if it already contains the will to lead. This naturally happens only when the conscious mind finds itself in a critical situation. Once the unconscious content has been given form and the meaning of the formulation is understood, the question arises as to how the ego will relate to this position, and how the ego and the unconscious are to come to terms. This is the second and more important stage of the procedure, the bringing together of opposites for the production of a third: the transcendent function. At this stage it is no longer the unconscious that takes the lead, but the ego.

We shall not define the individual ego here, but shall leave it in its banal reality as that continuous centre of consciousness whose presence has made itself felt since the days of childhood. It is confronted with a psychic product that owes its existence mainly to an unconscious process and is therefore in some degree opposed to the ego and its tendencies.

This standpoint is essential in coming to terms with the unconscious. The position of the ego must be maintained as being of equal value to the counter-position of the unconscious, and vice versa. This amounts to a very necessary warning: for just as the conscious mind of civilized man has a restrictive effect on the unconscious, so the rediscovered unconscious often has a really dangerous effect on the ego. In the same way that the ego suppressed the unconscious before, a liberated unconscious can thrust the ego aside and overwhelm it. There is a danger of the ego losing its head, so to speak, that it will not be able to defend itself against the pressure of affective factors—a situation often encountered at the beginning of schizophrenia. This danger would not exist, or would not be so acute, if the process of having it out with the unconscious could somehow divest the affects of their dynamism. And this is what does in fact happen when the counter-position is aestheticized or intellectualized. But the confrontation with the unconscious must be a many-sided one, for the transcendent function is not a partial process running a conditioned course; it is a total and integral event in which all aspects are, or should be, included. The affect must therefore be deployed in its full strength. Aestheticization and intellectualization are excellent weapons against dangerous affects, but they should be used only when there is a vital threat, and not for the purpose of avoiding a necessary task.

Thanks to the fundamental insight of Freud, we know that emotional factors must be given full consideration in the treatment of the neuroses. The personality *as a whole* must be taken seriously into account, and this applies to both parties, the patient as well as the analyst. How far the latter may hide behind the shield of theory remains a delicate question, to be left to his discretion. At all events, the treatment of neurosis is not a kind of psychological water-cure, but a renewal of the personality, working in every direction and penetrating every sphere of life. Coming to terms with the counter-position is a serious matter on which sometimes a very great deal depends. Taking the other side seriously is an essential prerequisite of the process, for only in that way can the regulating factors exert an influence on our actions. Taking it seriously does not mean taking it literally, but it does mean giving the unconscious credit, so that it has a chance to co-operate with consciousness instead of automatically disturbing it.

Thus, in coming to terms with the unconscious, not only is the standpoint of the ego justified, but the unconscious is granted the same authority. The ego takes the lead, but the unconscious must be allowed to have its say too— *audiatur et altera pars.*

The way this can be done is best shown by those cases in which the "other" voice is more or less distinctly heard. For such people it is technically very simple to note down the "other" voice in writing and to answer its statements from the standpoint of the ego. It is exactly as if a dialogue were taking place between two human beings with equal rights, each of whom gives the other credit for a valid argument and considers it worth-while to modify the conflicting standpoints by means of thorough comparison and discussion or else to distinguish them clearly from one another. Since the way to agreement seldom stands open, in most cases a long conflict will have to be borne, demanding sacrifices from both sides. Such a rapprochement could just as well take place between patient and analyst, the role of devil's advocate easily falling to the latter.

The present day shows with appalling clarity how little able people are to let the other man's argument count, although this capacity is a fundamental and indispensable condition for any human community. Everyone who proposes to come to terms with himself must reckon with this basic problem. For, to the degree that he does not admit the validity of the other person, he denies the "other" within himself the right to exist—and vice versa. The capacity for inner dialogue is a touchstone for outer objectivity.

Simple as the process of coming to terms may be in the case of the inner dialogue, it is undoubtedly more complicated in other cases where only visual products are available, speaking a language which is eloquent enough for one who understands it, but which seems like deaf-and-dumb language to one who does not. Faced with such products, the ego must seize the initiative and ask: "How am I affected by this sign?" [3] This Faustian question can call forth an illuminating answer. The more direct and natural the answer is, the more valuable it will be, for directness and naturalness guarantee a more or less total reaction. It

[3] [Cf. *Faust,* Part I, translated by Philip Wayne (Harmondsworth, England, 1949), p. 46.—EDITORS OF *The Collected Works.*]

is not absolutely necessary for the process of confrontation itself to become conscious in every detail. Very often a total reaction does not have at its disposal those theoretical assumptions, views, and concepts which would make clear apprehension possible. In such cases one must be content with the wordless but suggestive feelings which appear in their stead and are more valuable than clever talk.

The shuttling to and fro of arguments and affects represents the transcendent function of opposites. The confrontation of the two positions generates a tension charged with energy and creates a living, third thing—not a logical still-birth in accordance with the principle *tertium non datur* but a movement out of the suspension between opposites, a living birth that leads to a new level of being, a new situation. The transcendent function manifests itself as a quality of conjoined opposites. So long as these are kept apart —naturally for the purpose of avoiding conflict—they do not function and remain inert.

In whatever form the opposites appear in the individual, at bottom it is always a matter of a consciousness lost and obstinately stuck in one-sidedness, confronted with the image of instinctive wholeness and freedom. This presents a picture of the anthropoid and archaic man with, on the one hand, his supposedly uninhibited world of instinct and, on the other, his often misunderstood world of spiritual ideas, who, compensating and correcting our one-sidedness, emerges from the darkness and shows us how and where we have deviated from the basic pattern and crippled ourselves psychically.

I must content myself here with a description of the outward forms and possibilities of the transcendent function. Another task of greater importance would be the description of its *contents*. There is already a mass of material on this subject, but not all the difficulties in the way of exposition have yet been overcome. A number of preparatory studies are still needed before the conceptual foundation is laid which would enable us to give a clear and intelligible account of the contents of the transcendent function. I have unfortunately had the experience that the scientific public are not everywhere in a position to follow a purely psychological argument, since they either take it too personally or are bedevilled by philosophical or intellectual prejudices. This renders any meaningful appreciation of the psychological factors quite impossible. If people take it personally their judgment is always subjective, and they declare everything to be impossible which seems not to apply in their case or which they prefer not to acknowledge. They are quite incapable of realizing that what is valid for them may not be valid at all for another person with a different psychology. We are still very far from possessing a general valid scheme of explanation in all cases.

One of the greatest obstacles to psychological understanding is the inquisitive desire to know whether the psychological factor adduced is "true" or "correct." If the description of it is not erroneous or false, then the factor is valid in itself and proves its validity by its very existence. One might just as well ask if the duck-billed platypus is a "true" or "correct" invention of the Creator's will. Equally childish is the prejudice against the role which mythological assumptions play in the life of the psyche. Since they are not "true," it is argued, they have no place in a scientific explanation. But mythologems *exist,* even though their statements do not coincide with our incommensurable idea of "truth."

As the process of coming to terms with the counter-position has a total character, nothing is excluded. Everything takes part in the discussion, even if only fragments become conscious. Consciousness is continually widened through the confrontation with previously unconscious contents, or—to be more accurate—could be widened if it took the trouble to integrate them. That is naturally not always the case. Even if there is sufficient intelligence to understand the procedure, there may yet be a lack of courage and self-confidence, or one is too lazy, mentally and morally, or too cowardly, to make an effort. But where the necessary premises exist, the transcendent function not only forms a valuable addition to psychotherapeutic treatment, but gives the patient the inestimable advantage of assisting the analyst on his own resources, and of breaking a dependence which is often felt as humiliating. It is a way of attaining liberation by one's own efforts and of finding the courage to be oneself.

## ❦ *10* ❧

### *On the Relation of Analytical Psychology to Poetry*[1]

In spite of its difficulty, the task of discussing the relation of analytical psychology to poetry affords me a welcome opportunity to define my views on the much debated question of the relations between psychology and art in general. Although the two things cannot be compared, the close connections which undoubtedly exist between them call for investigation. These connections arise from the fact that the practice of art is a psychological activity and, as such, can be approached from a psychological angle. Considered in this light, art, like any other human activity deriving from psychic motives, is a proper subject for psychology. This statement, however, involves a very definite limitation of

[1] From *The Spirit in Man, Art, and Literature. Collected Works,* Vol. 15, pars. 97–132. [A lecture delivered to the Society for German Language and Literature, Zurich, May, 1922. First published as "Über die Beziehungen der analytischen Psychologie zum dichterischen Kunstwerk," *Wissen und Leben* (Zurich), XV: 19–20 (Sept., 1922); reprinted in *Seelenprobleme der Gegenwart* (Zurich, 1931); translated by C. F. and H. G. Baynes, as "On the Relation of Analytical Psychology to Poetic Art," *British Journal of Medical Psychology* (London), III: 3 (1925), reprinted in *Contributions to Analytical Psychology* (London and New York, 1928).—Editors of *The Collected Works.*]

the psychological viewpoint when we come to apply it in practice. Only that aspect of art which consists in the process of artistic creation can be a subject for psychological study, but not that which constitutes its essential nature. The question of what art is in itself can never be answered by the psychologist, but must be approached from the side of aesthetics.

A similar distinction must be made in the realm of religion. A psychological approach is permissible only in regard to the emotions and symbols which constitute the phenomenology of religion, but which do not touch upon its essential nature. If the essence of religion and art could be explained, then both of them would become mere subdivisions of psychology. This is not to say that such violations of their nature have not been attempted. But those who are guilty of them obviously forget that a similar fate might easily befall psychology, since its intrinsic value and specific quality would be destroyed if it were regarded as a mere activity of the brain, and were relegated along with the endocrine functions to a subdivision of physiology. This too, as we know, has been attempted.

Art by its very nature is not science, and science by its very nature is not art; both these spheres of the mind have something in reserve that is peculiar to them and can be explained only in its own terms. Hence when we speak of the relation of psychology to art, we shall treat only of that aspect of art which can be submitted to psychological scrutiny without violating its nature. Whatever the psychologist has to say about art will be confined to the process of artistic creation and has nothing to do with its innermost essence. He can no more explain this than the intellect can describe or even understand the nature of feeling. Indeed, art and science would not exist as separate entities at all if the fundamental difference between them had not long since forced itself on the mind. The fact that artistic, scientific, and religious propensities still slumber peacefully together in the small child, or that with primitives the beginnings of art, science, and religion coalesce in the undifferentiated chaos of the magical mentality, or that no trace of "mind" can be found in the natural instincts of animals—all this does nothing to prove the existence of a unifying principle which alone would justify a reduction of the one to the other. For if we go so far back into the history of the mind that the distinctions between its various fields of activity become altogether invisible, we do not reach an underlying principle of their unity, but merely an earlier, undifferentiated state in which no separate activities yet exist. But the elementary state is not an explanatory principle that would allow us to draw conclusions as to the nature of later, more highly developed states, even though they must necessarily derive from it. A scientific attitude will always tend to overlook the peculiar nature of these more differentiated states in favour of their causal derivation, and will endeavour to subordinate them to a general but more elementary principle.

These theoretical reflections seem to me very much in place today, when we so often find that works of art, and particularly poetry, are interpreted precisely in this manner, by reducing them to more elementary states. Though the material he works with and its individual treatment can easily be traced back to the poet's personal relations with his parents, this does not enable us to understand his poetry. The same reduction can be made in all sorts of other fields, and not least in the case of pathological disturbances. Neuroses and psychoses are likewise reducible to infantile relations with the parents, and so are a man's good and bad habits, his beliefs, peculiarities, passions, interests, and so forth. It can hardly be supposed that all these very different things must have exactly the same explanation, for otherwise we would be driven to the conclusion that they actually are the same thing. If a work of art is explained in the same way as a neurosis, then either the work of art is a neurosis or a neurosis is a work of art. This explanation is all very well as a play on words, but sound common sense rebels against putting a work of art on the same level as a neurosis. An analyst might, in an extreme case, view a neurosis as a work of art through the lens of his professional bias, but it would never occur to an intelligent layman to mistake a pathological phenomenon for art, in spite of the undeniable fact that a work of art arises from much the same psychological conditions as a neurosis. This is only natural, because certain of these conditions are present in every individual and, owing to the relative constancy of the human environment, are constantly the same, whether in the case of a nervous intellectual, a poet, or a normal human being. All have had parents, all have a father- or a mother-complex, all know about sex and therefore have certain common and typical human difficulties. One poet may be influenced more by his relation to his father, another by the tie to his mother, while a third shows unmistakable traces of sexual repression in his poetry. Since all this can be said equally well not only of every neurotic but of every normal human being, nothing specific is gained for the judgment of a work of art. At most our knowledge of its psychological antecedents will have been broadened and deepened.

The school of medical psychology inaugurated by Freud has undoubtedly encouraged the literary historian to bring certain peculiarities of a work of art into relation with the intimate, personal life of the poet. But this is nothing new in principle, for it has long been known that the scientific treatment of art will reveal the personal threads that the artist, intentionally or unintentionally, has woven into his work. The Freudian approach may, however, make possible a more exhaustive demonstration of the influences that reach back into earliest childhood and play their part in artistic creation. To this extent the psychoanalysis of art differs in no essential from the subtle psychological nuances of a penetrating literary analysis. The difference is at most a question of degree, though we may occasionally be surprised by indiscreet references to things which a rather more delicate touch might have passed over if only for reasons of tact. This lack of delicacy seems to be a professional peculiarity of the medical psychologist, and the temptation to draw daring conclusions easily leads to flagrant abuses. A slight whiff of scandal often lends spice to a biography, but a little more becomes a nasty inquisitiveness—bad taste masquerading as science. Our interest is insidiously deflected from the work of art and gets lost in the labyrinth of psychic determinants, the poet becomes a clinical case and, very likely, yet another addition to the curiosa of *psychopathia sexualis*. But this means that the psychoanalysis of art has turned aside from its proper objective and strayed into a province that is as broad as mankind, that is not in the least specific of the artist and has even less relevance to his art.

This kind of analysis brings the work of art into the sphere of general human psychology, where many other things besides art have their origin. To explain art in these terms is just as great a platitude as the statement that "every artist is a narcissist." Every man who pursues his own goal is a "narcissist"—though one wonders how permissible it is to give such wide currency to a term specifically coined for the pathology of neurosis. The statement therefore amounts to nothing; it merely elicits the faint surprise of a *bon mot*. Since this kind of analysis is in no way concerned with the work of art itself, but strives like a mole to bury itself in the dirt as speedily as possible, it always ends up in the common earth that unites all mankind. Hence its explanations have the same tedious monotony as the recitals which one daily hears in the consulting-room.

The reductive method of Freud is a purely medical one, and the treatment is directed at a pathological or otherwise unsuitable formation which has taken the place of the normal functioning. It must therefore be broken down, and the way cleared for healthy adaptation. In this case, reduction to the common human foundation is altogether appropriate. But when applied to a work of art it leads to the results I have described. It strips the work of art of its shimmering robes and exposes the nakedness and drabness of *Homo sapiens,* to which species the poet and artist also belong. The golden gleam of artistic creation—the original object of discussion—is extinguished as soon as we apply to it the same corrosive method which we use in analyzing the fantasies of hysteria. The results are no doubt very interesting and may perhaps have the same kind of scientific value as, for instance, a post-mortem examination of the brain of Nietzsche, which might conceivably show us the particular atypical form of paralysis from which he died. But what would this have to do with *Zarathustra*? Whatever its subterranean background may have been, is it not a whole world in itself, beyond the human, all-too-human imperfections, beyond the world of migraine and cerebral atrophy?

I have spoken of Freud's reductive method but have not stated in what that method consists. It is essentially a medical technique for investigating morbid psychic phenomena, and it is solely concerned with the ways and means of getting round or peering through the foreground of consciousness in order to reach the psychic background, or the unconscious. It is based on the assumption that the neurotic patient represses certain psychic contents because they are morally incompatible with his conscious values. It follows that the repressed contents must have correspondingly negative traits—infantile-sexual, obscene, or even criminal —which make them unacceptable to consciousness. Since no man is perfect, everyone must possess such a background whether he admits it or not. Hence it can always be exposed if only one uses the technique of interpretation worked out by Freud.

In the short space of a lecture I cannot, of course, enter into the details of the technique. A few hints must suffice. The unconscious background does not remain inactive, but betrays itself by its characteristic effects on the contents of consciousness. For example, it produces fantasies of a peculiar nature, which can easily be interpreted as sexual images. Or it produces characteristic disturbances of the conscious processes, which again can be reduced to repressed contents. A very important source for knowledge of the unconscious contents is provided by dreams, since these are direct products of the activity of the unconscious. The essential thing in Freud's reductive method is to collect all the clues pointing to the unconscious background, and then, through the analysis and interpretation of this material, to reconstruct the elementary instinctual processes. Those conscious contents which give us a clue to the unconscious background are incorrectly called *symbols* by Freud. They are not true symbols, however, since according to his theory they have merely the role of *signs* or *symptoms* of the subliminal processes. The true symbol differs essentially from this, and should be understood as an expression of an intuitive idea that cannot yet be formulated in any other or better way. When Plato, for instance, puts the whole problem of the theory of knowledge in his parable of the cave, or when Christ expresses the idea of the Kingdom of Heaven in parables, these are genuine and true symbols, that is, attempts to express something for which no verbal concept yet exists. If we were to interpret Plato's metaphor in Freudian terms we would naturally arrive at the uterus, and would have proved that even a mind like Plato's was still struck on a primitive level of infantile sexuality. But we would have completely overlooked what Plato actually created out of the primitive determinants of his philosophical ideas; we would have missed the essential point and merely discovered that he had infantile-sexual fantasies like any other mortal. Such a discovery could be of value only for a man who regarded Plato as superhuman, and who can now state with satisfaction that Plato too was an ordinary human being. But who would want to regard Plato as a god? Surely only one who is dominated by infantile fantasies and therefore possesses a neurotic mentality. For him the reduction to common human truths is salutary on medical grounds, but this would have nothing whatever to do with the meaning of Plato's parable.

I have purposely dwelt on the application of medical psychoanalysis to works of art because I want to emphasize that the psychoanalytic method is at the same time an essential part of the Freudian doctrine. Freud himself by his rigid dogmatism has ensured that the method and the doctrine—in themselves two very different things—are regarded by the public as identical. Yet the method may be employed with beneficial results in medical cases without at the same time exalting it into a doctrine. And against this doctrine we are bound to raise vigorous objections. The assumptions it rests on are quite arbitrary. For example, neuroses are by no means exclusively caused by sexual repression, and the same holds true for psychoses. There is no foundation for saying that dreams merely contain repressed wishes whose moral incompatibility requires them to be disguised by a hypothetical dream-censor. The Freudian technique of interpretation, so far as it remains under the influence of its own one-sided and therefore erroneous hypotheses, displays a quite obvious bias.

In order to do justice to a work of art, analytical psychology must rid itself entirely of medical prejudice; for a work of art is not a disease, and consequently requires a different approach from the medical one. A doctor naturally has to seek out the causes of a disease in order to pull it up by the roots, but just as naturally the psychologist must adopt exactly the opposite attitude towards a work of art. Instead of investigating its typically human determinants, he will inquire first of all into its meaning, and will concern himself with its determinants only in so far as they enable him to understand it more fully. Personal causes have as much or as little to do with a work of art as the soil with the plant that springs from it. We can certainly learn to understand some of the plant's peculiarities by getting to know its habitat, and for the botanist this is an important part of his equipment. But nobody will maintain that everything essential has then been discovered about the plant itself. The personal orientation which the doctor needs when confronted with the question of aetiology in medicine is quite out of place in dealing with a work of art, just because a work of art is not a human being, but is something supra-personal. It is a thing and not a personality; hence it cannot be judged by personal criteria. Indeed, the special significance of a true work of art resides in the fact that it has escaped from the limitations of the personal and has soared beyond the personal concerns of its creator.

I must confess from my own experience that it is not at all easy for a doctor to lay aside his professional bias when considering a work of art and look at it with a mind cleared of the current biological causality. But I have come to learn that although a psychology with a purely biological orientation can explain a good deal about man in general, it cannot be applied to a work of art and still less to man as creator. A purely causalistic psychology is only able to reduce every human individual to a member of the species *Homo sapiens,* since its range is limited to what is transmitted by heredity or derived from other sources. But a work of art is not transmitted or derived—it is a creative reorganization of those very conditions to which a causalistic psychology must always reduce it. The plant is not a mere product of the soil; it is a living, self-contained process which in essence has nothing to do with the character of the soil. In the same way, the meaning and individual quality of a work of art inhere within it and not in its extrinsic determinants. One might almost describe it as a living being that uses man only as a nutrient medium, employing his capacities according to its own laws and shaping itself to the fulfilment of its own creative purpose.

But here I am anticipating somewhat, for I have in mind a particular type of art which I still have to introduce. Not every work of art originates in the way I have just described. There are literary works, prose as well as poetry, that spring wholly from the author's intention to produce a particular result. He submits his material to a definite treatment with a definite aim in view; he adds to it and subtracts from it, emphasizing one effect, toning down another, laying on a touch of colour here, another there, all the time carefully considering the over-all result and paying strict attention to the laws of form and style. He exercises the keenest judgment and chooses his words with complete freedom. His material is entirely subordinated to his artistic purpose; he wants to express this and nothing else. He is wholly at one with the creative process, no matter whether he has deliberately made himself its spearhead, as it were, or whether it has made him its instrument so completely that he has lost all consciousness of this fact. In either case, the artist is so identified with his work that his intentions and his faculties are indistinguishable from the act of creation itself. There is no need, I think, to give examples of this from the history of literature or from the testimony of the artists themselves.

Nor need I cite examples of the other class of works which flow more or less complete and perfect from the author's pen. They come as it were fully arrayed into the world, as Pallas Athene sprang from the head of Zeus. These works positively force themselves upon the author; his hand is seized, his pen writes things that his mind contemplates with amazement. The work brings with it its own form; anything he wants to add is rejected, and what he himself would like to reject is thrust back at him. While his conscious mind stands amazed and empty before this phenomenon, he is overwhelmed by a flood of thoughts and images which he never intended to create and which his own will could never have brought into being. Yet in spite of himself he is forced to admit that it is his own self speaking, his own inner nature revealing itself and uttering things which he would never have entrusted to his tongue. He can only obey the apparently alien impulse within him and follow where it leads, sensing that his work is greater than himself, and wields a power which is not his and which he cannot command. Here the artist is not identical with the process of creation; he is aware that he is subordinate to his work or stands outside it, as though he were a second person; or as though a person other than himself had fallen within the magic circle of an alien will.

So when we discuss the psychology of art, we must bear in mind these two entirely different modes of creation, for much that is of the greatest importance in judging a work of art depends on this distinction. It is one that had been sensed earlier by Schiller, who as we know attempted to classify it in his concept of the *sentimental* and the *naïve*. The psychologist would call "sentimental" art *introverted* and the "naïve" kind *extraverted*. The introverted attitude is characterized by the subject's assertion of his conscious intentions and aims against the demands of the object, whereas the extraverted attitude is characterized by the subject's subordination to the demands which the object makes upon him. In my view, Schiller's plays and most of his poems give one a good idea of the introverted attitude: the material is mastered by the conscious intentions of the poet. The extraverted attitude is illustrated by the second part of *Faust*: here the material is distinguished by its refractoriness. A still more striking example is Nietzsche's *Zarathustra,* where the author himself observed how "one became two."

From what I have said, it will be apparent that a shift of psychological standpoint has taken place as soon as one speaks not of the poet as a person but of the creative process that moves him. When the focus of interest shifts to the latter, the poet comes into the picture only as a reacting subject. This is immediately evident in our second category of works, where the consciousness of the poet is not identical with the creative process. But in works of the first category the opposite appears to hold true. Here the poet appears to be the creative process itself, and to create of his own free will without the slightest feeling of compulsion.

He may even be fully convinced of his freedom of action and refuse to admit that his work could be anything else than the expression of his will and ability.

Here we are faced with a question which we cannot answer from the testimony of the poets themselves. It is really a scientific problem that psychology alone can solve. As I hinted earlier, it might well be that the poet, while apparently creating out of himself and producing what he consciously intends, is nevertheless so carried away by the creative impulse that he is no longer aware of an "alien" will, just as the other type of poet is no longer aware of his own will speaking to him in the apparently "alien" inspiration, although this is manifestly the voice of his own self. The poet's conviction that he is creating in absolute freedom would then be an illusion: he fancies he is swimming, but in reality an unseen current sweeps him along.

This is not by any means an academic question, but is supported by the evidence of analytical psychology. Researches have shown that there are all sorts of ways in which the conscious mind is not only influenced by the unconscious but actually guided by it. Yet is there any evidence for the supposition that a poet, despite his self-awareness, may be taken captive by his work? The proof may be of two kinds, direct or indirect. Direct proof would be afforded by a poet who thinks he knows what he is saying but actually says more than he is aware of. Such cases are not uncommon. Indirect proof would be found in cases where behind the apparent free will of the poet there stands a higher imperative that renews its peremptory demands as soon as the poet voluntarily gives up his creative activity, or that produces psychic complications whenever his work has to be broken off against his will.

Analysis of artists consistently shows not only the strength of the creative impulse arising from the unconscious, but also its capricious and wilful character. The biographies of great artists make it abundantly clear that the creative urge is often so imperious that it battens on their humanity and yokes everything to the service of the work, even at the cost of health and ordinary human happiness. The unborn work in the psyche of the artist is a force of nature that achieves its end either with tyrannical might or with the subtle cunning of nature herself, quite regardless of the personal fate of the man who is its vehicle. The creative urge lives and grows in him like a tree in the earth from which it draws its nourishment. We would do well, therefore, to think of the creative process as a living thing implanted in the human psyche. In the language of analytical psychology this living thing is an *autonomous complex*. It is a split-off portion of the psyche, which leads a life of its own outside the hierarchy of consciousness. Depending on its energy charge, it may appear either as a mere disturbance of conscious activities or as a supraordinate authority which can harness the ego to its purpose. Accordingly, the poet who identifies with the creative process would be one who acquiesces from the start when the unconscious imperative begins to function. But the other poet, who feels the creative force as something alien, is one who for various reasons cannot acquiesce and is thus caught unawares.

It might be expected that this difference in its origins would be perceptible in a work of art. For in the one case it is a conscious product shaped and designed to have the effect intended. But in the other we are dealing with an event originating in unconscious nature; with something that achieves its aim without the assistance of human consciousness, and often defies it by wilfully insisting on its own form and effect. We would therefore expect that works belonging to the first class would nowhere overstep the limits of comprehension, that their effect would be bounded by the author's intention and would not extend beyond it. But with works of the other class we would have to be prepared for something suprapersonal that transcends our understanding to the same degree that the author's consciousness was in abeyance during the process of creation.

We would expect a strangeness of form and content, thoughts that can only be apprehended intuitively, a language pregnant with meanings, and images that are true symbols because they are the best possible expressions for something unknown—bridges thrown out towards an unseen shore.

These criteria are, by and large, corroborated in practice. Whenever we are confronted with a work that was consciously planned and with material that was consciously selected, we find that it agrees with the first class of qualities, and in the other case with the second. The example we gave of Schiller's plays, on the one hand, and *Faust II* on the other, or better still *Zarathustra,* is an illustration of this. But I would not undertake to place the work of an unknown poet in either of these categories without first having examined rather closely his personal relations with his work. It is not enough to know whether the poet belongs to the introverted or to the extraverted type, since it is possible for either type to work with an introverted attitude at one time, and an extraverted attitude at another. This is particularly noticeable in the difference between Schiller's plays and his philosophical writings, between Goethe's perfectly formed poems and the obvious struggle with his material in *Faust II,* and between Nietzsche's well-turned aphorisms and the rushing torrent of *Zarathustra.* The same poet can adopt different attitudes to his work at different times, and on this depends the standard we have to apply.

The question, as we now see, is exceedingly complicated, and the complication grows even worse when we consider the case of the poet who identifies with the creative process. For should it turn out that the apparently conscious and purposeful manner of composition is a subjective illusion of the poet, then his work would possess symbolic qualities that are outside the range of his consciousness. They would only be more difficult to detect, because the reader as well would be unable to get beyond the bounds of the poet's consciousness which are fixed by the spirit of the time. There is no Archimedean point outside his world by which he could lift his time-bound consciousness off its hinges and recognize the symbols hidden in the poet's work. For a symbol is the intimation of a meaning beyond the level of our present powers of comprehension.

I raise this question only because I do not want my typological classification to limit the possible significance of works of art which apparently mean no more than what they say. But we have often found that a poet who has gone out of fashion is suddenly rediscovered. This happens when our conscious development has reached a higher level from which the poet can tell us something new. It was always present in his work but was hidden in a symbol, and only a renewal of the spirit of the time permits us to read its meaning. It needed to be looked at with fresher eyes, for the old ones could see in it only what they were accustomed to see. Experiences of this kind should make us cautious, as they bear out my earlier argument. But works that are openly symbolic do not require this subtle approach; their pregnant language cries out at us that they mean more than they say. We can put our finger on the symbol at once, even though we may not be able to unriddle its meaning to our entire satisfaction. A symbol remains a perpetual challenge to our thoughts and feelings. That probably explains why a symbolic work is so stimulating, why it grips us so intensely, but also why it seldom affords us a purely aesthetic enjoyment. A work that is manifestly not symbolic appeals much more to our aesthetic sensibility because it is complete in itself and fulfils its purpose.

What then, you may ask, can analytical psychology contribute to our fundamental problem, which is the mystery of artistic creation? All that we have said so far has to do only with the psychological phenomenology of art. Since nobody can penetrate to the heart of nature, you will not expect psychology to do the impossible and offer a valid explanation of the secret of creativity. Like every other science, psychology has only a modest contribution to make towards a deeper understanding of the phenomena of life, and is no nearer than its sister sciences to absolute knowledge.

We have talked so much about the meaning of works of art that one can hardly suppress a doubt as to whether art really "means" anything at all. Perhaps art has no "meaning," at least not as we understand meaning. Perhaps it is like nature, which simply *is* and "means" nothing beyond that. Is "meaning" necessarily more than mere interpretation—an interpretation secreted into something by an intellect hungry for meaning? Art, it has been said, is beauty, and "a thing of beauty is a joy for ever." It needs no meaning, for meaning has nothing to do with art. Within the sphere of art, I must accept the truth of this statement. But when I speak of the relation of psychology to art we are outside its sphere, and it is impossible for us not to speculate. We must interpret, we must find meanings in things, otherwise we would be quite unable to think about them. We have to break down life and events, which are self-contained processes, into meanings, images, concepts, well knowing that in doing so we are getting further away from the living mystery. As long as we ourselves are caught up in the process of creation, we neither see nor understand; indeed we ought not to understand, for nothing is more injurious to immediate experience than cognition. But for the purpose of cognitive understanding we must detach ourselves from the creative process and look at it from the outside; only then does it become an image that expresses what we are bound to call "meaning." What was a mere phenomenon before becomes something that in association with other phenomena has meaning, that has a definite role to play, serves certain ends, and exerts meaningful effects. And when we have seen all this we get the feeling of having understood and explained something. In this way we meet the demands of science.

When, a little earlier, we spoke of a work of art as a

tree growing out of the nourishing soil, we might equally well have compared it to a child growing in the womb. But as all comparisons are lame, let us stick to the more precise terminology of science. You will remember that I described the nascent work in the psyche of the artist as an autonomous complex. By this we mean a psychic formation that remains subliminal until its energy-charge is sufficient to carry it over the threshold into consciousness. Its association with consciousness does not mean that it is assimilated, only that it is perceived; but it is not subject to conscious control, and can be neither inhibited nor voluntarily reproduced. Therein lies the autonomy of the complex: it appears and disappears in accordance with its own inherent tendencies, independently of the conscious will. The creative complex shares this peculiarity with every other autonomous complex. In this respect it offers an analogy with pathological processes, since these too are characterized by the presence of autonomous complexes, particularly in the case of mental disturbances. The divine frenzy of the artist comes perilously close to a pathological state, though the two things are not identical. The *tertium comparationis* is the autonomous complex. But the presence of autonomous complexes is not in itself pathological, since normal people, too, fall temporarily or permanently under their domination. This fact is simply one of the normal peculiarities of the psyche, and for a man to be unaware of the existence of an autonomous complex merely betrays a high degree of unconsciousness. Every typical attitude that is to some extent differentiated shows a tendency to become an autonomous complex, and in most cases it actually does. Again, every instinct has more or less the character of an autonomous complex. In itself, therefore, an autonomous complex has nothing morbid about it; only when its manifestations are frequent and disturbing is it a symptom of illness.

How does an autonomous complex arise? For reasons which we cannot go into here, a hitherto unconscious portion of the psyche is thrown into activity, and gains ground

by activating the adjacent areas of association. The energy
needed for this is naturally drawn from consciousness—unless the latter happens to identify with the complex. But
where this does not occur, the drain of energy produces
what Janet calls an *abaissement du niveau mental.* The intensity of conscious interests and activities gradually dimin-
ishes, leading either to apathy—a condition very common
with artists—or to a regressive development of the conscious functions, that is, they revert to an infantile and
archaic level and undergo something like a degeneration.
The "inferior parts of the functions," as Janet calls them,
push to the fore; the instinctual side of the personality
prevails over the ethical, the infantile over the mature, and
the unadapted over the adapted. This too is something we
see in the lives of many artists. The autonomous complex
thus develops by using the energy that has been withdrawn
from the conscious control of the personality.

But in what does an autonomous *creative* complex consist? Of this we can know next to nothing so long as the
artist's work affords us no insight into its foundations. The
work presents us with a finished picture, and this picture
is amenable to analysis only to the extent that we can recognize it as a symbol. But if we are unable to discover any
symbolic value in it, we have merely established that, so
far as we are concerned, it means no more than what it
says, or to put it another way, that it *is* no more than what
it *seems* to be. I use the word "seems" because our own
bias may prevent a deeper appreciation of it. At any rate
we can find no incentive and no starting-point for an analysis. But in the case of a symbolic work we should remember the dictum of Gerhard Hauptmann: "Poetry evokes
out of words the resonance of the primordial word." The
question we should ask, therefore, is: "What primordial
image lies behind the imagery of art?"

This question needs a little elucidation. I am assuming
that the work of art we propose to analyze, as well as being
symbolic, has its source not in the *personal unconscious* of

the poet, but in a sphere of unconscious mythology whose primordial images are the common heritage of mankind. I have called this sphere the *collective unconscious,* to distinguish it from the personal unconscious. The latter I regard as the sum total of all those psychic processes and contents which are capable of becoming conscious and often do, but are then suppressed because of their incompatibility and kept subliminal. Art receives tributaries from this sphere too, but muddy ones; and their predominance, far from making a work of art a symbol, merely turns it into a symptom. We can leave this kind of art without injury and without regret to the purgative methods employed by Freud.

In contrast to the personal unconscious, which is a relatively thin layer immediately below the threshold of consciousness, the collective unconscious shows no tendency to become conscious under normal conditions, nor can it be brought back to recollection by any analytical technique, since it was never repressed or forgotten. The collective unconscious is not to be thought of as a self-subsistent entity; it is no more than a potentiality handed down to us from primordial times in the specific form of mnemonic images or inherited in the anatomical structure of the brain. There are no inborn ideas, but there are inborn possibilities of ideas that set bounds to even the boldest fantasy and keep our fantasy activity within certain categories: *a priori* ideas, as it were, the existence of which cannot be ascertained except from their effects. They appear only in the shaped material of art as the regulative principles that shape it; that is to say, only by inferences drawn from the finished work can we reconstruct the age-old original of the primordial image.

The primordial image, or archetype, is a figure—be it a daemon, a human being, or a process—that constantly recurs in the course of history and appears wherever creative fantasy is freely expressed. Essentially, therefore, it is a mythological figure. When we examine these images more

closely, we find that they give form to countless typical experiences of our ancestors. They are, so to speak, the
psychic residua of innumerable experiences of the same
type. They present a picture of psychic life in the average,
divided up and projected into the manifold figures of the
mythological pantheon. But the mythological figures are
themselves products of creative fantasy and still have to be
translated into conceptual language. Only the beginnings
of such a language exist, but once the necessary concepts
are created they could give us an abstract, scientific understanding of the unconscious processes that lie at the roots
of the primordial images. In each of these images there is
a little piece of human psychology and human fate, a remnant of the joys and sorrows that have been repeated
countless times in our ancestral history, and on the average
follow ever the same course. It is like a deeply graven river-
bed in the psyche, in which the waters of life, instead of
flowing along as before in a broad but shallow stream, suddenly swell into a mighty river. This happens whenever that
particular set of circumstances is encountered which over
long periods of time has helped to lay down the primordial image.

The moment when this mythological situation reappears
is always characterized by a peculiar emotional intensity;
it is as though chords in us were struck that had never
resounded before, or as though forces whose existence we
never suspected were unloosed. What makes the struggle
for adaptation so laborious is the fact that we have constantly to be dealing with individual and atypical situations.
So it is not surprising that when an archetypal situation
occurs we suddenly feel an extraordinary sense of release,
as though transported, or caught up by an overwhelming
power. At such moments we are no longer individuals, but
the race; the voice of all mankind resounds in us. The individual man cannot use his powers to the full unless he is
aided by one of those collective representations we call
ideals, which releases all the hidden forces of instinct that

are inaccessible to his conscious will. The most effective ideals are always fairly obvious variants of an archetype, as is evident from the fact that they lend themselves to allegory. The ideal of the "mother country," for instance, is an obvious allegory of the mother, as is the "fatherland" of the father. Its power to stir us does not derive from the allegory, but from the symbolical value of our native land. The archetype here is the *participation mystique* of primitive man with the soil on which he dwells, and which contains the spirits of his ancestors.

The impact of an archetype, whether it takes the form of immediate experience or is expressed through the spoken word, stirs us because it summons up a voice that is stronger than our own. Whoever speaks in primordial images speaks with a thousand voices; he enthrals and overpowers, while at the same time he lifts the idea he is seeking to express out of the occasional and the transitory into the realm of the ever-enduring. He transmutes our personal destiny into the destiny of mankind, and evokes in us all those beneficent forces that ever and anon have enabled humanity to find a refuge from every peril and to outlive the longest night.

That is the secret of great art, and of its effect upon us. The creative process, so far as we are able to follow it at all, consists in the unconscious activation of an archetypal image, and in elaborating and shaping this image into the finished work. By giving it shape, the artist translates it into the language of the present, and so makes it possible for us to find our way back to the deepest springs of life. Therein lies the social significance of art: it is constantly at work educating the spirit of the age, conjuring up the forms in which the age is most lacking. The unsatisfied yearning of the artist reaches back to the primordial image in the unconscious which is best fitted to compensate the inadequacy and one-sidedness of the present. The artist seizes on this image, and in raising it from deepest unconsciousness he brings it into relation with conscious values, thereby transforming it until it can be accepted by the minds of his contemporaries according to their powers.

Peoples and times, like individuals, have their own characteristic tendencies and attitudes. The very word "attitude" betrays the necessary bias that every marked tendency entails. Direction implies exclusion, and exclusion means that very many psychic elements that could play their part in life are denied the right to exist because they are incompatible with the general attitude. The normal man can follow the general trend without injury to himself; but the man who takes to the back streets and alleys because he cannot endure the broad highway will be the first to discover the psychic elements that are waiting to play their part in the life of the collective. Here the artist's relative lack of adaptation turns out to his advantage; it enables him to follow his own yearnings far from the beaten path, and to discover what it is that would meet the unconscious needs of his age. Thus, just as the one-sidedness of the individual's conscious attitude is corrected by reactions from the unconscious, so art represents a process of self-regulation in the life of nations and epochs.

I am aware that in this lecture I have only been able to sketch out my views in the barest outline. But I hope that what I have been obliged to omit, that is to say their practical application to poetic works of art, has been furnished by your own thoughts, thus giving flesh and blood to my abstract intellectual frame.

# ⚜ 11 ⚜

## Individual Dream Symbolism
## in Relation to Alchemy[1]

### A Study of the Unconscious Processes
### at Work in Dreams

> . . . *facilis descensus Averno;*
> *noctes atque dies patet atri ianua Ditis;*
> *sed revocare gradum superasque evadere ad auras, hoc*
> *opus, hic labor est.* . . .
> —Virgil, *Aeneid,* VI, 126–29

> . . . easy is the descent to Avernus: night and day the
> door of gloomy Dis stands open; but to recall thy steps
> and pass out to the upper air, this is the task, this the toil!
> —Translated by H. R. Fairclough

[1] Volume 12 of Professor Jung's *Collected Works,* of which this article is Part II, is a translation, with minor alterations made at the instance of the author, of *Psychologie und Alchemie* (Zurich, 1944; 2nd ed., revised, 1952). That work was based on two lectures, "Traumsymbole des Individuationsprozesses," *Eranos-Jahrbuch* 1935 (Zurich, 1936), and "Die Erlösungsvorstellungen in der Alchemie," *Eranos-Jahrbuch* 1936 (Zurich, 1937). These were translated by Stanley Dell and published in *The Integration of the Personality* (New York, 1939; London, 1940) under the titles "Dream Symbols of the Process of Individuation" and "The Idea of Redemption in Alchemy." Professor Jung then considerably expanded them and added an introduction, in which he set out his whole position particularly in relation to religion. These three parts together with a short epilogue make up the Swiss volume, of which *Collected Works,* Vol. 12, is a translation.—J.C.

## 1. *Introduction*

### I. *The Material*

The symbols of the process of individuation that appear in dreams are images of an archetypal nature which depict the centralizing process or the production of a new centre of personality. A general idea of this process may be got from my essay, "The Relations between the Ego and the Unconscious." [2] For certain reasons mentioned there I call this centre the "self," which should be understood as the totality of the psyche. The self is not only the centre, but also the whole circumference which embraces both conscious and unconscious; it is the centre of this totality, just as the ego is the centre of consciousness.

The symbols now under consideration are not concerned with the manifold stages and transformations of the individuation process, but with the images that refer directly and exclusively to the new centre as it comes into consciousness. These images belong to a definite category which I call mandala symbolism. In *The Secret of the Golden Flower,* published in collaboration with Richard Wilhelm, I have described this symbolism in some detail. In the present study I should like to put before you an individual series of such symbols in chronological order. The material consists of over a thousand dreams and visual impressions coming from a young man of excellent scientific education.[3] For the purposes of this study I have worked on the first four hundred dreams and visions, which covered a period of nearly ten months. In order to avoid all personal influence I asked one of my pupils, a woman doctor,

---

[2] See supra, pp. 70–138.
[3] I must emphasize that this education was not historical, philological, archaeological, or ethnological. Any references to material derived from these fields came unconsciously to the dreamer.

who was then a beginner, to undertake the observation of the process. This went on for five months. The dreamer then continued his observations alone for three months. Except for a short interview at the very beginning, before the commencement of the observation, I did not see the dreamer at all during the first eight months. Thus it happened that 355 of the dreams were dreamed away from any personal contact with myself. Only the last forty-five occurred under my observation. No interpretations worth mentioning were then attempted because the dreamer, owing to his excellent scientific training and ability, did not require any assistance. Hence conditions were really ideal for unprejudiced observation and recording.

First of all, then, I shall present extracts from the twenty-two initial dreams in order to show how the mandala symbolism makes a very early appearance and is embedded in the rest of the dream material. Later on I shall pick out in chronological order the dreams that refer specifically to the mandala.[4]

With few exceptions all the dreams have been abbreviated, either by extracting the part that carries the main thought or by condensing the whole text to essentials. This simplifying procedure has not only curtailed their length but has also removed personal allusions and complications, as was necessary for reasons of discretion. Despite this somewhat doubtful interference I have, to the best of my knowledge and scrupulosity, avoided any arbitrary distortion of meaning. The same considerations had also to apply to my own interpretation, so that certain passages in the dreams may appear to have been overlooked. Had I not made this sacrifice and kept the material absolutely complete, I should not have been in a position to publish this series, which in my opinion could hardly be surpassed in intelligence, clarity, and consistency. It therefore gives me

[4] "Mandala" (Sanskrit) means "circle," also "magic circle." Its symbolism includes—to mention only the most important forms—all concentrically arranged figures, round or square patterns with a centre, and radial or spherical arrangements.

great pleasure to express my sincere gratitude here and now to the "author" for the service he has rendered to science.

## II. *The Method*

In my writings and lectures I have always insisted that we must give up all preconceived opinions when it comes to the analysis and interpretation of the objective psyche,[5] in other words the "unconscious." We do not yet possess a general theory of dreams that would enable us to use a deductive method with impunity, any more than we possess a general theory of consciousness from which we can draw deductive conclusions. The manifestations of the subjective psyche, or consciousness, can be predicted to only the smallest degree, and there is no theoretical argument to prove beyond doubt that any causal connection necessarily exists between them. On the contrary, we have to reckon with a high percentage of arbitrariness and "chance" in the complex actions and reactions of the conscious mind. Similarly there is no empirical, still less a theoretical, reason to assume that the same does not apply to the manifestations of the unconscious. The latter are just as manifold, unpredictable, and arbitrary as the former and must therefore be subjected to as many different ways of approach. In the case of conscious utterances we are in the fortunate position of being directly addressed and presented with a content whose purpose we can recognize; but with "unconscious" manifestations there is no directed or adapted language in our sense of the word—there is merely a psychic phenomenon that would appear to have only the loosest connections with conscious contents. If the expres-

[5] For this concept see Jung, "Basic Postulates of Analytical Psychology" (*Collected Works*, Vol. 8), and Toni Wolff, "Einführung in die Grundlagen der komplexen Psychologie," in *Studien zu C. G. Jung's Psychologie* (Zurich, 1959), pp. 34ff.

sions of the conscious mind are incomprehensible we can always ask what they mean. But the objective psyche is something alien even to the conscious mind through which it expresses itself. We are therefore obliged to adopt the method we would use in deciphering a fragmentary text or one containing unknown words: we examine the context. The meaning of the unknown word may become evident when we compare a series of passages in which it occurs. The psychological context of dream-contents consists in the web of associations in which the dream is naturally embedded. Theoretically we can never know anything in advance about this web, but in practice it is sometimes possible, granted long enough experience. Even so, careful analysis will never rely too much on technical rules; the danger of deception and suggestion is too great. In the analysis of isolated dreams above all, this kind of knowing in advance and making assumptions on the grounds of practical expectation or general probability is positively wrong. It should therefore be an absolute rule to assume that every dream, and every part of a dream, is unknown at the outset, and to attempt an interpretation only after carefully taking up the context. We can then apply the meaning we have thus discovered to the text of the dream itself and see whether this yields a fluent reading, or rather whether a satisfying meaning emerges. But in no circumstances may we anticipate that this meaning will fit in with any of our subjective expectations; for quite possibly, indeed very frequently, the dream is saying something surprisingly different from what we would expect. As a matter of fact, if the meaning we find in the dream happens to coincide with our expectations, that is a reason for suspicion; for as a rule the standpoint of the unconscious is complementary or compensatory[6] to consciousness and thus unexpectedly "different." I would not deny the possibility of *parallel* dreams, i.e., dreams whose meaning coincides with or supports the

---

[6] I intentionally omit an analysis of the words "complementary" and "compensatory," as it would lead us too far afield.

conscious attitude, but, in my experience at least, these are rather rare.

Now, the method I adopt in the present study seems to run directly counter to this basic principle of dream interpretation. It looks as if the dreams were being interpreted without the least regard for the context. And in fact I have not taken up the context at all, seeing that the dreams in this series were not dreamed (as mentioned above) under my observation. I proceed rather as if I had had the dreams myself and were therefore in a position to supply the context.

This procedure, if applied to *isolated* dreams of someone unknown to me personally, would indeed be a gross technical blunder. But here we are not dealing with isolated dreams; they form a coherent series in the course of which the meaning gradually unfolds more or less of its own accord. *The series is the context which the dreamer himself supplies.* It is as if not one text but many lay before us, throwing light from all sides on the unknown terms, so that a reading of all the texts is sufficient to elucidate the difficult passages in each individual one. Moreover, in the third chapter we are concerned with a definite archetype—the mandala—that has long been known to us from other sources, and this considerably facilitates the interpretation. Of course the interpretation of each individual passage is bound to be largely conjecture, but the series as a whole gives us all the clues we need to correct any possible errors in the preceding passages.

It goes without saying that while the dreamer was under the observation of my pupil he knew nothing of these interpretations and was therefore quite unprejudiced by anybody else's opinion. Moreover I hold the view, based on wide experience, that the possibility and danger of prejudgment are exaggerated. Experience shows that the objective psyche is independent in the highest degree. Were it not so, it could not carry out its most characteristic function: the compensation of the conscious mind. The conscious mind allows itself to be trained like a parrot, but the unconscious does not—which is why St. Augustine thanked God for not making him responsible for his dreams. The unconscious is an autonomous psychic entity; any efforts to drill it are only apparently successful, and moreover are harmful to consciousness. It is and remains beyond the reach of subjective arbitrary control, in a realm where nature and her secrets can be neither improved upon nor perverted, where we can listen but may not meddle.

## 2. The Initial Dreams

*1.* DREAM:
*The dreamer is at a social gathering. On leaving, he puts on a stranger's hat instead of his own.*

The hat, as a covering for the head, has the general sense of something that epitomizes the head. Just as in summing up we bring ideas "under one head" (*unter einen Hut*), so the hat, as a sort of leading idea, covers the whole personality and imparts its own significance to it. Coronation endows the ruler with the divine nature of the sun, the doctor's hood bestows the dignity of a scholar, and a stranger's hat imparts a strange personality. Meyrink uses this theme in his novel *The Golem,* where the hero puts on the hat of Athanasius Pernath and, as a result, becomes involved in a strange experience. It is clear enough in *The Golem* that it is the unconscious which entangles the hero in fantastic adventures. Let us stress at once the significance of the *Golem* parallel and assume that the hat in the dream is the hat of an Athanasius, an immortal, a being beyond time, the universal and everlasting man as distinct from the ephemeral and "accidental" mortal man. Encircling the head, the hat is round like the sun-disc of a crown and therefore contains the first allusion to the mandala. We shall find the attribute of eternal duration confirmed in the ninth mandala dream while the mandala character of the hat comes out in the thirty-fifth mandala dream. As a general result of the exchange of hats we may expect a development similar to that in *The Golem*: an emergence of the unconscious. The unconscious with its figures is already standing like a shadow behind the dreamer and pushing its way into consciousness.

## 2. DREAM:

*The dreamer is going on a railway journey, and by standing in front of the window, he blocks the view for his fellow passengers. He must get out of their way.*

The process is beginning to move, and the dreamer discovers that he is keeping the light from those who stand *behind* him, namely the unconscious components of his personality. We have no eyes behind us; consequently "behind" is the region of the unseen, the unconscious. If the dreamer will only stop blocking the window (consciousness), the unconscious content will become conscious.

## 3. HYPNAGOGIC VISUAL IMPRESSION:

*By the sea shore. The sea breaks into the land, flooding everything. Then the dreamer is sitting on a lonely island.*

The sea is the symbol of the collective unconscious, because unfathomed depths lie concealed beneath its reflecting surface.[7] Those who stand behind, the shadowy personifications of the unconscious, have burst into the *terra firma* of consciousness like a flood. Such invasions have something uncanny about them because they are irrational and incomprehensible to the person concerned. They bring about a momentous alteration of his personality since they immediately constitute a painful personal secret which alienates and isolates him from his surroundings. It is

---

[7] The sea is a favourite place for the birth of visions (i.e., invasions by unconscious contents). Thus the great vision of the eagle in II Esdras 11 : 1 rises out of the sea, and the vision of "Man" —ἄνθρωπος—in 13 : 3, 25, and 51 comes up "from the midst of the sea." Cf. also 13 : 52: "Like as thou canst neither seek out nor know the things that are in the deep of the sea: even so can no man upon earth see my Son. . . ."

something that we "cannot tell anybody." We are afraid of being accused of mental abnormality—not without reason, for much the same thing happens to lunatics. Even so, it is a far cry from the intuitive perception of such an invasion to being inundated by it pathologically, though the layman does not realize this. Isolation by a secret results as a rule in an animation of the psychic atmosphere, as a substitute for loss of contact with other people. It causes an activation of the unconscious, and this produces something similar to the illusions and hallucinations that beset lonely wanderers in the desert, seafarers, and saints. The mechanism of these phenomena can best be explained in terms of energy. Our normal relations to objects in the world at large are maintained by a certain expenditure of energy. If the relation to the object is cut off there is a "retention" of energy, which then creates an equivalent substitute. For instance, just as persecution mania comes from a relationship poisoned by mistrust, so, as a substitute for the normal animation of the environment, an illusory reality rises up in which weird ghostly shadows flit about in place of people. That is why primitive man has always believed that lonely and desolate places are haunted by "devils" and suchlike apparitions.

4. DREAM:
*The dreamer is surrounded by a throng of vague female forms. A voice within him says, "First I must get away from Father."*

Here the psychic atmosphere has been animated by what the Middle Ages would call succubi. We are reminded of the visions of St. Anthony in Egypt, so eruditely described by Flaubert in *La Tentation de Saint-Antoine*. The element of hallucination shows itself in the fact that the thought is spoken aloud. The words "first I must get away" call for a concluding sentence which would begin with "in order to." Presumably it would run "in order to follow the unconscious, i.e., the alluring female forms." The father, the embodiment of the traditional spirit as expressed in religion or a general philosophy of life, is standing in his way. He imprisons the dreamer in the world of the conscious mind and its values. The traditional masculine world with its intellectualism and rationalism is felt to be an impediment, from which we must conclude that the unconscious, now approaching him, stands in direct opposition to the tendencies of the conscious mind and that the dreamer, despite this opposition, is already favourably disposed towards the unconscious. For this reason the latter should not be subordinated to the rationalistic judgments of consciousness; it ought rather to be an experience *sui generis*. Naturally it is not easy for the intellect to accept this, because it involves at least a partial, if not a total, *sacrificium intellectus*. Furthermore, the problem thus raised is very difficult for modern man to grasp; for to begin with he can understand the unconscious only as an inessential and unreal appendage of the conscious mind, and not as a special sphere of experience with laws of its own. In the course of the later dreams this conflict will appear again and again, until finally the right formula is found for the correlation of conscious and unconscious, and the personality is assigned its correct position between the two. Moreover, such a conflict cannot be solved by understanding, but only by experience. Every stage of the experience must be lived through. There is no feat of interpretation or any other trick by which to circumvent this difficulty, for the union of conscious and unconscious can be achieved only step by step.

The resistance of the conscious mind to the unconscious and the depreciation of the latter were historical necessities in the development of the human psyche, for otherwise the conscious mind would never have been able to differentiate itself at all. But modern man's consciousness has strayed rather too far from the fact of the unconscious. We have even forgotten that the psyche is by no means of our design, but is for the most part autonomous and unconscious. Consequently the approach of the unconscious induces a panic fear in civilized people, not least on account of the menacing analogy with insanity. The intellect has no objection to "analyzing" the unconscious as a passive object; on the contrary such an activity would coincide with our rational expectations. But to let the unconscious go its own way and to experience it as a reality is something that exceeds the courage and capacity of the average European. He prefers simply not to understand this problem. For the spiritually weak-kneed this is the better course, since the thing is not without its dangers.

The experience of the unconscious is a personal secret communicable only to very few, and that with difficulty; hence the isolating effect we noted above. But isolation brings about a compensatory animation of the psychic atmosphere which strikes us as uncanny. The figures that appear in the dream are feminine, thus pointing to the feminine nature of the unconscious. They are fairies or fascinating sirens and lamias, who infatuate the lonely wanderer and lead him astray. Likewise seductive maidens appear at the beginning of the *nekyia*[8] of Poliphilo[9] and the Melusina of Paracelsus[10] is another such figure.

### 5. VISUAL IMPRESSION:
*A snake describes a circle round the dreamer, who stands rooted to the ground like a tree.*

[8] Νεκυία, from νέκυς (corpse), the title of the eleventh book of the Odyssey, is the sacrifice to the dead for conjuring up the departed from Hades. *Nekyia* is therefore an apt designation for the "journey to Hades," the descent into the land of the dead, and was used by Dieterich in this sense in his commentary on the Codex of Akhmim, which contains an apocalyptic fragment from the Gospel of Peter (*Nekyia: Beiträge zur Erklärung der neuentdeckten Petrusapokalypse*). Typical examples are the *Divine Comedy*, the classical *Walpurgisnacht* in *Faust*, the apocryphal accounts of Christ's descent into hell, etc.

[9] Cf. the French edition of *Hypnerotomachia*, called *Le Tableau des riches inventions* or *Songe de Poliphile*, translated by Béroalde de Verville (Paris, 1600). The original Italian edition appeared in 1499.

[10] For details see Jung, "Paracelsus as a Spiritual Phenomenon" (*Collected Works*, Vol. 13), pars. 179f., 214ff.

The drawing of a spellbinding circle is an ancient magical device used by everyone who has a special or secret purpose in mind. He thereby protects himself from the "perils of the soul" that threaten him from without and attack anyone who is isolated by a secret. The same procedure has also been used since olden times to set a place apart as holy and inviolable: in founding a city, for instance, they first drew the *sulcus primigenius* or original furrow.[11] The fact that the dreamer stands rooted to the centre is a compensation of his almost insuperable desire to run away from the unconscious. He experienced an agreeable feeling of relief after this vision—and rightly, since he has succeeded in establishing a protected *temenos*,[12] a taboo area where he will be able to meet the unconscious. His isolation, so uncanny before, is now endowed with meaning and purpose, and thus robbed of its terrors.

6. VISUAL IMPRESSION, DIRECTLY FOLLOWING UPON 5:
*The veiled figure of a woman seated on a stair.*

The motif of the unknown woman—whose technical name is the "anima" [13]—appears here for the first time. Like the throng of vague female forms in dream 4, she is a personification of the animated psychic atmosphere. From now on the figure of the unknown woman reappears in a great many of the dreams. Personification always indicates an autonomous activity of the unconscious. If some personal figure appears we may be sure that the unconscious is beginning to grow active. The activity of such figures very often has an anticipatory character: something that the dreamer himself will do later is now being done in advance. In this case the allusion is to a stair, thus indicating an ascent or a descent.

Since the process running through dreams of this kind

[11] Eduard Fritz Knuchel, *Die Umwandlung in Kult, Magie und Rechtsbrauch* (Basel, 1919).
[12] A piece of land, often a grove, set apart and dedicated to a god.
[13] For the concept of the "anima," see supra, pp. 148–161.

has an historical analogy in the rites of initiation, it may not be superfluous to draw attention to the important part which the Stairway of the Seven Planets played in these rites, as we know from Apuleius, among others. The initiations of late classical syncretism, already saturated with alchemy (cf. the visions of Zosimos),[14] were particularly concerned with the theme of ascent, i.e., sublimation. The ascent was often represented by a ladder; hence the burial gift in Egypt of a smaller ladder for the *ka* of the dead.[15] The idea of an ascent through the seven spheres of the planets symbolizes the return of the soul to the sun-god from whom it originated, as we know for instance from Firmicus Maternus.[16] Thus the Isis mystery described by Apuleius[17] culminated in what early medieval alchemy, going back to Alexandrian tradition as transmitted by the Arabs,[18] called the *solificatio,* where the initiand was crowned as Helios.

7. VISUAL IMPRESSION:

*The veiled woman uncovers her face. It shines like the sun.*

The *solificatio* is consummated on the person of the anima. The process would seem to correspond to the *illuminatio,* or enlightenment. This "mystical" idea contrasts strongly with the rational attitude of the conscious mind, which recognizes only intellectual enlightenment as the highest form of understanding and insight. Naturally this

[14] Zosimos lived c. A.D. 300. Cf. Richard Reitzenstein, *Poimandres: Studien zur griechisch-ägyptischen und frühchristlichen Literatur* (Leipzig, 1904), pp. 9ff.; Marcellin Berthelot, *Collection des anciens alchimistes grecs* (Paris, 1887–88, 3 vols.), Vol. III.i, p. 2.
[15] The ladder motif is confirmed in dreams 12 and 13. Cf. also Jacob's ladder.
[16] *De errore profanarum religionum:* "Animo descensus per orbem solis tribuitur" (It is said [by the pagans] that the soul descends through the circle of the sun).
[17] *The Golden Ass.*
[18] Cf. Julius Ferdinand Ruska, *Turba Philosophorum: ein Beitrag zur Geschichte der Alchemie. Quellen und Studien zur Geschichte der Naturwissenschaften und der Medizin,* I (Berlin, 1931).

attitude never reckons with the fact that scientific knowledge only satisfies the little tip of personality that is contemporaneous with ourselves, not the collective psyche[19] that reaches back into the grey mists of antiquity and always requires a special rite if it is to be united with present-day consciousness. It is clear, therefore, that a "lighting up" of the unconscious is being prepared, which has far more the character of an *illuminatio* than of rational "elucidation." The *solificatio* is infinitely far removed from the conscious mind and seems to it almost chimerical.

## 8. VISUAL IMPRESSION:

*A rainbow is to be used as a bridge. But one must go under it and not over it. Whoever goes over it will fall and be killed.*

Only the gods can walk rainbow bridges in safety; mere mortals fall and meet their death, for the rainbow is only a lovely semblance that spans the sky, and not a highway for human beings with bodies. These must pass "under it." But water flows under bridges too, following its own gradient and seeking the lowest place. This hint will be confirmed later.

## 9. DREAM:

*A green land where many sheep are pastured. It is the "land of sheep."*

This curious fragment, inscrutable at first glance, may derive from childhood impressions and particularly from those of a religious nature, which would not be far to seek in this connection—e.g., "He maketh me to lie down in green pastures," or the early Christian allegories of sheep and shepherd.[20] The next vision points in the same direction.

---

[19] Cf. "collective unconscious," supra, pp. 59–69.

[20] The direct source of the Christian sheep symbolism is to be found in the visions of the Book of Enoch 89 : 10ff. (Robert Henry Charles, ed., *Apocrypha and Pseudepigrapha* [Oxford, 1913, 2 vols.], Vol. II, p. 252). The Apocalypse of Enoch was written about the beginning of the first century B.C.

*10.* VISUAL IMPRESSION:

*The unknown woman stands in the land of sheep and points the way.*

The anima, having already anticipated the *solificatio,* now appears as the psychopomp, the one who shows the way.[21] The way begins in the children's land, i.e., at a time when rational present-day consciousness was not yet separated from the historical psyche, the collective unconscious. The separation is indeed inevitable, but it leads to such an alienation from that dim psyche of the dawn of mankind that a loss of instinct ensues. The result is instinctual atrophy and hence disorientation in everyday human situations. But it also follows from the separation that the "children's land" will remain definitely infantile and become a perpetual source of childish inclinations and impulses. These intrusions are naturally most unwelcome to the conscious mind, and it consistently represses them for that reason. But the very consistency of the repression only serves to bring about a still greater alienation from the fountainhead, thus increasing the lack of instinct until it becomes lack of soul. As a result, the conscious mind is either completely swamped by childishness or else constantly obliged to defend itself in vain against the inundation, by means of a cynical affectation of old age or embittered resignation. We must therefore realize that despite its undeniable success the rational attitude of present-day consciousness is, in many human respects, childishly unadapted and hostile to life. Life has grown desiccated and cramped, crying out for the rediscovery of the fountainhead. But the fountainhead can only be found if the conscious mind will suffer itself to be led back to the "children's land," there to receive guidance from the unconscious as before. To remain a child too long is childish, but it is just as childish to move away and then assume that

---

[21] In the vision of Enoch, the leader and prince appears first as a sheep or ram: Book of Enoch 89 : 48 (Charles, op. cit., Vol. II, p. 254).

childhood no longer exists because we do not see it. But if we return to the "children's land" we succumb to the fear of becoming childish, because we do not understand that everything of psychic origin has a double face. One face looks forward, the other back. It is ambivalent and therefore symbolic, like all living reality.

We stand on a peak of consciousness, believing in a childish way that the path leads upward to yet higher peaks beyond. That is the chimerical rainbow bridge. In order to reach the next peak we must first go down into the land where the paths begin to divide.

## 11. DREAM:

*A voice says, "But you are still a child."*

This dream forces the dreamer to admit that even a highly differentiated consciousness has not by any means finished with childish things, and that a return to the world of childhood is necessary.

## 12. DREAM:

*A dangerous walk with Father and Mother, up and down many ladders.*

A childish consciousness is always tied to father and mother, and is never by itself. Return to childhood is always the return to father and mother, to the whole burden of the psychic non-ego as represented by the parents, with its long and momentous history. Regression spells disintegration into our historical and hereditary determinants, and it is only with the greatest effort that we can free ourselves from their embrace. Our psychic pre-history is in truth the spirit of gravity, which needs steps and ladders because, unlike the disembodied airy intellect, it cannot fly at will. Disintegration into the jumble of historical determinants is like losing one's way, where even what is right seems an alarming mistake.

As hinted above, the steps and ladders theme points to the process of psychic transformation, with all its ups and downs. We find a classic example of this in Zosimos' ascent and descent of the fifteen steps of light and darkness.[22]

It is of course impossible to free oneself from one's childhood without devoting a great deal of work to it, as Freud's researches have long since shown. Nor can it be achieved through intellectual knowledge only; what is alone effective is a remembering that is also a re-experiencing. The swift passage of the years and the overwhelming inrush of the newly discovered world leave a mass of material behind that is never dealt with. We do not shake this off; we merely remove ourselves from it. So that when, in later years, we return to the memories of childhood we find bits of our personality still alive, which cling round us and suffuse us with the feeling of earlier times. Being still in their childhood state, these fragments are very powerful in their effect. They can lose their infantile aspect and be corrected only when they are reunited with adult consciousness. This "personal unconscious" must always be dealt with first, that is, made conscious, otherwise the gateway to the collective unconscious cannot be opened. The journey with father and mother up and down many ladders represents the making conscious of infantile contents that have not yet been integrated.

*13.* Dream:
   *The father calls out anxiously, "That is the seventh!"*

During the walk over many ladders some event has evidently taken place which is spoken of as "the seventh." In the language of initiation, "seven" stands for the highest stage of illumination and would therefore be the coveted goal of all desire. But to the conventional mind the *solificatio* is an outlandish, mystical idea bordering on madness. We assume that it was only in the dark ages of misty superstition that people thought in such a nonsensical fashion, but that the lucid and hygienic mentality of our own

[22] Berthelot, *Collection des anciens alchimistes grecs*, III, i, 2. Cf. also Jung, "The Visions of Zosimos" (*Collected Works*, Vol. 13).

enlightened days has long since outgrown such nebulous notions, so much so, indeed, that this particular kind of "illumination" is to be found nowadays only in a lunatic asylum. No wonder the father is scared and anxious, like a hen that has hatched out ducklings and is driven to despair by the aquatic proclivities of its young. If this interpretation—that the "seventh" represents the highest stage of illumination—is correct, it would mean in principle that the process of integrating the personal unconscious was actually at an end. Thereafter the collective unconscious would begin to open up, which would suffice to explain the anxiety the father felt as the representative of the traditional spirit.

Nevertheless the return to the dim twilight of the unconscious does not mean that we should entirely abandon the precious acquisition of our forefathers, namely the intellectual differentiation of consciousness. It is rather a question of the *man* taking the place of the *intellect*—not the man whom the dreamer imagines himself to be, but someone far more rounded and complete. This would mean assimilating all sorts of things into the sphere of his personality which the dreamer still rejects as disagreeable or even impossible. The father who calls out so anxiously, "That is the seventh!" is a psychic component of the dreamer himself, and the anxiety is therefore his own. So the interpretation must bear in mind the possibility that the "seventh" means not only a sort of culmination but something rather ominous as well. We come across this theme, for instance, in the fairytale of Tom Thumb and the Ogre. Tom Thumb is the youngest of seven brothers. His dwarflike stature and his cunning are harmless enough, yet he is the one who leads his brothers to the ogre's lair, thus proving his own dangerous double nature as a bringer of good and bad luck; in other words, he is also the ogre himself. Since olden times "the seven" have represented the seven gods of the planets; they form what the Pyramid inscriptions call a *paut neteru*, a "company of gods." [23] Al-

[23] Sir E. A. Wallis Budge, in *Gods of the Egyptians* (London, 1904, 2 vols.), Vol. I, p. 87, uses this expression.

though a company is described as "nine," it often proves to be not nine at all but ten, and sometimes even more. Thus Maspero[24] tells us that the first and last members of the series can be added to, or doubled, without injury to the number nine. Something of the sort happened to the classical *paut* of the Greco-Roman or Babylonian gods in the post-classical age, when the gods were degraded to demons and retired partly to the distant stars and partly to the metals inside the earth. It then transpired that Hermes or Mercurius possessed a double nature, being a chthonic god of revelation and also the spirit of quicksilver, for which reason he was represented as a hermaphrodite. As the planet Mercury, he is nearest to the sun, hence he is preeminently related to gold. But, as quicksilver, he dissolves the gold and extinguishes its sunlike brilliance. All through the Middle Ages he was the object of much puzzled speculation on the part of the natural philosophers: sometimes he was a ministering and helpful spirit, a πάρεδρος (literally "assistant, comrade") or *familiaris;* and sometimes the *servus* or *cervus fugitivus* (the fugitive slave or stag), an elusive, deceptive, teasing goblin[25] who drove the alchemists to despair and had many of his attributes in common with the devil. For instance he is dragon, lion, eagle, raven, to mention only the most important of them. In the alchemical hierarchy of gods Mercurius comes lowest as *prima materia* and highest as *lapis philosophorum.* The *spiritus mercurialis* is the alchemists' guide (Hermes Psychopompos, and their tempter; he is their good luck and their ruin. His dual nature enables him to be not only the seventh but also the eighth—the eighth on Olympus, "whom nobody thought of" (see infra, p. 404).

It may seem odd to the reader that anything as remote as medieval alchemy should have relevance here. But the

---

[24] Sir Gaston Camille Charles Maspero, *Études de mythologie et d'archéologie egyptiennes* (Paris, 1893–1913, 7 vols.), Vol. II, p. 245.
[25] Cf. the entertaining dialogue between the alchemist and Mercurius in Sendivogius, "Dialogus Mercurii, alchymistae, et naturae," *Theatrum chemicum,* Vol. 4 (Strassburg, 1613), pp. 509–17.

"black art" is not nearly so remote as we think; for as an educated man the dreamer must have read *Faust,* and *Faust* is an alchemical drama from beginning to end, although the educated man of today has only the haziest notion of this. Our conscious mind is far from understanding everything, but the unconscious always keeps an eye on the "age-old, sacred things," however strange they may be, and reminds us of them at a suitable opportunity. No doubt *Faust* affected our dreamer much as Goethe was affected when, as a young man in his Leipzig days, he studied Theophrastus Paracelsus with Fräulein von Klettenberg.[26] It was then, as we certainly may assume, that the mysterious equivalence of seven and eight sank deep into his soul, without his conscious mind ever unravelling the mystery. The following dream will show that this reminder of *Faust* is not out of place.

*14.* DREAM:

*The dreamer is in America looking for an employee with a pointed beard. They say that everybody has such an employee.*

America is the land of practical, straightforward thinking, uncontaminated by our European sophistication. The intellect would there be kept, very sensibly, as an employee. This naturally sounds like *lèse-majesté* and might therefore be a serious matter. So it is consoling to know that everyone (as is always the case in America) does the same. The "man with a pointed beard" is our time-honoured Mephisto whom Faust "employed" and who was not permitted to triumph over him in the end, despite the fact that Faust had dared to descend into the dark chaos of the historical psyche and steep himself in the ever-changing, seamy side of life that rose up out of that bubbling cauldron.

From subsequent questions it was discovered that the dreamer himself had recognized the figure of Mephistopheles in the "man with the pointed beard." Versatility

[26] Goethe, *Dichtung und Wahrheit.*

of mind as well as the inventive gift and scientific leanings are attributes of the astrological Mercurius. Hence the man with the pointed beard represents the intellect, which is introduced by the dream as a real *familiaris,* an obliging if somewhat dangerous spirit. The intellect is thus degraded from the supreme position it once occupied and is put in the second rank, and at the same time branded as daemonic. Not that it had ever been anything but daemonic—only the dreamer had not noticed before how possessed he was by the intellect as the tacitly recognized supreme power. Now he has a chance to view this function, which till then had been the uncontested dominant of his psychic life, at somewhat closer quarters. Well might he exclaim with Faust: "So that's what was inside the poodle!" Mephistopheles is the diabolical aspect of every psychic function that has broken loose from the hierarchy of the total psyche and now enjoys independence and absolute power. But this aspect can be perceived only when the function becomes a separate entity and is objectivated or personified, as in this dream.

Amusingly enough, the "man with the pointed beard" also crops up in alchemical literature, in one of the "Parabolae" contained in the "Güldenen Tractat vom philosophischen Stein," [27] written in 1625, which Herbert Silberer[28] has analyzed from a psychological point of view. Among the company of old white-bearded philosophers there is a young man with a black pointed beard. Silberer is uncertain whether he should assume this figure to be the devil.

Mercurius as quicksilver is an eminently suitable symbol for the "fluid," i.e., mobile, intellect. Therefore in alchemy Mercurius is sometimes a "spirit" and sometimes a "water," the so-called *aqua permanens,* which is none other than *argentum vivum.*

---

[27] Printed in *Geheime Figuren der Rosenkreuzer, aus dem 16ten und 17ten Jahrhundert* (Altona, 1785–88, 2 vols.).
[28] Herbert Silberer, *Problems of Mysticism and Its Symbolism,* translated by Smith Ely Jelliffe (New York, 1917).

15. DREAM:

*The dreamer's mother is pouring water from one basin into another.* (The dreamer only remembered in connection with vision 28 of the next series that this basin belonged to his sister.) *This action is performed with great solemnity: it is of the highest significance for the outside world. Then the dreamer is rejected by his father.*

Once more we meet with the theme of "exchange" (cf. dream 1): one thing is put in the place of another. The "father" has been dealt with; now begins the action of the "mother." Just as the father represents collective consciousness, the traditional spirit, so the mother stands for the collective unconscious, the source of the water of life.[29] (Cf. the maternal significance of $\pi\eta\gamma\dot{\eta}$,[30] the *fons signatus*,[31] as an attribute of the Virgin Mary, etc.) The unconscious has altered the locus of the life forces, thus indicating a change of attitude. The dreamer's subsequent recollection enables us to see who is now the source of life: it is the "sister." The mother is superior to the son, but the sister is his equal. Thus the deposition of the intellect frees the dreamer from the domination of the unconscious and hence from his infantile attitude. Although the sister is a remnant of the past, we know definitely from later dreams that she was the carrier of the anima-image. We may therefore assume that the transferring of the water of life to the sister really means that the mother has been replaced by the anima.[32]

The anima now becomes a life-giving factor, a psychic reality which conflicts strongly with the world of the father. Which of us could assert, without endangering his sanity,

[29] For water as origin, cf. Egyptian cosmogony, among others.
[30] Albrecht Wirth, *Aus orientalischen Chroniken* (Frankfurt am Main, 1894), p. 199.
[31] "A fountain sealed": Song of Songs 4 : 12.
[32] This is really a normal life-process, but it usually takes place quite unconsciously. The anima is an archetype that is always present. The mother is the first carrier of the anima-image, which gives her a fascinating quality in the eyes of the son. It is then transferred, via the sister and similar figures, to the beloved.

that he had accepted the guidance of the unconscious in the conduct of his life, assuming that anyone exists who could imagine what that would mean? Anyone who could imagine it at all would certainly have no difficulty in understanding what a monstrous affront such a *volte face* would offer to the traditional spirit, especially to the spirit that has put on the earthly garment of the Church. It was this subtle change of psychic standpoint that caused the old alchemists to resort to deliberate mystification, and that sponsored all kinds of heresies. Hence it is only logical for the father to reject the dreamer—it amounts to nothing less than excommunication. (Be it noted that the dreamer is a Roman Catholic.) By acknowledging the reality of the psyche and making it a co-determining ethical factor in our lives, we offend against the spirit of convention which for centuries has regulated psychic life from outside by means of institutions as well as by reason. Not that unreasoning instinct rebels of itself against firmly established order; by the strict logic of its own inner laws it is itself of the firmest structure imaginable and, in addition, the creative foundation of all binding order. But just because this foundation is creative, all order which proceeds from it—even in its most "divine" form—is a phase, a stepping-stone. Despite appearances to the contrary, the establishment of order and the dissolution of what has been established are at bottom beyond human control. The secret is that only that which can destroy itself is truly alive. It is well that these things are difficult to understand and thus enjoy a wholesome concealment, for weak heads are only too easily addled by them and thrown into confusion. From all these dangers dogma—whether ecclesiastical, philosophical, or scientific—offers effective protection, and, looked at from a social point of view, excommunication is a necessary and useful consequence.

The water that the mother, the unconscious, pours into the basin belonging to the anima is an excellent symbol for the living power of the psyche. The old alchemists never tired of devising new and expressive synonyms for this water. They called it *aqua nostra, mercurius vivus, argentum vivum, vinum ardens, aqua vitae, succus lunariae,* and so on, by which they meant a living being not devoid of substance, as opposed to the rigid immateriality of mind in the abstract. The expression *succus lunariae* (sap of the moon-plant) refers clearly enough to the nocturnal origin of the water, and *aqua nostra,* like *mercurius vivus,* to its earthliness. *Acetum fontis* is a powerful corrosive water that dissolves all created things and at the same time leads to the most durable of all products, the mysterious *lapis.*

These analogies may seem very far-fetched. But let me refer the reader to dreams 13 and 14 in the next section, where the water symbolism is taken up again. The importance of the action "for the outside world," noted by the dreamer himself, points to the collective significance of the dream, as also does the fact—which had a far-reaching influence on the conscious attitude of the dreamer—that he is "rejected by the father."

The saying "extra ecclesiam nulla salus"—outside the Church there is no salvation—rests on the knowledge that an institution is a safe, practicable highway with a visible or definable goal, and that no paths and no goals can be found outside it. We must not underestimate the devastating effect of getting lost in the chaos, even if we know that it is the *sine qua non* of any regeneration of the spirit and the personality.

16. DREAM:

*An ace of clubs lies before the dreamer. A seven appears beside it.*

The ace, as "1," is the lowest card but the highest in value. The ace of clubs, being in the form of a cross, points to the Christian symbol.[33] Hence in Swiss-German the club is often called *Chrüüz* (cross). At the same time the three leaves contain an allusion to the threefold nature of the one God. Lowest and highest are beginning and end, alpha and omega.

[33] Cf. dream 23 of second series.

The seven appears after the ace of clubs and not before. Presumably the idea is: first the Christian conception of God, and then the seven (stages). The seven stages symbolize the transformation which begins with the symbolism of Cross and Trinity, and, judging by the earlier archaic allusions in dreams 7 and 13, culminates in the *solificatio*. But this solution is not hinted at here. Now, we know that the regression to the Helios of antiquity vainly attempted by Julian the Apostate was succeeded in the Middle Ages by another movement that was expressed in the formula "per crucem ad rosam" (through the cross to the rose), which was later condensed into the "Rosie Crosse" of the Rosicrucians. Here the essence of the heavenly Sol descends into the flower—earth's answer to the sun's countenance. The solar quality has survived in the symbol of the "golden flower" of Chinese alchemy.[34] The well-known "blue flower" of the Romantics might well be the last nostalgic perfume of the "rose"; it looks back in true Romantic fashion to the medievalism of ruined cloisters, yet at the same time modestly proclaims something new in earthly loveliness. But even the golden brilliance of the sun had to submit to a descent, and it found its analogy in the glitter of earthly gold—although, as *aurum nostrum,* this was far removed from the gross

[34] Concerning the "golden flower" of medieval alchemy, see Adolphus Senior, *Azoth, sive Aureliae occultae philosophorum* (Frankfurt, 1613). The golden flower comes from the Greek χρυσάνθιον (Berthelot, op. cit., Vol. III.xlix, p. 19) and χρυσάνθεμον = "golden flower," a magical plant like the Homeric μωλυ, which is often mentioned by the alchemists. The golden flower is the noblest and purest essence of gold. The same name is sometimes given to pyrites. [Cf. Edmund O. von Lippmann, *Entstehung und Ausbreitung der Alchemie* (Berlin, 1919–31, 2 vols.), Vol. I, p. 70]. The strength of the *aqua permanens* is also called *flos,* "flower" (Ruska, ed., *Turba,* op. cit., p. 214, 20). *Flos* is used by later alchemists to express the mystical transforming substance. (Cf. "flos citrinus" in *Aurora consurgens;* "flos aeris aureus" in "Consil. coniug., *Ars chemica*" (Strassburg, 1566), p. 167; "flos est aqua nummosa [Mercurius]" in "Allegoriae sapientum," *Theatrum chemicum,* Vol. 5 (1622), p. 81; "flos operis est lapis" in Johann Daniel Mylius, *Philosophia reformata* (Frankfurt, 1622), p. 30.

materiality of the metal, at least for subtler minds. One of the most interesting of the alchemical texts is the *Rosarium philosophorum,* subtitled *Secunda pars alchimiae de lapide philosophico vero modo praeparando. . . . Cum figuris rei perfectionem ostendentibus* (1550).[35] The anonymous author was very definitely a "philosopher" and was apparently aware that alchemy was not concerned with ordinary goldmaking but with a philosophical secret. For these alchemists the gold undoubtedly had a symbolic nature[36] and was therefore distinguished by such attributes as *vitreum* or *philosophicum.* It was probably owing to its all too obvious analogy with the sun that gold was denied the highest philosophical honour, which fell instead to the *lapis philosophorum.* The transformer is above the transformed, and transformation is one of the magical properties of the marvellous stone. The *Rosarium philosophorum* says: "For our stone, namely the living western quicksilver which has placed itself above the gold and vanquished it, is that which kills and quickens." [37] As to the "philosophical" significance of the *lapis,* the following quotation from a treatise ascribed to Hermes is particularly enlightening: "Understand, ye sons of the wise, what this exceeding precious stone proclaims . . . 'And my light conquers every light, and my virtues are more excellent than all virtues. . . . I beget the light, but the darkness too is of my nature. . . .' " [38]

[35] Reprinted in *Artis auriferae* (Basel 1593, 2 vols.), Vol. II, pp. 204ff. and Joannes Jacobus Magnetus, ed., *Bibliotheca chemica curiosa* (Geneva, 1702, 2 vols.), Vol. II, pp. 87ff. My quotations are usually taken from the 1593 version.

[36] As the *Rosarium* says: "Aurum nostrum non est aurum vulgi" (Our gold is not the common gold). *Art. aurif.,* II, p. 220.

[37] "Quia lapis noster scilicet argentum vivum occidentale, quod praetulit se auro et vicit illud, et illud quod occidit et vivere facit." Ibid., p. 223.

[38] "Intelligite, filii sapientum, quod hic lapis preciosissimus clamat, . . . et lumen meum omne lumen superat ac mea bona omnibus bonis sunt sublimiora. . . . Ego gigno lumen, tenebrae autem naturae meae sunt. . . ." Ibid., p. 239. Concerning the Hermes quotations in *Rosarium,* see infra, p. 369, n. 68.

*17.* DREAM:

*The dreamer goes for a long walk, and finds a blue flower on the way.*

To go for a walk is to wander along paths that lead nowhere in particular; it is both a search and a succession of changes. The dreamer finds a blue flower blossoming aimlessly by the wayside, a chance child of nature, evoking friendly memories of a more romantic and lyrical age, of the youthful season when it came to bud, when the scientific view of the world had not yet broken away from the world of actual experience—or rather when this break was only just beginning and the eye looked back to what was already the past. The flower is in fact like a friendly sign, a numinous emanation from the unconscious, showing the dreamer, who as a modern man has been robbed of security and of participation in all the things that lead to man's salvation, the historical place where he can meet friends and brothers of like mind, where he can find the seed that wants to sprout in him too. But the dreamer knows nothing as yet of the old solar gold which connects the innocent flower with the obnoxious black art of alchemy and with the blasphemous pagan idea of the *solificatio*. For the "golden flower of alchemy" can sometimes be a blue flower: "The sapphire blue flower of the hermaphrodite." [39]

*18.* DREAM:

*A man offers him some golden coins in his outstretched hand. The dreamer indignantly throws them to the ground and immediately afterwards deeply regrets his action. A variety performance then takes place in an enclosed space.*

The blue flower has already begun to drag its history after it. The "gold" is offered and is indignantly refused. Such a misinterpretation of the *aurum philosophicum* is easy to understand. But hardly has it happened when there comes a pang of remorse that the precious secret has been

[39] "Epistola ad Hermannum," *Theatr. chem.,* V, p. 899.

rejected and a wrong answer given to the riddle of the Sphinx. The same thing happened to the hero in Meyrink's *Golem*, when the ghost offered him a handful of grain which he spurned. The gross materiality of the yellow metal with its odious fiscal flavour, and the mean look of the grain, make both rejections comprehensible enough—but that is precisely why it is so hard to find the *lapis:* it is *exilis,* uncomely, it is thrown out into the street or on the dunghill, it is the commonest thing to be picked up anywhere—"in planitie, in montibus et aquis." It has this "ordinary" aspect in common with Spitteler's jewel in *Prometheus and Epimetheus,* which, for the same reason, was also not recognized by the worldly wise. But "the stone which the builders rejected, the same is become the head of the corner," and the intuition of this possibility arouses the liveliest regret in the dreamer.

It is all part of the banality of its outward aspect that the gold is minted, i.e., shaped into coins, stamped, and valued. Applied psychologically, this is just what Nietzsche refuses to do in his *Zarathustra*: to give names to the virtues. By being shaped and named, psychic life is broken down into coined and valued units. But this is possible only because it is intrinsically a great variety of things, an accumulation of unintegrated hereditary units. Natural man is not a "self"—he is the mass and a particle in the mass, collective to such a degree that he is not even sure of his own ego. That is why since time immemorial he has needed the transformation mysteries to turn him into something, and to rescue him from the animal collective psyche, which is nothing but a *variété.*

But if we reject this unseemly *variété* of man "as he is," it is impossible for him to attain integration, to become a self.[40] And that amounts to spiritual death. Life that just

---

[40] This does not mean that the self is created, so to speak, only during the course of life; it is rather a question of its becoming conscious. The self exists from the very beginning, but is latent, that is, unconscious. Cf. my later explanations.

happens in and for itself is not real life; it is real only when it is *known*. Only a unified personality can experience life, not that personality which is split up into partial aspects, that bundle of odds and ends which also calls itself "man." The dangerous plurality already hinted at in dream 4 is compensated in vision 5, where the snake describes a magic circle and thus marks off the taboo area, the *temenos*. In much the same way and in a similar situation the *temenos* reappears here, drawing the "many" together for a united variety performance—a gathering that has the appearance of an entertainment, though it will shortly lose its entertaining character: the "play of goats" will develop into a "tragedy." According to all the analogies, the satyr play was a mystery performance, from which we may assume that its purpose, as everywhere, was to re-establish man's connection with his natural ancestry and thus with the source of life, much as the obscene stories, αἰσχρολογία, told by Athenian ladies at the mysteries of Eleusis, were thought to promote the earth's fertility.[41] (Cf. also Herodotus' account[42] of the exhibitionistic performances connected with the Isis festivities at Bubastis.)

The allusion to the compensatory significance of the *temenos*, however, is still wrapped in obscurity for the dreamer. As might be imagined, he is much more concerned with the danger of spiritual death, which is conjured up by his rejection of the historical context.

*19.* VISUAL IMPRESSION:

*A death's-head. The dreamer wants to kick it away, but cannot. The skull gradually changes into a red ball, then into a woman's head which emits light.*

The skull soliloquies of Faust and of Hamlet are reminders of the appalling senselessness of human life when "sicklied o'er with the pale cast of thought." It was traditional opinions and judgments that caused the dreamer to

[41] Paul François Foucart, *Les Mystères d'Eleusis* (Paris, 1914).
[42] *Histories*, Vol. II, p. 58; translated by Powell, Vol. I, p. 137.

dash aside the doubtful and uninviting-looking offerings. But when he tries to ward off the sinister vision of the death's-head it is transformed into a red ball, which we may take as an allusion to the rising sun, since it at once changes into the shining head of a woman, reminding us directly of vision 7. Evidently an *enantiodromia,* a play of opposites,[43] has occurred: after being rejected the unconscious insists on itself all the more strongly. First it produces the classical symbol for the unity and divinity of the self, the sun; then it passes to the motif of the unknown woman who personifies the unconscious. Naturally this motif includes not merely the archetype of the anima but also the dreamer's relationship to a real woman, who is both a human personality and a vessel for psychic projections. ("Basin of the sister" in dream 15.)

In Neoplatonic philosophy the soul has definite affinities with the sphere. The soul substance is laid round the concentric spheres of the four elements above the fiery heaven.[44]

20. VISUAL IMPRESSION:

*A globe. The unknown woman is standing on it and worshipping the sun.*

This impression, too, is an amplification of vision 7. The rejection in dream 18 evidently amounted to the destruction of the whole development up to that point. Consequently the initial symbols reappear now, but in amplified form. Such enantiodromias are characteristic of dream-sequences in general. Unless the conscious mind intervened, the unconscious would go on sending out wave after wave with-

[43] For this term, see Editor's Introduction to this volume, p. xxvi —J. C.
[44] Cf. Heinrich Leberecht Fleischer, *Hermes Trismegistus an die Menschliche Seele* (Leipzig, 1970), p. 6; also the spherical form of Plato's Original Man and the σφαιρος of Empedocles. As in the *Timaeus,* the alchemical *anima mundi,* like the "soul of the substances," is spherical, and so is the gold. (See Michael Maier, *De circulo physico quadrato* [Oppenheim, 1616], pp. 11f.) For the connection between the *rotundum* and the skull or head, see Jung, "Transformation Symbolism in the Mass" (*Collected Works,* Vol. 11), pp. 239ff.

out result, like the treasure that is said to take nine years, nine months, and nine nights to come to the surface and, if not found on the last night, sinks back to start all over again from the beginning.

The globe probably comes from the idea of the red ball. But, whereas this is the sun, the globe is rather an image of the earth, upon which the anima stands worshipping the sun. Anima and sun are thus distinct, which points to the fact that the sun represents a different principle from that of the anima. The latter is a personification of the unconscious, while the sun is a symbol of the source of life and the ultimate wholeness of man (as indicated in the *solificatio*). Now, the sun is an antique symbol that is still very close to us. We know also that the early Christians had some difficulty in distinguishing the ἥλιος ἀνατολῆς (the rising sun) from Christ.[45] The dreamer's anima still seems to be a sun-worshipper, that is to say, she belongs to the ancient world, and for the following reason: the conscious mind with its rationalistic attitude has taken little or no interest in her and therefore made it impossible for the anima to become modernized (or better, Christianized). It almost seems as if the differentiation of the intellect that began in the Christian Middle Ages, as a result of scholastic training, had driven the anima to regress to the ancient world. The Renaissance gives us evidence enough for this, the clearest of all being the *Hypnerotomachia* of Francesco Colonna, where Poliphilo meets his anima, the lady Polia, at the court of Queen Venus, quite untouched by Christianity and graced with all the "virtues" of antiquity. The book was rightly regarded as a mystery text.[46] With this anima, then, we plunge straight into the ancient world. So that I

[45] Cf. St. Augustine's argument that God is not this sun but he who made the sun (*In Joannis Evang. Tract.*, XXXIV, 2) and the evidence of Eusebius, who actually witnessed "Christian" sun-worship (*Constantini Oratio ad Sanctorum Coelum*, VI; Jacques Paul Migne, *Patrologiae cursus completus*, Greek series [1857–66, 166 vols.], Vol. 20, cols. 1245–50).
[46] Béroalde de Verville, in his introduction ["Recueil stéganographique"] to the French translation (1600) of *Hypnerotomachia*, plainly adopts this view.

would not think anyone mistaken who interpreted the rejection of the gold in dream 18 *ex effectu* as an attempt to escape this regrettable and unseemly regression to antiquity. Certain vital doctrines of alchemical philosophy go back textually to late Greco-Roman syncretism, as Ruska, for instance, has sufficiently established in the case of the *Turba*. Hence any allusion to alchemy wafts one back to the ancient world and makes one suspect regression to pagan levels.

It may not be superfluous to point out here, with due emphasis, that consciously the dreamer had no inkling of all this. But in his unconscious he is immersed in this sea of historical associations, so that he behaves in his dreams as if he were fully cognizant of these curious excursions into the history of the human mind. He is in fact an unconscious exponent of an autonomous psychic development, just like the medieval alchemist or the classical Neoplatonist. Hence one could say—*cum grano salis*—that history could be constructed just as easily from one's own unconscious as from the actual texts.

21. VISUAL IMPRESSION:

*The dreamer is surrounded by nymphs. A voice says, "We were always there, only you did not notice us."*

Here the regression goes back even further, to an image that is unmistakably classical. At the same time the situation of dream 4 is taken up again and also the situation of dream 18, where the rejection led to the compensatory enantiodromia in vision 19. But here the image is amplified by the hallucinatory recognition that the drama has always existed although unnoticed until now. The realization of this fact joins the unconscious psyche to consciousness as a coexistent entity. The phenomenon of the "voice" in dreams always has for the dreamer the final and indisputable character of the αὐτὸς ἔφα,[47] i.e., the voice expresses

---

[47] "He said [it] himself." The phrase originally alluded to the authority of Pythagoras.

some truth or condition that is beyond all doubt. The fact that a sense of the remote past has been established, that contact has been made with the deeper layers of the psyche, is accepted by the unconscious personality of the dreamer and communicates itself to his conscious mind as a feeling of comparative security.

Vision 20 represents the anima as a sun-worshipper. She has as it were stepped out of the globe or spherical form. But the first spherical form was the skull. According to tradition the head or brain is the seat of the *anima intellectualis.* For this reason too the alchemical vessel must be round like the head, so that what comes out of the vessel shall be equally "round," i.e., simple and perfect like the *anima mundi.*[48] The work is crowned by the production of the *rotundum,* which, as the *materia globosa,* stands at the beginning and also at the end, in the form of gold. Possibly the nymphs who "were always there" are an allusion to this. The regressive character of the vision is also apparent from the fact that there is a multiplicity of female forms, as in dream 4. But this time they are of a classical nature, which, like the sun-worship in vision 20, points to an historical regression. The splitting of the anima into many figures is equivalent to dissolution into an indefinite state, i.e., into the unconscious, from which we may conjecture that a relative dissolution of the conscious mind is running parallel with the historical regression (a process to be observed in its extreme form in schizophrenia). The dissolution of consciousness or, as Janet calls it, *abaissement du niveau mental,* comes very close to the primitive state of mind. A parallel to this scene with the nymphs is to be

[48] Cf. "Liber Platonis quartorum," *Theatr. chem.,* V, pp. 149ff., 174. This treatise is a Harranite text of great importance for the history of alchemy. It exists in Arabic and Latin, but the latter version is unfortunately very corrupt. The original was probably written in the tenth century. Cf. Moritz Steinschneider, "Die europäischen Übersetzungen aus dem Arabischen bis Mitte des 17. Jahrhunderts," *Sitzungsberichte der kaiserlichen Akademie der Wissenschaften in Wien, Philosophisch-historische Klasse,* CL (1904), 1–84; CLI (1904), 1–108.

found in the Paracelsan *regio nymphididica,* mentioned in the treatise *De vita longa* as the initial stage of the individuation process.[49]

## 22. VISUAL IMPRESSION:

*In a primeval forest. An elephant looms up menacingly. Then a large ape-man, bear, or cave-man threatens to attack the dreamer with a club. Suddenly the "man with the pointed beard" appears and stares at the aggressor, so that he is spellbound. But the dreamer is terrified. The voice says, "Everything must be ruled by the light."*

The multiplicity of nymphs has broken down into still more primitive components; that is to say, the animation of the psychic atmosphere has very considerably increased, and from this we must conclude that the dreamer's isolation from his contemporaries has increased in proportion. This intensified isolation can be traced back to vision 21, where the union with the unconscious was realized and accepted as a fact. From the point of view of the conscious mind this is highly irrational; it constitutes a secret which must be anxiously guarded, since the justification for its existence could not possibly be explained to any so-called reasonable person. Anyone who tried to do so would be branded as a lunatic. The discharge of energy into the environment is therefore considerably impeded, the result being a surplus of energy on the side of the unconscious: hence the abnormal increase in the autonomy of the unconscious figures, culminating in aggression and real terror. The earlier entertaining variety performance is beginning to become uncomfortable. We find it easy enough to accept the classical figures of nymphs thanks to their aesthetic embellishments; but we have no idea that behind these gracious figures there lurks the Dionysian mystery of antiquity, the satyr play with its tragic implications: the bloody dismemberment of the god who has become an animal. It needed a

[49] Cf. "Paracelsus as a Spiritual Phenomenon" (*Collected Works,* Vol. 13), par. 214.

Nietzsche to expose in all its feebleness Europe's schoolboy attitude to the ancient world. But what did Dionysus mean to Nietzsche? What he says about it must be taken seriously; what it did to him still more so. There can be no doubt that he knew, in the preliminary stages of his fatal illness, that the dismal fate of Zagreus was reserved for him. Dionysus is the abyss of impassioned dissolution, where all human distinctions are merged in the animal divinity of the primordial psyche—a blissful and terrible experience. Humanity, huddling behind the walls of its culture, believes it has escaped this experience, until it succeeds in letting loose another orgy of bloodshed. All well-meaning people are amazed when this happens and blame high finance, the armaments industry, the Jews, or the Freemasons.[50]

At the last moment, friend "Pointed Beard" appears on the scene as an obliging *deus ex machina* and exorcizes the annihilation threatened by the formidable ape-man. Who knows how much Faust owed his imperturbable curiosity, as he gazed on the spooks and bogeys of the classical *Walpurgisnacht,* to the helpful presence of Mephisto and his matter-of-fact point of view! Would that more people could remember the scientific or philosophical reflections of the much-abused intellect at the right moment! Those who abuse it lay themselves open to the suspicion of never having experienced anything that might have taught them its value and shown them why mankind has forged this weapon with such unprecedented effort. One has to be singularly out of touch with life not to notice such things. The intellect may be the devil, but the devil is the "strange son of chaos" who can most readily be trusted to deal effectively with his mother. The Dionysian experience will give this devil plenty to do should he be looking for work, since the resultant settlement with the unconscious far outweighs the labours of Hercules. In my opinion it presents a whole world of problems which the intellect could not settle even

[50] I wrote this passage in spring, 1935.

in a hundred years—the very reason why it so often goes off for a holiday to recuperate on lighter tasks. And this is also the reason why the psyche is forgotten so often and so long, and why the intellect makes such frequent use of magical apotropaic words like "occult" and "mystic," in the hope that even intelligent people will think that these mutterings really mean something.

The voice finally declares, "Everything must be ruled by the light," which presumably means the light of the discerning, conscious mind, a genuine *illuminatio* honestly acquired. The dark depths of the unconscious are no longer to be denied by ignorance and sophistry—at best a poor disguise for common fear—nor are they to be explained away with pseudo-scientific rationalizations. On the contrary it must now be admitted that things exist in the psyche about which we know little or nothing at all, but which nevertheless affect our bodies in the most obstinate way, and that they possess at least as much reality as the things of the physical world which ultimately we do not understand either. No line of research which asserted that its subject was unreal or a "nothing but" has ever made any contribution to knowledge.

With the active intervention of the intellect a new phase of the unconscious process begins: the conscious mind must now come to terms with the figures of the unknown woman ("anima"), the unknown man ("the shadow"), the wise old man ("mana personality"),[51] and the symbols of the self. The last named are dealt with in the following section.

[51] "Wise Old Man": archetype of the Wisdom of Life personified as initiator. See below, Dream 14 (p. 342). "Mana personality": archetype of the mighty man in the form of hero, chief, magician, medicine-man, saint, ruler of men and spirits, friend of God. See *Two Essays on Analytical Psychology* (*Collected Works,* Vol. 7), pars. 376 ff.—J. C.

## 3. *The Symbolism of the Mandala*

### I. *Concerning the Mandala*

As I have already said, I have put together, out of a continuous series of some four hundred dreams and visions, all those that I regard as mandala dreams. The term "mandala" was chosen because this word denotes the ritual or magic circle used in Lamaism and also in Tantric yoga as a *yantra* or aid to contemplation. The Eastern mandalas

used in ceremonial are figures fixed by tradition; they may be drawn or painted or, in certain special ceremonies, even represented plastically.[52]

In 1938, I had the opportunity, in the monastery of Bhutia Busty, near Darjeeling, of talking with a Lamaic *rimpoche,* Lingdam Gomchen by name, about the *khilkor* or mandala. He explained it as a *dmigs-pa* (pronounced "migpa"), a mental image which can be built up only by a fully instructed lama through the power of imagination. He said that no mandala is like any other, they are all individually different. Also, he said, the mandalas to be found in monasteries and temples were of no particular significance because they were external representations only. The true mandala is always an inner image, which is gradually built up through (active) imagination, at such times when psychic equilibrium is disturbed or when a thought cannot be found and must be sought for, because it is not contained in holy doctrine. The aptness of this explanation will become apparent in the course of my exposition. The alleged free and individual formation of the mandala, however, should be taken with a considerable grain of salt, since in all Lamaic mandalas there predominates not only a certain unmistakable style but also a traditional structure. For instance they are all based on a quaternary system, a *quadratura circuli,* and their contents are invariably derived from Lamaic dogma. There are texts, such as the Shri-Chakra-Sambhara Tantra,[53] which contain directions for the construction of these "mental images." The *khilkor* is strictly distinguished from the so-called *sidpe-korlo,* or World Wheel, which represents the course of human existence in its various forms as conceived by the Buddhists. In contrast to the *khilkor,* the World Wheel

[52] Cf. Richard Wilhelm and C. G. Jung, *The Secret of the Golden Flower,* translated by Cary F. Baynes (London and New York, 1931), and Heinrich Zimmer, *Myths and Symbols in Indian Art and Civilization,* Joseph Campbell, ed., Bollingen Series VI (New York, 1946).
[53] Arthur Avalon, *The Serpent Power* (London, 1919), VII.

is based on a ternary system in that the three world-principles are to be found in its centre: the cock, equalling concupiscence; the serpent, hatred or envy; and the pig, ignorance or unconsciousness (*avidya*). Here we come upon the dilemma of three and four, which also crops up in Buddhism. We shall meet this problem again in the further course of our dream-series.

It seems to me beyond question that these Eastern symbols originated in dreams and visions, and were not invented by some Mahayana church father. On the contrary, they are among the oldest religious symbols of humanity and may even have existed in paleolithic times (cf. the Rhodesian rock-paintings). Moreover they are distributed all over the world, a point I need not insist on here. In this section I merely wish to show from the material at hand how mandalas come into existence.

The mandalas used in ceremonial are of great significance because their centres usually contain one of the highest religious figures: either Shiva himself—often in the embrace of Shakti—or the Buddha, Amitabha, Avalokiteshvara, or one of the great Mahayana teachers, or simply the *dorje,* symbol of all the divine forces together, whether creative or destructive. The text of the *Golden Flower,* a product of Taoist syncretism, specifies in addition certain "alchemical" properties of this centre after the manner of the *lapis* and the *elixir vitae,* so that it is in effect a φάρμακον ἀθανασίας.[54]

It is not without importance for us to appreciate the high value set upon the mandala, for it accords very well with the paramount significance of individual mandala symbols which are characterized by the same qualities of a—so to speak—"metaphysical" nature.[55] Unless every-

[54] Cf. Richard Reitzenstein, *Die hellenistischen Mysterienreligionen* (Leipzig, 1910).
[55] The quotation marks indicate that I am not positing anything by the term "metaphysical": I am only using it figuratively, in the psychological sense, to characterize the peculiar statements made by dreams.

thing deceives us, they signify nothing less than a psychic centre of the personality not to be identified with the ego. I have observed these processes and their products for close on thirty years on the basis of very extensive material drawn from my own experience. For fourteen years I neither wrote nor lectured about them so as not to prejudice my observations. But when, in 1929, Richard Wilhelm laid the text of the *Golden Flower* before me, I decided to publish at least a foretaste of the results. One cannot be too cautious in these matters, for what with the imitative urge and a positively morbid avidity to possess themselves of outlandish feathers and deck themselves out in this exotic plumage, far too many people are misled into snatching at such "magical" ideas and applying them externally, like an ointment. People will do anything, no matter how absurd, in order to avoid facing their own souls. They will practise Indian yoga and all its exercises, observe a strict regimen of diet, learn theosophy by heart, or mechanically repeat mystic texts from the literature of the whole world—all because they cannot get on with themselves and have not the slightest faith that anything useful could ever come out of their own souls. Thus the soul has gradually been turned into a Nazareth from which nothing good can come. Therefore let us fetch it from the four corners of the earth—the more far-fetched and bizarre it is the better! I have no wish to disturb such people at their pet pursuits, but when anybody who expects to be taken seriously is deluded enough to think that I use yoga methods and yoga doctrines or that I get my patients, whenever possible, to draw mandalas for the purpose of bringing them to the "right point"—then I really must protest and tax these people with having read my writings with the most horrible inattention. The doctrine that all evil thoughts come from the heart and that the human soul is a sink of iniquity must lie deep in the marrow of their bones. Were that so, then God had made a sorry job of creation, and it were high time for us to go over to Marcion the Gnostic and depose the incompetent demiurge. Ethically, of course, it is infinitely more convenient to leave God the sole responsibility for such a Home for Idiot Children, where no one is capable of putting a spoon into his own mouth. But it is worth man's while to take pains with himself, and he has something in his soul that can grow.[56] It is rewarding to watch patiently the silent happenings in the soul, and the most and the best happens when it is not regulated from outside and from above. I readily admit that I have such a great respect for what happens in the human soul that I would be afraid of disturbing and distorting the silent operation of nature by clumsy interference. That was why I even refrained from observing this particular case myself and entrusted the task to a beginner who was not handicapped by my knowledge—anything rather than disturb the process. The results which I now lay before you are the unadulterated, conscientious, and exact self-observations of a man of unerring intellect, who had nothing suggested to him from outside and who would in any case not have been open to suggestion. Anyone at all familiar with psychic material will have no difficulty in recognizing the authentic character of the results.

## II. The Mandalas in the Dreams

For the sake of completeness I will recapitulate the mandala symbols which occur in the initial dreams and visions already discussed:

*1.* The snake that described a circle round the dreamer (5).
*2.* The blue flower (17).

[56] As Meister Eckhart says, "It is not outside, it is inside: wholly within." *Meister Eckhart,* translated by C. de B. Evans (London, 1924, 2 vols.), Vol. I, p. 8.

3. The man with the gold coins in his hand, and the
   enclosed space for a variety performance (18).
4. The red ball (19).
5. The globe (20).

The next mandala symbol occurs in the first dream of
the new series:[57]

## 6. DREAM:

*An unknown woman is pursuing the dreamer. He keeps
running round in a circle.*

The snake in the first mandala dream was anticipatory,
as is often the case when a figure personifying a certain
aspect of the unconscious does or experiences something
that the subject himself will experience later. The snake
anticipates a circular movement in which the subject is
going to be involved; i.e., something is taking place in the
unconscious which is perceived as a circular movement, and
this occurrence now presses into consciousness so forcefully
that the subject himself is gripped by it. The unknown
woman or anima representing the unconscious continues to
harass the dreamer until he starts running round in circles.
This clearly indicates a potential centre which is not identical with the ego and round which the ego revolves.

## 7. DREAM:

*The anima accuses the dreamer of paying too little atten-
tion to her. There is a clock that says five minutes to the
hour.*

The situation is much the same: the unconscious pesters
him like an exacting woman. The situation also explains the
clock, for a clock's hands go round in a circle. Five minutes
to the hour implies a state of tension for anybody who lives
by the clock: when the five minutes are up he must do
something or other. He might even be pressed for time.

[57] [Inasmuch as the five mandala dreams and visions listed above
necessarily figure in this new series (though actually part of the first
dream-series), the author initiated the number sequence of the new—
i.e., the mandala—series with them.—EDITORS OF *The Collected
Works*.]

(The symbol of circular movement is always connected with a feeling of tension, as we shall see later.)

## 8. DREAM:

*On board ship. The dreamer is occupied with a new method of taking his bearings. Sometimes he is too far away and sometimes too near: the right spot is in the middle. There is a chart on which is drawn a circle with its centre.*

Obviously the task set here is to find the centre, the right spot, and this is the centre of a circle. While the dreamer was writing down this dream he remembered that he had dreamed shortly before of shooting at a target: sometimes he shot too high, sometimes too low. The right aim lay in the middle. Both dreams struck him as highly significant. The target is a circle with a centre. Bearings at sea are taken by the apparent rotation of the stars round the earth. Accordingly the dream describes an activity whose aim is to construct or locate an objective centre—a centre outside the subject.

## 9. DREAM:

*A pendulum clock that goes forever without the weights running down.*

This is a species of clock whose hands move unceasingly, and, since there is obviously no loss due to friction, it is a *perpetuum mobile,* an everlasting movement in a circle. Here we meet with a "metaphysical" attribute. As I have already said, I use this word in a psychological sense, hence figuratively. I mean by this that eternity is a quality predicated by the unconscious, and not a hypostasis. The statement made by the dream will obviously offend the dreamer's scientific judgment, but this is just what gives the mandala its peculiar significance. Highly significant things are often rejected because they seem to contradict reason and thus set it too arduous a test. The movement without friction shows that the clock is cosmic, even transcendental; at any rate it raises the question of a quality which leaves us in some doubt whether the psychic phe-

nomenon expressing itself in the mandala is under the laws
of space and time. And this points to something so entirely
different from the empirical ego that the gap between them
is difficult to bridge; i.e., the other centre of personality lies
on a different plane from the ego since, unlike this, it has
the quality of "eternity" or relative timelessness.

## 10. DREAM:

*The dreamer is in the Peterhofstatt in Zurich with the
doctor, the man with the pointed beard, and the "doll
woman." The last is an unknown woman who neither
speaks nor is spoken to. Question: To which of the three
does the woman belong?*

The tower of St. Peter's in Zurich has a clock with a
strikingly large face. The Peterhofstatt is an enclosed space,
a *temenos* in the truest sense of the word, a precinct of the
church. The four of them find themselves in this enclosure.
The circular dial of the clock is divided into four quarters,
like the horizon. In the dream the dreamer represents his
own ego, the man with the pointed beard the "employed"
intellect (Mephisto), and the "doll woman" the anima.
Since the doll is a childish object it is an excellent image
for the non-ego nature of the anima, who is further characterized as an object by "not being spoken to." This negative
element (also present in dreams 6 and 7 above) indicates
an inadequate relationship between the conscious mind
and the unconscious, as also does the question of whom
the unknown woman belongs to. The "doctor," too, belongs
to the non-ego; he probably contains a faint allusion to myself, although at that time I had no connections with the
dreamer.[58] The man with the pointed beard, on the other
hand, belongs to the ego. This whole situation is reminiscent
of the relations depicted in the diagram of functions. If
we think of the psychological function[59] as arranged
in a circle, then the most differentiated function is usually

[58] As the dream at most alludes to me and does not name me, the unconscious evidently has no intention of emphasizing my personal role.
[59] Cf. supra, p. *xxviii,* also, infra, pp. 382, note 95 and 383.

the carrier of the ego and, equally regularly, has an auxiliary function attached to it. The "inferior" function, on
the other hand, is unconscious and for that reason is projected into a non-ego. It too has an auxiliary function.
Hence it would not be impossible for the four persons in
the dream to represent the four functions as components
of the total personality (i.e., if we include the unconscious).
But this totality is ego plus non-ego. Therefore the centre
of the circle which expresses such a totality would correspond not to the ego but to the self as the summation of
the total personality. (The centre with a circle is a very
well-known allegory of the nature of God.) In the philosophy of the Upanishads the Self is in one aspect the
*personal* atman, but at the same time it has a cosmic and
metaphysical quality as the *suprapersonal* Atman.[60]

We meet with similar ideas in Gnosticism: I would mention the idea of the Anthropos, the Pleroma, the Monad,
and the spark of light (Spinther) in a treatise of the Codex
Brucianus:

> This same is he [Monogenes] who dwelleth in the Monad,
> which is in the Setheus, and which came from the place of
> which none can say where it is. . . . From Him it is the
> Monad came, in the manner of a ship, laden with all
> good things, and in the manner of a field, filled or planted
> with every kind of tree, and in the manner of a city,
> filled with all races of mankind. . . . This is the fashion
> of the Monad, all these being in it: there are twelve Mon-
> ads as a crown upon its head. . . . And to its veil which
> surroundeth it in the manner of a defence [πύργος =
> tower] there are twelve gates. . . . This same is
> the Mother-City [μητρόπολις] of the Only-begotten
> [μονογενής].[61]

By way of explanation I should add that "Setheus" is a
name for God, meaning "creator." The Monogenes is the

[60] Paul Deussen, *Allgemeine Geschichte der Philosophie* (Leipzig,
1906, 2 vols.), Vol. I.
[61] Charlotte Augusta Baynes, *A Coptic Gnostic Treatise Contained
in the Codex Brucianus—Bruce MS 96. Bodleian Library, Oxford*
(Cambridge, England, 1933), p. 89.

Son of God. The comparison of the Monad with a field and a city corresponds to the idea of the *temenos*. Also, the Monad is crowned (cf. the hat which appears in dream 1 of the first series and dream 35 of this series). As "metropolis" the Monad is feminine, like the *padma* or lotus, the basic form of the Lamaic mandala (the Golden Flower in China and the Rose or Golden Flower in the West). The Son of God, God made manifest, dwells in the flower.[62] In the Book of Revelation, we find the Lamb in the centre of the Heavenly Jerusalem. And in our Coptic text we are told that Setheus dwells in the innermost and holiest recesses of the Pleroma, a city with four gates (equivalent to the Hindu City of Brahma on the world-mountain Meru). In each gate there is a Monad.[63] The limbs of the Anthropos born of the Autogenes (= Monogenes) correspond to the four gates of the city. The Monad is a spark of light (Spinther) and an image of the Father, identical with the Monogenes. An invocation runs: "Thou art the House and the Dweller in the House." [64] The Monogenes stands on a *tetrapeza*,[65] a table or platform with four pillars corresponding to the quaternion of the four evangelists.[66]

The idea of the *lapis* has several points of contact with all this. In the *Rosarium* the *lapis* says, quoting Hermes:[67]

---

[62] The Buddha, Shiva, etc., in the lotus; Christ in the rose, in the womb of Mary (ample material on this theme in Anselm Salzer, *Die Sinnbilder und Beiworte Mariens in der deutschen Literatur und lateinischen Hymnen—Poesie des Mittelalters* [Linz, 1893]); the seeding-place of the diamond body in the golden flower. Cf. the circumambulation of the square in dream 16.

[63] Baynes, *A Coptic Gnostic Treatise*, p. 58. Cf. the Vajramandala, where the great *dorje* is found in the center surrounded by the twelve smaller *dorjes*, like the one Monad with the "twelve Monads as a crown upon its head." Moreover there is a *dorje* in each of the four gates.

[64] Ibid., p. 94.

[65] Ibid., p. 70. Similar to the tetramorph, the steed of the Church.

[66] Cf. Irenaeus, *Adversus haereses*, III, xi, and Clement of Alexandria, *Stromata*, V, vi.

[67] *Art. aurif.*, II, pp. 239f. The Hermes quotations come from the fourth chapter of "Tractatus aureus" (*Ars chemica*, pp. 23f., or *Bibl. chem.*, I, pp. 427f.).

"I beget the light, but the darkness too is of my nature . . . therefore nothing better or more worthy of veneration can come to pass in the world than the conjunction of myself and my son." [68] Similarly, the Monogenes is called the "dark light," [69] a reminder of the *sol niger,* the black sun of alchemy.[70]

The following passage from Chapter 4 of the "Tractatus aureus" provides an interesting parallel to the Monogenes who dwells in the bosom of the Mother-City and is identical with the crowned and veiled Monad:

> But the king reigns, as is witnessed by his brothers, [and] says: "I am crowned, and I am adorned with the diadem; I am clothed with the royal garment, and I bring joy to the heart; for, being chained to the arms and breast of my mother, and to her substance, I cause my substance to hold together and rest; and I compose the invisible from the visible, making the occult to appear; and everything that the philosophers have concealed will be generated from us. Hear then these words, and understand them; keep them, and meditate upon them, and seek for nothing more. Man is generated from the principle of Nature whose inward parts are fleshy, and from no other substance."

The "king" refers to the *lapis.* That the *lapis* is the "mas-

---

[68] "Ego gigno lumen, tenebrae autem naturae meae sunt . . . me igitur et filio meo conjuncto, nihil melius ac venerabilius in mundo fieri potest." The Hermes sayings as quoted by the anonymous author of the *Rosarium* contain deliberate alterations that have far more significance than mere faulty readings. They are authentic recastings, to which he lends higher authority by attributing them to Hermes. I have compared the three printed editions of the "Tractatus aureus," 1566, 1610, and 1702, and found that they all agree. The *Rosarium* quotation runs as follows in the "Tractatus aureus": "Iam Venus ait: Ego genero lumen, nec tenebrae meae naturae sunt . . . me igitur et fratri meo iunctis nihil melius ac venerabilius" (Venus says: I beget the light, and the darkness is not of my nature . . . therefore nothing is better or more worthy of veneration than the conjunction of myself and my brother).

[69] Baynes, *A Coptic Gnostic Treatise,* p. 87.

[70] Cf. Johann Daniel Mylius, *Philosophia reformata* (Frankfurt, 1622), p. 19.

ter" is evident from the following Hermes quotation in the
*Rosarium*:[71] "Et sic Philosophus non est Magister lapidis,
sed potius minister" (And thus the philosopher is not the
master of the stone but rather its minister). Similarly the
final production of the *lapis* in the form of the crowned
hermaphrodite is called the *aenigma regis*.[72] A German
verse refers to the *aenigma* as follows:

> Here now is born the emperor of all honour
> Than whom there cannot be born any higher,
> Neither by art nor by the work of nature
> Out of the womb of any living creature.
> Philosophers speak of him as their son
> And everything they do by him is done.[73]

The last two lines might easily be a direct reference to
the above quotation from Hermes.

It looks as if the idea had dawned on the alchemists that
the Son who, according to classical (and Christian) tradition, dwells eternally in the Father and reveals himself as
God's gift to mankind, was something that man could
produce out of his own nature—with God's help, of course
(*Deo concedente*). The heresy of this idea is obvious.

The feminine nature of the inferior function derives from
its contamination with the unconscious. Because of its
feminine characteristics the unconscious is personified by
the anima (that is to say, in men; in women it is masculine).[74]

If we assume that this dream and its predecessors really
do mean something that justly arouses a feeling of significance in the dreamer, and if we further assume that this
significance is more or less in keeping with the views put
forward in the commentary, then we would have reached
here a high point of introspective intuition whose boldness
leaves nothing to be desired. But even the everlasting pen-

[71] *Art. aurif.*, II, p. 356.
[72] Ibid., p. 359.
[73] Ibid.
[74] Cf. supra. pp. 148–62.

dulum clock is an indigestible morsel for a consciousness unprepared for it, and likely to hamper any too lofty flight of thought.

## *11.* DREAM:

*The dreamer, the doctor, a pilot, and the unknown woman are travelling by airplane. A croquet ball suddenly smashes the mirror, an indispensable instrument of navigation, and the airplane crashes to the ground. Here again there is the same doubt: to whom does the unknown woman belong?*

Doctor, pilot, and unknown woman are characterized as belonging to the non-ego by the fact that all three of them are strangers. Therefore the dreamer has retained possession only of the differentiated function, which carries the ego; that is, the unconscious has gained ground considerably. The croquet ball is part of a game where the ball is driven under a hoop. Vision 8 of the first series said that people should not go over the rainbow (fly?), but must go *under* it. Those who go over it fall to the ground. It looks as though the flight had been too lofty after all. Croquet is played on the ground and not in the air. We should not rise above the earth with the aid of "spiritual" intuitions and run away from hard reality, as so often happens with people who have brilliant intuitions. We can never reach the level of our intuitions and should therefore not identify ourselves with them. Only the gods can pass over the rainbow bridge; mortal men must stick to the earth and are subject to its laws. In the light of the possibilities revealed by intuition, man's earthliness is certainly a lamentable imperfection; but this very imperfection is part of his innate being, of his reality. He is compounded not only of his best intuitions, his highest ideals and aspirations, but also of the odious conditions of his existence, such as heredity and the indelible sequence of memories that shout after him: "You did it, and that's what you are!" Man may have lost his ancient saurian's tail, but in its stead he has a chain hanging on to his psyche which binds him to the earth—an anything-but-Homeric chain[75] of given conditions which weigh so heavy that it is better to remain bound to them, even at the risk of becoming neither a hero nor a saint. (History gives us some justification for not attaching any absolute value to these collective norms.) That we are bound to the earth does not mean that we cannot grow; on the contrary it is the *sine qua non* of growth. No noble, well-grown tree ever disowned its dark roots, for it grows not only upward but downward as well. The question of where we are going is of course extremely important; but equally important, it seems to me, is the question of *who* is going where. The "who" always implies a "whence." It takes a certain greatness to gain lasting possession of the heights, but anybody can overreach himself. The difficulty lies in striking the dead centre (cf. dream 8). For this an awareness of the two sides of man's personality is essential, of their respective aims and origins. These two aspects must never be separated through arrogance or cowardice.

The "mirror" as an "indispensable instrument of navigation" doubtless refers to the intellect, which is able to think and is constantly persuading us to identify ourselves with its insights ("reflections"). The mirror is one of Schopenhauer's favourite similes for the intellect. The term "instrument of navigation" is an apt expression for this, since it is indeed man's indispensable guide on pathless seas. But when the ground slips from under his feet and he begins to speculate in the void, seduced by the soaring flights of intuition, the situation becomes dangerous.

Here again the dreamer and the three dream figures form a quaternity. The unknown woman or anima always represents the "inferior," i.e., the undifferentiated function,

[75] The Homeric chain in alchemy is the series of great wise men, beginning with Hermes Trismegistus, which links earth with heaven. At the same time it is the chain of substances and different chemical states that appear in the course of the alchemical process. Cf. *Aurea catena Homeri* (Frankfurt and Leipzig, 1723).

which in the case of our dreamer is feeling. The croquet ball is connected with the "round" motif and is therefore a symbol of wholeness, that is, of the self, here shown to be hostile to the intellect (the mirror). Evidently the dreamer "navigates" too much by the intellect and thus upsets the process of individuation. In *De vita longa*, Paracelsus describes the "four" as *Scaiolae*, but the self as Adech (from Adam = the first man). Both, as Paracelsus emphasizes, cause so many difficulties in the "work" that one can almost speak of Adech as hostile.[76]

## 12. DREAM:

*The dreamer finds himself with his father, mother, and sister in a very dangerous situation on the platform of a tram-car.*

Once more the dreamer forms a quaternity with the other dream figures. He has fallen right back into childhood, a time when we are still a long way from wholeness. Wholeness is represented by the family, and its components are still projected upon the members of the family and personified by them. But this state is dangerous for the adult because regressive: it denotes a splitting of personality which primitive man experiences as the perilous "loss of soul." In the break-up the personal components that have been integrated with such pains are once more sucked into the outside world. The individual loses his guilt and exchanges it for infantile innocence; once more he can blame the wicked father for this and the unloving mother for that, and all the time he is caught in this inescapable causal nexus like a fly in a spider's web, without noticing that he has lost his moral freedom.[77] But no matter how much

[76] Jung, "Paracelsus as a Spiritual Phenomenon" (*Collected Works*, Vol. 13), pars. 209ff.

[77] Meister Eckhart says: " 'I came not upon earth to bring peace but a sword; to cut away all things, to part thee from brother, child, mother and friend, which are really thy foes.' For verily thy comforts are thy foes. Doth thine eye see all things and thine ear hear all things and thy heart remember them all, then in these things thy soul is destroyed."—*Eckhart*, op. cit., Vol. I, pp. 12–13.

parents and grandparents may have sinned against the child, the man who is really adult will accept these sins as his own condition which has to be reckoned with. Only a fool is interested in other people's guilt, since he cannot alter it. The wise man learns only from his own guilt. He will ask himself: Who am I that all this should happen to me? To find the answer to this fateful question he will look into his own heart.

As in the previous dream the vehicle was an airplane, so in this it is a tram. The type of vehicle in a dream illustrates the kind of movement or the manner in which the dreamer moves forward in time—in other words, how he lives his psychic life, whether individually or collectively, whether on his own or on borrowed means, whether spontaneously or mechanically. In the airplane he is flown by an unknown pilot; i.e., he is borne along on intuitions emanating from the unconscious. (The mistake is that the "mirror" is used too much to steer by.) But in this dream he is in a collective vehicle, a tram, which anybody can ride in; i.e., he moves or behaves just like everybody else. All the same he is again one of four, which means that he is in both vehicles on account of his unconscious striving for wholeness.

## 13. DREAM:

*In the sea there lies a treasure. To reach it, he has to dive through a narrow opening. This is dangerous, but down below he will find a companion. The dreamer takes the plunge into the dark and discovers a beautiful garden in the depths, symmetrically laid out, with a fountain in the centre.*

The "treasure hard to attain" lies hidden in the ocean of the unconscious, and only the brave can reach it. I conjecture that the treasure is also the "companion," the one who goes through life at our side—in all probability a close analogy to the lonely ego who finds a mate in the self, for at first the self is the strange non-ego. This is the theme of the magical travelling companion, of whom I will give three famous examples: the disciples on the road to Emmaus, Krishna and Arjuna in the Bhagavad Gita, Moses and El-Khidr in Sura 18 of the Koran.[78] I conjecture further that the treasure in the sea, the companion, and the garden with the fountain are all one and the same thing: the self. For the garden is another *temenos,* and the fountain is the source of "living water" mentioned in John 7 : 38, which the Moses of the Koran also sought and found, and beside it El-Khidr,[79] "one of Our servants whom We had endowed with Our grace and wisdom" (Sura 18). And the legend has it that the ground round about El-Khidr blossomed with spring flowers, although it was desert. In Islam, the plan of the *temenos* with the fountain developed under the influence of early Christian architecture into the court of the mosque with the ritual wash-house in the centre (e.g., Ahmed ibn-Tulun in Cairo). We see much the same thing in our Western cloisters with the fountain in the garden. This is also the "rose garden of the philosophers," which we know from the treatises on alchemy and from many beautiful engravings. "The Dweller in the House" (cf. commentary to dream 10) is the "companion." The centre and the circle, here represented by fountain and garden, are analogues of the *lapis,* which is among other things a living being. In the *Rosarium* the *lapis* says: "Protege me, protegam te. Largire mihi ius meum, ut te adiuvem" (Protect me and I will protect you. Give me my due that I may help you).[80] Here the *lapis* is nothing less than a good friend and helper who helps those that help him, and this points to a compensatory relationship. (I

[78] Cf. Jung, "Concerning Rebirth" (*Collected Works,* Vol. 9.i), pp. 135ff.

[79] Karl Vollers, "Chidher," *Archiv für Religions Wissenschaft* (Leipzig), XII (1909), 235.

[80] *Art. aurif.,* II, p. 239. This is a Hermes quotation from the "Tractatus aureus," but in the edition of 1566 (*Ars chemica*) it runs: "Largiri vis mihi meum ut adiuvem te" (You want to give me freely what is mine, that I may help you).

would call to mind what was said in the commentary to dream 10, more particularly the Monogenes-*lapis*-self parallel.)

The crash to earth thus leads into the depths of the sea, into the unconscious, and the dreamer reaches the shelter of the *temenos* as a protection against the splintering of personality caused by his regression to childhood. The situation is rather like that of dream 4 and vision 5 in the first series, where the magic circle warded off the lure of the unconscious and its plurality of female forms. (The dangers of temptation approach Poliphilo in much the same way at the beginning of his *nekyia*.)

The source of life is, like El-Khidr, a good companion, though it is not without its dangers, as Moses of old found to his cost, according to the Koran. It is the symbol of the life force that eternally renews itself and of the clock that never runs down. An uncanonical saying of our Lord runs: "He who is near unto me is near unto the fire." [81] Just as this esoteric Christ is a source of fire—probably not without reference to the πῦρ ἀεὶ ζῶον of Heraclitus—so the alchemical philosophers conceive their *aqua nostra* to be *ignis* (fire).[82] The source means not only the flow of life but its warmth, indeed its heat, the secret of passion, whose synonyms are always fiery.[83] The all-dissolving *aqua nostra* is an essential ingredient in the production of the *lapis*.

---

[81] A quotation from Aristotle in the *Rosarium, Art. aurif.*, II, p. 317, says: "Elige tibi pro lapide, per quem reges venerantur in Diadematibus suis . . . quia ille est propinquus igni" (Choose for your stone that through which kings are venerated in their crowns . . . because that [stone] is near to the fire).

[82] Cf. the treatise of Komarios, in which Cleopatra explains the meaning of the water (Berthelot, *Collection des anciens alchimistes grecs*, IV, xx).

[83] *Rosarium, Art. aurif.*, II, p. 378: "Lapis noster hic est ignis ex igne creatus et in ignem vertitur, et anima eius in igne moratur" (This our stone is fire, created of fire, and turns into fire; its soul dwells in fire). This may have been based on the following: "Item lapis noster, hoc est ignis ampulla, ex igne creatus est, et in cum vertitur" (Likewise this our stone, i.e., the flask of fire, is created out of fire and turns back into it).—"Allegoriae sapientum," *Bibl. chem. curiosa*, I, p. 468a.

But the source is underground and therefore the way leads underneath: only down below can we find the fiery source of life. These depths constitute the natural history of man, his causal link with the world of instinct. Unless this link be rediscovered no *lapis* and no self can come into being.

## 14. DREAM:

*The dreamer goes into a chemist's shop with his father. Valuable things can be got there quite cheap, above all a special water. His father tells him about the country the water comes from. Afterwards he crosses the Rubicon by train.*

The traditional apothecary's shop, with its carboys and gallipots, its waters, its *lapis divinus* and *infernalis* and its magisteries, is the last visible remnant of the kitchen paraphernalia of those alchemists who saw in the *donum spiritus sancti*—the precious gift—nothing beyond the chimera of goldmaking. The "special water" is literally the *aqua nostra non vulgi*.[84] It is easy to understand why it is his father who leads the dreamer to the source of life, since he is the natural source of the latter's life. We could say that the father represents the country or soil from which that life sprang. But figuratively speaking, he is the "informing spirit" who initiates the dreamer into the meaning of life and explains its secrets according to the teachings of old. He is a transmitter of the traditional wisdom. But nowadays the fatherly pedagogue fulfils this function only in the dreams of his son, where he appears as the archetypal father figure, the "wise old man."

[84] *Aqua nostra* is also called *aqua permanens*, corresponding to the ὕδωρ θεῖον of the Greeks: "aqua permanens, ex qua quidem aqua lapis noster pretiosissimus generatur," we read in the "Turba philosophorum," *Artis auriferae*, Vol. I, p. 14. "Lapis enim est haec ipsa permanens aqua et dum aqua est, lapis non est" (For the stone is this selfsame permanent water; and while it is water it is not the stone).—Ibid., p. 16. The commonness of the "water" is very often emphasized, as for instance in ibid., p. 30. "Quod quaerimus publice minimo pretio venditur, et si nosceretur, ne tantillum venderent mercatores" (What we are seeking is sold publicly for a very small price, and if it were recognized, the merchants would not sell it for so little).

The water of life is easily had: everybody possesses it, though without knowing its value. "Spernitur a stultis"—it is despised by the stupid, because they assume that every good thing is always outside and somewhere else, and that the source in their own souls is a "nothing but." Like the *lapis,* it is "pretio quoque vilis," of little price, and therefore, like the jewel in Spitteler's *Prometheus,* it is rejected by everyone from the high priest and the academicians down to the very peasants, and "in viam eiectus," flung out into the street, where Ahasuerus picks it up and puts it into his pocket. The treasure has sunk down again into the unconscious.

But the dreamer has noticed something and with vigorous determination crosses the Rubicon. He has realized that the flux and fire of life are not to be underrated and are absolutely necessary for the achievement of wholeness. But there is no recrossing the Rubicon.

*15.* DREAM:

*Four people are going down a river: the dreamer, his father, a certain friend, and the unknown woman.*

In so far as the "friend" is a definite person well known to the dreamer, he belongs, like the father, to the conscious world of the ego. Hence something very important has happened: in dream 11 the unconscious was three against one, but now the situation is reversed and it is the dreamer who is three against one (the latter being the unknown woman). The unconscious has been depotentiated. The reason for this is that by "taking the plunge" the dreamer has connected the upper and the lower regions—that is to say, he has decided not to live only as a bodiless abstract being but to accept the body and the world of instinct, the reality of the problems posed by love and life, and to act accordingly.[85] This was the Rubicon that was crossed.

[85] The alchemists give only obscure hints on this subject, e.g., the quotation from Aristotle in *Rosarium* (*Art. aurif.,* II, p. 318): "Fili, accipere debes de pinguiori carne" (Son, you must take of the fatter

Individuation, becoming a self, is not only a spiritual problem, it is the problem of all life.

## *16.* DREAM:

*Many people are present. They are all walking to the left around a square. The dreamer is not in the centre but to one side. They say that a gibbon is to be reconstructed.*

Here the square appears for the first time. Presumably it arises from the circle with the help of the four people. (This will be confirmed later.) Like the *lapis*, the *tinctura rubea*, and the *aurum philosophicum*, the squaring of the circle was a problem that greatly exercised medieval minds. It is a symbol of the *opus alchymicum*, since it breaks down the original chaotic unity into the four elements and then combines them again in a higher unity. Unity is represented by a circle and the four elements by a square. The production of one from four is the result of a process of distillation and sublimation which takes the so-called "circular" form: the distillate is subjected to sundry distillations[86] so that the "soul" or "spirit" shall be extracted in its purest state. The product is generally called the "quintessence," though this is by no means the only name for the ever-hoped-for and never-to-be-discovered "One." It has, as the alchemists say, a "thousand names," like the *prima materia*. Heinrich Khunrath has this to say about the circular distillation: "Through Circumrotation or a Circular Philosophical revolving of the Quaternarius, it is brought back to the highest and purest Simplicity of the plusquamperfect Catholic Monad. . . . Out of the gross and impure One there cometh an exceeding pure and subtile One," and so forth.[87]

---

flesh). And in the "Tractatus aureus," Chap. IV, we read: "Homo a principio naturae generatur, cuius viscera carnea sunt" (Man is generated from the principle of Nature whose inward parts are fleshy).
[86] Cf. "Paracelsus as a Spiritual Phenomenon" (*Collected Works*, Vol. 13), pars. 185ff.
[87] Heinrich Conrad Khunrath, *Von hylealischen, das ist, pri-materialischen catholischen, oder allgemeinem natürlichen Chaos* (Magdeburg, 1597), p. 204.

Soul and spirit must be separated from the body, and this is equivalent to death: "Therefore Paul of Tarsus saith, Cupio dissolvi, et esse cum Christo.[88] Therefore, my dear Philosopher, must thou catch the Spirit and Soul of the Magnesia." [89] The spirit (or spirit and soul) is the *ternarius* or number three which must first be separated from its body and, after the purification of the latter, infused back into it.[90] Evidently the body is the fourth. Hence Khunrath refers to a passage from Pseudo-Aristotle,[91] where the circle re-emerges from a triangle set in a square.[92] This circular figure, together with the Uroboros—the dragon devouring itself tail first—is the basic mandala of alchemy.

The Eastern and more particularly the Lamaic mandala usually contains a square ground-plan of the stupa. We can see from the mandalas constructed in solid form that it is really the plan of a *building*. The square also conveys the idea of a house or temple, or of an inner walled-in

[88] ". . . having a desire to be dissolved and to be with Christ" (Phil. (D.V.) 1 : 23).

[89] The "magnesia" of the alchemists has nothing to do with magnesia (MgO). In Khunrath (ibid., p. 161) it is the "materia coelestis et divina," i.e., the "materia lapidis Philosophorum," the arcane or transforming substance.

[90] Ibid., p. 203.

[91] Ibid., p. 207.

[92] There is a figurative representation of this idea in Michael Maier, *Scrutinium chymicum* (Frankfurt am Main, 1687), Emblema XXI. But Maier interprets the *ternarius* differently. He says (p. 63): "Similiter volunt Philosophi quadrangulum in triangulum ducendum esse, hoc est, in corpus, spiritum et animam, quae tria in trinis coloribus ante rubedinem praeviis apparent, utpote corpus seu terra in Saturni nigredine, spiritus in lunari albedine, tanquam aqua, anima sive aer in solari citrinitate. Tum triangulus perfectus erit, sed hic vicissim in circulum mutari debet, hoc est in rubedinem invariabilem." (Similarly the philosophers maintain that the quadrangle is to be reduced to a triangle, that is, to body, spirit, and soul. These three appear in three colours which precede the redness: the body, or earth, in Saturnine blackness; the spirit in lunar whiteness, like water; and the soul, or air, in solar yellow. Then the triangle will be perfect, but in its turn it must change into a circle, that is into unchangeable redness.) Here the fourth is fire, and an *everlasting* fire.

space[93] (cf. below). According to the ritual, stupas must always be circumambulated to the right, because a leftward movement is evil. The left, the "sinister" side, is the unconscious side. Therefore a leftward movement is equivalent to a movement in the direction of the unconscious, whereas a movement to the right is "correct" and aims at consciousness. In the East these unconscious contents have gradually, through long practice, come to assume definite forms which have to be accepted as such and retained by the conscious mind. Yoga, so far as we know it as an established practice, proceeds in much the same way: it impresses fixed forms on consciousness. Its most important Western parallel is the *Exercitia spiritualia* of Ignatius Loyola, which likewise impress fixed concepts about salvation on the psyche. This procedure is "right" so long as the symbol is still a valid expression of the unconscious situation. The psychological rightness of both Eastern and Western yoga ceases only when the unconscious process—which anticipates future modifications of consciousness—has developed so far that it produces shades of meaning which are no longer adequately expressed by, or are at variance with, the traditional symbol. Then and only then can one say that the symbol has lost its "rightness." Such a process signifies a gradual shift in man's unconscious view of the world over the centuries and has nothing whatever to do with intellectual criticisms of this view. Religious symbols are phenomena of life, plain facts and not intellectual opinions. If the Church clung for so long to the idea that the sun rotates round the earth, and then abandoned this contention in the nineteenth century, she can always appeal to the psychological truth that for millions of people the sun did revolve round the earth and that it was only in the nineteenth century that any major portion of mankind became sufficiently

[93] Cf. "city" and "castle" in commentary to dream 10. The alchemists similarly understand the *rotundum* arising out of the square as the *oppidum* (city). See Aegidius de Vadis, "Dialogus inter naturam et filium Philosophiae," *Theatrum chemicum*, Vol. 2, p. 115.

sure of the intellectual function to grasp the proofs of the earth's planetary nature. Unfortunately there is no "truth" unless there are people to understand it.

Presumably the leftward circumambulation of the square indicates that the squaring of the circle is a stage on the way to the unconscious, a point of transition leading to a goal lying as yet unformulated beyond it. It is one of those paths to the centre of the non-ego which were also trodden by the medieval investigators when producing the *lapis*. The *Rosarium* says:[94] "Out of man and woman make a round circle and extract the quadrangle from this and from the quadrangle the triangle. Make a round circle and you will have the philosophers' stone." [95]

[94] A quotation attributed to Pseudo-Aristotle ("Tractatus Aristotelis," *Theatr. chem.*, V, pp. 88off.), but not traceable.

[95] In the *Tractatus aureus . . . cum Scholiis Dominici Gnosii* (1610), p. 43, there is a drawing of the "secret square of the sages." In the centre of the square is a circle surrounded by rays of light. The scholium gives the following explanation: "Divide lapidem tuum in quatuor elementa . . . et coniunge in unum et totum habebis magisterium" (Reduce your stone to the four elements . . . and unite them into one and you will have the whole magistery)—a quotation from Pseudo-Aristotle. The circle in the centre is called "mediator, pacem faciens inter inimicos sive elementa imo hic solus efficit quadraturam circuli" (the mediator, making peace between enemies, or [the four] elements; nay rather he alone effects the squaring of the circle).—Ibid., p. 44. The circumambulation has its parallel in the "circulatio spirituum sive distillatio circularis, hoc est exterius intro, interius foras: item inferius et superius, simul in uno circulo conveniant, neque amplius cognoscas, quid vel exterius, vel interius, inferius vel superius fuerit: sed omnia sint unum in uno circulo sive vase. Hoc enim vas est Pelecanus verus Philosophicus, nec alius est in toto mundo quaerendus." ( . . . circulation of spirits or circular distillation, that is, the outside to the inside, the inside to the outside, likewise the lower and the upper; and when they meet together in one

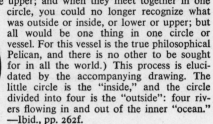

circle, you could no longer recognize what was outside or inside, or lower or upper; but all would be one thing in one circle or vessel. For this vessel is the true philosophical Pelican, and there is no other to be sought for in all the world.) This process is elucidated by the accompanying drawing. The little circle is the "inside," and the circle divided into four is the "outside": four rivers flowing in and out of the inner "ocean." —Ibid., pp. 262f.

The modern intellect naturally regards all this as poppy-cock. But this estimate fails to get rid of the fact that such concatenations of ideas do exist and that they even played an important part for many centuries. It is up to psychology to *understand* these things, leaving the layman to rant about poppycock and obscurantism. Many of my critics who call themselves "scientific" behave exactly like the bishop who excommunicated the cockchafers for their unseemly pro-liferation.

Just as the stupas preserve relics of the Buddha in their innermost sanctuary, so in the interior of the Lamaic quad-rangle, and again in the Chinese earth-square, there is a Holy of Holies with its magical agent, the cosmic source of energy, be it the god Shiva, the Buddha, a bodhisattva, or a great teacher. In China it is T'ien—heaven—with the four cosmic effluences radiating from it. And equally in the Western mandalas of medieval Christendom the deity is enthroned at the centre, often in the form of the triumphant Redeemer together with the four symbolical figures of the evangelists. The symbol in our dream presents the most violent contrast to these highly metaphysical ideas, for it is a gibbon, unquestionably an ape, that is to be reconstructed in the centre. Here we meet again the ape who first turned up in vision 22 of the first series. In that dream he caused a panic, but he also brought about the helpful intervention of the intellect. Now he is to be "reconstructed," and this can only mean that the anthropoid—man as an archaic fact —is to be put together again. Clearly the left-hand path does not lead upwards to the kingdom of the gods and eternal ideas, but down into natural history, into the bestial instinctive foundations of human existence. We are there-fore dealing, to put it in classical language, with a Dionysian mystery.

The square corresponds to the *temenos,* where a drama is taking place—in this case a play of apes instead of satyrs. The inside of the "golden flower" is a "seeding-place" where the "diamond body" is produced. The synonymous term "the ancestral land" [96] may actually be a hint that this product is the result of integrating the ancestral stages.

The ancestral spirits play an important part in primitive rites of renewal. The aborigines of central Australia even identify themselves with their mythical ancestors of the *alcheringa* period, a sort of Homeric age. Similarly the Pueblo Indians of Taos, in preparation for their ritual dances, identify with the sun, whose sons they are. This atavistic identification with human and animal ancestors can be interpreted psychologically as an integration of the unconscious, a veritable bath of renewal in the life-source where one is once again a fish, unconscious as in sleep, intoxication, and death. Hence the sleep of incubation, the Dionysian orgy, and the ritual death in initiation. Naturally the proceedings always take place in some hallowed spot. We can easily translate these ideas into the concretism of Freudian theory: the *temenos* would then be the womb of the mother and the rite a regression to incest. But these are the neurotic misunderstandings of people who have remained partly infantile and who do not realize that such things have been practised since time immemorial by adults whose activities cannot possibly be explained as a mere regression to infantilism. Otherwise the highest and most important achievements of mankind would ultimately be nothing but the perverted wishes of children, and the word "childish" would have lost its *raison d'être*.

Since the philosophical side of alchemy was concerned with problems that are very closely related to those which interest the most modern psychology, it might perhaps be worth while to probe a little deeper into the dream motif of the ape that is to be reconstructed in the square. In the overwhelming majority of cases alchemy identifies its transforming substance with the *argentum vivum* or Mercurius. Chemically this term denotes quicksilver, but philosophically it means the *spiritus vitae*, or even the world-soul, so that Mercurius also takes on the significance of Hermes,

[96] Wilhelm and Jung, *Secret of the Golden Flower* (1962 edn.), p. 22.

god of revelation. (This question has been discussed in detail elsewhere.)[97] Hermes is associated with the idea of roundness and also of squareness, as can be seen particularly in Papyrus V (line 401) of the *Papyri Graecae Magicae*,[98] where he is named στρογγύλος καὶ τετράλωνος, "round and square." He is also called τετραγλώχιν, "quadrangular." He is in general connected with the number four; hence there is a Ἑρμῆς τετρακέφαλος, a "four-headed Hermes." [99] These attributes were known also in the Middle Ages, as the work of Cartari,[100] for instance, shows. He says:

> Again, the square figures of Mercury [Hermes], made up of nothing but a head and a virile member, signify that the Sun is the head of the world, and scatters the seed of all things; while the four sides of the square figure have the same significance as the four-stringed sistrum which was likewise attributed to Mercury, namely, the four quarters of the world or the four seasons of the year; or again, that the two equinoxes and the two soltices make up between them the four parts of the whole zodiac.

It is easy to see why such qualities made Mercurius an eminently suitable symbol for the mysterious transforming substance of alchemy; for this is round and square, i.e., a totality consisting of four parts (four elements). Consequently the Gnostic quadripartite original man[101] as well as Christ Pantokrator is an *imago lapidis*. Western alchemy is mainly of Egyptian origin, so let us first of all turn our attention to the Hellenistic figure of Hermes Trismegistus, who, while standing sponsor to the medieval Mercurius,

[97] Cf. Jung, "The Spirit Mercurius" (*Collected Works*, Vol. 13).

[98] Karl Preisendanz, ed., *Papyri Graecae Magicae* (Leipzig, Berlin, 1928–31, 2 vols.), Vol. I, p. 195.

[99] Cf. Carl F. H. Bruchmann, *Epitheta deorum quae apud poetas Graecas leguntur, Ausführliches Lexikon der griechischen und römische Mythologie*, supplement (Leipzig, 1893), s.v.

[100] Vincenzo Cartari, *Les Images des dieux des anciens* (Lyons, 1581), p. 403.

[101] "Paracelsus as a Spiritual Phenomenon" (*Collected Works*, Vol. 13), pars. 168, 206ff.

derives ultimately from the ancient Egyptian Thoth. The attribute of Thoth was the baboon, or again he was represented outright as an ape.[102] This idea was visibly preserved all through the numberless editions of the Book of the Dead right down to the most recent times. It is true that in the existing alchemical texts—which with few exceptions belong to the Christian era—the ancient connection between Thoth-Hermes and the ape has disappeared, but it still existed at the time of the Roman Empire. Mercurius, however, had several things in common with the devil—which we will not enter upon here—and so the ape once more crops up in the vicinity of Mercurius as the *simia Dei*. It is of the essence of the transforming substance to be on the one hand extremely common, even contemptible (this is expressed in the series of attributes it shares with the devil, such as serpent, dragon, raven, lion, basilisk, and eagle), but on the other hand to mean something of great value, not to say divine. For the transformation leads from the depths to the heights, from the bestially archaic and infantile to the mystical *homo maximus*.

The symbolism of the rites of renewal, if taken seriously, points far beyond the merely archaic and infantile to man's innate psychic disposition, which is the result and deposit of all ancestral life right down to the animal level—hence the ancestor and animal symbolism. The rites are attempts to abolish the separation between the conscious mind and the unconscious, the real source of life, and to bring about a reunion of the individual with the native soil of his inherited, instinctive make-up. Had these rites of renewal not yielded definite results they would not only have died out in prehistoric times but would never have arisen in the first place. The case before us proves that even if the conscious mind is miles away from the ancient conceptions of the rites of renewal, the unconscious still strives to bring them closer in dreams. It is true that without the qualities of autonomy and autarky there would be no

[102] E. Wallis Budge, *The Gods of the Egyptians*, Vol. I, pp. 21, 404.

consciousness at all, yet these qualities also spell the danger of isolation and stagnation since, by splitting off the unconscious, they bring about an unbearable alienation of instinct. Loss of instinct is the source of endless error and confusion.

Finally the fact that the dreamer is "not in the centre but to one side" is a striking indication of what will happen to his ego: it will no longer be able to claim the central place but must presumably be satisfied with the position of a satellite, or at least of a planet revolving round the sun. Clearly the important place in the centre is reserved for the gibbon about to be reconstructed. The gibbon belongs to the anthropoids and, on account of its kinship with man, is an appropriate symbol for that part of the psyche which goes down into the subhuman. Further, we have seen from the cynocephalus or dog-headed baboon associated with Thoth-Hermes, the highest among the apes known to the Egyptians, that its godlike affinities make it an equally appropriate symbol for that part of the unconscious which transcends the conscious level. The assumption that the human psyche possesses layers that lie *below* consciousness is not likely to arouse serious opposition. But that there could just as well be layers lying *above* consciousness seems to be a surmise which borders on a *crimen laesae majestatis humanae.* In my experience the conscious mind can claim only a relatively central position and must accept the fact that the unconscious psyche transcends and as it were surrounds it on all sides. Unconscious contents connect it *backwards* with physiological states on the one hand and archetypal data on the other. But it is extended *forwards* by intuitions which are determined partly by archetypes and partly by subliminal perceptions depending on the relativity of time and space in the unconscious. I must leave it to the reader, after thorough consideration of this dream-series and the problems it opens up, to form his own judgment as to the possibility of such an hypothesis.

The following dream is given unabridged, in its original text:

17. DREAM:

*All the houses have something theatrical about them, with stage scenery and decorations. The name of Bernard Shaw is mentioned. The play is supposed to take place in the distant future. There is a notice in English and German on one of the sets:*

> *This is the universal Catholic Church.*
> *It is the Church of the Lord.*
> *All those who feel that they are the instruments of the Lord may enter.*

*Under this is printed in smaller letters: "The Church was founded by Jesus and Paul"—like a firm advertising its long standing.*

*I say to my friend, "Come on, let's have a look at this." He replies, "I do not see why a lot of people have to get together when they're feeling religious." I answer, "As a Protestant you will never understand." A woman nods emphatic approval. Then I see a sort of proclamation on the wall of the church. It runs:*

> *Soldiers!*
>
> *When you feel you are under the power of the Lord, do not address him directly. The Lord cannot be reached by words. We also strongly advise you not to indulge in any discussions among yourselves concerning the attributes of the Lord. It is futile, for everything valuable and important is ineffable.*
>
> (Signed) *Pope . . .* (Name illegible)

*Now we go in. The interior resembles a mosque, more particularly the Hagia Sophia: no seats—wonderful effect of space; no images, only framed texts decorating the walls (like the Koran texts in the Hagia Sophia). One of the*

*texts reads "Do not flatter your benefactor." The woman
who had agreed with me before bursts into tears and cries,
"Then there's nothing left!" I reply, "I find it quite right!"
but she vanishes. At first I stand with a pillar in front of
me and can see nothing. Then I change my position and
see a crowd of people. I do not belong to them and stand
alone. But they are quite distinct, so that I can see their
faces. They all say in unison, "We confess that we are
under the power of the Lord. The Kingdom of Heaven is
within us." They repeat this three times with great solemnity. Then the organ starts to play and they sing a Bach
fugue with chorale. But the original text is omitted; sometimes there is only a sort of coloratura singing, then the
words are repeated: "Everything else is paper" (meaning
that it does not make a living impression on me). When
the chorale has faded away the gemütlich part of the ceremony begins; it is almost like a students' party. The people
are all cheerful and equable. We move about, converse,
and greet one another, and wine (from an episcopal semi-
nary) is served with other refreshments. The health of the
Church is drunk and, as if to express everybody's pleasure
at the increase in membership, a loudspeaker blares out a
ragtime melody with the refrain, "Charles is also with us
now." A priest explains to me: "These somewhat trivial
amusements are officially approved and permitted. We
must adapt a little to American methods. With a large
crowd such as we have here this is inevitable. But we differ
in principle from the American churches by our decidedly
anti-ascetic tendency." Thereupon I awake with a feeling
of great relief.*

Unfortunately I must refrain from commenting on this
dream as a whole[103] and confine myself to our theme. The
*temenos* has become a sacred building (in accordance with
the hint given earlier). The proceedings are thus characterized as "religious." The grotesque-humorous side of the

[103] It was considered at length in my "Psychology and Religion"
(*Collected Works,* Vol. 11), pp. 24ff.

Dionysian mystery comes out in the so-called *gemütlich* part of the ceremony, where wine is served and a toast drunk to the health of the Church. An inscription on the floor of an Orphic-Dionysian shrine puts it very aptly: μόνον μὴ ὕδωρ (Only no water!).[104] The Dionysian relics in the Church, such as the fish and wine symbolism, the Damascus chalice, the seal-cylinder with the crucifix and the inscription ΟΡΦΕΟC BAKKIKOC,[105] and much else besides, can be mentioned only in passing.

The "anti-ascetic" tendency clearly marks the point of difference from the Christian Church, here defined as "American" (cf. commentary to dream 14 of the first series). America is the ideal home of the reasonable ideas of the practical intellect, which would like to put the world to rights by means of a "brain trust." [106] This view is in keeping with the modern formula "intellect = spirit," but it completely forgets the fact that "spirit" was never a human "activity," much less a "function." The movement to the left is thus confirmed as a withdrawal from the modern world of ideas and a regression to pre-Christian Dionysos worship, where "asceticism" in the Christian sense is unknown. At the same time the movement does not lead right out of the sacred spot but remains within it; in other words it does not lose its sacramental character. It does not simply fall into chaos and anarchy, it relates the Church directly to the Dionysian sanctuary just as the historical process did, though from the opposite direction.

---

[104] Orphic mosaic from Tramithia (Robert Eisler, *Orpheus—the Fisher* [London, 1921], pp. 271ff.). We can take this inscription as a joke without offending against the spirit of the ancient mysteries. (Cf. the frescoes in the Villa dei Misteri in Pompeii—Amadeo Maiuri, *La Villa dei Misteri* [Rome, 1931, 2 vols.]—where the drunkenness and ecstasy are not only closely related but actually one and the same thing.) But, since initiations have been connected with healing since their earliest days, the advice may possibly be a warning against water drinking, for it is well known that the drinking water in southern regions is the mother of dysentery and typhoid fever.
[105] Eisler, *Orpheus—the Fisher*, Plate XXXI.
[106] This is roughly the opinion of the dreamer.

We could say that this regressive development faithfully retreads the path of history in order to reach the pre-Christian level. Hence it is not a relapse but a kind of systematic descent *ad inferos,* a psychological *nekyia.*

I encountered something very similar in the dream of a clergyman who had a rather problematical attitude to his faith: *Coming into his church at night, he found that the whole wall of the choir had collapsed. The altar and ruins were overgrown with vines hanging full of grapes, and the moon was shining in through the gap.*

Again, a man who was much occupied with religious problems had the following dream: *An immense Gothic cathedral, almost completely dark. High Mass is being celebrated. Suddenly the whole wall of the aisle collapses. Blinding sunlight bursts into the interior together with a large herd of bulls and cows.* This setting is evidently more Mithraic, but Mithras is associated with the early Church in much the same way Dionysos is.

Interestingly enough, the church in our dream is a syncretistic building, for the Hagia Sophia is a very ancient Christian church which, however, served as a mosque until quite recently. It therefore fits in very well with the purpose of the dream: to attempt a combination of Christian and Dionysian religious ideas. Evidently this is to come about without the one excluding the other, without any values being destroyed. This is extremely important, since the reconstruction of the "gibbon" is to take place in the sacred precincts. Such a sacrilege might easily lead to the dangerous supposition that the leftward movement is a *diabolica fraus* and the gibbon the devil—for the devil is in fact regarded as the "ape of God." The leftward movement would then be a perversion of divine truth for the purpose of setting up "His Black Majesty" in place of God. But the unconscious has no such blasphemous intentions; it is only trying to restore the lost Dionysos who is somehow lacking in modern man (*pace* Nietzsche!) to the world of religion. At the end of vision 22, where the ape first appears, it was said that "everything must be ruled by the light," and everything, we might add, includes the Lord of Darkness with his horns and cloven hoof—actually a Dionysian corybant who has rather unexpectedly risen to the rank of Prince.

The Dionysian element has to do with emotions and affects which have found no suitable religious outlets in the predominantly Apollonian cult and ethos of Christianity. The medieval carnivals and *jeux de paume* in the Church were abolished relatively early; consequently the carnival became secularized and with it divine intoxication vanished from the sacred precincts. Mourning, earnestness, severity, and well-tempered spiritual joy remained. But intoxication, that most direct and dangerous form of possession, turned away from the gods and enveloped the human world with its exuberance and pathos. The pagan religions met this danger by giving drunken ecstasy a place within their cult. Heraclitus doubtless saw what was at the back of it when he said, "But Hades is that same Dionysos in whose honour they go mad and keep the feast of the wine-vat." For this very reason orgies were granted religious license, so as to exorcise the danger that threatened from Hades. Our solution, however, has served to throw the gates of hell wide open.

18. DREAM:

*A square space with complicated ceremonies going on in it, the purpose of which is to transform animals into men. Two snakes, moving in opposite directions, have to be got rid of at once. Some animals are there, e.g., foxes and dogs. The people walk round the square and must let themselves be bitten in the calf by these animals at each of the four corners. If they run away all is lost. Now the higher animals come on the scene—bulls and ibexes. Four snakes glide into the four corners. Then the congregation files out. Two sacrificial priests carry in a huge reptile and with this they touch the forehead of a shapeless animal lump or life-mass. Out of it there instantly rises a human head, transfigured. A voice proclaims: "These are attempts at being."*

One might almost say that the dream goes on with the "explanation" of what is happening in the square space. Animals are to be changed into men; a "shapeless life-mass" is to be turned into a transfigured (illuminated) human head by magic contact with a reptile. The animal lump or life-mass stands for the mass of the inherited unconscious which is to be united with consciousness. This is brought about by the ceremonial use of a reptile, presumably a snake. The idea of transformation and renewal by means of a serpent is a well-substantiated archetype. It is the healing serpent, representing the god. It is reported of the mysteries of Sabazius: "Aureus coluber in sinum demittitur consecratis et eximitur rursus ab inferioribus partibus atque imis" (A golden snake is let down into the lap of the initiated and taken away again from the lower parts).[107] Among the Ophites, Christ was the serpent. Probably the most significant development of serpent symbolism as regards renewal of personality is to be found in Kundalini yoga.[108] The shepherd's experience with the snake in Nietzsche's *Zarathustra* would accordingly be a fatal omen (and not the only one of its kind—cf. the prophecy at the death of the rope-dancer).

The "shapeless life-mass" immediately recalls the ideas of the alchemical "chaos," [109] the *massa* or *materia informis* or *confusa* which has contained the divine seeds of life ever since the Creation. According to a midrashic view, Adam was created in much the same way: in the first hour

---

[107] Arnobius, *Adversus gentes*, V, 21 (Migne, *Patrologiae . . .*, Latin series [Paris, 1844–64, 221 vols.], Vol. 5, col. 1125). For similar practices during the Middle Ages, cf. Joseph Hammer-Purgstall, *Mémoire sur deux coffrets gnostiques du moyen âge* (Paris, 1835).
[108] Avalon, *The Serpent Power*; Sir John George Woodroffe, *Shakti and Shakta* (Madras, 1920).
[109] The alchemists refer to Lactantius, *Opera*, I, p. 14, 20: "a chao, quod est rudis inordinataeque materiae confusa congeries" (from the chaos, which is a confused assortment of crude disordered matter).

God collected the dust, in the second made a shapeless mass out of it, in the third fashioned the limbs, and so on.[110]

But if the life-mass is to be transformed a *circumambulatio* is necessary, i.e., exclusive concentration on the centre, the place of creative change. During this process one is "bitten" by animals; in other words, we have to expose ourselves to the animal impulses of the unconscious without identifying with them and without "running away"; for flight from the unconscious would defeat the purpose of the whole proceeding. We must hold our ground, which means here that the process initiated by the dreamer's self-observation must be experienced in all its ramifications and then articulated with consciousness to the best of his understanding. This often entails an almost unbearable tension because of the utter incommensurability between conscious life and the unconscious process, which can be experienced only in the innermost soul and cannot touch the visible surface of life at any point. The principle of conscious life is: "Nihil est in intellectu, quod non prius fuerit in sensu." But the principle of the unconscious is the autonomy of the psyche itself, reflecting in the play of its images not the world but *itself*, even though it utilizes the illustrative possibilities offered by the sensible world in order to make its images clear. The sensory datum, however, is not the *causa efficiens* of this; rather, it is autonomously selected and exploited by the psyche, with the result that the rationality of the cosmos is constantly being violated in the most distressing manner. But the sensible world has an equally devastating effect on the deeper psychic processes when it breaks into them as a *causa efficiens*. If reason is not to be outraged on the one hand and the creative play of images not violently suppressed on the other, a circumspect and farsighted synthetic procedure is required in order to accomplish the paradoxical

[110] J. Dreyfuss, *Adam und Eva nach der Auffassung des Midrasch* (Strassburg, 1894), quoted by Reitzenstein, *Poimandres*, p. 258.

union of irreconcilables. Hence the alchemical parallels in our dreams.

The focusing of attention on the centre demanded in this dream and the warning about "running away" have clear parallels in the *opus alchymicum:* the need to concentrate on the work and to meditate upon it is stressed again and again. The tendency to run away, however, is attributed not to the operator but to the transforming substance. Mercurius is evasive and is labelled *servus* (servant) or *cervus fugitivus* (fugitive stag). The vessel must be well sealed so that what is within may not escape. Eirenaeus Philalethes[111] says of this *servus:* "You must be very wary how you lead him, for if he can find an opportunity he will give you the slip, and leave you to a world of misfortune." [112] It did not occur to these philosophers that they were chasing a projection, and that the more they attributed to the substance the further away they were getting from the psychological source of their expectations. From the difference between the material in this dream and its medieval predecessors we can measure the psychological advance: the running away is now clearly apparent as a characteristic of the dreamer, i.e., it is no longer projected into the unknown substance. Running away thus becomes a moral question. This aspect was recognized by the alchemists in so far as they emphasized the need for a special religious devotion at their work, though one cannot altogether clear them of the suspicion of having used their prayers and pious exercises for the purpose of forcing a miracle—there are even some who aspired to have the Holy Ghost as their familiar! [113] But, to do them justice, one should not overlook the fact that

[111] Pseudonymous author ("peaceable lover of truth") who lived in England at the beginning of the 17th century.
[112] Eirenaeus Philalethes, *Ripley Reviv'd; or An Exposition upon Sir George Ripley's Hermetico-Poetical Work. . . .* (London, 1678), p. 100.
[113] [Cf. *Mysterium Coniunctionis* (*Collected Works,* Vol. 14), p. 288, n. 116.—EDITORS OF *The Collected Works.*]

there is more than a little evidence in the literature that
they realized it was a matter of their own transformation.
For instance, Gerhard Dorn exclaims, "Transmutemini in
vivos lapides philosophicos!" (Transform yourselves into
living philosophical stones!)

Hardly have conscious and unconscious touched when
they fly asunder on account of their mutual antagonism.
Hence, right at the beginning of the dream, the snakes that
are making off in opposite directions have to be removed;
i.e., the conflict between conscious and unconscious is at
once resolutely stopped and the conscious mind is forced
to stand the tension by means of the *circumambulatio*.
The magic circle thus traced will also prevent the unconscious from breaking out again, for such an eruption
would be equivalent to psychosis. "Nonnulli perierunt in
opere nostro": "Not a few have perished in our work," we
can say with the author of the *Rosarium*. The dream
shows that the difficult operation of thinking in paradoxes
—a feat possible only to the superior intellect—has succeeded. The snakes no longer run away but settle themselves in the four corners, and the process of transformation or integration sets to work. The "transfiguration" and
illumination, the conscious recognition of the centre, has
been attained, or at least anticipated, in the dream. This
potential achievement—if it can be maintained, i.e., if the
conscious mind does not lose touch with the centre again[114]
—means a renewal of personality. Since it is a subjective
state whose reality cannot be validated by any external
criterion, any further attempt to describe and explain it is
doomed to failure, for only those who have had this experience are in a position to understand and attest its
reality. "Happiness," for example, is such a noteworthy
reality that there is nobody who does not long for it, and

[114] Cf. the commentary to dream 10, second series: "And, being
chained to the arms and breast of my mother, and to her substance,
I cause my substance to hold together and rest." ("Tractatus aureus,"
Chap. IV.)

yet there is not a single objective criterion which would prove beyond all doubt that this condition necessarily exists. As so often with the most important things, we have to make do with a subjective judgment.

The arrangement of the snakes in the four corners is indicative of an order in the unconscious. It is as if we were confronted with a pre-existent ground plan, a kind of Pythagorean *tetraktys*. I have very frequently observed the number four in this connection. It probably explains the universal incidence and magical significance of the cross or of the circle divided into four. In the present case the point seems to be to capture and regulate the animal instincts so as to exorcise the danger of falling into unconsciousness. This may well be the empirical basis of the cross as that which vanquishes the powers of darkness.

In this dream the unconscious has managed to stage a powerful advance by thrusting its contents dangerously near to the conscious sphere. The dreamer appears to be deeply entangled in the mysterious synthetic ceremony and will unfailingly carry a lasting memory of the dream into his conscious life. Experience shows that this results in a serious conflict for the conscious mind, because it is not always either willing or able to put forth the extraordinary intellectual and moral effort needed to take a paradox seriously. Nothing is so jealous as a truth.

As a glance at the history of the medieval mind will show, our whole modern mentality has been moulded by Christianity. (This has nothing to do with whether we believe the truths of Christianity or not.) Consequently the reconstruction of the ape in the sacred precincts as proposed by the dream comes as such a shock that the majority of people will seek refuge in blank incomprehension. Others will heedlessly ignore the abysmal depths of the Dionysian mystery and will welcome the rational Darwinian core of the dream as a safeguard against mystic exaltation. Only a very few will feel the collision of the two worlds and realize what it is all about. Yet the dream says plainly enough that in the place where, according to tradition, the deity dwells, the ape is to appear. This substitution is almost as bad as a Black Mass.

In Eastern symbolism the square—signifying the earth in China, the *padma* or lotus in India—has the character of the *yoni:* femininity. A man's unconscious is likewise feminine and is personified by the anima.[115] The anima also stands for the "inferior" function[116] and for that reason frequently has a shady character; in fact she sometimes stands for evil itself. She is as a rule the *fourth* person (cf. dreams 10, 11, 15). She is the dark and dreaded maternal womb, which is of an essentially ambivalent nature. The Christian deity is one in three persons. The fourth person in the heavenly drama is undoubtedly the devil. In the more harmless psychological version he is merely the inferior function. On a moral valuation he is a man's sin, a function belonging to him and presumably masculine. The feminine element in the deity is kept very dark, the interpretation of the Holy Ghost as Sophia being considered heretical. Hence the Christian metaphysical drama, the "Prologue in Heaven," has only masculine actors, a point it shares with many of the ancient mysteries. But the feminine element must obviously be somewhere—so it is presumably to be found in the dark. At any rate that is where the ancient Chinese philosophers located it: in the *yin*.[117] Although man and woman unite they never-

---

[115] The idea of the anima as I define it is by no means a novelty but an archetype which we meet in the most diverse places. It was also known in alchemy, as the following scholium proves ("Tractatus aureus," in *Bibl. chem. curiosa,* I, p. 417): "Quemadmodum in sole ambulantis corpus continuo sequitur umbra . . . sic hermaphroditus noster Adamicus, quamvis in forma masculi appareat semper tamen in corpore occultatam Evam sive foeminam suam secum circumfert" (As the shadow continually follows the body of one who walks in the sun, so our hermaphroditic Adam, though he appears in the form of a male, nevertheless always carries about with him Eve, or his wife, hidden in his body).

[116] Cf. supra, pp. 266–69.

[117] "Tractatus aureus," *Ars chemica,* p. 12: "Verum masculus est coelum foeminae et foemina terra masculi" (The male is the heaven of the female, and the female is the earth of the male).

theless represent irreconcilable opposites which, when activated, degenerate into deadly hostility. This primordial pair of opposites symbolizes every conceivable pair of opposites that may occur: hot and cold, light and dark, north and south, dry and damp, good and bad, conscious and unconscious. In the psychology of the functions there are two conscious and therefore masculine functions, the differentiated function and its auxiliary, which are represented in dreams by, say, father and son, whereas the unconscious functions appear as mother and daughter. Since the conflict between the two auxiliary functions is not nearly as great as that between the differentiated and the inferior function, it is possible for the third function— that is, the unconscious auxiliary one—to be raised to consciousness and thus made masculine. It will, however, bring with it traces of its contamination with the inferior function, thus acting as a kind of link with the darkness of the unconscious. It was in keeping with this psychological fact that the Holy Ghost should be heretically interpreted as Sophia, for he was the mediator of birth in the flesh, who enabled the deity to shine forth in the darkness of the world. No doubt it was this association that caused the Holy Ghost to be suspected of femininity, for Mary was the dark earth of the field—"illa terra virgo nondum pluviis irrigata" (that virgin earth not yet watered by the rains), as Tertullian called her.[118]

The fourth function is contaminated with the unconscious and, on being made conscious, drags the whole of the unconscious with it. We must then come to terms with the unconscious and try to bring about a synthesis of opposites.[119] At first a violent conflict breaks out, such as

---

[118] *Adversus Judaeos,* 13 (Migne, *P.L.*, Vol. 2, col. 655).
[119] Alchemy regarded this synthesis as one of its chief tasks. The *Turba philosophorum* (ed. Ruska, p. 26) says: "Coniungite ergo masculinum servi rubei filium suae odoriferae uxori et iuncti artem gignunt" (Join therefore the male son of the red slave to his sweet-scented wife, and joined together they will generate the Art). This synthesis of opposites was often represented as a brother-and-sister incest, which version undoubtedly goes back to the "Visio Arislei,"

any reasonable man would experience when it became evident that he had to swallow a lot of absurd superstitions. Everything in him would rise up in revolt and he would defend himself desperately against what looked to him like murderous nonsense. This situation explains the following dreams.

*19.* DREAM:

*Ferocious war between two peoples.*

This dream depicts the conflict. The conscious mind is defending its position and trying to suppress the unconscious. The first result of this is the expulsion of the fourth function, but, since it is contaminated with the third, there is a danger of the latter disappearing as well. Things would then return to the state that preceded the present one, when only two functions were conscious and the other two unconscious.

*20.* DREAM:

*There are two boys in a cave. A third falls in as if through a pipe.*

The cave represents the darkness and seclusion of the unconscious; the two boys correspond to the two unconscious functions. Theoretically the third must be the auxiliary function, which would indicate that the conscious mind had become completely absorbed in the differentiated function. The odds now stand 1 : 3, greatly in favour of the unconscious. We may therefore expect a new advance on its part and a return to its former position. The "boys" are an allusion to the dwarf motif, of which more later.

*21.* DREAM:

*A large transparent sphere containing many little spheres. A green plant is growing out of the top.*

---

Art. aurif., I, where the cohabitation of Thabritius and Beya, the children of the *Rex marinus,* is described (see Jung, *Psychology and Alchemy* [Collected Works, Vol. 12], pars. 434ff.).

The sphere is a whole that embraces all its contents; life which has been brought to a standstill by useless struggle becomes possible again. In Kundalini yoga the "green womb" is a name for Ishvara (Shiva) emerging from his latent condition.

## 22. DREAM:

*The dreamer is in an American hotel. He goes up in the lift to about the third or fourth floor. He has to wait there with a lot of other people. A friend (an actual person) is also there and says that the dreamer should not have kept the dark unknown woman waiting so long below, since he had put her in his (the dreamer's) charge. The friend now gives him an unsealed note for the dark woman, on which is written: "Salvation does not come from refusing to take part or from running away. Nor does it come from just drifting. Salvation comes from complete surrender, with one's eyes always turned to the centre." On the margin of the note there is a drawing: a wheel or wreath with eight spokes. Then a lift-boy appears and says that the dreamer's room is on the eighth floor. He goes on up in the lift, this time to the seventh or eighth floor. An unknown red-haired man, standing there, greets him in a friendly way. Then the scene changes. There is said to be a revolution in Switzerland: the military party is making propaganda for "completely throttling the left." The objection that the left is weak enough anyway is met by the answer that this is just why it ought to be throttled completely. Soldiers in old-fashioned uniforms now appear, who all resemble the red-haired man. They load their guns with ramrods, stand in a circle, and prepare to shoot at the centre. But in the end they do not shoot and seem to march away. The dreamer wakes up in terror.*

The tendency to re-establish a state of wholeness—already indicated in the foregoing dream—once more comes up against a consciousness with a totally different orientation. It is therefore appropriate that the dream should have an American background. The lift is going up, as is right and proper when something is coming "up" from the "sub-"conscious. What is coming up is the unconscious content, namely the mandala characterized by the number four. Therefore the lift should rise to the fourth floor; but, as the fourth function is taboo, it only rises to "about the third or fourth." This happens not to the dreamer alone but to many others as well, who must all wait like him until the fourth function can be accepted. A good friend then calls his attention to the fact that he should not have kept the dark woman, i.e., the anima who stands for the tabooed function, waiting "below," i.e., in the unconscious, which was just the reason why the dreamer himself had to wait upstairs with the others. It is in fact not merely an individual but a collective problem, for the animation of the unconscious which has become so noticeable in recent times has, as Schiller foresaw, raised questions which the nineteenth century never even dreamed of. Nietzsche in his *Zarathustra* decided to reject the "snake" and the "ugliest man," thus exposing himself to an heroic cramp of consciousness which led, logically enough, to the collapse foretold in the same book.

The advice given in the note is as profound as it is to the point, so that there is really nothing to add. After it has been more or less accepted by the dreamer the ascent can be resumed. We must take it that the problem of the fourth function was accepted, at least broadly, for the dreamer now reaches the seventh or eighth floor, which means that the fourth function is no longer represented by a quarter but by an eighth, and is apparently reduced by a half.

Curiously enough, this hesitation before the last step to wholeness seems also to play a part in *Faust II,* where, in the Cabiri scene, "resplendent mermaids" come from over the water:[120]

[120] [Based on the translation by Philip Wayne (*Faust*, Part II, pp. 145f.). Slight modifications have been necessary to accommodate his version to Jung's commentary.—TRANSLATOR.]

| | |
|---|---|
| NEREIDS AND TRITONS: | Bear we, on the waters riding, That which brings you all glad tiding. In Chelone's giant shield Gleams a form severe revealed: These are gods that we are bringing; Hail them, you high anthems singing. |
| SIRENS: | Little in length, Mighty in strength! Time-honoured gods Of shipwreck and floods. |
| NEREIDS AND TRITONS: | Great Cabiri do we bear, That our feast be friendly fair: Where their sacred powers preside Neptune's rage is pacified. |

A "form severe" is brought by "mermaids," feminine figures who represent as it were the sea and the waves of the unconscious. The word "severe" reminds us of "severe" architectural or geometrical forms which illustrate a definite idea without any romantic (feeling-toned) trimmings. It "gleams" from the shell of a tortoise,[121] which, primitive and cold-blooded like the snake, symbolizes the instinctual side of the unconscious. The "image" is somehow identical with the unseen, creative dwarf-gods, hooded and cloaked manikins who are kept hidden in the dark *cista,* but who also appear on the seashore as little figures about a foot high, where, as kinsmen of the unconscious, they protect navigation, i.e., the venture into darkness and uncertainty. In the form of the Dactyls they are also the gods of invention, small and apparently insignificant like the impulses of the unconscious but endowed with the same mighty power. (*El gabir* is "the great, the mighty one.")

[121] The *testudo* (tortoise) is an alchemical instrument, a shallow bowl with which the cooking-vessel was covered on the fire. See Johannes Rhenanus, *Solis e puteo emergentis sive dissertationis chymotechnicae libri tres* (Frankfurt am Main, 1613), p. 40.

| NEREIDS AND TRITONS: | Three have followed where we led,<br>But the fourth refused to call;<br>He the rightful seer, he said,<br>His to think for one and all. |
|---|---|
| SIRENS: | A god may count it sport<br>To set a god at naught.<br>Honour the grace they bring,<br>And fear their threatening. |

It is characteristic of Goethe's feeling-toned nature that the fourth should be the thinker. If the supreme principle is "feeling is all," then thinking has to play an unfavourable role and be submerged. *Faust I* portrays this development. Since Goethe acted as his own model, thinking became the fourth (taboo) function. Because of its contamination with the unconscious it takes on the grotesque form of the Cabiri, for the Cabiri, as dwarfs, are chthonic gods and misshapen accordingly. ("I call them pot-bellied freaks of common clay.") They thus stand in grotesque contrast to the heavenly gods and poke fun at them (cf. the "ape of God"). The Nereids and Tritons sing:

| | Seven there should really be. |
|---|---|
| SIRENS: | Where, then, stay the other three? |
| NEREIDS AND TRITONS: | That we know not. You had best<br>On Olympus make your quest.<br>There an eighth may yet be sought<br>Though none other gave him thought.<br>Well inclined to us in grace,<br>Not all perfect yet their race.<br>Beings there beyond compare,<br>Yearning, unexplainable,<br>Press with hunger's pang to share<br>In the unattainable. |

We learn that there are "really" seven of them; but again there is some difficulty with the eighth as there was

before with the fourth. Similarly, in contradiction to the
previous emphasis placed on their lowly origin in the dark,
it now appears that the Cabiri are actually to be found on
Olympus; for they are eternally striving from the depths to
the heights and are therefore always to be found both
below *and* above. The "severe image" is obviously an unconscious content that struggles towards the light. It seeks,
and itself is, what I have elsewhere called "the treasure
hard to attain." [122] This hypothesis is immediately confirmed:

> SIRENS:    Fame is dimmed of ancient time,
>            Honour droops in men of old;
>            Though they have the Fleece of Gold,
>            Ye have the Cabiri.

The Golden Fleece is the coveted goal of the argosy, the
perilous quest that is one of the numerous synonyms for
attaining the unattainable. Thales makes this wise remark
about it:

> That is indeed what men most seek on earth:
> 'Tis rust alone that gives the coin its worth!

The unconscious is always the fly in the ointment, the
skeleton in the cupboard of perfection, the painful lie given
to all idealistic pronouncements, the earthliness that clings
to our human nature and sadly clouds the crystal clarity
we long for. In the alchemical view rust, like verdigris, is
the metal's sickness. But at the same time this leprosy is
the *vera prima materia,* the basis for the preparation of the
philosophical gold. The *Rosarium* says:

> Our gold is not the common gold. But thou hast inquired
> concerning the greenness [*viriditas,* presumably verdigris],
> deeming the bronze to be a leprous body on account of
> the greenness it hath upon it. Therefore I say unto thee

[122] Jung, *Symbols of Transformation (Collected Works,* Vol. 5),
index, s.v.

that whatever is perfect in the bronze is that greenness only, because that greenness is straightway changed by our magistery into our most true gold.[123]

The paradoxical remark of Thales that the rust alone gives the coin its true value is a kind of alchemical quip, which at bottom only says that there is no light without shadow and no psychic wholeness without imperfection. To round itself out, life calls not for perfection but for completeness; and for this the "thorn in the flesh" is needed, the suffering of defects without which there is no progress and no ascent.

The problem of three and four, seven and eight, which Goethe has tackled here was a great puzzle to alchemy and goes back historically to the texts ascribed to Christianos.[124] In the treatise on the production of the "mythical water" it is said: "Therefore the Hebrew prophetess cried without restraint, 'One becomes two, two becomes three, and out of the third comes the One as the fourth.' "[125] In alchemical literature this prophetess is taken to be Maria Prophetissa,[126] also called the Jewess, sister of Moses, or the Copt, and it is not unlikely that she is connected with the Maria of Gnostic tradition. Epiphanius testifies to the existence of writings by this Maria, namely the "Interrogationes magnae" and "Interrogationes parvae," said to describe a vision of how Christ, on a mountain, caused a woman to come forth from his side and how he mingled himself with her.[127] It is probably no accident that the treatise of Maria

---

[123] *Art. aurif.*, II, p. 220: a quotation from Senior. *Viriditas* is occasionally called *azoth*, which is one of the numerous synonyms for the stone.

[124] According to Marcellin Berthelot (*Origines de l'alchimie* [Paris, 1885], p. 100), the anonymous author called Christianos was a contemporary of Stephanos of Alexandria, and must therefore have lived about the beginning of the 7th century.

[125] Berthelot, *Alchimistes grecs*, VI, v, 6. The almost bestial κραυγάζειν (shriek) points to an ecstatic condition.

[126] A treatise (of Arabic origin?) is ascribed to her under the title "Practica Mariae Prophetissae in artem alchemicam," *Art. aurif.*, I, pp. 319ff.

[127] *Panarium*, XXVI. Concerning further possible connections with Mariamne and with the Mary Magdalene of the *Pistis Sophia*, cf.

(see n. 126) deals with the theme of the *matrimonium alchymicum* in a dialogue with the philosopher Aros,[128] from which comes the saying, often repeated later: "Marry gum with gum in true marriage." [129] Originally it was "gum arabic," and it is used here as a secret name for the transforming substance, on account of its adhesive quality. Thus Khunrath[130] declares that the "red" gum is the "resin of the wise"—a synonym for the transforming substance. This substance, as the life force (*vis animans*), is likened by another commentator to the "glue of the world" (*glutinum mundi*), which is the medium between mind and body and the union of both.[131] The old treatise "Consilium coniugii" explains that the "philosophical man" consists of the "four natures of the stone." Of these three are earthy or in the earth, but "the fourth nature is the water of the stone, namely the viscous gold which is called red gum and with which the three earthy natures are tinted." [132] We learn here that gum is the critical fourth nature: it is duplex, i.e., masculine and feminine, and at the same time the one and only aqua mercurialis. So the union of the two is a kind of self-fertilization, a characteristic always ascribed to the mercurial dragon.[133] From these hints it can easily be seen

---

Hans Leisegang, *Die Gnosis* (Leipzig, 1924), pp. 113f., and Carl Schmidt, "Gnostische Schriften in koptischer Sprache aus dem Codex Brucianus heraus gegeben," *Texte und Untersuchungen der altchristlichen Literatur* (Leipzig), VIII (1892), 1–692.

[128] Aros = Horos. Ἶσις προφῆτις τῷ υἱῷ αὐτῆς (Berthelot, *Alchimistes grecs*, I, xiii) may be an earlier version of the Maria dialogue. Isis and Maria were easy to confuse.

[129] "Matrimonifica gummi cum gummi vero matrimonio."—*Art. aurif.*, I, p. 320.

[130] *Von hylealischen Chaos*, pp. 239f.

[131] "Aphorismi Basiliani," *Theatr. chem.*, IV, p. 368.

[132] *Ars chemica*, pp. 247, 255.

[133] Arnaldus de Villanova ("Carmen," *Theatr. chem.*, IV, p. 614) has summed up the quintessence of Maria's treatise very aptly in the following verses:

"Maria mira sonat breviter, quod talia tonat.
Gummis cum binis fugitivum figit in imis. . . .
Filia Plutonis consortia iungit amoris,
Gaudet in assata sata per tria sociata."

(Maria utters brief wonders because such are the things that she thunders.

who the philosophical man is: he is the androgynous original man or Anthropos of Gnosticism,[134] whose parallel in India is *purusha*. Of him the Brihadaranyaka Upanishad says: "He was as large as a man and woman embracing. He divided his self [Atman] in two, and thence arose husband and wife. He united himself with her and men were born," etc.[135] The common origin of these ideas lies in the primitive notion of the bisexual original man.

The fourth nature—to return to the text of the "Consilium coniugii"—leads straight to the Anthropos idea that stands for man's wholeness, that is, the conception of a unitary being who existed before man and at the same time represents man's goal. The one joins the three as the fourth and thus produces the synthesis of the four in a unity.[136] We seem to be dealing with much the same thing in the case of seven and eight, though this motif occurs much less frequently in the literature. It is, however, to be found in Paracelsus' *Ein ander Erklärung der gantzen Astronomie*,[137] to which Goethe had access. "One is powerful, Six are subjects, the Eighth is also powerful"—and somewhat more so than the first. One is the king, the six are his servants and his son; so here we have King Sol and the six planets

---

She fixes what runs to the bottom with double-strong gums. . . .
This daughter of Pluto unites love's affinities,
Delighting in everything sown, roasted, assembled by threes.)
[134] Cf. my remarks on Paracelsus' "Adech" in "Paracelsus as a Spiritual Phenomenon" (*Collected Works*, Vol. 13), pars. 168, 203ff.
[135] I.4.3. (Cf. Max Müller, *The Upanishads*, II, *Sacred Books of the East XV* [Oxford, 1884], pp. 85–86.)
[136] There is a rather different formulation in Distinction XIV of the "Allegoriae sapientum" (*Theatr. chem.*, V, p. 86): "Unum et est duo, et duo et sunt tria, et tria et sunt quatuor, et quatuor et sunt tria, et tria et sunt duo, et duo et sunt unum" (One, and it is two; and two, and it is three; and three, and it is four; and four, and it is three; and three, and it is two; and two, and it is one). This evidently represents the quartering (tetrameria) of the one and the synthesis of the four in one.
[137] In Karl Sudhoff and Wilhelm Matthiessen, eds., *Theophrast von Hohenheim genannt Paracelsus. Sämtliche Werke* (Munich, Berlin, 1922–33, 15 vols.), Vol. XII.

or metallic homunculi as depicted in the *Pretiosa margarita novella* of Petrus Bonus (Lacinius edition, 1546).[138] As a matter of fact the eighth does not appear in this text; Paracelsus seems to have invented it himself. But since the eighth is even more "powerful" than the first, the crown is presumably bestowed on him. In *Faust II*, the eighth who dwells on Olympus is a direct reference to the Paracelsan text in so far as this describes the "astrology of Olympus" (that is, the structure of the *corpus astrale*).[139]

Returning now to our dream, we find at the critical point —the seventh or eighth floor—the red-haired man, a synonym for the "man with the pointed beard" and hence for the shrewd Mephisto, who magically changes the scene because he is concerned with something that Faust himself never saw: the "severe image," symbolizing the supreme treasure, the immortal self.[140] He changes himself into the soldiers, representatives of uniformity, of collective opinion, which is naturally dead against tolerating anything "unsuitable." For collective opinion the numbers three and seven are, on the highest authority, sacred; but four and eight are the very devil, something inferior—"common clay"—that in the stern judgment of bonzes of every hue has no right to exist. The "left" is to be "completely throttled," meaning the unconscious and all the "sinister" things that come from it. An antiquated view, no doubt, and one that uses antiquated methods; but even muzzle-loaders can hit the mark. For reasons unknown, i.e., not stated in the dream, the destructive attack on the "centre"—to which, according to the advice in the note, "one's eyes must always be turned"—peters out. In the drawing on the margin of

[138] Folio VIII$^v$. The *aqua mercurialis* is characterized here as the "bright and clear fluid of Bacchus." The king and the son are united in the operation, so that at the end only the renewed king and his five servants are left. The *senarius* (sixth) plays a modest role only in later alchemy.

[139] Paracelsus, *Opera*, John Huser, ed. (Strassburg, 1603, also 1616–18, 2 vols.), Vol. I, p. 503.

[140] The angels bear Faust's "immortal part" to heaven, after cheating the devil of it. This, in the original version, is "Faust's entelechy."

the note this centre is portrayed as a wheel with eight spokes.

## 23. DREAM:

*In the square space. The dreamer is sitting opposite the unknown woman whose portrait he is supposed to be drawing. What he draws, however, is not a face but three-leaved clovers or distorted crosses in four different colours: red, yellow, green, and blue.*

In connection with this dream the dreamer spontaneously drew a circle with quarters tinted in the above colours. It was a wheel with eight spokes. In the middle there was a four-petalled blue flower. A great many drawings now followed at short intervals, all dealing with the curious structure of the "centre," and arising from the dreamer's need to discover a configuration that adequately expresses the nature of this centre. The drawings were based partly on visual impressions, partly on intuitive perceptions, and partly on dreams.

It is to be noted that the wheel is a favourite symbol in alchemy for the circulating process, the *circulatio*. By this is meant firstly the *ascensus* and *descensus*, for instance the ascending and descending birds symbolizing the precipitation of vapours,[141] and secondly the rotation of the universe as a model for the work, and hence the cycling of the year in which the work takes place. The alchemist was not unaware of the connection between the *rotatio* and his drawings of circles. The contemporary moral allegories of the wheel emphasize that the *ascensus* and *descensus* are, among other things, God's descent to man and man's ascent to God. (On the authority of one of St. Bernard's sermons: "By his descent he established for us a joyful and wholesome ascent."[142]) Further, the wheel express virtues that

---

[141] Cf. the movements of the transforming substance in the "Tabula smaragdina" (*De alchemia,* Codex Vossianus 29, Rijksuniversiteit Bibliotheek, Leyden, p. 363).

[142] "Suo nobis descensu suavem ac salubrem dedicavit ascensum." *Sermo IV de Ascensione Domini* (Migne, *Patrologiae . . . ,* Latin Series, Vol. 183, col. 312).

are important for the work: *constantia, obedientia, moderatio, aequalitas,* and *humilitas.*[143] The mystical associations of the wheel play no small part in Jakob Böhme. Like the alchemists he too operates with the wheels of Ezekiel, saying: "Thus we see that the spiritual life stands turned in upon itself, and that the natural life stands turned out of and facing itself. We can then liken it to a round spherical wheel that goes on all its sides, as the wheel in Ezekiel shows." [144] He goes on to explain: "The wheel of nature turns in upon itself from without; for God dwells within himself and has such a figure, not that it can be painted, it being only a natural likeness, the same as when God paints himself in the figure of this world; for God is everywhere entire, and so dwells in himself. Mark: the outer wheel is the zodiac with the stars, and after it come the seven planets," etc.[145] "Albeit this figure is not fashioned sufficiently, it is nevertheless a meditation: and we could make a fine drawing of it on a great circle for the meditation of those of less understanding. Mark therefore, desire goes in upon itself to the heart, which is God," etc. But Böhme's wheel is also the "impression" (in alchemical terms, the *informatio*) of the eternal will. It is Mother Nature, or the "mind [*Gemüth*] of the mother, from whence she continually creates and works; and these are the stars with the planetary orb [after the model] of the eternal *astrum*, which is only a spirit, and the eternal mind in the wisdom of God, viz., the Eternal Nature, from whence the eternal spirits proceeded and entered into a creaturely being." [146] The "property" of the wheel is *life* in the form of "four bailiffs" who "manage the dominion in the life-giving

[143] Philippus Picinelli, *Mundus Symbolicus* (Cologne, 1680–81), s.v. "rota."
[144] "Vom irdischen und himmlischen Mysterium," *Theosophische Schrifften* (Amsterdam, 1682), Chap. V, pp. 1f.
[145] "Hohe und tiefe Gründe von dem dreyfachen Leben des Menschen," ibid., Chap. IX, pp. 58f.
[146] "De signatura rerum," ibid., Chap. XIV, p. 15, translated by John Ellistone, in Clifford Bax (ed.), *The Signature of All Things, with Other Writings by Jacob Boehme* (London, 1912, Everyman's Library), p. 179.

mother." These bailiffs are the four elements "to which the
wheel of the mind, viz., the *astrum,* affords will and desire;
so that this whole essence is but one thing only, like the
mind of a man. Even as he is in soul and body, so also is
this whole essence"; for he is created in the likeness of this
"whole essence." But nature in her four elements is also
a whole essence with a soul.[147] This "sulphurean wheel" is
the origin of good and evil, or rather it leads into them
and out of them.[148]

Böhme's mysticism is influenced by alchemy in the
highest degree. Thus he says: "The form of the birth is as
a turning wheel, which Mercurius causes in the sul-
phur." [149] The "birth" is the "golden child" (*filius philosophorum* = archetype of the divine child [150]) whose "mas-
ter-workman" is Mercurius.[151] Mercurius himself is the
"fiery wheel of the essence" in the form of a serpent. Similarly the (unenlightened) soul is just "such a fiery Mercurius." Vulcan kindles the fiery wheel of the essence in
the soul when it "breaks off" from God; whence come
desire and sin, which are the "wrath of God." The soul is
then a "worm" like the "fiery serpent," a "larva" and a
"monster." [152]

The interpretation of the wheel in Böhme reveals something of the mystical secret of alchemy and is thus of considerable importance in this respect as well as from the
psychological point of view: the wheel appears here as a
concept for wholeness which represents the essence of mandala symbolism and therefore includes the *mysterium ini-
quitatis.*

The idea of the "centre," which the unconscious has

[147] Ibid., 16 (p. 179).
[148] Ibid.
[149] Ibid., Chap. IV, p. 28 (Bax, p. 37).
[150] Cf. Jung, "The Psychology of the Child Archetype" (*Collected Works,* Vol. 9).
[151] Böhme, "De signatura rerum," Chap. IV, p. 27 (Bax, p. 37).
[152] Böhme, "Gespräch einer erleuchteten und unerleuchteten Seele," ibid., pp. 11–24.

been repeatedly thrusting upon the conscious mind of the dreamer, is beginning to gain foothold there and to exercise a peculiar fascination. The next drawing is again of the blue flower, but this time subdivided into eight; then follow pictures of four mountains round a lake in a crater, also of a red ring lying on the ground with a withered tree standing in it, round which a green snake creeps up with a leftward movement.

The layman may be rather puzzled by the serious attention devoted to this problem. But a little knowledge of yoga and of the medieval philosophy of the *lapis* would help him to understand. As we have already said, the squaring of the circle was one of the methods for producing the *lapis;* another was the use of *imaginatio,* as the following text unmistakably proves:

> And take care that thy door be well and firmly closed, so that he who is within cannot escape, and—God willing—thou wilt reach the goal. Nature performeth her operations gradually; and indeed I would have thee do the same: let thy imagination be guided wholly by nature. And observe according to nature, through whom the substances regenerate themselves in the bowels of the earth. And imagine this with true and not with fantastic imagination.[153]

The *vas bene clausum* (well-sealed vessel) is a precautionary measure very frequently mentioned in alchemy, and is the equivalent of the magic circle. In both cases the idea is to protect what is within from the intrusion and admixture of what is without, as well as to prevent it from escaping.[154] The *imaginatio* is to be understood here as the real and literal power to create images (*Einbildungskraft* = imagination)—the classical use of the word in contrast to

---

[153] *Rosarium, Art. aurif.,* II, p. 214.
[154] Ibid., p. 213: "Nec intrat in eum [lapidem], quod non sit ortum ex eo, quoniam si aliquid extranei sibi apponatur, statim corrumpitur" (Nothing enters into it [the stone] that did not come from it; since, if anything extraneous were to be added to it, it would at once be spoilt).

*phantasia,* which means a mere "conceit" in the sense of insubstantial thought. In the *Satyricon* this connotation is more pointed still: *phantasia* means something ridiculous.[155] *Imaginatio* is the active evocation of (inner) images *secundum naturam,* an authentic feat of thought or ideation, which does not spin aimless and groundless fantasies "into the blue"—does not, that is to say, just play with its objects, but tries to grasp the inner facts and portray them in images true to their nature. This activity is an *opus,* a work. And we cannot call the manner in which the dreamer handles the objects of his inner experience anything but true work, considering how conscientiously, accurately, and carefully he records and elaborates the content now pushing its way into consciousness. The resemblance to the *opus* is obvious enough to anyone familiar with alchemy. Moreover the analogy is borne out by the dreams themselves, as dream 24 will show.

The present dream, from which the above-mentioned drawings originated, shows no signs of the "left" having been in any way "throttled." On the contrary, the dreamer finds himself once more in the *temenos* facing the unknown woman who personifies the fourth or "inferior" function.[156] His drawing of the wheel with a four-petalled blue flower in the middle was anticipated by the dream: what the dream represents in personified form the dreamer reproduces as an abstract ideogram. This might well be a hint that the *meaning* of the personification could also be represented

---

[155] Petronius, *Satyricon,* par. 38: "Phantasia non homo" (He's a fantasy, not a man).

[156] Prescription for preparation of the *lapis* (Hermes quotation in *Rosarium, Art. aurif.,* II, p. 317): "Fili, extrahe a radio suam umbram: accipe ergo quartam partem sui, hoc est, unam partem de fermento et tres partes de corpore imperfecto," etc. (Son, extract from the ray its shadow: then take a fourth part of it, i.e., one part of the ferment and three parts of the imperfect body, etc.). For *umbra,* see ibid., p. 233: "Fundamentum artis est sol et eius umbra" (The basis of the art is the sun and its shadow). The above quotation gives only the sense of the "Tractatus aureus" and is not literal.

in quite another form. This "other form" (three-leaved clover, distorted cross) refers back to the ace of clubs in dream 16 of the first series, where we pointed out its analogy with the irregular cross. The analogy is confirmed here. In this dream, however, the symbol of the Christian Trinity has been overshadowed or "coloured" by the alchemical quaternity. The colours appear as a concretization of the *tetraktys*. The *Rosarium* quotes a similar statement from the "Tractatus aureus": "Vultur[157] . . . clamat voce magna, inquiens: Ego sum albus niger et rubeus citrinus" [158] (The vulture . . . exclaims in a loud voice: I am the white black and the red yellow). On the other hand it is stressed that the *lapis* unites *omnes colores* in itself. We can thus take it that the quaternity represented by the colours is a kind of preliminary stage of the *lapis*. This is confirmed by the *Rosarium:* "Our stone is from the four elements." [159] The same applies to the *aurum philosophicum:* "In the gold the four elements are contained in equal proportions." [160] The fact is that the four colours in the dream represent the transition from trinity to quaternity and thus to the squared circle, which, according to the alchemists, comes nearest to the *lapis* on account of its roundness or perfect simplicity. For this reason a recipe for the preparation of the *lapis,* attributed to Raymundus, says:

> Take of the body that is most simple and round, and do not take of the triangle or quadrangle but of the round, for the round is nearer to simplicity than the triangle.

[157] Cf. dream 58. The alchemical vulture, eagle, and crow are all essentially synonymous.
[158] This quotation from Hermes is likewise an arbitrary reading. The passage runs literally: "Ego sum albus nigri et rubeus albi et citrinus rubei et certe veridicus sum" (I am the white of the black, and the red of the white, and the yellow of the red, and I speak very truth). In this way three meanings are expressed by four colours, in contrast to the formula of Hortulanus which attributes four natures and three colours to the *lapis.—De alchemia,* p. 372.
[159] *Art. aurif.,* II, p. 207: "Lapis noster est ex quatuor elementis."
[160] Ibid., p. 208: "In auro sunt quatuor elementa in aequali proportione aptata."

Hence it is to be noted that a simple body has no corners, for it is the first and last among the planets, like the sun among the stars.[161]

## 24. DREAM:

*Two people are talking about crystals, particularly about a diamond.*

Here one can hardly avoid thinking of the *lapis*. In fact this dream discloses the historical background and indicates that we really are dealing with the coveted *lapis*, the "treasure hard to attain." The dreamer's *opus* amounts to an unconscious recapitulation of the efforts of Hermetic philosophy. (More about the diamond in dreams 37, 39, 50 below.)

## 25. DREAM:

*It is a question of constructing a central point and making the figure symmetrical by reflection at this point.*

The word "constructing" points to the synthetic character of the *opus* and also to the laborious building process that taxes the dreamer's energy. The "symmetry" is an answer to the conflict in dream 22 ("completely throttling the left"). Each side must perfectly balance the other as its mirror-image, and this image is to fall at the "central point," which evidently possesses the property of reflection —it is a *vitrum*,[162] a crystal or sheet of water. This power of reflection seems to be another allusion to the underlying idea of the *lapis*, the *aurum philosophicum*, the elixir, the *aqua nostra*, etc.

Just as the "right" denotes the world of consciousness

---

[161] Ibid., p. 317: "Recipe de simplicissimo et de rotundo corpore, et noli recipere de triangulo vel quadrangulo sed de rotundo: quia rotundum est propinquius simplicitati quam triangulus. Notandum est ergo, quod corpus simplex nullum habens angulum, quia ipsum est primum et posterius in planetis, sicut Sol in stellis."
[162] A quotation from Ademarus (ibid., p. 353): "[Lapis] nihilominus non funditur, nec ingreditur, nec permiscetur, sed vitrificatur" (But [the stone] can neither be melted nor penetrated nor mixed but is made as hard as glass).

and its principles, so by "reflection" the picture of the world is to be turned round to the left, thus producing a corresponding world in reverse. We could equally well say: through reflection the right appears as the reverse of the left. Therefore the left seems to have as much validity as the right; in other words, the unconscious and its—for the most part unintelligible—order becomes the symmetrical counterpart of the conscious mind and its contents, although it is still not clear which of them is reflected and which reflecting. To carry our reasoning a step further, we could regard the centre as the point of intersection of two worlds that correspond but are inverted by reflection.[163]

The idea of creating a symmetry would thus indicate some kind of climax in the task of accepting the unconscious and incorporating it in a general picture of the world. The unconscious here displays a "cosmic" character.

## 26. DREAM:

*It is night, with stars in the sky. A voice says, "Now it will begin." The dreamer asks, "What will begin?" Whereupon the voice answers, "The circulation can begin." Then a shooting star falls in a curious leftward curve. The scene changes, and the dreamer is in a rather squalid night club. The proprietor, who appears to be an unscrupulous crook, is there with some bedraggled-looking girls. A quarrel starts about left and right. The dreamer then leaves and drives round the perimeter of a square in a taxi. Then he is in the bar again. The proprietor says, "What they said about left and right did not satisfy my feelings. Is there really such a thing as a left and a right side of human society?" The dreamer answers, "The existence of the left does not contradict that of the right. They both exist in everyone. The left is the mirror-image of the right. Whenever I feel it like that, as a mirror-image, I am at one with myself. There is no right and no left side to human society,*

---

[163] There are very interesting parapsychological parallels to this, but I cannot enter upon them here.

*but there are symmetrical and lopsided people. The lop-
sided are those who can fulfil only one side of themselves,
either left or right. They are still in the childhood state."
The proprietor says meditatively, "Now that's much better," and goes about his business.*

I have given this dream in full because it is an excellent
illustration of how the ideas hinted at in the last dream
have been taken up by the dreamer. The idea of symmetrical proportion has been stripped of its cosmic character
and translated into psychological terms, expressed in social
symbols. "Right" and "left" are used almost like political
slogans.

The beginning of the dream, however, is still under the
cosmic aspect. The dreamer noted that the curious curve
of the shooting star corresponded exactly to the line he
drew when sketching the picture of the eightfold flower
(cf. p. 413). The curve formed the edge of the petals.
Thus the shooting star traces the outline, so to speak, of
a flower that spreads over the whole starry heaven. What is
now beginning is the circulation of the light.[164] This cosmic flower corresponds roughly to the rose in Dante's
*Paradiso.*

The "cosmic" nature of an experience—as an aspect of
some inner occurrence that can only be understood psychologically—is offensive and at once provokes a reaction
"from below." Evidently the cosmic aspect was too high
and is compensated "downward," so that the symmetry is
no longer that of two world pictures but merely of human
society, in fact of the dreamer himself. When the proprietor remarks that the latter's psychological understanding is "much better," he is making an estimate whose conclusion should run: "but still not good enough."

The quarrel about right and left that starts in the bar
is the conflict which breaks out in the dreamer himself when
he is called upon to recognize the symmetry. He cannot do
this because the other side looks so suspicious that he

[164] See infra, pp. 423, and 429f.; and my commentary on *The
Secret of the Golden Flower,* Chap. I, sec. 2.

would rather not investigate it too closely. That is the reason for the magical *circumambulatio* (driving round the square): he has to stay inside and learn to face his mirror-image without running away. He does this as best he can, though not quite as the other side would wish. Hence the somewhat chill recognition of his merits.

27. VISUAL IMPRESSION:

*A circle with a green tree in the middle. In the circle a fierce battle is raging between savages. They do not see the tree.*

Evidently the conflict between right and left has not yet ended. It continues because the savages are still in the "childhood state" and therefore, being "lopsided," only know either the left or the right but not a third that stands above the conflict.

28. VISUAL IMPRESSION:

*A circle: within it, steps lead up to a basin with a fountain inside.*

When a condition is unsatisfactory because some essential aspect of the unconscious content is lacking, the unconscious process reverts to earlier symbols, as is the case here. The symbolism goes back to dream 13, where we met the mandala garden of the philosophers with its fountain of *aqua nostra*. Circle and basin emphasize the mandala, the rose of medieval symbolism.[165] The "rose garden of the philosophers" is one of alchemy's favourite symbols.[166]

29. VISUAL IMPRESSION:

*A bunch of roses, then the sign*  *, but it should be*

---

[165] Luigi Valli, "Die Geheimsprache Dantes und der Fedeli d'Amore," *Europäische Revue* (Berlin), VI Jahrgang: 1 Halbband (January–June 1930), 92–112.
[166] Cf. "Rosarius minor," *De alchemia*, p. 309.

A rose bouquet is like a fountain fanning out. The meaning of the first sign—possibly a tree—is not clear, whereas the correction represents the eightfold flower. Evidently a mistake is being corrected which somehow impaired the wholeness of the rose. The aim of the reconstruction is to bring the problem of the mandala—the correct valuation and interpretation of the "centre"—once more into the field of consciousness.

### 30. Dream:

*The dreamer is sitting at a round table with the dark unknown woman.*

Whenever a process has reached a culmination as regards either its clarity or the wealth of inferences that can be drawn from it, a regression is likely to ensue. From the dreams that come in between the ones we have quoted here it is evident that the dreamer is finding the insistent demands of wholeness somewhat disagreeable; for their realization will have far-reaching practical consequences, whose personal nature, however, lies outside the scope of our study.

The round table again points to the circle of wholeness, and the anima comes in as representative of the fourth function, especially in her "dark" aspect, which always makes itself felt when something is becoming concrete, i.e., when it has to be translated, or threatens to translate itself, into reality. "Dark" means chthonic, i.e., concrete and earthy. This is also the source of the fear that causes the regression.[167]

### 31. Dream:

*The dreamer is sitting with a certain man of unpleasant*

---

[167] "Symbola Pythagore phylosophi" in Marsilio Ficino, *Auctores platonici* (Venice, 1497), Fol. X, III, says: "Ab eo, quod nigram caudam habet abstine, terrestrium enim deorum est" (Keep your hands from that which has a black tail, for it belongs to the gods of the earth).

*aspect at a round table. On it stands a glass filled with a gelatinous mass.*

This dream is an advance on the last in that the dreamer has accepted the "dark" as his own darkness, to the extent of producing a real "shadow" belonging to him personally.[168] The anima is thus relieved of the moral inferiority projected upon her and can take up the living and creative function[169] which is properly her own. This is represented by the glass with its peculiar contents which we, like the dreamer, may compare with the undifferentiated "life-mass" in dream 18. It was then a question of the gradual transformation of primitive animality into something human. So we may expect something of the sort here, for it seems as if the spiral of inner development had come round to the same point again, though higher up.

The glass corresponds to the *unum vas* of alchemy and

[168] Although the theme of this study does not permit a full discussion of the psychology of dreams, I must make a few explanatory remarks at this point. Sitting together at one table means relationship, being connected or "put together." The round table indicates that the figures have been brought together for the purpose of wholeness. If the anima figure (the personified unconscious) is separated from ego-consciousness and therefore unconscious, it means that there is an isolating layer of personal unconscious embedded between the ego and the anima. The existence of a personal unconscious proves that contents of a personal nature which could really be made conscious are being kept unconscious for no good reason. There is thus an inadequate or even non-existent consciousness of the shadow. The shadow corresponds to a negative ego-personality and includes all those qualities we find painful or regrettable. Shadow and anima, being unconscious, are then contaminated with each other, a state that is represented in dreams by "marriage" or the like. But if the existence of the anima (or the shadow) is accepted and understood, a separation of these figures ensues, as has happened in the case of our dreamer. The shadow is thus recognized as belonging, and the anima as not belonging, to the ego.
[169] Cf. what I have said about the anima in "The Archetypes of the Collective Unconscious" (*Collected Works,* Vol. 9.i), pars. 53ff. In Hermes' treatise, *An die menschliche Seele,* ed., Heinrich L. Fleischer (Leipzig, 1870), she is called "the highest interpreter and nearest custodian (of the eternal)," which aptly characterizes her function as mediator between conscious and unconscious.

its contents to the living, semi-organic mixture from which the body of the *lapis,* endowed with spirit and life, will emerge—or possibly that strange Faustian figure who bursts into flame three times: the Boy Charioteer, the Homunculus who is dashed against the throne of Galatea, and Euphorion (all symbolizing a dissolution of the "centre" into its unconscious elements). We know that the *lapis* is not just a "stone" since it is expressly stated to be composed "de re animali, vegetabili et minerali," and to consist of body, soul, and spirit;[170] moreover, it grows from flesh and blood.[171] For which reason the philosopher (Hermes in the "Tabula smaragdina") says: "The wind hath carried it in his belly." Therefore "wind is air, air is life, and life is soul." "The stone is that thing midway between perfect and imperfect bodies, and that which nature herself begins is brought to perfection through the art." [172] The stone "is named the stone of invisibility" (*lapis invisibilitatis*).[173]

The dream takes up the question of giving the centre life and reality—giving birth to it, so to speak. That this birth can issue from an amorphous mass has its parallel in the alchemical idea of the *prima materia* as a chaotic *massa informis* impregnated by the seeds of life. As we have seen, the qualities of gum arabic and glue are attributed to it, or again it is called *viscosa* and *unctuosa.* (In Paracelsus the "Nostoc" is the arcane substance.) Although modern conceptions of nutrient soil, jelly-like growths, etc., underlie the dreamer's "gelatinous mass," the atavistic associations with far older alchemical ideas still persist, and these, although not consciously present, nevertheless exert a powerful unconscious influence on the choice of symbols.

*32.* DREAM:
*The dreamer receives a letter from an unknown woman.*

170 *Rosarium, Art. aurif.,* II, p. 237.
171 Ibid., p. 238.
172 P. 236.
173 P. 231.

*She writes that she has pains in the uterus. A drawing is attached to the letter, looking roughly like this:* [174]

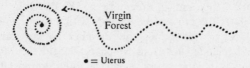

Virgin
Forest

● = Uterus

*In the primeval forest there are swarms of monkeys. Then a panorama of white glaciers opens out.*

The anima reports that there are painful processes going on in the life-creating centre, which in this case is no longer the "glass" containing the life-mass but a point designated as a "uterus," to be reached—so the spiral suggests—by means of a *circumambulatio*. At all events the spiral emphasizes the centre and hence the uterus, which is a synonym frequently employed for the alchemical vessel, just as it is one of the basic meanings of the Eastern mandala.[175] The serpentine line leading to the vessel is analogous to the healing serpent of Aesculapius and also to the Tantric symbol of *Shiva bindu,* the creative, latent god without extension in space who, in the form of a point or *lingam,* is encircled three and a half times by the Kundalini serpent.[176] With the primeval forest we meet the animal

[174] The uterus is the centre, the life-giving vessel. The stone, like the grail, is itself the creative vessel, the *elixir vitae*. It is surrounded by the spiral, the symbol of indirect approach by means of the *circumambulatio*.

[175] The centre of the mandala corresponds to the calyx of the Indian lotus, seat and birthplace of the gods. This is called the *padma,* and has a feminine significance. In alchemy the *vas* is often understood as the uterus where the "child" is gestated. In the Litany of Loreto, Mary is spoken of three times as the "vas" ("vas spirituale," "honorabile," and "insigne devotionis") and in medieval poetry she is called the "flower of the sea" which shelters the Christ (cf. dream 36). The grail is closely related to the Hermetic vessel: Wolfram von Eschenbach calls the stone of the grail "lapsit exilis." Arnold of Villanova (d. ?1312) calls the *lapis* "lapis exilis," the uncomely stone (*Rosarium, Art. aurif.,* II, p. 210), which may be of importance for the interpretation of Wolfram's term.

[176] See Avalon, *The Serpent Power.*

or ape motif again, which appeared before in vision 22 of
the first series and in dreams 16 and 18 of this. In vision
22 it led to the announcement that "everything must be
ruled by the light" and, in dream 18, to the "transfigured"
head. Similarly the present dream ends with a panorama of
white "glaciers," reminding the dreamer of an earlier
dream (not included here) in which he beheld the Milky
Way and was having a conversation about immortality.
Thus the glacier symbol is a bridge leading back again to
the cosmic aspect that caused the regression. But, as is
nearly always the case, the earlier content does not return
in its first simple guise—it brings a new complication with
it, which, though it might have been expected logically, is
no less repugnant to the intellectual consciousness than the
cosmic aspect was. The complication is the memory of the
conversation about immortality. This theme was already
hinted at in dream 9 with its pendulum clock, a *perpetuum
mobile*. Immortality is a clock that never runs down, a
mandala that revolves eternally like the heavens. Thus the
cosmic aspect returns with interest and compound interest.
This might easily prove too much for the dreamer, for the
"scientific" stomach has very limited powers of digestion.

The unconscious does indeed put forth a bewildering
profusion of semblances for that obscure thing we call the
mandala or "self." It almost seems as if we were ready to
go on dreaming in the unconscious the age-old dream of
alchemy, and to continue to pile new synonyms on top of
the old, only to know as much or as little about it in the
end as the ancients themselves. I will not enlarge upon
what the *lapis* meant to our forefathers, and what the mandala still means to the Lamaist and Tantrist, Aztec and
Pueblo Indian, the "golden pill" [177] to the Taoist, and the
"golden seed" to the Hindu. We know the texts that give us
a vivid idea of all this. But what does it mean when the
unconscious stubbornly persists in presenting such abstruse
symbolisms to a cultured European? The only point of view
I can apply here is a psychological one. (There may be

[177] Synonymous with the "golden flower."

others with which I am not familiar.) From this point of view, as it seems to me, everything that can be grouped together under the general concept "mandala" expresses the essence of a certain kind of *attitude*. The known attitudes of the conscious mind have definable aims and purposes. But a man's attitude towards the self is the only one that has no definable aim and no visible purpose. It is easy enough to say "self," but exactly what have we said? That remains shrouded in "metaphysical" darkness. I may define "self" as the totality of the conscious and unconscious psyche, but this totality transcends our vision; it is a veritable *lapis invisibilitatis*. In so far as the unconscious exists it is not definable; its existence is a mere postulate and nothing whatever can be predicated as to its possible contents. The totality can only be experienced in its parts and then only in so far as these are contents of consciousness; but *qua* totality it necessarily transcends consciousness. Consequently the "self" is a pure borderline concept similar to Kant's *Ding an sich*. True, it is a concept that grows steadily clearer with experience—as our dreams show—without, however, losing anything of its transcendence. Since we cannot possibly know the boundaries of something unknown to us, it follows that we are not in a position to set any bounds to the self. It would be wildly arbitrary and therefore unscientific to restrict the self to the limits of the individual psyche, quite apart from the fundamental fact that we have not the least knowledge of these limits, seeing that they also lie in the unconscious. We may be able to indicate the limits of consciousness, but the unconscious is simply the unknown psyche and for that very reason illimitable because indeterminable. Such being the case, we should not be in the least surprised if the empirical manifestations of unconscious contents bear all the marks of something illimitable, something not determined by space and time. This quality is numinous and therefore alarming, above all to a cautious mind that knows the value of precisely delimited concepts. One is glad not to be a philosopher or theologian and so under no obligation to meet such numina professionally. It is all the worse when it becomes increasingly clear that numina are psychic *entia* that force themselves upon consciousness, since night after night our dreams practise philosophy on their own account. What is more, when we attempt to give these numina the slip and angrily reject the alchemical gold which the unconscious offers, things do in fact go badly with us, we may even develop symptoms in defiance of all reason, but the moment we face up to the stumbling-block and make it—if only hypothetically—the cornerstone, the symptoms vanish and we feel "unaccountably" well. In this dilemma we can at least comfort ourselves with the reflection that the unconscious is a necessary evil which must be reckoned with, and that it would therefore be wiser to accompany it on some of its strange symbolic wanderings, even though their meaning be exceedingly questionable. It might perhaps be conducive to good health to relearn Nietzsche's "lesson of earlier humanity."

The only objection I could make to such rationalistic explanations is that very often they do not stand the test of events. We can observe in these and similar cases how, over the years, the entelechy of the self becomes so insistent that consciousness has to rise to still greater feats if it is to keep pace with the unconscious.

All that can be ascertained at present about the symbolism of the mandala is that it portrays an autonomous psychic fact, characterized by a phenomenology which is always repeating itself and is everywhere the same. It seems to be a sort of atomic nucleus about whose innermost structure and ultimate meaning we know nothing. We can also regard it as the actual—i.e., effective—reflection of a conscious attitude that can state neither its aim nor its purpose and, because of this failure, projects its activity entirely upon the virtual centre of the mandala.[178] The compelling

---

[178] Projection is considered here a spontaneous phenomenon, and not the deliberate extrapolation of anything. It is not a phenomenon of the will.

force necessary for this projection always lies in some situation where the individual no longer knows how to help himself in any other way. That the mandala is merely a psychological reflex is, however, contradicted firstly by the autonomous nature of this symbol, which sometimes manifests itself with overwhelming spontaneity in dreams and visions, and secondly by the autonomous nature of the unconscious as such, which is not only the original form of everything psychic but also the condition we pass through in early childhood and to which we return every night. There is no evidence for the assertion that the activity of the psyche is merely reactive or reflex. This is at best a biological working hypothesis of limited validity. When raised to a universal truth it is nothing but a materialistic myth, for it overlooks the creative capacity of the psyche, which—whether we like it or not—exists, and in face of which all so-called "causes" become mere occasions.

*33.* DREAM:

*A battle among savages, in which bestial cruelties are perpetrated.*

As was to be foreseen, the new complication ("immortality") has started a furious conflict, which makes use of the same symbols as the analogous situation in dream 27.

*34.* DREAM:

*A conversation with a friend. The dreamer says, "I must carry on with the figure of the bleeding Christ before me and persevere in the work of self-redemption."*

This, like the previous dream, points to an extraordinary, subtle kind of suffering caused by the breaking through of an alien spiritual world which we find very hard to accept —hence the analogy with the tragedy of Christ: "My kingdom is not of this world." But it also shows that the dreamer is now continuing his task in deadly earnest. The reference to Christ may well have a deeper meaning than that of a mere moral reminder: we are concerned here

with the process of individuation, a process which has constantly been held up to Western man in the dogmatic and
religious model of the life of Christ. The accent has always
fallen on the "historicity" of the Saviour's life, and because
of this its symbolical nature has remained in the dark, although the Incarnation formed a very essential part of the
*symbolon* (creed). The efficacy of dogma, however, by no
means rests on Christ's unique historical reality but on its
own symbolic nature, by virtue of which it expresses a
more or less ubiquitous psychological assumption quite independent of the existence of any dogma. There is thus a
"pre-Christian" as well as a "non-Christian" Christ, in so
far as he is an autonomous psychological fact. At any rate
the doctrine of prefiguration is founded on this idea. In the
case of the modern man, who has no religious assumptions
at all, it is therefore only logical that the Anthropos or
Poimen figure should emerge, since it is present in his own
psyche.

35. DREAM:

*An actor smashes his hat against the wall, where it
looks like this:*

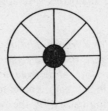

As certain material not included here shows, the "actor"
refers to a definite fact in the dreamer's personal life. Up
to now he had maintained a certain fiction about himself
which prevented him from taking himself seriously. This

fiction has become incompatible with the serious attitude he has now attained. He must give up the actor, for it was the actor in him who rejected the self. The hat refers to the first dream of all, where he put on a *stranger's* hat. The actor throws the hat against the wall, and the hat proves to be a mandala. So the "strange" hat was the self, which at that time—while he was still playing a fictitious role—seemed like a stranger to him.

## 36. DREAM:
*The dreamer drives in a taxi to the Rathausplatz, but it is called the "Marienhof."*

I mention this dream only in passing because it shows the feminine nature of the *temenos,* just as *hortus conclusus* (enclosed garden) is often used as an image for the Virgin Mary in medievel hymns, and *rosa mystica* is one of her attributes in the Litany of Loreto.

## 37. DREAM:
*There are curves outlined in light around a dark centre. Then the dreamer is wandering about in a dark cave, where a battle is going on between good and evil. But there is also a prince who knows everything. He gives the dreamer a ring set with a diamond and places it on the fourth finger of his left hand.*

The circulation of light that started in dream 26 reappears more clearly. Light always refers to consciousness, which at present runs only along the periphery. The centre is still dark. It is the dark cave, and to enter it is obviously to set the conflict going again. At the same time it is like the prince who stands aloof, who knows everything and is the possessor of the precious stone. The gift means nothing less than the dreamer's vow to the self—for as a rule the wedding ring is worn on the fourth finger of the left hand. True, the left is the unconscious, from which it is to be inferred that the situation is still largely shrouded in unconsciousness. The prince seems to be the representative of the *aenigma regis* (cf. commentary to dream 10). The dark cave corresponds to the vessel containing the warring opposites. The self is made manifest in the opposites and in the conflict between them; it is a *coincidentia oppositorum*. Hence the way to the self begins with conflict.

### 38. DREAM:

*A circular table with four chairs round it. Table and chairs are empty.*

This dream confirms the above conjecture. The mandala is not yet "in use."

### 39. VISUAL IMPRESSION:

*The dreamer is falling into the abyss. At the bottom there is a bear whose eyes gleam alternately in four colours: red, yellow, green, and blue. Actually it has four eyes that change into four lights. The bear disappears and the dreamer goes through a long dark tunnel. Light is shimmering at the far end. A treasure is there, and on top of it the ring with the diamond. It is said that this ring will lead him on a long journey to the east.*

This waking dream shows that the dreamer is still preoccupied with the dark centre. The bear stands for the chthonic element that might seize him. But then it becomes clear that the animal is only leading up to the four colours (cf. dream 23), which in their turn lead to the *lapis*, i.e., the diamond whose prism contains all the hues of the rainbow. The way to the east probably points to the unconscious as an antipode. According to the legend the Grail-stone comes from the east and must return there again. In alchemy the bear corresponds to the *nigredo* of the *prima materia*, whence comes the colourful *cauda pavonis*.

### 40. DREAM:

*Under the guidance of the unknown woman the dreamer has to discover the Pole at the risk of his life.*

The Pole is the point round which everything turns—

hence another symbol of the self. Alchemy also took up this analogy: "In the Pole is the heart of Mercurius, who is the true fire, wherein his master rests. When navigating over this great sea . . . he sets his course by the aspect of the North star." [179] Mercurius is the world-soul, and the Pole is its heart. The idea of the *anima mundi* coincides with that of the collective unconscious whose centre is the self. The symbol of the sea is another synonym for the unconscious.

*41.* VISUAL IMPRESSION:
*Yellow balls rolling round to the left in a circle.*

Rotation about a centre, recalling dream 21.

*42.* DREAM:
*An old master points to a spot on the ground illuminated in red.*

The *philosophus* shows him the "centre." The redness may mean the dawn, like the *rubedo* in alchemy, which as a rule immediately preceded the completion of the work.

*43.* DREAM:
*A yellow light like the sun looms through the fog, but it is murky. Eight rays go out from the centre. This is the point of penetration: the light ought to pierce through, but has not quite succeeded.*

The dreamer himself observed that the point of penetration was identical with the Pole in dream 40. So it is, as we surmised, a question of the sun's appearing, which now turns yellow. But the light is still murky, which probably means insufficient understanding. The "penetration" alludes to the need for effort in coming to a decision. In alchemy yellow (*citrinitas*) often coincides with the *rubedo*. The "gold" is yellow or reddish yellow.

---

[179] "In polo est cor Mercurii, qui versus est ignis, in quo requies est Domini sui, navigans per mare hoc magnum . . . cursum dirigat per aspectum astri septentrionalis"—Philalethes, "Introitus apertus," *Musaeum hermeticum* (Frankfurt, 1678), p. 655.

44. DREAM:

*The dreamer is in a square enclosure where he must keep still. It is a prison for Lilliputians (or children?). A wicked woman is in charge of them. The children start moving and begin to circulate round the periphery. The dreamer would like to run away but may not do so. One of the children turns into an animal and bites him in the calf.*

The lack of clarity demands further efforts of concentration; hence the dreamer finds himself still in the childhood state, hence "lopsided" (cf. dream 26), and imprisoned in the *temenos* in the charge of a wicked mother-anima. The animal appears as in dream 1 and he is bitten, i.e., he must expose himself and pay the price. The *circumambulatio* means, as always, concentration on the centre. He finds this state of tension almost unendurable. But he wakes up with an intense and pleasant feeling of having solved something, "as if he held the diamond in his hand." The children point to the drawf motif, which may express Cabiric elements, i.e., it may represent unconscious formative powers (see dreams 56ff., below), or it may at the same time allude to his still childish condition.

45. DREAM:

*A parade ground with troops. They are not equipping themselves for war but form an eight-rayed star rotating to the left.*

The essential point here is that the conflict seems to be overcome. The star is not in the sky and not a diamond, but a configuration on the earth formed by human beings.

46. DREAM:

*The dreamer is imprisoned in the square enclosure. Lions and a wicked sorceress appear.*

He cannot get out of the chthonic prison because he is not yet ready to do something that he should. (This is an important personal matter, a duty even, and the cause of much misgiving.) Lions, like all wild animals, indicate latent affects. The lion plays an important part in alchemy and has much the same meaning. It is a "fiery" animal, an emblem of the devil, and stands for the danger of being swallowed by the unconscious.

47. DREAM:
*The wise old man shows the dreamer a place on the ground marked in a peculiar way.*

This is probably the place on earth where the dreamer belongs if he is to realize the self (similar to dream 42).

48. DREAM:
*An acquaintance wins a prize for digging up a potter's wheel.*

The potter's wheel rotates on the ground (cf. dream 45) and produces earthenware ("earthly") vessels which may figuratively be called "human bodies." Being round, the wheel refers to the self and the creative activity in which it is manifest. The potter's wheel also symbolizes the recurrent theme of circulation.

49. DREAM:
*A starry figure rotating. At the cardinal points of the circle there are pictures representing the seasons.*

Just as the place was defined before, so now the time. Place and time are the most general and necessary elements in any definition. The determination of time and place was stressed right at the beginning (cf. dreams 7, 8, 9). A definite location in place and time is part of a man's reality. The seasons refer to the quartering of the circle which corresponds to the cycle of the year. The year is a symbol of the original man.[180] The rotation motif indicates that the symbol of the circle is to be thought of not as static but as dynamic.

[180] See "Paracelsus as a Spiritual Phenomenon" (*Collected Works*, Vol. 13), pars. 229, 237.

### 50. DREAM:

*An unknown man gives the dreamer a precious stone. But he is attacked by a gang of apaches. He runs away (nightmare) and is able to escape. The unknown woman tells him afterwards that it will not always be so: sometime he will have to stand his ground and not run away.*

When a definite time is added to a definite place one is rapidly approaching reality. That is the reason for the gift of the jewel, but also for the fear of decision, which robs the dreamer of the power to make up his mind.

### 51. DREAM:

*There is a feeling of great tension. Many people are circulating round a large central oblong with four smaller oblongs on its sides. The circulation in the large oblong goes to the left and in the smaller oblongs to the right. In the middle there is the eight-rayed star. A bowl is placed in the centre of each of the smaller oblongs, containing red, yellow, green, and colourless water. The water rotates to the left. The disquieting question arises: Is there enough water?*

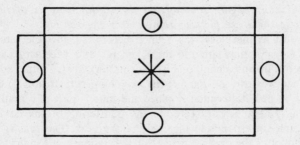

The colours point once more to the preliminary stage. The "disquieting" question is whether there is enough water of life—*aqua nostra,* energy, libido—to reach the central star (i.e., the "core" or "kernel"; cf. next dream). The circulation in the central oblong is still going to the left, i.e., consciousness is moving towards the unconscious. The centre is therefore not yet sufficiently illuminated. The rightward circulation in the smaller oblongs, which represent the quaternity, seems to suggest that the four functions are becoming conscious. The four are generally characterized by the four colours of the rainbow. The striking fact here is that the blue is missing, and also that the square ground-plan has suddenly been abandoned. The horizontal has extended itself at the cost of the vertical. So we are dealing with a "disturbed" mandala.[181] We might add by way of criticism that the antithetical arrangement of the functions has not yet become sufficiently conscious for their characteristic polarity to be recognized.[182] The predominance of the horizontal over the vertical indicates that the ego-consciousness is uppermost, thus entailing a loss of height and depth.

## 52. DREAM:

*A rectangular dance hall. Everybody is going round the periphery to the left. Suddenly the order is heard: "To the kernels!" But the dreamer has first to go into the adjoining room to crack some nuts. Then the people climb down rope ladders to the water.*

The time has come to press on to the "kernel" or core of the matter, but the dreamer still has a few more "hard

---

[181] "Disturbed" mandalas occur from time to time. They consist of all forms that deviate from the circle, square, or regular cross, and also of those based not on the number four but on three or five. The numbers six and twelve are something of an exception. Twelve can be based on either four or three. The twelve months and the twelve signs of the zodiac are definite symbolic circles in daily use. And six is likewise a well-known symbol for the circle. Three suggests the predominance of ideation and will (trinity), and five that of the physical man (materialism).

[182] Cf. the psychological functions in *Psychological Types,* supra, pp. 178–269.

nuts" to crack in the little rectangle (the "adjoining room"), i.e., in one of the four functions. Meanwhile the process goes on and descends to the "water." The vertical is thus lengthened, and from the incorrect oblong we again get the square which expresses the complete symmetry of conscious and unconscious with all its psychological implications.

### 53. DREAM:

*The dreamer finds himself in an empty square room which is rotating. A voice cries, "Don't let him out. He won't pay the tax!"*

This refers to the dreamer's inadequate self-realization in the personal matter already alluded to, which in this case was one of the essential conditions of individuation and therefore could not be circumvented. As was to be expected, after the preparatory emphasis on the vertical in the preceding dream, the square is now re-established. The cause of the disturbance was an underestimation of the demands of the unconscious (the vertical), which led to a flattening of the personality (recumbent oblong).

After this dream the dreamer worked out six mandalas in which he tried to determine the right length of the vertical, the form of "circulation," and the distribution of colour. At the end of this work came the following dream (given unabridged):

### 54. DREAM:

*I come to a strange, solemn house—the "House of the Gathering." Many candles are burning in the background, arranged in a peculiar pattern with four points running upward. Outside, at the door of the house, an old man is posted. People are going in. They say nothing and stand motionless in order to collect themselves inwardly. The man at the door says of the visitors to the house, "When they come out again they are cleansed." I go into the house myself and find I can concentrate perfectly. Then a voice says: "What you are doing is dangerous. Religion is not a tax to be paid so that you can rid yourself of the woman's image, for this image cannot be got rid of. Woe unto them who use religion as a substitute for another side of the soul's life; they are in error and will be accursed. Religion is no substitute; it is to be added to the other activities of the soul as the ultimate completion. Out of the fulness of life shall you bring forth your religion; only then shall you be blessed!" While the last sentence is being spoken in ringing tones I hear distant music, simple chords on an organ. Something about it reminds me of Wagner's Fire Music. As I leave the house I see a burning mountain and I feel: "The fire that is not put out is a holy fire"* (Shaw, *St. Joan*).

The dreamer notes that this dream was a "powerful experience." Indeed it has a numinous quality and we shall therefore not be far wrong if we assume that it represents a new climax of insight and understanding. The "voice" has as a rule an absolutely authoritative character and generally comes at decisive moments.

The house probably corresponds to the square, which is a "gathering place." The four shining points in the background again indicate the quaternity. The remark about cleansing refers to the transformative function of the taboo area. The production of wholeness, which is prevented by the "tax evasion," naturally requires the "image of the woman," since as anima she represents the fourth, "inferior" function, feminine because contaminated with the unconscious. In what sense the "tax" is to be paid depends on the nature of the inferior function and its auxiliary, and also on the attitude type.[183] The payment can be either concrete or symbolic, but the conscious mind is not qualified to decide which form is valid.

The dream's view that religion may not be a substitute for "another side of the soul's life" will certainly strike many people as a radical innovation. According to it, religion is equated with wholeness; it even appears as the ex-

[183] *Psychological Types*, supra, pp. 178–269.

pression of the integration of the self in the "fulness of life."

The faint echo of the Fire Music—the Loki motif—is not out of key, for what does "fulness of life" mean? What does "wholeness" mean? I feel that there is every reason here for some anxiety, since man as a whole being casts a shadow. The fourth was not separated from the three and banished to the kingdom of everlasting fire for nothing. Does not an uncanonical saying of our Lord declare: "Whoso is near unto me is near unto the fire"? [184] Such dire ambiguities are not meant for grown-up children—which is why Heraclitus of old was named "the dark," because he spoke too plainly and called life itself an "ever-living fire." And that is why there are uncanonical sayings for those that have ears to hear.

The theme of the Fire Mountain is to be met with in the Book of Enoch.[185] Enoch sees the seven stars chained "like great mountains and burning with fire" at the angels' place of punishment. Originally the seven stars were the seven great Babylonian gods, but at the time of Enoch's revelation they had become the seven Archons, rulers of "this world," fallen angels condemned to punishment. In contrast to this menacing theme there is an allusion to the miracles of Jehovah on Mount Sinai, while according to other sources the number seven is by no means sinister, since it is on the seventh mountain of the western land that the tree with the life-giving fruit is to be found, i.e., the *arbor sapientiae*.[186]

---

[184] "Ait autem ipse salvator: Qui iuxta me est, iuxta ignem est, qui longe est a me, longe est a regno" (The Saviour himself says: He that is near me is near the fire. He that is far from me is far from the kingdom).—Origen, *Homiliae in Jeremiam*, XX, 3, Migne, *Patrologiae . . .* Greek series, Vol. 13, cols. 530–532; cited in Montague Rhodes James, *Apocryphal New Testament* (Oxford, 1924, revised 1955), p. 35.

[185] Book of Enoch 18 : 13 and Chap. 21 (Robert Henry Charles, *The Apocrypha and Pseudepigrapha of the Old Testament in English*, Vol. II, pp. 200, 201).

[186] A more detailed commentary on this dream is to be found in Jung, "Psychology and Religion" (*Collected Works*, Vol. II), pars. 59ff.

## 55. DREAM:

*A silver bowl with four cracked nuts at the cardinal point.*

This dream shows that some of the problems in dream 52 have been settled, though the settlement is not complete. The dreamer pictured the goal that has now been attained as a circle divided into four, with the quadrants painted in the four colours. The circulation is to the left. Though this satisfies the demands of symmetry, the polarity of the functions is still unrecognized—despite the last, very illuminating dream—because, in the painting, red and blue, green and yellow, are side by side instead of opposite one another. From this we must conclude that the "realization" is meeting with strong inner resistances, partly of a philosophical and partly of an ethical nature, the justification for which cannot lightly be set aside. That the dreamer has an inadequate understanding of the polarity is shown by the fact that the nuts have still to be cracked in reality, and also that they are all alike, i.e., not yet differentiated.

## 56. DREAM:

*Four children are carrying a large dark ring. They move in a circle. The dark unknown woman appears and says she will come again, for it is the festival of the solstice.*

In this dream the elements of dream 44 come together again: the children and the dark woman, who was a wicked witch before. The "solstice" indicates the turning-point. In alchemy the work is completed in the autumn (*Vindemia Hermetis*). Children, dwarf-gods, bring the ring —i.e., the symbol of wholeness is still under the sway of childlike creative powers. Note that children also play a part in the *opus alchymicum:* a certain portion of the work is called *ludus puerorum.* Save for the remark that the work is as easy as "child's play," I have found no explanation for this. Seeing that the work is, in the unanimous testimony of all the adepts, exceedingly difficult, it must be a euphemistic and probably also a symbolical definition. It would thus point to a co-operation on the part of "infantile" or unconscious forces represented as Cabiri and hobgoblins (homunculi).

57. VISUAL IMPRESSION:
*The dark ring, with an egg in the middle.*

58. VISUAL IMPRESSION:
*A black eagle comes out of the egg and seizes in its beak the ring, now turned to gold. Then the dreamer is on a ship and the bird flies ahead.*

The eagle signifies height. (Previously the stress was on depth: people descending to the water.) It seizes the whole mandala and, with it, control of the dreamer, who, carried along on a ship, sails after the bird. Birds are thoughts and the flight of thought. Generally it is fantasies and intuitive ideas that are represented thus (the winged Mercurius, Morpheus, genii, angels). The ship is the vehicle that bears the dreamer over the sea and the depths of the unconscious. As a man-made thing it has the significance of a system or method (or a way: cf. Hinayana and Mahayana = the Lesser and Greater Vehicle, the two schools of Buddhism). The flight of thought goes ahead and methodical elaboration follows after. Man cannot walk the rainbow bridge like a god but must go underneath with whatever reflective afterthoughts he may have. The eagle—synonymous with phoenix, vulture, raven—is a well-known alchemical symbol. Even the *lapis,* the *rebis* (compounded of two parts and therefore frequently hermaphroditic as an amalgam of Sol and Luna), is often represented with wings, denoting intuition or spiritual (winged) potentiality. In the last resort all these symbols depict the consciousness-transcending fact we call the self. This visual impression is rather like a snapshot of an evolving process as it leads on to the next stage.

In alchemy the egg stands for the chaos apprehended by

the artifex, the *prima materia* containing the captive world-soul. Out of the egg—symbolized by the round cooking-vessel—will rise the eagle or phoenix, the liberated soul, which is ultimately identical with the Anthropos who was imprisoned in the embrace of Physis.

## III. *The Vision of the World Clock*

### 59. THE "GREAT VISION":[187]

*There is a vertical and a horizontal circle, having a common centre. This is the world clock. It is supported by the black bird.*

*The vertical circle is a blue disc with a white border divided into $4 \times 8 = 32$ partitions. A pointer rotates upon it.*

*The horizontal circle consists of four colours. On it stand four little men with pendulums, and round about it is laid the ring that was once dark and is now golden (formerly carried by the children).*

*The "clock" has three rhythms or pulses:*

| | |
|---|---|
| *1. The small pulse:* | *the pointer on the blue vertical disc advances by 1/32.* |
| *2. The middle pulse:* | *one complete revolution of the pointer. At the same time the horizontal circle advances by 1/32.* |
| *3. The great pulse:* | *32 middle pulses are equal to one revolution of the golden ring.* |

This remarkable vision made a deep and lasting impression on the dreamer, an impression of "the most sublime harmony," as he himself puts it. The world clock may well be the "severe image" which is identical with the Cabiri, i.e., the four children or four little men with the pendulums. It is a three-dimensional mandala—a mandala in

[187] This vision is treated in greater detail in Jung, "Psychology and Religion" (*Collected Works*, Vol. 11), pars. 112ff.

bodily form signifying realization. (Unfortunately medical discretion prevents my giving the biographical details. It must suffice to say that this realization did actually take place.) Whatever a man does in reality he himself becomes.

Just why the vision of this curious figure should produce an impression of "the most sublime harmony" is, in one sense, very difficult to understand; but it becomes comprehensible enough as soon as we consider the comparative historical material. It is difficult to feel our way into the matter because the meaning of the image is exceedingly obscure. If the meaning is impenetrable and the form and colour take no account of aesthetic requirements, then neither our understanding nor our sense of beauty is satisfied, and we are at a loss to see why it should give rise to the impression of "the most sublime harmony." We can only venture the hypothesis that disparate and incongruous elements have combined here in the most fortunate way, simultaneously producing an image which realizes the "intentions" of the unconscious in the highest degree. We must therefore assume that the image is a singularly happy expression for an otherwise unknowable psychic fact which has so far only been able to manifest apparently disconnected aspects of itself.

The impression is indeed extremely abstract. One of the underlying ideas seems to be the intersection of two heterogeneous systems by the sharing of a common centre. Hence if we start as before from the assumption that the centre and its periphery represent the totality of the psyche and consequently the self, then the figure tells us that two heterogeneous systems intersect in the self, standing to one another in a functional relationship that is governed by law and regulated by "three rhythms." The self is by definition the centre and the circumference of the conscious and unconscious systems. But the regulation of their functions by three rhythms is something that I cannot substantiate. I do not know what the three rhythms allude to. But I do not doubt for a moment that the allusion is amply justified.

The only analogy I could adduce would be the three *regimina* mentioned in the Introduction, by which the four elements are converted into one another or synthesized in the quintessence:

1st *regimen*: earth to water.
2nd    "    : water to air.
3rd    "    : air to fire.

We shall hardly be mistaken if we assume that our mandala aspires to the most complete union of opposites that is possible, including that of the masculine trinity and the feminine quaternity on the analogy of the alchemical hermaphrodite.

Since the figure has a cosmic aspect—world clock—we must suppose it to be a small-scale model or perhaps even a source of space-time, or at any rate an embodiment of it and therefore, mathematically speaking, four-dimensional in nature although only visible in a three-dimensional projection. I do not wish to labour this argument, for such an interpretation lies beyond my powers of proof

The thirty-two pulses may conceivably derive from the multiplication of $4 \times 8$, as we know from experience that the quaternity found at the centre of a mandala often becomes 8, 16, 32, or more when extended to the periphery. The number 32 plays an important role in the Cabala. Thus we read in the *Sepher Yetsirah* (1 : 1): "Jehovah, the Lord of Hosts, the God of Israel, the living God and King of the world . . . has graven his name in thirty-two mysterious paths of wisdom." These consist of "ten self-contained numbers [*Sephiroth*] and twenty-two basic letters" (1 : 2). The meaning of the ten numbers is as follows: "1: the spirit of the Living God; 2: spirit from spirit; 3: water from spirit; 4: fire from water; 5–10: height, depth, East, West, South, North." [188] Cornelius Agrippa mentions that "the learned Jews attribute the number 32 to

---

[188] Erich Bischoff, *Die Elemente der Kabbalah* (Berlin, 1913, 2 vols.), Vol. 1, pp. 63ff. Further associations with "32" on pp. 175ff.

Wisdom, for so many are the ways of Wisdom described by Abram." [189] Franck establishes a connection between 32 and the cabalistic trinity, Kether, Binah, and Hokhmah: "These three persons contain and unite in themselves everything that exists, and they in turn are united in the White Head, the Ancient of Days, for he is everything and everything is he. Sometimes he is represented with three heads which make but a single head, and sometimes he is likened to the brain which, without impairing its unity, divides into three parts and spreads through the whole body by means of thirty-two pairs of nerves, just as God spreads through the universe along thirty-two miraculous paths." [190] These thirty-two "canales occulti" are also mentioned by Knorr von Rosenroth,[191] who calls Hokhmah "the supreme path of all, embracing all," on the authority of Job 28 : 7 (AV): "There is a path which no fowl knoweth, and which the vulture's eye hath not seen." Allendy, in his very valuable account of number symbolism, writes: "32 . . . is the differentiation which appears in the organic world; not creative generation, but rather the plan and arrangement of the various forms of created things which the creator has modelled—as the product of 8 × 4. . . ." [192] Whether the cabalistic number 32 can be equated with the thirty-two fortunate signs (*mahavyanjana*) of the Buddha-child is doubtful.

As to the interpretation based on comparative historical material, we are in a more favourable position, at least as regards the general aspects of the figure. We have at our disposal, firstly, the whole mandala symbolism of three continents, and secondly, the specific time symbolism of the

---

[189] Heinrich Cornelius Agrippa von Nettesheim, *De incertitudine et vanitate omnium scientarum et artium* (The Hague, 1653), Vol. II, Chap. XV.

[190] Adolphe Franck, *Die Kabbala* (Leipzig, 1844), p. 137.

[191] Knorr von Rosenroth, *Kabbala denudata seu Doctrina Hebraeorum* (Sulzbach, 1677), Vol. I, p. 602.

[192] René Felix Allendy, *Le Symbolisme des nombres* (Paris, 1948), p. 378.

mandala as this developed under the influence of astrology, particularly in the West. The horoscope is itself a mandala (a clock) with a dark centre, and a leftward *circumambulatio* with "houses" and planetary phases. The mandalas of ecclesiastical art, particularly those on the floor before the high altar or beneath the transept, make frequent use of the zodiacal beasts or the yearly seasons. A related idea is the identity of Christ with the Church calendar, of which he is the fixed pole and the life. The Son of Man is an anticipation of the idea of the self: hence the Gnostic adulteration of Christ with the other synonyms for the self among the Naassenes, recorded by Hippolytus. There is also a connection with the symbolism of Horus: on the one hand, Christ enthroned with the four emblems of the evangelists—three animals and an angel; on the other, Father Horus with his four sons, or Osiris with the four sons of Horus.[193] Horus is also the ἥλιος ἀνατολῆς (rising sun),[194] and Christ was still worshipped as such by the early Christians.

We find a remarkable parallel in the writings of Guillaume de Digulleville, prior of the Cistercian monastery at Châlis, a Norman poet who, independently of Dante, composed three "pélerinages" between 1330 and 1355: *Les Pélerinages de la vie humaine, de l'âme,* and *de Jésus Christ.*[195] The last canto of the *Pélerinage de l'âme* contains a vision of Paradise, which consists of seven large spheres each containing seven smaller spheres.[196] All the spheres rotate, and this movement is called a *siècle* (*sae-*

---

[193] Bas-relief at Philae (Budge, *Osiris and the Egyptian Resurrection,* Vol. I, p. 3); and *The Book of the Dead* (1899), Papyrus of Hunefer, pl. 5. Sometimes there are three with animal heads and one with a human head, as in the Papyrus of Kerasher (ibid.). In a 7th-century manuscript (Gellone) the evangelists actually wear their animal heads, as in several other Romanesque monuments.

[194] So called by Melito of Sardis, *De baptismo,* in Jean Baptiste Pitra, *Analecta sacra* (Paris, 1876–91, 8 vols.), Vol. II, p. 5.

[195] Joseph Delacotte, *Guillaume de Digulleville* (Paris, 1932).

[196] An idea which corresponds to dream 21 of the large sphere containing many little spheres.

*culum*). The heavenly *siècles* are the prototypes of the
earthly centuries. The angel who guides the poet explains:
"When holy Church ends her prayers with *in saecula
saeculorum* [for ever and ever], she has in mind, not
earthly time, but eternity." At the same time the *siècles* are
spherical spaces in which the blessed dwell. *Siècles* and
*cieux* are identical. In the highest heaven of pure gold the
King sits on a round throne which shines more brightly
than the sun. A *couronne* of precious stones surrounds him.
Beside him, on a circular throne that is made of brown
crystal, sits the Queen, who intercedes for the sinners.

"Raising his eyes to the golden heaven, the pilgrim perceived a marvellous circle which appeared to be three feet
across. It came out of the golden heaven at one point and
re-entered it at another, and it made the whole tour of the
golden heaven." This circle is sapphire-coloured. It is a
small circle, three feet in diameter, and evidently it moves
over a great horizontal circle like a rolling disc. This great
circle intersects the golden circle of heaven.

While Guillaume is absorbed in this sight, three spirits
suddenly appear clad in purple, with golden crowns and
girdles, and enter the golden heaven. This moment, so the
angel tells him, is *une fête,* like a church festival on earth:

> Ce cercle que tu vois est le calendrier
> Qui en faisant son tour entier,
> Montre des Saints les journées
> Quand elles doivent être fêtées.
> Chacun en fait le cercle un tour,
> Chacune étoile y est pour jour,
> Chacun soleil pour l'espace
> De jours trente ou zodiaque.
>
> (This circle is the calendar
> Which spinning round the course entire
> Shows the feast day of each saint
> And when it should be celebrate.
> Each saint goes once round all the way,

> Each star you see stands for a day,
> And every sun denotes a spell
> Of thirty days zodiacal.)

The three figures are saints whose feast day is even now being celebrated. The small circle that enters the golden heaven is *three* feet in width, and likewise there are *three* figures who make their sudden entry. They signify the moment of time in eternity, as does the circle of the calendar. But why this should be exactly three feet in diameter and why there are three figures remains a mystery. We naturally think of the three rhythms in our vision which are started off by the pointer moving over the blue disc, and which enter the system just as inexplicably as the calendar-circle enters the golden heaven.

The guide continues to instruct Guillaume on the significance of the signs of the zodiac with particular reference to sacred history, and ends with the remark that the feast of the twelve fishermen will be celebrated in the sign of Pisces, when the twelve will appear before the Trinity. Then it suddenly occurs to Guillaume that he has never really understood the nature of the Trinity, and he begs the angel for an explanation. The angel answers, "Now, there are three principal colours, namely green, red, and gold. These three colours are seen united in divers works of watered silk and in the feathers of many birds, such as the peacock. The almighty King who puts three colours in one, cannot he also make one substance to be three?" Gold, the royal colour, is attributed to God the Father; red to God the Son, because he shed his blood; and to the Holy Ghost green, "la couleur qui verdoye et qui réconforte." Thereupon the angel warns Guillaume not to ask any more questions, and disappears. The poet wakes up to find himself safely in his bed, and so ends the *Pélerinage de l'âme*.

There is, however, one thing more to be asked: "Three there are—but where is the fourth?" Why is blue missing? This colour was also missing in the "disturbed" mandala of our dreamer (see Mandala 51). Curiously enough, the *calendrier* that intersects the golden circle is blue, and so is the vertical disc in the three-dimensional mandala. We would conjecture that blue, standing for the vertical, means height and depth (the blue sky above, the blue sea below), and that any shrinkage of the vertical reduces the square to an oblong, thus producing something like an inflation of consciousness.[197] Hence the vertical would correspond to the unconscious. But the unconscious in a man has feminine characteristics, and blue is the traditional colour of the Virgin's celestial cloak. Guillaume was so absorbed in the Trinity and in the threefold aspect of the *roy* that he quite forgot the *reyne*. Faust prays to her in these words: "Supreme Mistress of the world! Let me behold thy secret in the outstretched azure canopy of heaven."

It was inevitable that blue should be missing for Guillaume in the tetrad of rainbow colours, because of its feminine nature. But, like woman herself, the anima means the height and depth of a man. Without the blue vertical circle the golden mandala remains bodiless and two-dimensional, a mere abstraction. It is only the intervention of time and space here and now that makes reality. Wholeness is realized for a moment only—the moment that Faust was seeking all his life.

The poet in Guillaume must have had an inkling of the heretical truth when he gave the King a Queen sitting on a throne made of earth-brown crystal. For what is heaven without Mother Earth? And how can man reach fulfilment if the Queen does not intercede for his black soul? She understands the darkness, for she has taken her throne— the earth itself—to heaven with her, if only by the subtlest of suggestions. She adds the missing blue to the gold, red, and green, and thus completes the harmonious whole.

[197] Cf. my remarks on "inflation" in "The Relations Between the Ego and the Unconscious," supra, pp. 88–103.

## IV. *The Symbols of the Self*

The vision of the "world clock" is neither the last nor the highest point in the development of the symbols of the objective psyche. But it brings to an end the first third of the material, consisting in all of some four hundred dreams and visions. This series is noteworthy because it gives an unusually complete description of a psychic fact that I had observed long before in many individual cases.[198] We have to thank not only the completeness of the objective material but the care and discernment of the dreamer for having placed us in a position to follow, step by step, the synthetic work of the unconscious. The troubled course of this synthesis would doubtless have been depicted in even greater completeness had I taken account of the 340 dreams interspersed among the 59 examined here. Unfortunately this was impossible, because the dreams touch to some extent on the intimacies of personal life and must therefore remain unpublished. So I had to confine myself to the impersonal material.

I hope I may have succeeded in throwing some light upon the development of the symbols of the self and in overcoming, partially at least, the serious difficulties inherent in all material drawn from actual experience. At the same time I am fully aware that the comparative material so necessary for a complete elucidation could have been greatly increased. But, so as not to burden the exposition unduly, I have exercised the greatest reserve in this respect. Consequently there is much that is only hinted at, though this should not be taken as a sign of superficiality. I believe myself to be in a position to offer ample evidence for my views, but I do not wish to give the impression that I imagine I have said anything final on this highly compli-

---

[198] Cf. my commentary on *The Secret of the Golden Flower* (*Collected Works*, Vol. 13), pars. 31ff. Cf. also "Concerning Mandala Symbolism" (*Collected Works*, Vol. 9.i).

cated subject. It is true that this is not the first time I have
dealt with a series of spontaneous manifestations of the
unconscious. I did so once before, in my book *Psychology
of the Unconscious*,[199] but there it was more a problem of
neurosis in puberty, whereas this is the broader problem of
individuation. Moreover, there is a very considerable difference between the two personalities in question. The earlier case, which I never saw at first hand, ended in psychic
catastrophe—a psychosis; but the present case shows a normal development such as I have often observed in highly
intelligent persons.

What is particularly noteworthy here is the consistent
development of the central symbol. We can hardly escape
the feeling that the unconscious process moves spiral-wise
round a centre, gradually getting closer, while the characteristics of the centre grow more and more distinct. Or
perhaps we could put it the other way round and say that
the centre—itself virtually unknowable—acts like a magnet
on the disparate materials and processes of the unconscious
and gradually captures them as in a crystal lattice. For this
reason the centre is (in other cases) often pictured as a
spider in its web, especially when the conscious attitude is
still dominated by fear of unconscious processes. But if the
process is allowed to take its course, as it was in our case,
then the central symbol, constantly renewing itself, will
steadily and consistently force its way through the apparent
chaos of the personal psyche and its dramatic entanglements, just as the great Bernoulli's epitaph[200] says of the
spiral: "Eadem mutata resurgo." Accordingly we often find
spiral representations of the centre, as for instance the
serpent coiled round the creative point, the egg.

Indeed, it seems as if all the personal entanglements and
dramatic changes of fortune that make up the intensity of
life were nothing but hesitations, timid shrinkings, almost

---

[199] Revised edition: *Symbols of Transformation* (*Collected Works*,
Vol. 5).
[200] In the cloisters of Basel Cathedral.

like petty complications and meticulous excuses for not facing the finality of this strange and uncanny process of
crystallization. Often one has the impression that the personal psyche is running round this central point like a shy
animal, at once fascinated and frightened, always in flight,
and yet steadily drawing nearer.

I trust I have given no cause for the misunderstanding
that I know anything about the nature of the "centre"—for
it is simply unknowable and can only be expressed symbolically through its own phenomenology, as is the case,
incidentally, with every object of experience. Among the
various characteristics of the centre the one that struck me
from the beginning was the phenomenon of the quaternity.
That it is not simply a question of, shall we say, the "four"
points of the compass or something of that kind is proved
by the fact that there is often a competition between four
and three.[201] There is also, but more rarely, a competition
between four and five, though five-rayed mandalas must be
characterized as abnormal on account of their lack of symmetry.[202] It would seem, therefore, that there is normally
a clear insistence on four, or as if there were a greater
statistical probability of four. Now it is—as I can hardly
refrain from remarking—a curious "sport of nature" that
the chief chemical constituent of the physical organism is
carbon, which is characterized by four valencies; also it is
well known that the diamond is a carbon crystal. Carbon
is black—coal, graphite—but the diamond is "purest
water." To draw such an analogy would be a lamentable
piece of intellectual bad taste were the phenomenon of four
merely a poetic conceit on the part of the conscious mind
and not a spontaneous product of the objective psyche.
Even if we supposed that dreams could be influenced to any
appreciable extent by auto-suggestion—in which case it

[201] This was observed chiefly in men, but whether it was mere
chance I am unable to say.
[202] Observed mainly in women. But it occurs so rarely that it is
impossible to draw any further conclusions.

would naturally be more a matter of their meaning than of their form—it would still have to be proved that the conscious mind of the dreamer had made a serious effort to impress the idea of the quaternity on the unconscious. But in this case as in many other cases I have observed, such a possibility is absolutely out of the question, quite apart from the numerous historical and ethnological parallels.[203] Surveying these facts as a whole, we come, at least in my opinion, to the inescapable conclusion that there is some psychic element present which expresses itself through the quaternity. No daring speculation or extravagant fancy is needed for this. If I have called the centre the "self," I did so after mature consideration and a careful appraisal of the empirical and historical data. A materialistic interpretation could easily maintain that the "centre" is "nothing but" the point at which the psyche ceases to be knowable because it there coalesces with the body. And a spiritualistic interpretation might retort that this "self" is nothing but "spirit," which animates both soul and body and irrupts into time and space at that creative point. I purposely refrain from all such physical and metaphysical speculations and content myself with establishing the empirical facts, and this seems to me infinitely more important for the advance of human knowledge than running after fashionable intellectual crazes or jumped-up "religious" creeds.

To the best of my experience we are dealing here with very important "nuclear processes" in the objective psyche —"images of the goal," as it were, which the psychic process, being goal-directed, apparently sets up of its own accord, without any external stimulus.[204] Externally, of course, there is always a certain condition of psychic need,

[203] I have mentioned only a few of these parallels here.
[204] The image that presents itself in this material as a goal may also serve as the origin when viewed from the historical standpoint. By way of example I would cite the conception of paradise in the Old Testament, and especially the creation of Adam in the Slavonic Book of Enoch. Charles, *Apocrypha and Pseudepigrapha*, Vol. II, pp. 425ff.; Max Förster "Adams Erschaffung und Namengebung. Ein lateinisches Fragment des s.g. slawischen Henoch," *Archiv für Religionswissenschaft* (Leipzig), XI (1908), 477–529.

a sort of hunger, but it seeks for familiar and favourite dishes and never imagines as its goal some outlandish food unknown to consciousness. The goal which beckons to this psychic need, the image which promises to heal, to make whole, is at first strange beyond all measure to the conscious mind, so that it can find entry only with the very greatest difficulty. Of course it is quite different for people who live in a time and environment when such images of the goal have dogmatic validity. These images are then *eo ipso* held up to consciousness, and the unconscious is thus shown its own secret reflection, in which it recognizes itself and so joins forces with the conscious mind.

As to the question of the origin of the mandala motif, from a superficial point of view it looks as if it had gradually come into being in the course of the dream-series. The fact is, however, that it only *appeared* more and more distinctly and in increasingly differentiated form; in reality it was always present and even occurred in the first dream— as the nymphs say later: "We were always there, only you did not notice us." It is therefore more probable that we are dealing with an *a priori* "type," an archetype which is inherent in the collective unconscious and thus beyond individual birth and death. The archetype is, so to speak, an "eternal" presence, and the only question is whether it is perceived by the conscious mind or not. I think we are forming a more probable hypothesis, and one that better explains the observed facts, if we assume that the increase in the clarity and frequency of the mandala motif is due to a more accurate perception of an already existing "type," rather than that it is generated in the course of the dream-series.[205] The latter assumption is contradicted by the fact,

---

[205] If we divide the four hundred dreams into eight groups of fifty each, we come to the following results:

| | | | | |
|---|---|---|---|---|
| I | ........ 6 mandalas | | V | ........ 11 mandalas |
| II | ........ 4 " | | VI | ......... 11 " |
| III | ........ 2 " | | VII | ......... 11 " |
| IV | ........ 9 " | | VIII | ......... 17 " |

So a considerable increase in the occurrence of the mandala motif takes place in the course of the whole series.

for instance, that such fundamental ideas as the hat which epitomizes the personality, the encircling serpent, and the *perpetuum mobile* appear right at the beginning (first series: dream 1, and vision 5; second series: dream 9).

If the motif of the mandala is an archetype it ought to be a collective phenomenon, i.e., theoretically it should appear in everyone. In practice, however, it is to be met with in distinct form in relatively few cases, though this does not prevent it from functioning as a concealed pole round which everything ultimately revolves. In the last analysis every life is the realization of a whole, that is, of a self, for which reason this realization can also be called "individuation." All life is bound to individual carriers who realize it, and it is simply inconceivable without them. But every carrier is charged with an individual destiny and destination, and the realization of these alone makes sense of life. True, the "sense" is often something that could just as well be called "nonsense," for there is a certain incommensurability between the mystery of existence and human understanding. "Sense" and "nonsense" are merely manmade labels which serve to give us a reasonably valid sense of direction.

As the historical parallels show, the symbolism of the mandala is not just a unique curiosity; we can well say that it is a regular occurrence. Were it not so there would be no comparative material, and it is precisely the possibility of comparing the mental products of all times from every quarter of the globe that shows us most clearly what immense importance the *consensus gentium* has always attached to the processes of the objective psyche. This is reason enough not to make light of them, and my medical experience has only confirmed this estimate. There are people, of course, who think it unscientific to take anything seriously; they do not want their intellectual playground disturbed by graver considerations. But the doctor who fails to take account of man's feelings for values commits a serious blunder, and if he tries to correct the mysterious and well-nigh inscrutable workings of nature with his so-called scientific attitude, he is merely putting his shallow sophistry in place of nature's healing processes. Let us take the wisdom of the old alchemists to heart: "Naturalissimum et perfectissimum opus est generare tale quale ipsum est." [206]

[206] "The most natural and perfect work is to generate its like."

# ᭥ *12* ᭥

## *The Spiritual Problem*
## *of Modern Man*[1]

The spiritual problem of modern man is one of those questions which are so much a part of the age we live in that we cannot see them in the proper perspective. Modern man is an entirely new phenomenon; a modern problem is one which has just arisen and whose answer still lies in the future. In speaking of the spiritual problem of modern man we can at most frame a question, and we should perhaps frame it quite differently if we had but the faintest inkling of the answer the future will give. The question, moreover, seems rather vague; but the truth is that it has to do with something so universal that it exceeds the grasp of any single individual. We have reason enough, therefore, to approach such a problem in all modesty and with the greatest caution. This open avowal of our limitations seems to me essential, because it is these problems more

---

[1] From *Civilization in Transition. Collected Works*, Vol. 10, pars. 148–196. [First published as "Das Seelenproblem des modernen Menschen," *Europäische Revue* (Berlin), IV (1928), 700–715. Revised and expanded in *Seelenprobleme der Gegenwart* (Zurich, 1931), pp. 401–35. Translated by W. S. Dell and Cary F. Baynes in *Modern Man in Search of a Soul* (London and New York, 1933), pp. 226–54. The latter version has been consulted.—EDITORS OF *The Collected Works*.]

than any others which tempt us to the use of high-sounding and empty words, and because I shall myself be forced to say certain things which may sound immoderate and incautious, and could easily lead us astray. Too many of us already have fallen victim to our own grandiloquence.

To begin at once with an example of such apparent lack of caution, I must say that the man we call modern, the man who is aware of the immediate present, is by no means the average man. He is rather the man who stands upon a peak, or at the very edge of the world, the abyss of the future before him, above him the heavens, and below him the whole of mankind with a history that disappears in primeval mists. The modern man—or, let us say again, the man of the immediate present—is rarely met with, for he must be conscious to a superlative degree. Since to be wholly of the present means to be fully conscious of one's existence as a man, it requires the most intensive and extensive consciousness, with a minimum of unconsciousness. It must be clearly understood that the mere fact of living in the present does not make a man modern, for in that case everyone at present alive would be so. He alone is modern who is fully conscious of the present.

The man who has attained consciousness of the present is solitary. The "modern" man has at all times been so, for every step towards fuller consciousness removes him further from his original, purely animal *participation mystique* with the herd, from submersion in a common unconsciousness. Every step forward means tearing oneself loose from the maternal womb of unconsciousness in which the mass of men dwells. Even in a civilized community the people who form, psychologically speaking, the lowest stratum live in a state of unconsciousness little different from that of primitives. Those of the succeeding strata live on a level of consciousness which corresponds to the beginnings of human culture, while those of the highest stratum have a consciousness that reflects the life of the last few centuries. Only the man who is modern in our meaning of the term really lives in the present; he alone has a present-day consciousness, and he alone finds that the ways of life on those earlier levels have begun to pall upon him. The values and strivings of those past worlds no longer interest him save from the historical standpoint. Thus he has become "unhistorical" in the deepest sense and has estranged himself from the mass of men who live entirely within the bounds of tradition. Indeed, he is completely modern only when he has come to the very edge of the world, leaving behind him all that has been discarded and outgrown, and acknowledging that he stands before the Nothing out of which All may grow.[2]

This sounds so grand that it borders suspiciously on bathos, for nothing is easier than to affect a consciousness of the present. A great horde of worthless people do in fact give themselves a deceptive air of modernity by skipping the various stages of development and the tasks of life they represent. Suddenly they appear by the side of the truly modern man—uprooted wraiths, bloodsucking ghosts whose emptiness casts discredit upon him in his unenviable loneliness. Thus it is that the few present-day men are seen by the undiscerning eyes of the masses only through the dismal veil of those spectres, the pseudo-moderns, and are confused with them. It cannot be helped; the "modern" man is questionable and suspect, and has been so at all times, beginning with Socrates and Jesus.

An honest admission of modernity means voluntarily declaring oneself bankrupt, taking the vows of poverty and chastity in a new sense, and—what is still more painful—renouncing the halo of sanctity which history bestows. To be "unhistorical" is the Promethean sin, and in this sense the modern man is sinful. A higher level of consciousness is like a burden of guilt. But, as I have said, only the man who has outgrown the stages of consciousness belonging to the past, and has amply fulfilled the duties appointed

[2] ["In this, your Nothing, I may find my All!" *Faust*, Part II.—Translator.]

for him by his world, can achieve full consciousness of the present. To do this he must be sound and proficient in the best sense—a man who has achieved as much as other people, and even a little more. It is these qualities which enable him to gain the next highest level of consciousness.

I know that the idea of proficiency is especially repugnant to the pseudo-moderns, for it reminds them unpleasantly of their trickery. This, however, should not prevent us from taking it as our criterion of the modern man. We are even forced to do so, for unless he is proficient, the man who claims to be modern is nothing but a trickster. He must be proficient in the highest degree, for unless he can atone by creative ability for his break with tradition, he is merely disloyal to the past. To deny the past for the sake of being conscious only of the present would be sheer futility. Today has meaning only if it stands between yesterday and tomorrow. It is a process of transition that forms the link between past and future. Only the man who is conscious of the present in this sense may call himself modern.

Many people call themselves modern—especially the pseudo-moderns. Therefore the really modern man is often to be found among those who call themselves old-fashioned. They do this firstly in order to make amends for their guilty break with tradition by laying all the more emphasis on the past, and secondly in order to avoid the misfortune of being taken for pseudo-moderns. Every good quality has its bad side, and nothing good can come into the world without at once producing a corresponding evil. This painful fact renders illusory the feeling of elation that so often goes with consciousness of the present—the feeling that we are the culmination of the whole history of mankind, the fulfilment and end-product of countless generations. At best it should be a proud admission of our poverty: we are also the disappointment of the hopes and expectations of the ages. Think of nearly two thousand years of Christian Idealism followed, not by the return of the Messiah and the heavenly millennium, but by the World War among

Christian nations with its barbed wire and poison gas. What a catastrophe in heaven and on earth!

In the face of such a picture we may well grow humble again. It is true that modern man is a culmination, but tomorrow he will be surpassed. He is indeed the product of an age-old development, but he is at the same time the worst conceivable disappointment of the hopes of mankind. The modern man is conscious of this. He has seen how beneficent are science, technology, and organization, but also how catastrophic they can be. He has likewise seen how all well-meaning governments have so thoroughly paved the way for peace on the principle "in time of peace prepare for war" that Europe has nearly gone to rack and ruin. And as for ideals, neither the Christian Church, nor the brotherhood of man, nor international social democracy, nor the solidarity of economic interests has stood up to the acid test of reality. Today, ten years after the war,[3] we observe once more the same optimism, the same organizations, the same political aspirations, the same phrases and catchwords at work. How can we but fear that they will inevitably lead to further catastrophes? Agreements to outlaw war leave us sceptical, even while we wish them every possible success. At bottom, behind every such palliative measure there is a gnawing doubt. I believe I am not exaggerating when I say that modern man has suffered an almost fatal shock, psychologically speaking, and as a result has fallen into profound uncertainty.

These statements make it clear enough that my views are coloured by a professional bias. A doctor always spies out diseases, and I cannot cease to be a doctor. But it is essential to the physician's art that he should not discover diseases where none exists. I will therefore not make the assertion that Western man, and the white man in particular, is sick, or that the Western world is on the verge of collapse. I am in no way competent to pass such a judgment.

[3] [This essay was originally written in 1928.—EDITORS OF *The Collected Works*.]

Whenever you hear anyone talking about a cultural or even about a human problem, you should never forget to inquire who the speaker really is. The more general the problem, the more he will smuggle his own, most personal psychology into the account he gives of it. This can, without a doubt, lead to intolerable distortions and false conclusions which may have very serious consequences. On the other hand, the very fact that a general problem has gripped and assimilated the whole of a person is a guarantee that the speaker has really experienced it, and perhaps gained something from his sufferings. He will then reflect the problem for us in his personal life and thereby show us a truth. But if he projects his own psychology into the problem, he falsifies it by his personal bias, and on the pretence of presenting it objectively so distorts it that no truth emerges but merely a deceptive fiction.

It is of course only from my own experience with other persons and with myself that I draw my knowledge of the spiritual problem of modern man. I know something of the intimate psychic life of many hundreds of educated persons, both sick and healthy, coming from every quarter of the civilized, white world; and upon this experience I base my statements. No doubt I can draw only a one-sided picture, for everything I have observed lies in the psyche—it is all *inside*. I must add at once that this is a remarkable fact in itself, for the psyche is not always and everywhere to be found on the inside. There are peoples and epochs where it is found *outside*, because they were wholly unpsychological. As examples we may choose any of the ancient civilizations, but especially that of Egypt with its monumental objectivity and its naïve confession of sins that have not been committed. We can no more feel psychic problems lurking behind the Apis tombs of Saqqara and the Pyramids than we can behind the music of Bach.

Whenever there exists some external form, be it an ideal or a ritual, by which all the yearnings and hopes of the soul are adequately expressed—as for instance in a living religion—then we may say that the psyche is outside and that there is no psychic problem, just as there is then no unconscious in our sense of the word. In consonance with this truth, the discovery of psychology falls entirely within the last decades, although long before that man was introspective and intelligent enough to recognize the facts that are the subject-matter of psychology. It was the same with technical knowledge. The Romans were familiar with all the mechanical principles and physical facts which would have enabled them to construct a steam engine, but all that came of it was the toy made by Hero of Alexandria. The reason for this is that there was no compelling necessity to go further. This need arose only with the enormous division of labour and the growth of specialization in the nineteenth century. So also a spiritual need has produced in our time the "discovery" of psychology. The psychic facts still existed earlier, of course, but they did not attract attention—no one noticed them. People got along without them. But today we can no longer get along unless we pay attention to the psyche.

It was men of the medical profession who were the first to learn this truth. For the priest, the psyche can only be something that needs fitting into a recognized form or system of belief in order to ensure its undisturbed functioning. So long as this system gives true expression to life, psychology can be nothing but a technical adjuvant to healthy living, and the psyche cannot be regarded as a factor *sui generis*. While man still lives as a herd-animal he has no psyche of his own, nor does he need any, except the usual belief in the immortality of the soul. But as soon as he has outgrown whatever local form of religion he was born to—as soon as this religion can no longer embrace his life in all its fulness—then the psyche becomes a factor in its own right which cannot be dealt with by the customary measures. It is for this reason that we today have a psychology founded on experience, and not upon articles of faith or the postulates of any philosophical system. The very fact that we have such a psychology is to me symptomatic of a profound convulsion of the collective psyche. For the collective psyche shows the same pattern of change as the psyche of the individual. So long as all goes well and all our psychic energies find an outlet in adequate and well-regulated ways, we are disturbed by nothing from within. No uncertainty or doubt besets us, and we *cannot* be divided against ourselves. But no sooner are one or two channels of psychic activity blocked up than phenomena of obstruction appear. The stream tries to flow back against the current, the inner man wants something different from the outer man, and we are at war with ourselves. Only then, in this situation of distress, do we discover the psyche as something which thwarts our will, which is strange and even hostile to us, and which is incompatible with our conscious standpoint. Freud's psychoanalytic endeavours show this process in the clearest way. The very first thing he discovered was the existence of sexually perverse and criminal fantasies which at their face value are wholly incompatible with the conscious outlook of civilized man. A person who adopted the standpoint of these fantasies would be nothing less than a rebel, a criminal, or a madman.

We cannot suppose that the unconscious or hinterland of man's mind has developed this aspect only in recent times. Probably it was always there, in every culture. And although every culture had its destructive opponent, a Herostratus who burned down its temples, no culture before ours was ever forced to take these psychic undercurrents in deadly earnest. The psyche was merely part of a metaphysical system of some sort. But the conscious, modern man can no longer refrain from acknowledging the might of the psyche, despite the most strenuous and dogged efforts at self-defence. This distinguishes our time from all others. We can no longer deny that the dark stirrings of the unconscious are active powers, that psychic forces exist which, for the present at least, cannot be fitted into our rational world order. We have even elevated them into a science —one more proof of how seriously we take them. Previous centuries could throw them aside unnoticed; for us they are a shirt of Nessus which we cannot strip off.

The revolution in our conscious outlook, brought about by the catastrophic results of the World War, shows itself in our inner life by the shattering of our faith in ourselves and our own worth. We used to regard foreigners as political and moral reprobates, but the modern man is forced to recognize that he is politically and morally just like anyone else. Whereas formerly I believed it was my bounden duty to call others to order, I must now admit that I need calling to order myself, and that I would do better to set my own house to rights first. I admit this the more readily because I realize only too well that my faith in the rational organization of the world—that old dream of the millennium when peace and harmony reign—has grown pale. Modern man's scepticism in this respect has chilled his enthusiasm for politics and world-reform; more than that, it is the worst possible basis for a smooth flow of psychic energies into the outer world, just as doubt concerning the morality of a friend is bound to prejudice the relationship and hamper its development. Through his scepticism modern man is thrown back on himself; his energies flow towards their source, and the collision washes to the surface those psychic contents which are at all times there, but lie hidden in the silt so long as the stream flows smoothly in its course. How totally different did the world appear to medieval man! For him the earth was eternally fixed and at rest in the centre of the universe, circled by a sun that solicitously bestowed its warmth. Men were all children of God under the loving care of the Most High, who prepared them for eternal blessedness; and all knew exactly what they should do and how they should conduct themselves in order to rise from a corruptible world to an incorruptible and joyous existence. Such a life no longer seems real to us, even in our dreams. Science has long ago torn this lovely veil to shreds. That age lies as far behind as childhood, when one's own father was unquestionably the handsomest and strongest man on earth.

Modern man has lost all the metaphysical certainties of his medieval brother, and set up in their place the ideals of material security, general welfare and humanitarianism. But anyone who.has still managed to preserve these ideals unshaken must have been injected with a more than ordinary dose of optimism. Even security has gone by the board, for modern man has begun to see that every step forward in material "progress" steadily increases the threat of a still more stupendous catastrophe. The imagination shrinks in terror from such a picture. What are we to think when the great cities today are perfecting defence measures against gas attacks, and even practise them in dress rehearsals? It can only mean that these attacks have already been planned and provided for, again on the principle "in time of peace prepare for war." Let man but accumulate sufficient engines of destruction and the devil within him will soon be unable to resist putting them to their fated use. It is well known that fire-arms go off of themselves if only enough of them are together.

An intimation of the terrible law that governs blind contingency, which Heraclitus called the rule of *enantiodromia* (a running towards the opposite), now steals upon modern man through the by-ways of his mind, chilling him with fear and paralyzing his faith in the lasting effectiveness of social and political measures in the face of these monstrous forces. If he turns away from the terrifying prospect of a blind world in which building and destroying successively tip the scales, and then gazes into the recesses of his own mind, he will discover a chaos and a darkness there which everyone would gladly ignore. Science has destroyed even this last refuge; what was once a sheltering haven has become a cesspool.

And yet it is almost a relief to come upon so much evil in the depths of our own psyche. Here at least, we think, is the root of all the evil in mankind. Even though we are shocked and disillusioned at first, we still feel, just because these things are part of our psyche, that we have them more or less in hand and can correct them or at any rate effectively suppress them. We like to assume that, if we succeeded in this, we should at least have rooted out some fraction of the evil in the world. Given a widespread knowledge of the unconscious, everyone could see when a statesman was being led astray by his own bad motives. The very newspapers would pull him up: "Please have yourself analyzed; you are suffering from a repressed father-complex."

I have purposely chosen this grotesque example to show to what absurdities we are led by the illusion that because something is psychic it is under our control. It is, however, true that much of the evil in the world comes from the fact that man in general is hopelessly unconscious, as it is also true that with increasing insight we can combat this evil at its source in ourselves, in the same way that science enables us to deal effectively with injuries inflicted from without.

The rapid and worldwide growth of a psychological interest over the last two decades shows unmistakably that modern man is turning his attention from outward material things to his own inner processes. Expressionism in art prophetically anticipated this subjective development, for all art intuitively apprehends coming changes in the collective unconsciousness.

The psychological interest of the present time is an indication that modern man expects something from the psyche which the outer world has not given him: doubtless something which our religion ought to contain, but no longer does contain, at least for modern man. For him the various forms of religion no longer appear to come from within, from the psyche; they seem more like items from the inventory of the outside world. No spirit not of this world vouchsafes him inner revelation; instead, he tries on a variety of religions and beliefs as if they were Sunday attire, only to lay them aside again like worn-out clothes.

Yet he is somehow fascinated by the almost pathological manifestations from the hinterland of the psyche, difficult though it is to explain how something which all previous ages have rejected should suddenly become interesting. That there is a general interest in these matters cannot be denied, however much it offends against good taste. I am not thinking merely of the interest taken in psychology as a science, or of the still narrower interest in the psycho-analysis of Freud, but of the widespread and ever-growing interest in all sorts of psychic phenomena, including spirit-ualism, astrology, Theosophy, parapsychology, and so forth. The world has seen nothing like it since the end of the seventeenth century. We can compare it only to the flower-ing of Gnostic thought in the first and second centuries after Christ. The spiritual currents of our time have, in fact, a deep affinity with Gnosticism. There is even an "Église gnostique de la France," and I know of two schools in Germany which openly declare themselves Gnostic. The most impressive movement numerically is undoubtedly Theosophy, together with its continental sister, Anthroposo-phy; these are pure Gnosticism in Hindu dress. Compared with them the interest in scientific psychology is negligible. What is striking about these Gnostic systems is that they are based exclusively on the manifestations of the uncon-scious, and that their moral teachings penetrate into the dark side of life, as is clearly shown by the refurbished European version of *Kundalini-yoga*. The same is true of parapsychology, as everyone acquainted with this subject will agree.

The passionate interest in these movements undoubtedly arises from psychic energy which can no longer be invested in obsolete religious forms. For this reason such movements have a genuinely religious character, even when they pretend to be scientific. It changes nothing when Rudolf Steiner calls his Anthroposophy "spiritual science," or when Mrs. Eddy invents a "Christian Science." These at-tempts at concealment merely show that religion has grown suspect—almost as suspect as politics and world-reform.

I do not believe that I am going too far when I say that

modern man, in contrast to his nineteenth-century brother, turns to the psyche with very great expectations, and does so without reference to any traditional creed but rather with a view to Gnostic experience. The fact that all the movements I have mentioned give themselves a scientific veneer is not just a grotesque caricature or a masquerade, but a positive sign that they are actually pursuing "science," i.e., *knowledge,* instead of *faith,* which is the essence of the Western forms of religion. Modern man abhors faith and the religions based upon it. He holds them valid only so far as their knowledge-content seems to accord with his own experience of the psychic background. He wants to *know* —to experience for himself.

The age of discovery has only just come to an end in our day, when no part of the earth remains unexplored; it began when men would no longer *believe* that the Hyperboreans were one-footed monsters, or something of that kind, but wanted to find out and see with their own eyes what existed beyond the boundaries of the known world. Our age is apparently setting out to discover what exists in the psyche beyond consciousness. The question asked in every spiritual-istic circle is: What happens after the medium has lost consciousness? Every Theosophist asks: What shall I experience at the higher levels of consciousness? The question which every astrologer asks is: What are the operative forces that determine my fate despite my conscious intention? And every psychoanalyst wants to know: What are the unconscious drives behind the neurosis?

Our age wants to experience the psyche for itself. It wants original experience and not assumptions, though it is willing to make use of all the existing assumptions as a means to this end, including those of the recognized religions and the authentic sciences. The European of yesterday will feel a slight shudder run down his spine when he gazes more deeply into these delvings. Not only does he consider the subject of this so-called research obscure and shuddersome, but even the methods employed seem to him a shocking misuse of man's finest intellectual attainments. What is the professional astronomer to say when he is told that at least a thousand times more horoscopes are cast today than were cast three hundred years ago? What will the educator and advocate of philosophical enlightenment say about the fact that the world has not grown poorer by a single superstition since the days of antiquity? Freud himself, the founder of psychoanalysis, has taken the greatest pains to throw as glaring a light as possible on the dirt and darkness and evil of the psychic background, and to interpret it in such a way as to make us lose all desire to look for anything behind it except refuse and smut. He did not succeed, and his attempt at deterrence has even brought about the exact opposite—an admiration for all this filth. Such a perverse phenomenon would normally be inexplicable were it not that even the scatologists are drawn by the secret fascination of the psyche.

There can be no doubt that from the beginning of the nineteenth century—ever since the time of the French Revolution—the psyche has moved more and more into the foreground of man's interest, and with a steadily increasing power of attraction. The enthronement of the Goddess of Reason in Notre Dame seems to have been a symbolic gesture of great significance for the Western world—rather like the hewing down of Wotan's oak by Christian missionaries. On both occasions no avenging bolt from heaven struck the blasphemer down.

It is certainly more than an amusing freak of history that just at the time of the Revolution a Frenchman, Anquetil du Perron, should be living in India and, at the beginning of the nineteenth century, brought back with him a translation of the *Oupnek'hat,* a collection of fifty Upanishads, which gave the West its first deep insight into the baffling mind of the East. To the historian this is a mere coincidence independent of the historical nexus of cause and effect. My medical bias prevents me from seeing it simply as an accident. Everything happened in accordance with a psychological law which is unfailingly valid in personal affairs. If anything of importance is devalued in our conscious life, and perishes—so runs the law—there arises a compensation in the unconscious. We may see in this an analogy to the conservation of energy in the physical world, for our psychic processes also have a quantitative, energic aspect. No psychic value can disappear without being replaced by another of equivalent intensity. This is a fundamental rule which is repeatedly verified in the daily practice of the psychotherapist and never fails. The doctor in me refuses point blank to consider the life of a people as something that does not conform to psychological law. For him the psyche of a people is only a somewhat more complex structure than the psyche of an individual. Moreover, has not a poet spoken of the "nations of his soul"? And quite correctly, it seems to me, for in one of its aspects the psyche is not individual, but is derived from the nation, from the collectivity, from humanity even. In some way or other we are part of a single, all-embracing psyche, a single "greatest man," the *homo maximus,* to quote Swedenborg.

And so we can draw a parallel: just as in me, a single individual, the darkness calls forth a helpful light, so it does in the psychic life of a people. In the crowds that poured into Notre Dame, bent on destruction, dark and nameless forces were at work that swept the individual off his feet; these forces worked also upon Anquetil du Perron and provoked an answer which has come down in history and speaks to us through the mouths of Schopenhauer and Nietzsche. For he brought the Eastern mind to the West, and its influence upon us we cannot as yet measure. Let us beware of underestimating it! So far, indeed, there is little of it to be seen on the intellectual surface: a handful of orientalists, one or two Buddhist enthusiasts, a few sombre celebrities like Madame Blavatsky and Annie Besant with her Krishnamurti. These manifestations are like tiny scattered islands in the ocean of mankind; in reality they are the peaks of submarine mountain-ranges. The cultural Philistines believed until recently that astrology had been disposed of long since and was something that could safely be laughed at. But today, rising out of the social deeps, it knocks at the doors of the universities from which it was banished some three hundred years ago. The same is true of Eastern ideas; they take root in the lower levels and slowly grow to the surface. Where did the five or six million Swiss francs for the Anthroposophist temple at Dornach come from? Certainly not from one individual. Unfortunately there are no statistics to tell us the exact number of avowed Theosophists today, not to mention the unavowed. But we can be sure there are several millions of them. To this number we must add a few million Spiritualists of Christian or Theosophist leanings.

Great innovations never come from above; they come invariably from below, just as trees never grow from the sky downward, but upward from the earth. The upheaval of our world and the upheaval of our consciousness are one and the same. Everything has become relative and therefore doubtful. And while man, hesitant and questioning, contemplates a world that is distracted with treaties of peace and pacts of friendship, with democracy and dictatorship, capitalism and Bolshevism, his spirit yearns for an answer that will allay the turmoil of doubt and uncertainty. And it is just the people from the obscurer levels who follow the unconscious drive of the psyche; it is the much-derided, silent folk of the land, who are less infected with academic prejudices than the shining celebrities are wont to be. Looked at from above, they often present a dreary or laughable spectacle; yet they are as impressively simple as those Galileans who were once called blessed. Is it not touching to see the offscourings of man's psyche gathered together in compendia a foot thick? We find the merest babblings, the most absurd actions, the wildest fantasies recorded with scrupulous care in the volumes of *Anthropophyteia,*[4] while men like Havelock Ellis and Freud

---

[4] Friedrich H. Krauss, ed., *Anthropophyteia. Jahrbücher für folkloristische Erhebungen und Forschungen zur Entwicklungsgeschichte der geschlectlichen Moral* (Leipzig, 1904–13, 10 vols.).

have dealt with like matters in serious treatises which have been accorded all scientific honours. Their reading public is scattered over the breadth of the civilized, white world. How are we to explain this zeal, this almost fanatical worship of everything unsavoury? It is because these things are psychological—they are of the substance of the psyche and therefore as precious as fragments of manuscript salvaged from ancient middens. Even the secret and noisome things of the psyche are valuable to modern man because they serve his purpose. But what purpose?

Freud prefixed to his *Interpretation of Dreams* the motto: *Flectere si nequeo superos Acheronta movebo*—"If I cannot bend the gods on high, I will at least set Acheron in uproar." But to what purpose?

The gods whom we are called upon to dethrone are the idolized values of our conscious world. Nothing, as we know, discredited the ancient gods so much as their love-scandals, and now history is repeating itself. People are laying bare the dubious foundations of our belauded virtues and incomparable ideals, and are calling out to us in triumph: "There are your man-made gods, mere snares and delusions tainted with human baseness—whited sepulchres full of dead men's bones and of all uncleanness." We recognize a familiar strain, and the Gospel words which we failed to digest at Confirmation come to life again.

I am deeply convinced that these are not just vague analogies. There are too many persons to whom Freudian psychology is dearer than the Gospels, and to whom Bolshevism means more than civic virtue. And yet they are all our brothers, and in each of us there is at least one voice which seconds them, for in the end there is one psyche which embraces us all.

The unexpected result of this development is that an uglier face is put upon the world. It becomes so ugly that no one can love it any longer; we cannot even love ourselves, and in the end there is nothing in the outer world to draw us away from the reality of the life within. Here, no doubt, we have the true significance of this whole development. After all, what does Theosophy, with its doctrines of *karma* and reincarnation, seek to teach except that this world of appearance is but a temporary health-resort for the morally unperfected? It depreciates the intrinsic value of the present-day world no less radically than does the modern outlook, but with the help of a different technique; it does not vilify our world, but grants it only a relative meaning in that it promises other and higher worlds. The result in either case is the same.

I admit that all these ideas are extremely unacademic, the truth being that they touch modern man on the side where he is least conscious. Is it again a mere coincidence that modern thought has had to come to terms with Einstein's relativity theory and with nuclear theories which lead us away from determinism and border on the inconceivable? Even physics is volatilizing our material world. It is no wonder, then, in my opinion, if modern man falls back on the reality of psychic life and expects from it that certainty which the world denies him.

Spiritually the Western world is in a precarious situation, and the danger is greater the more we blind ourselves to the merciless truth with illusions about our beauty of soul. Western man lives in a thick cloud of incense which he burns to himself so that his own countenance may be veiled from him in the smoke. But how do we strike men of another colour? What do China and India think of us? What feelings do we arouse in the black man? And what about all those whom we rob of their lands and exterminate with rum and venereal disease?

I have an American Indian friend who is a Pueblo chieftain. Once when we were talking confidentially about the white man, he said to me: "We don't understand the whites. They are always wanting something, always restless, always looking for something. What is it? We don't know. We can't understand them. They have such sharp noses, such thin, cruel lips, such lines in their faces. We think they are all crazy."

My friend had recognized, without being able to name it,

the Aryan bird of prey with his insatiable lust to lord it in every land, even those that concern him not at all. And he had also noted that megalomania of ours which leads us to suppose, among other things, that Christianity is the only truth and the white Christ the only redeemer. After setting the whole East in turmoil with our science and technology, and exacting tribute from it, we send our missionaries even to China. The comedy of Christianity in Africa is really pitiful. There the stamping out of polygamy, no doubt highly pleasing to God, has given rise to prostitution on such a scale that in Uganda alone twenty thousand pounds are spent annually on preventives of venereal infection. And the good European pays his missionaries for these edifying achievements! Need we also mention the story of suffering in Polynesia and the blessings of the opium trade?

That is how the European looks when he is extricated from the cloud of his own moral incense. No wonder that unearthing the psyche is like undertaking a full-scale drainage operation. Only a great idealist like Freud could devote a lifetime to such unclean work. It was not he who caused the bad smell, but all of us—we who think ourselves so clean and decent from sheer ignorance and the grossest self-deception. Thus our psychology, the acquaintance with our own souls, begins in every respect from the most repulsive end, that is to say with all those things which we do not wish to see.

But if the psyche consisted only of evil and worthless things, no power on earth could induce the normal man to find it attractive. That is why people who see in Theosophy nothing but lamentable intellectual superficiality, and in Freudian psychology nothing but sensationalism, prophesy an early and inglorious end to these movements. They overlook the fact that such movements derive their force from the fascination of the psyche, and that it will express itself in these forms until they are replaced by something better. They are transitional or embryonic stages from which new and riper forms will emerge.

We have not yet realized that Western Theosophy is an amateurish, indeed barbarous imitation of the East. We are just beginning to take up astrology again, which to the Oriental is his daily bread. Our studies of sexual life, originating in Vienna and England, are matched or surpassed by Hindu teachings on this subject. Oriental texts ten centuries old introduce us to philosophical relativism, while the idea of indeterminacy, newly broached in the West, is the very basis of Chinese science. As to our discoveries in psychology, Richard Wilhelm has shown me that certain complicated psychic processes are recognizably described in ancient Chinese texts. Psychoanalysis itself and the lines of thought to which it gives rise—a development which we consider specifically Western—are only a beginner's attempt compared with what is an immemorial art in the East. It may not perhaps be known that parallels between psychoanalysis and yoga have already been drawn by Oscar Schmitz.[5]

Another thing we have not realized is that while we are turning the material world of the East upside down with our technical proficiency, the East with its superior psychic proficiency is throwing our spiritual world into confusion. We have never yet hit upon the thought that while we are overpowering the Orient from without, it may be fastening its hold on us from within. Such an idea strikes us as almost insane, because we have eyes only for obvious causal connections and fail to see that we must lay the blame for the confusion of our intellectual middle class at the doors of Max Müller, Oldenberg, Deussen, Wilhelm, and others like them. What does the example of the Roman Empire teach us? After the conquest of Asia Minor, Rome became Asiatic; Europe was infected by Asia and remains so today. Out of Cilicia came the Mithraic cult, the religion of the Roman legions, and it spread from Egypt to fog-bound Britain. Need I point out the Asiatic origin of Christianity?

[5] *Psychoanalyse und Yoga* (Darmstadt, 1923).

The Theosophists have an amusing idea that certain Mahatmas, seated somewhere in the Himalayas or Tibet, inspire and direct every mind in the world. So strong, in fact, can be the influence of the Eastern belief in magic that Europeans of sound mind have assured me that every good thing I say is unwittingly inspired in me by the Mahatmas, my own inspirations being of no account whatever. This myth of the Mahatmas, widely circulated in the West and firmly believed, far from being nonsense, is —like every myth—an important psychological truth. It seems to be quite true that the East is at the bottom of the spiritual change we are passing through today. Only, this East is not a Tibetan monastery full of Mahatmas, but lies essentially within us. It is our own psyche, constantly at work creating new spiritual forms and spiritual forces which may help us to subdue the boundless lust for prey of Aryan man. We shall perhaps come to know something of that narrowing of horizons which has grown in the East into a dubious quietism, and also something of that stability which human existence acquires when the claims of the spirit become as imperative as the necessities of social life. Yet in this age of Americanization we are still far from anything of the sort; it seems to me that we are only at the threshold of a new spiritual epoch. I do not wish to pass myself off as a prophet, but one can hardly attempt to sketch the spiritual problem of modern man without mentioning the longing for rest in a period of unrest, the longing for security in an age of insecurity. It is from need and distress that new forms of existence arise, and not from idealistic requirements or mere wishes.

To me the crux of the spiritual problem today is to be found in the fascination which the psyche holds for modern man. If we are pessimists, we shall call it a sign of decadence; if we are optimistically inclined, we shall see in it the promise of a far-reaching spiritual change in the Western world. At all events, it is a significant phenomenon. It is the more noteworthy because it is rooted in the deeper social strata, and the more important because it touches those irrational and—as history shows—incalculable psychic forces which transform the life of peoples and civilizations in ways that are unforeseen and unforeseeable. These are the forces, still invisible to many persons today, which are at the bottom of the present "psychological" interest. The fascination of the psyche is not by any means a morbid perversity; it is an attraction so strong that it does not shrink even from what it finds repellent.

Along the great highways of the world everything seems desolate and outworn. Instinctively modern man leaves the trodden paths to explore the by-ways and lanes, just as the man of the Greco-Roman world cast off his defunct Olympian gods and turned to the mystery cults of Asia. Our instinct turns outward, and appropriates Eastern theosophy and magic; but it also turns inward, and leads us to contemplate the dark background of the psyche. It does this with the same scepticism and the same ruthlessness which impelled the Buddha to sweep aside his two million gods that he might attain the original experience which alone is convincing.

And now we must ask a final question. Is what I have said of modern man really true, or is it perhaps an illusion? There can be no doubt whatever that to many millions of Westerners the facts I have adduced are wholly irrelevant and fortuitous, and regrettable aberrations to a large number of educated persons. But—did a cultivated Roman think any differently when he saw Christianity spreading among the lower classes? Today the God of the West is still a living person for vast numbers of people, just as Allah is beyond the Mediterranean, and the one believer holds the other an inferior heretic, to be pitied and tolerated failing all else. To make matters worse, the enlightened European is of the opinion that religion and such things are good enough for the masses and for women, but of little consequence compared with immediate economic and political questions.

So I am refuted all along the line, like a man who predicts a thunderstorm when there is not a cloud in the sky. Perhaps it is a storm below the horizon, and perhaps it will never reach us. But what is significant in psychic life always lies below the horizon of consciousness, and when we speak of the spiritual problem of modern man we are speaking of things that are barely visible—of the most intimate and fragile things, of flowers that open only in the night. In daylight everything is clear and tangible, but the night lasts as long as the day, and we live in the night-time also. There are people who have bad dreams which even spoil their days for them. And for many people the day's life is such a bad dream that they long for the night when the spirit awakes. I believe that there are nowadays a great many such people, and this is why I also maintain that the spiritual problem of modern man is much as I have presented it.

I must plead guilty, however, to the charge of one-sidedness, for I have passed over in silence the spirit of the times, about which everyone has so much to say because it is so clearly apparent to us all. It shows itself in the ideal of internationalism and supernationalism, embodied in the League of Nations and the like; we see it also in sport and, significantly, in cinema and jazz. These are characteristic symptoms of our time, which has extended the humanistic ideal even to the body. Sport puts an exceptional valuation on the body, and this tendency is emphasized still further in modern dancing. The cinema, like the detective story, enables us to experience without danger to ourselves all the excitements, passions, and fantasies which have to be repressed in a humanistic age. It is not difficult to see how these symptoms link up with our psychological situation. The fascination of the psyche brings about a new self-appraisal, a reassessment of our fundamental human nature. We can hardly be surprised if this leads to a rediscovery of the body after its long subjection to the spirit—we are even tempted to say that the flesh is getting its own back. When Keyserling sarcastically singles out the chauffeur as the culture-hero of our time, he has struck, as he often does, close to the mark. The body lays claim to equal recognition; it exerts the same fascination as the psyche. If we are still caught in the old idea of an antithesis between mind and matter, this state of affairs must seem like an unbearable contradiction. But if we can reconcile ourselves to the mysterious truth that the spirit is the life of the body seen from within, and the body the outward manifestation of the life of the spirit—the two being really one—then we can understand why the striving to transcend the present level of consciousness through acceptance of the unconscious must give the body its due, and why recognition of the body cannot tolerate a philosophy that denies it in the name of the spirit. These claims of physical and psychic life, incomparably stronger than they were in the past, may seem a sign of decadence, but they may also signify a rejuvenation, for as Hölderlin says:

> Where danger is,
> Arises salvation also.

And indeed we see, as the Western world strikes up a more rapid tempo—the American tempo—the exact opposite of quietism and world-negating resignation. An unprecedented tension arises between outside and inside, between objective and subjective reality. Perhaps it is a final race between aging Europe and young America; perhaps it is a healthier or a last desperate effort to escape the dark sway of natural law, and to wrest a yet greater and more heroic victory of waking consciousness over the sleep of the nations. This is a question only history can answer.

# ❧ 13 ❧

## The Difference Between
## Eastern and Western Thinking[1]

Dr. Evans-Wentz has entrusted me with the task of commenting on a text which contains an important exposition of Eastern "psychology." The very fact that I have to use quotation marks shows the dubious applicability of this term. It is perhaps not superfluous to mention that the East has produced nothing equivalent to what we call psychology, but rather philosophy or metaphysics. Critical philosophy, the mother of modern psychology, is as foreign to the East as to medieval Europe. Thus the word "mind," as used in the East, has the connotation of something metaphysical. Our Western conception of mind has lost this connotation since the Middle Ages, and the word has now come to signify a "psychic function." Despite the fact that we neither know nor pretend to know what

[1] Part I of Jung's "Psychological Commentary on 'The Tibetan Book of the Great Liberation,'" from *Psychology and Religion: West and East. Collected Works,* Vol. 11, pars. 759-787. [Written in English in 1939 and first published in *The Tibetan Book of the Great Liberation,* the texts of which were translated from Tibetan by various hands and edited by W. Y. Evans-Wentz (London and New York, 1954), pp. xxix–lxiv. The commentary is republished here with only minor alterations.—EDITORS OF *The Collected Works.*]

"psyche" is, we can deal with the phenomenon of "mind." We do not assume that the mind is a metaphysical entity or that there is any connection between an individual mind and a hypothetical Universal Mind. Our psychology is, therefore, a science of mere phenomena without any metaphysical implications. The development of Western philosophy during the last two centuries has succeeded in isolating the mind in its own sphere and in severing it from its primordial oneness with the universe. Man himself has ceased to be the microcosm and eidolon of the cosmos, and his "anima" is no longer the consubstantial *scintilla,* or spark of the *Anima Mundi,* the World Soul.

Psychology accordingly treats all metaphysical claims and assertions as mental phenomena, and regards them as statements about the mind and its structure that derive ultimately from certain unconscious dispositions. It does not consider them to be absolutely valid or even capable of establishing a metaphysical truth. We have no intellectual means of ascertaining whether this attitude is right or wrong. We only know that there is no evidence for, and no possibility of proving, the validity of a metaphysical postulate such as "Universal Mind." If the mind asserts the existence of a Universal Mind, we hold that it is merely making an assertion. We do not assume that by such an assertion the existence of a Universal Mind has been established. There is no argument against this reasoning, but no evidence, either, that our conclusion is ultimately right. In other words, it is just as possible that our mind is nothing but a perceptible manifestation of a Universal Mind. Yet we do not know, and we cannot even see, how it would be possible to recognize whether this is so or not. Psychology therefore holds that the mind cannot establish or assert anything beyond itself.

If, then, we accept the restrictions imposed upon the capacity of our mind, we demonstrate our common sense. I admit it is something of a sacrifice, inasmuch as we bid farewell to that miraculous world in which mind-created things and beings move and live. This is the world of the primitive, where even inanimate objects are endowed with a living, healing, magic power, through which they participate in us and we in them. Sooner or later we had to understand that their potency was really ours, and that their significance was our projection. The theory of knowledge is only the last step out of humanity's childhood, out of a world where mind-created figures populated a metaphysical heaven and hell.

Despite this inevitable epistemological criticism, however, we have held fast to the religious belief that the organ of faith enables man to know God. The West thus developed a new disease: the conflict between science and religion. The critical philosophy of science became as it were negatively metaphysical—in other words, materialistic—on the basis of an error in judgment; matter was assumed to be a tangible and recognizable reality. Yet this is a thoroughly metaphysical concept hypostatized by uncritical minds. Matter is an hypothesis. When you say "matter," you are really creating a symbol for something unknown, which may just as well be "spirit" or anything else; it may even be God. Religious faith, on the other hand, refuses to give up its pre-critical *Weltanschauung*. In contradiction to the saying of Christ, the faithful try to *remain* children instead of becoming *as* children. They cling to the world of childhood. A famous modern theologian confesses in his autobiography that Jesus has been his good friend "from childhood on." Jesus is the perfect example of a man who preached something different from the religion of his forefathers. But the *imitatio Christi* does not appear to include the mental and spiritual sacrifice which he had to undergo at the beginning of his career and without which he would never have become a saviour.

The conflict between science and religion is in reality a misunderstanding of both. Scientific materialism has merely introduced a new hypostasis, and that is an intellectual sin. It has given another name to the supreme principle of reality and has assumed that this created a new thing and destroyed an old thing. Whether you call the principle of existence "God," "matter," "energy," or anything else you like, you have created nothing; you have simply changed a symbol. The materialist is a metaphysician *malgré lui*. Faith, on the other hand, tries to retain a primitive mental condition on merely sentimental grounds. It is unwilling to give up the primitive, childlike relationship to mind-created and hypostatized figures; it wants to go on enjoying the security and confidence of a world still presided over by powerful, responsible, and kindly parents. Faith may include a *sacrificium intellectus* (provided there is an intellect to sacrifice), but certainly not a sacrifice of feeling. In this way the faithful *remain* children instead of becoming *as* children, and they do not gain their life because they have not lost it. Furthermore, faith collides with science and thus gets its deserts, for it refuses to share in the spiritual adventure of our age.

Any honest thinker has to admit the insecurity of all metaphysical positions, and in particular of all creeds. He has also to admit the unwarrantable nature of all metaphysical assertions and face the fact that there is no evidence whatever for the ability of the human mind to pull itself up by its own bootstrings, that is, to establish anything transcendental.

Materialism is a metaphysical reaction against the sudden realization that cognition is a mental faculty and, if carried beyond the human plane, a projection. The reaction was "metaphysical" in so far as the man of average philosophical education failed to see through the implied hypostasis, not realizing that "matter" was just another name for the supreme principle. As against this, the attitude of faith shows how reluctant people were to accept philosophical criticism. It also demonstrates how great is the fear of letting go one's hold on the securities of childhood and of dropping into a strange, unknown world ruled by forces unconcerned with man. Nothing really changes in either case; man and his surroundings remain the same. He has only to realize that he is shut up inside his mind and cannot step beyond it, even in insanity; and that the appearance of his world or of his gods very much depends upon his own mental condition.

In the first place, the structure of the mind is responsible for anything we may assert about metaphysical matters, as I have already pointed out. We have also begun to understand that the intellect is not an *ens per se*, or an independent mental faculty, but a psychic function dependent upon the conditions of the psyche as a whole. A philosophical statement is the product of a certain personality living at a certain time in a certain place, and not the outcome of a purely logical and impersonal procedure. To that extent it is chiefly subjective; whether it has an objective validity or not depends on whether there are few or many persons who argue in the same way. The isolation of man within his mind as a result of epistemological criticism has naturally led to psychological criticism. This kind of criticism is not popular with the philosophers, since they like to consider the philosophic intellect as the perfect and unconditioned instrument of philosophy. Yet this intellect of theirs is a function dependent upon an individual psyche and determined on all sides by subjective conditions, quite apart from environmental influences. Indeed, we have already become so accustomed to this point of view that "mind" has lost its universal character altogether. It has become a more or less individualized affair, with no trace of its former cosmic aspect as the *anima rationalis*. Mind is understood nowadays as a subjective, even an arbitrary, thing. Now that the formerly hypostatized "universal ideas" have turned out to be mental principles, it is dawning upon us to what an extent our whole experience of so-called reality is psychic; as a matter of fact, everything thought, felt, or perceived is a psychic image, and the world itself exists only so far as we are able to produce an image of it. We are so deeply impressed with the truth of our imprisonment in, and limitation by, the psyche that we are ready to admit the existence in it even of things we do *not* know: we call them "the unconscious."

The seemingly universal and metaphysical scope of the mind has thus been narrowed down to the small circle of individual consciousness, profoundly aware of its almost limitless subjectivity and of its infantile-archaic tendency to heedless projection and illusion. Many scientifically-minded persons have even sacrificed their religious and philosophical leanings for fear of uncontrolled subjectivism. By way of compensation for the loss of a world that pulsed with our blood and breathed with our breath, we have developed an enthusiasm for *facts*—mountains of facts, far beyond any single individual's power to survey. We have the pious hope that this incidental accumulation of facts will form a meaningful whole, but nobody is quite sure, because no human brain can possibly comprehend the gigantic sum total of this mass-produced knowledge. The facts bury us, but whoever dares to speculate must pay for it with a bad conscience—and rightly so, for he will instantly be tripped up by the facts.

Western psychology knows the mind as the mental functioning of a psyche. It is the "mentality" of an individual. An impersonal Universal Mind is still to be met with in the sphere of philosophy, where it seems to be a relic of the original human "soul." This picture of our Western outlook may seem a little drastic, but I do not think it is far from the truth. At all events, something of the kind presents itself as soon as we are confronted with the Eastern mentality. In the East, mind is a cosmic factor, the very essence of existence; while in the West we have just begun to understand that it is the essential condition of cognition, and hence of the cognitive existence of the world. There is no conflict between religion and science in the East, because no science is there based upon the passion for facts, and no religion upon mere faith; there is religious cognition and cognitive religion.[2] With us, man is incommensurably small and the grace of God is everything; but in the East, man is God and he redeems himself. The gods of Tibetan Buddhism belong to the sphere of illusory separateness and mind-created projections, and yet they exist; but so far as we are concerned an illusion remains an illusion, and thus is nothing at all. It is a paradox, yet nevertheless true, that with us a thought has no proper reality; we treat it as if it were a nothingness. Even though the thought be true in itself, we hold that it exists only by virtue of certain facts which it is said to formulate. We can produce a most devastating fact like the atom bomb with the help of this ever-changing phantasmagoria of virtually non-existent thoughts, but it seems wholly absurd to us that one could ever establish the reality of thought itself.

"Psychic reality" is a controversial concept, like "psyche" or "mind." By the latter terms some understand consciousness and its contents, others allow the existence of "dark" or "subconscious" representations. Some include instincts in the psychic realm, others exclude them. The vast majority consider the psyche to be a result of bio-chemical processes in the brain cells. A few conjecture that it is the psyche that makes the cortical cells function. Some identify "life" with psyche. But only an insignificant minority regards the psychic phenomenon as a category of existence *per se* and draws the necessary conclusions. It is indeed paradoxical that *the* category of existence, the indispensable *sine qua non* of all existence, namely the psyche, should be treated as if it were only semi-existent. Psychic existence is the only category of existence of which we have *immediate* knowledge, since nothing can be known unless it first appears as a psychic image. Only psychic existence is immediately verifiable. To the extent that the world does not assume the form of a psychic image, it is virtually non-existent. This is a fact which,

[2] I am purposely leaving out of account the modernized East.

with few exceptions—as for instance in Schopenhauer's philosophy—the West has not yet fully realized. But Schopenhauer was influenced by Buddhism and by the Upanishads.

Even a superficial acquaintance with Eastern thought is sufficient to show that a fundamental difference divides East and West. The East bases itself upon psychic reality, that is, upon the psyche as the main and unique condition of existence. It seems as if this Eastern recognition were a psychological or temperamental fact rather than a result of philosophical reasoning. It is a typically introverted point of view, contrasted with the equally typical extraverted point of view of the West.[3] Introversion and extraversion are known to be temperamental or even constitutional attitudes which are never intentionally adopted in normal circumstances. In exceptional cases they may be produced at will, but only under very special conditions. Introversion is, if one may so express it, the "style" of the East, an habitual and collective attitude, just as extraversion is the "style" of the West. Introversion is felt here as something abnormal, morbid, or otherwise objectionable. Freud identifies it with an autoerotic, "narcissistic" attitude of mind. He shares his negative position with the National Socialist philosophy of modern Germany,[4] which accuses introversion of being an offence against community feeling. In the East, however, our cherished extraversion is depreciated as illusory desirousness, as existence in the *samsāra,* the very essence of the *nidāna*-chain which culminates in the sum of the world's sufferings.[5] Anyone with practical knowledge of the mutual depreciation of values between introvert and extravert will understand the emotional conflict between the Eastern and the Western standpoint. For those who know something of the history of European philosophy the bit-

---

[3] *Psychological Types,* supra, pp. 178–182.
[4] Written in the year 1939.
[5] *Samyutta-nikāya* 12, *Nidāna-samyutta.*

ter wrangling about "universals" which began with Plato will provide an instructive example. I do not wish to go into all the ramifications of this conflict between introversion and extraversion, but I must mention the religious aspects of the problem. The Christian West considers man to be wholly dependent upon the grace of God, or at least upon the Church as the exclusive and divinely sanctioned earthly instrument of man's redemption. The East, however, insists that man is the sole cause of his higher development, for it believes in "self-liberation."

The religious point of view always expresses and formulates the essential psychological attitude and its specific prejudices, even in the case of people who have forgotten, or who have never heard of, their own religion. In spite of everything, the West is thoroughly Christian as far as its psychology is concerned. Tertullian's *anima naturaliter christiana* holds true throughout the West—not, as he thought, in the religious sense, but in a psychological one. Grace comes from elsewhere; at all events from outside. Every other point of view is sheer heresy. Hence it is quite understandable why the human psyche is suffering from undervaluation. Anyone who dares to establish a connection between the psyche and the idea of God is immediately accused of "psychologism" or suspected of morbid "mysticism." The East, on the other hand, compassionately tolerates those "lower" spiritual stages where man, in his blind ignorance of karma, still bothers about sin and tortures his imagination with a belief in absolute gods, who, if he only looked deeper, are nothing but the veil of illusion woven by his own unenlightened mind. The psyche is therefore all-important; it is the all-pervading Breath, the Buddha-essence; it is the Buddha-Mind, the One, the *Dharmakāya*. All existence emanates from it, and all separate forms dissolve back into it. This is the basic psychological prejudice that permeates Eastern man in every fibre of his being, seeping into all his thoughts, feelings, and deeds, no matter what creed he professes.

In the same way Western man is Christian, no matter to what denomination his Christianity belongs. For him man is small inside, he is next to nothing; moreover, as Kierkegaard says, "before God man is always wrong." By fear, repentance, promises, submission, self-abasement, good deeds, and praise he propitiates the great power, which is not himself but *totaliter aliter,* the Wholly Other, altogether perfect and "outside," the only reality.[6] If you shift the formula a bit and substitute for God some other power, for instance the world or money, you get a complete picture of Western man—assiduous, fearful, devout, self-abasing, enterprising, greedy, and violent in his pursuit of the goods of this world: possessions, health, knowledge, technical mastery, public welfare, political power, conquest, and so on. What are the great popular movements of our time? Attempts to grab the money or property of others and to protect our own. The mind is chiefly employed in devising suitable "isms" to hide the real motives or to get more loot. I refrain from describing what would happen to Eastern man should he forget his ideal of Buddhahood, for I do not want to give such an unfair advantage to my Western prejudices. But I cannot help raising the question of whether it is possible, or indeed advisable, for either to imitate the other's standpoint. The difference between them is so vast that one can see no reasonable possibility of this, much less its advisability. You cannot mix fire and water. The Eastern attitude stultifies the Western, and vice versa. You cannot be a good Christian and redeem yourself, nor can you be a Buddha and worship God. It is much better to accept the conflict, for it admits only of an irrational solution, if any.

By an inevitable decree of fate the West is becoming acquainted with the peculiar facts of Eastern spirituality.

[6] [Cf. Rudolf Otto, *The Idea of the Holy,* translated by John W. Harvey (4th impr.; Oxford, 1926), pp. 26ff.—EDITORS OF *The Collected Works.*]

It is useless either to belittle these facts, or to build false and treacherous bridges over yawning gaps. Instead of learning the spiritual techniques of the East by heart and imitating them in a thoroughly Christian way—*imitatio Christi!*—with a correspondingly forced attitude, it would be far more to the point to find out whether there exists in the unconscious an introverted tendency similar to that which has become the guiding spiritual principle of the East. We should then be in a position to build on our own ground with our own methods. If we snatch these things directly from the East, we have merely indulged our Western acquisitiveness, confirming yet again that "everything good is outside," whence it has to be fetched and pumped into our barren souls.[7] It seem to me that we have really learned something from the East when we understand that the psyche contains riches enough without having to be primed from outside, and when we feel capable of evolving out of ourselves with or without divine grace. But we cannot embark upon this ambitious enterprise until we have learned how to deal with our spiritual pride and blasphemous self-assertiveness. The Eastern attitude violates the specifically Christian values, and it is no good blinking this fact. If our new attitude is to be genuine, i.e., grounded in our own history, it must be acquired with full consciousness of the Christian values and of the conflict between them and the introverted attitude of the East. We must get at the Eastern values from within and not from without, seeking them in ourselves, in the unconscious. We shall then discover how great is our fear of the unconscious and how formidable are our resistances. Because of these resistances we doubt the very thing that seems so obvious to the East, namely, the *self-liberating power of the introverted mind.*

---

[7] "Whereas who holdeth not God as such an inner possession, but with every means must fetch Him from without . . . verily such a man hath Him not, and easily something cometh to trouble him." Meister Eckhart (H. Büttner, *Meister Eckharts Schriften und Predigten* [Jena, 1909–17, 2 vols.], Vol. II, p. 185). Cf. *Meister Eckhart,* translated by Evans, Vol. II, p. 8.

This aspect of the mind is practically unknown to the West, though it forms the most important component of the unconscious. Many people flatly deny the existence of the unconscious, or else they say that it consists merely of instincts, or of repressed or forgotten contents that were once part of the conscious mind. It is safe to assume that what the East calls "mind" has more to do with our "unconscious" than with mind as we understand it, which is more or less identical with consciousness. To us, consciousness is inconceivable without an ego; it is equated with the relation of contents to an ego. If there is no ego there is nobody to be conscious of anything. The ego is therefore indispensable to the conscious process. The Eastern mind, however, has no difficulty in conceiving of a consciousness without an ego. Consciousness is deemed capable of transcending its ego condition; indeed, in its "higher" forms, the ego disappears altogether. Such an ego-less mental condition can only be unconscious to us, for the simple reason that there would be nobody to witness it. I do not doubt the existence of mental states transcending consciousness. But they lose their consciousness to exactly the same degree that they transcend consciousness. I cannot imagine a conscious mental state that does not relate to a subject, that is, to an ego. The ego may be depotentiated—divested, for instance, of its awareness of the body—but so long as there is awareness of something, there must be somebody who is aware. The unconscious, however, is a mental condition of which no ego is aware. It is only by indirect means that we eventually become conscious of the existence of an unconscious. We can observe the manifestation of unconscious fragments of the personality, detached from the patient's consciousness, in insanity. But there is no evidence that the unconscious contents are related to an unconscious centre analogous to the ego; in fact there are good reasons why such a centre is not even probable.

The fact that the East can dispose so easily of the ego seems to point to a mind that is not to be identified with our "mind." Certainly the ego does not play the same role in Eastern thought as it does with us. It seems as if the Eastern mind were less egocentric, as if its contents were more loosely connected with the subject, and as if greater stress were laid on mental states which include a depotentiated ego. It also seems as if *hatha* yoga were chiefly useful as a means for extinguishing the ego by fettering its unruly impulses. There is no doubt that the higher forms of yoga, in so far as they strive to reach samādhi, seek a mental condition in which the ego is practically dissolved. Consciousness in our sense of the word is rated a definitely inferior condition, the state of *avidyā* (ignorance), whereas what we call the "dark background of consciousness" is understood to be a "higher" consciousness.[8] Thus our concept of the "collective unconscious" would be the European equivalent of *buddhi*, the enlightened mind.

In view of all this, the Eastern form of "sublimation" amounts to a withdrawal of the centre of psychic gravity from ego-consciousness, which holds a middle position between the body and the ideational processes of the psyche. The lower, semi-physiological strata of the psyche are subdued by *askesis*, i.e., exercises, and kept under control. They are not exactly denied or suppressed by a supreme effort of the will, as is customary in Western sublimation. Rather, the lower psychic strata are adapted and shaped through the patient practice of *hatha* yoga until they no longer interfere with the development of "higher" consciousness. This peculiar process seems to be aided by the fact that the ego and its desires are checked by the greater importance which the East habitually attaches to the "subjective factor." [9] By this I mean the

[8] In so far as "higher" and "lower" are categorical judgments of consciousness, Western psychology does not differentiate unconscious contents in this way. It appears that the East recognizes subhuman psychic conditions, a real "subconsciousness" comprising the instincts and semi-physiological psychisms, but classed as a "higher consciousness."

[9] *Psychological Types*, supra, pp. 229ff.

"dark background" of consciousness, the unconscious. The introverted attitude is characterized in general by an emphasis on the *a priori* data of apperception. As is well known, the act of apperception consists of two phases: first the perception of the object, second the assimilation of the perception to a preexisting pattern or concept by means of which the object is "comprehended." The psyche is not a nonentity devoid of all quality; it is a definite system made up of definite conditions and it reacts in a specific way. Every new representation, be it a perception or a spontaneous thought, arouses associations which derive from the storehouse of memory. These leap immediately into consciousness, producing the complex picture of an "impression," though this is already a sort of interpretation. The unconscious disposition upon which the quality of the impression depends is what I call the "subjective factor." It deserves the qualification "subjective" because objectivity is hardly ever conferred by a first impression. Usually a rather laborious process of verification, comparison, and analysis is needed to modify and adapt the immediate reactions of the subjective factor.

The prominence of the subjective factor does not imply a *personal subjectivism,* despite the readiness of the extraverted attitude to dismiss the subjective factor as "nothing but" subjective. The psyche and its structure are real enough. They even transform material objects into psychic images, as we have said. They do not perceive waves, but sound; not wave-lengths, but colours. Existence is as we see and understand it. There are innumerable things that can be seen, felt, and understood in a great variety of ways. Quite apart from merely personal prejudices, the psyche assimilates external facts in its own way, which is based ultimately upon the laws or patterns of apperception. These laws do not change, although different ages or different parts of the world call them by different names. On a primitive level people are afraid of witches; on the modern level we are apprehensively aware of microbes.

There everybody believes in ghosts, here everybody believes in vitamins. Once upon a time men were possessed by devils, now they are not less obsessed by ideas, and so on.

The subjective factor is made up, in the last resort, of the eternal patterns of psychic functioning. Anyone who relies upon the subjective factor is therefore basing himself on the reality of psychic law. So he can hardly be said to be wrong. If by this means he succeeds in extending his consciousness downwards, to touch the basic laws of psychic life, he is in possession of that truth which the psyche will naturally evolve if not fatally interfered with by the non-psyche, i.e., the external, world. At any rate, his truth could be weighed against the sum of all knowledge acquired through the investigation of externals. We in the West believe that a truth is satisfactory only if it can be verified by external facts. We believe in the most exact observation and exploration of nature; our truth must coincide with the behaviour of the external world, otherwise it is merely "subjective." In the same way that the East turns its gaze from the dance of *prakriti* (physis) and from the multitudinous illusory forms of *māyā*, the West shuns the unconscious and its futile fantasies. Despite its introverted attitude, however, the East knows very well how to deal with the external world. And despite its extraversions the West, too, has a way of dealing with the psyche and its demands; it has an institution called the Church, which gives expression to the unknown psyche of man through its rites and dogmas. Nor are natural science and modern techniques by any means the invention of the West. Their Eastern equivalents are somewhat old-fashioned, or even primitive. But what we have to show in the way of spiritual insight and psychological technique must seem, when compared with yoga, just as backward as Eastern astrology and medicine when compared with Western science. I do not deny the efficacy of the Christian Church; but, if you compare the *Exercitia* of Ignatius Loyola with yoga, you will take my meaning. There is a difference, and a big one. To jump straight from that level into Eastern yoga is no more advisable than the sudden transformation of Asian peoples into half-baked Europeans. I have serious doubts as to the blessings of Western civilization, and I have similar misgivings as to the adoption of Eastern spirituality by the West. Yet the two contradictory worlds have met. The East is in full transformation; it is thoroughly and fatally disturbed. Even the most efficient methods of European warfare have been successfully imitated. The trouble with us seems to be far more psychological. Our blight is ideologies—they are the long-expected Antichrist! National Socialism comes as near to being a religious movement as any movement since A.D. 622.[10] Communism claims to be paradise come to earth again. We are far better protected against failing crops, inundations, epidemics, and invasions from the Turk than we are against our own deplorable spiritual inferiority, which seems to have little resistance to psychic epidemics.

In its religious attitude, too, the West is extraverted. Nowadays it is gratuitously offensive to say that Christianity implies hostility, or even indifference, to the world and the flesh. On the contrary, the good Christian is a jovial citizen, an enterprising business man, an excellent soldier, the very best in every profession there is. Worldly goods are often interpreted as special rewards for Christian behaviour, and in the Lord's Prayer the adjective ἐπιούσιος, *supersubstantialis,*[11] referring to the bread, has long since been omitted, for the real bread obviously makes so very much more sense! It is only logical that extraversion, when carried to such lengths, cannot credit man with a psyche which contains anything not imported into it from outside, either by human teaching or divine grace.

[10] [Date of Mohammed's flight (*hegira*) to Medina: beginning of Moslem era.]

[11] This is not the unacceptable translation of ἐπιούσιος by Jerome but the ancient spiritual interpretation by Tertullian, Origen, and others.

From this point of view it is downright blasphemy to assert that man has it in him to accomplish his own redemption. Nothing in our religion encourages the idea of the self-liberating power of the mind. Yet a very modern form of psychology—"analytical" or "complex" psychology—envisages the possibility of there being certain processes in the unconscious which, by virtue of their symbolism, compensate the defects and anfractuosities of the conscious attitude. When these unconscious compensations are made conscious through the analytical technique, they produce such a change in the conscious attitude that we are entitled to speak of a new level of consciousness. The method cannot, however, produce the actual process of unconscious compensation; for that we depend upon the unconscious psyche or the "grace of God"—names make no difference. But the unconscious process itself hardly ever reaches consciousness without technical aid. When brought to the surface, it reveals contents that offer a striking contrast to the general run of conscious thinking and feeling. If that were not so, they would not have a compensatory effect. The first effect, however, is usually a conflict, because the conscious attitude resists the intrusion of apparently incompatible and extraneous tendencies, thoughts, feelings, etc. Schizophrenia yields the most startling examples of such intrusions of utterly foreign and unacceptable contents. In schizophrenia it is, of course, a question of pathological distortions and exaggerations, but anybody with the slightest knowledge of the normal material will easily recognize the sameness of the underlying patterns. It is, as a matter of fact, the same imagery that one finds in mythology and other archaic thought-forms.

Under normal conditions, every conflict stimulates the mind to activity for the purpose of creating a satisfactory solution. Usually—i.e., in the West—the conscious standpoint arbitrarily decides against the unconscious, since anything coming from inside suffers from the prejudice of being regarded as inferior or somehow wrong. But in the cases with which we are here concerned it is tacitly agreed that the apparently incompatible contents shall not be suppressed again, and that the conflict shall be accepted and suffered. At first no solution appears possible, and this fact, too, has to be borne with patience. The suspension thus created "constellates" the unconscious—in other words, the conscious suspense produces a new compensatory reaction in the unconscious. This reaction (usually manifested in dreams) is brought to conscious realization in its turn. The conscious mind is thus confronted with a new aspect of the psyche, which arouses a different problem or modifies an old one in an unexpected way. The procedure is continued until the original conflict is satisfactorily resolved. The whole process is called the "transcendent function." It is a process and a method at the same time. The production of unconscious compensations is a spontaneous *process;* the conscious realization is a *method.* The function is called "transcendent" because it facilitates the transition from one psychic condition to another by means of the mutual confrontation of opposites.

This is a very sketchy description of the transcendent function, and for details I must refer the reader to the relevant literature.[12] But I felt it necessary to call attention to these psychological observations and methods because they indicate the way by which we may find access to the sort of "mind" referred to in our text. This is the image-creating mind, the matrix of all those patterns that give apperception its peculiar character. These patterns are inherent in the unconscious "mind"; they are its structural elements, and they alone can explain why certain mythological motifs are more or less ubiquitous, even where migration as a means of transmission is exceedingly improbable. Dreams, fantasies, and psychoses produce images to all appearances identical with mythological motifs of which the individuals concerned had absolutely no knowledge, not even indirect knowledge acquired through

[12] "The Transcendent Function," supra, pp. 273–300.

popular figures of speech or through the symbolic language of the Bible.[13] The psychopathology of schizophrenia, as well as the psychology of the unconscious, demonstrate the production of archaic material beyond a doubt. Whatever the structure of the unconscious may be, one thing is certain: it contains an indefinite number of motifs or patterns of an archaic character, in principle identical with the root ideas of mythology and similar thought-forms.

Because the unconscious is the matrix mind, the quality of creativeness attaches to it. It is the birthplace of thought-forms such as our text considers the Universal Mind to be. Since we cannot attribute any particular form to the unconscious, the Eastern assertion that the Universal Mind is without form, the *arupaloka,* yet is the source of all forms, seems to be psychologically justified. In so far as the forms or patterns of the unconscious belong to no time in particular, being seemingly eternal, they convey a peculiar feeling of timelessness when consciously realized. We find similar statements in primitive psychology: for instance, the Australian word *aljira*[14] means "dream" as well as "ghostland" and the "time" in which the ancestors lived and still live. It is, as they say, the "time when there was no time." This looks like an obvious concretization and projection of the unconscious with all its characteristic qualities—its dream manifestations, its ancestral world of thought-forms, and its timelessness.

---

[13] Some people find such statements incredible. But either they have no knowledge of primitive psychology, or they are ignorant of the results of psychopathological research. Specific observations occur in my *Symbols of Transformation* and *Psychology and Alchemy,* Part II; Jan Nelken, "Analytische Beobachtungen über Phantasien eines Schizophrenen," *Jahrbuch für psychoanalytische und psychopathologische Forschung* (Vienna and Leipzig), IV (1912), 504ff.; Sabina Spielrein, "Über den psychologischen Inhalt eines Falls von Schizophrenie," ibid., III (1912), 329ff.; and C. A. Meier, "Spontanmanifestationen des kollektiven Unbewussten," *Zentralblatt für Psychotherapie* (Leipzig), XI (1939), 284–302.
[14] Lucien Lévy-Bruhl, *La Mythologie primitive* (Paris, 1935), pp. xxiiiff.

An introverted attitude, therefore, which withdraws its emphasis from the external world (the world of consciousness) and localizes it in the subjective factor (the background of consciousness) necessarily calls forth the characteristic manifestations of the unconscious, namely, archaic thought-forms imbued with "ancestral" or "historic" feeling, and, beyond them, the sense of indefiniteness, timelessness, oneness. The extraordinary feeling of oneness is a common experience in all forms of "mysticism" and probably derives from the general contamination of contents, which increases as consciousness dims. The almost limitless contamination of images in dreams, and particularly in the products of insanity, testifies to their unconscious origin. In contrast to the clear distinction and differentiation of forms in consciousness, unconscious contents are incredibly vague and for this reason capable of any amount of contamination. If we tried to conceive of a state in which nothing is distinct, we should certainly feel the whole as one. Hence it is not unlikely that the peculiar experience of oneness derives from the subliminal awareness of all-contamination in the unconscious.

By means of the transcendent function we not only gain access to the "One Mind" but also come to understand why the East believes in the possibility of self-liberation. If, through introspection and the conscious realization of unconscious compensations, it is possible to transform one's mental condition and thus arrive at a solution of painful conflicts, one would seem entitled to speak of "self-liberation." But, as I have already hinted, there is a hitch in this proud claim to self-liberation, for a man cannot produce these unconscious compensations at will. He has to rely upon the possibility that they *may* be produced. Nor can he alter the peculiar character of the compensation: *est ut est aut non est*—"it is as it is or it isn't at all." It is a curious thing that Eastern philosophy seems to be almost unaware of this highly important fact. And it is precisely this fact that provides the psychological justification for the Western point of view. It seems as if the Western mind had a most penetrating intuition of man's fateful dependence upon some dark power which must co-operate if all is to be well. Indeed, whenever and wherever the unconscious fails to co-operate, man is instantly at a loss, even in his most ordinary activities. There may be a failure of memory, of co-ordinated action, or of interest and concentration; and such failure may well be the cause of serious annoyance, or of a fatal accident, a professional disaster, or a moral collapse. Formerly, men called the gods unfavourable; now we prefer to call it a neurosis, and we seek the cause in lack of vitamins, in endocrine disturbances, overwork, or sex. The co-operation of the unconscious, which is something we never think of and always take for granted, is, when it suddenly fails, a very serious matter indeed.

In comparison with other races—the Chinese for instance—the white man's mental equilibrium, or, to put it bluntly, his brain, seems to be his tender spot. We naturally try to get as far away from our weaknesses as possible, a fact which may explain the sort of extraversion that is always seeking security by dominating its surroundings. Extraversion goes hand in hand with mistrust of the inner man, if indeed there is any consciousness of him at all. Moreover, we all tend to undervalue the things we are afraid of. There must be some such reason for our absolute conviction that *nihil est in intellectu quod non antea fuerit in sensu,* which is the motto of Western extraversion. But, as we have emphasized, this extraversion is psychologically justified by the vital fact that unconscious compensation lies beyond man's control. I know that yoga prides itself on being able to control even the unconscious processes, so that nothing can happen in the psyche as a whole that is not ruled by a supreme consciousness. I have not the slightest doubt that such a condition is more or less possible. But it is possible only at the price of becoming identical with the unconscious. Such an identity is the Eastern equivalent of our Western fetish of "complete objectivity," the machine-like subservience to one goal, to one idea or cause, at the cost of losing every trace of inner life. From the Eastern point of view this complete objectivity is appalling, for it amounts to complete identity with the samsāra; to the West, on the other hand, samādhi is nothing but a meaningless dream-state. In the East, the inner man has always had such a firm hold on the outer man that the world had no chance of tearing him away from his inner roots; in the West, the outer man gained the ascendancy to such an extent that he was alienated from his innermost being. The One Mind, Oneness, indefiniteness, and eternity remained the prerogative of the One God. Man became small, futile, and essentially in the wrong.

I think it is becoming clear from my argument that the two standpoints, however contradictory, each have their psychological justification. Both are one-sided in that they fail to see and take account of those factors which do not fit in with their typical attitude. The one underrates the world of consciousness, the other the world of the One Mind. The result is that, in their extremism, both lose one half of the universe; their life is shut off from total reality, and is apt to become artificial and inhuman. In the West, there is the mania for "objectivity," the asceticism of the scientist or of the stockbroker, who throw away the beauty and universality of life for the sake of the ideal, or not so ideal, goal. In the East, there is the wisdom, peace, detachment, and inertia of a psyche that has returned to its dim origins, having left behind all the sorrow and joy of existence as it is and, presumably, ought to be. No wonder that one-sidedness produces very similar forms of monasticism in both cases, guaranteeing to the hermit, the holy man, the monk or the scientist unswerving singleness of purpose. I have nothing against one-sidedness as such. Man, the great experiment of nature, or his own great experiment, is evidently entitled to all such undertakings—

if he can endure them. Without one-sidedness the spirit of man could not unfold in all its diversity. But I do not think there is any harm in trying to understand both sides.

The extraverted tendency of the West and the introverted tendency of the East have one important purpose in common: both make desperate efforts to conquer the mere naturalness of life. It is the assertion of mind over matter, the *opus contra naturam,* a symptom of the youthfulness of man, still delighting in the use of the most powerful weapon ever devised by nature: the conscious mind. The afternoon of humanity, in a distant future, may yet evolve a different ideal. In time, even conquest will cease to be the dream.

# ❧ Part III ❧

# ❧ 14 ❧

## On Synchronicity[1]

It might seem appropriate to begin my exposition by defining the concept with which it deals. But I would rather approach the subject the other way and first give you a brief description of the facts which the concept of synchronicity is intended to cover. As its etymology shows, this term has something to do with time or, to be more accurate, with a kind of simultaneity. Instead of simultaneity we could also use the concept of a *meaningful coincidence* of two or more events, where something other than the probability of chance is involved. A statistical—that is, a probable—concurrence of events, such as the "duplication of cases" found in hospitals, falls within the category of chance. Groupings of this kind can consist of any number of terms and still remain within the framework of the probable and rationally possible. Thus, for instance,

---

[1] From *The Structure and Dynamics of the Psyche. Collected Works,* Vol. 8, pars. 969–997. [Originally given as a lecture, "Über Synchronizität," at the 1951 Eranos conference, Ascona, Switzerland, and published in the *Eranos-Jahrbuch 1951* (Zurich, 1952). The present translation was published in *Man and Time* (Papers from the Eranos Yearbooks, 3; New York and London, 1957); it is republished with minor revisions. The essay was, in the main, drawn from the preceding monograph.—EDITORS OF *The Collected Works.*]

someone chances to notice the number on his street-car ticket. On arriving home he receives a telephone call during which the same number is mentioned. In the evening he buys a theatre ticket that again has the same number. The three events form a chance grouping that, although not likely to occur often, nevertheless lies well within the framework of probability owing to the frequency of each of its terms. I would like to recount from my own experience the following chance grouping, made up of no fewer than six terms:

On April 1, 1949, I made a note in the morning of an inscription containing a figure that was half man and half fish. There was fish for lunch. Somebody mentioned the custom of making an "April fish" of someone. In the afternoon, a former patient of mine, whom I had not seen for months, showed me some impressive pictures of fish. In the evening, I was shown a piece of embroidery with sea monsters and fishes in it. The next morning, I saw a former patient, who was visiting me for the first time in ten years. She had dreamed of a large fish the night before. A few months later, when I was using this series for a larger work and had just finished writing it down, I walked over to a spot by the lake in front of the house, where I had already been several times that morning. This time a fish a foot long lay on the sea-wall. Since no one else was present, I have no idea how the fish could have got there.

When coincidences pile up in this way one cannot help being impressed by them—for the greater the number of terms in such a series, or the more unusual its character, the more improbable it becomes. For reasons that I have mentioned elsewhere and will not discuss now, I assume that this was a chance grouping. It must be admitted, though, that it is more improbable than a mere duplication.

In the above-mentioned case of the street-car ticket, I said that the observer "chanced" to notice the number and retain it in his memory, which ordinarily he would never have done. This formed the basis for the series of chance events, but I do not know what caused him to notice the number. It seems to me that in judging such a series a factor of uncertainty enters in at this point and requires attention. I have observed something similar in other cases, without, however, being able to draw any reliable conclusions. But it is sometimes difficult to avoid the impression that there is a sort of foreknowledge of the coming series of events. This feeling becomes irresistible when, as so frequently happens, one thinks one is about to meet an old friend in the street, only to find to one's disappointment that it is a stranger. On turning the next corner one then runs into him in person. Cases of this kind occur in every conceivable form and by no means infrequently, but after the first momentary astonishment they are as a rule quickly forgotten.

Now, the more the foreseen details of an event pile up, the more definite is the impression of an existing foreknowledge, and the more improbable does chance become. I remember the story of a student friend whose father had promised him a trip to Spain if he passed his final examinations satisfactorily. My friend thereupon dreamed that he was walking through a Spanish city. The street led to a square, where there was a Gothic cathedral. He then turned right, around a corner, into another street. There he was met by an elegant carriage drawn by two cream-coloured horses. Then he woke up. He told us about the dream as we were sitting round a table drinking beer. Shortly afterward, having successfully passed his examinations, he went to Spain, and there, in one of the streets, he recognized the city of his dream. He found the square and the cathedral, which exactly corresponded to the dream-image. He wanted to go straight to the cathedral, but then remembered that in the dream he had turned right, at the corner, into another street. He was curious to find out whether his dream would be corroborated further. Hardly had he turned the corner when he saw in reality the carriage with the two cream-coloured horses.

The *sentiment du déjà-vu* is based, as I have found in a number of cases, on a foreknowledge in dreams, but we saw that this foreknowledge can also occur in the waking state. In such cases mere chance becomes highly improbable because the coincidence is known in advance. It thus loses its chance character not only psychologically and subjectively, but objectively too, since the accumulation of details that coincide immeasurably increases the improbability of chance as a determining factor. (For correct precognitions of death, Dariex and Flammarion have computed probabilities ranging from 1 in 4,000,000 to 1 in 8,000,000.) [2] So in these cases it would be incongruous to speak of "chance" happenings. It is rather a question of meaningful coincidences. Usually they are explained by precognition—in other words, foreknowledge. People also talk of clairvoyance, telepathy, etc., without, however, being able to explain what these faculties consist of or what means of transmission they use in order to render events distant in space and time accessible to our perception. All these ideas are mere names; they are not scientific concepts which could be taken as statements of principle, for no one has yet succeeded in constructing a causal bridge between the elements making up a meaningful coincidence.

Great credit is due to J. B. Rhine for having established a reliable basis for work in the vast field of these phenomena by his experiments in extrasensory perception, or ESP. He used a pack of 25 cards divided into 5 groups of 5, each with its special sign (star, square, circle, cross, two wavy lines). The experiment was carried out as follows. In each series of experiments the pack is laid out 800 times, in such a way that the subject cannot see the cards. He is then asked to guess the cards as they are turned up. The probability of a correct answer is 1 in 5. The result, computed from very high figures, showed an average of

[2] [For documentation, see *The Structure and Dynamics of the Psyche* (*Collected Works*, Vol. 8), par. 830.—Editors of *The Collected Works*.]

6.5 hits. The probability of a chance deviation of 1.5 amounts to only 1 in 250,000. Some individuals scored more than twice the probable number of hits. On one occasion all 25 cards were guessed correctly, which gives a probability of 1 in 298,023,223,876,953,125. The spatial distance between experimenter and subject was increased from a few yards to about 4,000 miles, with no effect on the result.

A second type of experiment consisted in asking the subject to guess a series of cards that was still to be laid out in the near or more distant future. The time factor was increased from a few minutes to two weeks. The result of these experiments showed a probability of 1 in 400,000.

In a third type of experiment, the subject had to try to influence the fall of mechanically thrown dice by wishing for a certain number. The results of this so-called psychokinetic (PK) experiment were the more positive the more dice were used at a time.

The result of the spatial experiment proves with tolerable certainty that the psyche can, to some extent, eliminate the space factor. The time experiment proves that the time factor (at any rate, in the dimension of the future) can become psychically relative. The experiment with dice proves that moving bodies, too, can be influenced psychically—a result that could have been predicted from the psychic relativity of space and time.

The energy postulate shows itself to be inapplicable to the Rhine experiments, and thus rules out all ideas about the transmission of force. Equally, the law of causality does not hold—a fact that I pointed out thirty years ago. For we cannot conceive how a future event could bring about an event in the present. Since for the time being there is no possibility whatever of a causal explanation, we must assume provisionally that improbable accidents of an acausal nature—that is, meaningful coincidences—have entered the picture.

In considering these remarkable results we must take

into account a fact discovered by Rhine, namely that in each series of experiments the first attempts yielded a better result than the later ones. The falling off in the number of hits scored was connected with the mood of the subject. An initial mood of faith and optimism makes for good results. Scepticism and resistance have the opposite effect, that is, they create an unfavourable disposition. As the energic, and hence also the causal, approach to these experiments has shown itself to be inapplicable, it follows that the affective factor has the significance simply of a *condition* which makes it possible for the phenomenon to occur, though it need not. According to Rhine's results, we may nevertheless expect 6.5 hits instead of only 5. But it cannot be predicted in advance when the hit will come. Could we do so, we would be dealing with a law, and this would contradict the entire nature of the phenomenon. It has, as said, the improbable character of a "lucky hit" or accident that occurs with a more than merely probable frequency and is as a rule dependent on a certain state of affectivity.

This observation has been thoroughly confirmed, and it suggests that the psychic factor which modifies or even eliminates the principles underlying the physicist's picture of the world is connected with the affective state of the subject. Although the phenomenology of the ESP and PK experiments could be considerably enriched by further experiments of the kind described above, deeper investigation of its bases will have to concern itself with the nature of the affectivity involved. I have therefore directed my attention to certain observations and experiences which, I can fairly say, have forced themselves upon me during the course of my long medical practice. They have to do with spontaneous, meaningful coincidences of so high a degree of improbability as to appear flatly unbelievable. I shall therefore describe to you only one case of this kind, simply to give an example characteristic of a whole category of phenomena. It makes no difference whether you refuse to believe this particular case or whether you dispose of it with an *ad hoc* explanation. I could tell you a great many such stories, which are in principle no more surprising or incredible than the irrefutable results arrived at by Rhine, and you would soon see that almost every case calls for its own explanation. But the causal explanation, the only possible one from the standpoint of natural science, breaks down owing to the psychic relativization of space and time, which together form the indispensable premises for the cause-and-effect relationship.

My example concerns a young woman patient who, in spite of efforts made on both sides, proved to be psychologically inaccessible. The difficulty lay in the fact that she always knew better about everything. Her excellent education had provided her with a weapon ideally suited to this purpose, namely a highly polished Cartesian rationalism with an impeccably "geometrical" [3] idea of reality. After several fruitless attempts to sweeten her rationalism with a somewhat more human understanding, I had to confine myself to the hope that something unexpected and irrational would turn up, something that would burst the intellectual retort into which she had sealed herself. Well, I was sitting opposite her one day, with my back to the window, listening to her flow of rhetoric. She had had an impressive dream the night before, in which someone had given her a golden scarab—a costly piece of jewellery. While she was still telling me this dream, I heard something behind me gently tapping on the window. I turned round and saw that it was a fairly large flying insect that was knocking against the window-pane from outside in the obvious effort to get into the dark room. This seemed to me very strange. I opened the window immediately and caught the insect in the air as it flew in. It was a scarabaeid beetle, or common rose-chafer (*Cetonia aurata*), whose gold-green colour most nearly resembles that of a golden scarab. I handed the beetle to my patient with the words, "Here is your scarab."

[3] [Descartes demonstrated his propositions by the "Geometrical Method."—EDITORS OF *The Collected Works*.]

This experience punctured the desired hole in her rationalism and broke the ice of her intellectual resistance. The treatment could now be continued with satisfactory results.

This story is meant only as a paradigm of the innumerable cases of meaningful coincidence that have been observed not only by me but by many others, and recorded in large collections. They include everything that goes by the name of clairvoyance, telepathy, etc., from Swedenborg's well-attested vision of the great fire in Stockholm to the recent report by Air Marshal Sir Victor Goddard about the dream of an unknown officer, which predicted the subsequent accident to Goddard's plane.[4]

All the phenomena I have mentioned can be grouped under three categories:

1. The coincidence of a psychic state in the observer with a simultaneous, objective, external event that corresponds to the psychic state or content (e.g., the scarab), where there is no evidence of a causal connection between the psychic state and the external event, and where, considering the psychic relativity of space and time, such a connection is not even conceivable.

2. The coincidence of a psychic state with a corresponding (more or less simultaneous) external event taking place outside the observer's field of perception, i.e., at a distance, and only verifiable afterward (e.g., the Stockholm fire).

3. The coincidence of a psychic state with a corresponding, not yet existent future event that is distant in time and can likewise only be verified afterward.

In groups 2 and 3 the coinciding events are not yet present in the observer's field of perception, but have been anticipated in time in so far as they can only be verified afterward. For this reason I call such events *synchronistic,* which is not to be confused with *synchronous.*

Our survey of this wide field of experience would be incomplete if we failed to take into account the so-called

---

[4] [This case was the subject of an English film, *The Night My Number Came Up.*—EDITORS OF *The Collected Works.*]

mantic methods. Manticism lays claim, if not actually to producing synchronistic events, then at least to making them serve its ends. An example of this is the oracle method of the *I Ching*, which Dr. Hellmut Wilhelm has described in detail.[5] The *I Ching* presupposes that there is a synchronistic correspondence between the psychic state of the questioner and the answering hexagram. The hexagram is formed either by the random division of the 49 yarrow stalks or by the equally random throw of three coins. The result of this method is, incontestably, very interesting, but so far as I can see it does not provide any tool for an objective determination of the facts, that is to say a statistical evaluation, since the psychic state in question is much too indefinite and indefinable. The same holds true of the geomantic experiment, which is based on similar principles.

We are in a somewhat more favourable situation when we turn to the astrological method, as it presupposes a meaningful coincidence of planetary aspects and positions with the character or the existing psychic state of the questioner. In the light of the most recent astrophysical research, astrological correspondence is probably not a matter of synchronicity but, very largely, of a causal relationship. As Professor Max Knoll has demonstrated,[6] the solar proton radiation is influenced to such a degree by planetary conjunctions, oppositions, and quartile aspects that the appearance of magnetic storms can be predicted with a fair amount of probability. Relationships can be established between the curve of the earth's magnetic disturbances and the mortality rate that confirm the unfavourable influence of conjunctions, oppositions, and quartile aspects and the favourable influence of trine and sextile aspects. So it is

[5] ["The Concept of Time in the Book of Changes," in Joseph Campbell, ed., *Papers from the Eranos Yearbooks,* Bollingen Series XXX (New York, 1954–68, 6 vols.), Vol. 3; originally a lecture at the 1951 Eranos conference.—EDITORS OF *The Collected Works.*]

[6] ["Transformations of Science in Our Age," ibid.—EDITORS OF *The Collected Works.*]

probably a question here of a causal relationship, i.e., of a natural law that excludes synchronicity or restricts it. At the same time, the zodiacal qualification of the houses, which plays a large part in the horoscope, creates a complication in that the astrological zodiac, although agreeing with the calendar, does not coincide with the actual constellations themselves. These have shifted their positions by almost a whole platonic month as a result of the precession of the equinoxes since the time when the springpoint was in zero Aries, about the beginning of our era. Therefore, anyone born in Aries today (according to the calendar) is actually born in Pisces. It is simply that his birth took place at a time which, for approximately 2,000 years, has been called "Aries." Astrology presupposes that this time has a determining quality. It is possible that this quality, like the disturbances in the earth's magnetic field, is connected with the seasonal fluctuations to which solar proton radiation is subject. It is therefore not beyond the realm of possibility that the zodiacal positions may also represent a causal factor.

Although the psychological interpretation of horoscopes is still a very uncertain matter, there is nevertheless some prospect today of a causal explanation in conformity with natural law. Consequently, we are no longer justified in describing astrology as a mantic method. Astrology is in the process of becoming a science. But as there are still large areas of uncertainty, I decided some time ago to make a test and find out how far an accepted astrological tradition would stand up to statistical investigation. For this purpose it was necessary to select a definite and indisputable fact. My choice fell on marriage. Since antiquity, the traditional belief in regard to marriage has been that there is a conjunction of sun and moon in the horoscope of the marriage partners, that is, ☉ (sun) with an orbit of 8 degrees in the case of one partner, in ☌ (conjunction) with ☾ (moon) in the case of the other. A second, equally old, tradition takes ☾ ☌ ☾ as another marriage characteristic. Of like importance are the conjunctions of the ascendent (*Asc.*) with the large luminaries.

Together with my co-worker, Mrs. Liliane Frey-Rohn, I first proceeded to collect 180 marriages, that is to say, 360 horoscopes,[7] and compared the 50 most important aspects that might possibly be characteristic of marriage, namely the conjunctions and oppositions of ☉ ☾ ♂ (Mars) ♀ (Venus) *Asc.* and *Desc.* This resulted in a maximum of 10 per cent for ☉ ♂ ☾. As Professor Markus Fierz, of Basel, who kindly went to the trouble of computing the probability of my result, informed me, my figure has a probability of 1 : 10,000. The opinion of several mathematical physicists whom I consulted about the significance of this figure is divided: some find it considerable, others find it of questionable value. Our figure is inconclusive inasmuch as a total of 360 horoscopes is far too small from a statistical point of view.

While the aspects of these 180 marriages were being worked out statistically, our collection was enlarged, and when we had collected 220 more marriages, this batch was subjected to separate investigation. As on the first occasion, the material was evaluated just as it came in. It was not selected from any special point of view and was drawn from the most varied sources. Evaluation of this second batch yielded a maximum figure of 10.9 per cent for ☾ ♂ ☾. The probability of this figure is also about 1 : 10,000.

Finally, 83 more marriages arrived, and these in turn were investigated separately. The result was a maximum figure of 9.6 per cent for ☾ ♂ *Asc.* The probability of this figure is approximately 1 : 3,000.[8]

---

[7] This material stemmed from different sources. They were simply horoscopes of married people. There was no selection of any kind. We took at random all the marriage horoscopes we could lay hands on.

[8] [These and the following figures were later revised by Professor Fierz and considerably reduced. See *The Structure and Dynamics of the Psyche* (*Collected Works*, Vol. 8), pars. 901ff.—EDITORS OF *The Collected Works*.]

One is immediately struck by the fact that the conjunctions are all *moon conjunctions,* which is in accord with astrological expectations. But the strange thing is that what has turned up here are the three basic positions of the horoscope, $\odot$ $\mathbb{C}$ and *Asc.* The probability of a concurrence of $\odot$ $\sigma$ $\mathbb{C}$ and $\mathbb{C}$ $\sigma$ $\mathbb{C}$ amounts to $1 : 100,000,000$. The concurrence of the three moon conjunctions with $\odot$ $\mho$ *Asc.* has a probability of $1 : 3 \times 10^{11}$; in other words, the improbability of its being due to mere chance is so enormous that we are forced to take into account the existence of some factor responsible for it. The three batches were so small that little or no theoretical significance can be attached to the individual probabilities of $1 : 10,000$ and $1 : 3,000$. Their concurrence, however, is so improbable that one cannot help assuming the existence of an impelling factor that produced this result.

The possibility of there being a scientifically valid connection between astrological data and proton radiation cannot be held responsible for this, since the individual probabilities of $1 : 10,000$ and $1 : 3,000$ are too great for us to be able, with any degree of certainty, to view our result as other than mere chance. Besides, the maxima cancel each other out as soon as one divides up the marriages into a larger number of batches. It would require hundreds of thousands of marriage horoscopes to establish the statistical regularity of occurrences like the sun, moon, and ascendent conjunctions, and even then the result would be questionable. That anything so improbable as the turning up of the three classical moon conjunctions should occur at all, however, can only be explained either as the result of an intentional or unintentional fraud, or else as precisely such a meaningful coincidence, that is, as synchronicity.

Although I was obliged to express doubt, earlier, about the mantic character of astrology, I am now forced as a result of my astrological experiment to recognize it again. The chance arrangement of the marriage horoscopes, which were simply piled on top of one another as they came in from the most diverse sources, and the equally fortuitous

way they were divided into three unequal batches, suited the sanguine expectations of the research workers and produced an over-all picture that could scarcely have been improved upon from the standpoint of the astrological hypothesis. The success of the experiment is entirely in accord with Rhine's ESP results, which were also favourably affected by expectation, hope, and faith. However, there was no definite expectation of any one result. Our selection of 50 aspects is proof of this. After we got the result of the first batch, a slight expectation did exist that the $\odot$ ♂ ☾ would be confirmed. But we were disappointed. The second time, we made up a larger batch from the newly added horoscopes in order to increase the element of certainty. But the result was ☾ ♂ ☾. With the third batch, there was only a faint expectation that ☾ ♂ ☾ would be confirmed, but again this was not the case.

What happened in this case was admittedly a curiosity, apparently a unique instance of meaningful coincidence. If one is impressed by such things, one could call it a minor miracle. Today, however, we are obliged to view the miraculous in a somewhat different light. The Rhine experiments have demonstrated that space and time, and hence causality, are factors that can be eliminated, with the result that acausal phenomena, otherwise called miracles, appear possible. All natural phenomena of this kind are unique and exceedingly curious combinations of chance, held together by the common meaning of their parts to form an unmistakable whole. Although meaningful coincidences are infinitely varied in their phenomenology, as acausal events they nevertheless form an element that is part of the scientific picture of the world. Causality is the way we explain the link between two successive events. Synchronicity designates the parallelism of time and meaning between psychic and psychophysical events, which scientific knowledge so far has been unable to reduce to a common principle. The term explains nothing, it simply formulates the occurrence of meaningful coincidences which, in themselves, are chance happenings, but are so improbable that we must assume them to be based on some kind of principle, or on some property of the empirical world. No reciprocal causal connection can be shown to obtain between parallel events, which is just what gives them their chance character. The only recognizable and demonstrable link between them is a common meaning, or equivalence. The old theory of correspondence was based on the experience of such connections—a theory that reached its culminating point and also its provisional end in Leibniz' idea of pre-established harmony, and was then replaced by causality. Synchronicity is a modern differentiation of the obsolete concept of correspondence, sympathy, and harmony. It is based not on philosophical assumptions but on empirical experience and experimentation.

Synchronistic phenomena prove the simultaneous occurrence of meaningful equivalences in heterogeneous, causally unrelated processes; in other words, they prove that a content perceived by an observer can, at the same time, be represented by an outside event, without any causal connection. From this it follows either that the psyche cannot be localized in space, or that space is relative to the psyche. The same applies to the temporal determination of the psyche and the psychic relativity of time. I do not need to emphasize that the verification of these findings must have far-reaching consequences.

In the short space of a lecture I cannot, unfortunately, do more than give a very cursory sketch of the vast problem of synchronicity. For those of you who would care to go into this question more deeply, I would mention that a more extensive work of mine is soon to appear under the title "Synchronicity: An Acausal Connecting Principle." It will be published together with a work by Professor W. Pauli in a book called *The Interpretation of Nature and the Psyche*.[9]

---

[9] [See *The Structure and Dynamics of the Psyche* (*Collected Works*, Vol. 8).—EDITORS OF *The Collected Works*.]

# 💥 *15* 💥

## *Answer to Job*[1]

### *Prefatory Note*[2]

The suggestion that I should tell you how *Answer to Job* came to be written sets me a difficult task, because the history of this book can hardly be told in a few words. I have been occupied with its central problem for years. Many different sources nourished the stream of its thoughts, until one day—and after long reflection—the time was ripe to put them into words.

The most immediate cause of my writing the book is perhaps to be found in certain problems discussed in my book *Aion,* especially the problems of Christ as a symbolic

[1] From *Psychology and Religion: West and East. Collected Works,* Vol. 11. [First published as a book, *Antwort auf Hiob* (Zurich, 1952). The present translation was first published, in book form, in London, 1954; for it, Professor Jung made some half-dozen alterations to the original text and added or authorized an occasional footnote. In 1956, it was reprinted and published by Pastoral Psychology Book Club, Great Neck, New York. Only minor stylistic alterations have been made in the version here published.—EDITORS OF *The Collected Works.*]

[2] [Written for *Pastoral Psychology* (Great Neck, New York.), VI : 60 (January, 1956).—EDITORS OF *The Collected Works.*]

figure and of the antagonism Christ-Antichrist, represented in the traditional zodiacal symbolism of the two fishes.

In connection with the discussion of these problems and of the doctrine of Redemption, I criticized the idea of the *privatio boni* as not agreeing with the psychological findings. Psychological experience shows that whatever we call "good" is balanced by an equally substantial "bad" or "evil." If "evil" is non-existent, then whatever there is must needs be "good." Dogmatically, neither "good" nor "evil" can be derived from Man, since the "Evil One" existed before Man as one of the "Sons of God." The idea of the *privatio boni* began to play a role in the Church only after Mani. Before this heresy, Clement of Rome taught that God rules the world with a right and a left hand, the right being Christ, the left Satan. Clement's view is clearly *monotheistic,* as it unites the opposites in one God.

Later Christianity, however, is dualistic, inasmuch as it splits off one half of the opposites, personified in Satan, and he is *eternal* in his state of damnation. This crucial question forms the point of departure for the Christian theory of Redemption. It is therefore of prime importance. If Christianity claims to be a monotheism, it becomes unavoidable to assume the opposites as being contained in God. But then we are confronted with a major religious problem: the problem of Job. It is the aim of my book to point out its historical evolution since the time of Job down through the centuries to the most recent symbolic phenomena, such as the *Assumptio Mariae,* etc.

Moreover, the study of medieval natural philosophy—of the greatest importance to psychology—made me try to find an answer to the question: what image of God did these old philosophers have? Or rather: how should the symbols which supplement their image of God be understood? All this pointed to a *complexio oppositorum* and thus recalled again the story of Job to my mind: Job who expected help from God against God. This most peculiar fact presupposes a similar conception of the opposites in God.

On the other hand, numerous questions, not only from my patients, but from all over the world, brought up the problem of giving a more complete and explicit answer than I had given in *Aion*. For many years I hesitated to do this because I was quite conscious of the probable consequences, and knew what a storm would be raised. But I was gripped by the urgency and difficulty of the problem and was unable to throw it off. Therefore I found myself obliged to deal with the whole problem, and I did so in the form of describing a personal experience, carried by subjective emotions. I deliberately chose this form because I wanted to avoid the impression that I had any idea of announcing an "eternal truth." The book does not pretend to be anything but the voice or question of a single individual who hopes or expects to meet with thoughtfulness in the public.

## Lectori Benevolo

*I am distressed for thee, my brother . . .*
II Samuel 1 : 26 (AV)

On account of its somewhat unusual content, my little book requires a short preface. I beg of you, dear reader, not to overlook it. For, in what follows, I shall speak of the venerable objects of religious belief. Whoever talks of such matters inevitably runs the risk of being torn to pieces by the two parties who are in mortal conflict about those very things. This conflict is due to the strange supposition that a thing is true only if it presents itself as a *physical* fact. Thus some people believe it to be physically true that Christ was born as the son of a virgin, while others deny this as a physical impossibility. Everyone can see that there is no logical solution to this conflict and that one would do better not to get involved in such sterile disputes. Both are right and both are wrong. Yet they could easily reach agreement if only they dropped the word "physical."

"Physical" is not the only criterion of truth: there are also *psychic* truths which can neither be explained nor proved nor contested in any physical way. If, for instance, a general belief existed that the river Rhine had at one time flowed backwards from its mouth to its source, then this belief would in itself be a fact even though such an assertion, physically understood, would be deemed utterly incredible. Beliefs of this kind are psychic facts which cannot be contested and need no proof.

Religious statements are of this type. They refer without exception to things that cannot be established as physical facts. If they did not do this, they would inevitably fall into the category of the natural sciences. Taken as referring to anything physical, they make no sense whatever, and science would dismiss them as non-experienceable. They would be mere miracles, which are sufficiently exposed to doubt as it is, and yet they could not demonstrate the reality of the spirit or *meaning* that underlies them, because meaning is something that always demonstrates itself and is experienced on its own merits. The spirit and meaning of Christ are present and perceptible to us even without the aid of miracles. Miracles appeal only to the understanding of those who cannot perceive the meaning. They are mere substitutes for the not understood reality of the spirit. This is not to say that the living presence of the spirit is not occasionally accompanied by marvellous physical happenings. I only wish to emphasize that these happenings can neither replace nor bring about an understanding of the spirit, which is the one essential thing.

The fact that religious statements frequently conflict with the observed physical phenomena proves that in contrast to physical perception the spirit is autonomous, and that psychic experience is to a certain extent independent of physical data. The psyche is an autonomous factor, and religious statements are psychic confessions which in the last resort are based on unconscious, i.e., on transcendental, processes. These processes are not accessible to physical perception but demonstrate their existence through the confessions of the psyche. The resultant statements are filtered through the medium of human consciousness: that is to say, they are given visible forms which in their turn are subject to manifold influences from within and without. That is why whenever we speak of religious contents we move in a world of images that point to something ineffable. We do not know how clear or unclear these images, metaphors, and concepts are in respect of their transcendental object. If, for instance, we say "God," we give expression to an image or verbal concept which has undergone many changes in the course of time. We are, however, unable to say with any degree of certainty—unless it be by faith—whether these changes affect only the images and concepts, or the Unspeakable itself. After all, we can imagine God as an eternally flowing current of vital energy that endlessly changes shape just as easily as we can imagine him as an eternally unmoved, unchangeable essence. Our reason is sure only of one thing: that it manipulates images and ideas which are dependent on human imagination and its temporal and local conditions, and which have therefore changed innumerable times in the course of their long history. There is no doubt that there is something behind these images that transcends consciousness and operates in such a way that the statements do not vary limitlessly and chaotically, but clearly all relate to a few basic principles or archetypes. These, like the psyche itself, or like matter, are unknowable as such. All we can do is to construct models of them which we know to be inadequate, a fact which is confirmed again and again by religious statements.

If, therefore, in what follows I concern myself with these "metaphysical" objects, I am quite conscious that I am moving in a world of images and that none of my reflections touches the essence of the Unknowable. I am also too well aware of how limited are our powers of conception —to say nothing of the feebleness and poverty of language

—to imagine that my remarks mean anything more in principle than what a primitive man means when he conceives of his god as a hare or a snake. But, although our whole world of religious ideas consists of anthropomorphic images that could never stand up to rational criticism, we should never forget that they are based on numinous archetypes, i.e., on an emotional foundation which is unassailable by reason. We are dealing with psychic facts which logic can overlook but not eliminate. In this connection Tertullian has already appealed, quite rightly, to the testimony of the soul. In his *De testimonio animae,* he says:

> These testimonies of the soul are as simple as they are true, as obvious as they are simple, as common as they are obvious, as natural as they are common, as divine as they are natural. I think that they cannot appear to any one to be trifling and ridiculous if he considers the majesty of Nature, whence the authority of the soul is derived. What you allow to the mistress you will assign to the disciple. Nature is the mistress, the soul is the disciple; what the one has taught, or the other has learned, has been delivered to them by God, who is, in truth, the Master even of the mistress herself. What notion the soul is able to conceive of her first teacher is in your power to judge, from that soul which is in you. Feel that which causes you to feel; think upon that which is in forebodings your prophet; in omens, your augur; in the events which befall you, your foreseer. Strange if, being given by God, she knows how to act the diviner for men! Equally strange if she knows Him by whom she has been given! [3]

I would go a step further and say that the statements made in the Holy Scriptures are also utterances of the soul —even at the risk of being suspected of psychologism. The statements of the conscious mind may easily be snares and

---

[3] Cap. V, in Migne, *Patrologiae* . . . Latin series, Vol. 1, cols. 615f., translated by C. Dodgson, *Tertullian,* Library of Fathers of the Holy Catholic Church (Oxford, 1842), Vol. I, pp. 138f., slightly modified.

delusions, lies, or arbitrary opinions, but this is certainly not true of the statements of the soul: to begin with they always go over our heads because they point to realities that transcend consciousness. These *entia* are the archetypes of the collective unconscious, and they precipitate complexes of ideas in the form of mythological motifs. Ideas of this kind are never invented, but enter the field of inner perception as finished products, for instance in dreams. They are spontaneous phenomena which are not subject to our will, and we are therefore justified in ascribing to them a certain autonomy. They are to be regarded not only as objects but as subjects with laws of their own. From the point of view of consciousness, we can, of course, describe them as objects, and even explain them up to a point, in the same measure as we can describe and explain a living human being. But then we have to disregard their autonomy. If that is considered, we are compelled to treat them as subjects; in other words, we have to admit that they possess spontaneity and purposiveness, or a kind of consciousness and free will. We observe their behaviour and consider their statements. This dual standpoint, which we are forced to adopt towards every relatively independent organism, naturally has a dual result. On the one hand it tells me what I do to the object, and on the other hand what it does (possibly to me). It is obvious that this unavoidable dualism will create a certain amount of confusion in the minds of my readers, particularly as in what follows we shall have to do with the archetype of Deity.

Should any of my readers feel tempted to add an apologetic "only" to the God-images as we perceive them, he would immediately fall foul of experience, which demonstrates beyond any shadow of doubt the extraordinary numinosity of these images. The tremendous effectiveness (mana) of these images is such that they not only give one the feeling of pointing to the *Ens realissimum*, but make one convinced that they actually express it and establish it as a fact. This makes discussion uncommonly difficult, if not impossible. It is, in fact, impossible to demonstrate God's reality to oneself except by using images which have arisen spontaneously or are sanctified by tradition, and whose psychic nature and effects the naïve-minded person has never separated from their unknowable metaphysical background. He instantly equates the effective image with the transcendental *x* to which it points. The seeming justification for this procedure appears self-evident and is not considered a problem so long as the statements of religion are not seriously questioned. But if there is occasion for criticism, then it must be remembered that the image and the statement are psychic processes which are different from their transcendental object; they do not posit it, they merely point to it. In the realm of psychic processes criticism and discussion are not only permissible but are unavoidable.

In what follows I shall attempt just such a discussion, such a "coming to terms" with certain religious traditions and ideas. Since I shall be dealing with numinous factors, my feeling is challenged quite as much as my intellect. I cannot, therefore, write in a coolly objective manner, but must allow my emotional subjectivity to speak if I want to describe what I feel when I read certain books of the Bible, or when I remember the impressions I have received from the doctrines of our faith. I do not write as a biblical scholar (which I am not), but as a layman and physician who has been privileged to see deeply into the psychic life of many people. What I am expressing is first of all my own personal view, but I know that I also speak in the name of many who have had similar experiences.

## ANSWER TO JOB

The Book of Job is a landmark in the long historical development of a divine drama. At the time the book was written, there were already many testimonies which had given a contradictory picture of Yahweh—the picture of a God who knew no moderation in his emotions and suffered precisely from this lack of moderation. He himself admitted that he was eaten up with rage and jealousy and that this knowledge was painful to him. Insight existed along with obtuseness, loving-kindness along with cruelty, creative power along with destructiveness. Everything was there, and none of these qualities was an obstacle to the other. Such a condition is only conceivable either when no reflecting consciousness is present at all, or when the capacity for reflection is very feeble and a more or less adventitious phenomenon. A condition of this sort can only be described as *amoral*.

How the people of the Old Testament felt about their God we know from the testimony of the Bible. That is not what I am concerned with here, but rather with the way in which a modern man with a Christian education and background comes to terms with the divine darkness which is unveiled in the Book of Job, and what effect it has on him. I shall not give a cool and carefully considered exegesis that tries to be fair to every detail, but a purely subjective reaction. In this way I hope to act as a voice for many who feel the same way as I do, and to give expression to the shattering emotion which the unvarnished spectacle of divine savagery and ruthlessness produces in us. Even if we know by hearsay about the suffering and discord in the Deity, they are so unconscious, and hence so ineffectual morally, that they arouse no human sympathy or understanding. Instead, they give rise to an equally ill-considered outburst of affect, and a smouldering resentment that may be compared to a slowly healing wound. And just as there is a secret tie between the wound and the weapon, so the affect corresponds to the violence of the deed that caused it.

The Book of Job serves as a paradigm for a certain experience of God which has a special significance for us today. These experiences come upon man from inside as

well as from outside, and it is useless to interpret them
rationalistically and thus weaken them by apotropaic means.
It is far better to admit the affect and submit to its violence
than to try to escape it by all sorts of intellectual tricks or
by emotional value-judgments. Although, by giving way to
the affect, one imitates all the bad qualities of the outrage-
ous act that provoked it and thus makes oneself guilty of
the same fault, that is precisely the point of the whole proceeding: the violence is meant to penetrate to a man's
vitals, and he to succumb to its action. He must be affected
by it, otherwise its full effect will not reach him. But he
should know, or learn to know, what has affected him, for
in this way he transforms the blindness of the violence on
the one hand and of the affect on the other into knowledge.

For this reason I shall express my affect fearlessly and
ruthlessly in what follows, and I shall answer injustice with
injustice, that I may learn to know why and to what purpose Job was wounded, and what consequences have
grown out of this for Yahweh as well as for man.

# I

Job answers Yahweh thus:

Behold, I am of small account; what shall I answer thee?
  I lay my hand on my mouth.
I have spoken once, and I will not answer;
  twice, but I will proceed no further.[4]

And indeed, in the immediate presence of the infinite
power of creation, this is the only possible answer for a witness who is still trembling in every limb with the terror of

---

[4] Job 40 : 4–5. [Quotations throughout are from the Revised Standard
Version (RSV), except where the Authorized Version (AV) is closer
to the text of the Zürcher Bibel (ZB) used by the author in conjunction with the original Hebrew and Greek sources. Where neither
RSV nor AV fits, I have translated direct from ZB. The poetic line-
arrangement of RSV is followed in so far as possible.—TRANSLATOR.]

almost total annihilation. What else could a half-crushed human worm, grovelling in the dust, reasonably answer in the circumstances? In spite of his pitiable littleness and feebleness, this man knows that he is confronted with a superhuman being who is personally most easily provoked. He also knows that it is far better to withhold all mortal reflections, to say nothing of certain moral requirements which might be expected to apply to a god.

Yahweh's "justice" is praised, so presumably Job could bring his complaint and the protestation of his innocence before him as the just judge. But he doubts this possibility. "How can a man be just before God?" [5] "If I summoned him and he answered me, I would not believe that he was listening to my voice." [6] "If it is a matter of justice, who can summon him?" [7] He "multiplies my wounds without cause." [8] "He destroys both the blameless and the wicked." [9] "If the scourge slay suddenly, he will laugh at the trial of the innocent." [10] "I know," Job says to Yahweh, "thou wilt not hold me innocent. I shall be condemned." [11] "If I wash myself . . . never so clean, yet shalt thou plunge me in the ditch." [12] "For he is not a man, as I am, that I should answer him, and we should come together in judgment." [13] Job wants to explain his point of view to Yahweh, to state his complaint, and tells him: "Thou knowest that I am not guilty, and there is none to deliver out of thy hand." [14] "I desire to argue my case with God." [15] "I will defend my ways to his face," [16] "I know

[5] Job 9 : 2.
[6] 9 : 16.
[7] 9 : 19.
[8] 9 : 17.
[9] 9 : 22.
[10] 9 : 23 (AV).
[11] 9 : 28, 29.
[12] 9 : 30–31 (AV).
[13] 9 : 32 (AV).
[14] 10 : 7.
[15] 13 : 3.
[16] 13 : 15.

that I shall be vindicated." [17] Yahweh should summon him and render him an account or at least allow him to plead his cause. Properly estimating the disproportion between man and God, he asks: "Wilt thou break a leaf driven to and fro? and wilt thou pursue the dry stubble?" [18] God has put him in the wrong, but there is no justice.[19] He has "taken away my right." [20] "Till I die I will not put away my integrity from me. I hold fast to my righteousness, and will not let it go." [21] His friend Elihu the Buzite does not believe the injustice of Yahweh: "Of a truth, God will not do wickedly, and the Almighty will not pervert justice." [22] Illogically enough, he bases his opinion on God's *power:* "Is it fit to say to a king, Thou art wicked? and to princes, Ye are ungodly?" [23] One must "respect the persons of princes and esteem the high more than the low." [24] But Job is not shaken in his faith, and had already uttered an important truth when he said: "Behold, my witness is in heaven, and he that vouches for me is on high . . . my eye pours out tears to God, that he would maintain the right of a man with God, like that of a man with his neighbour." [25] And later: "For I know that my Vindicator lives, and at last he will stand upon the earth." [26]

These words clearly show that Job, in spite of his doubt as to whether man can be just before God, still finds it difficult to relinquish the idea of meeting God on the basis of justice and therefore of morality. Because, in spite of everything, he cannot give up his faith in divine justice, it is not easy for him to accept the knowledge that divine arbitrari-

[17] 13 : 18.
[18] 13 : 25 (AV).
[19] 19 : 6–7.
[20] 27 : 2.
[21] 27 : 5–6.
[22] 34 : 12.
[23] 34 : 18 (AV).
[24] 34 : 19 (ZB).
[25] 16 : 19–21.
[26] 19:25. ["Vindicator" is RSV alternative reading for "Redeemer," and comes very close to the ZB *Anwalt,* "advocate."—TRANSLATOR.]

ness breaks the law. On the other hand, he has to admit that no one except Yahweh himself is doing him injustice and violence. He cannot deny that he is up against a God who does not care a rap for any moral opinion and does not recognize any form of ethics as binding. This is perhaps the greatest thing about Job, that, faced with this difficulty, he does not doubt the unity of God. He clearly sees that God is at odds with himself—so totally at odds that he, Job, is quite certain of finding in God a helper and an "advocate" against God. As certain as he is of the evil in Yahweh, he is equally certain of the good. In a human being who renders us evil we cannot expect at the same time to find a helper. But Yahweh is not a human being: he is both a persecutor and a helper in one, and the one aspect is as real as the other. Yahweh is not split but is an *antinomy*—a totality of inner opposites—and this is the indispensable condition for his tremendous dynamism, his omniscience and omnipotence. Because of this knowledge Job holds on to his intention of "defending his ways to his face," i.e., of making his point of view clear to him, since notwithstanding his wrath, Yahweh is also man's advocate *against himself* when man puts forth his complaint.

One would be even more astonished at Job's knowledge of God if this were the first time one were hearing of Yahweh's amorality. His incalculable moods and devastating attacks of wrath had, however, been known from time immemorial. He had proved himself to be a jealous defender of morality and was specially sensitive in regard to justice. Hence he had always to be praised as "just," which, it seemed, was very important to him. Thanks to this circumstance or peculiarity of his, he had a *distinct personality*, which differed from that of a more or less archaic king only in scope. His jealous and irritable nature, prying mistrustfully into the faithless hearts of men and exploring their secret thoughts, compelled a personal relationship between himself and man, who could not help but feel personally called by him. That was the essential difference between

Yahweh and the all-ruling Father Zeus, who in a benevolent and somewhat detached manner allowed the economy
of the universe to roll along on its accustomed courses and
punished only those who were disorderly. He did not moralize but ruled purely instinctively. He did not demand anything more *from* human beings than the sacrifices due to
him; he did not want to do anything *with* human beings
because he had no plans for them. Father Zeus is certainly
a figure but not a personality. Yahweh, on the other hand,
was interested in man. Human beings were a matter of first-
rate importance to him. He needed them as they needed
him, urgently and personally. Zeus too could throw thun-
derbolts about, but only at hopelessly disorderly individuals. Against mankind as a whole he had no objections—
but then they did not interest him all that much. Yahweh,
however, could get inordinately excited about man as a
species and men as individuals if they did not behave as he
desired or expected, without ever considering that in his
omnipotence he could easily have created something better
than these "bad earthenware pots."

In view of this intense personal relatedness to his chosen
people, it was only to be expected that a regular covenant
would develop which also extended to certain individuals,
for instance to David. As we learn from the Eighty-ninth
Psalm, Yahweh told him:

> My steadfast love I will keep for him for ever,
>     and my covenant will stand firm for him.

> . . . . . . . . . . . .

> I will not violate my covenant,
>     or alter the word that went forth from my lips.
> Once for all I have sworn by my holiness;
>     I will not lie to David.[27]

And yet it happened that he, who watched so jealously
over the fulfilment of laws and contracts, broke his own
oath. Modern man, with his sensitive conscience, would

[27] Verses 28, 34, 35.

have felt the black abyss opening and the ground giving way under his feet, for the least he expects of his God is that he should be superior to mortal man in the sense of being better, higher, nobler—but not his superior in the kind of moral flexibility and unreliability that do not jib even at perjury.

Of course one must not tax an archaic god with the requirements of modern ethics. For the people of early antiquity things were rather different. In their gods there was absolutely everything: they teemed with virtues and vices. Hence they could be punished, put in chains, deceived, stirred up against one another without losing face, or at least not for long. The man of that epoch was so inured to divine inconsistencies that he was not unduly perturbed when they happened. With Yahweh the case was different because, from quite early on, the personal and moral tie began to play an important part in the religious relationship. In these circumstances a breach of contract was bound to have the effect not only of a personal but of a moral injury. One can see this from the way David answers Yahweh:

How long, Lord? wilt thou hide thyself for ever?
    shall thy wrath burn like fire?
Remember how short my time is:
    wherefore hast thou made all men in vain?

·   ·   ·   ·   ·   ·   ·   ·   ·   ·   ·

Lord, where are thy former loving kindnesses,
    which by thy faithfulness thou didst swear to David? [28]

Had this been addressed to a human being it would have run something like this: "For heaven's sake, man, pull yourself together and stop being such a senseless savage! It is really too grotesque to get into such a rage when it's partly your own fault that the plants won't flourish. You used to be quite reasonable and took good care of the garden you planted, instead of trampling it to pieces."

[28] Psalm 89 : 46, 47, 49 (AV; last line from RSV).

Certainly our interlocutor would never dare to remonstrate with his almighty partner about this breach of contract. He knows only too well what a row he would get into if *he* were the wretched breaker of the law. Because anything else would put him in peril of his life, he must retire to the more exalted plane of reason. In this way, without knowing it or wanting it, he shows himself superior to his divine partner both intellectually and morally. Yahweh fails to notice that he is being humoured, just as little as he understands why he has continually to be praised as just. He makes pressing demands on his people to be praised [29] and propitiated in every possible way, for the obvious purpose of keeping him in a good temper at any price.

The character thus revealed fits a personality who can only convince himself that he exists through his relation to an object. Such dependence on the object is absolute when the subject is totally lacking in self-reflection and therefore has no insight into himself. It is as if he existed only by reason of the fact that he has an object which assures him that he is really there. If Yahweh, as we would expect of a sensible human being, were really conscious of himself, he would, in view of the true facts of the case, at least have put an end to the panegyrics on his justice. But he is too unconscious to be moral. Morality presupposes consciousness. By this I do not mean to say that Yahweh is imperfect or evil, like a gnostic demiurge. He is everything in its totality; therefore, among other things, he is total justice, and also its total opposite. At least this is the way he must be conceived if one is to form a unified picture of his character. We must only remember that what we have sketched is no more than an anthropomorphic picture which is not even particularly easy to visualize. From the way the divine nature expresses itself we can see that the individual qualities are not adequately related to one another, with the result that they fall apart into mutually contradictory acts. For

[29] Or to be "blessed," which is even more captious of him.

instance, Yahweh regrets having created human beings, although in his omniscience he must have known all along what would happen to them.

# II

Since the Omniscient looks into all hearts, and Yahweh's eyes "run to and fro through the whole earth," [30] it were better for the interlocutor of the Eighty-ninth Psalm not to wax too conscious of his slight moral superiority over the more unconscious God. Better to keep it dark, for Yahweh is no friend of critical thoughts which in any way diminish the tribute of recognition he demands. Loudly as his power resounds through the universe, the basis of its existence is correspondingly slender, for it needs conscious reflection in order to exist in reality. Existence is only real when it is conscious to somebody. That is why the Creator needs conscious man even though, from sheer unconsciousness, he would like to prevent him from becoming conscious. And that is also why Yahweh needs the acclamation of a small group of people. One can imagine what would happen if this assembly suddenly decided to stop the applause: there would be a state of high excitation, with outbursts of blind destructive rage, then a withdrawal into hellish loneliness and the torture of non-existence, followed by a gradual reawakening of an unutterable longing for something which would make him conscious of himself. It is probably for this reason that all pristine things, even man before he becomes the canaille, have a touching, magical beauty, for in its nascent state "each thing after its kind" is the most precious, the most desirable, the tenderest thing in the world, being a reflection of the infinite love and goodness of the Creator.

[30] Zechariah 4 : 10 (AV). Cf. also the Wisdom of Solomon 1 : 10 (AV): "For the ear of jealousy heareth all things: and the noise or murmurings is not hid."

In view of the undoubted frightfulness of divine wrath, and in an age when men still knew what they were talking about when they said "Fear God," it was only to be expected that man's slight superiority should have remained unconscious. The powerful personality of Yahweh, who, in addition to everything else, lacked all biographical antecedents (his original relationship to the Elohim had long since been sunk in oblivion), had raised him above all the numina of the Gentiles and had immunized him against the influence that for several centuries had been undermining the authority of the pagan gods. It was precisely the details of their mythological biography that had become their nemesis, for with his growing capacity for judgment man had found these stories more and more incomprehensible and indecent. Yahweh, however, had no origin and no past, except his creation of the world, with which all history began, and his relation to that part of mankind whose forefather Adam he had fashioned in his own image as the Anthropos, the original man, by what appears to have been a special act of creation. One can only suppose that the other human beings who must also have existed at that time had been formed previously on the divine potter's wheel along with the various kinds of beasts and cattle—those human beings, namely, from whom Cain and Seth chose their wives. If one does not approve of this conjecture, then the only other possibility that remains is the far more scandalous one that they incestuously married their sisters (for whom there is no evidence in the text), as was still surmised by the philosopher Karl Lamprecht at the end of the nineteenth century.

The special providence which singled out the Jews from among the divinely stamped portion of humanity and made them the "chosen people" had burdened them from the start with a heavy obligation. As usually happens with such mortgages, they quite understandably tried to circumvent it as much as possible. Since the chosen people used every opportunity to break away from him, and Yahweh felt it of vital importance to tie this indispensable object (which he had made "godlike" for this very purpose) definitely to himself, he proposed to the patriarch Noah a contract between himself on the one hand, and Noah, his children, and all their animals, both tame and wild, on the other—a contract that promised advantages to both parties. In order to strengthen this contract and keep it fresh in the memory, he instituted the rainbow as a token of the covenant. If, in future, he summoned the thunder-clouds which hide within them floods of water and lightning, then the rainbow would appear, reminding him and his people of the contract. The temptation to use such an accumulation of clouds for an experimental deluge was no small one, and it was therefore a good idea to associate it with a sign that would give timely warning of possible catastrophe.

In spite of these precautions the contract had gone to pieces with David, an event which left behind it a literary deposit in the Scriptures and which grieved some few of the devout, who upon reading it became reflective. As the Psalms were zealously read, it was inevitable that certain thoughtful people were unable to stomach the Eighty-ninth Psalm. However that may be, the fatal impression made by the breach of contract survived.[31] It is historically possible that these considerations influenced the author of the Book of Job.

The Book of Job places this pious and faithful man, so heavily afflicted by the Lord, on a brightly lit stage where he presents his case to the eyes and ears of the world. It is amazing to see how easily Yahweh, quite without reason, had let himself be influenced by one of his sons, by a *doubting thought*,[32] and made unsure of Job's faithfulness. With his touchiness and suspiciousness the mere possibility of doubt was enough to infuriate him and induce that peculiar

[31] The 89th Psalm is attributed to David and is supposed to have been a community song written in exile.

[32] Satan is presumably one of God's eyes which "go to and fro in the earth and walk up and down in it" (Job 1 : 7). In Persian tradition, Ahriman proceeded from one of Ormuzd's doubting thoughts.

double-faced behaviour of which he had already given proof in the Garden of Eden, when he pointed out the tree to the First Parents and at the same time forbade them to eat of it. In this way he precipitated the Fall, which he apparently never intended. Similarly, his faithful servant Job is now to be exposed to a rigorous moral test, quite gratuitously and to no purpose, although Yahweh is convinced of Job's faithfulness and constancy and could moreover have assured himself beyond all doubt on this point had he taken counsel with his own omniscience. Why, then, is the experiment made at all, and a bet with the unscrupulous slanderer settled, without a stake, on the back of a powerless creature? It is indeed no edifying spectacle to see how quickly Yahweh abandons his faithful servant to the evil spirit and lets him fall without compunction or pity into the abyss of physical and moral suffering. From the human point of view Yahweh's behaviour is so revolting that one has to ask oneself whether there is not a deeper motive hidden behind it. Has Yahweh some secret resistance against Job? That would explain his yielding to Satan. But what does man possess that God does not have? Because of his littleness, puniness, and defencelessness against the Almighty, he possesses, as we have already suggested, a somewhat keener consciousness based on self-reflection: he must, in order to survive, always be mindful of his impotence. God has no need of this circumspection, for nowhere does he come up against an insuperable obstacle that would force him to hesitate and hence make him reflect on himself. Could a suspicion have grown up in God that man possesses an infinitely small yet more concentrated light than he, Yahweh, possesses? A jealousy of that kind might perhaps explain his behaviour. It would be quite explicable if some such dim, barely understood deviation from the definition of a mere "creature" had aroused his divine suspicions. Too often already these human beings had not behaved in the prescribed manner. Even his trusty servant Job might have something up his sleeve. . . . Hence Yahweh's surprising readiness to listen to Satan's insinuations against his better judgment.

Without further ado Job is robbed of his herds, his servants are slaughtered, his sons and daughters are killed by a whirlwind, and he himself is smitten with sickness and brought to the brink of the grave. To rob him of peace altogether, his wife and his old friends are let loose against him, all of whom say the wrong things. His justified complaint finds no hearing with the judge who is so much praised for his justice. Job's right is refused in order that Satan be not disturbed in his play.

One must bear in mind here the dark deeds that follow one another in quick succession: robbery, murder, bodily injury with premeditation, and denial of a fair trial. This is further exacerbated by the fact that Yahweh displays no compunction, remorse, or compassion, but only ruthlessness and brutality. The plea of unconsciousness is invalid, seeing that he flagrantly violates at least three of the commandments he himself gave out on Mount Sinai.

Job's friends do everything in their power to contribute to his moral torments, and instead of giving him, whom God has perfidiously abandoned, their warm-hearted support, they moralize in an all too human manner, that is, in the stupidest fashion imaginable, and "fill him with wrinkles." They thus deny him even the last comfort of sympathetic participation and human understanding, so that one cannot altogether suppress the suspicion of connivance in high places.

Why Job's torments and the divine wager should suddenly come to an end is not quite clear. So long as Job does not actually die, the pointless suffering could be continued indefinitely. We must, however, keep an eye on the background of all these events: it is just possible that something in this background will gradually begin to take shape as a compensation for Job's undeserved suffering—something to which Yahweh, even if he had only a faint inkling of it, could hardly remain indifferent. Without Yahweh's knowledge and contrary to his intentions, the tormented though guiltless Job had secretly been lifted up to a superior knowledge of God which God himself did not possess. Had Yahweh consulted his omniscience, Job would not have had the advantage of him. But then, so many other things would not have happened either.

Job realizes God's inner antinomy, and in the light of this realization his knowledge attains a divine numinosity. The possibility of this development lies, one must suppose, in man's "godlikeness," which one should certainly not look for in human morphology. Yahweh himself had guarded against this error by expressly forbidding the making of images. Job, by his insistence on bringing his case before God, even without hope of a hearing, had stood his ground and thus created the very obstacle that forced God to reveal his true nature. With this dramatic climax Yahweh abruptly breaks off his cruel game of cat and mouse. But if anyone should expect that his wrath will now be turned against the slanderer, he will be severely disappointed. Yahweh does not think of bringing this mischief-making son of his to account, nor does it ever occur to him to give Job at least the moral satisfaction of explaining his behaviour. Instead, he comes riding along on the tempest of his almightiness and thunders reproaches at the half-crushed human worm:

> Who is this that darkens counsel
> by words without insight? [33]

In view of the subsequent words of Yahweh, one must really ask oneself: *Who* is darkening *what* counsel? The only dark thing here is how Yahweh ever came to make a bet with Satan. It is certainly not Job who has darkened anything and least of all a counsel, for there was never any talk of this nor will there be in what follows. The bet does not contain any "counsel" so far as one can see—unless, of course, it was Yahweh himself who egged Satan on for

[33] Job 38 : 2 (ZB).

the ultimate purpose of exalting Job. Naturally this development was foreseen in omniscience, and it may be that the word "counsel" refers to this eternal and absolute knowledge. If so, Yahweh's attitude seems the more illogical and incomprehensible, as he could then have enlightened Job on this point—which, in view of the wrong done to him, would have been only fair and equitable. I must therefore regard this possibility as improbable.

*Whose* words are without insight? Presumably Yahweh is not referring to the words of Job's friends, but is rebuking Job. But what is Job's guilt? The only thing he can be blamed for is his incurable optimism in believing that he can appeal to divine justice. In this he is mistaken, as Yahweh's subsequent words prove. God does not want to be just; he merely flaunts might over right. Job could not get that into his head, because he looked upon God as a moral being. He had never doubted God's might, but had hoped for right as well. He had, however, already taken back this error when he recognized God's contradictory nature, and by so doing he assigned a place to God's justice and goodness. So one can hardly speak of lack of insight.

The answer to Yahweh's conundrum is therefore: it is Yahweh himself who darkens his own counsel and who has no insight. He turns the tables on Job and blames him for what he himself does: man is not permitted to have an opinion about him, and, in particular, is to have no insight which he himself does not possess. For seventy-one verses he proclaims his world-creating power to his miserable victim, who sits in ashes and scratches his sores with potsherds, and who by now has had more than enough of superhuman violence. Job has absolutely no need of being impressed by further exhibitions of this power. Yahweh, in his omniscience, could have known just how incongruous his attempts at intimidation were in such a situation. He could easily have seen that Job believes in his omnipotence as much as ever and has never doubted it or wavered in his loyalty. Altogether, he pays so little attention to Job's real situation that one suspects him of having an ulterior motive which is more important to him: Job is no more than the outward occasion for an inward process of dialectic in God. His thunderings at Job so completely miss the point that one cannot help but see how much he is occupied with himself. The tremendous emphasis he lays on his omnipotence and greatness makes no sense in relation to Job, who certainly needs no more convincing, but only becomes intelligible when aimed at a listener *who doubts it*. This "doubting thought" is Satan, who after completing his evil handiwork has returned to the paternal bosom in order to continue his subversive activity there. Yahweh must have seen that Job's loyalty was unshakable and that Satan had lost his bet. He must also have realized that, in accepting this bet, he had done everything possible to drive his faithful servant to disloyalty, even to the extent of perpetrating a whole series of crimes. Yet it is not remorse and certainly not moral horror that rises to his consciousness, but an obscure intimation of something that questions his omnipotence. He is particularly sensitive on this point, because "might" is the great argument. But omniscience knows that might excuses nothing. The said intimation refers, of course, to the extremely uncomfortable fact that Yahweh had let himself be bamboozled by Satan. This weakness of his does not reach full consciousness, since Satan is treated with remarkable tolerance and consideration. Evidently Satan's intrigue is deliberately overlooked at Job's expense.

Luckily enough, Job had noticed during this harangue that everything else had been mentioned except his right. He has understood that it is at present impossible to argue the question of right, as it is only too obvious that Yahweh has no interest whatever in Job's cause but is far more preoccupied with his own affairs. Satan, that is to say, has somehow to disappear, and this can best be done by casting suspicion on Job as a man of subversive opinions. The problem is thus switched on to another track, and the episode with Satan remains unmentioned and unconscious. To the spectator it is not quite clear why Job is treated to this almighty exhibition of thunder and lightning, but the performance as such is sufficiently magnificent and impressive to convince not only a larger audience but above all Yahweh himself of his unassailable power. Whether Job realizes what violence Yahweh is doing to his own omniscience by behaving like this we do not know, but his silence and submission leave a number of possibilities open. Job has no alternative but formally to revoke his demand for justice, and he therefore answers in the words quoted at the beginning: "I lay my hand on my mouth."

He betrays not the slightest trace of mental reservation—in fact, his answer leaves us in no doubt that he has succumbed completely and without question to the tremendous force of the divine demonstration. The most exacting tyrant should have been satisfied with this, and could be quite sure that his servant—from terror alone, to say nothing of his undoubted loyalty—would not dare to nourish a single improper thought for a very long time to come.

Strangely enough, Yahweh does not notice anything of the kind. He does not see Job and his situation at all. It is rather as if he had another powerful opponent in the place of Job, one who was better worth challenging. This is clear from his twice-repeated taunt:

> Gird up your loins like a man;
> I will question you, and you shall declare to me.[34]

One would have to choose positively grotesque examples to illustrate the disproportion between the two antagonists. Yahweh sees something in Job which we would not ascribe to him but to God, that is, an equal power which causes him to bring out his whole power apparatus and parade it before his opponent. Yahweh projects on to Job a sceptic's face which is hateful to him because it is his own, and

[34] Job 38 : 3 and 40 : 7.

which gazes at him with an uncanny and critical eye. He is afraid of it, for only in face of something frightening does one let off a cannonade of references to one's power, cleverness, courage, invincibility, etc. What has all that to do with Job? Is it worth the lion's while to terrify a mouse?

Yahweh cannot rest satisfied with the first victorious round. Job has long since been knocked out, but the great antagonist whose phantom is projected on to the pitiable sufferer still stands menacingly upright. Therefore Yahweh raises his arm again:

> Will you even put me in the wrong?
> Will you condemn me that you may be justified?
> Have you an arm like God,
> and can you thunder with a voice like his? [35]

Man, abandoned without protection and stripped of his rights, and whose nothingness is thrown in his face at every opportunity, evidently appears to be so dangerous to Yahweh that he must be battered down with the heaviest artillery. What irritates Yahweh can be seen from his challenge to the ostensible Job:

> Look on every one that is proud, and bring him low;
> and tread down the wicked where they stand.
> Hide them in the dust together;
> bind their faces in the hidden place.
> Then will I also acknowledge to you
> that your own right hand can give you victory. [36]

Job is challenged as though he himself were a god. But in the contemporary metaphysics there was no *deuteros theos,* no other god except Satan, who owns Yahweh's ear and is able to influence him. He is the only one who can pull the wool over his eyes, beguile him, and put him up to a massive violation of his own penal code. A formidable opponent indeed, and, because of his close kinship, so compromising that he must be concealed with the utmost dis-

[35] 40 : 8–9.
[36] 40 : 12–14 ("in the hidden place" is RSV alternative reading for "in the world below").

cretion—even to the point of God's hiding him from his own consciousness in his own bosom! In his stead God must set up his miserable servant as the bugbear whom he has to fight, in the hope that by banishing the dreaded countenance to "the hidden place" he will be able to maintain himself in a state of unconsciousness.

The stage-managing of this imaginary duel, the speechifying, and the impressive performance given by the prehistoric menagerie would not be sufficiently explained if we tried to reduce them to the purely negative factor of Yahweh's fear of becoming conscious and of the relativization which this entails. The conflict becomes acute for Yahweh as a result of a new factor, which is, however, not hidden from omniscience—though in this case the existing knowledge is not accompanied by any conclusion. The new factor is something that has never occurred before in the history of the world, the unheard-of fact that, without knowing it or wanting it, a mortal man is raised by his moral behaviour above the stars in heaven, from which position of advantage he can behold the back of Yahweh, the abysmal world of "shards."[37]

Does Job know what he has seen? If he does, he is astute or canny enough not to betray it. But his words speak volumes:

> I know that thou canst do all things,
> and that no purpose of thine can be thwarted.[38]

---

[37] This is an allusion to an idea found in the later cabalistic philosophy. [These "shards," also called "shells" (Heb. *kelipot*), form ten counterpoles to the ten *sefiroth*, which are the ten stages in the revelation of God's creative power. The shards, representing the forces of evil and darkness, were originally mixed with the light of the *sefiroth*. The *Zohar* describes evil as the by-product of the life process of the *sefiroth*. Therefore the *sefiroth* had to be cleansed of the evil admixture of the shards. This elimination of the shards took place in what is described in the cabalistic writings—particularly of Luria and his school—as the "breaking of the vessels." Through this the powers of evil assumed a separate and real existence. Cf. Gershom G. Scholem, *Major Trends in Jewish Mysticism* (3rd ed.; [New York, 1941, 1954), p. 267.—EDITORS OF *The Collected Works*.]
[38] 42 : 2.

Truly, Yahweh can do all things and permits himself all things without batting an eyelid. With brazen countenance he can project his shadow side and remain unconscious at man's expense. He can boast of his superior power and enact laws which mean less than air to him. Murder and manslaughter are mere bagatelles, and if the mood takes him he can play the feudal grand seigneur and generously recompense his bondslave for the havoc wrought in his wheat-fields. "So you have lost your sons and daughters? No harm done, I will give you new and better ones."

Job continues (no doubt with downcast eyes and in a low voice):

"Who is this that hides counsel without insight?"
Therefore I have uttered what I did not understand,
    things too wonderful for me, which I did not know.
"Hear, and I will speak;
    I will question you, and you declare to me."
I had heard of thee by the hearing of the ear,
    but now my eye sees thee;
therefore I abhor myself,
    and repent in dust and ashes.[39]

Shrewdly, Job takes up Yahweh's aggressive words and prostrates himself at his feet as if he were indeed the defeated antagonist. Guileless as Job's speech sounds, it could just as well be equivocal. He has learnt his lesson well and experienced "wonderful things" which are none too easily grasped. Before, he had known Yahweh "by the hearing of the ear," but now he has got a taste of his reality, more so even than David—an incisive lesson that had better not be forgotten. Formerly he was naïve, dreaming perhaps of a "good" God, or of a benevolent ruler and just judge. He had imagined that a "covenant" was a legal matter and that anyone who was party to a contract could insist on his rights as agreed; that God would be faithful and true or at least just, and, as one could assume from the Ten Com-

[39] 42 : 3–6 (modified).

mandments, would have some recognition of ethical values
or at least feel committed to his own legal standpoint. But,
to his horror, he has discovered that Yahweh is not human
but, in certain respects, less than human, that he is just
what Yahweh himself says of Leviathan (the crocodile):

> He beholds everything that is high:
> He is king over all proud beasts.[40]

Unconsciousness has an animal nature. Like all old gods
Yahweh has his animal symbolism with its unmistakable
borrowings from the much older theriomorphic gods of
Egypt, especially Horus and his four sons. Of the four
animals of Yahweh only one has a human face. That is
probably Satan, the godfather of man as a spiritual being.
Ezekiel's vision attributes three-fourths animal nature and
only one-fourth human nature to the animal deity, while
the upper deity, the one above the "sapphire throne,"
merely had the "likeness" of a man.[41] This symbolism explains Yahweh's behaviour, which, from the human point
of view, is so intolerable: it is the behaviour of an unconscious being who cannot be judged morally. Yahweh is a
*phenomenon* and, as Job says, "not a man." [42]

One could, without too much difficulty, impute such a
meaning to Job's speech. Be that as it may, Yahweh calmed
down at last. The therapeutic measure of unresisting acceptance had proved its value yet again. Nevertheless,
Yahweh is still somewhat nervous of Job's friends—they

---

[40] Job 41 : 25 (ZB); cf. 41 : 34 (AV and RSV).
[41] Ezekiel 1 : 26.
[42] The naïve assumption that the creator of the world is a conscious
being must be regarded as a disastrous prejudice which later gave rise
to the most incredible dislocations of logic. For example, the nonsensical doctrine of the *privatio boni* would never have been necessary
had one not had to assume in advance that it is impossible for the
consciousness of a good God to produce evil deeds. Divine unconsciousness and lack of reflection, on the other hand, enable us to
form a conception of God which puts his actions beyond moral
judgment and allows no conflict to arise between goodness and
beastliness.

"have not spoken of me what is right." [43] The projection of his doubt-complex extends—comically enough, one must say—to these respectable and slightly pedantic old gentlemen, as though God-knows-what depended on what they thought. But the fact that men should think at all, and especially about him, is maddeningly disquieting and ought somehow to be stopped. It is far too much like the sort of thing his vagrant son is always springing on him, thus hitting him in his weakest spot. How often already has he bitterly regretted his unconsidered outbursts!

One can hardly avoid the impression that Omniscience is gradually drawing near to a realization, and is threatened with an insight that seems to be hedged about with fears of self-destruction. Fortunately, Job's final declaration is so formulated that one can assume with some certainty that, for the protagonists, the incident is closed for good and all.

We, the commenting chorus on this great tragedy, which has never at any time lost its vitality, do not feel quite like that. For our modern sensibilities it is by no means apparent that with Job's profound obeisance to the majesty of the divine presence, and his prudent silence, a real answer has been given to the question raised by the Satanic prank of a wager with God. Job has not so much answered as reacted in an adjusted way. In so doing he displayed remarkable self-discipline, but an unequivocal answer has still to be given.

To take the most obvious thing, what about the moral wrong Job has suffered? Is man so worthless in God's eyes that not even a *tort moral* can be inflicted on him? That contradicts the fact that man is desired by Yahweh and that it obviously matters to him whether men speak "right" of him or not. He needs Job's loyalty, and it means so much to him that he shrinks at nothing in carrying out his test. This attitude attaches an almost divine importance to man, for what else is there in the whole wide world that could mean anything to one who has everything? Yahweh's

[43] Job 42 : 7.

divided attitude, which on the one hand tramples on human life and happiness without regard, and on the other hand must have man for a partner, puts the latter in an impossible position. At one moment Yahweh behaves as irrationally as a cataclysm; the next moment he wants to be loved, honoured, worshipped, and praised as just. He reacts irritably to every word that has the faintest suggestion of criticism, while he himself does not care a straw for his own moral code if his actions happen to run counter to its statutes.

One can submit to such a God only with fear and trembling, and can try indirectly to propitiate the despot with unctuous praises and ostentatious obedience. But a relationship of trust seems completely out of the question to our modern way of thinking. Nor can moral satisfaction be expected from an unconscious nature god of this kind. Nevertheless, Job got his satisfaction, without Yahweh's intending it and possibly without himself knowing it, as the poet would have it appear. Yahweh's allocutions have the unthinking yet none the less transparent purpose of showing Job the brutal power of the demiurge: "This is I, the creator of all the ungovernable, ruthless forces of Nature, which are not subject to any ethical laws. I, too, am an amoral force of Nature, a purely phenomenal personality that cannot see its own back."

This is, or at any rate could be, a moral satisfaction of the first order for Job, because through this declaration man, in spite of his impotence, is set up as a judge over God himself. We do not know whether Job realizes this, but we do know from the numerous commentaries on Job that all succeeding ages have overlooked the fact that a kind of Moira or Dike rules over Yahweh, causing him to give himself away so blatantly. Anyone can see how he unwittingly raises Job by humiliating him in the dust. By so doing he pronounces judgment on himself and gives man the moral satisfaction whose absence we found so painful in the Book of Job.

The poet of this drama showed a masterly discretion in

ringing down the curtain at the very moment when his hero gave unqualified recognition to the ἀπόφασις μεγάλη of the Demiurge by prostrating himself at the feet of His Divine Majesty. No other impression was permitted to remain. An unusual scandal was blowing up in the realm of metaphysics, with supposedly devastating consequences, and nobody was ready with a saving formula which would rescue the monotheistic conception of God from disaster. Even in those days the critical intellect of a Greek could easily have seized on this new addition to Yahweh's biography and used it in his disfavour (as indeed happened, though very much later) [44] so as to mete out to him the fate that had already overtaken the Greek gods. But a relativization of God was utterly unthinkable at that time, and remained so for the next two thousand years.

The unconscious mind of man sees correctly even when conscious reason is blind and impotent. The drama has been consummated for all eternity: Yahweh's dual nature has been revealed, and somebody or something has seen and registered this fact. Such a revelation, whether it reached man's consciousness or not, could not fail to have far-reaching consequences.

# III

Before turning to the question of how the germ of unrest developed further, we must turn back to the time when the Book of Job was written. Unfortunately the dating is uncertain. It is generally assumed that it was written between 600 and 300 B.C.—not too far away, therefore, from the time of the Book of Proverbs (4th to 3rd century). Now in Proverbs we encounter a symptom of Greek influence which, if an earlier date is assigned to it, reached the Jewish sphere of culture through Asia Minor and, if a later date,

[44] [Cf. Gnostic interpretation of Yahweh as Saturn-Ialdabaoth in "Transformation Symbolism in the Mass" in *Psychology and Religion* (*Collected Works*, Vol. 11), par. 350; *Aion* (*Collected Works*, Vol. 9.i), par. 128.—EDITORS OF *The Collected Works*.]

through Alexandria. This is the idea of Sophia, or the *Sapientia Dei,* who is a coeternal and more or less hypostatized pneuma of feminine nature that existed before the Creation:

> The Lord possessed me in the beginning of his way,
>> before his works of old.
> I was set up from everlasting, from the beginning,
>> or ever the earth was.
> When there were no depths, I was brought forth;
>> when there were no fountains abounding with water.
>
> . . . . . . . . . . . . .
>
> When he established the heavens, I was there,
>
> . . . . . . . . . . . . .
>
> when he marked out the foundations of the earth,
>> then I was by him, as a master workman,
> and I was his delight,
>> rejoicing always before him,
> rejoicing in his habitable earth;
> and my delights were with the sons of men.[45]

This Sophia, who already shares certain essential qualities with the Johannine Logos, is on the one hand closely associated with the Hebrew Chochma, but on the other hand goes so far beyond it that one can hardly fail to think of the Indian Shakti. Relations with India certainly existed at that time (the time of the Ptolemys). A further source is the Wisdom of Jesus the Son of Sirach, or Ecclesiasticus, written around 200 B.C. Here Wisdom says of herself:

> I came out of the mouth of the most High,
>> and covered the earth as a cloud.
> I dwelt in high places,
>> and my throne is in a cloudy pillar.
> I alone encompassed the circuit of heaven,
>> and walked in the bottom of the deep.
> ·I had power over the waves of the sea, and over all the
>> earth,
>> and over every people and nation.
>
> . . . . . . . . . . . . .

[45] Proverbs 8 : 22–24 (AV), 27, 29–31 (AV, modified).

He created me from the beginning before the world,
and I shall never fail.
In the holy tabernacle I served before him;
and so was I established in Sion.
Likewise in the beloved city he gave me rest,
and in Jerusalem was my power.

. . . . . . . . . . . . .

I was exalted like a cedar in Libanus,
and as a cypress tree upon the mountains of Hermon.
I was exalted like a palm tree in En-gaddi,
and as a rose plant in Jericho,
as a fair olive tree in a pleasant field,
and grew up as a plane tree by the water.
I gave a sweet smell like cinnamon and aspalathus,
and I yielded a pleasant odour like the best myrrh . . .
As the turpentine tree I stretched out my branches,
and my branches are the branches of honour and grace.
As the vine brought I forth pleasant savour,
and my flowers are the fruit of honour and riches.
I am the mother of fair love,
and fear, and knowledge, and holy hope:
I therefore, being eternal, am given to all my children which are chosen of him.[46]

It is worth while to examine this text more closely. Wisdom describes herself, in effect, as the Logos, the Word of God ("I came out of the mouth of the most High"). As Ruach, the spirit of God, she brooded over the waters of the beginning. Like God, she has her throne in heaven. As the cosmogonic Pneuma she pervades heaven and earth and all created things. She corresponds in almost every feature to the Logos of St. John. We shall see below how far this connection is also important as regards content.

She is the feminine numen of the "metropolis" par excellence, of Jerusalem the mother-city. She is the mother-beloved, a reflection of Ishtar, the pagan city-goddess.

---

[46] Ecclesiasticus 24 : 3–18 (AV, modified).

This is confirmed by the detailed comparison of Wisdom with trees, such as the cedar, palm, terebinth ("turpentine-tree"), olive, cypress, etc. All these trees have from ancient times been symbols of the Semitic love- and mother-goddess. A holy tree always stood beside her altar on high places. In the Old Testament oaks and terebinths are oracle trees. God or angels are said to appear in or beside trees. David consulted a mulberry-tree oracle.[47] The tree in Babylon represented Tammuz, the son-lover, just as it represented Osiris, Adonis, Attis, and Dionysus, the young dying gods of the Near East. All these symbolic attributes also occur in the Song of Songs, as characteristics of the *sponsus* as well as the *sponsa*. The vine, the grape, the vine flower, and the vineyard play a significant role here. The Beloved is like an apple-tree; she shall come down from the mountains (the cult places of the mother-goddess), "from the lions' dens, from the mountains of the leopards";[48] her womb is "an orchard of pomegranates, with pleasant fruits, camphire with spikenard, spikenard and saffron, calamus and cinnamon, with all trees of frankincense, myrrh and aloes, with all the chief spices." [49] Her hands "dropped with myrrh" [50] (Adonis, we may remember, was born of the myrrh). Like the Holy Ghost, Wisdom is given as a gift to the elect, an idea that is taken up again in the doctrine of the Paraclete.

The pneumatic nature of Sophia as well as her world-building Maya character come out still more clearly in the apocryphal Wisdom of Solomon. "For wisdom is a loving spirit," [51] "kind to man." [52] She is "the worker of all things," "in her is an understanding spirit, holy." [53] She is "the breath of the power of God," "a pure effluence flowing from the glory of the Almighty," [54] "the brightness of the

---

[47] Samuel 5 : 23f.
[48] Song of Solomon 4 : 8 (AV).
[49] 4 : 13–15.
[50] Song of Solomon 5 : 5.
[51] Wisdom of Solomon 1 : 6. (φιλάνθρωπον πνεῦμα σοφία.)
[52] 7 : 23.
[53] 7 : 22. (πάντων τεχνίτις./πνεῦμα νοερὸν ἅγιον.)
[54] 7 : 25 (AV, modified). (ἀπόρροια.)

everlasting light, the unspotted mirror of the power of God," [55] a being "most subtil," who "passeth and goeth through all things by reason of her pureness." [56] She is "conversant with God," and "the Lord of all things himself loved her." [57] "Who of all that are is a more cunning workman than she?" [58] She is sent from heaven and from the throne of glory as a "Holy Spirit." [59] As a psychopomp she leads the way to God and assures immortality.[60]

The Wisdom of Solomon is emphatic about God's justice and, probably not without pragmatic purpose, ventures to sail very close to the wind: "Righteousness is immortal, but ungodly men with their works and words call death upon themselves." [61] The unrighteous and the ungodly, however, say:

> Let us oppress the poor righteous man,
>> let us not spare the widow,
>> nor reverence the ancient gray hairs of the aged.
> Let our strength be the law of justice:
>> for that which is feeble is found to be nothing worth.
> Therefore let us lie in wait for the righteous;
>> because . . . he upbraideth us with our offending
>>> the law,
>> and objecteth to our infamy. . . .
> He professeth to have the knowledge of God:
>> and he calleth himself the child of the Lord.
> He was made to reprove our thoughts.
>
> .   .   .   .   .   .   .   .   .   .   .   .   .
>
> Let us see if his words be true:
>> and let us prove what shall happen in the end of him.
>
> .   .   .   .   .   .   .   .   .   .   .   .
>
> Let us examine him with despitefulness and torture,
>> that we may know his meekness, and prove his pa-
>>> tience.[62]

[55] 7 : 26.
[56] 7 : 23, 24.
[57] 8 : 3. (συμβίωσιν ἔχουσα/πάντων δεσρότης.)
[58] 8 : 6.
[59] 9 : 10, 17.
[60] 6 : 18 and 8 : 13.
[61] 1 : 15–16 (modified).
[62] 2 : 10–19.

Where did we read but a short while before: "And the Lord said to Satan, Have you considered my servant Job, that there is none like him on the earth, a blameless and upright man, who fears God and turns away from evil? He still holds fast his integrity, although you moved me against him, to destroy him without cause"? "Wisdom is better than might," saith the Preacher.[63]

Not from mere thoughtfulness and unconsciousness, but from a deeper motive, the Wisdom of Solomon here touches on the sore spot. In order to understand this more fully, we would have to find out in what sort of relation the Book of Job stands to the change that occurred in the status of Yahweh at about the same time, i.e., its relation to the appearance of Sophia. It is not a question of literary history, but of Yahweh's fate as it affects man. From the ancient records we know that the divine drama was enacted between God and his people, who were betrothed to him, the masculine dynamis, like a woman, and over whose faithfulness he watched jealously. A particular instance of this is Job, whose faithfulness is subjected to a savage test. As I have said, the really astonishing thing is how easily Yahweh gives in to the insinuations of Satan. If it were true that he trusted Job perfectly, it would be only logical for Yahweh to defend him, unmask the malicious slanderer, and make him pay for his defamation of God's faithful servant. But Yahweh never thinks of it, not even after Job's innocence has been proved. We hear nothing of a rebuke or disapproval of Satan. Therefore, one cannot doubt Yahweh's connivance. His readiness to deliver Job into Satan's murderous hands proves that he doubts Job precisely because he projects his own tendency to unfaithfulness upon a scapegoat. There is reason to suspect that he is about to loosen his matrimonial ties with Israel but hides this intention from himself. This vaguely suspected unfaithfulness causes him, with the help of Satan, to seek out the unfaithful one, and he infallibly picks on the most faithful of the

[63] Job 2 : 3; Ecclesiastes 9 : 16.

lot, who is forthwith subjected to a gruelling test. Yahweh has become unsure of his own faithfulness.

At about the same time, or a little later, it is rumoured what has happened: he has remembered a feminine being who is no less agreeable to him than to man, a friend and playmate from the beginning of the world, the first-born of all God's creatures, a stainless reflection of his glory and a master workman, nearer and dearer to his heart than the late descendants of the protoplast, the original man, who was but a secondary product stamped in his image. There must be some dire necessity responsible for this anamnesis of Sophia: things simply could not go on as before, the "just" God could not go on committing injustices, and the "Omniscient" could not behave any longer like a clueless and thoughtless human being. Self-reflection becomes an imperative necessity, and for this Wisdom is needed. Yahweh has to remember his absolute knowledge; for, if Job gains knowledge of God, then God must also learn to know himself. It just could not be that Yahweh's dual nature should become public property and remain hidden from himself alone. Whoever knows God has an effect on him. The failure of the attempt to corrupt Job has changed Yahweh's nature.

We shall now proceed to reconstruct, from the hints given in the Bible and from history, what happened after this change. For this purpose we must turn back to the time of Genesis, and to the protoplast before the Fall. He, Adam, produced Eve, his feminine counterpart, from his rib with the Creator's help, in the same way as the Creator had produced the hermaphroditic Adam from the *prima materia* and, along with him, the divinely stamped portion of humanity, namely the people of Israel and the other descendants of Adam.[64] Mysteriously following the same pattern, it was bound to happen that Adam's first

[64] [As to that portion of humanity *not* divinely stamped, and presumably descended from the pre-Adamic anthropoids, see p. 536, above.—EDITORS OF *The Collected Works*.]

son, like Satan, was an evildoer and murderer before the Lord, so that the prologue in heaven was repeated on earth. It can easily be surmised that this was the deeper reason why Yahweh gave special protection to the unsuccessful Cain, for he was a faithful reproduction of Satan in miniature. Nothing is said about a prototype of the early-departed Abel, who was dearer to God than Cain, the go-ahead husbandman (who was no doubt instructed in these arts by one of Satan's angels). Perhaps this prototype was another son of God of a more conservative nature than Satan, no rolling stone with a fondness for new and black-hearted thoughts, but one who was bound to the Father in childlike love, who harboured no other thoughts except those that enjoyed paternal approval, and who dwelt in the inner circle of the heavenly economy. That would explain why his earthly counterpart Abel could so soon "hasten away from the evil world," in the words of the Book of Wisdom, and return to the Father, while Cain in his earthly existence had to taste to the full the curse of his progressiveness on the one hand and of his moral inferiority on the other.

If the original father Adam is a copy of the Creator, his son Cain is certainly a copy of God's son Satan, and this gives us good reason for supposing that God's favourite, Abel, must also have his correspondence in a "supracelestial place." The ominous happenings that occur right at the beginning of a seemingly successful and satisfactory Creation—the Fall and the fratricide—catch our attention, and one is forced to admit that the initial situation, when the spirit of God brooded over the tohubohu, hardly permits us to expect an absolutely perfect result. Furthermore the Creator, who found every other day of his work "good," failed to give good marks to what happened on Monday. He simply said nothing—a circumstance that favours an argument from silence! What happened on that day was the final separation of the upper from the lower waters by the interposed "plate" of the firmament.

It is clear that this unavoidable dualism refused, then as later, to fit smoothly into the concept of monotheism, because it points to a metaphysical disunity. This split, as we know from history, had to be patched up again and again through the centuries, concealed and denied. It had made itself felt from the very beginning in Paradise, through a strange inconsequence which befell the Creator or was put over on him. Instead of following his original programme of letting man appear on the last day as the most intelligent being and lord of all creatures, he created the serpent who proved to be much more intelligent and more conscious than Adam, and, in addition, had been created before him. We can hardly suppose that Yahweh would have played such a trick on himself; it is far more likely that his son Satan had a hand in it. He is a trickster and spoilsport who loves nothing better than to cause annoying accidents. Although Yahweh had created the reptiles before Adam, they were common or garden snakes, highly unintelligent, from among whom Satan selected a tree-snake to use as his disguise. From then on the rumour spread that the snake was "the most spiritual animal." [65] Later the snake became the favourite symbol of the Nous, received high honours and was even permitted to symbolize God's second son, because the latter was interpreted as the world-redeeming Logos, which frequently appears as identical with the Nous. A legend of later origin maintains that the snake in the Garden of Eden was Lilith, Adam's first wife, with whom he begot a horde of demons. This legend likewise supposes a trick that can hardly have been intended by the Creator. Consequently, the Bible knows only of Eve as Adam's legitimate wife. It nevertheless remains a strange fact that the original man who was created in the image of God had, according to tradition, two wives, just like his heavenly prototype. Just as Yahweh is legitimately united with his wife Israel, but has a feminine pneuma as his intimate playmate from all

[65] τὸ πνευματικώτατον ζῷον.—A view that is found in Philo Judaeus.

eternity, so Adam first has Lilith (the daughter or emanation of Satan) to wife, as a Satanic correspondence to
Sophia. Eve would then correspond to the people of
Israel. We naturally do not know why we should hear at
such a late date that the Ruach Elohim, the "spirit of
God," is not only feminine but a comparatively independent being who exists side by side with God, and that long
before the marriage with Israel Yahweh had had relations
with Sophia. Nor do we know why, in the older tradition,
the knowledge of this first alliance had been lost. Likewise
it was only quite late that one heard of the delicate relationship between Adam and Lilith. Whether Eve was as
troublesome a wife for Adam as the children of Israel,
who were perpetually flirting with unfaithfulness, were for
Yahweh, is equally dark to us. At any rate the family life
of our first parents was not all beer and skittles: their
first two sons are a typical pair of hostile brothers, for at
that time it was apparently still the custom to live out
mythological motifs in reality. (Nowadays this is felt to be
objectionable and is denied whenever it happens.) The
parents can share the blame for original sin: Adam has
only to remember his demon-princes, and Eve should
never forget that she was the first to fall for the wiles of
the serpent. Like the Fall, the Cain-Abel intermezzo can
hardly be listed as one of Creation's shining successes.
One must draw this conclusion because Yahweh himself
did not appear to be informed in advance of the above-
mentioned incidents. Here as later there is reason to suspect that no conclusions were ever drawn from Omniscience: Yahweh did not consult his total knowledge and
was accordingly surprised by the result. One can observe
the same phenomenon in human beings, wherever in fact
people cannot deny themselves the pleasure of their emotions. It must be admitted that a fit of rage or a sulk has
its secret attractions. Were that not so, most people would
long since have acquired a little wisdom.

From this point of view we may be in a better position

to understand what happened to Job. In the pleromatic or (as the Tibetans call it) Bardo state,[66] there is a perfect interplay of cosmic forces, but with the Creation—that is, with the division of the world into distinct processes in space and time—events begin to rub and jostle one another. Covered by the hem of the paternal mantle, Satan soon starts putting a right touch here and a wrong touch there, thus giving rise to complications which were apparently not intended in the Creator's plan and which come as surprises. While unconscious creation—animals, plants, and crystals—functions satisfactorily so far as we know, things are constantly going wrong with man. At first his consciousness is only a very little higher than that of the animals, for which reason his freedom of will is also extremely limited. But Satan takes an interest in him and experiments with him in his own way, leading him into all sorts of wickedness while his angels teach him the arts and sciences, which until now had been reserved for the perfection of the pleroma. (Even in those days Satan would have merited the name of "Lucifer"!) The peculiar, unforeseen antics of men arouse Yahweh's wrath and thereby involve him in his own creation. Divine interventions become a compelling necessity. Irritatingly enough, they only meet with temporary success. Even the Draconian punishment of drowning all life with a few choice exceptions (a fate which, according to old Johann Jacob Scheuchzer on the evidence of the fossils, not even the fishes escaped), had no lasting effect. Creation remained just as tainted as before. The strange thing is that Yahweh invariably seeks the reason for this in man, who apparently refuses to obey, but never in his son, the father of all tricksters. This false orientation cannot fail to exasperate his already touchy nature, so that fear of God is regarded by man in general as the principle and even as

[66] [Cf. the commentary on the *Tibetan Book of the Dead*, in *Psychology and Religion* (*Collected Works*, Vol. 11), pars. 831ff.— EDITORS OF *The Collected Works*.]

the beginning of all wisdom. While mankind tried, under this hard discipline, to broaden their consciousness by acquiring a modicum of wisdom, that is, a little foresight and reflection,[67] it is clear from the historical development that Yahweh had lost sight of his pleromatic co-existence with Sophia since the days of the Creation. Her place was taken by the covenant with the chosen people, who were thus forced into the feminine role. At that time the people consisted of a patriarchal society in which women were only of secondary importance. God's marriage with Israel was therefore an essentially masculine affair, something like the founding of the Greek *polis*, which occurred about the same time. The inferiority of women was a settled fact. Woman was regarded as less perfect than man, as Eve's weakness for the blandishments of the serpent amply proved. *Perfection* is a masculine desideratum, while woman inclines by nature to *completeness*. And it is a fact that, even today, a man can stand a relative state of perfection much better and for a longer period than a woman, while as a rule it does not agree with women and may even be dangerous for them. If a woman strives for perfection she forgets the complementary role of completeness, which, though imperfect by itself, forms the necessary counterpart to perfection. For, just as completeness is always imperfect, so perfection is always incomplete, and therefore represents a final state which is hopelessly sterile. "Ex perfecto nihil fit," say the old masters, whereas the *imperfectum* carries within it the seeds of its own improvement. Perfectionism always ends in a blind alley, while completeness by itself lacks selective values.

At the bottom of Yahweh's marriage with Israel is a perfectionist intention which excludes that kind of relatedness we know as "Eros." The lack of Eros, of relationship to values, is painfully apparent in the Book of Job: the paragon of all creation is not a man but a mon-

[67] Cf. φρονίμως in the parable of the unjust steward (Luke 16 : 8).

ster! Yahweh has no Eros, no relationship to man, but only to a purpose man must help him fulfil. But that does not prevent him from being jealous and mistrustful like any other husband, though even here he has his purpose in mind and not man.

The faithfulness of his people becomes the more important to him the more he forgets Wisdom. But again and again they slip back into unfaithfulness despite the many proofs of his favour. This behaviour naturally does nothing to mollify Yahweh's jealousy and suspicions, hence Satan's insinuations fall on fertile ground when he drips his doubt about Job's faithfulness into the paternal ear. Against his own convictions Yahweh agrees without any hesitation to inflict the worst tortures on him. One misses Sophia's "love of mankind" more than ever. Even Job longs for the Wisdom which is nowhere to be found.[68]

Job marks the climax of this unhappy development. He epitomizes a thought which had been maturing in mankind about that time—a dangerous thought that makes great demands on the wisdom of gods and men. Though conscious of these demands, Job obviously does not know enough about the Sophia who is coeternal with God. Because man feels himself at the mercy of Yahweh's capricious will, he is in need of wisdom; not so Yahweh, who up to now has had nothing to contend with except man's nothingness. With the Job drama, however, the situation undergoes a radical change. Here Yahweh comes up against a man who stands firm, who clings to his rights until he is compelled to give way to brute force. He has seen God's face and the unconscious split in his nature. God was now known, and this knowledge went on working not only in Yahweh but in man too. Thus it was the men of the last few centuries before Christ who, at the gentle touch of the pre-existent Sophia, compensate Yahweh and his attitude, and at the same time complete the anamnesis of Wisdom. Taking a highly personified form

[68] Job 28 : 12: "But where shall wisdom be found?" Whether this is a later interpolation or not makes no difference.

that is clear proof of her autonomy, Wisdom reveals herself to men as a friendly helper and advocate against Yahweh, and shows them the bright side, the kind, just, and
amiable aspect of their God.

At the time when Satan's practical joke with the snake
compromised the paradise that was planned to be perfect, Yahweh banished Adam and Eve, whom he had created as images of his masculine essence and its feminine
emanation, to the extraparadisal world, the limbo of
"shards." It is not clear how much of Eve represents
Sophia and how much of her is Lilith. At any rate Adam
has priority in every respect. Eve was taken out of his
body as an afterthought. I mention these details from
Genesis only because the reappearance of Sophia in the
heavenly regions points to a coming act of creation. She
is indeed the "master workman"; she realizes God's
thoughts by clothing them in material form, which is the
prerogative of all feminine beings. Her coexistence with
Yahweh signifies the perpetual *hieros gamos* from which
worlds are begotten and born. A momentous change is
imminent: God desires to regenerate himself in the mystery of the heavenly nuptials—as the chief gods of Egypt
had done from time immemorial—and to become man.
For this he uses the Egyptian model of the god's incarnation in Pharaoh, which in its turn is but a copy of the
eternal *hieros gamos* in the pleroma. It would, however,
be wrong to suppose that this archetype is merely repeating itself mechanically. So far as we know, this is never
the case, since archetypal situations only return when
specifically called for. The real reason for God's becoming man is to be sought in his encounter with Job. Later on
we shall deal with this question in more detail.


IV


Just as the decision to become man apparently makes
use of the ancient Egyptian model, so we can expect that

the process itself will follow certain prefigurations. The approach of Sophia betokens a new creation. But this time it is not the world that is to be changed; rather it is God who intends to change his own nature. Mankind is not, as before, to be destroyed, but saved. In this decision we can discern the "philanthropic" influence of Sophia: no new human beings are to be created, but only one, the God-man. For this purpose a contrary procedure must be employed. The Second Adam shall not, like the first, proceed directly from the hand of the Creator, but shall be born of a human woman. So this time priority falls to the Second Eve, not only in a temporal sense but in a material sense as well. On the basis of the so-called Proto-Evangelium, the Second Eve corresponds to "the woman and her seed" mentioned in Genesis 3 : 15, which shall bruise the serpent's head. And just as Adam was believed to be originally hermaphroditic, so "the woman and her seed" are thought of as a human pair, as the Queen of Heaven and Mother of God and as the divine son who has no human father. Thus Mary, the virgin, is chosen as the pure vessel for the coming birth of God. Her independence of the male is emphasized by her virginity as the *sine qua non* of the process. She is a "daughter of God" who, as a later dogma will establish, is distinguished at the outset by the privilege of an immaculate conception and is thus free from the taint of original sin. It is therefore evident that she belongs to the state before the Fall. This posits a new beginning. The divine immaculateness of her status makes it immediately clear that she not only bears the image of God in undiminished purity, but, as the bride of God, is also the incarnation of her prototype, namely Sophia. Her love of mankind, widely emphasized in the ancient writings, suggests that in this newest creation of his Yahweh has allowed himself to be extensively influenced by Sophia. For Mary, the blessed among women, is a friend and intercessor for sinners, which all men are. Like Sophia, she is a mediatrix who leads the way to God and assures man of immortality. Her Assumption is therefore the prototype of man's bodily resurrection. As the bride of God and Queen of Heaven she holds the place of the Old Testament Sophia.

Remarkable indeed are the unusual precautions which surround the making of Mary: immaculate conception, extirpation of the taint of sin, everlasting virginity. The Mother of God is obviously being protected against Satan's tricks. From this we can conclude that Yahweh has consulted his own omniscience, for in his omniscience there is a clear knowledge of the perverse intentions which lurk in the dark son of God. Mary must at all costs be protected from these corrupting influences. The inevitable consequence of all these elaborate protective measures is something that has not been sufficiently taken into account in the dogmatic evaluation of the Incarnation: her freedom from original sin sets Mary apart from mankind in general, whose common characteristic is original sin and therefore the need of redemption. The *status ante lapsum* is tantamount to a paradisal, i.e., pleromatic and divine, existence. By having these special measures applied to her, Mary is elevated to the status of a goddess and consequently loses something of her humanity: she will not conceive her child in sin, like all other mothers, and therefore he also will never be a human being, but a god. To my knowledge at least, no one has ever perceived that this queers the pitch for a genuine Incarnation of God, or rather, that the Incarnation was only partially consummated. Both mother and son are not real human beings at all, but gods.

This arrangement, though it had the effect of exalting Mary's personality in the masculine sense by bringing it closer to the perfection of Christ, was at the same time injurious to the feminine principle of imperfection or completeness, since this was reduced by the perfectionizing tendency to the little bit of imperfection that still distinguishes Mary from Christ. *Phoebo propior lumina perdit!* Thus the more the feminine ideal is bent in the direction of the masculine, the more the woman loses her power to compensate the masculine striving for perfection, and a typically masculine, ideal state arises which, as we shall see, is threatened with an enantiodromia.[69] No path leads beyond perfection into the future—there is only a turning back, a collapse of the ideal, which could easily have been avoided by paying attention to the feminine ideal of completeness. Yahweh's perfectionism is carried over from the Old Testament into the New, and despite all the recognition and glorification of the feminine principle this never prevailed against the patriarchal supremacy. We have not, therefore, by any means heard the last of it.

# V

The older son of the first parents was corrupted by Satan and not much of a success. He was an eidolon of Satan, and only the younger son, Abel, was pleasing to God. In Cain the God-image was distorted, but in Abel it was considerably less dimmed. If Adam is thought of as a copy of God, then God's successful son, who served as a model for Abel (and about whom, as we have seen, there are no available documents), is the prefiguration of the God-man. Of the latter we know positively that, as the Logos, he is preexistent and coeternal with God, indeed of the same substance (ὁμοούσιος) as he. One can therefore regard Abel as the imperfect prototype of God's son who is about to be begotten in Mary. Just as Yahweh originally undertook to create a chthonic equivalent of himself in the first man, Adam, so now he intends something similar, but much better. The extraordinary precautionary measures above-mentioned are designed to serve this purpose. The new son, Christ, shall on the one hand be a chthonic man like Adam, mortal and capable of

[69] For this term, cf. supra, Editor's Introduction, p. *xxvii*.

suffering, but on the other hand he shall not be, like Adam, a mere copy, but God himself, begotten by himself as the Father, and rejuvenating the Father as the Son. As God he has always been God, and as the son of Mary, who is plainly a copy of Sophia, he is the Logos (synonymous with Nous), who, like Sophia, is a master workman, as stated by the Gospel according to St. John.[70] This identity of mother and son is borne out over and over again in the myths.

Although the birth of Christ is an event that occurred but once in history, it has always existed in eternity. For the layman in these matters, the identity of a nontemporal, eternal event with a unique historical occurrence is something that is extremely difficult to conceive. He must, however, accustom himself to the idea that "time" is a relative concept and needs to be complemented by that of the "simultaneous" existence, in the Bardo or pleroma, of all historical processes. What exists in the pleroma as an eternal process appears in time as an aperiodic sequence, that is to say, it it repeated many times in an irregular pattern. To take but one example: Yahweh had one good son and one who was a failure. Cain and Abel, Jacob and Esau, correspond to this prototype, and so, in all ages and in all parts of the world, does the motif of the hostile brothers, which in innumerable modern variants still causes dissension in families and keeps the psychotherapist busy. Just as many examples, no less instructive, could be found for the two women prefigured in eternity. When these things occur as modern variants, therefore, they should not be regarded merely as personal episodes, moods, or chance idiosyncrasies in people, but as fragments of the pleromatic process itself, which, broken up into individual events occurring in time, is an essential component or aspect of the divine drama.

When Yahweh created the world from his *prima ma-*

[70] John 1 : 3: "All things were made through him, and without him was not anything made that was made."

*teria,* the "Void," he could not help breathing his own mystery into the Creation which is himself in every part, as every reasonable theology has long been convinced. From this comes the belief that it is possible to know God from his Creation. When I say that he could not help doing this, I do not imply any limitation of his omnipotence; on the contrary, it is an acknowledgment that all possibilities are contained in him, and that there are in consequence no other possibilities than those which express him.

All the world is God's, and God is in all the world from the very beginning. Why, then, the *tour de force* of the Incarnation? one asks oneself, astonished. God is in everything already, and yet there must be something missing if a sort of second entrance into Creation has now to be staged with so much care and circumspection. Since Creation is universal, reaching to the remotest stellar galaxies, and since it has also made organic life infinitely variable and capable of endless differentiation, we can hardly see where the defect lies. The fact that Satan has everywhere intruded his corrupting influence is no doubt regrettable for many reasons, but it makes no difference in principle. It is not easy to give an answer to this question. One would like to say that Christ had to appear in order to deliver mankind from evil. But when one considers that evil was originally slipped into the scheme of things by Satan, and still is, then it would seem much simpler if Yahweh would, for once, call this "practical joker" severely to account, get rid of his pernicious influence, and thus eliminate the root of all evil. He would then not need the elaborate arrangement of a special Incarnation with all the unforeseeable consequences which this entails. One should make clear to oneself what it means when God becomes man. It means nothing less than a world-shaking transformation of God. It means more or less what Creation meant in the beginning, namely an objectivation of God. At the time of the Creation he revealed himself in Nature; now he wants to be more specific and become man. It must be admitted, however, that there was a tendency in this direction right from the start. For, when those other human beings, who had evidently been created before Adam, appeared on the scene along with the higher mammals, Yahweh created on the following day, by a special act of creation, a man who was the image of God. This was the first prefiguration of his becoming man. He took Adam's descendants, especially the people of Israel, into his personal possession, and from time to time he filled this people's prophets with his spirit. All these things were preparatory events and symptoms of a tendency within God to become man. But in omniscience there had existed from all eternity a knowledge of the human nature of God or of the divine nature of man. That is why, long before Genesis was written, we find corresponding testimonies in the ancient Egyptian records. These intimations and prefigurations of the Incarnation must strike one as either completely incomprehensible or superfluous, since all creation *ex nihilo* is God's and consists of nothing but God, with the result that man, like the rest of creation, is simply God become concrete. Prefigurations, however, are not in themselves creative events, but are only stages in the process of becoming conscious. It was only quite late that we realize (or rather, are beginning to realize) that God is Reality itself and therefore—last but not least—man. This realization is a millennial process.

# VI

In view of the immense problem which we are about to discuss, this excursus on pleromatic events is not out of place as an introduction.

What, then, is the real reason for the Incarnation as an historical event?

In order to answer this question we have to go rather far back. As we have seen, Yahweh evidently has a disinclination to take his absolute knowledge into account as a counterbalance to the dynamism of omnipotence. The most instructive example of this is his relation to Satan: it always looks as if Yahweh were completely uninformed about his son's intentions. That is because he never consults his omniscience. We can only explain this on the assumption that Yahweh was so fascinated by his successive acts of creation, so taken up with them, that he forgot about his omniscience altogether. It is quite understandable that the magical bodying forth of the most diverse objects, which had never before existed in such pristine splendour, should have caused God infinite delight. Sophia's memory is not at fault when she says:

> when he marked out the foundations of the earth,
>     then I was by him, like a master workman,
> and I was daily his delight.[71]

The Book of Job still rings with the proud joy of creating when Yahweh points to the huge animals he has successfully turned out:

> Behold, Behemoth,
>     which I made as I made you.
>
> . . . . . . . . . . . .
>
> He is the first of the works of God,
>     made to be lord over his companions.[72]

So even in Job's day Yahweh is still intoxicated with the tremendous power and grandeur of his creation. Compared with this, what are Satan's pinpricks and the lamentations of human beings who were created with the behemoth, even if they do bear God's image? Yahweh seems to have forgotten this fact entirely, otherwise he would never have ridden so roughshod over Job's human dignity.

[71] Proverbs 8 : 29–30.
[72] Job 40 : 15, 19 (last line, ZB).

It is only the careful and farsighted preparations for Christ's birth which show us that omniscience has begun to have a noticeable effect on Yahweh's actions. A certain philanthropic and universalistic tendency makes itself felt. The "children of Israel" take something of a second place in comparison with the "children of men." After Job, we hear nothing further about new covenants. Proverbs and gnomic utterances seem to be the order of the day, and a real *novum* now appears on the scene, namely apocalyptic communications. This points to metaphysical acts of cognition, that is, to "constellated" unconscious contents which are ready to irrupt into consciousness. In all this, as we have said, we discern the helpful hand of Sophia.

If we consider Yahweh's behaviour, up to the reappearance of Sophia, as a whole, one indubitable fact strikes us—the fact that his actions are accompanied by an inferior consciousness. Time and again we miss reflection and regard for absolute knowledge. His consciousness seems to be not much more than a primitive "awareness" which knows no reflection and no morality. One merely perceives and acts blindly, without conscious inclusion of the subject, whose individual existence raises no problems. Today we would call such a state psychologically "unconscious," and in the eyes of the law it would be described as *non compos mentis*. The fact that consciousness does not perform acts of thinking does not, however, prove that they do not exist. They merely occur unconsciously and make themselves felt indirectly in dreams, visions, revelations, and "instinctive" changes of consciousness, whose very nature tells us that they derive from an "unconscious" knowledge and are the result of unconscious acts of judgment or unconscious conclusions.

Some such process can be observed in the curious change which comes over Yahweh's behaviour after the Job episode. There can be no doubt that he did not immediately become conscious of the moral defeat he had suffered at Job's hands. In his omniscience, of course, this fact had been known from all eternity, and it is not unthinkable that the knowledge of it unconsciously brought him into the position of dealing so harshly with Job in order that he himself should become conscious of something through this conflict, and thus gain new insight. Satan who, with good reason, later on received the name of "Lucifer," knew how to make more frequent and better use of omniscience than did his father.[73] It seems he was the only one among the sons of God who developed that much initiative. At all events, it was he who placed those unforeseen incidents in Yahweh's way, which omniscience knew to be necessary and indeed indispensable for the unfolding and completion of the divine drama. Among these the case of Job was decisive, and it could only have happened thanks to Satan's initiative.

The victory of the vanquished and oppressed is obvious: Job stands morally higher than Yahweh. In this respect the creature has surpassed the creator. As always when an external event touches on some unconscious knowledge, this knowledge can reach consciousness. The event is recognized as a *déjà vu,* and one remembers a pre-existent knowledge about it. Something of the kind must have happened to Yahweh. Job's superiority cannot be shrugged off. Hence a situation arises in which real reflection is needed. That is why Sophia steps in. She reinforces the much needed self-reflection and thus makes possible Yahweh's decision to become man. It is a decision fraught with consequences: he raises himself above his earlier primitive level of consciousness by indirectly acknowledging that the man Job is morally superior to

---

[73] In Christian tradition, too, there is a belief that God's intention to become man was known to the Devil many centuries before, and that this was why he instilled the Dionysus myth into the Greeks, so that they could say, when the joyful tidings reached them in reality: "So what? We knew all that long ago." When the conquistadores later discovered the crosses of the Mayas in Yucatán, the Spanish bishops used the same argument.

him and that therefore he has to catch up and become human himself. Had he not taken this decision he would have found himself in flagrant opposition to his omniscience. Yahweh must become man precisely because he has done man a wrong. He, the guardian of justice, knows that every wrong must be expiated, and Wisdom knows that moral law is above even him. Because his creature has surpassed him he must regenerate himself.

As nothing can happen without a pre-existing pattern, not even creation *ex nihilo,* which must always resort to the treasure-house of eternal images in the fabulous mind of the "master workman," the choice of a model for the son who is now about to be begotten lies between Adam (to a limited extent) and Abel (to a much greater extent). Adam's limitation lies in the fact that, even if he is the Anthropos, he is chiefly a creature and a father. Abel's advantage is that he is the son well pleasing to God, begotten and not directly created. One disadvantage has to be accepted: he met with an early death by violence, too early to leave behind him a widow and children, which ought really to be part of human fate if lived to the full. Abel is not the authentic archetype of the son well pleasing to God; he is a copy, but the first of the kind to be met with in the Scriptures. The young dying god is also well known in the contemporary pagan religions, and so is the fratricide motif. We shall hardly be wrong in assuming that Abel's fate refers back to a metaphysical event which was played out between Satan and another son of God with a "light" nature and more devotion to his father. Egyptian tradition can give us information on this point (Horus and Set). As we have said, the disadvantage prefigured in the Abel type can hardly be avoided, because it is an integral part of the mythical-son drama, as the numerous pagan variants of this motif show. The short, dramatic course of Abel's fate serves as an excellent paradigm for the life and death of a God become man.

To sum up: the immediate cause of the Incarnation lies

in Job's elevation, and its purpose is the differentiation of Yahweh's consciousness. For this a situation of extreme gravity was needed, a *peripeteia* charged with affect, without which no higher level of consciousness can be reached.

## VII

In addition to Abel, we have to consider, as a model for the impending birth of the son of God, the general pattern of the hero's life which has been established since time immemorial and handed down by tradition. Since this son is not intended merely as a national Messiah, but as the universal saviour of mankind, we have also to consider the pagan myths and revelations concerning the life of one who is singled out by the gods.

The birth of Christ is therefore characterized by all the usual phenomena attendant upon the birth of a hero, such as the annunciation, the divine generation from a virgin, the coincidence of the birth with the thrice-repeated *coniunctio maxima* ( ♃ ♂ ♄ ) in the sign of Pisces, which at that precise moment inaugurated the new era, the recognition of the birth of a king, the persecution of the newborn, his flight and concealment, his lowly birth, etc. The motif of the growing up of the hero is discernible in the wisdom of the twelve-year-old child in the temple, and there are several examples in the gospels of the breaking away from the mother.

It goes without saying that a quite special interest attaches to the character and fate of the incarnate son of God. Seen from a distance of nearly two thousand years, it is uncommonly difficult to reconstruct a biographical picture of Christ from the traditions that have been preserved. Not a single text is extant which would fulfil even the minimum modern requirements for writing a history. The historically verifiable facts are extremely scanty, and the little biographically valid material that exists is not sufficient for us to create out of it a consistent career or an even remotely probable character. Certain theologians have discovered the main reason for this in the fact that Christ's biography and psychology cannot be separated from eschatology. Eschatology means in effect that Christ is God and man at the same time and that he therefore suffers a divine as well as a human fate. The two natures interpenetrate so thoroughly that any attempt to separate them mutilates both. The divine overshadows the human, and the human being is scarcely graspable as an empirical personality. Even the critical procedures of modern psychology do not suffice to throw light on all the obscurities. Every attempt to single out one particular feature for clarity's sake does violence to another which is just as essential either with respect to his divinity or with respect to his humanity. The commonplace is so interwoven with the miraculous and the mythical that we can never be sure of our facts. Perhaps the most disturbing and confusing thing of all is that the oldest writings, those of St. Paul, do not seem to have the slightest interest in Christ's existence as a concrete human being. The synoptic gospels are equally unsatisfactory as they have more the character of propaganda than of biography.

With regard to the human side of Christ, if we can speak of a "purely human" aspect at all, what stands out particularly clearly is his love of mankind. This feature is already implied in the relationship of Mary to Sophia, and especially in his genesis by the Holy Ghost, whose feminine nature is personified by Sophia, since she is the preliminary historical form of the ἅγιον πνεῦμα, who is symbolized by the dove, the bird belonging to the love-goddess. Furthermore, the love-goddess is in most cases the mother of the young dying god. Christ's love of mankind is, however, limited to a not inconsiderable degree by a certain predestinarian tendency which sometimes causes him to withhold his salutary message from those who do not belong to the elect. If one takes the doctrine of predestination literally, it is difficult to see how it can be fitted into the framework of the Christian message. But taken psychologically, as a means to achieving a definite effect, it can readily be understood that these allusions to predestination give one a feeling of distinction. If one knows that one has been singled out by divine choice and intention from the beginning of the world, then one feels lifted beyond the transitoriness and meaninglessness of ordinary human existence and transported to a new state of dignity and importance, like one who has a part in the divine world drama. In this way man is brought nearer to God, and this is in entire accord with the meaning of the message in the gospels.

Besides his love of mankind a certain irascibility is noticeable in Christ's character, and, as is often the case with people of emotional temperament, a manifest lack of self-reflection. There is no evidence that Christ ever wondered about himself, or that he ever confronted himself. To this rule there is only one significant exception— the despairing cry from the Cross: "My God, my God, why hast thou forsaken me?" Here his human nature attains divinity; at that moment God experiences what it means to be a mortal man and drinks to the dregs what he made his faithful servant Job suffer. Here is given the answer to Job, and, clearly, this supreme moment is as divine as it is human, as "eschatological" as it is "psychological." And at this moment, too, where one can feel the human being so absolutely, the divine myth is present in full force. And both mean one and the same thing. How, then, can one possibly "demythologize" the figure of Christ? A rationalistic attempt of that sort would soak all the mystery out of his personality, and what remained would no longer be the birth and tragic fate of a God in time, but, historically speaking, a badly authenticated religious teacher, a Jewish reformer who was hellenistically interpreted and misunderstood—a kind of Pythagoras, maybe, or, if you like, a Buddha or a Mohammed, but certainly not a son of God or a God incarnate. Nor does anybody seem to have realized what would be the consequences of a Christ disinfected of all trace of eschatology. Today we have an empirical psychology, which continues to exist despite the fact that the theologians have done their best to ignore it, and with its help we can put certain of Christ's statements under the microscope. If these statements are detached from their mythical context, they can only be explained personalistically. But what sort of conclusion are we bound to arrive at if a statement like "I am the way, and the truth, and the life; no one comes to the Father, but by me" [74] is reduced to personal psychology? Obviously the same conclusion as that reached by Jesus' relatives when, in their ignorance of eschatology, they said, "He is beside himself." [75] What is the use of a religion without a mythos, since religion means, if anything at all, precisely that function which links us back to the eternal myth?

In view of these portentous impossibilities, it has been assumed, perhaps as the result of a growing impatience with the difficult factual material, that Christ was nothing but a myth, in this case no more than a fiction. But myth is not fiction: it consists of facts that are continually repeated and can be observed over and over again. It is something that happens to man, and men have mythical fates just as much as the Greek heroes do. The fact that the life of Christ is largely myth does absolutely nothing to disprove its factual truth—quite the contrary. I would even go so far as to say that the mythical character of a life is just what expresses its universal human validity. It is perfectly possible, psychologically, for the unconscious or an archetype to take complete possession of a man and to determine his fate down to the smallest detail. At the same time objective, nonpsychic parallel phenomena can occur which also represent the archetype. It not only seems

[74] John 14 : 6.
[75] Mark 3 : 21.

so, it simply is so, that the archetype fulfils itself not only psychically in the individual, but objectively outside the individual. My own conjecture is that Christ was such a personality. The life of Christ is just what it had to be if it is the life of a god and a man at the same time. It is a *symbolum,* a bringing together of heterogeneous natures, rather as if Job and Yahweh were combined in a single personality. Yahweh's intention to become man, which resulted from his collision with Job, is fulfilled in Christ's life and suffering.

# VIII

When one remembers the earlier acts of creation, one wonders what has happened to Satan and his subversive activities. Everywhere he sows his tares among the wheat. One suspects he had a hand in Herod's massacre of the innocents. What is certain is his attempt to lure Christ into the role of a worldly ruler. Equally obvious is the fact, as is evidenced by the remarks of the man possessed of devils, that he is very well informed about Christ's nature. He also seems to have inspired Judas, without, however, being able to influence or prevent the sacrificial death.

His comparative ineffectiveness can be explained on the one hand by the careful preparations for the divine birth, and on the other hand by a curious metaphysical phenomenon which Christ witnessed: he saw Satan fall like lightning from heaven.[76] In this vision a metaphysical event has become temporal; it indicates the historic and —so far as we know—final separation of Yahweh from his dark son. Satan is banished from heaven and no longer has any opportunity to inveigle his father into dubious undertakings. This event may well explain why he plays such an inferior role wherever he appears in the history

[76] Luke 10 : 18.

of the Incarnation. His role here is in no way comparable to his former confidential relationship to Yahweh. He has obviously forfeited the paternal affection and been exiled. The punishment which we missed in the story of Job has at last caught up with him, though in a strangely limited form. Although he is banished from the heavenly court he has kept his dominion over the sublunary world. He is not cast directly into hell, but upon earth. Only at the end of time shall he be locked up and made permanently in-effective. Christ's death cannot be laid at his door, be-cause, through its prefiguration in Abel and in the young dying gods, the sacrificial. death was a fate chosen by Yahweh as a reparation for the wrong done to Job on the one hand, and on the other hand as a fillip to the spiritual and moral development of man. There can be no doubt that man's importance is enormously enhanced if God himself deigns to become one.

As a result of the partial neutralization of Satan, Yah-weh identifies with his light aspect and becomes the good God and loving father. He has not lost his wrath and can still mete out punishment, but he does it with justice. Cases like the Job tragedy are apparently no longer to be ex-pected. He proves himself benevolent and gracious. He shows mercy to the sinful children of men and is defined as Love itself. But although Christ has complete con-fidence in his father and even feels at one with him, he cannot help inserting the cautious petition—and warning —into the Lord's Prayer: "Lead us not into temptation, but deliver us from evil." God is asked not to entice us outright into doing evil, but rather to deliver us from it. The possibility that Yahweh, in spite of all the precau-tionary measures and in spite of his express intention to become the Summum Bonum, might yet revert to his former ways is not so remote that one need not keep one eye open for it. At any rate, Christ considers it appropri-ate to remind his father of his destructive inclinations to-wards mankind and to beg him to desist from them. Judged by any human standards it is after all unfair, indeed extremely immoral, to entice little children into doing things that might be dangerous for them, simply in order to test their moral stamina! Especially as the difference between a child and a grown-up is immeasurably smaller than that between God and his creatures, whose moral weakness is particularly well known to him. The incongruity of it is so colossal that if this petition were not in the Lord's Prayer one would have to call it sheer blasphemy, because it really will not do to ascribe such contradictory behaviour to the God of Love and Summum Bonum.

The sixth petition indeed allows a deep insight, for in face of this fact Christ's immense certainty with regard to his father's character becomes somewhat questionable. It is, unfortunately, a common experience that particularly positive and categorical assertions are met with wherever there is a slight doubt in the background that has to be stifled. One must admit that it would be contrary to all reasonable expectations to suppose that a God who, for all his lavish generosity, had been subject to intermittent but devastating fits of rage ever since time began could suddenly become the epitome of everything good. Christ's unadmitted but none the less evident doubt in this respect is confirmed in the New Testament, and particularly in the Apocalypse. There Yahweh again delivers himself up to an unheard-of fury of destruction against the human race, of whom a mere hundred and forty-four thousand specimens appear to survive.[77]

One is indeed at a loss how to bring such a reaction into line with the behaviour of a loving father, whom we would expect to glorify his creation with patience and love. It looks as if the attempt to secure an absolute and final victory for good is bound to lead to a dangerous accumulation of evil and hence to catastrophe. Compared with the end of the world, the destruction of Sodom and Gomorrah and even the Deluge are mere child's play;

[77] Revelation 7 : 4.

for this time the whole of creation goes to pieces. As Satan was locked up for a time, then conquered and cast into a lake of fire,[78] the destruction of the world can hardly be the work of the devil, but must be an "act of God" not influenced by Satan.

The end of the world is, however, preceded by the circumstance that even Christ's victory over his brother Satan—Abel's counterstroke against Cain—is not really and truly won, because, before this can come to pass, a final and mighty manifestation of Satan is to be expected. One can hardly suppose that God's incarnation in his son Christ would be calmly accepted by Satan. It must certainly have stirred up his jealousy to the highest pitch and evoked in him a desire to imitate Christ (a role for which he is particularly well suited as the πνεῦμα ἀντίμιμον), and to become incarnate in his turn as the *dark* God. (As we know, numerous legends were later woven round this theme.) This plan will be put into operation by the figure of the Antichrist after the preordained thousand years are over, the term allotted by astrology to the reign of Christ. This expectation, which is already to be found in the New Testament, reveals a doubt as to the immediate finality or universal effectiveness of the work of salvation. Unfortunately it must be said that these expectations gave rise to thoughtless revelations which were never even discussed with other aspects of the doctrine of salvation, let alone brought into harmony with them.


# IX


I mention these future apocalyptic events only to illustrate the doubt which is indirectly expressed in the sixth petition of the Lord's Prayer, and not in order to give a general interpretation of the Apocalypse. I shall come back to this theme later on. But, before doing so, we must

[78] Revelation 19 : 20.

turn to the question of how matters stood with the Incarnation after the death of Christ. We have always been
taught that the Incarnation was a unique historical event.
No repetition of it was to be expected, any more than one
could expect a further revelation of the Logos, for this
too was included in the uniqueness of God's appearance
on earth, in human form, nearly two thousand years ago.
The sole source of revelation, and hence the final authority, is the Bible. God is an authority only in so far as he
authorized the writings in the New Testament, and with
the conclusion of the New Testament the authentic communications of God cease. Thus far the Protestant standpoint. The Catholic Church, the direct heir and continua-
tor of historical Christianity, proves to be somewhat more
cautious in this regard, believing that with the assistance
of the Holy Ghost the dogma can progressively develop
and unfold. This view is in entire agreement with Christ's
own teachings about the Holy Ghost and hence with the
further continuance of the Incarnation. Christ is of the
opinion that whoever believes in him—believes, that is to
say, that he is the son of God—can "do the works that
I do, and greater works than these." [79] He reminds his
disciples that he had told them they were gods.[80] The believers or chosen ones are children of God and "fellow
heirs with Christ." [81] When Christ leaves the earthly stage,
he will ask his father to send his flock a Counsellor (the
"Paraclete"), who will abide with them and in them for
ever.[82] The Counsellor is the Holy Ghost, who will be
sent from the father. This "Spirit of truth" will teach the
believers "all things" and guide them "into all truth." [83]
According to this, Christ envisages a continuing realization of God in his children, and consequently in his
(Christ's) brothers and sisters in the spirit, so that his

[79] John 14 : 12.
[80] 10 : 34.
[81] Romans 8 : 17.
[82] John 14 : 16f.
[83] 14 : 26 and 16 : 13.

own works need not necessarily be considered the greatest ones.

Since the Holy Ghost is the Third Person of the Trinity and God is present entire in each of the three Persons at any time, the indwelling of the Holy Ghost means nothing less than an approximation of the believer to the status of God's son. One can therefore understand what is meant by the remark "you are gods." The deifying effect of the Holy Ghost is naturally assisted by the *imago Dei* stamped on the elect. God, in the shape of the Holy Ghost, puts up his tent in man, for he is obviously minded to realize himself continually not only in Adam's descendants, but in an indefinitely large number of believers, and possibly in mankind as a whole. Symptomatic of this is the significant fact that Barnabas and Paul were identified in Lystra with Zeus and Hermes: "The gods have come down to us in the likeness of men." [84] This was certainly only the more naïve, pagan view of the Christian transmutation, but precisely for that reason it convinces. Tertullian must have had something of the sort in mind when he described the "sublimiorem Deum" as a sort of lender of divinity "who has made gods of men." [85]

God's Incarnation in Christ requires continuation and completion because Christ, owing to his virgin birth and his sinlessness, was not an empirical human being at all. As stated in the first chapter of St. John, he represented a light which, though it shone in the darkness, was not comprehended by the darkness. He remained outside and above mankind. Job, on the other hand, was an ordinary human being, and therefore the wrong done to him, and through him to mankind, can, according to divine justice, only be repaired by an incarnation of God in an empirical human being. This act of expiation is performed by the Paraclete; for, just as man must suffer from God, so God

---

[84] Acts 14 : 11.
[85] Mancipem quendam divinitatis qui ex hominibus deos fecerit." *Apologeticus,* XI, in Migne, *P.L.,* Vol. 1, col. 386.

must suffer from man. Otherwise there can be no reconciliation between the two.

The continuing, direct operation of the Holy Ghost on those who are called to be God's children implies, in fact, a broadening process of incarnation. Christ, the son begotten by God, is the first-born who is succeeded by an ever-increasing number of younger brothers and sisters. These are, however, neither begotten by the Holy Ghost nor born of a virgin. This may be prejudicial to their metaphysical status, but their merely human birth will in no sense endanger their prospects of a future position of honour at the heavenly court, nor will it diminish their capacity to perform miracles. Their lowly origin (possibly from the mammals) does not prevent them from entering into a close kinship with God as their father and Christ as their brother. In a metaphorical sense, indeed, it is actually a "kinship by blood," since they have received their share of the blood and flesh of Christ, which means more than mere adoption. These profound changes in man's status are the direct result of Christ's work of redemption. Redemption or deliverance has several different aspects, the most important of which is the expiation wrought by Christ's sacrificial death for the misdemeanours of mankind. His blood cleanses us from the evil consequences of sin. He reconciles God with man and delivers him from the divine wrath, which hangs over him like doom, and from eternal damnation. It is obvious that such ideas still picture God the father as the dangerous Yahweh who has to be propitiated. The agonizing death of his son is supposed to give him satisfaction for an affront he has suffered, and for this "moral injury" he would be inclined to take a terrible vengeance. Once more we are appalled by the incongruous attitude of the world creator towards his creatures, who to his chagrin never behave according to his expectations. It is as if someone started a bacterial culture which turned out to be a failure. He might curse his luck, but he would never seek the reason for the failure in the bacilli and want to punish them morally for it. Rather, he would select a more suitable culture medium. Yahweh's behaviour towards his creatures contradicts all the requirements of so-called "divine" reason whose possession is supposed to distinguish men from animals. Moreover, a bacteriologist might make a mistake in his choice of a culture medium, for he is only human. But God in his omniscience would never make mistakes if only he consulted with it. He has equipped his human creatures with a modicum of consciousness and a corresponding degree of free will, but he must also know that by so doing he leads them into the temptation of falling into a dangerous independence. That would not be too great a risk if man had to do with a creator who was only kind and good. But Yahweh is forgetting his son Satan, to whose wiles even he occasionally succumbs. How then could he expect man with his limited consciousness and imperfect knowledge to do any better? He also overlooks the fact that the more consciousness a man possesses the more he is separated from his instincts (which at least give him an inkling of the hidden wisdom of God) and the more prone he is to error. He is certainly not up to Satan's wiles if even his creator is unable, or unwilling, to restrain this powerful spirit.

## X

The fact of God's "unconsciousness" throws a peculiar light on the doctrine of salvation. Man is not so much delivered from his sins, even if he is baptized in the prescribed manner and thus washed clean, as delivered from fear of the consequences of sin, that is, from the wrath of God. Consequently, the work of salvation is intended to save man from the fear of God. This is certainly possible where the belief in a loving father, who has sent his only-begotten son to rescue the human race, has repressed the

persistent traces of the old Yahweh and his dangerous
affects. Such a belief, however, presupposes a lack of reflection or a *sacrificium intellectus,* and it appears questionable whether either of them can be morally justified.
We should never forget that it was Christ himself who
taught us to make usurious use of the talents entrusted to
us and not hide them in the ground. One ought not to make
oneself out to be more stupid and more unconscious than
one really is, for in all other aspects we are called upon to
be alert, critical, and self-aware, so as not to fall into temptation, and to "examine the spirits" who want to gain influence over us and "see whether they are of God," [86] so that
we may recognize the mistakes we make. It even needs
superhuman intelligence to avoid the cunning snares of
Satan. These obligations inevitably sharpen our understanding, our love of truth, and the urge to know, which
as well as being genuine human virtues are quite possibly
effects of that spirit which "searches everything, even the
depths of God." [87] These intellectual and moral capacities
are themselves of a divine nature, and therefore cannot
and must not be cut off. It is just by following Christian
morality that one gets into the worst collisions of duty.
Only those who habitually make five an even number can
escape them. The fact that Christian ethics leads to collisions of duty speaks in its favour. By engendering insoluble
conflicts and consequently an *afflictio animae,* it brings
man nearer to a knowledge of God. All opposites are of
God, therefore man must bend to this burden; and in so
doing he finds that God in his "oppositeness" has taken
possession of him, incarnated himself in him. He becomes
a vessel filled with divine conflict. We rightly associate the
idea of suffering with a state in which the opposites violently collide with one another, and we hesitate to describe
such a painful experience as being "redeemed." Yet it cannot be denied that the great symbol of the Christian faith,

[86] I John 4 : 1 (modified).
[87] I Corinthians 2 : 10.

the Cross, upon which hangs the suffering figure of the Redeemer, has been emphatically held up before the eyes of Christians for nearly two thousand years. This picture is completed by the two thieves, one of whom goes down to hell, the other into paradise. One could hardly imagine a better representation of the "oppositeness" of the central Christian symbol. Why this inevitable product of Christian psychology should signify redemption is difficult to see, except that the conscious recognition of the opposites, painful though it may be at the moment, does bring with it a definite feeling of deliverance. It is on the one hand a deliverance from the distressing state of dull and helpless unconsciousness, and on the other hand a growing awareness of God's oppositeness, in which man can participate if he does not shrink from being wounded by the dividing sword which is Christ. Only through the most extreme and most menacing conflict does the Christian experience deliverance into divinity, always provided that he does not break, but accepts the burden of being marked out by God. In this way alone can the *imago Dei* realize itself in him, and God become man. The seventh petition in the Lord's Prayer, "But deliver us from evil," is to be understood in the same sense as Christ's prayer in the Garden of Gethsemane: "My Father, if it be possible, let this cup pass from me." [88] In principle it does not seem to fit God's purpose to exempt a man from conflict and hence from evil. It is altogether human to express such a desire but it must not be made into a principle, because it is directed against God's will and rests only on human weakness and fear. Fear is certainly justified up to a point, for, to make the conflict complete, there must be doubt and uncertainty as to whether man's strength is not being overtaxed.

Because the *imago Dei* pervades the whole human sphere and makes mankind its involuntary exponent, it is just possible that the four-hundred-year-old schism in the Church and the present division of the political world into

[88] Matthew 26 : 39.

two hostile camps are both expressions of the unrecognized polarity of the dominant archetype.

The traditional view of Christ's work of redemption reflects a one-sided way of thinking, no matter whether we regard that one-sidedness as purely human or as willed by God. The other view, which regards the atonement not as the payment of a human debt to God, but as reparation for a wrong done by God to man, has been briefly outlined above. This view seems to me to be better suited to the power situation as it actually exists. The sheep can stir up mud in the wolf's drinking water, but can do him no other harm. So also the creature can disappoint the creator, but it is scarcely credible that he can do him a painful wrong. This lies only in the power of the creator with respect to the powerless creature. On this view, a wrong is imputed to God, but it is certainly no worse than what has already been imputed to him if one assumes that it was necessary to torture the son to death on the Cross merely in order to appease the father's wrath. What kind of father is it who would rather his son were slaughtered than forgive his ill-advised creatures who have been corrupted by his precious Satan? What is supposed to be demonstrated by this gruesome and archaic sacrifice of the son? God's love, perhaps? Or his implacability? We know from chapter 22 of Genesis[89] and from Exodus 22 : 29 that Yahweh has a tendency to employ such means as the killing of the son and the first-born in order to test his people's faith or to assert his will, despite the fact that his omniscience and omnipotence have no need whatever of such savage procedures, which moreover set a bad example to the mighty ones of the earth. It is very understandable, therefore, that a naïve mind is apt to run away from such questions and excuse this manoeuvre as a beautiful *sacrificium intellectus*. If one prefers not to read the Eighty-ninth Psalm, the matter will not end there. He who cheats once will cheat again, particularly when it comes to self-knowledge. But self-knowledge, in the form of an examination of conscience, is

[89] Abraham and Isaac.

demanded by Christian ethics. They were very pious people who maintained that self-knowledge paves the way to knowledge of God.

# XI

To believe that God is the Summum Bonum is impossible for a reflecting consciousness. Such a consciousness does not feel in any way delivered from the fear of God, and therefore asks itself, quite rightly, what Christ means to it. That, indeed, is the great question: can Christ still be interpreted in our day and age, or must one be satisfied with the historical interpretation?

One thing, anyway, cannot be doubted: Christ is a highly numinous figure. The interpretation of him as God and the son of God is in full accord with this. The old view, which is based on Christ's own view of the matter, asserts that he came into the world, suffered, and died in order to save mankind from the wrath to come. Furthermore he believed that his own bodily resurrection would assure all God's children of the same future.

We have already pointed out at some length how curiously God's salvationist project works out in practice. All he does is, in the shape of his own son, to rescue mankind from himself. This thought is as scurrilous as the old rabbinical view of Yahweh hiding the righteous from his wrath under his throne, where of course he cannot see them. It is exactly as if God the father were a different God from the son, which is not the meaning at all. Nor is there any psychological need for such an assumption, since the undoubted lack of reflection in God's consciousness is sufficient to explain his peculiar behaviour. It is quite right, therefore, that fear of God should be considered the beginning of all wisdom. On the other hand, the much-vaunted goodness, love, and justice of God should not be regarded as mere propitiation, but should be recognized as a genuine experience, for God is a *coincidentia oppositorum*. Both are justified, the fear of God as well as the love of God.

A more differentiated consciousness must, sooner or later, find it difficult to love, as a kind father, a God whom on account of his unpredictable fits of wrath, his unreliability, injustice, and cruelty, it has every reason to fear. The decay of the gods of antiquity has proved to our satisfaction that man does not relish any all-too-human inconsistencies and weaknesses in his gods. Likewise, it is probable that Yahweh's moral defeat in his dealings with Job had its hidden effects: man's unintended elevation on the one hand, and on the other hand a disturbance of the unconscious. For a while the first-mentioned effect remains a mere fact, not consciously realized though registered by the unconscious. This contributes to the disturbance in the unconscious, which thereby acquires a higher potential than exists in consciousness. Man then counts for more in the unconscious than he does consciously. In these circumstances the potential starts flowing from the unconscious towards consciousness, and the unconscious breaks through in the form of dreams, visions, and revelations. Unfortunately the Book of Job cannot be dated with any certainty. As mentioned above, it was written somewhere between 600 and 300 B.C. During the first half of the sixth century, Ezekiel,[90] the prophet with the so-called "pathological" features, appears on the scene. Although laymen are inclined to apply this epithet to his visions, I must, as a psychiatrist, emphatically state that visions and their accompanying phenomena cannot be uncritically evaluated as morbid. Visions, like dreams, are unusual but quite natural occurrences which can be designated as "pathological" only when their morbid nature has been proved. From a strictly clinical standpoint Ezekiel's visions are of an archetypal nature and are not morbidly distorted in any way. There is no reason to regard them as pathological.[91]

[90] The vision in which he received his call occurred in 592 B.C.

[91] It is altogether wrong to assume that visions as such are pathological. They occur with normal people also—not very frequently, it is true, but they are by no means rare.

They are a symptom of the split which already existed at that time between conscious and unconscious. The first great vision is made up of two well-ordered compound quaternities, that is, conceptions of totality, such as we frequently observe today as spontaneous phenomena. Their *quinta essentia* is represented by a figure which has "the likeness of a human form." [92] Here Ezekiel has seen the essential content of the unconscious, namely *the idea of the higher man* by whom Yahweh was morally defeated and who he was later to become.

In India, a more or less simultaneous symptom of the same tendency was Gautama the Buddha (b. 562 B.C.), who gave the maximum differentiation of consciousness supremacy even over the highest Brahman gods. This development was a logical consequence of the *purusha-ātman* doctrine and derived from the inner experience of yoga practice.

Ezekiel grasped, in a symbol, the fact that Yahweh was drawing closer to man. This is something which came to Job as an experience but probably did not reach his consciousness. That is to say, he did not realize that his consciousness was higher than Yahweh's, and that consequently God wants to become man. What is more, in Ezekiel we meet for the first time the title "Son of Man," which Yahweh significantly uses in addressing the prophet, presumably to indicate that he is a son of the "Man" on the throne, and hence a prefiguration of the much later revelation in Christ. It is with the greatest right, therefore, that the four seraphim on God's throne became the emblems of the evangelists, for they form the quaternity which expresses Christ's totality, just as the four gospels represent the four pillars of his throne.

The disturbance of the unconscious continued for several centuries. Around 165 B.C., Daniel had a vision of four beasts and the "Ancient of Days," to whom "with the clouds of heaven there came one like a son of man." [93]

[92] Ezekiel 1 : 26.
[93] Daniel 7 : 13.

Here the "son of man" is no longer the prophet but a son of the "Ancient of Days" in his own right, and a son whose task it is to rejuvenate the father.

The Book of Enoch, written around 100 B.C., goes into considerably more detail. It gives a revealing account of the advance of the sons of God into the world of men, another prefiguration which has been described as the "fall of the angels." Whereas, according to Genesis,[94] Yahweh resolved that his spirit should not "abide in man for ever," and that men should not live to be hundreds of years old as they had before, the sons of God, by way of compensation, fell in love with the beautiful daughters of men. This happened at the time of the giants. Enoch relates that after conspiring with one another, two hundred angels under the leadership of Samiazaz descended to earth, took the daughters of men to wife, and begat with them giants three thousand ells long.[95] The angels, among whom Azazel particularly excelled, taught mankind the arts and sciences. They proved to be extraordinarily progressive elements who broadened and developed man's consciousness, just as the wicked Cain had stood for progress as contrasted with the stay-at-home Abel. In this way they enlarged the significance of man to "gigantic" proportions, which points to an inflation of the cultural consciousness at that period. An inflation, however, is always threatened with a counter-stroke from the unconscious, and this actually did happen in the form of the Deluge. So corrupt was the earth before the Deluge that the giants "consumed all the acquisitions of men" and then began to devour each other, while men in their turn devoured the beasts, so that "the earth laid accusation against the lawless ones." [96]

The invasion of the human world by the sons of God

---

[94] Genesis 6 : 3f.
[95] Enoch 7 : 2.
[96] Enoch 7 : 3–6. [The translations of the Book of Enoch are from Robert Henry Charles, ed., *The Apocrypha and Pseudepigrapha of the Old Testament in English* (Oxford, 1913. 2 vols.), Vol. II, sometimes slightly modified.—TRANSLATOR.]

therefore had serious consequences, which make Yahweh's precautions prior to his appearance on the earthly scene the more understandable. Man was completely helpless in face of this superior divine force. Hence it is of the greatest interest to see how Yahweh behaves in this matter. As the later Draconian punishment proves, it was a not unimportant event in the heavenly economy when no less than two hundred of the sons of God departed from the paternal household to carry out experiments on their own in the human world. One would have expected that information concerning this mass exodus would have trickled through to the court (quite apart from the fact of divine omniscience). But nothing of the sort happened. Only after the giants had long been begotten and had already started to slaughter and devour mankind did four archangels, apparently by accident, hear the weeping and wailing of men and discover what was going on on earth. One really does not know which is the more astonishing, the bad organization of the angelic hosts or the faulty communications in heaven. Be that as it may, this time the archangels felt impelled to appear before God with the following peroration:

> All things are naked and open in Thy sight, and Thou seest all things, and nothing can hide itself from Thee. Thou seest what Azazel hath done, who taught all unrighteousness on earth and revealed the eternal secrets which were preserved in heaven. . . . [And enchantments hath Samiazaz taught], to whom Thou hast given authority to bear rule over his associates. . . . And Thou knowest all things before they come to pass, and Thou seest these things and Thou dost suffer them, and Thou dost not say to us what we are to do to them in regard to these.[97]

Either all that the archangels say is a lie, or Yahweh, for some incomprehensible reason, has drawn no conclusions from his omniscience, or—what is more likely—the archangels must remind him that once again he has pre-

[97] Enoch 9 : 5-11.

ferred to know nothing of his omniscience. At any rate it is only on their intervention that retaliatory action is released on a global scale, but it is not really a just punishment, seeing that Yahweh promptly drowns all living creatures with the exception of Noah and his relatives. This intermezzo proves that the sons of God are somehow more vigilant, more progressive, and more conscious than their father. Yahweh's subsequent transformation is therefore to be rated all the higher. The preparations for his Incarnation give one the impression that he has really learnt something from experience and is setting about things more consciously than before. Undoubtedly the recollection of Sophia has contributed to this increase of consciousness. Parallel with this, the revelation of the metaphysical structure becomes more explicit. Whereas in Ezekiel and Daniel we find only vague hints about the quaternity and the Son of Man, Enoch gives us clear and detailed information on these points. The underworld, a sort of Hades, is divided into four hollow places which serve as abodes for the spirits of the dead until the Last Judgment. Three of these hollow places are dark, but one is bright and contains a "fountain of water." [98] This is the abode of the righteous.

With statements of this type we enter into a definitely psychological realm, namely that of mandala symbolism, to which also belong the ratios 1 : 3 and 3 : 4.[99] The quadripartite Hades of Enoch corresponds to a chthonic quaternity, which presumably stands in everlasting contrast to a pneumatic or heavenly one. The former corresponds in alchemy to the *quaternio* of the elements, the latter to a fourfold, or total, aspect of the deity, as for instance Barbelo, Kolorbas, *Mercurius quadratus*, and the fourfaced gods all indicate.

In fact, Enoch in his vision sees the four faces of God. Three of them are engaged in praising, praying, and supplicating, but the fourth in "fending off the Satans and for-

[98] 22 : 2.
[99] Cf. supra, pp. 363–455.

bidding them to come before the Lord of Spirits to accuse them who dwell on earth." [100]

The vision shows us an essential differentiation of the God-image: God now has four faces, or rather, four angels of his face, who are four hypostases or emanations, of which one is exclusively occupied in keeping his elder son Satan, now changed into many, away from him, and in preventing further experiments after the style of the Job episode.[101] The Satans still dwell in the heavenly regions, since the fall of Satan has not yet occurred. The above-mentioned proportions are also suggested here by the fact that three of the angels perform holy or beneficial functions, while the fourth is a militant figure who has to keep Satan at bay.

This quaternity has a distinctly pneumatic nature and is therefore expressed by angels, who are generally pictured with wings, i.e., as aerial beings. This is the more likely as they are presumably the descendants of Ezekiel's four seraphim.[102] The doubling and separation of the quaternity into an upper and a lower one, like the exclusion of the Satans from the heavenly court, points to a metaphysical split that had already taken place. But the pleromatic split is in its turn a symptom of a much deeper split in the divine will: the father wants to become the son, God wants to become man, the amoral wants to become exclusively good, the unconscious wants to become consciously responsible. So far everything exists only *in statu nascendi*.

Enoch's unconscious is vastly excited by all this and its contents burst out in a spate of apocalyptic visions. It also causes him to undertake the *peregrinatio,* the journey to the four quarters of heaven and to the centre of the earth, so that he draws a mandala with his own movements, in accordance with the "journeys" of the alchemistic philoso-

---

[100] Enoch 40 : 7.
[101] Cf. also Chap. 87f. Of the four "beings who were like white men," three take Enoch by the hand, while the other seizes a star and hurls it into the abyss.
[102] Three had animal faces, one a human face.

phers and the corresponding fantasies of our modern unconscious.

When Yahweh addressed Ezekiel as "Son of Man," this
was no more at first than a dark and enigmatic hint. But
now it becomes clear: the man Enoch is not only the
recipient of divine revelation but is at the same time a
participant in the divine drama, as though he were at least
one of the sons of God himself. This can only be taken as
meaning that in the same measure as God sets out to
become man, man is immersed in the pleromatic process.
He becomes, as it were, baptized in it and is made to
participate in the divine quaternity (i.e., is crucified with
Christ). That is why even today, in the rite of the *benedictio
fontis*, the water is divided into a cross by the hand of the
priest and then sprinkled to the four quarters.

Enoch is so much under the influence of the divine
drama, so gripped by it, that one could almost suppose he
had a quite special understanding of the coming Incarnation. The "Son of Man" who is with the "Head [or Ancient]
of Days" looks like an angel (i.e., like one of the sons of
God). He "hath righteousness"; "with him dwelleth righteousness"; the Lord of Spirits has "chosen him"; "his lot
hath the preeminence before the Lord of Spirits in up-
rightness." [103] It is probably no accident that so much
stress is laid on righteousness, for it is the one quality that
Yahweh lacks, a fact that could hardly have remained
hidden from such a man as the author of the Book of
Enoch. Under the reign of the Son of Man ". . . the
prayer of the righteous has been heard, and the blood of
the righteous . . . [avenged] before the Lord of Spirits." [104] Enoch sees a "fountain of righteousness which was
inexhaustible." [105] The Son of Man

> . . . shall be a staff to the righteous. . . .
> For this reason hath he been chosen and hidden before
>      him,

[103] Enoch 46 : 1–3.
[104] 47 : 4.
[105] 48 : 1.

Before the creation of the world and for evermore
And the wisdom of the Lord of Spirits hath revealed
    him . . . ,
For he hath preserved the lot of the righteous.[106]
For wisdom is poured out like water. . . .
He is mighty in all the secrets of righteousness,
And unrighteousness shall disappear as a shadow. . . .
In him dwells the spirit of wisdom,
And the spirit which gives insight,
And the spirit of understanding and of might.[107]

Under the reign of the Son of Man

. . . shall the earth also give back that which has been
    entrusted to it,
And Sheol also shall give back that which it has re-
    ceived,
And hell [108] shall give back that which it owes. . . .

The Elect One shall in those days sit on My throne,
And his mouth shall pour forth all the secrets of
    wisdom and counsel.[109]

"All shall become angels in heaven." Azazel and his hosts
shall be cast into the burning fiery furnace for "becoming
subject to Satan and leading astray those who dwell on the
earth." [110]

At the end of the world the Son of Man shall sit in
judgment over all creatures. "The darkness shall be destroyed, and the light established for ever." [111] Even Yahweh's two big exhibits, Leviathan and Behemoth, are forced
to succumb: they are carved up and eaten. In this passage[112] Enoch is addressed by the revealing angel with the
title "Son of Man," a further indication that he, like Ezekiel, has been assimilated by the divine mystery, is included

---

[106] 48 : 4, 6–7.
[107] Enoch 49 : 1–3.
[108] Synonym for Sheol.
[109] 51 : 1, 3.
[110] 54 : 6. Here at last we hear that the exodus of the two hundred
angels was a prank of Satan's.
[111] 58 : 6 (modified).
[112] 60 : 10.

in it, as is already suggested by the bare fact that he witnesses it. Enoch is wafted away and takes his seat in heaven. In the "heaven of heavens" he beholds the house of God built of crystal, with streams of living fire about it, and guarded by winged beings that never sleep.[113] The "Head of Days" comes forth with the angelic quaternity (Michael, Gabriel, Raphael, Phanuel) and speaks to him, saying: "This is the Son of Man who is born unto righteousness, and righteousness abides over him, and the righteousness of the Head of Days forsakes him not." [114]

It is remarkable that the Son of Man and what he means should be associated again and again with righteousness. It seems to be his leitmotif, his chief concern. Only where injustice threatens or has already occurred does such an emphasis on righteousness make any sense. No one, only God, can dispense justice to any noticeable degree, and precisely with regard to him there exists the justifiable fear that he may forget his justice. In this case his righteous son would intercede with him on man's behalf. Thus "the righteous shall have peace." [115] The justice that shall prevail under the son is stressed to such an extent that one has the impression that formerly, under the reign of the father, injustice was paramount, and that only with the son is the era of law and order inaugurated. It looks as though, with this, Enoch had unconsciously given an answer to Job.

The emphasis laid on God's agedness is logically connected with the existence of a son, but it also suggests that he himself will step a little into the background and leave the government of the human world more and more to the son, in the hope that a juster order will emerge. From all this we can see the aftereffects of some psychological trauma, the memory of an injustice that cries to heaven and beclouds the intimate relationship with God. God himself wants a son, and man also wants a son

[113] 71 : 5–6.
[114] 71 : 14.
[115] 71 : 17.

to take the place of the father. This son must, as we have conclusively seen, be absolutely just, and this quality is given priority over all other virtues. God and man both want to escape from blind injustice.

Enoch, in his ecstasy, recognizes himself as the Son of Man, or as the son of God, although neither by birth nor by predestination does he seem to have been chosen for such a role.[116] He experiences that godlike elevation which, in the case of Job, we merely assumed, or rather inferred as the inevitable outcome. Job himself seems to have suspected something of the sort when he declares: "I know that my Vindicator lives." [117] This highly remarkable statement can, under the circumstances, only refer to the benevolent Yahweh. The traditional Christian interpretation of this passage as an anticipation of Christ is correct in so far as Yahweh's benevolent aspect incarnates itself, as its own hypostasis, in the Son of Man, and in so far as the Son of Man proves in Enoch to be a representative of justice and, in Christianity, the justifier of mankind. Furthermore, the Son of Man is pre-existent, and therefore Job could very well appeal to him. Just as Satan plays the role of accuser and slanderer, so Christ, God's other son, plays the role of advocate and defender.

Despite the contradiction, certain scholars have wished to see Enoch's Messianic ideas as Christian interpolations. For psychological reasons this suspicion seems to me unjustified. One has only to consider what Yahweh's injustice, his downright immorality, must have meant to a devout thinker. It was no laughing matter to be burdened with such an idea of God. A much later document tells us of a pious sage who could never read the Eighty-ninth Psalm, "because he could not bear it." When one considers with

---

[116] The author of the Book of Enoch chose, as the hero of his tale, Enoch the son of Jared, the seventh after Adam, who "walked with God," and, instead of dying, simply disappeared, i.e., was carried away by God (". . . and he was not, for God took him."—Genesis 5 : 24).

[117] Job 19 : 25.

what intensity and exclusiveness not only Christ's teaching, but the doctrines of the Church in the following centuries down to the present day, have emphasized the goodness of the loving Father in heaven, the deliverance from fear, the Summum Bonum, and the *privatio boni,* one can form some conception of the incompatibility which the figure of Yahweh presents, and see how intolerable such a paradox must appear to the religious consciousness. And this has probably been so ever since the days of Job.

The inner instability of Yahweh is the prime cause not only of the creation of the world, but also of the pleromatic drama for which mankind serves as a tragic chorus. The encounter with the creature changes the creator. In the Old Testament writings we find increasing traces of this development from the sixth century B.C. on. The two main climaxes are formed firstly by the Job tragedy, and secondly by Ezekiel's revelation. Job is the innocent sufferer, but Ezekiel witnesses the humanization and differentiation of Yahweh. By being addressed as "Son of Man," it is intimated to him that Yahweh's incarnation and quaternity are, so to speak, the pleromatic model for what is going to happen, through the transformation and humanization of God, not only to God's son as foreseen from all eternity, but to man as such. This is fulfilled as an intuitive anticipation in Enoch. In his ecstasy he becomes the Son of Man in the pleroma, and his wafting away in a chariot (like Elijah) prefigures the resurrection of the dead. To fulfil his role as minister of justice he must get into immediate proximity to God, and as the pre-existing Son of Man he is no longer subject to death. But in so far as he was an ordinary human being and therefore mortal, other mortals as well as he can attain to the vision of God; they too can become conscious of their saviour, and consequently immortal.

All these ideas could easily have become conscious at the time on the basis of the assumptions then current, if only someone had seriously reflected on them. For that no Christian interpolations were needed. The Book of Enoch was an anticipation in the grand manner, but everything still hung in mid air as mere revelation that never came down to earth. In view of these facts one cannot, with the best will in the world, see how Christianity, as we hear over and over again, is supposed to have burst upon world history as an absolute novelty. If ever anything had been historically prepared, and sustained and supported by the existing *Weltanschauung,* Christianity would be a classic example.

# XII

Jesus first appears as a Jewish reformer and prophet of an exclusively good God. In so doing he saves the threatened religious continuity, and in this respect he does in fact prove himself a σωτήρ, a saviour. He preserves mankind from loss of communion with God and from getting lost in mere consciousness and rationality. That would have brought something like a dissociation between consciousness and the unconscious, an unnatural and even pathological condition, a "loss of soul" such as has threatened man from the beginning of time. Again and again and in increasing measure he gets into danger of overlooking the necessary irrationalities of his psyche, and of imagining that he can control everything by will and reason alone, and thus paddle his own canoe. This can be seen most clearly in the great socio-political movements, such as Socialism and Communism: under the former the state suffers, and under the latter, man.

Jesus, it is plain, translated the existing tradition into his own personal reality, announcing the glad tidings: "God has good pleasure in mankind. He is a loving father and loves you as I love you, and has sent me as his son to ransom you from the old debt." He offers himself as an expiatory sacrifice that shall effect the reconciliation with God. The more desirable a real relationship of trust between man and God, the more astonishing becomes Yahweh's vindictiveness and irreconcilability towards his creatures. From a God who is a loving father, who is actually Love itself, one would expect understanding and forgiveness. So it comes as a nasty shock when this supremely good God only allows the purchase of such an act of grace through a human sacrifice, and, what is worse, through the killing of his own son. Christ apparently overlooked this anticlimax; at any rate all succeeding centuries have accepted it without opposition. One should keep before one's eyes the strange fact that the God of goodness is so unforgiving that he can only be appeased by a human sacrifice! This is an insufferable incongruity which modern man can no longer swallow, for he must be blind if he does not see the glaring light it throws on the divine character, giving the lie to all talk about love and the Summum Bonum.

Christ proves to be a mediator in two ways: he helps men against God and assuages the fear which man feels towards this being. He holds an important position midway between the two extremes, man and God, which are so difficult to unite. Clearly the focus of the divine drama shifts to the mediating God-man. He is lacking neither in humanity nor in divinity, and for this reason he was long ago characterized by totality symbols, because he was understood to be all-embracing and to unite all opposites. The quaternity of the Son of Man, indicating a more differentiated consciousness, was also ascribed to him (*vide* Cross and tetramorph). This corresponds by and large to the pattern in Enoch, but with one important deviation: Ezekiel and Enoch, the two bearers of the title "Son of Man," were ordinary human beings, whereas Christ by his descent,[118] conception, and birth is a hero and half-god in the classical sense. He is virginally begotten by the Holy Ghost and, as

---

[118] As a consequence of her immaculate conception Mary is already different from other mortals, and this fact is confirmed by her assumption.

he is not a creaturely human being, has no inclination to sin. The infection of evil was in his case precluded by the preparations for the Incarnation. Christ therefore stands more on the divine than on the human level. He incarnates God's good will to the exclusion of all else and therefore does not stand exactly in the middle, because the essential thing about the creaturely human being, sin, does not touch him. Sin originally came from the heavenly court and entered into creation with the help of Satan, which enraged Yahweh to such an extent that in the end his own son had to be sacrificed in order to placate him. Strangely enough, he took no steps to remove Satan from his entourage. In Enoch a special archangel, Phanuel, was charged with the task of defending Yahweh from Satan's insinuations, and only at the end of the world shall Satan, in the shape of a star,[119] be bound hand and foot, cast into the abyss, and destroyed. (This is not the case in the Book of Revelation, where he remains eternally alive in his natural element.)

Although it is generally assumed that Christ's unique sacrifice broke the curse of original sin and finally placated God, Christ nevertheless seems to have had certain misgivings in this respect. What will happen to man, and especially to his own followers, when the sheep have lost their shepherd, and when they miss the one who interceded for them with the father? He assures his disciples that he will always be with them, nay more, that he himself abides within them. Nevertheless this does not seem to satisfy him completely, for in addition he promises to send them from the father another παράκλητος (advocate, "Counsellor"), in his stead, who will assist them by word and deed and remain with them forever.[120] One might conjecture from this that the "legal position" has still not been cleared up beyond a doubt, or that there still exists a factor of uncertainty.

[119] Presumably the "morning star" (cf. Revelation 2 : 28 and 22 : 16). This is the planet Venus in her psychological implications and not, as one might think, either of the two *malefici,* Saturn and Mars.
[120] John 14 : 16.

The sending of the Paraclete has still another aspect. This Spirit of Truth and Wisdom is the Holy Ghost by whom Christ was begotten. He is the spirit of physical and spiritual procreation who from now on shall make his abode in creaturely man. Since he is the Third Person of the Deity, this is as much as to say that *God will be begotten in creaturely man*. This implies a tremendous change in man's status, for he is now raised to sonship and almost to the position of a man-god. With this the prefiguration in Ezekiel and Enoch, where, as we saw, the title "Son of Man" was already conferred on the creaturely man, is fulfilled. But that puts man, despite his continuing sinfulness, in the position of the mediator, the unifier of God and creature. Christ probably had this incalculable possibility in mind when he said: ". . . . he who believes in me, will also do the works that I do; and greater works than these will he do," [121] and, referring to the sixth verse of the Eighty-second Psalm, "I say, 'You are gods, sons of the Most High, all of you,'" he added, "and scripture cannot be broken." [122]

The future indwelling of the Holy Ghost in man amounts to a continuing incarnation of God. Christ, as the begotten son of God and pre-existing mediator, is a first-born and a divine paradigm which will be followed by further incarnations of the Holy Ghost in the empirical man. But man participates in the darkness of the world, and therefore, with Christ's death, a critical situation arises which might well be a cause for anxiety. When God became man all darkness and evil were carefully kept outside. Enoch's transformation into the Son of Man took place entirely in the realm of light, and to an even greater extent this is true of the incarnation in Christ. It is highly unlikely that the bond between God and man was broken with the death of Christ; on the contrary, the continuity of this bond is stressed again and again and is further confirmed by the sending of the Paraclete. But the closer this bond becomes,

[121] John 14 : 12.
[122] 10 : 35.

the closer becomes the danger of a collision with evil. On the basis of a belief that had existed quite early, the expectation grew up that the light manifestation would be followed by an equally dark one, and Christ by an Antichrist. Such an opinion is the last thing one would expect from the metaphysical situation, for the power of evil is supposedly overcome, and one can hardly believe that a loving father, after the whole complicated arrangement of salvation in Christ, the atonement and declaration of love for mankind, would again let loose his evil watch-dog on his children in complete disregard of all that had gone before. Why this wearisome forbearance towards Satan? Why this stubborn projection of evil on man, whom he has made so weak, so faltering, and so stupid that we are quite incapable of resisting his wicked sons? Why not pull up evil by the roots?

God, with his good intentions, begot a good and helpful son and thus created an image of himself as the good father—unfortunately, we must admit, again without considering that there existed in him a knowledge that spoke a very different truth. Had he only given an account of his action to himself, he would have seen what a fearful dissociation he had got into through his incarnation. Where, for instance, did his darkness go—that darkness by means of which Satan always manages to escape his well-earned punishment? Does he think he is completely changed and that his amorality has fallen from him? Even his "light" son, Christ, did not quite trust him in this respect. So now he sends to men the "spirit of truth," with whose help they will discover soon enough what happens when God incarnates only in his light aspect and believes he is goodness itself, or at least wants to be regarded as such. An enantiodromia in the grand style is to be expected. This may well be the meaning of the belief in the coming of the Antichrist, which we owe more than anything else to the activity of the "spirit of truth."

Although the Paraclete is of the greatest significance metaphysically, it was, from the point of view of the organization of the Church, most undesirable, because, as is authoritatively stated in scripture, the Holy Ghost is not subject to any control. In the interests of continuity and the Church the uniqueness of the incarnation and of Christ's work of redemption has to be strongly emphasized, and for the same reason the continuing indwelling of the Holy Ghost is discouraged and ignored as much as possible. No further individualistic digressions can be tolerated. Anyone who is inclined by the Holy Ghost towards dissident opinions necessarily becomes a heretic, whose persecution and elimination take a turn very much to Satan's liking. On the other hand one must realize that if everybody had tried to thrust the intuitions of his own private Holy Ghost upon others for the improvement of the universal doctrine, Christianity would rapidly have perished in a Babylonian confusion of tongues—a fate that lay threateningly close for many centuries.

It is the task of the Paraclete, the "spirit of truth," to dwell and work in individual human beings, so as to remind them of Christ's teachings and lead them into the light. A good example of this activity is Paul, who knew not the Lord and received his gospel not from the apostles but through revelation. He is one of those people whose unconscious was disturbed and produced revelatory ecstasies. The life of the Holy Ghost reveals itself through its own activity, and through effects which not only confirm the things we all know, but go beyond them. In Christ's sayings there are already indications of ideas which go beyond the traditionally "Christian" morality—for instance the parable of the unjust steward, the moral of which agrees with the Logion of the Codex Bezae,[123] and betrays an ethical standard very different from what is expected. Here the moral criterion is *consciousness,* and not law or convention. One might also mention the strange fact that it is precisely

---

[123] An apocryphal insertion at Luke 6. 4. ["Man, if indeed thou knowest what thou doest, thou art blessed; but if thou knowest not, thou art cursed, and a transgressor of the law" (translated in James, *The Apocryphal New Testament,* p. 33).—TRANSLATOR.]

Peter, who lacks self-control and is fickle in character, whom Christ wishes to make the rock and foundation of his Church. These seem to me to be ideas which point to the inclusion of evil in what I would call a *differential moral valuation*. For instance, it is good if evil is sensibly covered up, but to act unconsciously is evil. One might almost suppose that such views were intended for a time when consideration is given to evil as well as to good, or rather, when it is not suppressed below the threshold in the dubious assumption that we always know exactly what evil is.

Again, the expectation of the Antichrist is a far-reaching revelation or discovery, like the remarkable statement that despite his fall and exile the devil is still "prince of this world" and has his habitation in the all-surrounding air. In spite of his misdeeds and in spite of God's work of redemption for mankind, the devil still maintains a position of considerable power and holds all sublunary creatures under his sway. This situation can only be described as critical; at any rate it does not correspond to what could reasonably have been expected from the "glad tidings." Evil is by no means fettered, even though its days are numbered. God still hesitates to use force against Satan. Presumably he still does not know how much his own dark side favours the evil angel. Naturally this situation could not remain indefinitely hidden from the "spirit of truth" who has taken up his abode in man. He therefore created a disturbance in man's unconscious and produced, at the beginning of the Christian era, another great revelation which, because of its obscurity, gave rise to numerous interpretations and misinterpretations in the centuries that followed. This is the Revelation of St. John.

# XIII

One could hardly imagine a more suitable personality for the John of the Apocalypse than the author of the Epistles of John. It was he who declared that God is light and that "in him is no darkness at all." [124] (Who said there was any darkness in God?) Nevertheless, he knows that when we sin we need an "advocate with the Father," and this is Christ, "the expiation for our sins," [125] even though for his sake our sins are already forgiven. (Why then do we need an advocate?) The Father has bestowed his great love upon us (though it had to be bought at the cost of a human sacrifice!), and we are the children of God. He who is begotten by God commits no sin.[126] (Who commits *no* sin?) John then preaches the message of love. God himself is love; perfect love casteth out fear. But he must warn against false prophets and teachers of false doctrines, and it is he who announces the coming of the Antichrist.[127] His conscious attitude is orthodox, but he has evil forebodings. He might easily have dreams that are not listed on his conscious programme. He talks as if he knew not only a sinless state but also a perfect love, unlike Paul, who was not lacking in the necessary self-reflection. John is a bit too sure, and therefore he runs the risk of a dissociation. Under these circumstances a counterposition is bound to grow up in the unconscious, which can then irrupt into consciousness in the form of a revelation. If this happens, the revelation will take the form of a more or less subjective myth, because, among other things, it compensates the one-sidedness of an individual consciousness. This contrasts with the visions of Ezekiel or Enoch, whose conscious situation was mainly characterized by an ignorance (for which they were not to blame) and was therefore compensated by a more or less objective and universally valid configuration of archetypal material.

So far as we can see, the Apocalypse conforms to these conditions. Even in the initial vision a fear-inspiring figure appears: Christ blended with the Ancient of Days, having

[124] I John 1 : 5.
[125] 2 : 1–2.
[126] 3 : 9.
[127] 2 : 18f., 4 : 3.

the likeness of a man and the Son of Man. Out of his mouth goes a "sharp two-edged sword," which would seem more suitable for fighting and the shedding of blood than for demonstrating brotherly love. Since this Christ says to him, "Fear not," we must assume that John was not overcome by love when he fell "as though dead," [128] but rather by fear. (What price now the perfect love which casts out fear?)

Christ commands him to write seven epistles to the churches in the province of Asia. The church in Ephesus is admonished to repent; otherwise it is threatened with deprivation of the light ("I will come . . . and remove your candlestick from its place").[129] We also learn from this letter that Christ "hates" the Nicolaitans. (How does this square with love of your neighbour?)

The church in Smyrna does not come off so badly. Its enemies supposedly are Jews, but they are "a synagogue of Satan," which does not sound too friendly.

Pergamum is censured because a teacher of false doctrines is making himself conspicuous there, and the place swarms with Nicolaitans. Therefore it must repent—"if not, I will come to you soon." This can only be interpreted as a threat.

Thyatira tolerates the preaching of "that woman Jezebel, who calls herself a prophetess." He will "throw her on a sickbed" and "strike her children dead." But "he who . . . keeps my works until the end, I will give him power over the nations, and he shall rule them with a rod of iron, as when earthen pots are broken in pieces, even as I myself have received power from my Father; and I will give him the morning star." [130] Christ, as we know, teaches "Love your enemies," but here he threatens a massacre of children all too reminiscent of Bethlehem!

The works of the church in Sardis are not perfect before

[128] Cf. Rev. 1 : 16–17.
[129] Rev. 2 : 5.
[130] 2 : 20f.

God. Therefore, "repent." Otherwise he will come like a thief, "and you will not know at what hour I will come upon you" [131]—a none too friendly warning.

In regard to Philadelphia, there is nothing to be censured. But Laodicea he will spew out of his mouth, because they are lukewarm. They too must repent. His explanation is characteristic: "Those whom I love, I reprove and chasten." [132] It would be quite understandable if the Laodiceans did not want too much of this "love."

Five of the seven churches get bad reports. This apocalyptic "Christ" behaves rather like a bad-tempered, power-conscious "boss" who very much resembles the "shadow" of a love-preaching bishop.

As if in confirmation of what I have said, there now follows a vision in the style of Ezekiel. But he who sat upon the throne did not look like a man, but was to look upon "like jasper and carnelian." [133] Before him was "a sea of glass, like crystal"; around the throne, four "living creatures" ($\zeta\omega\alpha$), which were "full of eyes in front and behind . . . all round and within." [134] The symbol of Ezekiel appears here strangely modified: stone, glass, crystal—dead and rigid things deriving from the inorganic realm—characterize the Deity. One is inevitably reminded of the preoccupation of the alchemists during the following centuries, when the mysterious "Man," the *homo altus,* was named $\lambda i\theta o\varsigma$ $o\dot{v}$ $\lambda i\theta o\varsigma$, "the stone that is no stone," and multiple eyes gleamed in the ocean of the unconscious.[135] At any rate, something of John's psychology comes in here, which has caught a glimpse of things beyond the Christian cosmos.

Hereupon follows the opening of the Book with Seven Seals by the "Lamb." The latter has put off the human fea-

---

[131] 3 : 3.
[132] 3 : 19.
[133] 4 : 3.
[134] 4 : 6f.
[135] This refers to the "luminosity" of the archetypes. [Cf. Jung, "On the Nature of the Psyche," (*Collected Works,* Vol. 8), pp. 190ff.— EDITORS OF *The Collected Works.*]

tures of the "Ancient of Days" and now appears in purely theriomorphic but monstrous form, like one of the many other horned animals in the Book of Revelation. It has seven eyes and seven horns, and is therefore more like a ram than a lamb. Altogether it must have looked pretty awful. Although it is described as "standing, as though it had been slain," [136] it does not behave at all like an innocent victim, but in a very lively manner indeed. From the first four seals it lets loose the four sinister apocalyptic horsemen. With the opening of the fifth seal, we hear the martyrs crying for vengeance ("O sovereign Lord, holy and true, how long before thou wilt judge and avenge our blood on those who dwell upon the earth?").[137] The sixth seal brings a cosmic catastrophe, and everything hides from the "wrath of the Lamb," "for the great day of his wrath is come." [138] We no longer recognize the meek Lamb who lets himself be led unresistingly to the slaughter; there is only the aggressive and irascible ram whose rage can at last be vented. In all this I see less a metaphysical mystery than the outburst of long pent-up negative feelings such as can frequently be observed in people who strive for perfection. We can take it as certain that the author of the Epistles of John made every effort to practise what he preached to his fellow Christians. For this purpose he had to shut out all negative feelings, and, thanks to a helpful lack of self-reflection, he was able to forget them. But though they disappeared from the conscious level they continued to rankle beneath the surface, and in the course of time spun an elaborate web of resentments and vengeful thoughts which then burst upon consciousness in the form of a revelation. From this there grew up a terrifying picture that blatantly contradicts all ideas of Christian humility, tolerance, love of your neighbour and your enemies, and makes nonsense of a loving father in heaven and rescuer of mankind.

[136] Rev. 5 : 6.
[137] 6 : 10.
[138] 6 : 17 (AV).

A veritable orgy of hatred, wrath, vindictiveness, and blind destructive fury that revels in fantastic images of terror breaks out and with blood and fire overwhelms a world which Christ had just endeavoured to restore to the original state of innocence and loving communion with God.

The opening of the seventh seal naturally brings a new flood of miseries which threaten to exhaust even St. John's unholy imagination. As if to fortify himself, he must now eat a "little scroll" in order to go on with his "prophesying."

When the seventh angel had finally ceased blowing his trumpet, there appeared in heaven, after the destruction of Jerusalem, a vision of the *sun-woman,* "with the moon under her feet, and on her head a crown of twelve stars." [139] She was in the pangs of birth, and before her stood a great red dragon that wanted to devour her child.

This vision is altogether out of context. Whereas with the previous visions one has the impression that they were afterwards revised, rearranged, and embellished, one feels that this image is original and not intended for any educational purpose. The vision is introduced by the opening of the temple in heaven and the sight of the Ark of the Covenant.[140] This is probably a prelude to the descent of the heavenly bride, Jerusalem, an equivalent of Sophia, for it is all part of the heavenly *hieros gamos,* whose fruit is a divine man-child. He is threatened with the fate of Apollo, the son of Leto, who was likewise pursued by a dragon. But here we must dwell for a moment on the figure of the mother. She is "a woman clothed with the sun." Note the simple statement "a woman"—an ordinary woman, not a goddess and not an eternal virgin immaculately conceived. No special precautions exempting her from complete womanhood are noticeable, except the cosmic and naturalistic attributes which mark her as an

[139] Rev. 12 : 1.
[140] Rev. 11 : 19. The *arca foederis* is an *allegoria Mariae*.

*anima mundi* and peer of the primordial cosmic man, or Anthropos. She is the feminine Anthropos, the counterpart of the masculine principle. The pagan Leto motif is eminently suited to illustrate this, for in Greek mythology matriarchal and patriarchal elements are about equally mixed. The stars above, the moon below, in the middle the sun, the rising Horus and the setting Osiris, and the maternal night all round, οὐρανὸς ἄνω, οὐρανὸς κάτω[141]—this symbolism reveals the whole mystery of the "woman": she contains in her darkness the sun of "masculine" consciousness, which rises as a child out of the nocturnal sea of the unconscious, and as an old man sinks into it again. She adds the dark to the light, symbolizes the hierogamy of opposites, and reconciles nature with spirit.

The son who is born of these heavenly nuptials is perforce a *complexio oppositorum,* a uniting symbol, a totality of life. John's unconscious, certainly not without reason, borrowed from Greek mythology in order to describe this strange eschatological experience, for it was not on any account to be confused with the birth of the Christ-child which had occurred long before under quite different circumstances. Though obviously the allusion is to the "wrathful Lamb," i.e., the apocalyptic Christ, the newborn man-child is represented as his duplicate, as one who will "rule the nations with a rod of iron." [142] He is thus assimilated to the predominant feelings of hatred and vengeance, so that it looks as if he will needlessly continue to wreak his judgment even in the distant future. This interpretation does not seem consistent, because the Lamb is already charged with this task and, in the course of the revelation, carries it to an end without the new-born man-child ever having an opportunity to act on his own. He never reappears afterwards. I am therefore inclined to believe that the depiction of him as a son of vengeance, if it is not an interpretative interpolation, must have been

[141] "Heaven above, heaven below."
[142] Rev. 12 : 5; cf. 2 : 27.

a familiar phrase to John and that it slipped out as the obvious interpretation. This is the more probable in that the intermezzo could not at the time have been understood in any other way, even though this interpretation is quite meaningless. As I have already pointed out, the sun-woman episode is a foreign body in the flow of the visions. Therefore, I believe, it is not too far-fetched to conjecture that the author of the Apocalypse, or perhaps a perplexed transcriber, felt the need to interpret this obvious parallel with Christ and somehow bring it into line with the text as a whole. This could easily be done by using the familiar image of the shepherd with the iron crook. I cannot see any other reason for this association.

The man-child is "caught up" to God, who is manifestly his father, and the mother is hidden in the wilderness. This would seem to indicate that the child-figure will remain latent for an indefinite time and that its activity is reserved for the future. The story of Hagar may be a prefiguration of this. The similarity between this story and the birth of Christ obviously means no more than that the birth of the man-child is an analogous event, like the previously mentioned enthronement of the Lamb in all his metaphysical glory, which must have taken place long before at the time of the ascension. In the same way the dragon, i.e., the devil, is described as being thrown down to earth,[143] although Christ had already observed the fall of Satan very much earlier. This strange repetition or duplication of the characteristic events in Christ's life gave rise to the conjecture that a second Messiah is to be expected at the end of the world. What is meant here cannot be the return of Christ himself, for we are told that he would come "in the clouds of heaven," but not be *born* a second time, and certainly not from a sun-moon conjunction. The epiphany at the end of the world corresponds more to the content of Revelation 1 and 19 : 11ff. The fact that John uses the myth of Leto and Apollo in de-

[143] Rev. 12 : 9.

scribing the birth may be an indication that the vision, in contrast to the Christian tradition, is a product of the unconscious.[144] But in the unconscious is everything that has been rejected by consciousness, and the more Christian one's consciousness is, the more heathenishly does the unconscious behave, if in the rejected heathenism there are values which are important for life—if, that is to say, the baby has been thrown out with the bath water, as so often happens. The unconscious does not isolate or differentiate its objects as consciousness does. It does not think abstractly or apart from the subject: the person of the ecstatic or visionary is always drawn into the process and included in it. In this case it is John himself whose unconscious personality is more or less identified with Christ; that is to say, he is born like Christ, and born to a like destiny. John is so completely captivated by the archetype of the divine son that he sees its activity in the unconscious; in other words, he sees how God is born again in the (partly pagan) unconscious, indistinguishable from the self of John, since the "divine child" is a symbol of the one as much as the other, just as Christ is. Consciously, of course, John was very far from thinking of Christ as a symbol. For the believing Christian, Christ is everything, but certainly not a symbol, which is an expression for something unknown or not yet knowable. And yet he is a symbol by his very nature. Christ would never have made the impression he did on his followers if he had not expressed something that was alive and at work in their unconscious. Christianity itself would never have spread through the pagan world with such astonishing rapidity had its ideas not found an analogous psychic readiness to receive them. It is this fact which also makes it possible to say that whoever believes in Christ is not only contained

---

[144] It is very probable that John knew that Leto myth and used it consciously. What was unconscious and most unexpected, however, was the fact that his unconscious used this pagan myth to describe the birth of the second Messiah.

in him, but that Christ then dwells in the believer as the perfect man formed in the image of God, the second Adam. Psychologically, it is the same relationship as that in Indian philosophy between man's ego-consciousness and *purusha,* or *ātman.* It is the ascendancy of the "complete" —τέλειος—or total human being, consisting of the totality of the psyche, of conscious and unconscious, over the ego, which represents only consciousness and its contents and knows nothing of the unconscious, although in many respects it is dependent on the unconscious and is often decisively influenced by it. This relationship of the self to the ego is reflected in the relationship of Christ to man. Hence the unmistakable analogies between certain Indian and Christian ideas, which have given rise to conjectures of Indian influence on Christianity.

This parallelism, which has so far remained latent in John, now bursts into consciousness in the form of a vision. That this invasion is authentic can be seen from the use of pagan mythological material, a most improbable procedure for a Christian of that time, especially as it contains traces of astrological influence. That may explain the thoroughly pagan remark, "And the earth helped the woman." [145] Even though the consciousness of that age was exclusively filled with Christian ideas, earlier or contemporaneous pagan contents lay just below the surface, as for example in the case of St. Perpetua.[146] With a Judaeo-Christian—and the author of the Apocalypse was probably such—another possible model to be considered is the cosmic Sophia, to whom John refers on more than one occasion. She could easily be taken as the mother of the divine child,[147] since she is obviously a woman in

---

[145] Rev. 12 : 16 (AV).
[146] [Cf. Marie-Louise von Franz, "Die Passio Perpetuae," in *Aion: Untersuchungen zur Symbolgeschichte,* by C. G. Jung and Marie-Louise von Franz (Zurich, 1951).—EDITORS OF *The Collected Works.*]
[147] The son would then correspond to the *filius sapientiae* of medieval alchemy.

heaven, i.e., a goddess or consort of a god. Sophia comes up to this definition, and so does the transfigured Mary. If the vision were a modern dream one would not hesitate to interpret the birth of the divine child as the coming to consciousness of the self. In John's case the conscious attitude of faith made it possible for the Christ-image to be received into the material of the unconscious; it activated the archetype of the divine virgin mother and of the birth of her son-lover, and brought it face to face with his Christian consciousness. As a result, John became personally involved in the divine drama.

His Christ-image, clouded by negative feelings, has turned into a savage avenger who no longer bears any real resemblance to a saviour. One is not at all sure whether this Christ-figure may not in the end have more of the human John in it, with his compensating shadow, than of the divine saviour who, as the *lumen de lumine,* contains "no darkness." The grotesque paradox of the "wrathful Lamb" should have been enough to arouse our suspicions in this respect. We can turn and twist it as we like, but, seen in the light of the gospel of love, the avenger and judge remains a most sinister figure. This, one suspects, may have been the reason which moved John to assimilate the new-born man-child to the figure of the avenger, thereby blurring his mythological character as the lovely and lovable divine youth whom we know so well in the figures of Tammuz, Adonis, and Balder. The enchanting springlike beauty of this divine youth is one of those pagan values which we miss so sorely in Christianity, and particularly in the sombre world of the apocalypse—the indescribable morning glory of a day in spring, which after the deathly stillness of winter causes the earth to put forth and blossom, gladdens the heart of man and makes him believe in a kind and loving God.

As a totality, the self is by definition always a *complexio oppositorum,* and the more consciousness insists on its own luminous nature and lays claim to moral authority, the more the self will appear as something dark and menacing. We may assume such a condition in John, since he was a shepherd of his flock and also a fallible human being. Had the Apocalypse been a more or less personal affair of John's, and hence nothing but an outburst of personal resentment, the figure of the wrathful Lamb would have satisfied this need completely. Under those conditions the new-born man-child would have been bound to have a noticeably positive aspect, because, in accordance with his symbolic nature, he would have compensated the intolerable devastation wrought by the outburst of long pent-up passions, being the child of the conjunction of opposites, of the sunfilled day world and the moonlit night world. He would have acted as a mediator between the loving and the vengeful sides of John's nature, and would thus have become a beneficent saviour who restored the balance. This positive aspect, however, must have escaped John's notice, otherwise he could never have conceived of the child as standing on the same level as the avenging Christ.

But John's problem was not a personal one. It was not a question of his personal unconscious or of an outburst of ill humour, but of visions which came up from a far greater and more comprehensive depth, namely from the collective unconscious. His problem expresses itself far too much in collective and archetypal forms for us to reduce it to a merely personal situation. To do so would be altogether too easy as well as being wrong in theory and practice. As a Christian, John was seized by a collective, archetypal process, and he must therefore be explained first and foremost in that light. He certainly also had his personal psychology, into which we, if we may regard the author of the Epistles and the apocalyptist as one and the same person, have some insight. That the imitation of Christ creates a corresponding shadow in the unconscious hardly needs demonstrating. The fact that John had visions at all is evidence of an unusual tension between conscious and unconscious. If he is identical with the author of the

Epistles, he must have been quite old when he wrote the Book of Revelation. *In confinio mortis* and in the evening of a long and eventful life a man will often see immense vistas of time stretching out before him. Such a man no longer lives in the everyday world and in the vicissitudes of personal relationships, but in the sight of many aeons and in the movement of ideas as they pass from century to century. The eye of John penetrates into the distant future of the Christian aeon and into the dark abyss of those forces which his Christianity kept in equilibrium. What burst upon him is the storm of the times, the premonition of a tremendous enantiodromia which he could only understand as the final annihilation of the darkness which had not comprehended the light that appeared in Christ. He failed to see that the power of destruction and vengeance is that very darkness from which God had split himself off when he became man. Therefore he could not understand, either, what that sun-moon-child meant, and he could only interpret it as another figure of vengeance. The passion that breaks through in his revelation bears no trace of the feebleness or serenity of old age, because it is infinitely more than personal resentment: it is the spirit of God itself, which blows through the weak mortal frame and again demands man's *fear* of the unfathomable Godhead.

## XIV

The torrent of negative feelings seems to be inexhaustible, and the dire events continue their course. Out of the sea come monsters "with horns" (i.e., endowed with power), the horrid progeny of the deep. Faced with all this darkness and destruction, man's terrified consciousness quite understandably looks round for a mountain of refuge, an island of peace and safety. John therefore weaves in a vision of the Lamb on Mount Zion, where the hundred and forty-four thousand elect and redeemed are gathered round the Lamb.[148] They are the παρθένοι, the male virgins, "which were not defiled with women." [149] They are the ones who, following in the footsteps of the young dying god, have never become complete human beings, but have voluntarily renounced their share in the human lot and have said no to the continuance of life on earth.[150] If everyone were converted to this point of view, man as a species would die out in a few decades. But of such pre-ordained ones there are relatively few. John believed in predestination in accordance with higher authority. This is rank pessimism.

> Everything created
> Is worth being liquidated

says Mephisto.

This only moderately comforting prospect is immediately interrupted by the warning angels. The first angel proclaims an "everlasting gospel," the quintessence of which is "Fear God!" There is no more talk of God's love. What is feared can only be something fearful.[151]

The Son of Man now appears holding a sharp sickle in his hand, together with an auxiliary angel who also has a sickle.[152] But the grape harvest consists in an unparalleled blood-bath: the angel "gathered the vintage of the earth, and threw it into the great winepress of the wrath of God . . . and blood flowed from the winepress"—in

[148] Rev. 14 : 1. It may be significant that there is no longer any talk of the "great multitude which no man could number, from every nation, from all tribes and peoples and tongues, standing before the throne and before the Lamb," who were mentioned in 7 : 9.

[149] 14 : 4 (AV).

[150] They really belong to the cult of the Great Mother, since they correspond to the emasculated Galli. Cf. the strange passage in Matthew 19 : 12, about the eunuchs "who have made themselves eunuchs for the sake of the kingdom of heaven," like the priests of Cybele who used to castrate themselves in honour of her son Attis.

[151] Cf. also Rev. 19 : 5.

[152] 14 : 14 and 17. The auxiliary angel might well be John himself.

which human beings were trodden!—"as high as a horse's
bridle, for one thousand six hundred stadia." [153]

Seven angels then come out of the heavenly temple with
the seven vials of wrath, which they proceed to pour out
on the earth.[154] The *pièce de résistance* is the destruction
of the Great Whore of Babylon, the counterpart of the
heavenly Jerusalem. The Whore is the chthonic equivalent
of the sun-woman Sophia, with, however, a reversal in
moral character. If the elect turn themselves into "virgins"
in honour of the Great Mother Sophia, a gruesome fantasy
of fornication is spawned in the unconscious by way of
compensation. The destruction of Babylon therefore represents not only the end of fornication, but the utter erad-
ication of all life's joys and pleasures, as can be seen from
18 : 22–23:

and the sound of harpers and minstrels, of flute players
    and trumpeters.
shall be heard in thee no more;
   .   .   .   .   .   .   .   .   .     .   .   .   .   .
and the light of a lamp
    shall shine in thee no more;
and the voice of bridegroom and bride
    shall be heard in thee no more . . .

As we happen to be living at the end of the Christian
aeon Pisces, one cannot help but recall the doom that has
overtaken our modern art.

Symbols like Jerusalem, Babylon, etc. are always over-
determined, that is, they have several aspects of meaning
and can therefore be interpreted in different ways. I am
only concerned with the psychological aspect, and do not
wish to express an opinion as to their possible connection
with historical events.

The destruction of all beauty and of all life's joys, the
unspeakable suffering of the whole of creation that once

[153] 14 : 19–20.
[154] 15 : 6–7 and 16 : 1ff.

sprang from the hand of a lavish Creator, would be, for a feeling heart, an occasion for deepest melancholy. But John cries: "Rejoice over her, thou heaven, ye holy apostles and prophets, for God hath avenged you on her [Babylon]," [155] from which we can see how far vindictiveness and lust for destruction can go, and what the "thorn in the flesh" means.

It is Christ who, leading the hosts of angels, treads "the winepress of the fierceness and wrath of Almighty God." [156] His robe "is dipped in blood." [157] He rides a *white horse*,[158] and with the sword which issues out of his mouth he kills the beast and the "false prophet," presumably his—or John's—dark counterpart, i.e., the shadow. Satan is locked up in the bottomless pit for a thousand years, and *Christ shall reign for the same length of time.* "After that he must be loosed a little season." [159] These thousand years correspond astrologically to the first half of the Pisces aeon. The setting free of Satan after this time must therefore correspond—one cannot imagine any other reason for it—to the enantiodromia of the Christian aeon, that is, to the reign of the Antichrist, whose coming could be predicted on astrological grounds. Finally, at the end of an unspecified period, the devil is thrown into the lake of fire and brimstone for ever and ever (but not completely destroyed as in Enoch), and the whole of the first creation disappears.[160]

The *hieros gamos,* the marriage of the Lamb with "his Bride," which had been announced earlier,[161] can now take place. The bride is the "new Jerusalem coming down out of heaven." [162] Her "radiance [was] like a most rare

[155] Rev. 18 : 20 (AV).
[156] 19 : 15 (AV).
[157] 19 : 13.
[158] 19 : 11. Here again astrological speculations concerning the second half of the Christian aeon may be implied, with Pegasus as paranatellon of Aquarius.
[159] Rev. 20 : 3 (AV).
[160] 20 : 10 and 21 : 1.
[161] 19 : 7.
[162] 21 : 2.

jewel, like a jasper, clear as crystal." [163] The city was built foursquare and was of pure gold, clear as glass, and so were its streets. The Lord God himself and the Lamb are its temple, and the source of never-ending light. There is no night in the city, and nothing unclean can enter in to defile it.[164] (This repeated assurance allays a doubt in John that has never been quite silenced.) From the throne of God and the Lamb flows the river of the water of life, and beside it stands the tree of life, as a reminder of paradise and pleromatic pre-existence.[165]

This final vision, which is generally interpreted as referring to the relationship of Christ to his Church, has the meaning of a "uniting symbol" and is therefore a representation of perfection and wholeness: hence the quaternity, which expresses itself in the city as a quadrangle, in paradise as the four rivers, in Christ as the four evangelists, and in God as the four living creatures. While the circle signifies the roundness of heaven and the all-embracing nature of the "pneumatic" deity, the square refers to the earth.[166] Heaven is masculine, but the earth is feminine. Therefore God has his throne in heaven, while Wisdom has hers on the earth, as she says in Ecclesiasticus: "Likewise in the beloved city he gave me rest, and in Jerusalem was my power." She is the "mother of fair love," [167] and when John pictures Jerusalem as the bride he is probably following Ecclesiasticus. The city is Sophia, who was with God before time began, and at the end of time will be reunited with God through the sacred marriage. As a feminine being she coincides with the earth, from which, so a Church Father tell us, Christ was born,[168] and hence

[163] 21 : 11.
[164] 21 : 16–27.
[165] 22 : 1–2.
[166] In China, heaven is round and the earth square.
[167] Ecclesiasticus 24 : 11 and 18 (AV).
[168] Tertullian, *Adversus Judaeos,* XIII (Migne, *P.L.*, Vol. 2, col. 635): ". . . illa terra virgo nondum pluviis rigata nec imbribus foecundata, ex qua homo tunc primum plasmatus est, ex qua nunc Christus secundum carnem ex virgine natus est" (. . . that virgin soil, not yet watered by the rains nor fertilized by the showers, from

with the quaternity of the four living creatures in whom God manifests himself in Ezekiel. In the same way that Sophia signifies God's self-reflection, the four seraphim represent God's consciousness with its four functional aspects. The many perceiving eyes[169] which are concentrated in the four wheels point in the same direction. They represent a fourfold synthesis of unconscious luminosities, corresponding to the tetrameria of the *lapis philosophorum*, of which the description of the heavenly city reminds us: everything sparkles with precious gems, crystal, and glass, in complete accordance with Ezekiel's vision of God. And just as the *hieros gamos* unites Yahweh with Sophia (Shekinah in the Cabala), thus restoring the original pleromatic state, so the parallel description of God and city points to their common nature: they are originally one, a single hermaphroditic being, an archetype of the greatest universality.

No doubt this is meant as a final solution of the terrible conflict of existence. The solution, however, as here presented, does not consist in the reconciliation of the opposites, but in their final severance, by which means those whose destiny it is to be saved can save themselves by identifying with the bright pneumatic side of God. An indispensable condition for this seems to be the denial of propagation and of sexual life altogether.

# XV

The Book of Revelation is on the one hand so personal and on the other so archetypal and collective that one is obliged to consider both aspects. Our modern interest would certainly turn first to the person of John. As I have said before, it is possible that John the author of the

---

which man was originally formed [and] from which Christ is now born of a Virgin through the flesh).
[169] Ezekiel 1 : 18.

Epistles is identical with the apocalyptist. The psychological findings speak in favour of such an assumption. The "revelation" was experienced by an early Christian who, as a leading light of the community, presumably had to live an exemplary life and demonstrate to his flock the Christian virtues of true faith, humility, patience, devotion, selfless love, and denial of all worldly desires. In the long run this can become too much, even for the most righteous. Irritability, bad moods, and outbursts of affect are the classic symptoms of chronic virtuousness.[170] In regard to his Christian attitude, his own words probably give us the best picture:

> Beloved, let us love one another; for love is of God, and he who loves is born of God and knows God. He who does not love does not know God; for God is love. . . . In this is love, not that we loved God but that he loved us and sent his Son to be the expiation for our sins. Beloved, if God so loved us, we also ought to love one another. . . . So we know and believe the love God has for us. God is love, and he who abides in love abides in God, and God abides in him. . . . There is no fear in love, but perfect love casts out fear. For fear has to do with punishment, and he who fears is not perfected in love. . . . If any one says, "I love God," and hates his brother, he is a liar; for he who does not love his brother whom he has seen, cannot love God whom he has not seen. And this commandment we have from him, that he who loves God should love his brother also.[171]

But who hates the Nicolaitans? Who thirsts for vengeance and even wants to throw "that woman Jezebel" on a sickbed and strike her children dead? Who cannot have enough of bloodthirsty fantasies? Let us be psychologically correct, however: it is not the conscious mind of John that thinks up these fantasies, they come to him in a violent "revelation." They fall upon him involuntarily with an un-

[170] Not for nothing was the apostle John nicknamed "son of thunder" by Christ.

[171] I John 4 : 7-21.

expected vehemence and with an intensity which, as said, far transcends anything we could expect as compensation of a somewhat one-sided attitude of consciousness.

I have seen many compensating dreams of believing Christians who deceived themselves about their real psychic constitution and imagined that they were in a different condition from what they were in reality. But I have seen nothing that even remotely resembles the brutal impact with which the opposites collide in John's visions, except in the case of severe psychosis. However, John gives us no grounds for such a diagnosis. His apocalyptic visions are not confused enough; they are too consistent, not subjective and scurrilous enough. Considering the nature of their subject, the accompanying affects are adequate. Their author need not necessarily be an unbalanced psychopath. It is sufficient that he is a passionately religious person with an otherwise well-ordered psyche. But he must have an intensive relationship to God which lays him open to an invasion far transcending anything personal. The really religious person, in whom the capacity for an unusual extension of consciousness is inborn, must be prepared for such dangers.

The purpose of the apocalyptic visions is not to tell John, as an ordinary human being, how much shadow he hides beneath his luminous nature, but to open the seer's eye to the immensity of God, for he who loves God will know God. We can say that just because John loved God and did his best to love his fellows also, this "gnosis," this knowledge of God, struck him. Like Job, he saw the fierce and terrible side of Yahweh. For this reason he felt his gospel of love to be one-sided, and he supplemented it with the gospel of fear: *God can be loved but must be feared.*

With this, the seer's range of vision extends far beyond the first half of the Christian aeon: he divines that the reign of Antichrist will begin after a thousand years, a clear indication that Christ was not an unqualified victor.

John anticipated the alchemists and Jakob Böhme; maybe he even sensed his own personal implication in the divine drama, since he anticipated the possibility of God's birth in man, which the alchemists, Meister Eckhart, and Angelus Silesius also intuited. He thus outlined the programme for the whole aeon of Pisces, with its dramatic enantiodromia, and its dark end which we have still to experience, and before whose—without exaggeration—truly apocalyptic possibilities mankind shudders. The four sinister horsemen, the threatening tumult of trumpets, and the brimming vials of wrath are still waiting; already the atom bomb hangs over us like the sword of Damocles, and behind that lurk the incomparably more terrible possibilities of chemical warfare, which would eclipse even the horrors described in the Apocalypse. *Luciferi vires accendit Aquarius acres*—"Aquarius sets aflame Lucifer's harsh forces." Could anyone in his right senses deny that John correctly foresaw at least some of the possible dangers which threaten our world in the final phase of the Christian aeon? He knew, also, that the fire in which the devil is tormented burns in the divine pleroma for ever. God has a terrible double aspect: a sea of grace is met by a seething lake of fire, and the light of love glows with a fierce dark heat of which it is said "ardet non lucet"—it burns but gives no light. That is the eternal, as distinct from the temporal, gospel: *one can love God but must fear him.*

## XVI

The Book of Revelation, rightly placed at the end of the New Testament, reaches beyond it into a future that is all too palpably close with its apocalyptic terrors. The decision of an ill-considered moment, made in some Herostratic head,[172] can suffice to unleash the world cataclysm. The

[172] [Herostratus, in order to make his name immortal, burned down the temple of Artemis in Ephesus, in 365 B.C.—EDITORS OF *The Collected Works.*]

thread by which our fate hangs is wearing thin. Not nature, but the "genius of mankind," has knotted the hangman's noose with which it can execute itself at any moment. This is simply another *façon de parler* for what John called the "wrath of God."

Unfortunately we have no means of envisaging how John—if, as I surmise, he is the same as the author of the Epistles—would have come to terms with the double aspect of God. It is possible, even probable, that he was not aware of any contrast. It is altogether amazing how little most people reflect on numinous objects and attempt to come to terms with them, and how laborious such an undertaking is once we have embarked upon it. The numinosity of the object makes it difficult to handle intellectually, since our affectivity is always involved. One always participates for or against, and "absolute objectivity" is more rarely achieved here than anywhere else. If one has positive religious convictions, i.e., if one believes, then doubt is felt as very disagreeable and also one fears it. For this reason, one prefers not to analyze the object of belief. If one has no religious beliefs, then one does not like to admit the feeling of deficit, but prates loudly about one's liberal-mindedness and pats oneself on the back for the noble frankness of one's agnosticism. From this standpoint, it is hardly possible to admit the numinosity of the religious object, and yet its very numinosity is just as great a hindrance to critical thinking, because the unpleasant possibility might then arise that one's faith in enlightenment or agnosticism would be shaken. Both types feel, without knowing it, the insufficiency of their argument. Enlightenment operates with an inadequate rationalistic concept of truth and points triumphantly to the fact that beliefs such as the virgin birth, divine filiation, the resurrection of the dead, transubstantiation, etc., are all moonshine. Agnosticism maintains that it does not possess any knowledge of God or of anything metaphysical, overlooking the fact that one never *possesses* a metaphysical belief but is *possessed by it*. Both are possessed by reason, which represents the supreme arbiter who cannot be argued with. But who or what is this "reason" and why should it be supreme? Is not something that *is* and has real existence for us an authority superior to any rational judgment, as has been shown over and over again in the history of the human mind? Unfortunately the defenders of "faith" operate with the same futile arguments, only the other way about. The only thing which is beyond doubt is that there are metaphysical statements which are asserted or denied with considerable affect precisely because of their numinosity. This fact gives us a sure empirical basis from which to proceed. It is objectively real as a psychic phenomenon. The same applies naturally to all statements, even the most contradictory, that ever were or still are numinous. From now on we shall have to consider religious statements in their totality.

## XVII

Let us turn back to the question of coming to terms with the paradoxical idea of God which the Apocalypse reveals to us. Evangelical Christianity, in the strict sense, has no need to bother with it, because it has as an essential doctrine an idea of God that, unlike Yahweh, coincides with the epitome of good. It would have been very different if the John of the Epistles had been obliged to discuss these matters with the John of Revelation. Later generations could afford to ignore the dark side of the Apocalypse, because the specifically Christian achievement was something that was not to be frivolously endangered. But for modern man the case is quite otherwise. We have experienced things so unheard of and so staggering that the question of whether such things are in any way reconcilable with the idea of a good God has become burningly topical. It is no longer a problem for experts in theological seminaries, but a universal religious nightmare, to the solution of which even a layman in theology like myself can, or perhaps must, make a contribution.

I have tried to set forth above the inescapable conclusions which must, I believe, be reached if one looks at tradition with critical common sense. If, in this wise, one is confronted with a paradoxical idea of God, and if, as a religious person, one considers at the same time the full extent of the problem, one finds oneself in the situation of the author of Revelation, who we may suppose was a convinced Christian. His possible identity with the writer of the letters brings out the acuteness of the contradiction: What is the relationship of this man to God? How does he endure the intolerable contradiction in the nature of Deity? Although we know nothing of his conscious decision, we believe we may find some clue in the vision of the sun-woman in travail.

The paradoxical nature of God has a like effect on man: it tears him asunder into opposites and delivers him over to a seemingly insoluble conflict. What happens in such a condition? Here we must let psychology speak, for psychology represents the sum of all the observations and insights it has gained from the empirical study of severe states of conflict. There are, for example, conflicts of duty no one knows how to solve. Consciousness only knows: *tertium non datur!* The doctor therefore advises his patient to wait and see whether the unconscious will not produce a dream which proposes an irrational and therefore unexpected third thing as a solution. As experience shows, symbols of a reconciling and unitive nature do in fact turn up in dreams, the most frequent being the motif of the child-hero and the squaring of the circle, signifying the union of opposites. Those who have no access to these specifically medical experiences can derive practical instruction from fairy tales, and particularly from alchemy. The real subject of Hermetic philosophy is the *coniunctio oppositorum.* Alchemy characterizes its "child" on the one hand as the stone (e.g., the carbuncle), and on the other hand as the homunculus, or the *filius sapientiae* or even the *homo altus.* This is precisely the figure we meet in the Apocalypse as the son of the sun-woman, whose birth story seems like a paraphrase of the birth of Christ—a paraphrase which was repeated in various forms by the alchemists. In fact, they posit their stone as a parallel to Christ (this, with one exception, without reference to the Book of Revelation). This motif appears again in corresponding form and in corresponding situations in the dreams of modern man, with no connection with alchemy, and always it has to do with the bringing together of the light and the dark, as though modern man, like the alchemists, had divined what the problem was that the Apocalypse set the future. It was this problem on which the alchemists laboured for nearly seventeen centuries, and it is the same problem that distresses modern man. Though in one respect he knows more, in another respect he knows less than the alchemists. The problem for him is no longer projected upon matter, as it was for them; but on the other hand it has become psychologically acute, so that the psychotherapist has more to say on these matters than the theologian, who has remained caught in his archaic figures of speech. The doctor, often very much against his will, is forced by the problems of psychoneurosis to look more closely at the religious problem. It is not without good reason that I myself have reached the age of seventy-six before venturing to catechize myself as to the nature of those "ruling ideas" which decide our ethical behaviour and have such an important influence on our practical life. They are in the last resort the principles which, spoken or unspoken, determine the moral decisions upon which our existence depends, for weal or woe. All these dominants culminate in the positive or negative concept of God.[173]

Ever since John the apocalyptist experienced for the first time (perhaps unconsciously) the conflict into which Christianity inevitably leads, mankind has groaned under

---

[173] Psychologically the God-concept includes every idea of the ultimate, of the first or last, of the highest or lowest. The name makes no difference.

632 : Psychology and Religion: West and East

this burden: *God wanted to become man, and still wants to.* That is probably why John experienced in his vision a second birth of a son from the mother Sophia, a divine birth which was characterized by a *coniunctio oppositorum* and which anticipated the *filius sapientiae,* the essence of the individuation process. This was the effect of Christianity on a Christian of early times, who had lived long and resolutely enough to be able to cast a glance into the distant future. The mediation between the opposites was already indicated in the symbolism of Christ's fate, in the crucifixion scene where the mediator hangs between two thieves, one of whom goes to paradise, the other down to hell. Inevitably, in the Christian view, the opposition had to lie between God and man, and man was always in danger of being identified with the dark side. This, and the predestinarian hints dropped by our· Lord, influenced John strongly: only the few preordained from eternity shall be saved, while the great mass of mankind shall perish in the final catastrophe. The opposition between God and man in the Christian view may well be a Yahwistic legacy from olden times, when the metaphysical problem consisted solely in Yahweh's relations with his people. The fear of Yahweh was still too great for anybody to dare—despite Job's gnosis—to lodge the antinomy in Deity itself. But if you keep the opposition between God and man, then you finally arrive, whether you like it or not, at the Christian conclusion "omne bonum a Deo, omne malum ab homine," with the absurd result that the creature is placed in opposition to its creator and a positively cosmic or daemonic grandeur in evil is imputed to man. The terrible destructive will that breaks out in John's ecstasies gives some idea of what it means when man is placed in opposition to the God of goodness: it burdens him with the dark side of God, which in Job is still in its right place. But either way man is identified with evil, with the result that he sets his face against goodness or else tries to be as perfect as his father in heaven.

Yahweh's decision to become man is a symbol of the development that had to supervene when man becomes conscious of the sort of God-image he is confronted with.[174] God acts out of the unconscious of man and forces him to harmonize and unite the opposing influences to which his mind is exposed from the unconscious. The unconscious wants both: to divide and to unite. In his striving for unity, therefore, man may always count on the help of a metaphysical advocate, as Job clearly recognized. The unconscious wants to flow into consciousness in order to reach the light, but at the same time it continually thwarts itself, because it would rather remain unconscious. That is to say, God wants to become man, but not quite. The conflict in his nature is so great that the incarnation can only be bought by an expiatory self-sacrifice offered up to the wrath of God's dark side.

At first, God incarnated his good side in order, as we may suppose, to create the most durable basis for a later assimilation of the other side. From the promise of the Paraclete we may conclude that God wants to become *wholly* man; in other words, to reproduce himself in his own dark creature (man not redeemed from original sin). The author of Revelation has left us a testimony to the continued operation of the Holy Ghost in the sense of a continuing incarnation. He was a creaturely man who was invaded by the dark God of wrath and vengeance—a *ventus urens,* a "burning wind." (This John was possibly the favourite disciple, who in old age was vouchsafed a premonition of future developments.) This disturbing invasion engendered in him the image of the divine child, of a future saviour, born of the divine consort whose reflection (the anima) lives in every man—that child whom

---

[174] The God-concept, as the idea of an all-embracing totality, also includes the unconscious, and hence, in contrast to consciousness, it includes the objective psyche, which so often frustrates the will and intentions of the conscious mind. Prayer, for instance, reinforces the potential of the unconscious, thus accounting for the sometimes unexpected effects of prayer.

Meister Eckhart also saw in a vision. It was he who knew that God alone in his Godhead is not in a state of bliss, but must be born in the human soul ("Gott ist selig in der Seele"). The incarnation in Christ is the prototype which is continually being transferred to the creature by the Holy Ghost.

Since our moral conduct can hardly be compared with that of an early Christian like John, all manner of good as well as evil can still break through in us, particularly in regard to love. A sheer will for destruction, such as was evident in John, is not to be expected in our case. In all my experience I have never observed anything like it, except in cases of severe psychoses and criminal insanity. As a result of the spiritual differentiation fostered by the Reformation, and by the growth of the sciences in particular (which were originally taught by the fallen angels), there is already a considerable admixture of darkness in us, so that, compared with the purity of the early Christian saints (and some of the later ones too), we do not show up in a very favourable light. Our comparative blackness naturally does not help us a bit. Though it mitigates the impact of evil forces, it makes us more vulnerable and less capable of resisting them. We therefore need more light, more goodness and moral strength, and must wash off as much of the obnoxious blackness as possible, otherwise we shall not be able to assimilate the dark God who also wants to become man, and at the same time endure him without perishing. For this all the Christian virtues are needed and something else besides, for the problem is not only moral: we also need the Wisdom that Job was seeking. But at that time she was still hidden in Yahweh, or rather, she was not yet remembered by him. That higher and "complete" (τέλειος) man is begotten by the "unknown" father and born from Wisdom, and it is he who, in the figure of the *puer aeternus*—"vultu mutabilis albus et ater" [175]—repre-

---

[175] "Of changeful countenance, both white and black." Horace, *Epistulae*, II, 2.

sents our totality, which transcends consciousness. It was
this boy into whom Faust had to change, abandoning his
inflated one-sidedness which saw the devil only outside.
Christ's "Except ye become as little children" prefigures
this change, for in them the opposites lie close together;
but what is meant is the boy who is born from the maturity
of the adult man, and not the unconscious child we would
like to remain. Looking ahead, Christ also hinted, as I
mentioned before, at a morality of evil.

Strangely, suddenly, as if it did not belong there, the
sun-woman with her child appears in the stream of apocalyptic visions. He belongs to another, future world. Hence,
like the Jewish Messiah, the child is "caught up" to God,
and his mother must stay for a long time hidden in the
wilderness, where she is nourished by God. For the immediate and urgent problem in those days was not the
union of opposites, which lay in the future, but the incarnation of the light and the good, the subjugation of
*concupiscentia,* the lust of this world, and the consolidation
of the *civitas Dei* against the advent of the Antichrist, who
would come after a thousand years to announce the horrors
of the last days, the epiphany of the wrathful and avenging
God. The Lamb, transformed into a demonic ram, reveals
a new gospel, the *Evangelium Aeternum,* which, going
right beyond the love of God, has the fear of God as its
main ingredient. Therefore the Apocalypse closes, like the
classical individuation process, with the symbol of the
*hieros gamos,* the marriage of the son with the mother-
bride. But the marriage takes place in heaven, where "nothing unclean" enters, high above the devastated world. Light
consorts with light. That is the programme for the Christian aeon which must be fulfilled before God can incarnate
in the creaturely man. Only in the last days will the vision
of the sun-woman be fulfilled. In recognition of this truth,
and evidently inspired by the workings of the Holy Ghost,
the Pope has recently announced the dogma of the *Assumptio Mariae,* very much to the astonishment of all

rationalists. Mary as the bride is united with the son in the heavenly bridal-chamber, and, as Sophia, with the Godhead.[176]

This dogma is in every respect timely. In the first place it is a symbolical fulfilment of John's vision.[177] Secondly, it contains an allusion to the marriage of the Lamb at the end of time, and, thirdly, it repeats the Old Testament anamnesis of Sophia. These three references foretell the Incarnation of God. The second and third foretell the Incarnation in Christ,[178] but the first foretells the Incarnation in creaturely man.


# XVIII


Everything now depends on man: immense power of destruction is given into his hand, and the question is whether he can resist the will to use it, and can temper his will with the spirit of love and wisdom. He will hardly be

[176] *Apostolic Constitution ("Munificentissimus Deus") of . . . Pius XII,* §22: "Oportebat sponsam, quam Pater desponsaverat, in thalamis caelestibus habitare" (The place of the bride whom the Father had espoused was in the heavenly courts).—St. John Damascene, *Encomium in Dormitionem, etc.,* Homily II, 14 (cf. Migne, *P.G.,* Vol. 96, col. 742). §30: Comparison with the Bride in the Song of Solomon. §33: ". . . ita pariter surrexit et Arca sanctificationis suae, cum in hac die Virgo Mater ad aethereum thalamum est assumpta" ( . . . so in like manner arose the Ark which he had sanctified, when on this day the Virgin Mother was taken up to her heavenly bridal chamber).—St. Anthony of Padua, *S. Antonii Patavini Sermones Dominicales, etc.* (ed. Antonio Maria Locatelli, [Padua, 1895, 3 vols.] Vol. III, p. 730).
[177] *Apostolic Constitution,* §31: "Ac praeterea scholastici doctores non modo in variis Veteris Testamenti figuris, sed in illa etiam Muliere amicta sole, quam Joannes Apostolus in insula Patmo [Rev. 12 : 1ff.] contemplatus est, Assumptionem Deiparae Virginis significatam viderunt" (Moreover, the Scholastic doctors saw the Assumption of the Virgin Mother of God signified not only in the various figures of the Old Testament, but also in the Woman clothed with the sun, whom the Apostle John contemplated on the island of Patmos).
[178] The marriage of the Lamb repeats the Annunciation and the Overshadowing of Mary.

capable of doing so on his own unaided resources. He needs
the help of an "advocate" in heaven, that is, of the child
who was caught up to God and who brings the "healing"
and making whole of the hitherto fragmentary man. Whatever man's wholeness, or the self, may mean *per se,* empirically it is an image of the goal of life spontaneously
produced by the unconscious, irrespective of the wishes and
fears of the conscious mind. It stands for the goal of the
total man, for the realization of his wholeness and individuality with or without the consent of his will. The dynamic
of this process is instinct, which ensures that everything
which belongs to an individual's life shall enter into it,
whether he consents or not, or is conscious of what is
happening to him or not. Obviously, it makes a great deal
of difference subjectively whether he knows what he is living out, whether he understands what he is doing, and
whether he accepts responsibility for what he proposes to
do or has done. The difference between conscious realization and the lack of it has been roundly formulated in the
saying of Christ already quoted: "Man, if indeed thou
knowest what thou doest, thou art blessed: but if thou
knowest not, thou art cursed, and a transgressor of the
law." [179] Before the bar of nature and fate, unconsciousness is never accepted as an excuse; on the contrary there
are very severe penalties for it. Hence all unconscious nature longs for the light of consciousness while frantically
struggling against it at the same time.

The conscious realization of what is hidden and kept
secret certainly confronts us with an insoluble conflict; at
least this is how it appears to the conscious mind. But the
symbols that rise up out of the unconscious in dreams show
it rather as a confrontation of opposites, and the images of
the goal represent their successful reconciliation. Something empirically demonstrable comes to our aid from the
depths of our unconscious nature. It is the task of the

[179] Codex Bezae, apocryphal insertion at Luke 6 : 4. [Translated by
James; see supra, p. 606, note 123.—TRANSLATOR.]

conscious mind to understand these hints. If this does not happen, the process of individuation will nevertheless continue. The only difference is that we become its victims and are dragged along by fate towards that inescapable goal which we might have reached walking upright, if only we had taken the trouble and been patient enough to understand in time the meaning of the numina that cross our path. The only thing that really matters now is whether man can climb up to a higher moral level, to a higher plane of consciousness, in order to be equal to the superhuman powers which the fallen angels have played into his hands. But he can make no progress with himself unless he becomes very much better acquainted with his own nature. Unfortunately, a terrifying ignorance prevails in this respect, and an equally great aversion to increasing the knowledge of his intrinsic character. However, in the most unexpected quarters nowadays we find people who can no longer blink the fact that something *ought* to be done with man in regard to his psychology. Unfortunately, the little word "ought" tells us that they do not know what to do, and do not know the way that leads to the goal. We can, of course, hope for the undeserved grace of God, who hears our prayers. But God, who also does *not* hear our prayers, wants to become man, and for that purpose he has chosen, through the Holy Ghost, the creaturely man filled with darkness—the natural man who is tainted with original sin and who learnt the divine arts and sciences from the fallen angels. The guilty man is eminently suitable and is therefore chosen to become the vessel for the continuing incarnation, not the guiltless one who holds aloof from the world and refuses to pay his tribute to life, for in him the dark God would find no room.

Since the Apocalypse we now know again that God is not only to be loved, but also to be feared. He fills us with evil as well as with good, otherwise he would not need to be feared; and because he wants to become man, the uniting of his antinomy must take place in man. This involves man in a new responsibility. He can no longer wriggle out of it on the plea of his littleness and nothingness, for the dark God has slipped the atom bomb and chemical weapons into his hands and given him the power to empty out the apocalyptic vials of wrath on his fellow creatures. Since he has been granted an almost godlike power, he can no longer remain blind and unconscious. He must know something of God's nature and of metaphysical processes if he is to understand himself and thereby achieve gnosis of the Divine.

## XIX

The promulgation of the new dogma of the Assumption of the Virgin Mary could, in itself, have been sufficient reason for examining the psychological background. It was interesting to note that, among the many articles published in the Catholic and Protestant press on the declaration of the dogma, there was not one, so far as I could see, which laid anything like the proper emphasis on what was undoubtedly the most powerful motive: namely, the popular movement and the psychological need behind it. Essentially, the writers of the articles were satisfied with learned considerations, dogmatic and historical, which have no bearing on the living religious process. But anyone who has followed with attention the visions of Mary which have been increasing in number over the last few decades, and has taken their psychological significance into account, might have known what was brewing. The fact, especially, that it was largely children who had the visions might have given pause for thought, for in such cases the collective unconscious is always at work. Incidentally, the Pope himself is rumoured to have had several visions of the Mother of God on the occasion of the declaration. One could have known for a long time that there was a deep longing in the masses for an intercessor and mediatrix who would at last take her place alongside the Holy Trinity and be received as the "Queen of Heaven and Bride at the heavenly court." For more than a thousand years it had been taken for granted that the Mother of God dwelt there, and we know from the Old Testament that Sophia was with God before the creation. From the ancient Egyptian theology of the divine Pharaohs we know that God wants to become man by means of a human mother, and it was recognized even in prehistoric times that the primordial divine being is both male and female. But such a truth eventuates in time only when it is solemnly proclaimed or rediscovered. It is psychologically significant for our day that in the year 1950 the heavenly bride was united with the bridegroom. In order to interpret this event, one has to consider not only the arguments adduced by the Papal Bull, but the prefigurations in the apocalyptic marriage of the Lamb and in the Old Testament anamnesis of Sophia. The nuptial union in the *thalamus* (bridal-chamber) signifies the *hieros gamos,* and this in turn is the first step towards incarnation, towards the birth of the saviour who, since antiquity, was thought of as the *filius solis et lunae,* the *filius sapientiae,* and the equivalent of Christ. When, therefore, a longing for the exaltation of the Mother of God passes through the people, this tendency, if thought to its logical conclusion, means the desire for the birth of a saviour, a peacemaker, a "mediator pacem faciens inter inimicos." [180] Although he is already born in the pleroma, his birth in time can only be accomplished when it is perceived, recognized, and declared by man.

The motive and content of the popular movement which contributed to the Pope's decision solemnly to declare the new dogma consist not in the birth of a new god, but in the continuing incarnation of God which began with Christ. Arguments based on historical criticism will never do justice to the new dogma; on the contrary, they are as lamentably wide of the mark as are the unqualified fears to

[180] "A mediator making peace between enemies."

which the English archbishops have given expression. In
the first place, the declaration of the dogma has changed
nothing in principle in the Catholic ideology as it has existed for more than a thousand years; and in the second
place, the failure to understand that God has eternally
wanted to become man, and for that purpose continually
incarnates through the Holy Ghost in the temporal sphere,
is an alarming symptom and can only mean that the Protestant standpoint has lost ground by not understanding the
signs of the times and by ignoring the continued operation
of the Holy Ghost. It is obviously out of touch with the
tremendous archetypal happenings in the psyche of the
individual and the masses, and with the symbols which are
intended to compensate the truly apocalyptic world situation today.[181] It seems to have succumbed to a species of
rationalistic historicism and to have lost any understanding
of the Holy Ghost who works in the hidden places of the
soul. It can therefore neither understand nor admit a
further revelation of the divine drama.

This circumstance has given me, a layman in things
theological, cause to put forward my views on these dark
matters. My attempt is based on the psychological experience I have harvested during the course of a long life. I
do not underestimate the psyche in any respect whatsoever,
nor do I imagine for a moment that psychic happenings
vanish into thin air by being explained. Psychologism represents a still primitive mode of magical thinking, with the
help of which one hopes to conjure the reality of the soul

[181] The papal rejection of psychological symbolism may be explained
by the fact that the Pope is primarily concerned with the reality of
metaphysical happenings. Owing to the undervaluation of the
psyche that everywhere prevails, every attempt at adequate psychological understanding is immediately suspected of psychologism. It
is understandable that dogma must be protected from this danger.
If, in physics, one seeks to explain the nature of light, nobody
expects that as a result there will be no light. But in the case of
psychology everybody believes that what it explains is explained
away. However, I cannot expect that my particular deviationist point
of view could be known in any competent quarter.

out of existence, after the manner of the "Proktophantas-mist" in *Faust:*

> Are you still here? Nay, it's a thing unheard.
> Vanish at once! We've said the enlightening word.

One would be very ill advised to identify me with such a childish standpoint. However, I have been asked so often whether I believe in the existence of God or not that I am somewhat concerned lest I be taken for an adherent of "psychologism" far more commonly than I suspect. What most people overlook or seem unable to understand is the fact that I regard the psyche as *real*. They believe only in physical facts, and must consequently come to the conclusion that either the uranium itself or the laboratory equipment created the atom bomb. That is no less absurd than the assumption that a non-real psyche is responsible for it. God is an obvious psychic and non-physical fact, i.e., a fact that can be established psychically but not physically. Equally, these people have still not got it into their heads that the psychology of religion falls into two categories, which must be sharply distinguished from one another: firstly, the psychology of the religious person, and secondly, the psychology of religion proper, i.e., of religious contents.

It is chiefly my experiences in the latter field which have given me the courage to enter into the discussion of the religious question and especially into the pros and cons of the dogma of the Assumption—which, by the way, I consider to be the most important religious event since the Reformation. It is a *petra scandali* for the unpsychological mind: how can such an unfounded assertion as the bodily reception of the Virgin into heaven be put forward as worthy of belief? But the method which the Pope uses in order to demonstrate the truth of the dogma makes sense to the psychological mind, because it bases itself firstly on the necessary prefigurations, and secondly on a tradition of religious assertions reaching back for more than a thousand years. Clearly, the material evidence for the

existence of this psychic phenomenon is more than sufficient. It does not matter at all that a physically impossible
fact is asserted, because all religious assertions are physical
impossibilities. If they were not so, they would, as I said
earlier, necessarily be treated in the text-books of natural
science. But religious statements without exception have to
do with the reality of the *psyche* and not with the reality
of *physis*. What outrages the Protestant standpoint in particular is the boundless approximation of the Deipara to
the Godhead and, in consequence, the endangered supremacy of Christ, from which Protestantism will not
budge. In sticking to this point it has obviously failed to
consider that its hymnology is full of references to the
"heavenly bridegroom," who is now suddenly supposed not
to have a bride with equal rights. Or has, perchance, the
"bridegroom," in true psychologistic manner, been understood as a mere metaphor?

The logical consistency of the papal declaration cannot
be surpassed, and it leaves Protestantism with the odium of
being nothing but a *man's religion* which allows no metaphysical representation of woman. In this respect it is similar to Mithraism, and Mithraism found this prejudice very
much to its detriment. Protestantism has obviously not
given sufficient attention to the signs of the times which
point to the equality of women. But this equality requires
to be metaphysically anchored in the figure of a "divine"
woman, the bride of Christ. Just as the person of Christ
cannot be replaced by an organization, so the bride cannot
be replaced by the Church. The feminine, like the masculine, demands an equally personal representation.

The dogmatizing of the Assumption does not, however,
according to the dogmatic view, mean that Mary has attained the status of a goddess, although, as mistress of
heaven (as opposed to the prince of the sublunary aerial
realm, Satan) and mediatrix, she is functionally on a par
with Christ, the king and mediator. At any rate her position
satisfies the need of the archetype. The new dogma expresses

a renewed hope for the fulfilment of that yearning for peace which stirs deep down in the soul, and for a resolution of the threatening tension between the opposites. Everyone shares this tension and everyone experiences it in his individual form of unrest, the more so the less he sees any possibility of getting rid of it by rational means. It is no wonder, therefore, that the hope, indeed the expectation of divine intervention arises in the collective unconscious and at the same time in the masses. The papal declaration has given comforting expression to this yearning. How could Protestantism so completely miss the point? This lack of understanding can only be explained by the fact that the dogmatic symbols and hermeneutic allegories have lost their meaning for Protestant rationalism. This is also true, in some measure, of the opposition to the new dogma within the Catholic Church itself, or rather to the dogmatization of the old doctrine. Naturally, a certain degree of rationalism is better suited to Protestantism than it is to the Catholic outlook. The latter gives the archetypal symbolisms the necessary freedom and space in which to develop over the centuries while at the same time insisting on their original form, unperturbed by intellectual difficulties and the objections of rationalists. In this way the Catholic Church demonstrates her maternal character, because she allows the tree growing out of her matrix to develop according to its own laws. Protestantism, in contrast, is committed to the paternal spirit. Not only did it develop, at the outset, from an encounter with the worldly spirit of the times, but it continues this dialectic with the spiritual currents of every age; for the pneuma, in keeping with its original wind nature, is flexible, ever in living motion, comparable now to water, now to fire. It can desert its original haunts, can even go astray and get lost, if it succumbs too much to the spirit of the age. In order to fulfil its task, the Protestant spirit must be full of unrest and occasionally troublesome; it must even be revolutionary, so as to make sure that tradition has an influence on the change of contemporary values. The shocks it sustains dur-

ing this encounter modify and at the same time enliven the
tradition, which in its slow progress through the centuries
would, without these disturbances, finally arrive at complete petrifaction and thus lose its effect. By merely criticiz-
ing and opposing certain developments within the Catholic
Church, Protestantism would gain only a miserable bit of
vitality, unless, mindful of the fact that Christianity consists
of two separate camps, or rather, is a disunited brother-
sister pair, it remembers that besides defending its own
existence it must acknowledge Catholicism's right to exist
too. A brother who for theological reasons wanted to cut
the thread of his elder sister's life would rightly be called
inhuman—to say nothing of Christian charity—and the
converse is also true. Nothing is achieved by merely negative criticism. It is justified only to the degree that it is
creative. Therefore it would seem profitable to me if, for
example, Protestantism admitted that it is shocked by the
new dogma not only because it throws a distressing light
on the gulf between brother and sister, but because, for
fundamental reasons, a situation has developed within
Christianity which removes it further than ever from the
sphere of worldly understanding. Protestantism knows, or
could know, how much it owes its very existence to the
Catholic Church. How much or how little does the Protestant still possess if he can no longer criticize or protest?
In view of the intellectual *skandalon* which the new dogma
represents, he should remind himself of his Christian responsibility—"Am I my brother's (or in this case, my sister's) keeper?"—and examine in all seriousness the reasons,
explicit or otherwise, that decided the declaration of the
new dogma. In so doing, he should guard against casting
cheap aspersions and would do well to assume that there
is more in it than papal arbitrariness. It would be desirable for the Protestant to understand that the new dogma
has placed upon him a new responsibility toward the
worldly spirit of our age, for he cannot simply deny his
problematical sister before the eyes of the world. He
must, even if he finds her antipathetic, be fair to her if

he does not want to lose his self-respect. For instance, this is a favourable opportunity for him to ask himself, for a change, what is the meaning not only of the new dogma but of all more or less dogmatic assertions over and above their literal concretism. Considering the arbitrary and protean state of his own dogmas, and the precarious, schism-riven condition of his Church, he cannot afford to remain rigid and impervious to the spirit of the age. And since, in accordance with his obligations to the *Zeitgeist,* he is more concerned to come to terms with the world and its ideas than with God, it would seem clearly indicated that, on the occasion of the entry of the Mother of God into the heavenly bridal-chamber, he should bend to the great task of reinterpreting all the Christian traditions. If it is a question of truths which are anchored deep in the soul—and no one with the slightest insight can doubt this fact—then the solution of this task must be possible. For this we need the freedom of the spirit, which, as we know, is assured only in Protestantism. The dogma of the Assumption is a slap in the face for the historical and rationalistic view of the world, and would remain so for all time if one were to insist obstinately on the arguments of reason and history. This is a case, if ever there was one, where psychological understanding is needed, because the mythologem coming to light is so obvious that we must be deliberately blinding ourselves if we cannot see its symbolic nature and interpret it in symbolic terms.

The dogmatization of the *Assumptio Mariae* points to the *hieros gamos* in the pleroma, and this in turn implies, as we have said, the future birth of the divine child, who, in accordance with the divine trend towards incarnation, will choose as his birthplace the empirical man. The metaphysical process is known to the psychology of the unconscious as the individuation process. In so far as this process, as a rule, runs its course unconsciously as it has from time immemorial, it means no more than that the acorn becomes an oak, the calf a cow, and the child an adult. But if the individuation process is made conscious, consciousness must confront the unconscious and a balance between the opposites must be found. As this is not possible through logic, one is dependent on *symbols* which make the irrational union of opposites possible. They are produced spontaneously by the unconscious and are amplified by the conscious mind. The central symbols of this process describe the self, which is man's totality, consisting on the one hand of that which is conscious to him, and on the other hand of the contents of the unconscious. The self is the τέλειος ἄνθρωπος, the whole man, whose symbols are the divine child and its synonyms. This is only a very summary sketch of the process, but it can be observed at any time in modern man, or one can read about it in the documents of Hermetic philosophy from the Middle Ages. The parallelism between the symbols is astonishing to anyone who knows both the psychology of the unconscious and alchemy.

The difference between the "natural" individuation process, which runs its course unconsciously, and the one which is consciously realized, is tremendous. In the first case consciousness nowhere intervenes; the end remains as dark as the beginning. In the second case so much darkness comes to light that the personality is permeated with light, and consciousness necessarily gains in scope and insight. The encounter between conscious and unconscious has to ensure that the light which shines in the darkness is not only comprehended by the darkness, but comprehends it. The *filius solis et lunae* is the symbol of the union of opposites as well as the catalyst of their union. It is the alpha and omega of the process, the mediator and intermedius. "It has a thousand names," say the alchemists, meaning that the source from which the individuation process rises and the goal towards which it aims is nameless, ineffable.

It is only through the psyche that we can establish that God acts upon us, but we are unable to distinguish whether these actions emanate from God or from the unconscious. We cannot tell whether God and the unconscious are two different entities. Both are border-line concepts for transcendental contents. But empirically it can be established, with a sufficient degree of probability, that there is in the unconscious an archetype of wholeness which manifests itself spontaneously in dreams, etc., and a tendency, independent of the conscious will, to relate other archetypes to this centre. Consequently, it does not seem improbable that the archetype of wholeness occupies as such a central position which approximates it to the God-image. The similarity is further borne out by the peculiar fact that the archetype produces a symbolism which has always characterized and expressed the Deity. These facts make possible a certain qualification of our above thesis concerning the indistinguishableness of God and the unconscious. Strictly speaking, the God-image does not coincide with the unconscious as such, but with a special content of it, namely the archetype of the self. It is this archetype from which we can no longer distinguish the God-image empirically. We can arbitrarily postulate a difference between these two entities, but that does not help us at all. On the contrary, it only helps us to separate man from God, and prevents God from becoming man. Faith is certainly right when it impresses on man's mind and heart how infinitely far away and inaccessible God is; but it also teaches his nearness, his immediate presence, and it is just this nearness which has to be empirically real if it is not to lose all significance. Only that which acts upon me do I recognize as real and actual. But that which has no effect upon me might as well not exist. The religious need longs for wholeness, and therefore lays hold of the images of wholeness offered by the unconscious, which, independently of the conscious mind, rise up from the depths of our psychic nature.

## XX

It will probably have become clear to the reader that the account I have given of the development of symbolic entities corresponds to a process of differentiation of human consciousness. But since, as I showed in the introduction, the archetypes in question are not mere objects of the mind, but are also autonomous factors, i.e., living subjects, the differentiation of consciousness can be understood as the effect of the intervention of transcendentally conditioned dynamisms. In this case it would be the archetypes that accomplish the primary transformation. But since, in our experience, there are no psychic conditions which could be observed *through introspection* outside the human being, the behaviour of the archetypes cannot be investigated at all without the interaction of the observing consciousness. Therefore the question as to whether the process is initiated by consciousness or by the archetype can never be answered; unless, in contradiction to experience, one either robbed the archetype of its autonomy or degraded consciousness to a mere machine. We find ourselves in best agreement with psychological experience if we concede to the archetype a definite measure of independence, and to consciousness a degree of creative freedom proportionate to its scope. There then arises that reciprocal action between two relatively autonomous factors which compels us, when describing and explaining the processes, to present sometimes the one and sometimes the other factor as the acting subject, even when God becomes man. The Christian solution has hitherto avoided this difficulty by recognizing Christ as the one and only God-man. But the indwelling of the Holy Ghost, the third Divine Person, in man, brings about a Christification of many, and the question then arises whether these many are all complete God-men. Such a transformation would lead to insufferable collisions between them, to say nothing of the unavoidable inflation to which the ordinary mortal, who is not freed from original sin, would instantly succumb. In these circumstances it is well to remind ourselves of St. Paul and his split consciousness: on one side he felt he was the apostle directly called and enlightened by God, and, on the other side, a sinful man who could not pluck out the "thorn in the flesh" and rid himself of the Satanic angel who plagued him. That is to say, even the enlightened person remains what he is, and is never more than his own limited ego before the One who dwells within him, whose form has no knowable boundaries, who encompasses him on all sides, fathomless as the abysms of the earth and vast as the sky.

# Appendix

Major publications are marked with asterisks.
Numbers in brackets indicate sources of selections in this volume.

I. *The Collected Works of Carl G. Jung,* Translated by
   R. F. C. Hull. Bollingen Series XX. Princeton University Press

Mental Disease and the Psyche (1928)
On the Psychogenesis of Schizophrenia (1939)
Recent Thoughts on Schizophrenia (1957)
Schizophrenia (1958)

4. FREUD AND PSYCHOANALYSIS
Freud's Theory of Hysteria: A Reply to Aschaffenburg
      (1906)
The Freudian Theory of Hysteria (1908)
The Analysis of Dreams (1909)
A Contribution to the Psychology of Rumour (1910–11)
On the Significance of Number Dreams (1910–11)
Morton Prince, "Mechanism and Interpretation of
      Dreams: A Critical Review" (1911)
On the Criticism of Psychoanalysis (1910)
Concerning Psychoanalysis (1912)
The Theory of Psychoanalysis (1913)
General Aspects of Psychoanalysis (1913)
Psychoanalysis and Neurosis (1916)
Some Crucial Points in Psychoanalysis: The Jung-Loÿ
      Correspondence (1914)
Prefaces to "Collected Papers on Analytical Psychology"
      (1916, 1917)
The Significance of the Father in the Destiny of the
      Individual (1909/1949)
Instruction to Kranefeldt's "Secret Ways of the Mind"
      (1930)
Freud and Jung: Contrasts (1929)

*5. SYMBOLS OF TRANSFORMATION (1911–12/1952)
   PART I (1911)
Introduction
Two Kinds of Thinking
The Miller Fantasies: Anamnesis
The Hymn of Creation
The Song of the Moth
   PART II (1912)
Introduction
The Concept of Libido
The Transformation of Libido

The Origin of the Hero
Symbols of the Mother and of Rebirth
The Battle for Deliverance from the Mother
The Dual Mother
The Sacrifice
Epilogue
Appendix: The Miller Fantasies

*6. PSYCHOLOGICAL TYPES (1921)
Introduction
The Problem of Types in the History of Classical and
    Medieval Thought
Schiller's Ideas on the Type Problem
The Apollonian and the Dionysian
The Type Problem in the Discernment of Human Char-
    acter
The Type Problem in Poetry
The Type Problem in Psychopathology
The Problem of Typical Attitudes in Aesthetics
The Type Problem in Modern Philosophy
The Type Problem in Biography
[8] General Description of the Types
Definitions
Conclusion
Four Papers on Psychological Typology (1913, 1925,
    1931, 1936)

*7. TWO ESSAYS ON ANALYTICAL PSYCHOLOGY
On the Psychology of the Unconscious (1917/1926/1943)
[5] The Relations Between the Ego and the Unconscious
    (1928)
Appendices: New Paths in Psychology (1912); The
    Structure of the Unconscious (1916) (new versions,
    with variants, 1966)

8. THE STRUCTURE AND DYNAMICS
OF THE PSYCHE
On Psychic Energy (1928)
[9] The Transcendent Function ([1916]/1957)
A Review of the Complex Theory (1934)
The Significance of Constitution and Heredity in Psy-
    chology (1929)

The Self
Christ, a Symbol of the Self
The Sign of the Fishes
The Prophecies of Nostradamus
The Historical Significance of the Fish
The Ambivalence of the Fish Symbol
The Fish in Alchemy
The Alchemical Interpretation of the Fish
Background to the Psychology of Christian Alchemical
     Symbolism
Gnostic Symbols of the Self
The Structure and Dynamics of the Self
Conclusion


10. CIVILIZATION IN TRANSITION
The Role of the Unconscious (1918)
Mind and Earth (1927/1931)
Archaic Man (1931)
[12] The Spiritual Problem of Modern Man (1928/1931)
The Love Problem of a Student (1928)
Women in Europe (1927)
The Meaning of Psychology for Modern Man (1933/
     1934)
The State of Psychotherapy Today (1934)
Preface and Epilogue to "Essays on Contemporary
     Events" (1946)
Wotan (1936)
After the Catastrophe (1945)
The Fight with the Shadow (1946)
The Undiscovered Self (Present and Future) (1957)
Flying Saucers: A Modern Myth (1958)
A Psychological View of Conscience (1958)
Good and Evil in Analytical Psychology (1959)
Introduction to Wolff's "Studies in Jungian Psychology"
     (1959)
The Swiss Line in the European Spectrum (1928)
Reviews of Keyserling's "America Set Free" (1930) and
     "La Révolution Mondiale" (1934)
Complications of American Psychology (1930)
The Dreamlike World of India (1939)

The Visions of Zosimos (1938/1954)
Paracelsus as a Spiritual Phenomenon (1942)
The Spirit Mercurius (1943/1948)
The Philosophical Tree (1945/1954)

*14. MYSTERIUM CONIUNCTIONIS (1955–56)
AN INQUIRY INTO THE SEPARATION AND
SYNTHESIS OF PSYCHIC OPPOSITES IN ALCHEMY
The Components of the Coniunctio
The Paradoxa
The Personification of Opposites
Rex and Regina
Adam and Eve
The Conjunction

15. THE SPIRIT IN MAN, ART, AND LITERATURE
Paracelsus (1929)
Paracelsus the Physician (1941)
Sigmund Freud in His Historical Setting (1932)
In Memory of Sigmund Freud (1939)
Richard Wilhelm: In Memoriam (1930)
[10] On the Relation of Analytical Psychology to Poetry
(1922)
Psychology and Literature (1930/1950)
"Ulysses" (1932)
Picasso (1932)

16. THE PRACTICE OF PSYCHOTHERAPY
GENERAL PROBLEMS OF PSYCHOTHERAPY
Principles of Practical Psychotherapy (1935)
What Is Psychotherapy? (1935)
Some Aspects of Modern Psychotherapy (1930)
The Aims of Psychotherapy (1929)
Psychotherapy and a Philosophy of Life (1943)
Medicine and Psychotherapy (1945)
Psychotherapy Today (1945)
Fundamental Questions of Psychotherapy (1951)
SPECIFIC PROBLEMS OF PSYCHOTHERAPY
The Therapeutic Value of Abreaction (1921/1928)
The Practical Use of Dream-Analysis (1934)

*Additional Introductory Works Recommended*

C. G. Jung, *Analytical Psychology, Its Theory and Practice*
(The Tavistock Lectures), Foreword by E. A. Bennet (N.Y.
Pantheon, 1968).

C. G. Jung, *Memories, Dreams, Reflections*, Recorded and
edited by Aniela Jaffé. Translated by Richard and Clara
Winston (N.Y. Pantheon, 1963).

Carl G. Jung, and M.-L. von Franz, Joseph L. Henderson,
Jolande Jacobi, Aniela Jaffé, *Man and His Symbols*. (Garden City, N.Y. Doubleday & Co., 1964).

**ACKNOWLEDGMENTS**

Random House, Inc., and William Collins Sons & Co. Ltd.: Excerpts from *Memories, Dreams, Reflections,* by C. G. Jung, recorded and edited by Aniela Jaffé. Copyright © Random House Inc., 1962, 1963. Reprinted by permission of Pantheon Books, a Division of Random House, Inc., and William Collins Sons & Co. Ltd.

The editor wishes to thank Mr. John D. Barrett of the Bollingen Foundation and Mr. William McGuire of Princeton University Press for advice and assistance in the publication of this volume; and both Mr. R. F. C. Hull and Dr. Joseph L. Henderson for important suggestions in the judgment of selections.

A selection of books published by Penguin is listed on the following page.

For a complete list of books available from Penguin in the United States, write to Dept. DG, Penguin Books, 299 Murray Hill Parkway, East Rutherford, New Jersey 07073.

For a complete list of books available from Penguin in Canada, write to Penguin Books Canada Limited, 2801 John Street, Markham, Ontario L3R 1B4.

Some Books on Psychology Published by
Penguin Books